Ideas and American Foreign Policy

Ideas and American Foreign Policy

A READER

EDITED BY

Andrew J. Bacevich

OXFORD
UNIVERSITY PRESS

Oxford University Press is a department of the University of Oxford. It furthers
the University's objective of excellence in research, scholarship, and education
by publishing worldwide. Oxford is a registered trade mark of Oxford University
Press in the UK and certain other countries.

Published in the United States of America by Oxford University Press
198 Madison Avenue, New York, NY 10016, United States of America.

CIP data is on file at the Library of Congress
ISBN 978–0–19–064539–7 (hbk.)
ISBN 978–0–19–064540–3 (pbk.)

1 3 5 7 9 8 6 4 2

Paperback printed by LSC Communications, United States of America
Hardback printed by Bridgeport National Bindery, Inc., United States of America

CONTENTS

INTRODUCTION

Many factors influence the formulation and implementation of US foreign policy. Among the most prominent are history and habit, interests and ambitions, partisan politics and bureaucratic rivalries. Groups and institutions external to the government also play a role: old media and new, think tanks and universities, lobbies and interest groups, corporations and labor unions, churches and civic organizations. Other nations, both allies and adversaries, also matter. So too do the personal characteristics of policymakers—their character, temperament, background, upbringing, and prior experience.

The premise of this reader is that *ideas* also play a prominent—indeed, central—role in shaping the way that Americans, members of the foreign policy establishment as well as ordinary citizens, see the world and America's role in it. The purpose of *Ideas and American Foreign Policy* is to survey the evolution of those ideas across time as expressed in contemporaneous documents.

The survey begins with the founding of Anglo-America, a century and a half prior to the establishment of the United States as an independent nation. It concludes in the first decades of the twenty-first century, with the United States having achieved superpower status and wrestling with the burdens of global leadership.

The documents included below and the ideas they express chronicle the transformation of the United States from a small and fragile republic into the preeminent power of the present age. The documents tell two parallel stories. The first is a story of opportunistic expansion, promoted and justified by an enduring belief in American exceptionalism—the conviction that Americans are a chosen people and that the United States is called upon to remake the world in its own image.

Yet the documents also chart a second parallel story of critics finding fault with America's quest for global power and offering an alternative interpretation of the nation's true calling.

Both camps in this ongoing debate asserted the prerogative of interpreting America's destiny. Each mobilized specific claims and convictions to argue its case. The items included in this anthology, ranging from policy statements and speeches to poems and song lyrics, invite us to reflect on those claims and convictions, to weigh their impact, and to evaluate their validity.

Andrew J. Bacevich
Professor of History and
International Relations Emeritus
Boston University

I.

FOUNDING TRADITION

During the interval between the colonization of North America by subjects of the English king and their establishment of an independent republic, the people who took to calling themselves "Americans" evolved a collective sense of where they stood in relation to history itself. Central to their self-image was a conviction that they had been summoned to perform a uniquely redemptive mission. Chosenness conferred both responsibilities and privileges, exercised in the name of advancing the cause of true freedom.

The documents in this section span over a century and a half of American history. The section begins in the early seventeenth century with the founding of Anglo-America as a colonial enterprise—a political, religious, and cultural extension of England. The section ends with the United States having successfully waged a violent revolution to become an independent republic in a world of monarchies. In the interim, American colonists waged wars against those that they perceived to be threats or obstacles, most notably Native Americans and "papists"—French or Spanish Roman Catholics engaged in their own efforts to colonize North America.

By 1776, "freedom" had emerged as a core value of the American enterprise. So it would remain in perpetuity. Yet not all those residing within the boundaries of the United States enjoyed equal access to freedom. Women, religious nonconformists, and poor whites were allowed limited rights. Enslaved blacks imported from Africa were allowed none at all.

Relative to the established European powers, the newly independent Republic was weak and fragile. Yet it also stood at a distance from Europe. From a security perspective, this was a great advantage. The immediate challenge facing the young nation was to set a course enabling it to gain strength while avoiding involvement in needless quarrels. By the end of the eighteenth century, the principles allowing for just such policies were in place.

JOHN WINTHROP, "A MODEL OF CHRISTIAN CHARITY" (1630)

A founder of Massachusetts Bay Colony, John Winthrop (1587–1649) here explains the purposes of the enterprise that he and the members of his community are about to undertake in establishing a Christian community in the New World. Central to that enterprise is a profoundly intimate relationship with God.

It rests now to make some application of this discourse, by the present design, which gave the occasion of writing of it. Herein are four things to be propounded; first the persons, secondly, the work, thirdly the end, fourthly the means.

First, for the persons. We are a company professing ourselves fellow members of Christ, in which respect only, though we were absent from each other many miles, and had our employments as far distant, yet we ought to account ourselves knit together by this bond of love and live in the exercise of it, if we would have comfort of our being in Christ. This was notorious in the practice of the Christians in former times; as is testified of the Waldenses, from the mouth of one of the adversaries Aeneas Sylvius "mutuo ament pene antequam norunt"—they use to love any of their own religion even before they were acquainted with them.

Secondly for the work we have in hand. It is by a mutual consent, through a special overvaluing providence and a more than an ordinary approbation of the churches of Christ, to seek out a place of cohabitation and consortship under a due form of government both civil and ecclesiastical. In such cases as this, the care of the public must oversway all private respects, by which, not only conscience, but mere civil policy, doth bind us. For it is a true rule that particular estates cannot subsist in the ruin of the public.

Thirdly, the end is to improve our lives to do more service to the Lord; the comfort and increase of the body of Christ, whereof we are members, that ourselves and posterity may be the better preserved from the common corruptions of this evil world, to serve the Lord and work out our salvation under the power and purity of his holy ordinances.

Fourthly, for the means whereby this must be effected. They are twofold, a conformity with the work and end we aim at. These we see are extraordinary, therefore we must not content ourselves with usual ordinary means. Whatsoever we did, or ought to have done, when we lived in England, the same must we do, and more also, where we go.

That which the most in their churches maintain as truth in profession only, we must bring into familiar and constant practice; as in this duty of love, we must love brotherly without dissimulation, we must love one another with a pure heart fervently. We must bear one another's burdens. We must not look only on our own things, but also on the things of our brethren.

Neither must we think that the Lord will bear with such failings at our hands as he doth from those among whom we have lived; and that for these three reasons:

First, in regard of the more near bond of marriage between Him and us, wherein He hath taken us to be His, after a most strict and peculiar manner, which will make Him the more jealous of our love and obedience. So He tells the people of Israel, you only have I known of all the families of the earth, therefore will I punish you for your transgressions.

Secondly, because the Lord will be sanctified in them that come near Him. We know that there were many that corrupted the service of the Lord; some setting up altars before his own; others offering both strange fire and strange sacrifices also; yet there came no fire from heaven, or other sudden judgment upon them, as did upon Nadab and Abihu, whom yet we may think did not sin presumptuously.

Thirdly, when God gives a special commission He looks to have it strictly observed in every article; When He gave Saul a commission to destroy Amaleck, He indented with him upon certain articles, and because he failed in one of the least, and that upon a fair pretense, it lost him the kingdom, which should have been his reward, if he had observed his commission.

Thus stands the cause between God and us. We are entered into covenant with Him for this work. We have taken out a commission. The Lord hath given us leave to draw our own articles. We have professed to enterprise these and those accounts, upon these and those ends. We have hereupon besought Him of favor and blessing. Now if the Lord shall please to hear us, and bring us in peace to the place we desire, then hath He ratified this covenant and sealed our commission, and will expect a strict performance of the articles contained in it; but if we shall neglect the observation of these articles which are the ends we have propounded, and, dissembling with our God, shall fall to embrace this present world and prosecute our carnal intentions, seeking great things for ourselves and our posterity, the Lord will surely break out in wrath against us, and be revenged of such a people, and make us know the price of the breach of such a covenant.

Now the only way to avoid this shipwreck, and to provide for our posterity, is to follow the counsel of Micah, to do justly, to love mercy, to walk humbly with our God. For this end, we must be knit together, in this work, as one man. We must entertain each other in brotherly affection. We must be willing to abridge ourselves of our superfluities, for the supply of others' necessities. We must uphold a familiar commerce together in all meekness, gentleness, patience and liberality. We must delight in each other; make others' conditions our own; rejoice together, mourn together, labor and suffer together, always having before our eyes our commission and community in the work, as members of the same body. So shall we keep the unity of the spirit in the bond of peace. The Lord will be our God, and delight to dwell among us, as His own people, and will command a blessing upon us in all our ways, so that we shall see much more of His wisdom, power, goodness and truth, than formerly we have been acquainted with. We shall find that the God of Israel is among us, when ten of us shall be able to resist a thousand of our enemies; when He shall make us a praise and glory that men shall say of succeeding plantations, "may the Lord make it like that of New England." For we must consider that we shall be as a city upon a hill. The eyes of all people are upon us. So that if we shall deal falsely with our God in this work we have undertaken, and so cause Him to withdraw His present help from us, we shall be made a story and a by-word through the world. We shall open the mouths of enemies to speak evil of the ways of God, and all professors for God's sake. We shall shame the faces of many of God's worthy servants, and cause their prayers to be turned into curses upon us till we be consumed out of the good land whither we are going.

And to shut this discourse with that exhortation of Moses, that faithful servant of the Lord, in his last farewell to Israel, Deut. 30. "Beloved, there is now set before us life and death, good and evil," in that we are commanded this day to love the Lord our God, and to love one another, to walk in his ways and to keep his Commandments and his ordinance and his laws, and the articles of our Covenant with Him, that we may live and be multiplied, and that the Lord our God may bless us in the land whither we go to possess it. But if our hearts shall turn away, so that we will not obey, but shall be seduced, and worship other Gods, our pleasure and profits, and serve them; it is propounded unto us this day, we shall surely perish out of the good land whither we pass over this vast sea to possess it.

> Therefore let us choose life,
> that we and our seed may live,
> by obeying His voice and cleaving to Him,
> for He is our life and our prosperity.

COTTON MATHER, "THEOPOLIS AMERICANA" (1709)

Born in Boston, Cotton Mather (1663–1728) was an influential clergyman and writer. In this sermon, he affirms that Americans are God's new chosen people destined to play a central role in the salvation of all humankind.

I have been Surprised at the Reading of a Passage in a Pagan Writer, who flourished more than Fifteen Hundred years ago. Tis Ælian, a Grecian Writer, who sayes, That in Times long preceding his, there was a Tradition, that Europe and Asia and Africa, were encompassed by the Ocean; But without and beyond the Ocean, there was a great Island, as big as They. And in that Other

World, there was an huge CITY, called Ευσεβυς. The Godly City. In that City, Sayes he, they enjoy all Possible Peace and Health, and Plenty: And, he Sayes, They are without Controversy a very Righteous People; So Righteous, that they have God marvellously coming down among them.

I know not what well to make of a Tradition so very Ancient, and yet having Such an American Face upon it. All I will say, is thus much. There are many Arguments to perswade us, That our Glorious LORD, will have an Holy City in AMERICA; a City, the Street whereof will be Pure Gold. We cannot imagine, that the brave Countries and Gardens which fill the American Hemisphere, were made for nothing but a Place for Dragons. We may not imagine, That when the Kingdom of God is come, and His Will is done on Earth as it is done in Heaven, which we had never been taught to Pray for, if it must not one day be accomplished, a Ballancing Half of the Globe, shall remain in the Hands of the Devil, who is then to be Chained up from deceiving the Nations.

Has it not been promised our Great Saviour? Psal. 2. 8. I will give thee the uttermost parts of the Earth for thy Possession. And, Psal. 86. 9. All Nations whom thou hast made, shall come and worship before thee, O Lord, and shall glorify thy Name. And, has it not been promised? Mal. 1. 11. From the Rising of the Sun even unto the going down of the same, my Name shall be great among the Gentiles. AMERICA is Legible in these Promises. But if it be not here plainly enough expressed, what can be more plain, than the Prophecy, concerning the Kingdom of our Saviour? Dan. 2. 44. It shall brake in Pieces, and consume all those Kingdoms, and it shall stand for ever. The Kingdom of our Saviour becoming a Great Mountain, that must fill the WHOLE EARTH, does particularly fill, and Change, and Bless those Countries, which belong to the Ten Kingdoms of the Roman Empire, in the Papal and Final Edition of it. Now, the American Countries, do belong to some of those Kingdoms, are become a considerable part of their Dominion; And therefore, tis most certain, the Glorious Holy Mountain, will some of it stand in these Countries, as well as in the European.

There have been Martyrs of CHRIST in America. The Blood of the Martyrs here, is an Omen that the Truths for which they Suffer are to Rise, and Live, and carry all before them, in the Land that has been so Marked for the Lord. Such men as they will doubtless have some Glorious Power over the Nations, where they have been Such Overcomers; They that are to Shine as the Stars, will turn many unto Righteousneß; bring many to believe on the Sun of Righteousneß, in these Goings down of the Sun.

. . . O AMERICA, will no Share of the Lords Garments, and Glories, and the Righteousneß of the Saints, fall to thee, who art a Part of the World singly almost as great as the Other Three? Yea, the Day is at hand, when that Voice will be heard concerning thee, Put on thy beautiful Garments, O America, the Holy City! Certainly, It was never intended, that the Church of our Lord, should be confined always within the Dimensions of Strabo's Cloak; and that, All the World, should always be no more, than it was, when Augustus taxed it. We are Sorry, we are Troubled, That the Good Seed of the WORD, falling on the other Three Soyls, has brought forth so little Good Fruit, and for so little a while. But our Glorious LORD, will order that Good Seed ere long, to be cast, upon the Fertile Regions of America, and it shall here find a Good Ground, where it shall bring forth Fruit unto Astonishments; and unto Perpetuity!

When our Lord uttered the Parable, to which I have now alluded, we read, He went into a Ship, and from thence instructed the Multitude that stood on the shore. I will believe, that in this very Action, there was a Parable and a Prophesy. By Navigation, there will be brought the Word of a Glorious CHRIST, unto a Multitude afar off; and as the Ships cover the Sea, the Earth, and thou, AMERICA, too, Shall be filled with the knowledge of the Glorious Lord. The Fall of Old Pagan Babylon, was brought about, by the Diversion of her Euphrates from her. The Fall of the New Popish Babylon, will be accompanied with the Loss of her American Interest: But when 'tis diverted from her, certainly it will then serve the City of God. . . .

Tis thought by Some, that America might be intended, as a Place where the Worshippers of the Glorious JESUS, may be Sheltered, while fearful Things are doing in the European World, and, [as 'tis foretold it shall be!] The Land shall be fearfully Emptied and Spoiled; The Curse will devour the Earth, and they that dwell therein will be desolate; the Inhabitants of the Earth will be burned, and few men will be left. [See the XXIV. of Isaiah.] Whether it shall be so, or no; we are sure, there is a Day at hand, When the Lord of Hosts will Reign among His Ancient People Gloriously. In that Day, it will be impossible, for the Holy People, and the Teachers and Rulers of the Reformed World in the other Hemisphere, to leave America unvisited. It will be impossible for a People, so inspired from Heaven for the Propagation of true Christianity as will then be the Stars of that Hemisphere, to be unconcerned about America, and all the Ends of the World that are to turn unto the Lord; all the Kindreds of the Nations that are to Worship before Him. It will be impossible, that the Effect of the Essayes used, by Men filled with the SPIRIT of CHRIST, and able to do more than all that was done in the Primitive Times, [For, When He gives the Word, Great will be the Army of them that so Publish it!] Should not be, a conquest of America, ten thousand times more glorious, than all that ever any Cortez pretended unto; The Kingdom here will be the Lords, and the Lord will be Governour among the Nations. When the Holy SPIRIT of God, that River, the Streams whereof are to Make glad the City of God, shall, as He will, Run down into, and thorough the World, and make the World become a Watered Garden, and an Eden for the Lord from Heaven, and God shall dwell with men, by His Holy Spirit marvellously Possessing, and Purifying, and Enlightening of them; can you think, that America, shall be nothing but Miery Places and Marishes, given to Salt? By no means. O wide Atlantick, Thou shalt not stand in the way as any Hindrance of those Communications!

Verily, Our Glorious LORD will have Dominion from Sea to Sea. In those Days will the Righteous flourish. Then they who dwell in the Wilderneß, & even in this also, Shall bow before Him. They that are of the City, shall have something to do here for Him. O NEW-ENGLAND, There is Room to hope, That thou also shalt belong to the CITY. Thou hast already made a Seisin of America, on behalf of thy Glorious LORD. It is in some sort His Primier Seisin. The Seisin in Fact, which the Son of GOD, has taken of these American Territories, is, we hope, a Seisin in Law for all the rest. And certainly, Thou shalt not be cast off, when He comes into the Actual Possession of all the rest. Thy Name shall then be, Jehovah Shammah, THE LORD IS THERE. And, As we have heard, so shall we see, in the City of the Lord of Hosts, in the City of our God: GOD will establish it for ever more.

SAMUEL DAVIES, "RELIGION AND PATRIOTISM THE CONSTITUENTS OF A GOOD SOLDIER" (1755)

Prior to mounting a revolution to throw off English rule, Americans participated in a series of wars aimed establishing British control of North America. Here Samuel Davies (1723–1761), a Presbyterian clergyman, urges members of the Virginia militia to do God's work by eliminating the threat posed by French "papists" in league with Indian "savages."

AN Hundred Years of Peace and Liberty in such a World as this, is a very unusual Thing; and yet our Country has been the happy Spot that has been distinguished with such a long Series of Blessings, with little or no Interruption. Our Situation in the Middle of the *British* Colonies, and our Separation from the *French,* those *eternal* Enemies of Liberty and *Britons,* on the one Side by the vast *Atlantic,* and on the other by a long Ridge of Mountains, and a wide, extended Wilderness, have for many Years been a Barrier to us; and while other Nations have been involved in War, we have not been alarmed with the Sound of the Trumpet, nor seen *Garments rolled in Blood.*

But now the Scene is changed: Now we begin to experience in our Turn the Fate of the Nations of the Earth. Our Territories are invaded by the Power and Perfidy of *France;* our Frontiers ravaged by merciless Savages, and our Fellow-Subjects there murdered with all the horrid Arts of *Indian* and Popish Torture. . . .

These Calamities have not come upon us without Warnings. We were long ago apprized of the ambitious Schemes of our Enemies, and their Motions to carry them into Execution: And had we taken timely Measures, they might have been crushed, before they could arrive at such a formidable Height. But how have we generally behaved in such a critical Time; Alas! our Country has been sunk in a deep Sleep: A stupid Security has unmanned the Inhabitants: They could not realize a Danger at the Distance of 2 or 300 Miles: They would not be persuaded, that even *French Papists* could seriously design us an Injury: And hence little or nothing has been done for the Defence of our Country in Time, except by the Compulsion of Authority. And now, when the Cloud thickens over our Heads, and alarms every thoughtful Mind with its near Approach, Multitudes, I am afraid, are still dissolved in careless Security, or enervated with an effeminate, cowardly Spirit. . . . We have also *suffered our poor Fellow-Subjects in the Frontier Counties to fall a helpless Prey to Blood-thirsty Savages, without affording them proper Assistance,* which as Members of the same Body Politic, they had a Right to expect. They might as well have continued *in a State of Nature,* as be united *in Society,* if in such an Article of extreme Danger, they are left to shift for themselves. The bloody Barbarians have exercised on some of them the most unnatural and leisurely Tortures; and others they have butchered in their Beds, or in some unguarded Hour. Can human Nature bear the Horror of the Sight! See yonder! the hairy Scalps, clotted with Gore! the mangled Limbs! the ript-up Women! the Heart and Bowels, still palpitating with Life, smoking on the Ground! See the Savages swilling their Blood, and imbibing a more outragious Fury with the inhuman Draught! Sure these are not *Men;* they are not *Beasts of Prey;* they are something worse; they must be *infernal Furies* in human Shape. And have we tamely looked on, and suffered them to exercise these hellish Barbarities upon our Fellow-Men, our Fellow-Subjects, our Brethren?

Alas! with what Horror must we look upon ourselves, as being little better than Accessaries to their Blood?

And shall these Ravages go on unchecked? Shall *Virginia* incur the Guilt and the everlasting Shame, of tamely exchanging her Liberty, her Religion, and her All, for arbitrary *Gallic* Power, and for Popish Slavery, Tyranny and Massacre? Alas! are there none of her Children, that enjoyed all the Blessings of her Peace, that will espouse her Cause, and befriend her now in the Time of her Danger? Are *Britons* utterly degenerated by so short a Remove from their Mother-Country? Is the Spirit of Patriotism entirely extinguished among us? And must I give thee up for lost, O my Country . . .?

No; I am agreeably checked by the happy, encouraging Prospect now before me. Is it a pleasing Dream? Or do I really see a Number of brave Men, without the Compulsion of Authority, without the Prospect of Gain, voluntarily associated in a Company, to march over horrendous Rocks and Mountains, into an hideous Wilderness, to succour their helpless Fellow-Subjects, and guard their Country? Yes, Gentlemen, I see you here upon this Design; and were you all united to my Heart by the most endearing Ties of Nature, or Friendship, I could not wish to see you engaged in a nobler Cause. . . .

Our Continent is like to become the Seat of War; and we, for the future (till the sundry *European* Nations that have planted Colonies in it, have fixed their Boundaries by the Sword) have no other Way left to defend our Rights and Privileges. And has God been pleased to diffuse some Sparks of this Martial Fire through our Country? I hope he has: And though it has been almost extinguished by so long a Peace, and a Deluge of Luxury and Pleasure, now I hope it begins to kindle. . . .

The Equity of our Cause is most evident. The *Indian* Savages have certainly no Right to murder our Fellow-subjects, living quiet and inoffensive in their Habitations; nor have the *French* any Power to hound them out upon us, nor to invade the Territories belonging to the *British* Crown, and secured to it by the Faith of Treaties. This is a clear Case. And it is equally clear, that you are engaged in a Cause of the utmost Importance.

To protect your Brethren from the most bloody Barbarities—to defend the Territories of the best of Kings against the Oppression and Tyranny of arbitrary Power, to secure the inestimable Blessings of Liberty, *British Liberty,* from the Chains of *French* Slavery—to preserve your Estates, for which you have sweat and toiled, from falling a Prey to greedy Vultures, *Indians,* Priests, Friers, and hungry *Gallic* Slaves, or not-more-devouring Flames—to guard your Religion, the pure *Religion of Jesus,* streaming uncorrupted from the sacred Fountain of the Scriptures . . ., against Ignorance, Superstition, Idolatry, Tyranny over Conscience, Massacre, Fire and Sword, and all the Mischiefs, beyond Expression, with which Popery is pregnant—to keep from the cruel Hands of Barbarians and Papists, your Wives, your Children, your Parents, your Friends—to secure the Liberties conveyed to you by your brave Fore-Fathers, and bought with their Blood, that you may transmit them uncurtailed to your Posterity. . . .

If You believe that God governs the World, if You do not abjure him from being the Ruler of Your Country, You must acknowledge that all the Calamities of War, and the threatening Appearances of Famine, are ordered by his Providence; *There is no Evil in a City or Country, but the Lord hath done it.* And if You believe that he is a just and Righteous Ruler, You must also believe, that he would not thus punish a righteous or a penitent People. We and our Countrymen are Sinners, aggravated Sinners: God proclaims that we are such by his Judgments now upon us, by withering Fields and scanty Harvests, by the Sound of the Trumpet and the Alarm of War. . . . O my Country, is *not thy Wickedness great, and thine Iniquities infinite?* Where is there a more sinful Spot to be found upon our guilty Globe? Pass over the Land, take a Survey of the Inhabitants, inspect into their Conduct, and what do you see? what do you hear? You see gigantic Forms of Vice braving the Skies, and bidding Defiance to Heaven and Earth, while Religion and Virtue is obliged to retire, to avoid public Contempt and Insult— You see Herds of Drunkards swilling down their Cups, and drowning all *the Man* within them. You hear the Swearer venting his Fury against God and Man, trifling with than Name which prostrate

Angels adore, and imprecating that Damnation, under which the hardiest Devil in Hell trembles and groans. You see Avarice hoarding up her useless Treasures, dishonest Craft planning her Schemes of unlawful Gain, and Oppression unmercifully grinding the Face of the Poor. You see Prodigality squandering her Stores, Luxury spreading her Table, and unmanning her Guests; Vanity laughing aloud, and dissolving in empty, unthinking Mirth, regardless of God and our Country, of Time and Eternity; Sensuality wallowing in brutal Pleasures, and aspiring with inverted Ambition, to sink as low as her four-footed Brethren of the Stall. . . . . You see Thousands of poor Slaves in a Christian Country, the Property of Christian Masters, and they will be called, almost as ignorant of Christianity, as when they left the Wilds of *Africa*. . . . . You see Crowds of professed Believers, that are practical Athiests; nominal Christians, that are real Heathens. . . .

My first and leading Advice to you is, Labour to conduct this Expedition in a Religious Manner. Methinks this should not seem strange Counsel to Creatures, entirely dependent upon God, and at his Disposal. As you are an Independent Company of Volunteers under Officers of your own chusing, you may manage your Affairs more according to your own Inclinations, than if you had enlisted upon the ordinary Footing. . . . You are engaged in a good Cause, the Cause of your People, and the Cities of your God; and therefore you may the more boldly commit it to him, and pray and hope for his Blessing.

And now, my dear Friends, and the Friends of you neglected Country, *In the Name of the Lord lift up your Banners: Be of good Courage, and play the Men for the People and the Cities of your God; and the Lord do what seemeth him good.* . . . May the Lord of Hosts, the God of the Armies of *Israel,* go forth along with you! *May he teach your Hands to War, and gird you with Strength to Battle!* May he bless you with a safe Return, and long Life, or a glorious Death in the Bed of Honour, and a happy Immortality! May he guard and support your anxious Families and Friends at home, and return you victorious to their longing Arms! May all the Blessings your Hearts can wish attend you wherever you go!

PATRICK HENRY, "GIVE ME LIBERTY OR GIVE ME DEATH" (1775)

By the 1770s, prominent colonists were concluding that fulfilling America's destiny required that it separate itself from the mother country. Here Patrick Henry (1736–1799), a member of the Virginia House of Burgesses, defines the issue as a choice between "freedom or slavery." Himself a slaveholder and an ardent exponent of liberty, Henry sees no contradiction between the two.

No man thinks more highly than I do of the patriotism, as well as abilities, of the very worthy gentlemen who have just addressed the House. But different men often see the same subject in different lights; and, therefore, I hope it will not be thought disrespectful to those gentlemen if, entertaining as I do opinions of a character very opposite to theirs, I shall speak forth my sentiments freely and without reserve. This is no time for ceremony. The question before the House is one of awful moment to this country. For my own part, I consider it as nothing less than a question of freedom or slavery; and in proportion to the magnitude of the subject ought to be the freedom of the debate. It is only in this way that we can hope to arrive at truth, and fulfill the great responsibility which we hold to God and our country. Should I keep back my opinions at such a time, through fear of giving offense, I should consider myself as guilty of treason towards my country, and of an act of disloyalty toward the Majesty of Heaven, which I revere above all earthly kings.

Mr. President, it is natural to man to indulge in the illusions of hope. We are apt to shut our eyes against a painful truth, and listen to the song of that siren till she transforms us into beasts. Is this the part of wise men, engaged in a great and arduous struggle for liberty? Are we disposed to be of the number of those who, having eyes, see not, and, having ears, hear not, the things which so nearly concern their temporal salvation? For my part, whatever anguish of spirit it may cost, I am willing to know the whole truth; to know the worst, and to provide for it.

I have but one lamp by which my feet are guided, and that is the lamp of experience. I know of no way of judging of the future but by the past. And judging by the past, I wish to know what there has been in the conduct of the British ministry for the last ten years to justify those hopes with which gentlemen have been pleased to solace themselves and the House. Is it that insidious smile with which our petition has been lately received? Trust it not, sir; it will prove a snare to your feet. Suffer not yourselves to be betrayed with a kiss. Ask yourselves how this gracious reception of our petition comports with those warlike preparations which cover our waters and darken our land. Are fleets and armies necessary to a work of love and reconciliation? Have we shown ourselves so unwilling to be reconciled that force must be called in to win back our love? Let us not deceive ourselves, sir. These are the implements of war and subjugation; the last arguments to which kings resort. I ask gentlemen, sir, what means this martial array, if its purpose be not to force us to submission? Can gentlemen assign any other possible motive for it? Has Great Britain any enemy, in this quarter of the world, to call for all this accumulation of navies and armies? No, sir, she has none. They are meant for us: they can be meant for no other. They are sent over to bind and rivet upon us those chains which the British ministry have been so long forging. And what have we to oppose to them? Shall we try argument? Sir, we have been trying that for the last ten years. Have we anything new to offer upon the subject? Nothing. We have held the subject up in every light of which it is capable; but it has been all in vain. Shall we resort to entreaty and humble supplication? What terms shall we find which have not been already exhausted? Let us not, I beseech you, sir, deceive ourselves. Sir, we have done everything that could be done to avert the storm which is now coming on. We have petitioned; we have remonstrated; we have supplicated; we have prostrated ourselves before the throne, and have implored its interposition to arrest the tyrannical hands of the ministry and Parliament. Our petitions have been slighted; our remonstrances have produced additional violence and insult; our supplications have been disregarded; and we have been spurned, with contempt, from the foot of the throne! In vain, after these things, may we indulge the fond hope of peace and reconciliation. There is no longer any room for hope. If we wish to be free—if we mean to preserve inviolate those inestimable privileges for which we have been so long contending—if we mean not basely to abandon the noble struggle in which we have been so long engaged, and which we have pledged ourselves never to abandon until the glorious object of our contest shall be obtained—we must fight! I repeat it, sir, we must fight! An appeal to arms and to the God of hosts is all that is left us!

They tell us, sir, that we are weak; unable to cope with so formidable an adversary. But when shall we be stronger? Will it be the next week, or the next year? Will it be when we are totally disarmed, and when a British guard shall be stationed in every house? Shall we gather strength by irresolution and inaction? Shall we acquire the means of effectual resistance by lying supinely on our backs and hugging the delusive phantom of hope, until our enemies shall have bound us hand and foot? Sir, we are not weak if we make a proper use of those means which the God of nature hath placed in our power. The millions of people, armed in the holy cause of liberty, and in such a country as that which we possess, are invincible by any force which our enemy can send against us. Besides, sir, we shall not fight our battles alone. There is a just God who presides over the destinies of nations, and who will raise up friends to fight our battles for us. The battle, sir, is not to the strong alone; it is to the vigilant, the active, the brave. Besides, sir, we have no election. If we were base enough to desire it, it is now too late to retire from the contest. There is no retreat but in submission and slavery! Our chains are forged! Their clanking may be heard on the plains of Boston! The war is inevitable—and let it come! I repeat it, sir, let it come.

It is in vain, sir, to extenuate the matter. Gentlemen may cry, Peace, Peace— but there is no peace. The war is actually begun! The next gale that sweeps from the north will bring to our ears the clash of resounding arms! Our brethren are already in the field! Why stand we here idle? What is it that gentlemen wish? What would they have? Is life so dear, or peace so sweet, as to be purchased at the price of chains and slavery? Forbid it, Almighty God! I know not what course others may take; but as for me, give me liberty or give me death!

Tom Paine, "Common Sense" (1776)

"Common Sense," written by the radical pamphleteer Tom Paine (1737–1809), swept through the American colonies when it appeared in January 1776. America, Paine insists, is called upon to "begin the world over again." Accomplishing that providentially assigned mission requires revolution.

IN the following pages I offer nothing more than simple facts, plain arguments, and common sense: and have no other preliminaries to settle with the reader, than that he will divest himself of prejudice and prepossession, and suffer his reason and his feelings to determine for themselves that he will put on, or rather that he will not put off, the true character of a man, and generously enlarge his views beyond the present day.

Volumes have been written on the subject of the struggle between England and America. Men of all ranks have embarked in the controversy, from different motives, and with various designs; but all have been ineffectual, and the period of debate is closed. Arms as the last resource decide the contest; the appeal was the choice of the King, and the Continent has accepted the challenge. . . .

The Sun never shined on a cause of greater worth. 'Tis not the affair of a City, a County, a Province, or a Kingdom; but of a Continent—of at least one-eighth part of the habitable Globe. 'Tis not the concern of a day, a year, or an age; posterity are virtually involved in the contest, and will be more or less affected even to the end of time, by the proceedings now. Now is the seed-time of Continental union, faith and honour. The least fracture now will be like a name engraved with the point of a pin on the tender rind of a young oak; the wound would enlarge with the tree, and posterity read in it full grown characters.

By referring the matter from argument to arms, a new era for politics is struck—a new method of thinking hath arisen. All plans, proposals, &c. prior to the nineteenth of April, i.e. to the commencement of hostilities, are like the almanacks of the last year; which tho' proper then, are superseded and useless now. Whatever was advanced by the advocates on either side of the question then, terminated in one and the same point, viz. a union with Great Britain; the only difference between the parties was the method of effecting it; the one proposing force, the other friendship; but it hath so far happened that the first hath failed, and the second hath withdrawn her influence.

As much hath been said of the advantages of reconciliation, which, like an agreeable dream, hath passed away and left us as we were, it is but right that we should examine the contrary side of the argument, and enquire into some of the many material injuries which these Colonies sustain, and always will sustain, by being connected with and dependent on Great Britain. To examine that connection and dependence, on the principles of nature and common sense, to see what we have to trust to, if separated, and what we are to expect, if dependent.

I have heard it asserted by some, that as America has flourished under her former connection with Great Britain, the same connection is necessary towards her future happiness, and will always have the same effect. Nothing can be more fallacious than this kind of argument. We may as well assert that because a child has thrived upon milk, that it is never to have meat, or that the first twenty years of our lives is to become a precedent for the next twenty. But even this is admitting more than is true; for I answer roundly that America would have flourished as much, and probably much more, had no European power taken any notice of her. The commerce by which she hath enriched herself are the necessaries of life, and will always have a market while eating is the custom of Europe.

But she has protected us, say some. That she hath engrossed us is true, and defended the Continent at our expense as well as her own, is admitted; and she would have defended Turkey from the same motive, viz.—for the sake of trade and dominion.

Alas! we have been long led away by ancient prejudices and made large sacrifices to superstition. We have boasted the protection of Great Britain, without considering, that her motive was INTEREST not ATTACHMENT; and that she did not protect us from OUR ENEMIES on OUR ACCOUNT; but from HER ENEMIES on HER OWN ACCOUNT, from those who had no quarrel with us on any OTHER ACCOUNT, and who will always be our enemies on the SAME ACCOUNT. Let Britain waive her pretensions to the Continent, or the Continent throw off the dependence, and we should be at peace with France and Spain, were they at war with Britain. . . .

It hath lately been asserted in parliament, that the Colonies have no relation to each other but through the Parent Country, i.e. that Pennsylvania and the Jerseys and so on for the rest, are sister Colonies by the way of England; this is certainly a very roundabout way of proving relationship, but it is the nearest and only true way of proving enmity (or enemyship, if I may so call it.) France and Spain never were, nor perhaps ever will be, our enemies as AMERICANS, but as our being the SUBJECTS OF GREAT BRITAIN.

But Britain is the parent country, say some. Then the more shame upon her conduct. Even brutes do not devour their young, nor savages make war upon their families. Wherefore, the assertion, if true, turns to her reproach; but it happens not to be true, or only partly so, and the phrase PARENT OR MOTHER COUNTRY hath been jesuitically adopted by the King and his parasites, with a low papistical design of gaining an unfair bias on the credulous weakness of our minds. Europe, and not England, is the parent country of America. This new World hath been the asylum for the persecuted lovers of civil and religious liberty from EVERY PART of Europe. Hither have they fled, not from the tender embraces of the mother, but from the cruelty of the monster; and it is so far true of England, that the same tyranny which drove the first emigrants from home, pursues their descendants still.

In this extensive quarter of the globe, we forget the narrow limits of three hundred and sixty miles (the extent of England) and carry our friendship on a larger scale; we claim brotherhood with every European Christian, and triumph in the generosity of the sentiment. . . .

But, admitting that we were all of English descent, what does it amount to? Nothing. Britain, being now an open enemy, extinguishes every other name and title: and to say that reconciliation is our duty, is truly farcical. The first king of England, of the present line (William the Conqueror) was a Frenchman, and half the peers of England are descendants from the same country; wherefore, by the same method of reasoning, England ought to be governed by France.

Much hath been said of the united strength of Britain and the Colonies, that in conjunction they might bid defiance to the world. But this is mere presumption; the fate of war is uncertain, neither do the expressions mean anything; for this continent would never suffer itself to be drained of inhabitants, to support the British arms in either Asia, Africa, or Europe.

Besides, what have we to do with setting the world at defiance? Our plan is commerce, and that, well attended to, will secure us the peace and friendship of all Europe; because it is the interest of all Europe to have America a free port. Her trade will always be a protection, and her barrenness of gold and silver secure her from invaders.

I challenge the warmest advocate for reconciliation to show a single advantage that this continent can reap by being connected with Great Britain. I repeat the challenge; not a single advantage is derived. Our corn will fetch its price in any market in Europe, and our imported goods must be paid for buy them where we will.

But the injuries and disadvantages which we sustain by that connection, are without number; and our duty to mankind at large, as well as to ourselves, instruct us to renounce the alliance: because, any submission to, or dependence on, Great Britain, tends directly to involve this Continent in European wars and quarrels, and set us at variance with nations who would otherwise seek our friendship, and against whom we have neither anger nor complaint. As Europe is

our market for trade, we ought to form no partial connection with any part of it. It is the true interest of America to steer clear of European contentions, which she never can do, while, by her dependence on Britain, she is made the makeweight in the scale of British politics.

Europe is too thickly planted with Kingdoms to be long at peace, and whenever a war breaks out between England and any foreign power, the trade of America goes to ruin, BECAUSE OF HER CONNECTION WITH BRITAIN. The next war may not turn out like the last, and should it not, the advocates for reconciliation now will be wishing for separation then, because neutrality in that case would be a safer convoy than a man of war. Every thing that is right or reasonable pleads for separation. The blood of the slain, the weeping voice of nature cries, 'TIS TIME TO PART. Even the distance at which the Almighty hath placed England and America is a strong and natural proof that the authority of the one over the other, was never the design of Heaven. The time likewise at which the Continent was discovered, adds weight to the argument, and the manner in which it was peopled, encreases the force of it. The Reformation was preceded by the discovery of America: As if the Almighty graciously meant to open a sanctuary to the persecuted in future years, when home should afford neither friendship nor safety.

The authority of Great Britain over this continent, is a form of government, which sooner or later must have an end: And a serious mind can draw no true pleasure by looking forward, under the painful and positive conviction that what he calls "the present constitution" is merely temporary. As parents, we can have no joy, knowing that this government is not sufficiently lasting to ensure any thing which we may bequeath to posterity: And by a plain method of argument, as we are running the next generation into debt, we ought to do the work of it, otherwise we use them meanly and pitifully. In order to discover the line of our duty rightly, we should take our children in our hand, and fix our station a few years farther into life; that eminence will present a prospect which a few present fears and prejudices conceal from our sight.

Though I would carefully avoid giving unnecessary offence, yet I am inclined to believe, that all those who espouse the doctrine of reconciliation, may be included within the following descriptions. Interested men, who are not to be trusted, weak men who CANNOT see, prejudiced men who will not see, and a certain set of moderate men who think better of the European world than it deserves; and this last class, by an ill-judged deliberation, will be the cause of more calamities to this Continent than all the other three. . . .

Men of passive tempers look somewhat lightly over the offences of Great Britain, and, still hoping for the best, are apt to call out, "Come, come, we shall be friends again for all this." But examine the passions and feelings of mankind: bring the doctrine of reconciliation to the touchstone of nature, and then tell me whether you can hereafter love, honour, and faithfully serve the power that hath carried fire and sword into your land? If you cannot do all these, then are you only deceiving yourselves, and by your delay bringing ruin upon posterity. . . .

This is not inflaming or exaggerating matters, but trying them by those feelings and affections which nature justifies, and without which, we should be incapable of discharging the social duties of life, or enjoying the felicities of it. I mean not to exhibit horror for the purpose of provoking revenge, but to awaken us from fatal and unmanly slumbers, that we may pursue determinately some fixed object. It is not in the power of Britain or of Europe to conquer America, if she do not conquer herself by *delay* and *timidity*. . . .

It is repugnant to reason, to the universal order of things to all examples from former ages, to suppose, that this continent can longer remain subject to any external power. The most sanguine in Britain does not think so. The utmost stretch of human wisdom cannot, at this time, compass a plan short of separation, which can promise the continent even a year's security. Reconciliation is *now* a falacious dream. Nature hath deserted the connexion, and Art cannot supply her place. For, as Milton wisely expresses, "never can true reconcilement grow where wounds of deadly hate have pierced so deep."

Every quiet method for peace hath been ineffectual. Our prayers have been rejected with disdain; and only tended to convince us, that nothing flatters vanity, or confirms obstinacy in Kings more than repeated petitioning—and nothing hath contributed more than that very measure to make the Kings of Europe absolute. . . .

Small islands not capable of protecting themselves, are the proper objects for kingdoms to take under their care; but there is something very absurd, in supposing a continent to be perpetually governed by an island. In no instance hath nature made the satellite larger than its primary planet, and as England and America, with respect to each other, reverses the common order of nature, it is evident they belong to different systems: England to Europe, America to itself.

I am not induced by motives of pride, party, or resentment to espouse the doctrine of separation and independence; I am clearly, positively, and conscientiously persuaded that it is the true interest of this continent to be so; that every thing short of *that* is mere patchwork, that it can afford no lasting felicity,—that it is leaving the sword to our children, and shrinking back at a time, when, a little more, a little farther, would have rendered this continent the glory of the earth. . . .

But the most powerful of all arguments, is, that nothing but independence, i.e. a continental form of government, can keep the peace of the continent and preserve it inviolate from civil wars. I dread the event of a reconciliation with Britain now, as it is more than probable, that it will be followed by a revolt somewhere or other, the consequences of which may be far more fatal than all the malice of Britain.

Thousands are already ruined by British barbarity; (thousands more will probably suffer the same fate.) Those men have other feelings than us who have nothing suffered. All they *now* possess is liberty, what they before enjoyed is sacrificed to its service, and having nothing more to lose, they disdain submission. . . .

But where says some is the King of America? I'll tell you Friend, he reigns above, and doth not make havoc of mankind like the Royal Brute of Britain. Yet that we may not appear to be defective even in earthly honors, let a day be solemnly set apart for proclaiming the charter; let it be brought forth placed on the divine law, the word of God; let a crown be placed thereon, by which the world may know, that so far as we approve as monarchy, that in America THE LAW IS KING. For as in absolute governments the King is law, so in free countries the law *ought* to be King; and there ought to be no other. . . .

A government of our own is our natural right: And when a man seriously reflects on the precariousness of human affairs, he will become convinced, that it is infinitely wiser and safer, to form a constitution of our own in a cool deliberate manner, while we have it in our power, than to trust such an interesting event to time and chance. . . .

Ye that oppose independence now, ye know not what ye do; ye are opening a door to eternal tyranny, by keeping vacant the seat of government. There are thousands, and tens of thousands, who would think it glorious to expel from the continent, that barbarous and hellish power, which hath stirred up the Indians and Negroes to destroy us, the cruelty hath a double guilt, it is dealing brutally by us, and treacherously by them.

To talk of friendship with those in whom our reason forbids us to have faith, and our affections wounded through a thousand pores instruct us to detest, is madness and folly. Every day wears out the little remains of kindred between us and them, and can there be any reason to hope, that as the relationship expires, the affection will increase, or that we shall agree better, when we have ten times more and greater concerns to quarrel over than ever?

Ye that tell us of harmony and reconciliation, can ye restore to us the time that is past? Can ye give to prostitution its former innocence? Neither can ye reconcile Britain and America. The last cord now is broken, the people of England are presenting addresses against us. There are injuries which nature cannot forgive; she would cease to be nature if she did. As well can the lover forgive the ravisher of his mistress, as the continent forgive the murders of Britain. The Almighty hath implanted in us these unextinguishable feelings for good and wise purposes. They are the guardians of his image in our hearts. They distinguish us from the herd of common animals. The social compact would dissolve, and justice be extirpated from the earth, or have only a casual existence were we callous to the touches of affection. The robber, and the murderer, would often escape unpunished, did not the injuries which our tempers sustain, provoke us into justice.

O ye that love mankind! Ye that dare oppose, not only the tyranny, but the tyrant, stand forth! Every spot of the old world is overrun with oppression. Freedom hath been hunted round the globe. Asia, and Africa, have long expelled her.—Europe regards her like a stranger, and England hath given her warning to depart. O! receive the fugitive, and prepare in time an asylum for mankind. . . .

We ought to reflect, that there are three different ways by which an independency may hereafter be effected, and that one of those three, will, one day or other, be the fate of America, viz. By the legal voice of the people in Congress; by a military power, or by a mob: It may not always happen that our soldiers are citizens, and the multitude a body of reasonable men; virtue, as I have already remarked, is not hereditary, neither is it perpetual. Should an independency be brought about by the first of those means, we have every opportunity and every encouragement before us, to form the noblest, purest constitution on the face of the earth. We have it in our power to begin the world over again. A situation, similar to the present, hath not happened since the days of Noah until now.

The birthday of a new world is at hand, and a race of men, perhaps as numerous as all Europe contains, are to receive their portion of freedom from the events of a few months. The reflection is awful, and in this point of view, how trifling, how ridiculous, do the little paltry cavilings of a few weak or interested men appear, when weighed against the business of a world.

EZRA STILES, "THE UNITED STATES ELEVATED TO GLORY AND HONOR" (1783)

Ezra Stiles (1727–1795) was serving as the seventh president of Yale College when he made this presentation to the Connecticut legislature. With American independence now won, Stiles offers assurances that the newly created republic is destined to serve as a divine instrument, "illuminating the world with truth and liberty."

Taught by the omniscient Deity, Moses foresaw and predicted the capital events relative to Israel, through the successive changes of depression and glory, until their final elevation to the first dignity and eminence among the empires of the world. . . .

However it may be doubted whether political communities are rewarded and punished in this world only, and whether the prosperity and decline of other empires have corresponded with their moral state as to virtue and vice, yet the history of the Hebrew theocracy shows that the secular welfare of God's ancient people depended upon their virtue, their religion, their observance of that holy covenant which Israel entered into with God on the plains at the foot of Nebo, on the other side Jordan. Here Moses, the man of God, assembled three million of people—the number of the United States—recapitulated and gave them a second publication of the sacred jural institute, delivered thirty-eight years before, with the most awful solemnity, at Mount Sinai. A law dictated with sovereign authority by the Most High to a people, to a world, a universe, becomes of invincible force and obligation without any reference to the consent of the governed. . . . Thereupon this great prophet, whom God had raised up for so solemn a transaction, declared in the name of the Lord that the Most High avouched, acknowledged, and took them for a peculiar people to Himself; promising to be their God and Protector, and upon their obedience to make them prosperous and happy. He foresaw, indeed, their rejection of God, and predicted the judicial chastisement of apostasy—a chastisement involving the righteous with the wicked. But, as well to comfort and support the righteous in every age, and under every calamity, as to make his power known among all nations, God determined that a remnant should be saved. . . . and become a very distinguished and glorious people, under the great Messiah, the Prince of Peace. He will then "make them high above all nations which he hath made, in praise, and in name, and in honor, and they shall become a holy people unto the Lord their God."

I shall enlarge no further upon the primary sense and literal accomplishment of this and numerous other prophecies respecting of both Jews and Gentiles in the latter-day glory of the church; for I have assumed the text only as introductory to a discourse upon the political welfare of God's American Israel, and as allusively

prophetic of the future prosperity and splendor of the United States. . . .

It gives me pleasure to find that public liberty is effectually secured in each and all the policies of the United States, though somewhat differently modeled. Not only the polity, or exterior system of government, but the laws and interior regulations of each state, are already excellent, surpassing the institutions of Lycurgus or Plato; and by the annual appeals to the public a power is reserved to the people to remedy any corruptions or errors in government. And even if the people should sometimes err, yet each assembly of the states, and the body of the people, always embosom wisdom sufficient to correct themselves; so that a political mischief cannot be durable. Herein we far surpass any states on earth. We can correct ourselves, if in the wrong. . . .

Besides a happy policy as to civil government, it is necessary to institute a system of law and jurisprudence founded in justice, equity, and public right. The American codes of law, and the *lex non scripta*, the *senatus consulta*, and the common law, are already advanced to great perfection—far less complicated and perplexed than the jural systems of Europe. . . .

Our trade opens to all the world. We shall doubtless at first overtrade ourselves everywhere, and be in danger of incurring heavy mortgages, unless prevented. The nations will not at first know how far they may safely trade with us. But commerce will find out its own system, and regulate itself in time. It will be governed on the part of America by the cheapest foreign markets; on the part of Europe, by our ability and punctuality of remittance. We can soon make a remittance of three or four million a year, in a circuitous trade, exclusive of the iniquitous African trade.

If Europe should indulge us beyond this, our failures and disappointments might lay the foundation of national animosities. Great wisdom is therefore necessary to regulate the commerce of America. The caution with which we are to be treated may occasion and originate a commercial system among the maritime nations on both sides of the Atlantic, founded in justice and reciprocity of interest, which will establish the benevolence as well as the opulence of nations, and advance the progress of society to civil perfection.

It is certainly for the benefit of every community that it be transfused with the efficacious motives of universal industry. This will take place if everyone can enjoy the fruits of his labor and activity unmolested. All the variety of labor in a well-regulated state will be so ordered and encouraged as that all will be employed, in a just proportion, in agriculture, mechanic arts, commerce, and the literary professions. It has been a question whether agriculture or commerce needs most encouragement in these states. But the motives for both seem abundantly sufficient. Never did they operate more strongly than at present. . . .

I have thus shown wherein consists the true political welfare of a civil community or sovereignty. The foundation is laid . . . in a good system of polity and jurisprudence, on which will arise, under a truly patriotic, upright, and firm administration, the beautiful superstructure of a well-governed and prosperous empire.

Already does the new constellation of the United States begin to realize this glory. It has already risen to an acknowledged sovereignty among the republics and kingdoms of the world. And we have reason to hope, and, I believe, to expect, that God has still greater blessings in store for this vine which His own right hand has planted, to make us high among the nations in praise, and in name, and in honor. The reasons are very numerous, weighty, and conclusive.

In our civil constitutions, those impediments are removed which obstruct the progress of society toward perfection, such, for instance, as respect the tenure of estates, and arbitrary government. . . .

Liberty, civil and religious, has sweet and attractive charms. The enjoyment of this, with property, has filled the English settlers in America with a most amazing spirit, which has operated, and still will operate, with great energy. Never before has the experiment been so effectually tried of every man's reaping the fruits of his labor and feeling his share in the aggregate system of power. The ancient republics did not stand on the people at large, and therefore no example or precedent can be taken from them. Even men of arbitrary principles will be obliged, if they would figure in these states, to assume the patriot so long that they will at length become charmed with the sweets of liberty.

Our degree of population is such as to give us reason to expect that this will become a great people. It is probable that within a century from our independence the sun will shine on fifty millions of inhabitants in the United States. This will be a great, a very great nation, nearly equal to half Europe. Already has our colonization extended down the Ohio, and to Koskaseah on the Mississippi. And if the present ratio of increase should be rather diminished in some of the other settlements, yet an accelerated multiplication will attend our general propagation, and overspread the whole territory westward for ages. So that before the millennium the English settlements in America may become more numerous millions than that greatest dominion on earth, the Chinese Empire. Should this prove a future fact, how applicable would be the text, when the Lord shall have made His American Israel high above all nations which He has made, in numbers, and in praise, and in name, and in honor!

I am sensible some will consider these as visionary, utopian ideas; and so they would have judged had they lived in the apostolic age, and been told that by the time of Constantine, the Empire would have become Christian. As visionary that the twenty thousand souls which first settled New England should be multiplied to near a million in a century and a half. . . . . As utopian would it have been to the loyalists, at the battle of Lexington, that in less than eight years the independence and sovereignty of the United States should be acknowledged by four European sovereignties, one of which should be Britain herself. How wonderful the revolutions, the events of Providence! We live in an age of wonders; we have lived an age in a few years; we have seen more wonders accomplished in eight years than are usually unfolded in a century.

God be thanked, we have lived to see peace restored to this bleeding land, at least a general cessation of hostilities among the belligerent powers. And on this occasion does it not become us to reflect how wonderful, how gracious, how glorious has been the good hand of our God upon us, in carrying us through so tremendous a warfare! We have sustained a force brought against us which might have made any empire on earth to tremble; and yet our bow has abode in strength, and, having obtained help of God, we continue unto this day. Forced unto the last solemn appeal, America watched for the first blood; this was shed by Britons on the nineteenth of April, 1775, which instantly sprung an army of twenty thousand into spontaneous existence, with the enterprising and daring, if imprudent, resolution of entering Boston and forcibly disburdening it of its bloody legions. Every patriot trembled till we had proved our armor, till it could be seen whether this hasty concourse was susceptible of exercitual arrangement, and could face the enemy with firmness. They early gave us the decided proof of this in the memorable battle of Bunker Hill. We were satisfied. This instantly convinced us, and for the first time convinced Britons themselves, that Americans both would and could fight with great effect. Whereupon Congress put at the head of this spirited army the only man on whom the eyes of all Israel were placed. Posterity, I apprehend, and the world itself, inconsiderate and incredulous as they may be of the dominion of Heaven, will yet do so much justice to the divine moral government as to acknowledge that this American Joshua was raised up by God, and divinely formed, by a peculiar influence of the Sovereign of the universe, for the great work of leading the armies of this American Joseph (now separated from his brethren), and conducting this people through the severe, the arduous conflict, to liberty and independence. Surprising was it with what instant celerity men ascended and rose into generals, and officers of every subordination, formed chiefly by the preparatory discipline of only the preceding year 1774, when the ardor and spirit of military discipline was by Heaven, and without concert, sent through the continent like lightning. Surprising was it how soon the army was organized, took its formation, and rose into firm system and impregnable arrangement.

To think of withstanding and encountering Britain by land was bold, and much more bold and daring by sea; yet we immediately began a navy, and built ships of war with an unexampled

expedition. . . . . Soon had we got, though small, a very gallant initial navy, which fought gallantly, and wanted nothing but numbers of ships for successful operations against that superior naval force before which we fell. We have, however, exhibited proof to posterity and the world that a powerful navy may be originated, built, and equipped for service in a much shorter period than was before imagined. . . .

What but a miracle has preserved the union of the States, the purity of Congress, and the unshaken patriotism of every General Assembly? It is God, who has raised up for us a great and powerful ally—an ally which sent us a chosen army and a naval force. . . . It is God who so ordered the balancing interests of nations as to produce an irresistible motive in the European maritime powers to take our part. . . .

But the time would fail me to recount the wonder-working providence of God in the events of this war. Let these serve as a specimen, and lead us to hope that God will not forsake this people for whom He has done such marvelous things— whereof we are glad, and rejoice this day—having at length brought us to the dawn of peace. O Peace, thou welcome guest, all hail! Thou heavenly visitant, calm the tumult of nations, and wave thy balmy wing to perpetuity over this region of liberty! Let there be a tranquil period for the unmolested accomplishment of the *Magnalia Dei*—the great events in God's moral government designed from eternal ages to be displayed in these ends of the earth.

And here I beg leave to congratulate my country upon the termination of this cruel and unnatural war, the cessation of hostilities, and the prospect of peace. May this great event excite and elevate our first, our highest acknowledgments to the Sovereign Monarch of universal nature, to the Supreme Disposer and Controller of all events! Let this, our pious, sincere, and devout gratitude, ascend in one general effusion of heartfelt praise and hallelujah, in one united cloud of incense, even the incense of universal joy and thanksgiving, to God, from the collective body of the United States.

And while we render our supreme honors to the Most High, the God of armies, let us recollect with affectionate honor the bold and brave sons of freedom who willingly offered themselves and bled in the defense of their country. Our fellow citizens, the officers and soldiers of the patriot army, who, with . . . other gallant commanders and brave seamen of the American navy, have heroically fought the war by sea and by land, merit of their once bleeding but now triumphant country laurels, crowns, rewards, and the highest honors. Never was the profession of arms used with more glory, or in a better cause. . . .

Great and extensive will be the happy effects of this warfare, in which we have been called in Providence to fight out not the liberties of America only, but the liberties of the world itself. The spirited and successful stand which we have made against tyranny will prove the salvation of England and Ireland, and, by teaching all sovereigns the danger of irritating and trifling with the affections and loyalty of their subjects, introduce clemency, moderation, and justice into public government at large through Europe. . . .

We shall have a communication with all nations in commerce, manners, and science, beyond anything heretofore known in the world. Manufacturers and artisans, and men of every description, may perhaps come and settle among us. They will be few indeed in comparison with the annual thousands of our natural increase, and will be incorporated with the prevailing hereditary complexion of the first settlers—we shall not be assimilated to them, but they to us, especially in the second and third generations. This fermentation and communion of nations will doubtless produce something very new, singular, and glorious. . . . . So all the arts may be transplanted from Europe and Asia, and flourish in America with an augmented luster. . . .

The rough, sonorous diction of the English language may here take its Athenian polish, and receive its attic urbanity, as it will probably become the vernacular tongue of more numerous millions than ever yet spoke one language on earth. It may continue for ages to be the prevailing and general language of North America. The intercommunion of the United States with all the world in travels, trade, and politics, and the infusion of letters into our infancy, will probably preserve us from the provincial dialects, risen into inexterminable habit before the

invention of printing. . . . Different from these, the English language will grow up with the present American population into great purity and elegance, unmutilated by the foreign dialects of foreign conquests. . . .

The great American Revolution, this recent political phenomenon of a new sovereignty arising among the sovereign powers of the earth, will be attended to and contemplated by all nations. Navigation will carry the American flag around the globe itself, and display the thirteen stripes and new constellation at Bengal and Canton, on the Indus and Ganges, on the Whang-ho and the Yang-tse-kiang, and with commerce will import the wisdom and literature of the East. That prophecy of Daniel is now literally fulfilling—there shall be a universal traveling to and fro, and knowledge shall be increased. This knowledge will be brought home and treasured up in America, and, being here digested and carried to the highest perfection, may reblaze back from America to Europe, Asia, and Africa, and illumine the world with truth and liberty. . . .

The most ample religious liberty will also probably obtain among all nations. Benevolence and religious lenity are increasing among the nations. . . . An emulation for liberty and science is enkindled among the nations, and will doubtless produce something very liberal and glorious in this age of science, this period of the empire of reason. . . .

Little would civilians have thought ages ago that the world should ever look to America for models of government and polity; little did they think of finding this most perfect polity among the poor outcasts, the contemptible people of New England, and particularly in the long despised civil polity of Connecticut. . . . And while Europe and Asia may hereafter learn that the most liberal principles of law and civil polity are to be found on this side the Atlantic, they may also find the true religion here depurated from the rust and corruption of ages, and learn from us to reform and restore the church to its primitive purity. It will be long before the ecclesiastical pride of the splendid European hierarchies can submit to learn wisdom from those whom they have been inured to look upon with

sovereign contempt. But candid and liberal disquisition will, sooner or later, have a great effect.
Removed from the embarrassments of corrupt
systems, and the dignities and blinding opulence
connected with them, the unfettered mind can
think with a noble enlargement, and, with an
unbounded freedom, go wherever the light of
truth directs. Here will be no bloody tribunals,
no cardinal's inquisitors-general, to bend the
human mind, forcibly to control the understanding, and put out the light of reason, the
candle of the Lord, in man—to force an innocent Galileo to renounce truths demonstrable
as the light of day. Religion may here receive
its last, most liberal, and impartial examination.
Religious liberty is peculiarly friendly to fair
and generous disquisition. . . .

There are three coetaneous events to take place,
whose futurition is certain from prophecy—the
annihilation of the pontificate, the reassembling
of the Jews, and the fulness of the Gentiles. That
liberal and candid disquisition of Christianity
which will most assuredly take place in America,
will prepare Europe for the first event, with which
the other will be connected, when, especially on
the return of the Twelve Tribes to the Holy Land,
there will burst forth a degree of evidence hitherto unperceived, and of efficacy to convert a
world. More than three quarters of mankind yet
remain heathen. Heaven put a stop to the propagation of Christianity when the church became
corrupted with the adoration of numerous dei-
ties and images, because this would have been
only exchanging an old for a new idolatry. Nor
is Christendom now larger than it was nine centuries ago. . . . . It may have been of the Lord
that Christianity is to be found in such greater
purity in this church exiled into the wildernesses
of America, and that its purest body should be
evidently advancing forward, by an augmented
natural increase and spiritual edification, into a
singular superiority, with the ultimate subserviency to the glory of God in converting the world.

And when the set time to favor Zion shall
come in God's good and holy providence, while
Christendom may no longer disdain to adopt a
reformation from us, the then newly gospelized
heathen may light up their candle at America.
In this country, out of sight of mitres and the
purple, and removed from systems of corruption
confirmed for ages and supported by the spiritual janizaries of an ecclesiatical hierarchy, aided
and armed by the secular power, religion may
be examined with the noble Berean freedom,
the freedom of American-born minds. And rev-
elation, both as to the true evangelical doctrines
and church polity, may be settled here before they
shall have undergone a thorough discussion, and
been weighed with a calm and unprejudiced candor elsewhere. Great things are to be effected in
the world before the millennium, which I do not
expect to commence under seven or eight hundred years hence; and perhaps the liberal and candid disquisitions in America are to be rendered
extensively subservient to some of the most glorious designs of Providence, and particularly in
the propagation and diffusion of religion through
the earth, in filling the whole earth with the
knowledge of the glory of the Lord. A time will
come when six hundred millions of the human
race shall be ready to drop their idolatry and all
false religion, when Christianity shall triumph
over superstition, as well as Deism, and Gentilism,
and Mohammedanism. They will then search
all Christendom for the best model, the purest
exemplification of the Christian church, with the
fewest human mixtures. And when God in His
providence shall convert the world, should the
newly-Christianized nations assume our form of
religion, should American missionaries be blessed
to succeed in the work of Christianizing the
heathen—in which the Romanists and foreign
Protestants have very much failed—it would be
an unexpected wonder, and a great honor to the
United States. And thus the American Republic,
by illuminating the world with truth and liberty, would be exalted and made high among
the nations, in praise, and in name, and in honor.
I doubt not this is the honor reserved for us . . . .

How infinitely happier they who, believing the
record which God gives of His Son, have received
Him, and have become the sons of God! . . . But
I must desist, with only observing that the United
States are under peculiar obligations to become a
holy people unto the Lord our God, on account
of the late eminent deliverance, salvation, peace,
and glory with which he has now crowned our
new sovereignty.

PUBLIUS [ALEXANDER HAMILTON], "THE FEDERALIST NO. 11" (1787)

The Federalist Papers were essays written by Alexander Hamilton, John Jay, and James Madison to persuade residents of New York to ratify the Constitution. In "Federalist No. 11," Hamilton (1755–1804) provides his own vision of American greatness—a commercial republic mighty enough "to dictate the terms of the connection between the old and the new world!"

To the People of the State of New York:

THE importance of the Union, in a commercial light, is one of those points about which there is least room to entertain a difference of opinion, and which has, in fact, commanded the most general assent of men who have any acquaintance with the subject. This applies as well to our intercourse with foreign countries as with each other.

There are appearances to authorize a supposition that the adventurous spirit, which distinguishes the commercial character of America, has already excited uneasy sensations in several of the maritime powers of Europe. They seem to be apprehensive of our too great interference in that carrying trade, which is the support of their navigation and the foundation of their naval strength. Those of them which have colonies in America look forward to what this country is capable of becoming, with painful solicitude. They foresee the dangers that may threaten their American dominions from the neighborhood of States, which have all the dispositions, and would possess all the means, requisite to the creation of a powerful marine. Impressions of this kind will naturally indicate the policy of fostering divisions among us, and of depriving us, as far as possible, of an ACTIVE COMMERCE in our own bottoms. This would answer the threefold purpose of preventing our interference in their navigation, of monopolizing the profits of our trade, and of clipping the wings by which we might soar to a dangerous greatness. Did not prudence forbid the detail, it would not be difficult to trace, by facts, the workings of this policy to the cabinets of ministers.

If we continue united, we may counteract a policy so unfriendly to our prosperity in a variety of ways. By prohibitory regulations, extending, at the same time, throughout the States, we may oblige foreign countries to bid against each other, for the privileges of our markets. This assertion will not appear chimerical to those who are able to appreciate the importance of the markets of three millions of people—increasing in rapid progression, for the most part exclusively addicted to agriculture, and likely from local circumstances to remain so—to any manufacturing nation; and the immense difference there would be to the trade and navigation of such a nation, between a direct communication in its own ships, and an indirect conveyance of its products and returns, to and from America, in the ships of another country. Suppose, for instance, we had a government in America, capable of excluding Great Britain (with whom we have at present no treaty of commerce) from all our ports; what would be the probable operation of this step upon her politics? Would it not enable us to negotiate, with the fairest prospect of success, for commercial privileges of the most valuable and extensive kind, in the dominions of that kingdom? When these questions have been asked, upon other occasions, they have received a plausible, but not a solid or satisfactory answer. It has been said that prohibitions on our part would produce no change in the system of Britain, because she could prosecute her trade with us through the medium of the Dutch, who would be her immediate customers and paymasters for those articles which were wanted for the supply of our markets. But would not her navigation be materially injured by the loss of the important advantage of being her own carrier in that trade? Would not the principal part of its profits be intercepted by the Dutch, as a compensation for their agency and risk? Would not the mere circumstance of freight occasion a considerable deduction? Would not so circuitous an intercourse facilitate the competitions of other nations, by enhancing the price of British commodities in our markets, and by transferring to other hands the management of this interesting branch of the British commerce?

A mature consideration of the objects suggested by these questions will justify a belief that the real disadvantages to Britain from such a state of things, conspiring with the pre-possessions of a great part of the nation in favor of the American trade, and with the importunities of the West India islands, would produce a relaxation in her present system, and would let us into the enjoyment of privileges in the markets of those islands elsewhere, from which our trade would derive the most substantial benefits. Such a point gained from the British government, and which could not be expected without an equivalent in exemptions and immunities in our markets, would be likely to have a correspondent effect on the conduct of other nations, who would not be inclined to see themselves altogether supplanted in our trade.

A further resource for influencing the conduct of European nations toward us, in this respect, would arise from the establishment of a federal navy. There can be no doubt that the continuance of the Union under an efficient government would put it in our power, at a period not very distant, to create a navy which, if it could not vie with those of the great maritime powers, would at least be of respectable weight if thrown into the scale of either of two contending parties. This would be more peculiarly the case in relation to operations in the West Indies. A few ships of the line, sent opportunely to the reinforcement of either side, would often be sufficient to decide the fate of a campaign, on the event of which interests of the greatest magnitude were suspended. Our position is, in this respect, a most commanding one. And if to this consideration we add that of the usefulness of supplies from this country, in the prosecution of military operations in the West Indies, it will readily be perceived that a situation so favorable would enable us to bargain with great advantage for commercial privileges. A price would be set not only upon our friendship, but upon our neutrality. By a steady adherence to the Union we may hope, erelong, to become the arbiter of Europe in America, and to be able to incline the balance of European competitions in this part of the world as our interest may dictate.

But in the reverse of this eligible situation, we shall discover that the rivalships of the parts would make them checks upon each other, and would frustrate all the tempting advantages which nature has kindly placed within our reach. In a state so insignificant our commerce would be a prey to the wanton intermeddlings of all nations at war with each other; who, having nothing to fear from us, would with little scruple or remorse, supply their wants by depredations on our property as often as it fell in their way. The rights of neutrality will only be respected when they are defended by an adequate power. A nation, despicable by its weakness, forfeits even the privilege of being neutral.

Under a vigorous national government, the natural strength and resources of the country, directed to a common interest, would baffle all the combinations of European jealousy to restrain our growth. This situation would even take away the motive to such combinations, by inducing an impracticability of success. An active commerce, an extensive navigation, and a flourishing marine would then be the offspring of moral and physical necessity. We might defy the little arts of the little politicians to control or vary the irresistible and unchangeable course of nature.

But in a state of disunion, these combinations might exist and might operate with success. It would be in the power of the maritime nations, availing themselves of our universal impotence, to prescribe the conditions of our political existence; and as they have a common interest in being our carriers, and still more in preventing our becoming theirs, they would in all probability combine to embarrass our navigation in such a manner as would in effect destroy it, and confine us to a PASSIVE COMMERCE. We should then be compelled to content ourselves with the first price of our commodities, and to see the profits of our trade snatched from us to enrich our enemies and persecutors. That unequaled spirit of enterprise, which signalizes the genius of the American merchants and navigators, and which is in itself an inexhaustible mine of national wealth, would be stifled and lost, and poverty and disgrace would overspread a country which, with wisdom, might make herself the admiration and envy of the world.

There are rights of great moment to the trade of America which are rights of the Union—I allude to the fisheries, to the navigation of the Western lakes, and to that of the Mississippi. The dissolution of the Confederacy would give room for delicate questions concerning the future existence of these rights; which the interest of more powerful partners would hardly fail to solve to our disadvantage. The disposition of Spain with regard to the Mississippi needs no comment. France and Britain are concerned with us in the fisheries, and view them as of the utmost moment to their navigation. They, of course, would hardly remain long indifferent to that decided mastery, of which experience has shown us to be possessed in this valuable branch of traffic, and by which we are able to undersell those nations in their own markets. What more natural than that they should be disposed to exclude from the lists such dangerous competitors?

This branch of trade ought not to be considered as a partial benefit. All the navigating States may, in different degrees, advantageously participate in it, and under circumstances of a greater extension of mercantile capital, would not be unlikely to do it. As a nursery of seamen, it now is, or when time shall have more nearly assimilated the principles of navigation in the several States, will become, a universal resource. To the establishment of a navy, it must be indispensable.

To this great national object, a NAVY, union will contribute in various ways. Every institution will grow and flourish in proportion to the quantity and extent of the means concentred towards its formation and support. A navy of the United States, as it would embrace the resources of all, is an object far less remote than a navy of any single State or partial confederacy, which would only embrace the resources of a single part. It happens, indeed, that different portions of confederated America possess each some peculiar advantage for this essential establishment. The more southern States furnish in greater abundance certain kinds of naval stores—tar, pitch, and turpentine. Their wood for the construction of ships is also of a more solid and lasting texture. The difference in the duration of the ships of which the navy might be composed, if chiefly constructed of Southern wood, would be of signal importance, either in the view of naval strength or of national economy. Some of the Southern and of the Middle States yield a greater plenty of iron, and of better quality. Seamen must chiefly be drawn from the Northern hive. The necessity of naval protection to external

or maritime commerce does not require a particular elucidation, no more than the conduciveness of that species of commerce to the prosperity of a navy.

An unrestrained intercourse between the States themselves will advance the trade of each by an interchange of their respective productions, not only for the supply of reciprocal wants at home, but for exportation to foreign markets. The veins of commerce in every part will be replenished, and will acquire additional motion and vigor from a free circulation of the commodities of every part. Commercial enterprise will have much greater scope, from the diversity in the productions of different States. When the staple of one fails from a bad harvest or unproductive crop, it can call to its aid the staple of another. The variety, not less than the value, of products for exportation contributes to the activity of foreign commerce. It can be conducted upon much better terms with a large number of materials of a given value than with a small number of materials of the same value; arising from the competitions of trade and from the fluctations of markets. Particular articles may be in great demand at certain periods, and unsalable at others; but if there be a variety of articles, it can scarcely happen that they should all be at one time in the latter predicament, and on this account the operations of the merchant would be less liable to any considerable obstruction or stagnation. The speculative trader will at once perceive the force of these observations, and will acknowledge that the aggregate balance of the commerce of the United States would bid fair to be much more favorable than that of the thirteen States without union or with partial unions.

It may perhaps be replied to this, that whether the States are united or disunited, there would still be an intimate intercourse between them which would answer the same ends; this intercourse would be fettered, interrupted, and narrowed by a multiplicity of causes, which in the course of these papers have been amply detailed. A unity of commercial, as well as political, interests, can only result from a unity of government.

There are other points of view in which this subject might be placed, of a striking and animating kind. But they would lead us too far into the regions of futurity, and would involve topics not proper for a newspaper discussion. I shall briefly observe, that our situation invites and our interests prompt us to aim at an ascendant in the system of American affairs. The world may politically, as well as geographically, be divided into four parts, each having a distinct set of interests. Unhappily for the other three, Europe, by her arms and by her negotiations, by force and by fraud, has, in different degrees, extended her dominion over them all. Africa, Asia, and America, have successively felt her domination. The superiority she has long maintained has tempted her to plume herself as the Mistress of the World, and to consider the rest of mankind as created for her benefit. Men admired as profound philosophers have, in direct terms, attributed to her inhabitants a physical superiority, and have gravely asserted that all animals, and with them the human species, degenerate in America—that even dogs cease to bark after having breathed awhile in our atmosphere. Facts have too long supported these arrogant pretensions of the Europeans. It belongs to us to vindicate the honor of the human race, and to teach that assuming brother, moderation. Union will enable us to do it. Disunion will will add another victim to his triumphs. Let Americans disdain to be the instruments of European greatness! Let the thirteen States, bound together in a strict and indissoluble Union, concur in erecting one great American system, superior to the control of all transatlantic force or influence, and able to dictate the terms of the connection between the old and the new world!

GEORGE WASHINGTON, "FAREWELL ADDRESS" (1796)

History remembers George Washington (1732–1799) more for what he accomplished than for what he wrote or said. Yet this document, issued as he was completing his term as the first US president, has remained central to his legacy. In it, Washington spells out the principles he believes should guide relations between the young American republic and the world beyond its borders.

Friends and Citizens:

The period for a new election of a citizen to administer the executive government of the United States being not far distant, and the time actually arrived when your thoughts must be employed in designating the person who is to be clothed with that important trust, it appears to me proper, especially as it may conduce to a more distinct expression of the public voice, that I should now apprise you of the resolution I have formed, to decline being considered among the number of those out of whom a choice is to be made.

I beg you, at the same time, to do me the justice to be assured that this resolution has not been taken without a strict regard to all the considerations appertaining to the relation which binds a dutiful citizen to his country; and that in withdrawing the tender of service, which silence in my situation might imply, I am influenced by no diminution of zeal for your future interest, no deficiency of grateful respect for your past kindness, but am supported by a full conviction that the step is compatible with both.

The acceptance of, and continuance hitherto in, the office to which your suffrages have twice called me have been a uniform sacrifice of inclination to the opinion of duty and to a deference for what appeared to be your desire. I constantly hoped that it would have been much earlier in my power, consistently with motives which I was not at liberty to disregard, to return to that retirement from which I had been reluctantly drawn. The strength of my inclination to do this, previous to the last election, had even led to the preparation of an address to declare it to you; but mature reflection on the then perplexed and critical posture of our affairs with foreign nations, and the unanimous advice of persons entitled to my confidence, impelled me to abandon the idea.

I rejoice that the state of your concerns, external as well as internal, no longer renders the pursuit of inclination incompatible with the sentiment of duty or propriety, and am persuaded, whatever partiality may be retained for my services, that, in the present circumstances of our country, you will not disapprove my determination to retire. . . .

Here, perhaps, I ought to stop. But a solicitude for your welfare, which cannot end but with my life, and the apprehension of danger, natural to that solicitude, urge me, on an occasion like the present, to offer to your solemn contemplation, and to recommend to your frequent review, some sentiments which are the result of much reflection, of no inconsiderable observation, and which appear to me all-important to the permanency of your felicity as a people. . . .

Interwoven as is the love of liberty with every ligament of your hearts, no recommendation of mine is necessary to fortify or confirm the attachment.

The unity of government which constitutes you one people is also now dear to you. It is justly so, for it is a main pillar in the edifice of your real independence, the support of your tranquility at home, your peace abroad; of your safety; of your prosperity; of that very liberty which you so highly prize. But as it is easy to foresee that, from different causes and from different quarters, much pains will be taken, many artifices employed to weaken in your minds the conviction of this truth; as this is the point in your political fortress against which the batteries of internal and external enemies will be most constantly and actively (though often covertly and insidiously) directed, it is of infinite moment that you should properly estimate the immense value of your national union to your collective and individual happiness; that you should cherish a cordial, habitual, and immovable attachment to it; accustoming yourselves to think and speak of it as of the palladium of your political safety and prosperity; watching for its preservation with jealous anxiety; discountenancing whatever may suggest even a suspicion that it can in any event be abandoned; and indignantly frowning upon the first dawning of every attempt to alienate any portion of our country from the rest, or to enfeeble the sacred ties which now link together the various parts.

For this you have every inducement of sympathy and interest. Citizens, by birth or choice, of a common country, that country has a right to concentrate your affections. The name of American, which belongs to you in your national capacity, must always exalt the just pride of patriotism more than any appellation derived from local discriminations. With slight shades of difference, you have the same religion, manners, habits, and political principles. You have in a common cause fought and triumphed together; the independence and liberty you possess are the work of joint counsels, and joint efforts of common dangers, sufferings, and successes.

But these considerations, however powerfully they address themselves to your sensibility, are greatly outweighed by those which apply more immediately to your interest. Here every portion of our country finds the most commanding motives for carefully guarding and preserving the union of the whole. . . .

While, then, every part of our country thus feels an immediate and particular interest in union, all the parts combined cannot fail to find in the united mass of means and efforts greater strength, greater resource, proportionably greater security from external danger, a less frequent interruption of their peace by foreign nations; and, what is of inestimable value, they must derive from union an exemption from those broils and wars between themselves, which so frequently afflict neighboring countries not tied together by the same governments, which their own rival ships alone would be sufficient to produce, but which opposite foreign alliances, attachments, and intrigues would stimulate and embitter. Hence, likewise, they will avoid the necessity of those overgrown military establishments which, under any form of government, are inauspicious to liberty, and which are to be regarded as particularly hostile to republican liberty. In this sense it is that your union ought to be considered as a main prop of your liberty, and that the love of the one ought to endear to you the preservation of the other.

These considerations speak a persuasive language to every reflecting and virtuous mind, and exhibit the continuance of the Union as a primary object of patriotic desire. Is there a doubt whether a common government can embrace so large a sphere? Let experience solve it. To listen to mere speculation in such a case were criminal. We are authorized to hope that a proper organization of the whole with the auxiliary agency of governments for the respective subdivisions, will afford a happy issue to the experiment. . . .

The basis of our political systems is the right of the people to make and to alter their constitutions of government. But the Constitution which at any time exists, till changed by an explicit and authentic act of the whole people, is sacredly obligatory upon all. The very idea of the power and the right of the people to establish government presupposes the duty of every individual to obey the established government. . . .

I have already intimated to you the danger of parties in the State, with particular reference to the founding of them on geographical discriminations. Let me now take a more comprehensive view, and warn you in the most solemn manner against the baneful effects of the spirit of party generally.

This spirit, unfortunately, is inseparable from our nature, having its root in the strongest passions of the human mind. It exists under different shapes in all governments, more or less stifled, controlled, or repressed; but, in those of the popular form, it is seen in its greatest rankness, and is truly their worst enemy.

The alternate domination of one faction over another, sharpened by the spirit of revenge, natural to party dissension, which in different ages and countries has perpetrated the most horrid enormities, is itself a frightful despotism. But this leads at length to a more formal and permanent despotism. The disorders and miseries which result gradually incline the minds of men to seek security and repose in the absolute power of an individual; and sooner or later the chief of some prevailing faction, more able or more fortunate than his competitors, turns this disposition to the purposes of his own elevation, on the ruins of public liberty.

Without looking forward to an extremity of this kind (which nevertheless ought not to be entirely out of sight), the common and continual mischiefs of the spirit of party are sufficient to make it the interest and duty of a wise people to discourage and restrain it.

It serves always to distract the public councils and enfeeble the public administration. It agitates the community with ill-founded jealousies and false alarms, kindles the animosity of one part against another, foments occasionally riot and insurrection. It opens the door to foreign influence and corruption, which finds a facilitated access to the government itself through the channels of party passions. Thus the policy and the will of one country are subjected to the policy and will of another. . . .

Of all the dispositions and habits which lead to political prosperity, religion and morality are indispensable supports. In vain would that man claim the tribute of patriotism, who should labor to subvert these great pillars of human happiness, these firmest props of the duties of men and citizens. The mere politician, equally with the pious man, ought to respect and to cherish them. A volume could not trace all their connections with private and public felicity. Let it simply be asked: Where is the security for property, for reputation, for life, if the sense of religious obligation desert the oaths which are the instruments of investigation in courts of justice? And let us with caution indulge the supposition that morality can be maintained without religion. Whatever may be conceded to the influence of refined education on minds of peculiar structure, reason and experience both forbid us to expect that national morality can prevail in exclusion of religious principle. . . .

Observe good faith and justice towards all nations; cultivate peace and harmony with all. Religion and morality enjoin this conduct; and can it be, that good policy does not equally enjoin it—It will be worthy of a free, enlightened, and at no distant period, a great nation, to give to mankind the magnanimous and too novel example of a people always guided by an exalted justice and benevolence. Who can doubt that, in the course of time and things, the fruits of such a plan would richly repay any temporary advantages which might be lost by a steady adherence to it? Can it be that Providence has not connected the permanent felicity of a nation with its virtue? The experiment, at least, is recommended by every sentiment which ennobles human nature. Alas! is it rendered impossible by its vices?

In the execution of such a plan, nothing is more essential than that permanent, inveterate antipathies against particular nations, and passionate attachments for others, should be excluded; and that, in place of them, just and amicable feelings towards all should be cultivated. The nation which indulges towards another a habitual hatred or a habitual fondness is in some degree a slave. It is a slave to its animosity or to its affection, either of which is sufficient to lead it astray from its duty and its interest. Antipathy in one nation against another disposes each more readily to offer insult and injury, to lay hold of slight causes of umbrage, and to be haughty and intractable, when accidental or trifling occasions of dispute occur. Hence, frequent collisions, obstinate, envenomed, and bloody contests. The nation, prompted by ill-will and resentment, sometimes impels to war the government, contrary to the best calculations of policy. The government sometimes participates in the national propensity, and adopts through passion what reason would reject; at other times it makes the animosity of the nation subservient to projects of hostility instigated by pride, ambition, and other sinister and pernicious motives. The peace often, sometimes perhaps the liberty, of nations, has been the victim.

So likewise, a passionate attachment of one nation for another produces a variety of evils. Sympathy for the favorite nation, facilitating the illusion of an imaginary common interest in cases where no real common interest exists, and infusing into one the enmities of the other, betrays the former into a participation in the quarrels and wars of the latter without adequate inducement or justification. It leads also to concessions to the favorite nation of privileges denied to others which is apt doubly to injure the nation making the concessions; by unnecessarily parting with what ought to have been retained, and by exciting jealousy, ill-will, and a disposition to retaliate, in the parties from whom equal privileges are withheld. And it gives to ambitious, corrupted, or deluded citizens (who devote themselves to the favorite nation), facility to betray or sacrifice the interests of their own country, without odium, sometimes even with popularity; gilding, with the appearances of a virtuous sense of obligation, a commendable deference for public opinion, or a laudable zeal for public good, the base or foolish compliances of ambition, corruption, or infatuation.

As avenues to foreign influence in innumerable ways, such attachments are particularly alarming to the truly enlightened and independent patriot. How many opportunities do they afford to tamper with domestic factions, to practice the arts of seduction, to mislead public opinion, to influence or awe the public councils. Such an attachment of a small or weak towards a great and powerful nation dooms the former to be the satellite of the latter.

Against the insidious wiles of foreign influence (I conjure you to believe me, fellow-citizens) the jealousy of a free people ought to be constantly awake, since history and experience prove that foreign influence is one of the most baneful foes of republican government. But that jealousy to be useful must be impartial; else it becomes the instrument of the very influence to be avoided, instead of a defense against it. Excessive partiality for one foreign nation and excessive dislike of another cause those whom they actuate to see danger only on one side, and serve to veil and even second the arts of influence on the other. Real patriots who may resist the intrigues of the favorite are liable to become suspected and odious, while its tools and dupes usurp the applause and confidence of the people, to surrender their interests.

The great rule of conduct for us in regard to foreign nations is in extending our commercial relations, to have with them as little political connection as possible. So far as we have already formed engagements, let them be fulfilled with perfect good faith. Here let us stop. Europe has a set of primary interests which to us have none; or a very remote relation. Hence she must be engaged in frequent controversies, the causes of which are essentially foreign to our concerns. Hence, therefore, it must be unwise in us to implicate ourselves by artificial ties in the ordinary vicissitudes of her politics, or the ordinary combinations and collisions of her friendships or enmities.

Our detached and distant situation invites and enables us to pursue a different course. If we remain one people under an efficient government, the period is not far off when we may defy material injury from external annoyance; when we may take such an attitude as will cause the neutrality we may at any time resolve upon to be scrupulously respected; when belligerent nations, under the impossibility of making acquisitions upon us, will not lightly hazard the giving us provocation; when we may choose peace or war, as our interest, guided by justice, shall counsel.

Why forego the advantages of so peculiar a situation? Why quit our own to stand upon foreign ground? Why, by interweaving our destiny with that of any part of Europe, entangle our peace and prosperity in the toils of European ambition, rivalship, interest, humor or caprice?

It is our true policy to steer clear of permanent alliances with any portion of the foreign world; so far, I mean, as we are now at liberty to do it; for let me not be understood as capable of patronizing infidelity to existing engagements. I hold the maxim no less applicable to public than to private affairs, that honesty is always the best policy. I repeat it, therefore, let those engagements be observed in their genuine sense. But, in my opinion, it is unnecessary and would be unwise to extend them.

Taking care always to keep ourselves by suitable establishments on a respectable defensive posture, we may safely trust to temporary alliances for extraordinary emergencies.

Harmony, liberal intercourse with all nations, are recommended by policy, humanity, and interest. But even our commercial policy should hold an equal and impartial hand; neither seeking nor granting exclusive favors or preferences; consulting the natural course of things; diffusing and diversifying by gentle means the streams of commerce, but forcing nothing; establishing (with powers so disposed, in order to give trade a stable course, to define the rights of our merchants, and to enable the government to support them) conventional rules of intercourse, the best that present circumstances and mutual opinion will permit, but temporary, and liable to be from time to time abandoned or varied, as experience and circumstances shall dictate; constantly keeping in view that it is folly in one nation to look for disinterested favors from another; that it must pay with a portion of its independence for whatever it may accept under that character; that, by such acceptance, it may place itself in the condition of having given equivalents for nominal favors, and yet of being reproached with ingratitude for not giving more. There can be no greater error than to expect or calculate upon real favors from nation to nation. It is an illusion, which experience must cure, which a just pride ought to discard.

In offering to you, my countrymen, these counsels of an old and affectionate friend, I dare not hope they will make the strong and lasting impression I could wish; that they will control the usual current of the passions, or prevent our nation from running the course which has hitherto marked the destiny of nations. But, if I may even flatter myself that they may be productive of some partial benefit, some occasional good; that they may now and then recur to moderate the fury of party spirit, to warn against the mischiefs of foreign intrigue, to guard against the impostures of pretended patriotism; this hope will be a full recompense for the solicitude for your welfare, by which they have been dictated. . . .

II.

YOUNG REPUBLIC

Accomplishing its mission would require the United States to establish itself among the world's great nations. In the near term, that meant enhancing American wealth and power without being drawn into counterproductive foreign wars. Expansion, both territorial and commercial, was essential. So too was keeping faith with prevailing republican values. Striking a balance between competing imperatives became a central preoccupation of American statesmen.

The documents in this section, drawn from the period between the start of the nineteenth century and the Civil War, illustrate the tension between efforts to preserve the vision of America as a "city upon a hill" and the urge to expand. Central to that tension were controversies involving the expulsion of Native Americans and the perpetuation of slavery. The most important of those controversies related to the annexation of Texas and the conquest of California and the Southwest, all accomplished through military means at the expense of Mexico. In the end, in the formulation of US policy, moral considerations took a back seat to pragmatic ones, and ideals to ambition.

By the time the Civil War erupted in 1861, the United States stretched from "sea to shining sea," its geographic area having increased by several orders of magnitude since 1776. Although the war itself momentarily disrupted the process of expansion, President Lincoln and others attributed to the conflict a transcendent significance. Much more was at stake than ending slavery and restoring the Union.

THOMAS JEFFERSON, "THIRD ANNUAL MESSAGE" (1803)

The Louisiana Purchase, engineered by President Thomas Jefferson (1743–1826), exemplifies the opportunistic expansionism that was central to US policy during the nineteenth century. To avoid involvement in European wars was not "isolationism" but prudence.

In calling you together, fellow citizens, at an earlier day than was contemplated by the act of the last session of Congress, I have not been insensible to the personal inconveniences necessarily resulting from an unexpected change in your arrangements. But matters of great public concernment have rendered this call necessary, and the interest you feel in these will supersede in your minds all private considerations.

Congress witnessed, at their last session, the extraordinary agitation produced in the public mind by the suspension of our right of deposit at the port of New Orleans, no assignment of another place having been made according to treaty. They were sensible that the continuance of that privation would be more injurious to our nation than any consequences which could flow from any mode of redress, but reposing just confidence in the good faith of the government whose officer had committed the wrong, friendly and reasonable representations were resorted to, and the right of deposit was restored.

Previous, however, to this period, we had not been unaware of the danger to which our peace would be perpetually exposed while so important a key to the commerce of the western country remained under foreign power. Difficulties, too, were presenting themselves as to the navigation of other streams, which, arising within our territories, pass through those adjacent. Propositions had, therefore, been authorized for obtaining, on fair conditions, the sovereignty of New Orleans, and of other possessions in that quarter interesting to our quiet, to such extent as was deemed practicable; and the provisional appropriation of two millions of dollars, to be applied and accounted for by the president of the United States, intended as part of the price, was considered as conveying the sanction of Congress to the acquisition proposed. The enlightened government of France saw, with just discernment, the importance to both nations of such liberal arrangements as might best and permanently promote the peace, friendship, and interests of both; and the property and sovereignty of all Louisiana, which had been restored to them, have on certain conditions been transferred to the United States by instruments bearing date the 30th of April last. When these shall have received the constitutional sanction of the senate, they will without delay be communicated to the representatives also, for the exercise of their functions, as to those conditions which are within the powers vested by the constitution in Congress. While the property and sovereignty of the Mississippi and its

waters secure an independent outlet for the produce of the western States, and an uncontrolled navigation through their whole course, free from collision with other powers and the dangers to our peace from that source, the fertility of the country, its climate and extent, promise in due season important aids to our treasury, an ample provision for our posterity, and a wide-spread field for the blessings of freedom and equal laws.

With the wisdom of Congress it will rest to take those ulterior measures which may be necessary for the immediate occupation and temporary government of the country; for its incorporation into our Union; for rendering the change of government a blessing to our newly-adopted brethren; for securing to them the rights of conscience and of property: for confirming to the Indian inhabitants their occupancy and self-government, establishing friendly and commercial relations with them, and for ascertaining the geography of the country acquired. Such materials for your information, relative to its affairs in general, as the short space of time has permitted me to collect, will be laid before you when the subject shall be in a state for your consideration.

Another important acquisition of territory has also been made since the last session of Congress. The friendly tribe of Kaskaskia Indians with which we have never had a difference, reduced by the wars and wants of savage life to a few individuals unable to defend themselves against the neighboring tribes, has transferred its country to the United States, reserving only for its members what is sufficient to maintain them in an agricultural way. The considerations stipulated are, that we shall extend to them our patronage and protection, and give them certain annual aids in money, in implements of agriculture, and other articles of their choice. This country, among the most fertile within our limits, extending along the Mississippi from the mouth of the Illinois to and up the Ohio, though not so necessary as a barrier since the acquisition of the other bank, may yet be well worthy of being laid open to immediate settlement, as its inhabitants may descend with rapidity in support of the lower country should future circumstances expose that to foreign enterprise. As the stipulations in this treaty also involve matters within the competence of both houses only, it will be laid before Congress as soon as the senate shall have advised its ratification.

With many other Indian tribes, improvements in agriculture and household manufacture are advancing, and with all our peace and friendship are established on grounds much firmer than heretofore. The measure adopted of establishing trading houses among them, and of furnishing them necessaries in exchange for their commodities, at such moderated prices as leave no gain, but cover us from loss, has the most conciliatory and useful effect upon them, and is that which will best secure their peace and good will.

The small vessels authorized by Congress with a view to the Mediterranean service, have been sent into that sea, and will be able more effectually to confine the Tripoline cruisers within their harbors, and supersede the necessity of convoy to our commerce in that quarter. They will sensibly lessen the expenses of that service the ensuing year.

A further knowledge of the ground in the north-eastern and north-western angles of the United States has evinced that the boundaries established by the treaty of Paris between the British territories and ours in those parts, were too imperfectly described to be susceptible of execution. It has therefore been thought worthy of attention, for preserving and cherishing the harmony and useful intercourse subsisting between the two nations, to remove by timely arrangements what unfavorable incidents might otherwise render a ground of future misunderstanding. A convention has therefore been entered into, which provides for a practicable demarkation of those limits to the satisfaction of both parties.

An account of the receipts and expenditures of the year ending 30th September last, with the estimates for the service of the ensuing year, will be laid before you by the secretary of the treasury so soon as the receipts of the last quarter shall be returned from the more distant States. It is already ascertained that the amount paid into the treasury for that year has been between eleven and twelve millions of dollars, and that the revenue accrued during the same term exceeds the sum counted on as sufficient for our current expenses, and to extinguish the public debt within the period heretofore proposed.

The amount of debt paid for the same year is about three millions one hundred thousand dollars, exclusive of interest, and making, with the payment of the preceding year, a discharge of more than eight millions and a half of dollars of the principal of that debt, besides the accruing interest; and there remain in the treasury nearly six millions of dollars. . . .

Should the acquisition of Louisiana be constitutionally confirmed and carried into effect, a sum of nearly thirteen millions of dollars will then be added to our public debt, most of which is payable after fifteen years; before which term the present existing debts will all be discharged by the established operation of the sinking fund. When we contemplate the ordinary annual augmentation of imposts from increasing population and wealth, the augmentation of the same revenue by its extension to the new acquisition, . . . I cannot but hope that Congress in reviewing their resources will find means to meet the intermediate interests of this additional debt without recurring to new taxes. . . .

We have seen with sincere concern the flames of war lighted up again in Europe, and nations with which we have the most friendly and useful relations engaged in mutual destruction. While we regret the miseries in which we see others involved let us bow with gratitude to that kind Providence which, inspiring with wisdom and moderation our late legislative councils while placed under the urgency of the greatest wrongs, guarded us from hastily entering into the sanguinary contest, and left us only to look on and to pity its ravages. These will be heaviest on those immediately engaged. Yet the nations pursuing peace will not be exempt from all evil. In the course of this conflict, let it be our endeavor, as it is our interest and desire, to cultivate the friendship of the belligerent nations by every act of justice and of incessant kindness; to receive their armed vessels with hospitality from the distresses of the sea, but to administer the means of annoyance to none; to establish in our harbors such a police as may maintain law and order; to restrain our citizens from embarking individually in a war in which their country takes no part; to punish severely those persons, citizen or alien, who shall usurp the cover of our flag for vessels not entitled to it, infecting thereby with suspicion those of real

Americans, and committing us into controversies for the redress of wrongs not our own; to exact from every nation the observance, toward our vessels and citizens, of those principles and practices which all civilized people acknowledge; to merit the character of a just nation, and maintain that of an independent one, preferring every consequence to insult and habitual wrong. Congress will consider whether the existing laws enable us efficaciously to maintain this course with our citizens in all places, and with others while within the limits of our jurisdiction, and will give them the new modifications necessary for these objects. Some contraventions of right have already taken place, both within our jurisdictional limits and on the high seas. The friendly disposition of the governments from whose agents they have proceeded, as well as their wisdom and regard for justice, leave us in reasonable expectation that they will be rectified and prevented in future; and that no act will be countenanced by them which threatens to disturb our friendly intercourse.

Separated by a wide ocean from the nations of Europe, and from the political interests which entangle them together, with productions and wants which render our commerce and friendship useful to them and theirs to us, it cannot be the interest of any to assail us, nor ours to disturb them. We should be most unwise, indeed, were we to cast away the singular blessings of the position in which nature has placed us, the opportunity she has endowed us with of pursuing, at a distance from foreign contentions, the paths of industry, peace, and happiness; of cultivating general friendship, and of bringing collisions of interest to the umpirage of reason rather than of force. How desirable then must it be, in a government like ours, to see its citizens adopt individually the views, the interests, and the conduct which their country should pursue, divesting themselves of those passions and partialities which tend to lessen useful friendships, and to embarrass and embroil us in the calamitous scenes of Europe. Confident, fellow citizens, that you will duly estimate the importance of neutral dispositions toward the observance of neutral conduct, that you will be sensible how much it is our duty to look on the bloody arena spread before us with commiseration indeed, but with no other wish than to see it closed, I am persuaded you will cordially cherish these dispositions in all discussions among yourselves, and in all communications with your constituents; and I anticipate with satisfaction the measures of wisdom which the great interests now committed to *you* will give you an opportunity of providing, and *myself* that of approving and carrying into execution with the fidelity I owe to my country.

JOHN QUINCY ADAMS, "SPEECH ON INDEPENDENCE DAY" (1821)

Son of the second American president and himself destined to become the sixth chief executive of the United States, John Quincy Adams (1767–1848) served with distinction as secretary of state to James Monroe. Here he argues that for the United States to fulfill its destiny it must chart an independent course, always keeping its own interests paramount.

Fellow Citizens, UNTIL within a few days before that which we have again assembled to commemorate, our fathers, the people of this Union, had constituted a portion of the British nation; a nation, renowned in arts and arms, who, from a small Island in the Atlantic ocean, had extended their dominion over considerable parts of every quarter of the globe. Governed themselves by a race of kings, whose title to sovereignty had originally been founded on conquest, spell-bound, for a succession of ages, under that portentous system of despotism and of superstition which, in the name of the meek and humble Jesus, had been spread over the christian world, the history of this nation had, for a period of seven hundred years, from the days of the conquest till our own, exhibited a conflict almost continued, between the oppressions of power and the claims of right. In the theories of the crown and the mitre, man had no rights. Neither the body nor the soul of the individual was his own. From the impenetrable gloom of this intellectual darkness, and the deep degradation of this servitude, the British nation had partially emerged. The martyrs of religious freedom had consumed to ashes at the stake; the champions of temporal liberty had bowed their heads upon the scaffold; and the spirits of many a bloody day had left their earthly vesture upon the field of battle, and soared to plead the cause of liberty before the throne of heaven. Through long ages of civil war the people of Britain had extorted from their tyrants, not acknowledgments, but grants of right. With this concession they had been content to stop in the progress of human improvement. . . .

From the earliest ages of their recorded history, the inhabitants of the British islands have been distinguished for their intelligence and their spirit. How much of these two qualities, the fountains of all amelioration in the condition of men, was stifled by these two principles of subserviency to ecclesiastical usurpation, and of holding rights as the donations of kings, this is not the occasion to inquire. Of their tendency to palsy the vigor, and enervate the faculties of man, all philosophical reasoning, and all actual experience concur in testimony. . . .

The triumph of reason was the result of inquiry and discussion. Centuries of desolating wars have succeeded, and oceans of human blood have flowed, for the final establishment of this principle; but it was from the darkness of the cloister that the first spark was emitted, and from the arches of a university that it first kindled into day. From the discussion of religious rights and duties, the transition to that of the political and civil relations of men with one another was natural and unavoidable; in both, the reformers were met by the weapons of temporal power. At the same glance of reason, the tiara would have fallen from the brow of priesthood, and the despotic sceptre would have departed from the hand of royalty, but for the sword, by which they were protected. . . .

The double contest against the oppressors of church and state was too appalling for the vigor, or too comprehensive for the faculties of the reformers of the European continent. In Britain alone was it undertaken, and in Britain but partially succeeded. . . .

[R]eleased from the fetters of ecclesiastical domination, the minds of men began to investigate the foundations of civil government. But the mass of the nation surveyed the fabric of their Institutions as it existed in fact. It had been founded in conquest; it had been cemented in servitude; and so broken and moulded had been the minds of this brave and intelligent people to their actual condition, that instead of solving civil society into its first elements in search of their rights, they looked back only to conquest as the origin of their liberties, and claimed their rights but as donations from their kings. . . .

Fellow citizens, it was in the heat of this war of moral elements . . . that our forefathers sought refuge from its fury, in the then wilderness of this Western World. They were willing exiles from a country dearer to them than life. But they were the exiles of liberty and of conscience: dearer to them even than their country. They came too, with charters from their kings; for even in removing to another hemisphere, they "cast longing, lingering looks behind," and were anxiously desirous of retaining ties of connexion with their country, which, in the solemn compact of a charter, they hoped by the corresponding links of allegiance and protection to preserve. But to their sense of right, the charter was only the ligament between them, their country, and their king. Transported to a new world, they had relations with one another, and relations with the aboriginal inhabitants of the country to which they came; for which no royal charter could provide. The first settlers of the Plymouth colony, at the eve of landing from their ship, therefore, bound themselves together by a written covenant; and immediately after landing, purchased from the Indian natives the right of settlement upon the soil.

Thus was a social compact formed upon the elementary principles of civil society, in which conquest and servitude had no part. The slough of brutal force was entirely cast off; all was voluntary; all was unbiased consent; all was the agreement of soul with soul.

Other colonies were successively founded, and other charters granted, until in the compass of a century and a half, thirteen distinct British provinces peopled the Atlantic shores of the North American continent with two millions of freemen; possessing by their charters the rights

of British subjects, and nurtured by their position and education, in the more comprehensive
and original doctrines of human rights. From
their infancy they had been treated by the parent
state with neglect, harshness and injustice. Their
charters had often been disregarded and violated;
their commerce restricted and shackled; their
interest wantonly or spitefully sacrificed; so that
the hand of the parent had been scarcely ever
felt, but in the alternate application of whips and
scorpions.

When in spite of all these persecutions, by
the natural vigor of their constitution, they were
just attaining the maturity of political manhood,
a British parliament, in contempt of the clearest
maxims of natural equity, in defiance of the fundamental principle upon which British freedom
itself had been cemented with British blood; on
the naked, unblushing allegation of absolute and
un-controllable power, undertook by their act to
levy, without representation and without consent,
taxes upon the people of America for the benefit
of the people of Britain. This enormous project of
public robbery was no sooner made known, than
it excited, throughout the colonies, one general
burst of indignant resistance. . . .

Long before the Declaration of Independence,
the great mass of the people of America and of
the people of Britain had become total strangers to each other. The people of America were
known to the people of Britain only by the
transactions of trade; by shipments of lumber and
flax-seed, indigo and tobacco. They were known
to the government only by half a dozen colonial
agents, humble, and often spurned suitors at the
feet of power, and by royal governors, minions
of patronage, sent from the footstool of a throne
beyond the seas, to rule a people of whom they
knew nothing; as if an inhabitant of the moon
should descend to give laws to the dwellers upon
earth. . . . The sympathies therefore most essential
to the communion of country were, between the
British and American people, extinct. Those most
indispensable to the just relation between sovereign and subject, had never existed and could not
exist between the British government and the
American people. The connexion was unnatural;
and it was in the moral order no less than in the
positive decrees of Providence, that it should be
dissolved. . . .

Then it was that the thirteen United Colonies
of North America, by their delegates in Congress
assembled, exercising the first act of sovereignty
by a right ever inherent in the people, but never
to be resorted to, save at the awful crisis when civil
society is solved into its first elements, declared
themselves free and independent states. . . .

The interest, which in this paper has survived
the occasion upon which it was issued; the interest
which is of every age and every clime; the interest
which quickens with the lapse of years, spreads
as it grows old, and brightens as it recedes, is in
the principles which it proclaims. It was the first
solemn declaration by a nation of the only legitimate foundation of civil government. It was the
corner stone of a new fabric, destined to cover
the surface of the globe. It demolished at a stroke
the lawfulness of all governments founded upon
conquest. It swept away all the rubbish of accu-
mulated centuries of servitude. It announced in
practical form to the world the transcendent truth
of the unalienable sovereignty of the people. It
proved that the social compact was no figment
of the imagination; but a real, solid, and sacred
bond of the social union. From the day of this
declaration, the people of North America were no
longer the fragment of a distant empire, imploring
justice and mercy from an inexorable master in
another hemisphere. They were no longer children appealing in vain to the sympathies of a heart-
less mother; no longer subjects leaning upon the
shattered columns of royal promises, and invoking
the faith of parchment to secure their rights. They
were a nation, asserting as of right, and maintaining by war, its own existence. A nation was born
in a day. . . .

"How many ages hence shall this their lofty
scene be acted o'er in states unborn, and accents
yet unknown?"

It will be acted o'er, fellow-citizens, but it can
never be repeated. It stands, and must forever stand
alone, a beacon on the summit of the mountain,
to which all the inhabitants of the earth may turn
their eyes for a genial and saving light, till time
shall be lost in eternity, and this globe itself dissolve, nor leave a wreck behind. It stands forever,
a light of admonition to the rulers of men; a light
of salvation and redemption to the oppressed. So
long as this planet shall be inhabited by human
beings, so long as man shall be of social nature, so

long as government shall be necessary to the great moral purposes of society, and so long as it shall be abused to the purposes of oppression, so long shall this declaration hold out to the sovereign and to the subject the extent and the boundaries of their respective rights and duties; founded in the laws of nature and of nature's God. Five and forty years have passed away since this Declaration was issued by our fathers; and here are we, fellow-citizens, assembled in the full enjoyment of its fruits, to bless the Author of our being for the bounties of his providence, in casting our lot in this favored land; to remember with effusions of gratitude the sages who put forth, and the heroes who bled for the establishment of this Declaration; and, by the communion of soul in the reperusal and hearing of this instrument, to renew the genuine Holy Alliance of its principles, to recognize them as eternal truths, and to pledge ourselves and bind our posterity to a faithful and undeviating adherence to them.

Fellow-citizens, our fathers have been faithful to them before us. When the little band of their Delegates, "with a firm reliance on the protection of Divine Providence, for the support of this declaration, mutually pledged to each other their lives, their fortunes, and their sacred honor," from every dwelling, street, and square of your populous cities, it was re-echoed with shouts of joy and gratulation! and if the silent language of the heart could have been heard, every hill upon the surface of this continent which had been trodden by the foot of civilized man, every valley in which the toil of your fathers had opened a paradise upon the wild, would have rung, with one accordant voice, louder than the thunders, sweeter than the harmonies of the heavens, with the solemn and responsive words, "We swear."

The pledge has been redeemed. Through six years of devastating but heroic war, through nearly forty years of more heroic peace, the principles of this declaration have been supported by the toils, by the vigils, by the blood of your fathers and of yourselves. The conflict of war had begun with fearful odds of apparent human power on the side of the oppressor. He wielded at will the collective force of the mightiest nation in Europe. He with more than poetic truth asserted the dominion of the waves. The power, to whose unjust usurpation your fathers hurled the gauntlet of defiance, baffled and vanquished by them, has even since, stripped of all the energies of this continent, been found adequate to give the law to its own quarter of the globe, and to mould the destinies of the European world. It was with a sling and a stone, that your fathers went forth to encounter the massive vigor of this Goliath. They slung the heaven-directed stone, and "With heaviest sound, the giant monster fell."

Amid the shouts of victory your cause soon found friends and allies in the rivals of your enemies. France recognized your independence as existing in fact, and made common cause with you for its support. Spain and the Netherlands, without adopting your principles, successively flung their weight into your scale . . .

The Declaration of Independence pronounced the irrevocable decree of political separation, between the United States and their people on the one part, and the British king, government, and nation on the other. It proclaimed the first principles on which civil government is founded, and derived from them the justification before earth and heaven of this act of sovereignty. But it left the people of this union, collective and individual, without organized government. In contemplating this state of things, one of the profoundest of British statesmen, in an ecstacy of astonishment exclaimed, "Anarchy is found tolerable!" But there was no anarchy. From the day of the Declaration, the people of the North American union, and of its constituent states, were associated bodies of civilized men and christians, in a state of nature, but not of anarchy. They were bound by the laws of God, which they all, and by the laws of the gospel, which they nearly all, acknowledged as the rules of their conduct. They were bound by the principles which they themselves had proclaimed in the declaration. They were bound by all those tender and endearing sympathies, the absence of which, in the British government and nation, towards them, was the primary cause of the distressing conflict in which they had been precipitated by the headlong rashness and unfeeling insolence of their oppressors. They were bound by all the beneficent laws and institutions, which their forefathers had brought with them from their mother country, not as servitudes but as rights. They were bound by habits of hardy industry, by frugal and hospitable manners, by the general sentiments of social equality, by pure and virtuous morals; and lastly they were bound by the grappling-hooks of common suffering under the scourge of oppression. Where then, among such a people, were the materials for anarchy! Had there been among them no other law, they would have been a law unto themselves.

They had before them in their new position, besides the maintenance of the independence which they had declared, three great objects to attain; the first, to cement and prepare for perpetuity their common union and that of their posterity; the second, to erect and organize civil and municipal governments in their respective states: and the third, to form connexions of friendship and of commerce with foreign nations. For all these objects, the same Congress which issued the Declaration, and at the same time with it, had provided. They recommended to the several states to form civil governments for themselves; with guarded and cautious deliberation they matured a confederation for the whole Union; and they prepared treaties of commerce, to be offered to the principal maritime nations of the world. All these objects were in a great degree accomplished amid the din of arms, and while every quarter of our country was ransacked by the fury of invasion. The states organized their governments, all in republican forms, all on the principles of the Declaration. The confederation was unanimously accepted by the thirteen states: and treaties of commerce were concluded with France and the Netherlands, in which, for the first time, the same just and magnanimous principles, consigned in the Declaration of Independence, were, so far as they could be applicable to the intercourse between nation and nation, solemnly recognized. When experience had proved that the confederation was not adequate to the national purposes of the country, the people of the United States, without tumult, without violence, by their delegates all chosen upon principles of equal right, formed a more perfect union, by the establishment of the federal constitution. This has already passed the ordeal of one human generation. In all the changes of men and of parties through which it has passed, it has been administered on the same fundamental principles. Our manners, our habits, our feelings, are all republican; and if our principles had been, when first proclaimed, doubtful to

the ear of reason or the sense of humanity, they would have been reconciled to our understanding and endeared to our hearts by their practical operation. In the progress of forty years since the acknowledgment of our Independence, we have gone through many modifications of internal government, and through all the vicissitudes of peace and war, with other mighty nations. But never, never for a moment have the great principles, consecrated by the Declaration of this day, been renounced or abandoned.

And now, friends and countrymen, if the wise and learned philosophers of the older world, the first observers of mutation and aberration, the discoverers of maddening ether and invisible planets, the inventors of Congreve rockets and shrapnel shells, should find their hearts disposed to inquire, what has America done for the benefit of mankind? Let our answer be this—America, with the same voice which spoke herself into existence as a nation, proclaimed to mankind the inextinguishable rights of human nature, and the only lawful foundations of government. America, in the assembly of nations, since her admission among them, has invariably, though often fruitlessly, held forth to them the hand of honest friendship, of equal freedom, of generous reciprocity. She has uniformly spoken among them, though often to heedless and often to disdainful ears, the language of equal liberty, equal justice, and equal rights. She has, in the lapse of nearly half a century, without a single exception, respected the independence of other nations, while asserting and maintaining her own. She has abstained from interference in the concerns of others, even when the conflict has been for principles to which she clings, as to the last vital drop that visits the heart. She has seen that probably for centuries to come, all the contests of that Aceldama, the European World, will be contests between inveterate power, and emerging right. Wherever the standard of freedom and independence has been or shall be unfurled, there will her heart, her benedictions and her prayers be. But she goes not abroad in search of monsters to destroy. She is the well-wisher to the freedom and independence of all. She is the champion and vindicator only of her own. She will recommend the general cause, by the countenance of her voice, and the benignant sympathy of her example. She well knows that by once enlisting under other banners than her own, were they even the banners of foreign independence, she would involve herself, beyond the power of extrication, in all the wars of interest and intrigue, of individual avarice, envy, and ambition, which assume the colors and usurp the standard of freedom. The fundamental maxims of her policy would insensibly change from liberty to force. The frontlet upon her brows would no longer beam with the ineffable splendor of freedom and independence; but in its stead would soon be substituted an imperial diadem, flashing in false and tarnished lustre the murky radiance of dominion and power. She might become the dictatress of the world: she would be no longer the ruler of her own spirit.

Stand forth, ye champions of Britannia, ruler of the waves! Stand forth, ye chivalrous knights of chartered liberties and the rotten borough! Enter the lists, ye, boasters of inventive genius! ye mighty masters of the palette and the brush! ye improvers upon the sculpture of the Elgin marbles! ye spawners of fustian romance and lascivious lyrics! Come, and inquire what has America done for the benefit of mankind! In the half century which has elapsed since the declaration of American independence, what have you done for the benefit of mankind? When Themistocles was sarcastically asked by some great musical genius of his age whether he knew how to play upon the lute, he answered, No! but he knew how to make a great city of a small one. We shall not contend with you for the prize of music, painting, or sculpture. We shall not disturb the ecstatic trances of your chemists, nor call from the heavens the ardent gaze of your astronomers. We will not ask you who was the last president of your Royal Academy. We will not inquire by whose mechanical combinations it was, that your steam-boats stem the currents of your rivers, and vanquish the opposition of the winds themselves upon your seas. We will not name the inventor of the cotton-gin, for we fear that you would ask us the meaning of the word, and pronounce it a provincial barbarism. We will not name to you him, whose graver defies the imitation of forgery, and saves the labor of your executioner, by taking from your greatest geniuses of robbery the power of committing the crime. He is now among yourselves; and since your philosophers have permitted him to prove to them the compressibility of water, you may perhaps claim him for your own. Would you soar to fame upon a rocket, or burst into glory from a shell? We shall leave you to inquire of your naval heroes their opinion of the steam-battery and the torpedo. It is not by the contrivance of agents of destruction, that America wishes to commend her inventive genius to the admiration or the gratitude of after times; nor is it even by the detection of the secrets or the composition of new modifications of physical nature.

"Excudent alii spirantia mollius aera."

Nor even is her purpose the glory of Roman ambition; nor "tu regere imperio populosa" her memento to her sons. Her glory is not dominion, but liberty. Her march is the march of mind. She has a spear and a shield; but the motto upon her shield is Freedom, Independence, Peace. This has been her declaration: this has been, as far as her necessary intercourse with the rest of mankind would permit, her practice. . . .

James Monroe, "The Monroe Doctrine" (1823)

The Monroe Doctrine, largely the handiwork of Secretary of State Adams, marked an essential first step toward establishing US primacy over the Western Hemisphere as a whole.

The people being with us exclusively the sovereign, it is indispensable that full information be laid before them on all important subjects, to enable them to exercise that high power with complete effect. If kept in the dark, they must be incompetent to it. We are all liable to error, and those who are engaged in the management of public affairs are more subject to excitement and to be led astray by their particular interests and passions than the great body of our constituents, who, living at home in the pursuit of their ordinary avocations, are calm but deeply interested spectators of events and of the conduct of those who are parties to them.

To the people every department of the Government and every individual in each are responsible, and the more full their information the better they can judge of the wisdom of the policy pursued and of the conduct of each in regard to it. From their dispassionate judgment much aid may always be obtained, while their approbation will form the greatest incentive and most gratifying reward for virtuous actions, and the dread of their censure the best security against the abuse of their confidence. . . .

A precise knowledge of our relations with foreign powers as respects our negotiations and transactions with each is thought to be particularly necessary. . . .

It appearing from long experience that no satisfactory arrangement could be formed of the commercial intercourse between the United States and the British colonies in this hemisphere by legislative acts while each party pursued its own course without agreement or concert with the other, a proposal has been made to the British Government to regulate this commerce by treaty, as it has been to arrange in like manner the just claim of the citizens of the United States inhabiting the States and Territories bordering on the lakes and rivers which empty into the St. Lawrence to the navigation of that river to the ocean. . . .

At the proposal of the Russian Imperial Government, made through the minister of the Emperor residing here, a full power and instructions have been transmitted to the minister of the United States at St. Petersburg to arrange by amicable negotiation the respective rights and interests of the two nations on the North West coast of this continent. A similar proposal had been made by His Imperial Majesty to the Government of Great Britain, which has likewise been acceded to. . . . In the discussions to which this interest has given rise and in the arrangements by which they may terminate the occasion has been judged proper for asserting, as a principle in which the rights and interests of the United States are involved, that the American continents, by the free and independent condition which they have assumed and maintain, are henceforth not to be considered as subjects for future colonization by any European powers. . . .

In compliance with a resolution of the House of Representatives adopted at their last session, instructions have been given to all the ministers of the United States accredited to the powers of Europe and America to propose the proscription of the African slave trade by classing it under the denomination, and inflicting on its perpetrators the punishment, of piracy. Should this proposal be acceded to, it is not doubted that this odious and criminal practice will be promptly and entirely suppressed. . . .

The state of the Army in its organization and discipline has been gradually improving for several years, and has now attained a high degree of perfection. . . .

I transmit a return of the militia of the several States according to the last reports which have been made by the proper officers in each to the Department of War. . . . As the defense and even the liberties of the country must depend in times of imminent danger on the militia, it is of the highest importance that it be well organized, armed, and disciplined throughout the Union. . . .

The usual force has been maintained in the Mediterranean Sea, the Pacific Ocean, and along the Atlantic coast, and has afforded the necessary protection to our commerce in those seas. . . .

It is a source of great satisfaction that we are always enabled to recur to the conduct of our Navy with price and commendation. As a means of national defense it enjoys the public confidence, and is steadily assuming additional importance. . . .

A strong hope has been long entertained, founded on the heroic struggle of the Greeks, that they would succeed in their contest and resume their equal station among the nations of the earth. It is believed that the whole civilized world take a deep interest in their welfare. . . . From the facts which have come to our knowledge there is good cause to believe that their enemy has lost forever all dominion over them; that Greece will become again an independent nation. That she may obtain that rank is the object of our most ardent wishes.

It was stated at the commencement of the last session that a great effort was then making in Spain and Portugal to improve the condition of the people of those countries, and that it appeared to be conducted with extraordinary moderation. It need scarcely be remarked that the result has been so far very different from what was then anticipated. Of events in that quarter of the globe, with which we have so much intercourse and from which we derive our origin, we have always been anxious and interested spectators.

The citizens of the United States cherish sentiments the most friendly in favor of the liberty and happiness of their fellow men on that side of the Atlantic. In the wars of the European powers in matters relating to themselves we have never taken any part, nor does it comport with our policy so to do.

It is only when our rights are invaded or seriously menaced that we resent injuries or make preparation for our defense. With the movements in this hemisphere we are of necessity more immediately connected, and by causes which must be obvious to all enlightened and impartial observers.

The political system of the allied powers is essentially different in this respect from that of America. This difference proceeds from that which exists in their respective Governments; and to the defense of our own, which has been achieved by the loss of so much blood and treasure, and matured by the wisdom of their most enlightened citizens, and under which we have enjoyed unexampled felicity, this whole nation is devoted.

We owe it, therefore, to candor and to the amicable relations existing between the United States and those powers to declare that we should consider any attempt on their part to extend their system to any portion of this hemisphere as dangerous to our peace and safety. With the existing colonies or dependencies of any European power we have not interfered and shall not interfere, but with the Governments who have declared their independence and maintained it, and whose independence we have, on great consideration and on just principles, acknowledged, we could not view any interposition for the purpose of oppressing them, or controlling in any other manner their destiny, by any European power in any other light than as the manifestation of an unfriendly disposition toward the United States.

In the war between those new Governments and Spain we declared our neutrality at the time of their recognition, and to this we have adhered, and shall continue to adhere, provided no change shall occur which, in the judgment of the competent authorities of this Government, shall make a corresponding change on the part of the United States indispensable to their security. . . .

Our policy in regard to Europe, which was adopted at an early stage of the wars which have so long agitated that quarter of the globe, nevertheless remains the same, which is, not to interfere in the internal concerns of any of its powers; to consider the government de facto as the legitimate government for us; to cultivate friendly relations with it, and to preserve those relations by a frank, firm, and manly policy, meeting in all instances the just claims of every power, submitting to injuries from none.

But in regard to those continents circumstances are eminently and conspicuously different. It is impossible that the allied powers should extend their political system to any portion of either continent without endangering our peace and happiness; nor can anyone believe that our southern brethren, if left to themselves, would adopt it of their own accord. It is equally impossible, therefore, that we should behold such interposition in any form with indifference. If we look to the comparative strength and resources of Spain and those new Governments, and their distance from each other, it must be obvious that she can never subdue them. It is still the true policy of the United States to leave the parties to themselves, in the hope that other powers will pursue the same course. . . .

At the first epoch half the territory within our acknowledged limits was uninhabited and a wilderness. Since then new territory has been acquired of vast extent, comprising within it many rivers, particularly the Mississippi, the navigation of which to the ocean was of the highest importance to the original States. Over this territory our population has expanded in every direction, and new States have been established almost equal in number to those which formed the first bond of our Union. This expansion of our population and accession of new States to our Union have had the happiest effect on all its highest interests.

That it has eminently augmented our resources and added to our strength and respectability as a power is admitted by all, but it is not in these important circumstances only that this happy effect is felt. It is manifest that by enlarging the basis of our system and increasing the number of States the system itself has been greatly strengthened in both its branches. Consolidation and disunion have thereby been rendered equally impracticable.

Each Government, confiding in its own strength, has less to apprehend from the other, and in consequence each, enjoying a greater freedom of action, is rendered more efficient for all the purposes for which it was instituted.

ANDREW JACKSON, "ON INDIAN REMOVAL" (1830)

As the United States incorporated into the Union vast tracts of additional territory, successive administrations set about the work of consolidating and exploiting the new holdings. Among other things, that meant eliminating inhabitants deemed likely to interfere with the advance of civilization, defined as white and Christian. Here, President Andrew Jackson (1767–1845) orders the expulsion of Native Americans. As implemented, the process was anything but benevolent.

It gives me pleasure to announce to Congress that the benevolent policy of the Government, steadily pursued for nearly thirty years, in relation to the removal of the Indians beyond the white settlements is approaching to a happy consummation. Two important tribes have accepted the provision made for their removal at the last session of Congress, and it is believed that their example will induce the remaining tribes also to seek the same obvious advantages.

The consequences of a speedy removal will be important to the United States, to individual States, and to the Indians themselves. The pecuniary advantages which it promises to the Government are the least of its recommendations. It puts an end to all possible danger of collision between the authorities of the General and State Governments on account of the Indians. It will place a dense and civilized population in large tracts of country now occupied by a few savage hunters. By opening the whole territory between Tennessee on the north and Louisiana on the south to the settlement of the whites it will incalculably strengthen the southwestern frontier and render the adjacent States strong enough to repel future invasions without remote aid. It will relieve the whole State of Mississippi and the western part of Alabama of Indian occupancy, and enable those States to advance rapidly in population, wealth, and power. It will separate the Indians from immediate contact with settlements of whites; free them from the power of the States; enable them to pursue happiness in their own way and under their own rude institutions; will retard the progress of decay, which is lessening their numbers, and perhaps cause them gradually, under the protection of the Government and through the influence of good counsels, to cast off their savage habits and become an interesting, civilized, and Christian community.

What good man would prefer a country covered with forests and ranged by a few thousand savages to our extensive Republic, studded with cities, towns, and prosperous farms embellished with all the improvements which art can devise or industry execute, occupied by more than 12,000,000 happy people, and filled with all the blessings of liberty, civilization and religion?

The present policy of the Government is but a continuation of the same progressive change by a milder process. The tribes which occupied the countries now constituting the Eastern States were annihilated or have melted away to make room for the whites. The waves of population and civilization are rolling to the westward, and we now propose to acquire the countries occupied by the red men of the South and West by a fair exchange, and, at the expense of the United States, to send them to land where their existence may be prolonged and perhaps made perpetual. Doubtless it will be painful to leave the graves of their fathers; but what do they more than our ancestors did or than our children are now doing? To better their condition in an unknown land our forefathers left all that was dear in earthly objects. Our children by thousands yearly leave the land of their birth to seek new homes in distant regions. Does Humanity weep at these painful separations from everything, animate and inanimate, with which the young heart has become entwined? Far from it. It is rather a source of joy that our country affords scope where our young population may range unconstrained in body or in mind, developing the power and facilities of man in their highest perfection. These remove hundreds and almost thousands of miles at their own expense, purchase the lands they occupy, and support themselves at their new homes from the moment of their arrival. Can it be cruel in this Government when, by events which it can not control, the Indian is made discontented in his ancient home to purchase his lands, to give him a new and extensive territory, to pay the expense of his removal, and support him a year in his new abode? How many thousands of our own people would gladly embrace the opportunity of removing to the West on such conditions! If the offers made to the Indians were extended to them, they would be hailed with gratitude and joy.

And is it supposed that the wandering savage has a stronger attachment to his home than the settled, civilized Christian? Is it more afflicting to him to leave the graves of his fathers than it is to our brothers and children? Rightly considered, the policy of the General Government toward the red man is not only liberal, but generous. He is unwilling to submit to the laws of the States and mingle with their population. To save him from this alternative, or perhaps utter annihilation, the General Government kindly offers him a new home, and proposes to pay the whole expense of his removal and settlement.

WILLIAM PENN [JEREMIAH EVERTS], "PRESENT CRISIS IN THE CONDITION OF THE AMERICAN INDIANS" (1830)

Jeremiah Everts (1781–1831), a Christian missionary, denounced the policy of Native American removal.

Every careful observer of events must have seen, that a crisis has been rapidly approaching, for several years past, in reference to the condition, relations, and prospects of the Indian tribes, in the southwestern parts of the United States. The attention of many of our most intelligent citizens has been fixed upon the subject with great interest. Many others are beginning to inquire. . . .

Still, however, the mass of the community possess but little information on the subject; and even among the best informed, scarcely a man can be found, who is thoroughly acquainted with the questions at issue. . . .

[T]he people of the United States owe it to themselves and to mankind, to form a correct judgment in this matter. The questions have forced themselves upon us as a nation:—*What is to become of the Indians? Have they any rights?* If they have, *What are these rights? and how are they to be secured?* These questions must receive a practical answer; and that very soon. . . .

The character of our government, and of our country, may be deeply involved. Most certainly an indelible stigma will be fixed upon us, if, in the plenitude of our power, and in the pride of our superiority, we shall be guilty of manifest injustice to our weak and defenseless neighbors. . . .

It should be remembered, by our rulers as well as others, that this controversy . . . will ultimately be well understood by the whole civilized world. No subject, not even war, nor slavery, nor the nature of free institutions, will be more thoroughly canvased. The voice of mankind will be pronounced upon it. . . .

Any course of action, in regard to the Indians, which is manifestly fair, and generous, and benevolent, will command the warm and decided approbation of intelligent men, not only in the present age, but in all succeeding times. And with equal confidence it may be said, if, in the phraseology of Mr. Jefferson, the people of the United States should "feel power, and forget right;"—if they should resemble a man, who, abounding in wealth of every kind, and assuming the office of lawgiver and judge, first declares himself to be the owner of his poor neighbor's little farm, and then ejects the same neighbor as a troublesome incumbrance;—if, with land enough, now in the undisputed possession of the whites, to sustain ten times our present population, we should compel the tribes to leave the places, which, received by inheritance from their fathers and never alienated, they have long regarded as their permanent homes;—if, when asked to explain the treaties, which we first proposed, then solemnly executed, and have many times ratified, we stammer and prevaricate, and complete our disgrace by an unsuccessful attempt to stultify, not merely ourselves, but the ablest and wisest statesmen, whom our country has produced; and if, in pursuance of a narrow and selfish policy, we should at this day, in a time of profound peace and great national prosperity, amidst all our professions of magnanimity and benevolence, and in the blazing light of the nineteenth century, drive away these remnants of tribes, in such a manner, and under such auspices as to insure their destruction;—if all this should hereafter appear to be a fair statement of the case;—then the sentence of an indignant world will be uttered in thunder, which will roll and reverberate for ages after the present actors in human affairs shall have passed away. . . .

There is a higher consideration still. The Great Arbiter of Nations never fails to take cognizance of national delinquencies. No sophistry can elude his scrutiny; no array of plausible arguments, or of smooth but hollow professions, can bias his judgment; and he has at his disposal most abundant means of executing his decisions. In many forms, and with awful solemnity, he has declared his abhorrence of oppression in every shape; and especially of injustice perpetrated against the weak by the strong, *when strength is in fact made the only rule of action.* . . .

[I]t is very clear, that our government and our people should be extremely cautious, lest, in judging between ourselves and the Indians, and carrying our own judgment into execution with a strong hand, we incur the displeasure of the Most High. . . .

JOHN ROSS, "LETTER TO CONGRESS" (1836)

Chief of the Cherokee Nation, John Ross (1790–1866) mounted an eloquent protest against the injustice done to his people by the United States government.

It is well known that for a number of years past we have been harassed by a series of vexations, which it is deemed unnecessary to recite in detail, but the evidence of which our delegation will be prepared to furnish. . . .

By the stipulations of this instrument, we are despoiled of our private possessions, the indefeasible property of individuals. We are stripped of every attribute of freedom and eligibility for legal self-defence. Our property may be plundered before our eyes; violence may be committed on our persons; even our lives may be taken away, and there is none to regard our complaints. We are denationalized; we are disfranchised. We are deprived of membership in the human family! We have neither land nor home, nor resting place that can be called our own. And this is effected by the provisions of a compact which assumes the venerated, the sacred appellation of treaty.

We are overwhelmed! Our hearts are sickened, our utterance is paralized, when we reflect on the condition in which we are placed, by the audacious practices of unprincipled men, who have managed their stratagems with so much dexterity as to impose on the Government of the United States, in the face of our earnest, solemn, and reiterated protestations.

The instrument in question is not the act of our Nation; we are not parties to its covenants; it has not received the sanction of our people. The makers of it sustain no office nor appointment in our Nation, under the designation of Chiefs, Head men, or any other title, by which they hold, or could acquire, authority to assume the reins of

Government, and to make bargain and sale of our rights, our possessions, and our common country. And we are constrained solemnly to declare, that we cannot but contemplate the enforcement of the stipulations of this instrument on us, against our consent, as an act of injustice and oppression, which, we are well persuaded, can never knowingly be countenanced by the Government and people of the United States; nor can we believe it to be the design of these honorable and high-minded individuals, who stand at the head of the Govt., to bind a whole Nation, by the acts of a few unauthorized individuals. And, therefore, we, the parties to be affected by the result, appeal with confidence to the justice, the magnanimity, the compassion, of your honorable bodies, against the enforcement, on us, of the provisions of a compact, in the formation of which we have had no agency.

In truth, our cause is your own; it is the cause of liberty and of justice; it is based upon your own principles, which we have learned from yourselves; for we have gloried to count your [George] Washington and your [Thomas] Jefferson our great teachers; we have read their communications to us with veneration; we have practised their precepts with success. And the result is manifest. The wildness of the forest has given place to comfortable dwellings and cultivated fields, stocked with the various domestic animals. Mental culture, industrious habits, and domestic enjoyments, have succeeded the rudeness of the savage state.

We have learned your religion also. We have read your Sacred books. Hundreds of our people have embraced their doctrines, practised the virtues they teach, cherished the hopes they awaken, and rejoiced in the consolations which they afford. To the spirit of your institutions, and your religion, which has been imbibed by our community, is mainly to be ascribed that patient endurance which has characterized the conduct of our people, under the laceration of their keenest woes. For assuredly, we are not ignorant of our condition; we are not insensible to our sufferings. We feel them! We groan under their pressure! And anticipation crowds our breasts with sorrows yet to come. We are, indeed, an afflicted people! Our spirits are subdued! Despair has well nigh seized upon our energies! But we speak to the representatives of a Christian country; the friends of justice; the patrons of the oppressed. And our hopes revive, and our prospects brighten, as we indulge the thought. On your sentence, our fate is suspended; prosperity or desolation depends on your word. To you, therefore, we look! Before your august assembly we present ourselves, in the attitude of deprecation, and of entreaty. On your kindness, on your humanity, on your compassion, on your benevolence, we rest our hopes. To you we address our reiterated prayers. Spare our people! Spare the wreck of our prosperity! Let not our deserted homes become the monuments of our desolation! But we forbear! We suppress the agonies which wring our hearts, when we look at our wives, our children, and our venerable sires! We restrain the forebodings of anguish and distress, of misery and devastation and death, which must be the attendants on the execution of this ruinous compact.

William Wirt, "The Triumph of Liberty in France" (1830)

Any distant uprising against tyranny will persuade at least some Americans that they are witnessing a reenactment of their own struggle for liberty. Here an oration by William Wirt (1772–1834), the longest serving attorney general in US history, makes the case that political upheaval in France represents a continuation of the work begun by Americans in 1776.

We have met, fellow citizens, to give public expression to the feelings which animate every bosom in our society, and to unite our congratulations on the triumph of liberty in France. On this subject, there is but one heart, one voice among us, and that a heart and voice of universal joy.

Had this great event occurred even in a land of strangers, unendeared to us by any previous act of kindness, and having no other claim upon our sympathies than that they belonged to the same family of human beings with ourselves, it would still have been cause of private joy to each individual among us; for it would have borne evidence of the progress of liberty in the world. But it is not in a land of strangers, it is not in a country unendeared to us by previous acts of kindness that it has occurred. It is in France, our ancient friend and ally: in France, who stood by us in the darkest days of our own revolution; in France, by the powerful aid of whose fleets and armies, the last ensign of British authority was struck in our land, and we took our undisputed place among the nations of the earth. Yes, it is in France, the land of our benefactors and friends, that this spectacle has been exhibited. . . .

In the stern decision, in the rapid and resistless execution, in the thorough accomplishment of the purpose, and in the sudden and perfect calm that succeeded, tyrants may read a lesson that may well make them tremble on their thrones; for they see that it is only for the people to resolve, and it is done. . . .

Very much, indeed every thing, depends upon the prudence of France herself. If she shall stop where she is, remain quiet, united and happy at home, and avoid all interference with other governments, the work is done. If, on the other hand, storms should arise within to drive her from her present anchorage, and set the revolution afloat again on a sea of anarchy, every thing is to be feared for herself and for Europe. . . .

The great security of France arises from her past experience, which must make her distrust all counsels tending to disunion and disorganization. There is, moreover, an efficient and watchful government in being, under whose jealous vigilance these incendiaries will have to carry on their machinations. What theme can they find of sufficient power to persuade the people of France to leave the port in which they now find themselves safe and happy, and to commit themselves again to those seas of whose dangers they have heretofore had such dreadful experience. . . .

The people of France finding themselves at once in the actual enjoyment of the sweets of peace and freedom, under the protection of a government mild, conciliating and efficient—open,

moreover, to such amendments as experience shall suggest, will hardly be persuaded to go again in quest of anarchy and confusion, with the horrors and the catastrophe of the former revolution full in their view. No: they have not forgotten that fearful lesson: and to suppose them ready, without any necessity, to re-enact that tragedy, is to suppose them madmen, without any other claim upon the sympathies of the world than such as are felt for the inmates of a lunatic asylum. . . .

Let us not fear that the light which has already gone forth will be extinguished. Tyrants might as well attempt to blot the sun from the firmament. They may attempt it; but "He that sitteth in the heavens shall laugh them to scorn." The creatures formed for his worship will be permitted to worship him with exalted faculties and full liberty of conscience. Placed here for their common good and happiness, and indued with minds and affections fitted for enlightened intercourse, and the mutual interchange of kind offices, let us not be so impious as to fear that the light which has arisen will be suffered to be put out and the world replunged in darkness and barbarity.

Fellow citizens, this light was first struck in our land. The sacred trust is still among us. Let us take care how we guard the holy fire. We stand under a fearful responsibility to our Creator and our fellow creatures. It has been his divine pleasure that we should be sent forth as the harbingers of free government on the earth, and in this attitude we are now before the world. The eyes of the world are upon us; and our example will probably be decisive of the cause of human liberty.

The great argument of despots against free governments is, that large bodies of men are incapable of self-rule, and that the inevitable and rapid tendency of such a government as ours is to faction, strife, anarchy and dissolution. Let it be our effort to give, to the expecting world, a great, practical and splendid refutation of this charge. If we cannot do this, the world may despair. To what other nation can we look to do it? We claim no natural superiority to other nations. We have not the folly to think of it. We claim nothing more than a natural equality. But circumstances have conspired to give us an advantage in making this great political experiment which no other modern nation enjoys. . . . . If, therefore, our experiment shall fail,

I say again that the world may well despair. Warned as we are by the taunts of European monarchists, and by the mournful example of all the ancient republics, are we willing to split on the same rock on which we have seen them shipwrecked? Are we willing to give our enemies such a triumph as to fulfil their prophecy and convince the world that self-government is impracticable—a mere chimera—and that man is fit only to be a slave to his fellow man? Are we willing to teach the nations of the earth to despair, and resign themselves at once to the power that crushes them? Shall we forfeit all the bright honors that we have hitherto won by our example, and now admit by our conduct, that, although free government may subsist for a while, under the pressure of extrinsic and momentary causes, yet that it cannot bear a long season of peace and prosperity; but that as soon as thus left to itself, it speedily hastens to faction, demoralization, anarchy and ruin? Are we prepared to make this practical admission by our conduct, and extinguish, ourselves, the sacred light of liberty which has been entrusted to our keeping? Or, shall we not rather show ourselves worthy of this high trust, maintain the advanced post which we have hitherto occupied with so much honor, prove, by our example, that a free government is the best pledge for peace and order and human happiness, and thus continue to light the other nations of the earth on their way to liberty? Who can hesitate between these two alternatives? Who . . . is willing to admit that men are incapable of self-government, and unworthy of the blessing of liberty? No man, I am sure, who has an American heart in his bosom.

Away, then, with all faction, strife and uncharitableness from our land. We are brothers. Let no angry feelings enter our political dwellings. If we differ about measures or about men, (as, from the constitution of our nature, differ we must,) let us remember that we are all but fallible men, and extend to others that charity of which the best of us cannot but feel that we stand in need. We owe this good temper and indulgence to each other as members of the same family, as all interested, and deeply interested, in the preservation of the Union and of our political institutions: and we owe it to the world as the van-couriers of free government on earth, and the guardians of the

first altar that has been erected to Liberty in modern times. . . .

Friends and fellow-citizens, "our lines have fallen to us in pleasant places: yea, we have a goodly heritage." Let us not mar it by vindictive altercations among ourselves, and offend the shades of our departed fathers who left this rich inheritance to us. . . . Let us not disappoint the world which still looks to us for a bright example, and is manifestly preparing to follow our steps. Let us not offend that Almighty Being who gave us all these blessings, and who has a right to expect that we will enjoy them in peace and brotherly love. It is His will that we should so enjoy them; and may His will be done. . . .

With no pretence of right, and no wish to interfere with the political institutions of other countries, but, on the contrary, holding it to be the right of all to pursue their own happiness, in their own way, and under the form of government which they deem most conducive to that end—yet believing, as we do, that civil and religious freedom are essential to the happiness of man, and to the development of the high capacities, mental and moral, with which his Creator has endowed him, it is natural for us to rejoice when we see any nation, and more especially one so endeared to us as France, coming, of her own accord, into the fold of free governments. If there be any people who believe that their peace and order and happiness require the curb of a despotic government, be it so: their believing it, is proof enough to us that it is so, with regard to them: And however much we may regret, it is not for us to disturb their repose. Free government is good only for those who understand its value and are prepared for its enjoyment. It cannot be forced, with advantage, upon any people who are not yet ripe for its reception. Nations yet in darkness require, like children, to be disciplined and instructed before they can act with advantage for themselves. Their best instruction from abroad, is the example of other nations; their only proper teachers at home, are their own enlightened patriots; and the wisest process, the gradual diffusion of light among them. . . . It is only by such a revolution as this that the cause of liberty can present an attraction to the world. It is only in such a revolution that the humane and benevolent can take delight.

ALEXIS DE TOCQUEVILLE, "CONDUCT OF FOREIGN AFFAIRS BY THE AMERICAN DEMOCRACY," *DEMOCRACY IN AMERICA* (1835)

Enduringly famous as the author of *Democracy in America,* Alexis de Tocqueville (1805–1859) offered a European perspective on US foreign policy. Diplomacy, he argues, is rightly the province of a trained elite, its members devoid of the passions and prejudices to which ordinary citizens are susceptible.

Direction given to the foreign policy of the United States by Washington and Jefferson—Almost all the defects inherent in democratic institutions are brought to light in the conduct of foreign affairs; their advantages are less perceptible.

We have seen that the Federal Constitution entrusts the permanent direction of the external interests of the nation to the President and the Senate, which tends in some degree to detach the general foreign policy of the Union from the direct control of the people. It cannot, therefore, be asserted with truth that the foreign affairs of the state are conducted by the democracy.

There are two men who have imparted to American foreign policy a tendency that is still being followed today; the first is Washington and the second Jefferson. Washington said, in the admirable Farewell Address which he made to his fellow citizens, and which may be regarded as his political testament:

"The great rule of conduct for us in regard to foreign nations is, in extending our commercial relations, to have with them as little political connection as possible. So far as we have already formed engagements, let them be fulfilled with perfect good faith. Here let us stop." [Further extracts from Washington's Farewell Address reprinted above follow].

In a previous part of the same address Washington makes this admirable and just remark: "The nation which indulges towards another an habitual hatred, or an habitual fondness, is in some degree a slave. It is a slave to its animosity or to its affection, either of which is sufficient to lead it astray from its duty and its interest."

The political conduct of Washington was always guided by these maxims. He succeeded in maintaining his country in a state of peace while all the other nations of the globe were at war; and he laid it down as a fundamental doctrine that the true interest of the Americans consisted in a perfect neutrality with regard to the internal dissensions of the European powers.

Jefferson went still further and introduced this other maxim into the policy of the Union, that "the Americans ought never to solicit any privileges from foreign nations, in order not to be obliged to grant similar privileges themselves."

These two principles, so plain and just as to be easily understood by the people, have greatly simplified the foreign policy of the United States. As the Union takes no part in the affairs of Europe, it has, properly speaking, no foreign interests to discuss, since it has, as yet, no powerful neighbors on the American continent. The country is as much removed from the passions of the Old World by its position as by its wishes, and it is called upon neither to repudiate nor to espouse them; while the dissensions of the New World are still concealed within the bosom of the future.

The Union is free from all pre-existing obligations, it can profit by the experience of the old nations of Europe, without being obliged, as they are, to make the best of the past and to adapt it to their present circumstances. It is not, like them, compelled to accept an immense inheritance bequeathed by their forefathers an inheritance of glory mingled with calamities, and of alliances conflicting with national antipathies. The foreign policy of the United States is eminently expectant; it consists more in abstaining than in acting.

It is therefore very difficult to ascertain, at present, what degree of sagacity the American democracy will display in the conduct of the foreign policy of the country; upon this point its adversaries as well as its friends must suspend their judgment. As for myself I do not hesitate to say that it is especially in the conduct of their foreign relations that democracies appear to me decidedly inferior to other governments. Experience, instruction, and habit almost always succeed in creating in a democracy a homely species of practical wisdom and that science of the petty occurrences of life which is called good sense. Good sense may suffice to direct

Alexis de Tocqueville, *Democracy in America.* London, England: Saunders and Otley (1835).

the ordinary course of society; and among a people whose education is completed, the advantages of democratic liberty in the internal affairs of the country may more than compensate for the evils inherent in a democratic government. But it is not always so in the relations with foreign nations.

Foreign politics demand scarcely any of those qualities which are peculiar to a democracy; they require, on the contrary, the perfect use of almost all those in which it is deficient. Democracy is favorable to the increase of the internal resources of a state, it diffuses wealth and comfort, promotes public spirit, and fortifies the respect for law in all classes of society: all these are advantages which have only an indirect influence over the relations which one people bears to another. But a democracy can only with great difficulty regulate the details of an important undertaking, persevere in a fixed design, and work out its execution in spite of serious obstacles. It cannot combine its measures with secrecy or await their consequences with patience. These are qualities which more especially belong to an individual or an aristocracy; and they are precisely the qualities by which a nation, like an individual, attains a dominant position.

If, on the contrary, we observe the natural defects of aristocracy, we shall find that, comparatively speaking, they do not injure the direction of the external affairs of the state. The capital fault of which aristocracies may be accused is that they work for themselves and not for the people. In foreign politics it is rare for the interest of the aristocracy to be distinct from that of the people.

The propensity that induces democracies to obey impulse rather than prudence, and to abandon a mature design for the gratification of a momentary passion, was clearly seen in America on the breaking out of the French Revolution. It was then as evident to the simplest capacity as it is at the present time that the interest of the Americans forbade them to take any part in the contest which was about to deluge Europe with blood, but which could not injure their own country. But the sympathies of the people declared themselves with so much violence in favor of France that nothing but the inflexible character of Washington and the immense popularity which he enjoyed could have prevented the Americans from declaring war against England. And even then the exertions which the austere reason of that great man made to repress the generous but imprudent passions of his fellow citizens nearly deprived him of the sole recompense which he ever claimed, that of his country's love. The majority reprobated his policy, but it was afterwards approved by the whole nation.

If the Constitution and the favor of the public had not entrusted the direction of the foreign affairs of the country to Washington it is certain that the American nation would at that time have adopted the very measures which it now condemns.

Almost all the nations that have exercised a powerful influence upon the destinies of the world, by conceiving, following out, and executing vast designs, from the Romans to the English, have been governed by aristocratic institutions. Nor will this be a subject of wonder when we recollect that nothing in the world is so conservative in its views as an aristocracy. The mass of the people may be led astray by ignorance or passion, the mind of a king may be biased and made to vacillate in his designs, and, besides, a king is not immortal. But an aristocratic body is too numerous to be led astray by intrigue, and yet not numerous enough to yield readily to the intoxication of unreflecting passion. An aristocracy is a firm and enlightened body that never dies.

WILLIAM ELLERY CHANNING, "A LETTER TO THE HONORABLE HENRY CLAY" (1837)

In 1835–1836, Americans living in Texas, then a province of Mexico, mounted a revolt, claimed independence, and petitioned Congress for statehood. The proposed annexation of Texas divided Americans. Here William Ellery Channing (1780–1842), a prominent Unitarian minister and abolitionist, rejects any comparison between the American Revolution and the Texas Revolution, which he describes as promoting the perpetuation of slavery.

Should Texas be annexed to our country, I feel that I could not forgive myself, if, with my deep, solemn impressions, I should do nothing to avert the evil. I cannot easily believe, that this disastrous measure is to be adopted, especially at the present moment. The annexation of Texas under existing circumstances, would be more than rashness; it would be madness. . . .

The Texan insurrection is seriously regarded by many among us as a struggle of the oppressed for freedom. The Texan revolution is thought to resemble our own. Our own is contaminated by being brought into such relationship, and we owe to our fathers and ourselves a disclaimer of affinity with this new republic. The Texan revolt, if regarded in its causes and its means of success, is criminal; and we ought in no way to become partakers in its guilt. . . .

I ask you, Sir, whether it is not your deliberate conviction, that Mexico, from the beginning of her connexion with the colonists, has been more sinned against than sinning. But allowing that the violent means, used by Mexico for enforcing her authority, were less provoked than we believe them to have been; did not the Texans enter the country with a full knowledge of its condition? Did they not become citizens of a state, just escaped from a grinding despotism, just entered into the school of freedom, which had been inured for ages to abuses of military power, and whose short republican history had been made up of civil agitation? In swearing allegiance to such a state, did they not consent to take their chance of the evils, through which it must have been expected to pass in its way to firm and free institutions? Was there, or could there be in so unsettled a society, that deliberate, settled, inflexible purpose of spoiling the colonists of their rights, which alone absolves a violation of allegiance from the guilt of treason. Some of the grounds, on which the Texans justify their conflict for independence, are so glaringly deficient in truth and reason, that it is hard to avoid suspicion of every defence set up for their revolt. . . .

The United States did not throw off the British yoke, because every human right, which could be demonstrated by moral science, was not granted them; but because they were denied the rights which their fathers had enjoyed, and which had been secured to the rest of the empire. They began with pleading precedent. They took their first stand on the British constitution. They claimed the rights of Englishmen. They set up the case of peculiar oppression; and did not appeal to arms, until they had sought redress for years by patient and respectful remonstrance; until they had exhausted every means of conciliation which wisdom could devise or a just self-respect would allow. Such was the code of national morality to which our fathers bowed; and in so doing they acknowledged the sacredness of allegiance, and manifested their deep conviction of the fearful responsibility of subverting a government and of rupturing national ties. A province, in estimating its grievances, should have respect to the general condition of the country to which it belongs. A colony, emigrating from a highly civilized country, has no right to expect in a less favored state the privileges it has left behind. The Texans must have been insane, if, on entering Mexico, they looked for an administration as faultless as that under which they had lived. . . .

I proceed to another cause of the revolt, and this was the resolution to throw Texas open to slaveholders and slaves. Mexico, at the moment of throwing off the Spanish yoke, gave a noble testimony of her loyalty to free principles, by decreeing, "that no person thereafter should be born a slave or introduced as such into the Mexican States; that all slaves then held, should receive stipulated wages, and be subject to no punishment but on trial and judgment by the magistrate." The subsequent acts of the government carried out fully these constitutional provisions. It is matter of deep grief and humiliation, that the emigrants from this country, whilst boasting of superior civilization, refused to second this honorable policy, intended to set limits to one of the greatest social evils. Slaves were brought into Texas with their masters from the neighboring States of this country. . . .

The project of dismembering a neighboring republic, that slaveholders and slaves might overspread a region which had been consecrated to a free population, was discussed in newspapers as coolly as if it were a matter of obvious right and unquestionable humanity. A powerful interest was thus created for severing from Mexico her distant province. We have here a powerful incitement to the Texan revolt, and another explanation of the eagerness, with which men and money were thrown from the United States into that region to carry on the war of revolution.

Such were the chief excitements to the revolt. Undoubtedly, the Texans were instigated by the idea of wrongs, as well as by mercenary hopes. But had they yielded true obedience to the country of which they had, with their own free will, become a part; had they submitted to the laws relating to the revenue, to the sale of lands, and to slavery; the wrongs of which they complained might never have been experienced, or might never have been construed into a plea for insurrection. The great motives to revolt on which I have insisted are so notorious, that it is wonderful that any among us could be cheated into sympathy with the Texan cause, as the cause of freedom. Slavery and fraud lay at its very foundation. It is notorious, that land speculators, slaveholders, and selfish adventurers were among the foremost to proclaim and engage in the crusade for "Texan liberties." From the hands of these we are invited to receive a province, torn from a country to which we have given pledges of amity and peace. . . .

Having considered the motives of the revolution, I proceed to inquire, how was it accomplished? The answer to this question will show more fully the criminality of the enterprise. The Texans, we have seen, were a few thousands, as unfit for sovereignty as one of our towns; and, if left to themselves, must have utterly despaired of achieving independence. They looked abroad; and to whom did they look? To any foreign state? To the government under which they had formerly lived? No; their whole reliance was placed on selfish individuals in a neighboring republic at peace with Mexico. They looked wholly to private individuals, to citizens of this country, to such among us, as, defying the laws of the land, and hungry for sudden gain, should be lured by the scent of this mighty prey, and should be ready to stain their hands with blood for spoil. They held out a country as a prize to the reckless, lawless, daring, avaricious, and trusted to the excitements of intoxicated imagination and insatiable cupidity, to supply them with partners in their scheme of violence.

By whom has Texas been conquered? By the colonists? By the hands which raised the standard of revolt? By foreign governments espousing their cause? No; it has been conquered by your and my countrymen, by citizens of the United States, in violation of our laws and of the laws of nations.

We, we have filled the ranks which have wrested Texas from Mexico. In the army of eight hundred men who won the victory which scattered the Mexican force, and made its chief a prisoner, "not more than fifty were citizens of Texas having grievances of their own to seek relief from, on that field." The Texans in this warfare are little more than a name, a cover, under which selfish adventurers from another country have prosecuted their work of plunder. Some crimes, by their magnitude, have a touch of the sublime; and to this dignity the seizure of Texas by our citizens is entitled. Modern times furnish no example of individual rapine on so grand a scale. It is nothing less than the robbery of a realm. The pirate seizes a ship. The colonists and their coadjutors can satisfy themselves with nothing short of an empire. . . .

Let me now ask, are the United States prepared to receive from these hands the gift of Texas? In annexing it to this country, shall we not appropriate to ourselves the fruits of a rapine which we ought to have suppressed? We certainly should shrink from a proposition to receive a piratical state into our confederacy. And of whom does Texas consist? Very much of our own citizens, who have won a country by waging war against a foreign nation, to which we owed protection against such assaults. Does it consist with national honor, with national virtue, to receive to our embrace men who have prospered by crimes which we were bound to reprobate and repress? . . . .

The United States have not been just to Mexico. Our citizens did not steal singly, silently, in disguise into that land. Their purpose of dismembering Mexico, and attaching her distant province to this country, was not wrapt in mystery. It was proclaimed in our public prints. Expeditions were openly fitted out within our borders for the Texan war. Troops were organized, equipped, and marched for the scene of action. Advertisements for volunteers to be enrolled and conducted to Texas at the expense of that territory, were inserted in our newspapers. The government, indeed, issued its proclamation, forbidding these hostile preparations; but this was a dead letter. Military companies, with officers and standards, in defiance of proclamations, and in the face of day, directed their steps to the revolted province. We had, indeed, an army near the frontiers of Mexico. Did it turn back these invaders of a land with which we were at peace? On the contrary, did not its presence give confidence to the revolters? After this, what construction of our conduct shall we force on the world, if we proceed, especially at this moment, to receive into our Union the territory, which, through our neglect, has fallen a prey to lawless invasion? Are we willing to take our place among robber-states? As a people, have we no self-respect? Have we no reverence for national morality? Have we no feeling of responsibility to other nations, and to Him by whom the fates of nations are disposed?

Having unfolded the argument against the annexation of Texas from the criminality of the revolt, I proceed to a second very solemn consideration, namely, that by this act our country will enter on a career of encroachment, war, and crime, and will merit and incur the punishment and woe of aggravated wrong doing. The seizure of Texas will not stand alone. It will darken our future history. It will be linked by an iron necessity to long continued deeds of rapine and blood. Ages may not see the catastrophe of the tragedy, the first scene of which we are so ready to enact. It is strange that nations should be so much more rash than individuals; and this, in the face of experience, which has been teaching from the beginning of society, that, of all precipitate and criminal deeds, those perpetrated by nations are the most fruitful of misery. Did this country know itself, or were it disposed to profit by self-knowledge, it would feel the necessity of laying an immediate curb on its passion for extended territory. It would not trust itself to new acquisitions. It would shrink from the temptation to conquest. We are a restless people, prone to encroachment, impatient of the ordinary laws of progress, less anxious to consolidate and perfect, than to extend our institutions, more ambitious of spreading ourselves over a wide space, than of diffusing beauty and fruitfulness over a narrower field. We boast of our rapid growth, forgetting that, throughout nature, noble growths are slow. Our people throw themselves beyond the bounds of civilization, and expose themselves to relapses into a semi-barbarous state, under the impulse of wild imagination, and for the name of great possessions. Perhaps there is no people on earth, on whom the ties of local attachment sit so loosely. . . .

It is full time, that we should lay on ourselves serious, resolute restraint. Possessed of a domain, vast enough for the growth of ages, it is time for us to stop in the career of acquisition and conquest. Already endangered by our greatness, we cannot advance without imminent peril to our institutions, union, prosperity, virtue, and peace. Our former additions of territory have been justified by the necessity of obtaining outlets for the population of the South and the West. No such pretext exists for the occupation of Texas. We cannot seize upon or join to ourselves that territory, without manifesting and strengthening the purpose of setting no limits to our empire. We give ourselves an impulse, which will and must precipitate us into new invasions of our neighbors' soil. Is it by pressing forward in this course that we are to learn self-restraint? Is cupidity to be appeased by gratification? Is it by unrighteous grasping, that an impatient people will be instructed how to hem themselves within the rigid bounds of justice? Texas is a country conquered by our citizens; and the annexation of it to our Union will be the beginning of conquests, which, unless arrested and beaten back by a just and kind Providence, will stop only at the Isthmus of Darien. Henceforth, we must cease to cry peace, peace. Our Eagle will whet, not gorge its appetite on its first victim. . . .

Hitherto, I have spoken of the annexation of Texas as embroiling us with Mexico; but it will not stop here. It will bring us into collision with other states. It will, almost of necessity, involve us in hostility with European powers.

Such are now the connexions of nations, that Europe must look with jealousy on a country, whose ambition, seconded by vast resources, will seem to place within her grasp the empire of the new world. And not only general considerations of this nature, but the particular relation of certain foreign states to this continent, must tend to destroy the peace now happily subsisting between us and the kingdoms of Europe. England, in particular, must watch us with suspicion, and cannot but resist our appropriation of Texas to ourselves. She has at once a moral and political interest in this question, which demands, and will justify interference. . . . . .

It is of great and manifest importance, that we should use every just means to separate this continent from the politics of Europe, that we should prevent, as far as possible, all connexion, except commercial, between the old and the new world, that we should give to foreign states no occasion or pretext for insinuating themselves into our affairs. For this end, we should maintain towards our sister republics a more liberal policy than was ever adopted by nation towards nation. We should strive to appease their internal divisions, and to reconcile them to each other. We should even make sacrifices to build up their strength. Weak and divided, they cannot but lean on foreign support. No pains should be spared to prevent or allay the jealousies, which the great superiority of this country is suited to awaken. By an opposite policy we shall favor foreign interference. By encroaching on Mexico, we shall throw her into the arms of European States, shall compel her to seek defence in transatlantic alliance. How plain is it, that alliance with Mexico will be hostility to the United States, that her defenders will repay themselves by making her subservient to their views, that they will thus strike root in her soil, monopolize her trade and control her resources. And with what face can we resist the aggressions of others on our neighbor, if we give an example of aggression? . . .

In attaching Texas to ourselves, we provoke hostilities, and at the same time expose new points of attack to our foes. Vulnerable at so many points, we shall need a vast military force. Great armies will require great revenues, and raise up great chieftains. Are we tired of freedom, that we are prepared to place it under such guardians? Is the republic bent on dying by its own hands? Does not every man feel, that, with war for our habit, our institutions cannot be preserved? If ever a country were bound to peace, it is this. Peace is our great interest. In peace our resources are to be developed, the true interpretation of the constitution to be established, and the interfering claims of liberty and order to be adjusted. In peace we are to discharge our great debt to the human race, and to diffuse freedom by manifesting its fruits. A country has no right to adopt a policy, however gainful, which, as it may foresee, will determine it to a career of war. A nation, like an individual, is bound to seek even by sacrifices a position, which will favor peace, justice, and the exercise of a beneficent influence on the world. A nation, provoking war by cupidity, by encroachment, and above all by efforts to propagate the curse of slavery, is alike false to itself, to God, and to the human race.

I proceed now to a consideration of what is to me the strongest argument against annexing Texas to the United States. This measure will extend and perpetuate slavery. . . .

The great argument for annexing Texas is, that it will strengthen "the peculiar institutions" of the South, and open a new and vast field for slavery. By this act, slavery will be spread over regions to which it is now impossible to set limits. Texas, I repeat it, is but the first step of aggressions. I trust, indeed, that Providence will beat back and humble our cupidity and ambition. But one guilty success is often suffered to be crowned, as men call it, with greater; in order that a more awful retribution may at length vindicate the justice of God, and the rights of the oppressed. Texas, smitten with slavery, will spread the infection beyond herself. We know that the tropical regions have been found most propitious to this pestilence; nor can we promise ourselves, that its expulsion from them for a season forbids its return. By annexing Texas, we may send this scourge to a distance, which, if now revealed, would appal us, and through these vast regions every cry of the injured will invoke wrath on our heads. By this act, slavery will be perpetuated in the old states as well as spread over new. . . .

I now ask, whether as a people, we are prepared to seize on a neighboring territory for the end of extending slavery? I ask, whether, as a people, we can stand forth in the sight of God, in the sight of the nations, and adopt this atrocious policy? Sooner perish! Sooner be our name blotted out from the record of nations! . . .

We do not belong to the dark ages, or to heathenism. We have not grown up under the prejudices of a blinding, crushing tyranny. We live under free institutions and under the broad light of Christianity. Every principle of our government and religion condemns slavery. The spirit of our age condemns it. The decree of the civilized world has gone out against it. . . .

And is this an age in which a free and Christian people shall deliberately resolve to extend and perpetuate the evil? In so doing, we cut ourselves off from the communion of the nations. We sink below the civilization of our age. We invite the scorn, indignation, and abhorrence of the world. Let it not be said, that this opposition of our times to slavery is an accident, a temporary gust of opinion, an eddy in the current of human thought, a fashion to pass away with the present actors on the stage. He, who so says, must have read history with a superficial eye, and is strangely blind to the deepest and most powerful influences which are moulding society. Christianity has done more than all things to determine the character and direction of our present civilization; and who can question or overlook the tendency and design of this religion? Christianity has no plainer purpose, than to unite all men as brethren, to make man unutterably dear to man, to pour contempt on outward distinctions, to raise the fallen, to league all in efforts for the elevation of all. . . .

Our mission is to elevate society through all its conditions, to secure to every human being the means of progress, to substitute the government of equal laws for that of irresponsible individuals, to prove that, under popular institutions, the people may be carried forward, that the multitude who toil are capable of enjoying the noblest blessings of the social state. The prejudice, that labor is a degradation, one of the worst prejudices handed down from barbarous ages, is to receive here, a practical refutation. The power of liberty to raise up the whole people, this is the great Idea, on which our institutions rest, and which is to be wrought out in our history. . . .

But a nation devoting itself to the work of spreading and perpetuating slavery, stamps itself with a guilt and shame, which generations may not be able to efface. The plea on which we have rested, that slavery was not our choice, but a sad necessity bequeathed us by our fathers, will avail us no longer. The whole guilt will be assumed by ourselves. . . .

A community, acknowledging the evils of slavery, and continuing it only because the first law of nature, self-preservation, seems to require gradual processes of change, may retain the respect of those who deem their fears unfounded. But a community, wedding itself to slavery inseparably, with choice and affection, and with the purpose of spreading the plague far and wide, must become a byword among the nations; and the friend of humanity will shake off the dust of his feet against it, in testimony of his reprobation.

I proceed now to the last head of this communication. I observe that the cause of Liberty, of free institutions, a cause more sacred than Union, forbids the annexation of Texas. It is plain from the whole preceding discussion, that this measure will exert a disastrous influence on the moral sentiments and principles of this country, by sanctioning plunder,

by inflaming cupidity, by encouraging lawless speculation, by bringing into the confederacy a community whose whole history and circumstances are adverse to moral order and wholesome restraint, by violating national faith, by proposing immoral and inhuman ends, by placing us as a people in opposition to the efforts of philanthropy, and the advancing movements of the civilized world. It will spread a moral corruption, already too rife among us, and in so doing, it will shake the foundations of freedom at home, and bring reproach on it abroad. It will be treachery to the great cause which has been confided to this above all nations. The dependence of freedom on morals is an old subject, and I have no thought of enlarging on the general truth. I wish only to say, that it is one which needs to be brought home to us at the present moment, and that it cannot be trifled with but to our great peril.

There are symptoms of corruption amongst us, which show us that we cannot enter on a new career of crime without peculiar hazard. I cannot do justice to this topic without speaking freely of our country, as freely as I should of any other; and unhappily, we are so accustomed, as a people, to receive incense, to be soothed by flattery, and to account reputation as a more important interest than morality, that my freedom may be construed into a kind of disloyalty. But it would be wrong to make concessions to this dangerous weakness.

I believe that morality is the first interest of a people, and that this requires self-knowledge in nations, as truly as in individuals. He who helps a community to comprehend itself, and to apply to itself a higher rule of action, is the truest patriot, and contributes most to its enduring fame. I have said, that we shall expose our freedom to great peril by entering a new career of crime.

We are corrupt enough already. In one respect, our institutions have disappointed us all. They have not wrought out for us that elevation of character, which is the most precious, and in truth, the only substantial blessing of liberty. Our progress in prosperity has indeed been the wonder of the world; but this prosperity has done much to counteract the ennobling influence of free institutions. The peculiar circumstances of the country and of our times, have poured in upon us a torrent of wealth; and human nature has not been strong enough for the assault of such severe temptation. Prosperity has become dearer than freedom. Government is regarded more as a means of enriching the country, than of securing private rights. We have become wedded to gain, as our chief good. That under the predominance of this degrading passion, the higher virtues, the moral independence, the simplicity of manners, the stern uprightness, the self-reverence, the respect for man as man, which are the ornaments and safe-guards of a republic, should wither, and give place to selfish calculation and indulgence, to show and extravagance, to anxious, envious, discontented strivings, to wild adventure, and to the gambling spirit of speculation, will surprise no one who has studied human nature.

The invasion of Texas by our citizens is a mournful comment on our national morality. Whether without some fiery trial, some signal prostration of our prosperity, we can rise to the force and self-denial of freemen, is a question not easily solved. There are other alarming views. A spirit of lawlessness pervades the community, which, if not repressed, threatens the dissolution of our present forms of society. . . .

Freedom is fighting her battles in the world with sufficient odds against her. Let us not give new chances to her foes. That the cause of republicanism is suffering abroad through the defects and crimes of our countrymen, is as true, as that it is regarded with increased skepticism among ourselves. . . .

Shall we make the name of republic "a stench in the nostrils" of all nations, by employing our power to build up and spread slavery, by resist-ing the efforts of other countries for its aboli-tion, by falling behind monarchies in reverence for the rights of men? When we look forward to the probable growth of this country; when we think of the millions of human beings who are to spread over our present territory; of the career

of improvement and glory opened to this new people; of the impulses which free institutions, if prosperous, may be expected to give to phi-losophy, religion, science, literature, and arts; of the vast field in which the experiment is to be made of what the unfettered powers of man may achieve; of the bright page of history which our fathers have filled, and of the advantages under which their toils and virtues have placed us for carrying on their work; when we think of all this, can we help for a moment surrendering ourselves to bright visions of our country's glory, before which all the glories of the past are to fade away?

Is it presumption to say, that, if just to our-selves and all nations, we shall be felt through this whole continent, that we shall spread our language, institutions, and civilization through a wider space than any nation has yet ruled with a like beneficent influence? And are we prepared to barter these hopes, this sublime moral empire, for conquests by force? Are we prepared to sink to the level of unprincipled nations, to content ourselves with a vulgar, guilty greatness, to adopt in our youth maxims and ends which must brand our future with sordidness, oppression, and shame? This country cannot without peculiar infamy run the common race of national rapacity. Our origin, institutions, and position are peculiar, and all favor an upright, honorable course. We have not the apologies of nations hemmed in by nar-row bounds or threatened by the overshadowing power of ambitious neighbors. If we surrender ourselves to a selfish policy, we shall sin almost without temptation, and forfeit opportunities of greatness vouchsafed to no other people, for a prize below contempt.

JOHN L. O'SULLIVAN, "THE GREAT NATION OF FUTURITY," *THE UNITED STATES MAGAZINE AND DEMOCRATIC REVIEW* (NOVEMBER 1839)

For editor and journalist John O'Sullivan (1813–1895) Americans would achieve the greatness to which they are called only by pushing westward, to Texas and beyond. Through overspreading the continent, the United States serves the cause of freedom itself.

The American people having derived their origin from many other nations, and the Declaration of National Independence being entirely based on

the great principle of human equality, these facts demonstrate at once our disconnected position as regards any other nation; that we have, in reality, but little connection with the past history of any of them, and still less with all antiquity, its glories, or its crimes. On the contrary, our national birth was the beginning of a new history, the formation and progress of an untried political system, which separates us from the past and connects us with the future only; and so far as regards the entire development of the natural rights of man, in moral, political, and national life, we may confidently assume that our country is destined to be *the great nation* of futurity.

It is so destined, because the principle upon which a nation is organized fixes its destiny, and that of equality is perfect, is universal. It presides in all the operations of the physical world, and it is also the conscious law of the soul—the self-evident dictate of morality, which accurately defines the duty of man to man, and consequently man's rights as man. Besides, the truthful annals of any nation furnish abundant evidence, that its happiness, its greatness, its duration, were always proportionate to the democratic equality in its system of government.

How many nations have had their decline and fall, because the equal rights of the minority were trampled on by the despotism of the majority; or the interests of the many sacrificed to the aristocracy of the few; or the rights and interests of all given up to the monarchy of one? These three kinds of government have figured so frequently and so largely in the ages that have passed away, that their history, through all time to come, can only furnish a resemblance. Like causes produce like effects, and the true philosopher of history will easily discern the principle of equality, or of privilege, working out its inevitable result. The first is regenerative, because it is natural and right; the latter is destructive to society, because it is unnatural and wrong.

What friend of human liberty, civilization, and refinement, can cast his view over the past history of the monarchies and aristocracies of antiquity, and not deplore that they ever existed? What philanthropist can contemplate the oppressions, the cruelties, and injustice inflicted by them on the masses of mankind, and not turn with moral horror from the retrospect?

America is destined for better deeds. It is our unparalleled glory that we have no reminiscences of battle fields, but in defence of humanity, of the oppressed of all nations, of the rights of conscience, the rights of personal enfranchisement. Our annals describe no scenes of horrid carnage, where men were led on by hundreds of thousands to slay one another, dupes and victims to emperors, kings, nobles, demons in the human form called heroes. We have had patriots to defend our homes, our liberties, but no aspirants to crowns or thrones; nor have the American people ever suffered themselves to be led on by wicked ambition to depopulate the land, to spread desolation far and wide, that a human being might be placed on a seat of supremacy.

We have no interest in the scenes of antiquity, only as lessons of avoidance of nearly all their examples. The expansive future is our arena, and for our history. We are entering on its untrodden space, with the truths of God in our minds, beneficent objects in our hearts, and with a clear conscience unsullied by the past. We are the nation of human progress, and who will, what can, set limits to our onward march? Providence is with us, and no earthly power can. We point to the everlasting truth on the first page of our national declaration, and we proclaim to the millions of other lands, that "the gates of hell"—the powers of aristocracy and monarchy—"shall not prevail against it."

The far-reaching, the boundless future will be the era of American greatness. In its magnificent domain of space and time, the nation of many nations is destined to manifest to mankind the excellence of divine principles; to establish on earth the noblest temple ever dedicated to the worship of the Most High—the Sacred and the True. Its floor shall be a hemisphere—its roof the firmament of the star-studded heavens, and its congregation an Union of many Republics, comprising hundreds of happy millions, calling, owning no man master, but governed by God's natural and moral law of equality, the law of brotherhood—of "peace and good will amongst men."

But although the mighty constituent truth upon which our social and political system is founded will assuredly work out the glorious destiny herein shadowed forth, yet there are many untoward circumstances to retard our progress, to procrastinate the entire fruition of the greatest good to the human race. There is a tendency to imitativeness, prevailing amongst our professional and literary men, subversive of originality of thought, and wholly unfavorable to progress. Being in early life devoted to the study of the laws, institutions, and antiquities of other nations, they are far behind the mind and movement of the age in which they live: so much so, that the spirit of improvement, as well as of enfranchisement, exists chiefly in the great masses—the agricultural and mechanical population.

This propensity to imitate foreign nations is absurd and injurious. It is absurd, for we have never yet drawn on our mental resources that we have not found them ample and of unsurpassed excellence; witness our constitutions of government, where we had no foreign ones to imitate. It is injurious, for never have we followed foreign examples in legislation; witness our laws, our charters of monopoly, that we did not inflict evil on ourselves, subverting common right, in violation of common sense and common justice. The halls of legislation and the courts of law in a Republic are necessarily the public schools of the adult population. If, in these institutions, foreign precedents are legislated, and foreign decisions adjudged over again, is it to be wondered at that an imitative propensity predominates amongst professional and business men. Taught to look abroad for the highest standards of law, judicial wisdom, and literary excellence, the native sense is subjugated to a most obsequious idolatry of the tastes, sentiments, and prejudices of Europe. Hence our legislation, jurisprudence, literature, are more reflective of foreign aristocracy than of American democracy.

European governments have plunged themselves in debt, designating burthens on the people "national blessings." Our State Legislatures, humbly imitating their pernicious example, have pawned, bonded the property, labor, and credit of their constituents to the subjects of monarchy. It is by our own labor, and with our own materials, that our internal improvements are constructed, but our British-law-trained legislators have enacted that we shall be in debt for them, paying interest, but never to become owners. With various climates, soils, natural resources, and products, beyond any other country, and producing more real capital annually than any other sixteen millions of people on earth, we are, nevertheless, borrowers, paying tribute to the money powers of Europe. . . .

And our literature!—Oh, when will it breathe the spirit of our republican institutions? When will it be imbued with the God-like aspiration of intellectual freedom—the elevating principle of equality? When will it assert *its* national independence, and speak the soul—the heart of the American people? Why cannot our literati comprehend the matchless sublimity of our position amongst the nations of the world—our high destiny—and cease bending the knee to foreign idolatry, false tastes, false doctrines, false principles? When will they be inspired by the magnificent scenery of our own world, imbibe the fresh enthusiasm of a new heaven and a new earth, and soar upon the expanded wings of truth and liberty? Is not nature as original—her truths as captivating—her aspects as various, as lovely, as grand—her Promethean fire as glowing in this, our Western hemisphere, as in that of the East? And above all, is not our private life as morally beautiful and good—is not our public life as politically right, as indicative of the brightest prospects of humanity, and therefore as inspiring of the highest conceptions? Why, then, do our authors aim at no higher degree of merit, than a successful imitation of English writers of celebrity?

But with all the retrograde tendencies of our laws, our judicature, our colleges, our literature, still they are compelled to follow the mighty impulse of the age; they are carried onward by the increasing tide of progress; and though they cast many a longing look behind, they cannot stay the glorious movement of the masses, nor induce them to venerate the rubbish, the prejudices, the superstitions of other times and other lands, the theocracy of priests, the divine right of kings, the aristocracy of blood, the metaphysics of colleges, the irrational stuff of law libraries. Already the brightest hopes of philanthropy, the most enlarged speculations of true philosophy, are inspired by the indications perceptible amongst the mechanical and agricultural population. There, with predominating influence, beats the vigorous national heart of America, propelling the onward march of the multitude, propagating and extending, through the present and the future, the powerful purpose of soul, which, in the seventeenth century, sought a refuge among savages, and reared in the wilderness the sacred altars of intellectual freedom. This was the seed that produced individual equality, and political liberty, as its natural fruit; and this is our true nationality. American patriotism is not of soil; we are not aborigines, nor of ancestry, for we are of all nations; but it is essentially personal enfranchisement, for "where liberty dwells," said Franklin, the sage of the Revolution, "there is my country."

Such is our distinguishing characteristic, our popular instinct, and never yet has any public functionary stood forth for the rights of conscience against any, or all, sects desirous of predominating over such right, that he was not sustained by the people. And when a venerated patriot of the Revolution appealed to his fellow-citizens against the overshadowing power of a monarch institution, they came in their strength, and the moneyed despot was brought low. Corporate powers and privileges shrink to nothing when brought in conflict against the rights of individuals. Hence it is that our professional, literary, or commercial aristocracy, have no faith in the virtue, intelligence or capability of the people. The latter have never responded to their exotic sentiments nor promoted their views of a strong government irresponsible to the popular majority, to the will of the masses.

Yes, we are the nation of progress, of individual freedom, of universal enfranchisement. Equality of rights is the cynosure of our union of States, the grand exemplar of the correlative equality of individuals; and while truth sheds its effulgence, we cannot retrograde, without dissolving the one and subverting the other. We must onward to the fulfilment of our mission—to the entire development of the principle of our organization—freedom of conscience, freedom of person, freedom of trade and business pursuits, universality of freedom and equality. This is our high destiny, and in nature's eternal, inevitable decree of cause and effect we must accomplish it. All this will be our future history, to establish on earth the moral dignity and salvation of man—the immutable truth and beneficence of God. For this blessed mission to the nations of the world, which are shut out from the life-giving light of truth, has America been chosen; and her high example shall smite unto death the tyranny of kings, hierarchs, and oligarchs, and carry the glad tidings of peace and good will where myriads now endure an existence scarcely more enviable than that of beasts of the field. Who, then, can doubt that our country is destined to be the great nation of futurity?

JOHN L. O'SULLIVAN, "ANNEXATION," *THE UNITED STATES MAGAZINE AND DEMOCRATIC REVIEW* (JULY–AUGUST 1845)

For O'Sullivan, the time for talk has passed. It is America's "manifest destiny" to take not only Texas but also California and everything else in between.

It is now time for the opposition to the Annexation of Texas to cease, all further agitation of the waters of bitterness and strife, at least in connexion with this question—even though it may perhaps be required of us as a necessary condition of the freedom of our institutions, that we must live on for ever in a state of unpausing struggle and excitement upon some subject of party division or other. But, in regard to Texas, enough has now been given to party. It is time for the common duty of Patriotism to the Country to succeed—or if this claim will not be recognized, it is at least time for common sense

to acquiesce with decent grace in the inevitable and the irrevocable.

Texas is now ours. Already, before these words are written, her Convention has undoubtedly ratified the acceptance, by her Congress, of our proffered invitation into the Union; and made the requisite changes in her already republican form of constitution to adapt it to its future federal relations. Her star and her stripe may already be said to have taken their place in the glorious blazon of our common nationality; and the sweep of our eagle's wing already includes within its circuit the wide extent of her fair and fertile land. She is no longer to us a mere geographical space—a certain combination of coast, plain, mountain, valley, forest and stream. She is no longer to us a mere country on the map. She comes within the dear and sacred designation of Our Country; no longer a *"pays,"* she is a part of *"la patrie;"* and that which is at once a sentiment and a virtue, Patriotism, already begins to thrill for her too within the national heart. It is time then that all should cease to treat her as alien, and even adverse—cease to denounce and vilify all and everything connected with her accession—cease to thwart and oppose the remaining steps for its consummation; or where such efforts are felt to be unavailing, at least to embitter the hour of reception by all the most ungracious frowns of aversion and words of unwelcome. There has been enough of all this. It has had its fitting day during the period when, in common with every other possible question of practical policy that can arise, it unfortunately became one of the leading topics of party division, of presidential electioneering. But that period has passed, and with it let its prejudices and its passions, its discords and its denunciations, pass away too. The next session of Congress will see the representatives of the new young State in their places in both our halls of national legislation, side by side with those of the old Thirteen. Let their reception into "the family" be frank, kindly, and cheerful, as befits such an occasion, as comports not less with our own self-respect than patriotic duty towards them. Ill betide those foul birds that delight to file their own nest, and disgust the ear with perpetual discord of ill-omened croak.

Why, were other reasoning wanting, in favor of now elevating this question of the reception of Texas into the Union, out of the lower region of our past party dissensions, up to its proper level of a high and broad nationality, it surely is to be found, found abundantly, in the manner in which other nations have undertaken to intrude themselves into it, between us and the proper parties to the case, in a spirit of hostile interference against us, for the avowed object of thwarting our policy and hampering our power, limiting our greatness and checking the fulfillment of our manifest destiny to overspread the continent allotted by Providence for the free development of our yearly multiplying millions. . . .

It is wholly untrue, and unjust to ourselves, the pretence that the Annexation has been a measure of spoliation, unrightful and unrighteous—of military conquest under forms of peace and law—of territorial aggrandizement at the expense of justice, and justice due by a double sanctity to the weak. This view of the question is wholly unfounded, and has been before so amply refuted in these pages, as well as in a thousand other modes, that we shall not again dwell upon it. The independence of Texas was complete and absolute. It was an independence, not only in fact, but of right. No obligation of duty towards Mexico tended in the least degree to restrain our right to effect the desired recovery of the fair province once our own—whatever motives of policy might have prompted a more deferential consideration of her feelings and her pride, as involved in the question. If Texas became peopled with an American population, it was by no contrivance of our government, but on the express invitation of that of Mexico herself; accompanied with such guaranties of State independence, and the maintenance of a federal system analogous to our own, as constituted a compact fully justifying the strongest measures of redress on the part of those afterwards deceived in this guaranty, and sought to be enslaved under the yoke imposed by its violation. She was released, rightfully and absolutely released, from all Mexican allegiance, or duty of cohesion to the Mexican political body, by the acts and fault of Mexico herself, and Mexico alone. There never was a clearer case. It was not revolution; it was resistance to revolution: and resistance under such circumstances as left independence the necessary resulting state, caused by the abandonment of those with whom her former federal association had existed. What then can be more preposterous than all this clamor by Mexico and the Mexican interest, against Annexation, as a violation of any rights of hers, any duties of ours? . . .

California probably, next fall away from the loose adhesion which, in such a country as Mexico, holds a remote province in a slight equivocal kind of dependence on the metropolis. Imbecile and distracted, Mexico never can exert any real governmental authority over such a country. The impotence of the one and the distance of the other, must make the relation one of virtual independence; unless, by stunting the province of all natural growth, and forbidding that immigration which can alone develop its capabilities and fulfil the purposes of its creation, tyranny may retain a military dominion, which is no government in the legitimate sense of the term. In the case of California this is now impossible. The Anglo-Saxon foot is already on its borders. Already the advance guard of the irresistible army of Anglo-Saxon emigration has begun to pour down upon it, armed with the plough and the rifle, and marking its trail with schools and colleges, courts and representative halls, mills and meeting-houses. A population will soon be in actual occupation of California, over which it will be idle for Mexico to dream of dominion. They will necessarily become independent. All this without agency of our government, without responsibility of our people—in the natural flow of events, the spontaneous working of principles, and the adaptation of the tendencies and wants of the human race to the elemental circumstances in the midst of which they find themselves placed. And they will have a right to independence—to self-government—to the possession of the homes conquered from the wilderness by their own labors and dangers, sufferings and sacrifices—a better and a truer right than the artificial tide of sovereignty in Mexico, a thousand miles distant, inheriting from Spain a title good only against those who have none better. Their right to independence will be the natural right of self-government belonging to any community strong enough to maintain it—distinct in position, origin and character, and free from any mutual obligations of membership of a common political body, binding it to others by the duty of loyalty and compact of public faith. This will be their title to independence; and by this title, there can be no doubt that the population now fast streaming down upon California will both assert and maintain that independence. Whether they will then attach themselves to our Union or not, is not to be predicted with any certainty. Unless the projected railroad across the continent to the Pacific be carried into effect, perhaps they

may not; though even in that case, the day is not distant when the Empires of the Atlantic and Pacific would again flow together into one, as soon as their inland border should approach each other. But that great work, colossal as appears the plan on its first suggestion, cannot remain long unbuilt. Its necessity for this very purpose of binding and holding together in its iron clasp our fast-settling Pacific region with that of the Mississippi valley—the natural facility of the route—the ease with which any amount of labor for the construction can be drawn in from the overcrowded populations of Europe, to be paid in the lands made valuable by the progress of the work itself—and its immense utility to the commerce of the world with the whole eastern Asia, alone almost sufficient for the support of such a road—these coast of considerations give assurance that the day cannot be distant which shall witness the conveyance of the representatives from Oregon and California to Washington within less time than a few years ago was devoted to a similar journey by those from Ohio; while the magnetic telegraph will enable the editors of the "San Francisco Union," the "Astoria Evening Post," or the "Nootka Morning News," to set up in type the first half of the President's Inaugural before the echoes of the latter half shall have died away beneath the lofty porch of the Capitol, as spoken from his lips.

Away, then, with all idle French talk of *balances of power* on the American Continent. There is no growth in Spanish America! Whatever progress of population there may be in the British Canadas, is only for their own early severance of their present colonial relation to the little island three thousand miles across the Atlantic; soon to be followed by Annexation, and destined to swell the still accumulating momentum of our progress. And whosoever may hold the balance, though they should cast into the opposite scale all the bayonets and cannon, not only of France and England, but of Europe entire, how would it kick the beam against the simple, solid weight of the two hundred and fifty, or three hundred millions—and American millions—destined to gather beneath the flutter of the stripes and stars, in the fast hastening year of the Lord 1845!

Walt Whitman, "Our Territory on the Pacific" *Brooklyn Daily Eagle* (July 7, 1846)

In an editorial for the *Brooklyn Daily Eagle*, Walt Whitman (1819–1892), better known as a poet than for his journalism, calls for the United States to liberate California from the grasp of "miserable, inefficient" Mexico.

However soon the passage-at-arms between this republic and Mexico, be closed, we hope—since things have resolved themselves into the state they now hold—that the United States will, (in some way,) fix their mark of ownership on the American coast of the Pacific. . . .

We love to indulge in thoughts of the future extent and power of this republic—because all its increase is the increase of human happiness and liberty. Therefore hope we that the U.S. will keep a fast grip on California. What has miserable, inefficient Mexico—with her superstition, her burlesque upon freedom, her actual tyranny by the few over the many—what has she to do with the great mission of peopling the new world with a noble race? Be it ours, to achieve that mission! Be it ours to roll down all of the upstart leaven of old despotism, that comes in our way!

Thomas Corwin, "On the Mexican War" (1847)

John L. O'Sullivan and Walt Whitman got the war of conquest that they wanted. Here Thomas Corwin (1794–1865), then serving as U.S. senator from Ohio, denounces the dismemberment of Mexico under President James Knox Polk as illegal, immoral, and un-American.

THE PRESIDENT has said he does not expect to hold Mexican territory by conquest. Why then conquer it? Why waste thousands of lives and millions of money fortifying towns and creating governments, if, at the end of the war, you retire from the graves of your soldiers and the desolated country of your foes, only to get money from Mexico for the expense of all your toil and sacrifice? Who ever heard, since Christianity was propagated among men, of a nation taxing its people, enlisting its young men, and marching off two thousand miles to fight a people merely to be paid for it in money? What is this but hunting a market for blood, selling the lives of your young men, marching them in regiments to be slaughtered and paid for like oxen and brute beasts?

Sir, this is, when stripped naked, that atrocious idea first promulgated in the president's message, and now advocated here, of fighting on till we can get our indemnity for the past as well as the present slaughter. We have chastised Mexico, and if it were worth while to do so, we have, I dare say, satisfied the world that we can fight.

Sir, I have no patience with this flagitious notion of fighting for indemnity, and this under the equally absurd and hypocritical pretense of securing an honorable peace. An honorable peace! If you have accomplished the objects of the war— if indeed you had an object which you dare to avow—cease to fight and you will have peace. Conquer your insane love of false glory, and you will "conquer a peace."

But now you have overrun half of Mexico, you have exasperated and irritated her people, you claim indemnity for all expenses incurred in doing this mischief and boldly ask her to give up New Mexico and California; and, as a bribe to her patriotism, seizing on her property, you offer three millions to pay the soldiers she has called out to repel your invasion on condition that she will give up to you at least one-third of her whole territory. This is the modest—I should say, the monstrous— proposition now before us. . . .

You may wrest provinces from Mexico by war—you may hold them by the right of the strongest—you may rob her; but a treaty of peace to that effect with the people of Mexico, legitimately and freely made, you never will have! I thank God that it is so, as well for the sake of the Mexican people as ourselves; for, unlike the senator from Alabama, I do not value the life of a citizen of the United States above the lives of a hundred thousand Mexican women and children—a rather cold sort of philanthropy, in my judgment. For the sake of Mexico, then, as well as our own country, I rejoice that it is an impossibility that you can obtain by treaty from her those territories under the existing state of things.

You have taken from Mexico one-fourth of her territory, and you now propose to run a line comprehending about another third, and for what? I ask, Mr. President, for what? What has Mexico got from you for parting with two-thirds of her domain? She has given you ample redress for every injury of which you have complained. She has submitted to the award of your commissioners, and up to the time of the rupture with Texas faithfully paid it. And for all that she has lost (not through or by you, but which loss has been your gain) what requital do we, her strong, rich, robust neighbor, make? Do we send our missionaries there "to point the way to heaven?" Or do we send the schoolmasters to pour daylight into her dark places, to aid her infant strength to conquer freedom and reap the fruit of the independence herself alone had won?

No, no, none of this do we! But we send regiments, storm towns, and our colonels prate of liberty in the midst of the solitudes their ravages have made. They proclaim the empty forms of social compact to a people bleeding and maimed with wounds received in defending their hearthstones against the invasion of these very men who shoot them down and then exhort them to be free.

What is the territory, Mr. President, which you propose to wrest from Mexico? It is consecrated to the heart of the Mexican by many a well-fought battle with his old Castilian master. His Bunker Hills, and Saratogas, and Yorktowns are there. The Mexican can say, "There I bled for liberty! and shall I surrender that consecrated home of my affections to the Anglo-Saxon invaders? What do they want with it? They have Texas already. They have possessed themselves of the territory between the Nueces and the Rio Grande. What else do they want? To what shall I point my children as memorials of that independence which I bequeath to them when those battlefields shall have passed from my possession?"

Sir, had one come and demanded Bunker Hill of the people of Massachusetts, had England's lion ever showed himself there, is there a man over thirteen and under ninety who would not have been ready to meet him; is there a river on this continent that would not have run red with blood; is there a field but would have been piled high with the unburied bones of slaughtered Americans before these consecrated battlefields of liberty should have been wrested from us? But this same American goes into a sister republic and says to poor, weak Mexico, "Give up your territory—you are unworthy to possess it—I have got one-half already—all I ask of you is to give up the other!"

Sir, I have read in some account of your Battle of Monterey, of a lovely Mexican girl, who, with the benevolence of an angel in her bosom and the robust courage of a hero in her heart, was busily engaged during the bloody conflict, amid the crash of falling houses, the groans of the dying, and the wild shriek of battle, in carrying, water to slake the burning thirst of the wounded of either host. While bending over a wounded American soldier a cannon-ball struck her and blew her to atoms! Sir, I do not charge my brave, generous-hearted countrymen who fought that fight with this. No, no! We who send them—we who know that scenes like this, which might send tears of sorrow "down Pluto's iron cheek," are the invariable, inevitable attendants on war—we are accountable for this. And this—this is the way we are to be made known to Europe. This—this is to be the undying renown of free, republican America! "She has stormed a city—killed many of its inhabitants of both sexes—she has room!" So it will read. Sir, if this were our only history, then may God of His mercy grant that its volume may speedily come to a close.

Why is it, sir, that we, the United States, a people of yesterday compared with the older nations of the world, should be waging war for territory—for "room?" Look at your country, extending from the Alleghany Mountains to the Pacific Ocean, capable itself of sustaining in comfort a larger population than will be in the whole Union for one hundred years to come. Over this vast expanse of territory your population is now so sparse that I believe we provided, at the last session, a regiment of mounted men to guard the mail from the frontier of Missouri to the mouth of the Columbia; and yet you persist in the ridiculous assertion, "I want room." One would imagine, from the frequent reiteration of the complaint, that you had a bursting, teeming population, whose energy was paralyzed, whose enterprise was crushed, for want of space. Why should we be so weak or wicked as to offer this idle apology for ravaging a neighboring Republic? It will impose on no one at home or abroad.

Do we not know, Mr. President, that it is a law never to be repealed that falsehood shall be short-lived? Was it not ordained of old that truth only shall abide for ever? Whatever we may say to-day, or whatever we may write in our books, the stern tribunal of history will review it all, detect falsehood, and bring us to judgment before that posterity which shall bless or curse us, as we may act now, wisely or otherwise. We may hide in the grave (which awaits us all) in vain; we may hope there, like the foolish bird that hides its head in the sand, in the vain belief that its body is not seen; yet even there this preposterous excuse of want of "room" shall be laid bare and the quick-coming future will decide that it was a hypocritical pretense under which we sought to conceal the avarice which prompted us to covet and to seize by force that which was not ours.

ABRAHAM LINCOLN, "THE WAR WITH MEXICO" (1848)

As a first-term congressman from Illinois, Abraham Lincoln (1809–1865) registers his dissent.

Some, if not all, of the gentlemen on the other side of the House, who have addressed the committee within the last two days, have spoken rather complainingly, if I have rightly understood them, of the vote given a week or ten days ago, declaring that the war with Mexico was unnecessarily and unconstitutionally commenced by the President. I admit that such a vote should not be given in mere party wantonness, and that the one given is justly censurable, if it have no other or better foundation. I am one of those who joined in that vote; and I did so under my best impression of the *truth* of the case. How I got this impression, and how it may possibly be removed, I will now try to show. When the war began, it was my opinion that all those who, because of knowing too *little*, or because of knowing too *much*, could not conscientiously approve the conduct of the President, (in the beginning of it,) should, nevertheless, as good citizens and patriots, remain silent on that point, at least till the war should be ended. . . .

The President, in his first message of May, 1846, declares that the soil was *ours* on which hostilities were commenced by Mexico; and he repeats that declaration, almost in the same language, in each successive annual message—thus showing that he esteems that point a highly essential one. In the importance of that point, I entirely agree with the President. To my judgment, it is the *very point* upon which he should be justified or condemned. In his message of December, 1846, it seems to have occurred to him, as is certainly true, that title, ownership to soil or anything else, is not a simple fact, but is a conclusion following one or more simple facts; and that it was incumbent upon him to present the facts from which he concluded the soil was ours, on which the first blood of the war was shed. . . .

Now, I propose to try to show that the whole of this—issue and evidence—is, from beginning to end, the sheerest deception. The issue, as he presents it, is in these words: "But there are those who, conceding all this to be true, assume the ground that the true western boundary of Texas is the Nueces, instead of the Rio Grande; and that, therefore, in marching our army to the east bank of the latter river, we passed the Texan line, and invaded the territory of Mexico." Now, this issue is made up of two affirmatives and no negative. The main deception of it is, that it assumes as true, that *one* river or the *other* is necessarily the boundary; and cheats the superficial thinker entirely out of the idea that possibly the boundary is somewhere *between* the two, and not actually at either. A further deception is, that it will let in *evidence* which a true issue would exclude. A true issue, made by the President, would be about as follows "I say, the soil was *ours* on which the first blood was shed; there are those who say it was not."

. . . it is a singular fact, that if any one should declare the President sent the army into the midst of a settlement of Mexican people, who had never submitted, by consent or by force to the authority of Texas or of the United States, and that *there*, and thereby, the first blood of the war was shed, there is not one word in all the President has said which would either admit or deny the declaration. In this strange omission chiefly consists the deception of the President's evidence—an omission which, it does seem to me, could scarcely have occurred but by design. My way of living leads me to be about the courts of justice; and there I have sometimes seen a good lawyer, struggling for his client's neck, in a desperate case, employing every artifice to work round, befog, and cover up with many words some point arising in the case, which he *dared* not admit, and yet *could* not deny. Party bias may help to make it appear so; but, with all the allowance I can make for such bias, it still does appear to me that just such, and from just such necessity, is the President's struggle in this case.

Some time after my colleague [Mr. Richardson] introduced the resolutions I have mentioned, I introduced a preamble, resolution, and interrogatories, intended to draw the President out, if possible, on this hitherto untrodden ground. To show their relevancy, I propose to state my understanding of the true rule for ascertaining the boundary between Texas and Mexico. It is, that *wherever* Texas was *exercising* jurisdiction was hers; and *wherever* Mexico was exercising jurisdiction, was hers; and that *whatever* separated the actual exercise of jurisdiction of the one from that of the other, was the true boundary between them. . . .

Now, sir, . . . let the President answer the interrogatories I proposed, as before mentioned, or some other similar ones. Let him answer fully, fairly, and candidly. Let him answer with *facts*, and not with arguments. Let him remember he sits where Washington sat; and, so remembering, let him answer as Washington would answer. As a nation *should* not, and the Almighty *will* not, be evaded, so let him attempt no evasion, no equivocation. And if, so answering, he can show that the soil was ours where the first blood of the war was shed . . . then I am with him for his justification. In that case I, shall be most happy to reverse the vote I gave the other day. . . . But if he *cannot*, or *will not* do this—if, on any pretence, or no pretence, he shall refuse or omit it, then I shall be fully convinced, of what I more than suspect already, that he is deeply conscious of being in the wrong; that he feels the blood of this war, like the blood of Abel, is crying to Heaven against him; that he ordered General Taylor into the midst of a peaceful Mexican settlement, purposely to bring on a war; that originally having some strong motive—what I will not stop now to give my opinion concerning—to involve the two countries in a war, and trusting to escape scrutiny by fixing the public gaze upon the exceeding brightness of military glory—that attractive rainbow that rises in showers of blood—that serpent's eye that charms to destroy—he plunged into it, and has swept *on* and *on*, till disappointed in his calculation of the ease with which Mexico might be subdued, he now finds himself he knows not where. How like the half insane mumbling of a fever-dream is the whole war part of his late message! At one time telling us that Mexico has nothing whatever that we can get but territory; at another, showing us how we can support the war by levying contributions on Mexico. At one time urging the national honor, the security of the future, the prevention of foreign interference, and even the good of Mexico herself, as among the objects of the war; at another, telling us that, "to reject indemnity, by refusing to accept a cession of territory, would be to abandon all our just demands, and to wage the war, bearing all its expenses, *without a purpose or definite object*." So, then, the national honor, security of the future, and every thing but territorial indemnity, may be considered the *no-purposes* and *indefinite* objects of the war! But, having it now settled that territorial indemnity is the only object, we are urged to seize, by legislation here, all that he was content to take a few months ago, and the whole province of Lower California to boot, and to still carry on the war—to take *all* we are fighting for, and *still* fight on. . . .

The war has gone on some twenty months; for the expenses of which, together with an inconsiderable old score, the President now claims about one half of the Mexican territory, and that by far the better half, so far as concerns our ability to make any thing out of it. It *is* comparatively uninhabited; so that we could establish land offices in it, and raise some money in that way. But the other half is already inhabited, as I understand it, tolerably densely for the nature of the country; and all its lands, or all that are valuable, already appropriated as private property. How, then, are we to make any thing out of these lands with this encumbrance on them, or how remove the encumbrance? I suppose no one will say we should kill the people, or drive them out, or make slaves of them, or even confiscate their property? How, then, can we make much out of this part of the territory? If the prosecution of the war has, in expenses, already equalled the *better* half of the country, how long its future prosecution will be in equaling the less valuable half is not a *speculative*, but a *practical* question, pressing closely upon us; And yet it is a question which the President seems to never have thought of.

As to the mode of terminating the war and securing peace, the President is equally wandering and indefinite. First, it is to be done by a more vigorous prosecution of the war in the vital parts of the enemies country; and, after apparently talking himself tired on this point, the President drops down into a half despairing tone, and tells us, that "with a people distracted and divided by contending factions, and a government subject to constant changes, by successive revolutions, *the continued success of our arms may fail to secure a satisfactory peace*." Then he suggests the propriety of wheedling the Mexican people to desert the counsels of their own leaders, and trusting in our protection, to set up a government from which we can secure a satisfactory peace telling us that "*this may become the only mode of obtaining such a peace*." But soon he falls into doubt of this too, and then drops back on to the already half abandoned ground of "more vigorous prosecution." All this shows that the President is in no wise satisfied with his own positions. First, he takes up one, and, in attempting to argue us *into* it, he argues himself *out* of it; then seizes another, and goes through the same process; and then, confused at being able to think of nothing new, he snatches up the old one again, which he has some time before cast off. His mind, tasked beyond its power, is running hither and thither, like some tortured creature on a burning surface, finding no position on which it can settle down and be at ease.

Again, it is a singular omission in this message, that it no where intimates when the President expects the war to terminate. At its beginning, General Scott was, by this same President, driven into disfavor, if not disgrace, for intimating that peace could not be conquered in less than three or four months. But now, at the end of about twenty months, during which time our arms have given us the most splendid successes—every department, and every part, land and water, officers and privates, regulars and volunteers, doing all that men *could* do, and hundreds of things which it had ever before been thought men *could not* do; after all this, this same President gives us a long message, without showing us that, as to the end, he himself has even an imaginary conception. As I have before said, he knows not where he is. He is a bewildered, confounded, and miserably perplexed man. God grant he may be able to show there is not something about his conscious more painful than all his mental perplexity!

Millard Fillmore, "Letter to the Emperor of Japan" (1853)

A flotilla of U.S. Navy warships dispatched by President Millard Fillmore (1800–1874) invites the emperor of Japan to accommodate friendly American demands.

Great and Good Friend! I send you this public letter by Commodore Matthew C. Perry, an officer of the highest rank in the navy of the United States, and commander of the squadron now visiting Your imperial majesty's dominions. I have directed Commodore Perry to assure your imperial majesty that I entertain the kindest feelings toward your majesty's person and government, and that I have no other object in sending him to Japan but to propose to your imperial majesty that the United States and Japan should live in friendship and have commercial intercourse with each other. The Constitution and laws of the United States forbid all interference with the religious or political concerns of other nations. I have particularly charged Commodore Perry to abstain from every act which could possibly disturb the tranquillity of your imperial majesty's dominions. The United States of America reach from ocean to ocean, and our Territory of Oregon and State of California lie directly opposite to the dominions of your imperial majesty. Our steamships can go from California to Japan in eighteen days. Our great State of California produces about sixty millions of dollars in gold every year, besides silver, quicksilver, precious stones, and many other valuable articles. Japan is also a rich and fertile country, and produces many very valuable articles. Your imperial majesty's subjects are skilled in many of the arts. I am desirous that our two countries should trade with each other, for the benefit both of Japan and the United States. We know that the ancient laws of your imperial majesty's government do not allow of foreign trade, except with the Chinese and the Dutch; but as the state of the world changes and new governments are formed, it seems to be wise, from time to time, to make new laws. There was a time when the ancient laws of your imperial majesty's government were first made. About the same time America, which is sometimes called the New World, was first discovered and settled by the Europeans. For a long time there were but a few people, and they were poor. They have now become quite numerous; their commerce is very extensive; and they think that if your imperial majesty were so far to change the ancient laws as to allow a free trade between the two countries it would be extremely beneficial to both. If your imperial majesty is not satisfied that it would be safe altogether to abrogate the ancient laws which forbid foreign trade,

they might be suspended for five or ten years, so as to try the experiment. If it does not prove as beneficial as was hoped, the ancient laws can be restored. The United States often limit their treaties with foreign States to a few years, and then renew them or not, as they please. I have directed Commodore Perry to mention another thing to your imperial majesty. Many of our ships pass every year from California to China; and great numbers of our people pursue the whale fishery near the shores of Japan. It sometimes happens, in stormy weather, that one of our ships is wrecked on your imperial majesty's shores. In all such cases we ask, and expect, that our unfortunate people should be treated with kindness, and that their property should be protected, till we can send a vessel and bring them away. We are very much in earnest in this. Commodore Perry is also directed by me to represent to your imperial majesty that we understand there is a great abundance of coal and provisions in the Empire of Japan. Our steamships, in crossing the great ocean, burn a great deal of coal, and it is not convenient to bring it all the way from America. We wish that our steamships and other vessels should be allowed to stop in Japan and supply themselves with coal, provisions, and water. They will pay for them in money, or anything else your imperial majesty's subjects may prefer; and we request your imperial majesty to appoint a convenient port, in the southern part of the Empire, where our vessels may stop for this purpose. We are very desirous of this. These are the only objects for which I have sent Commodore Perry, with a powerful squadron, to pay a visit to your imperial majesty's renowned city of Yedo: friendship, commerce, a supply of coal and provisions, and protection for our shipwrecked people. We have directed Commodore Perry to beg your imperial majesty's acceptance of a few presents. They are of no great value in themselves; but some of them may serve as specimens of the articles manufactured in the United States, and they are intended as tokens of our sincere and respectful friendship. May the Almighty have your imperial majesty in His great and holy keeping!

WALT WHITMAN, "A BROADWAY PAGEANT," *LEAVES OF GRASS (1860)*

The poet sees in the opening of Japan a portent of bigger and better things to come, a "greater supremacy" certain to encompass all of Asia.

1

Over the Western sea hither from Niphon come,
Courteous, the swart-cheek'd two-sworded envoys,
Leaning back in their open barouches, bareheaded, impassive,
Ride to-day through Manhattan.

Libertad! I do not know whether others behold what I behold,
In the procession along with the nobles of Niphon, the errand-bearers,
Bringing up the rear, hovering above, around, or in the ranks marching,
But I will sing you a song of what I behold Libertad.

When million-footed Manhattan unpent descends to her pavements,
When the thunder-cracking guns arouse me with the proud roar love,
When the round-mouth'd guns out of the smoke and smell I love spit their salutes,
When the fire-flashing guns have fully alerted me, and heaven-clouds canopy my city with a delicate thin haze,
When gorgeous the countless straight stems, the forests at the wharves, thicken with colors,
When every ship richly drest carries her flag at the peak,
When pennants trail and street-festoons hang from the windows,
When Broadway is entirely given up to foot-passengers and foot-standers, when the mass is densest,
When the facades of the houses are alive with people, when eyes gaze riveted tens of thousands at a time,

When the guests from the islands advance, when the pageant moves forward visible,
When the summons is made, when the answer that waited thousands of years answers,
I too arising, answering, descend to the pavements, merge with the crowd, and gaze with them.

_= ==

2

Superb-faced Manhattan!
Comrade Americanos! to us, then at last the Orient comes.

To us, my city,
Where our tall-topt marble and iron beauties range on opposite sides, to walk in the space between,
To-day our Antipodes comes.

The Originatress comes,
The nest of languages, the bequeather of poems, the race of eld,
Florid with blood, pensive, rapt with musings, hot with passion,
Sultry with perfume, with ample and flowing garments,
With sunburnt visage, with intense soul and glittering eyes,
The race of Brahma comes.

See my cantabile! these and more are flashing to us from the procession,
As it moves changing, a kaleidoscope divine it moves changing before us.
For not the envoys nor the tann'd Japanee from his island only,
Lithe and silent the Hindoo appears, the Asiatic continent itself appears, the past, the dead,
The murky night-morning of wonder and fable inscrutable,
The envelop'd mysteries, the old and unknown hive-bees,

Walt Whitman, *Leaves of Grass.* Boston: Thayer and Eldridge (1860).

The north, the sweltering south, eastern Assyria, the Hebrews, the ancient of ancients,
Vast desolated cities, the gliding present, all of these and more are in the pageant-procession.

Geography, the world, is in it,
The Great Sea, the brood of islands, Polynesia, the coast beyond,
The coast you henceforth are facing—you Libertad! from your Western golden shores,
The countries there with their populations, the millions en-masse are curiously here,
The swarming market-places, the temples with idols ranged along the sides or at the end, bonze, brahmin, and llama,
Mandarin, farmer, merchant, mechanic, and fisherman,
The singing-girl and the dancing-girl, the ecstatic persons, the secluded emperors,
Confucius himself, the great poets and heroes, the warriors, the castes, all,
Trooping up, crowding from all directions, from the Altay mountains,
From Thibet, from the four winding and far-flowing rivers of China,
From the southern peninsulas and the demi-continental islands, from Malaysia,
These and whatever belongs to them palpable show forth to me, and are seiz'd by me,
And I am seiz'd by them, and friendlily held by them,
Till as here them all I chant, Libertad! for themselves and for you.

For I too raising my voice join the ranks of this pageant,
I am the chanter, I chant aloud over the pageant,
I chant the world on my Western sea,
I chant copious the islands beyond, thick as stars in the sky,
I chant the new empire grander than any before, as in a vision it comes to me,
I chant America the mistress, I chant a greater supremacy,
I chant projected a thousand blooming cities yet in time on those groups of sea-islands,

My sail-ships and steam-ships threading the archipelagoes,
My stars and stripes fluttering in the wind,
Commerce opening, the sleep of ages having done its work, races reborn, refresh'd,
Lives, works resumed—the object I know not—but the old, the Asiatic renew'd as it must be,
Commencing from this day surrounded by the world.

3
And you Libertad of the world!
You shall sit in the middle well-pois'd thousands and thousands of years,
As to-day from one side the nobles of Asia come to you,
As to-morrow from the other side the queen of England sends her eldest son to you.

The sign is reversing, the orb is enclosed,
The ring is circled, the journey is done,
The box-lid is but perceptibly open'd, nevertheless the perfume pours copiously out of the whole box.

Young Libertad! with the venerable Asia, the all-mother,
Be considerate with her now and ever hot Libertad, for you are all,
Bend your proud neck to the long-off mother now sending messages over the archipelagoes to you,
Bend your proud neck low for once, young Libertad.

Were the children straying westward so long? so wide the tramping?
Were the precedent dim ages debouching westward from Paradise so long?
Were the centuries steadily footing it that way, all the while unknown, for you, for reasons?

They are justified, they are accomplish'd, they shall now be turn'd the other way also, to travel toward you thence,
They shall now also march obediently eastward for your sake Libertad.

Abraham Lincoln, "Gettysburg Address" (1863)

In the midst of a brutal and bloody civil war, the nation's sixteenth president affirms that the purpose of the American experiment extends far beyond the United States itself.

Fourscore and seven years ago our fathers brought forth on this continent a new nation, conceived in liberty and dedicated to the proposition that all men are created equal.

Now we are engaged in a great civil war, testing whether that nation or any nation so conceived and so dedicated can long endure. We are met on a great battlefield of that war. We have come to dedicate a portion of that field as a final resting-place for those who here gave their lives that that nation might live. It is altogether fitting and proper that we should do this. But in a larger sense, we cannot dedicate, we cannot consecrate, we cannot hallow this ground. The brave men, living and dead who struggled here have consecrated it far above our poor power to add or detract. The world will little note nor long remember what we say here, but it can never forget what they did here. It is for us the living rather to be dedicated here to the unfinished work which they who fought here have thus far so nobly advanced.

It is rather for us to be here dedicated to the great task remaining before us—that from these honored dead we take increased devotion to that cause for which they gave the last full measure of devotion—that we here highly resolve that these dead shall not have died in vain, that this nation under God shall have a new birth of freedom, and that government of the people, by the people, for the people shall not perish from the earth.

III.

TOWARD EMPIRE

Once the Civil War concluded, consolidating and exploiting a vast transcontinental expanse of territory became for a time the nation's overarching priority. The United States was fast transforming itself into an industrial powerhouse. As the end of the nineteenth century approached, it had become the world's wealthiest nation.

Yet with success came fresh ambitions along with anxieties and discontent. These combined by century's end to inspire a new surge of expansionism, this time reaching beyond North America itself. In 1898, declaring its intention of liberating Cuba, the United States went to war with Spain. By the time this brief conflict ended, the United States itself had become a colonial master, absorbing Puerto Rico, the Hawaiian Islands, the Philippines, and several lesser possessions in a sprawling maritime empire. Cuba itself became the first of several U.S. protectorates or quasi-colonies in the Caribbean.

Although critics protested these developments with great vigor, a people devoutly opposed to imperialism had fallen prey to its allure. The documents provided in this section survey the various motives that informed this outward thrust as well as the arguments mustered against it.

JOHN FISKE, "MANIFEST DESTINY," *HARPER'S NEW MONTHLY MAGAZINE* (MARCH 1885)

Although a historian of some note, John Fiske (1842–1901) made his impact by promoting social Darwinism. Here he explains how a collaboration between the United States and the British Empire holds the promise of lasting dominion for English-speaking whites.

Among the legends of our late Civil War there is a story of a dinner-party given by the Americans residing in Paris, at which were propounded sundry toasts concerning not so much the past and present as the expected glories of the great American nation. In the general character of these toasts geographical considerations were very prominent, and the principal fact which seemed to occupy the minds of the speakers was the unprecedented *bigness* of our country. "Here's to the United States," said the first speaker, "bounded on the north by British America, on the south by the Gulf of Mexico, on the east by the Atlantic, and on the west by the Pacific, Ocean." "But," said the second speaker, "this is far too limited a view of the subject: in assigning our boundaries we must look to the great and glorious future which is prescribed for us by the Manifest Destiny of the Anglo-Saxon Race. Here's to the United States,—bounded on the north by the North Pole, on the south by the South Pole, on the east by the rising and on the west by the setting sun." Emphatic applause greeted this aspiring prophecy. But here arose the third speaker—a very serious gentleman from the Far West. "If we are going," said this truly patriotic American, "to leave the historic past and present, and take our manifest destiny into the account, why restrict ourselves within the narrow limits assigned by our fellow-countryman who has just sat down? I give you the United States,—bounded on the north by the Aurora Borealis, on the south by the precession of the equinoxes, on the east by the primeval chaos, and on the west by the Day of Judgment!". . . .

Our eloquent friends of the Paris dinner-party seem to have been strongly impressed with the excellence of enormous political aggregates. We, too, approaching the subject from a different point of view, have been led to see how desirable it is that self-governing groups of men should be enabled to work together in permanent harmony and on a great scale. In this kind of political integration the work of civilization very largely consists. We have seen how in its most primitive form political society is made up of small self-governing groups that are perpetually at war with one another. Now the process of change which we call civilization means quite a number of things. But there is no doubt that on its political side it means primarily the gradual substitution of a state of peace for a state of war. This change is the condition precedent for all the other kinds of improvement that are connoted by such a term as "civilization." Manifestly the development of industry is largely dependent upon the cessation or restriction of warfare; and furthermore, as the industrial phase of civilization

slowly supplants the military phase, men's characters undergo, though very slowly, a corresponding change. Men become less inclined to destroy life or to inflict pain; or—to use the popular terminology which happens here to coincide precisely with that of the Doctrine of Evolution—they become less *brutal* and more *humane*. Obviously then the prime feature of the process called civilization is the general diminution of warfare. But we have seen that a general diminution of warfare is rendered possible only by the union of small political groups into larger groups that are kept together by community of interests, and that can adjust their mutual relations by legal discussion without coming to blows. . . .

In order that the pacific community may be able to go on doing its work, it must be strong enough and warlike enough to overcome its barbaric neighbours who have no notion whatever of keeping peace. This is another of the seeming paradoxes of the history of civilization, that for a very long time the possibility of peace can be guaranteed only through war. Obviously the permanent peace of the world can be secured only through the gradual concentration of the preponderant military strength into the hands of the most pacific communities. With infinite toil and trouble this point has been slowly gained by mankind, through the circumstance that the very same political aggregation of small primitive communities which makes them less disposed to quarrel among themselves tends also to make them more than a match for the less coherent groups of their more barbarous neighbours. The same concert of action which tends towards internal harmony tends also towards external victory, and both ends are promoted by the co-operation of the same sets of causes. But for a long time all the political problems of the civilized world were complicated by the fact that the community had to fight for its life. . . .

I think we may safely lay it down, as a large and general rule, that all this prodigious warfare required to free the civilized world from peril of barbarian attack served greatly to increase the difficulty of solving the great initial problem of civilization. . . . . It is a very difficult thing for a free people to maintain its free constitution if it has to keep perpetually fighting for its life. The "one-man-power" less fit for carrying on the peaceful pursuits of life is sure to be brought into the foreground in a state of endless warfare. It is a still more difficult thing for a free people to maintain its free constitution when it undertakes to govern a dependent people despotically, as has been wont to happen when a portion of the barbaric world has been overcome and annexed to the civilized world. . . .

I am fully prepared to show that the conquest of the North American continent by men of English race was unquestionably the most prodigious event in the political annals of mankind. . . .

Chronologically the discovery of America coincides precisely with the close of the Middle Ages, and with the opening of the drama of what is called *modern* history. The coincidence is in many ways significant. . . .

It was for Spain, France, and England to contend for the possession of this vast region, and to prove by the result of the struggle which kind of civilization was endowed with the higher and sturdier political life. The race which here should gain the victory was clearly destined hereafter to take the lead in the world, though the rival powers could not in those days fully appreciate this fact. . . . It was not until the American Resolution that this began to be dimly realized by a few prescient thinkers. It is by no means so fully realized even now that a clear and thorough-going statement of it has not somewhat an air of novelty. When the highly-civilized community, representing the ripest political ideas of England, was planted in America, removed from the manifold and complicated checks we have just been studying in the history of the Old World, the growth was portentously rapid and steady. . . .

Let us consider now to what conclusions the rapidity and unabated steadiness of the increase of the English race in America must lead us as we go on to forecast the future. Carlyle somewhere speaks slightingly of the fact that the Americans double their numbers every twenty years, as if to have forty million dollar-hunters in the world were any better than to have twenty million dollar-hunters! The implication that Americans are nothing but dollar-hunters, and are thereby distinguishable from the rest of mankind, would not perhaps bear too elaborate scrutiny. But during the present lecture we have been considering the gradual transfer of the preponderance of

physical strength from the hands of the war-loving portion of the human race into the hands of the peace-loving portion,—into the hands of the dollar-hunters, if you please, but out of the hands of the scalp-hunters. Obviously to double the numbers of a pre-eminently industrious, peaceful, orderly, and free-thinking community, is somewhat to increase the weight in the world of the tendencies that go towards making communities free and orderly and peaceful and industrious. . . .

And now we may begin to see distinctly what it was that the American government fought for in the late civil war,—a point which at the time was by no means clearly apprehended outside the United States. We used to hear it often said, while that war was going on, that we were fighting not so much for the emancipation of the negro as for the maintenance of our federal union; and I well remember that to many who were burning to see our country purged of the folly and iniquity of negro slavery this used to seem like taking a low and unrighteous view of the case. From the standpoint of universal history it was nevertheless the correct and proper view. The emancipation of the negro, as an incidental result of the struggle, was a priceless gain which was greeted warmly by all right-minded people. But deeper down than this question, far more subtly interwoven with the innermost fibres of our national well-being, far heavier laden too with weighty consequences for the future weal of all mankind, was the question whether this great pacific principle of union joined with independence should be overthrown by the first deep-seated social difficulty it had to encounter, or should stand as an example of priceless value to other ages and to other lands. The solution was well worth the effort it cost. There have been many useless wars, but this was not one of them, for more than most wars that have been, it was fought in the direct interest of peace, and the victory so dearly purchased and so humanely used was an earnest of future peace and happiness for the world. . . .

In the United States of America a century hence we shall therefore doubtless have a political aggregation immeasurably surpassing in power and in dimensions any empire that has as yet existed. But we must now consider for a moment the probable future career of the English race in other parts of the world. The colonization of North America by

Englishmen had its direct effects upon the eastern as well as upon the western side of the Atlantic. . . . . These circumstances reacted powerfully upon the material development of England, multiplying manifold the dimensions of her foreign trade, increasing proportionately her commercial marine, and giving her in the eighteenth century the dominion over the seas. Endowed with this maritime supremacy, she has with an unerring instinct proceeded to seize upon the keys of empire in all parts of the world,—Gibraltar, Malta, the isthmus of Suez, Aden, Ceylon, the coasts of Australia, island after island in the Pacific,—every station, in short, that commands the pathways of maritime commerce, or guards the approaches to the barbarous countries which she is beginning to regard as in some way her natural heritage. . . . No one can carefully watch what is going on in Africa to-day without recognizing it as the same sort of thing which was going on in North America in the seventeenth century; and it cannot fail to bring forth similar results in course of time. Here is a vast country, rich in beautiful scenery and in resources of timber and minerals, with a salubrious climate and fertile soil, with great navigable rivers and inland lakes, which will not much longer be left in control of tawny lions and long-eared elephants and negro fetish-worshippers. . . . . Who can doubt that within two or three centuries the African continent will be occupied by a mighty nation of English descent, and covered with populous cities and flourishing farms, with railroads and telegraphs and other devices of civilization as yet undreamed of?

If we look next to Australia, we find a country of more than two-thirds the area of the United States, with a temperate climate and immense resources, agricultural and mineral,—a country sparsely peopled by a race of irredeemable savages hardly above the level of brutes. Here England within the present century has planted six greatly thriving states. . . Then there is New Zealand, with its climate of perpetual spring, where the English race is now multiplying faster than anywhere else in the world. . . . And there are in the Pacific Ocean many rich and fertile spots where we shall very soon see the same things going on.

It is not necessary to dwell upon such considerations as these. It is enough to point to the general conclusion, that the work which the English race began when it colonized North America is destined to go on until every land on the earth's surface that is not already the seat of an old civilization shall become English in its language, in its political habits and traditions, and to a predominant extent in the blood of its people. The day is at hand when, four-fifths of the human race will trace its pedigree to English forefathers, as four-fifths of the white people in the United States trace their pedigree to-day. The race thus spread over both hemispheres, and from the rising to the setting sun, will not fail to keep that sovereignty of the sea and that commercial supremacy which it began to acquire when England first stretched its arm across the Atlantic to the shores of Virginia and Massachusetts. The language spoken by these great communities will not be sundered into dialects like the language of the ancient Romans, but perpetual intercommunication and the universal habit of reading and writing will preserve its integrity; and the world's business will be transacted by English-speaking people to so great an extent, that whatever language any man may have learned in his infancy he will find it necessary sooner or later to learn to express his thoughts in English. . . .

Now a century hence, with a population of six hundred millions in the United States, and a hundred and fifty millions in Australia and New Zealand, to say nothing of the increase of power in other parts of the English-speaking world, the relative weights will be very different from what they were in 1788. The population of Europe will not increase in anything like the same proportion, and a very considerable part of the increase will be transferred by emigration to the English-speaking world outside of Europe. By the end of the twentieth century such nations as France and Germany can only claim such a relative position in the political world as Holland and Switzerland now occupy. . . . It will then become as desirable for the states of Europe to enter into a federal union as it was for the states of North America a century ago.

It is only by thus adopting the lesson of federalism that Europe can do away with the chances of useless warfare which remain so long as its different states own no allegiance to any common authority. War, as we have seen, is with barbarous races both a necessity and a favourite occupation.

As long as civilization comes into contact with barbarism, it remains a too frequent necessity. But as between civilized and Christian nations it is a wretched absurdity. . . .

Already in America, as we have seen, it has become customary to deal with questions between states just as we would deal with questions between individuals. This we have seen to be the real purport of American federalism. To have established such a system over one great continent is to have made a very good beginning towards establishing it over the world. To establish such a system in Europe will no doubt be difficult, for here we have to deal with an immense complication of prejudices, intensified by linguistic and ethnological differences. Nevertheless the pacific pressure exerted upon Europe by America is becoming so great that it will doubtless before long overcome all these obstacles. . . .

The disparity between the United States, with a standing army of only twenty-five thousand men withdrawn from industrial pursuits, and the states of Europe, with their standing armies amounting to four millions of men, is something that cannot possibly be kept up. The economic competition will become so keen that European armies will have to be disbanded, the swords will have to be turned into ploughshares, and *thus* the victory of the industrial over the military type of civilization will at last become complete. . . .

Thus we may foresee in general outline how, through the gradual concentration of the preponderance of physical power into the hands of the most pacific communities, the wretched business of warfare must finally become obsolete all over the globe. The element of distance is now fast becoming eliminated from political problems, and the history of human progress politically will continue in the future to be what it has been in the past—the history of the successive union of groups of men into larger and more complex aggregates. As this process goes on, it may after many more ages of political experience become apparent that there is really no reason, in the nature of things, why the whole of mankind should not constitute politically one huge federation—each little group managing its local affairs in entire independence, but relegating all questions of international interest to the decision of one central tribunal supported by the public opinion of the entire human race. I believe that the time will come when such a state of things will exist upon the earth, when it will be possible (with our friends of the Paris dinner-party) to speak of the UNITED STATES as stretching from pole to pole—or, with Tennyson, to celebrate the "parliament of man and the federation of the world." Indeed, only when such a state of things has begun to be realized, can Civilization, as sharply demarcated from Barbarism, be said to have fairly begun. Only then can the world be said to have become truly Christian. Many ages of toil and doubt and perplexity will no doubt pass by before such a desideratum is reached. Meanwhile it is pleasant to feel that the dispassionate contemplation of great masses of historical facts goes far towards confirming our faith in this ultimate triumph of good over evil. Our survey began with pictures of horrid slaughter and desolation: it ends with the picture of a world covered with cheerful homesteads, blessed with a sabbath of perpetual peace.

JOSIAH STRONG, *OUR COUNTRY* (1885)

A Protestant clergyman and best-selling author, the Reverend Josiah Strong (1847–1916) believed it incumbent upon "Anglo-Saxons" to spread the blessings of liberty and convert the world to Christ. Here he anoints the United States as the leader of this great cause.

Every race which has deeply impressed itself on the human family has been the representative of some great idea—one or more—which had given direction to the nation's life and form to its civilization. Among the Egyptians this seminal idea was life, among the Persians it was light, among the

Josiah Strong, *Our Country*, New York: Baker and Taylor, 1885.

Hebrews it was purity, among the Greeks it was beauty, among the Romans it was law. The Anglo-Saxon is the representative of two great ideas, which are closely related. One of them is that of civil liberty. Nearly all of the civil liberty in the world is enjoyed by Anglo-Saxons: the English, the British colonists, and the people of the United States. . . . The noblest races have always been lovers of liberty. That love ran strong in early German blood, and has profoundly influenced the institutions of all the branches of the great German family; but it was left for the Anglo-Saxon branch fully to recognize the right of the individual to himself, and formally to declare it the foundation stone of government.

The other great idea of which the Anglo-Saxon is the exponent is that of a pure spiritual Christianity. It was no accident that the great reformation of the sixteenth century originated among a Teutonic, rather than a Latin people. It was the fire of liberty burning in the Saxon heart that flamed up against the absolutism of the Pope. . . .

It is not necessary to argue to those for whom I write that the two great needs of mankind, that all men may be lifted up into the light of the highest Christian civilization, are, first, a pure, spiritual Christianity, and, second, civil liberty. Without controversy, these are the forces which, in the past, have contributed most to the elevation of the human race, and they must continue to be, in the future, the most efficient ministers to its progress. It follows, then, that the Anglo-Saxon, as the great representative of these two ideas, the depository of these two greatest blessings, sustains peculiar relations to the world's future, is divinely commissioned to be, in a peculiar sense, his brother's keeper. . . .

There can be no reasonable doubt that North America is to be the great home of the Anglo-Saxon, the principal seat of his power, the center of his life and influence. Not only does it constitute seven-elevenths of his possessions, but this empire is unsevered, while the remaining four-elevenths are fragmentary and scattered over the earth. Australia will have a great population; but its disadvantages, as compared with North America, are too manifest to need mention. Our continent has room and resources and climate, it lies in the pathway of the nations, it belongs to the zone of power, and already, among Anglo-Saxons, do we lead in population and wealth.

Mr. Darwin is not only disposed to see, in the superior vigor of our people, an illustration of his favorite theory of natural selection, but even intimates that the world's history thus far has been simply preparatory for our future, and tributary to it. He says: "There is apparently much truth in the belief that the wonderful progress of the United States, as well as the character of the people, are the results of natural selection; for the more energetic, restless, and courageous men from all parts of Europe have emigrated during the last ten or twelve generations to that great country, and have there succeeded best. . . ."

The time is coming when the pressure of population on the means of subsistence will be felt there as it is now felt in Europe and Asia. Then will the world enter upon a new stage of its history—the final competition of races, for which the Anglo-Saxon is being schooled. Long before the thousands millions are here, the mighty centrifugal tendency, inherent in this stock and strengthened in the United States, will assert itself. Then this race of unequaled energy, with all the majesty of numbers and the might of wealth behind it—the representative, let us hope, of the largest liberty, the purest Christianity, the highest civilization—having developed peculiarly aggressive traits calculated to impress its institutions upon mankind, will spread itself over the earth. If I read not amiss, this powerful race will move down upon Mexico, down upon Central and South America, out upon the islands of the sea, over upon Africa and beyond. And can anyone doubt that the result of this competition of races will be the "survival of the fittest"?. . . .

In my own mind, there is no doubt that the Anglo-Saxon is to exercise the commanding influence in the world's future; but the exact nature of that influence is, as yet, undetermined. How far his civilization will be materialistic and atheistic, and how long it will take thoroughly to Christianize and sweeten it, how rapidly he will hasten the coming of the kingdom wherein dwelleth righteousness, or how many ages he may retard it, is still uncertain; but it is now being swiftly determined. . . .

Notwithstanding the great perils which threaten it, I cannot think our civilization will perish; but I believe it is fully in the hand of the

Christians of the United States, during the next fifteen or twenty years, to hasten or retard the coming of Christ's kingdom in the world by hundreds, and perhaps thousands, of years. We of this generation and nation occupy the Gibraltar of the ages which command the world's future.

Alfred Thayer Mahan, "The United States Looking Outward," *The Atlantic Monthly* (December 1890)

A graduate of the US Naval Academy and a career naval officer, Alfred Thayer Mahan (1840–1914) was an indifferent sailor. As a proponent of what he called "sea power," however, he greatly influenced US strategic thought. In this essay, he explains why the United States has no alternative but to become a great naval power.

Indications are not wanting of an approaching change in the thoughts and policy of Americans as to their relations with the world outside their own borders. For the past quarter of a century, the predominant idea, which has successfully asserted itself at the polls and shaped the course of the government, has been to preserve the home market for the home industries. The employer and the workman have alike been taught to look at the various economical measures proposed from this point of view, to regard with hostility any step favoring the intrusion of the foreign producer upon their own domain, and rather to demand increasingly rigorous measures of exclusion than to acquiesce in any loosening of the chain that binds the consumer to them. The inevitable consequence has followed, as in all eases when the mind or the eye is exclusively fixed in one direction, that the danger of loss or the prospect of advantage in another quarter has been overlooked; and although the abounding resources of the country have maintained the exports at a high figure, this flattering result has been due more to the superabundant bounty of Nature than to the demand of other nations for our protected manufactures.

For nearly the lifetime of a generation, therefore, American industries have been thus protected, until the practice has assumed the force of a tradition, and is clothed in the mail of conservatism. In their mutual relations, these industries resemble the activities of a modern ironclad that has heavy armor, but an inferior engine and no guns; mighty for defense, weak for offense. Within, the home market is secured; but outside, beyond the broad seas, there are the markets of the world, that can be entered and controlled only by a vigorous contest, to which the habit of trusting to protection by statute does not conduce.

At bottom, however, the temperament of the American people is essentially alien to such a sluggish attitude. Independently of all bias for or against protection, it is safe to predict that, when the opportunities for gain abroad are understood, the course of American enterprise will cleave a channel by which to reach them. . . .

The interesting and significant feature of this changing attitude is the turning of the eyes outward, instead of inward only, to seek the welfare of the country. To affirm the importance of distant markets, and the relation to them of our own immense powers of production, implies logically the recognition of the link that joins the products and the markets—that is, the carrying trade; the three together constituting that chain of maritime power to which Great Britain owes her wealth and greatness. Further, is it too much to say that, as two of these links, the shipping and the markets, are exterior to our own borders, the acknowledgment of them carries with it a view of the relations of the United States to the world radically distinct from the simple idea of self-sufficingness? We shall not follow far this line of thought before there will dawn the realization of America's unique position, facing the older worlds of the East and West, her shores lapped by the oceans which touch the one or the other, but which are common to her alone.

Coincident with these signs of change in our own policy there is a restlessness in the world at large which is deeply significant, if not ominous. It is beside our purpose to dwell upon the internal state of Europe, whence, if disturbances arise, the effect upon us may be but partial and indirect. But the great seaboard powers there do not only stand on guard against their continental rivals; they cherish also aspirations for commercial extension, for colonies, and for influence in distant regions, which may bring, and, even under our present contracted policy, have already brought them into collision with ourselves. . . .

There is no sound reason for believing that the world has passed into a period of assured peace outside the limits of Europe. Unsettled political conditions, such as exist in Hayti, Central America, and many of the Pacific islands, especially the Hawaiian group, when combined with great military or commercial importance, as is the case with most of these positions, involve, now as always, dangerous germs of quarrel, against which it is at least prudent to be prepared. Undoubtedly, the general temper of nations is more averse from war than it was of old. If no less selfish and grasping than our predecessors, we feel more dislike to the discomforts and sufferings attendant upon a breach of peace; but to retain that highly valued repose and the undisturbed enjoyment of the returns of commerce, it is necessary to argue upon somewhat equal terms of strength with an adversary. It is the preparedness of the enemy, and not acquiescence in the existing state of things, that now holds back the armies of Europe.

On the other hand, neither the sanctions of international law nor the justice of a cause can be depended upon for a fair settlement of differences, when they come into conflict with a strong political necessity on the one side opposed to comparative weakness on the other. In our still-pending dispute over the seal-fishing of Bering Sea, whatever may be thought of the strength of our argument, in view of generally admitted principles of international law, it is beyond doubt that our contention is reasonable, just, and in the interest of the world generally. But in the attempt to enforce it we have come into collision not only with national susceptibilities as to the honor of the flag, which we ourselves very strongly share, but also with a state governed by a powerful necessity, and exceedingly strong where we are particularly weak and exposed. Not only has Great Britain a mighty navy and we a long, defenseless seacoast, but it is a great commercial and political advantage to her that her larger

colonies, and above all Canada, should feel that the power of the mother country is something which they need, and upon which they can count. The dispute is between the United States and Canada, not the United States and England; but it has been ably used by the latter to promote the solidarity of sympathy between herself and her colony. . . .

This dispute, seemingly paltry, yet really serious, sudden in its appearance, and dependent for its issue upon other considerations than its own merits, may serve to convince us of many latent and yet unforeseen dangers to the peace of the western hemisphere, attendant upon the opening of a canal through the Central American Isthmus. In a general way, it is evident enough that this canal, by modifying the direction of trade routes, will induce a great increase of commercial activity and carrying trade throughout the Caribbean Sea; and that this now comparatively deserted nook of the ocean will, like the Red Sea, become a great thoroughfare of shipping, and attract, as never before in our day, the interest and ambition of maritime nations. Every position in that sea will have enhanced commercial and military value, and the canal itself will become a strategic centre of the most vital importance. . . .

Militarily speaking, the piercing of the Isthmus is nothing but a disaster to the United States, in the present state of her military and naval preparation. It is especially dangerous to the Pacific coast; but the increased exposure of one part of our seaboard reacts unfavorably upon the whole military situation. Despite a certain great original superiority conferred by our geographical nearness and immense resources—due, in other words, to our natural advantages, and not to our intelligent preparations—the United States is wofully unready, not only in fact, but in purpose, to assert in the Caribbean and Central America a weight of influence proportioned to the extent of her interests. We have not the navy, and, what is worse, we are not willing to have the navy, that will weigh seriously in any disputes with those nations whose interests will there conflict with our own. We have not, and we are not anxious to provide, the defense of the seaboard which will leave the navy free for its work at sea. We have not, but many other powers have, positions, either within or on the borders of the Caribbean, which not only possess great natural advantages for the control of that sea, but have received and are receiving that artificial strength of fortification and armament which will make them practically inexpugnable. On the contrary, we have not on the Gulf of Mexico even the beginning of a navy yard which could serve as the base of our operations. Let me not be misunderstood. I am not regretting that we have not the means to meet on terms of equality the great navies of the Old World. I recognize, what few at least say, that, despite its great surplus revenue, this country is poor in proportion to its length of seaboard and its exposed points. That which I deplore, and which is a sober, just, and reasonable cause of deep national concern, is that the nation neither has nor cares to have its sea frontier so defended, and its navy of such power, as shall suffice, with the advantages of our position, to weigh seriously when inevitable discussions arise,—such as we have recently had about Samoa and Bering Sea, and which may at any moment come up about the Caribbean Sea or the canal. . . .

It is perfectly reasonable and legitimate, in estimating our needs of military preparation, to take into account the remoteness of the chief naval and military nations from our shores, and the consequent difficulty of maintaining operations at such a distance. It is equally proper, in framing our policy, to consider the jealousies of the European family of states, and their consequent unwillingness to incur the enmity of a people so strong as ourselves; their dread of our revenge in the future, as well as their inability to detach more than a certain part of their forces to our shores without losing much of their own weight in the councils of Europe. In truth, a careful determination of the force that Great Britain or France could probably spare for operations against our coasts, if the latter were suitably defended, without weakening their European position or unduly exposing their colonies and commerce, is the starting-point from which to calculate the strength of our own navy. . . .

While, therefore, the advantages of our own position in the western hemisphere, and the disadvantages under which the operations of a European state would labor, are undeniable and just elements in the calculations of the statesman, it is folly to look upon them as sufficient for our security. Much more needs to be cast into the scale that it may incline in favor of our strength. They are mere defensive factors, and partial at that. Though distant, our shores can be reached; being defenseless, they can detain but a short time a force sent against them. With a probability of three months' peace in Europe, no maritime power would now fear to support its demands by a number of ships with which it would be loath indeed to part for a year.

Yet, were our sea frontier as strong as it now is weak, passive self-defense, whether in trade or war, would be but a poor policy, so long as this world continues to be one of struggle and vicissitude. All around us now is strife; "the struggle of life," "the race of life," are phrases so familiar that we do not feel their significance till we stop to think about them. Everywhere nation is arrayed against nation; our own no less than others. . . .

Our self-imposed isolation in the matter of markets, and the decline of our shipping interest in the last thirty years, have coincided singularly with an actual remoteness of this continent from the life of the rest of the world. . . .

When the Isthmus is pierced this isolation will pass away, and with it the indifference of foreign nations. From wheresoever they come and whithersoever they afterward go, all ships that use the canal will pass through the Caribbean. Whatever the effect produced upon the prosperity of the adjacent continent and islands by the thousand wants attendant upon maritime activity, around such a focus of trade will centre large commercial and political interests. To protect and develop its own, each nation will seek points of support and means of influence in a quarter where the United States has always been jealously sensitive to the intrusion of European powers. The precise value of the Monroe doctrine is very loosely understood by most Americans, but the effect of the familiar phrase has been to develop a national sensitiveness, which is a more frequent cause of war than material interests. . . .

Whether they will or no, Americans must now begin to look outward. The growing production of the country demands it. An increasing volume of public sentiment demands it. The position of the United States, between the two Old Worlds and the two great oceans, makes the same claim, which will soon be strengthened by the creation of the new link joining the Atlantic and Pacific. The tendency will be maintained and increased by the growth of the European colonies in the

Pacific, by the advancing civilization of Japan, and by the rapid peopling of our Pacific States with men who have all the aggressive spirit of the advanced line of national progress. Nowhere does a vigorous foreign policy find more favor than among the people west of the Rocky Mountains.

It has been said that, in our present state of unpreparedness, a trans-isthmian canal will be a military disaster to the United States, and especially to the Pacific coast. When the canal is finished the Atlantic seaboard will be neither more nor less exposed than it now is; it will merely share with the country at large the increased danger of foreign complications with inadequate means to meet them. The danger of the Pacific coast will be greater by so much as the way between it and Europe is shortened through a passage which the stronger maritime power can control. The danger lies not merely in the greater facility for dispatching a hostile squadron from Europe, but also in the fact that a more powerful fleet than formerly can be maintained on that coast by a European power, because it can be so much more promptly called home in case of need. The greatest weakness of the Pacific ports, however, if wisely met by our government, will go far to insure our naval superiority there. . . .

The military needs of the Pacific States, as well as their supreme importance to the whole country, are yet a matter of the future, but of a future so near that provision should immediately begin. . . . . But such influence, to work without jar and friction, requires underlying military readiness, like the proverbial iron hand under the velvet glove. To provide this, three things are needful: First, protection of the chief harbors by fortifications and coast-defense ships, which gives defensive strength, provides security to the community within, and supplies the bases necessary to all military operations. Secondly, naval force, the arm of offensive power, which alone enables a country to extend its influence outward. Thirdly, it should be an inviolable resolution of our national policy that no European state should henceforth acquire a coaling position within three thousand miles of San Francisco,—a distance which includes the Sandwich and Galapagos islands and the coast of Central America. For fuel is the life of modern naval war; it is the food of the ship; without it the modern monsters of the deep die of inaction. Around it, therefore, cluster some of the most important considerations of naval strategy. In the Caribbean and the Atlantic we are confronted with many a foreign coal depot, and perhaps it is not an unmitigated misfortune that we, like Rome, find Carthage at our gates bidding us stand to our arms; but let us not acquiesce in an addition to our dangers, a further diversion of our strength, by being forestalled in the North Pacific.

In conclusion, while Great Britain is undoubtedly the most formidable of our possible enemies, both by her great navy and the strong positions she holds near our coasts, it must be added that a cordial understanding with that country is one of the first of our external interests. Both nations, doubtless, and properly, seek their own advantage; but both, also, are controlled by a sense of law and justice drawn from the same sources, and deep-rooted in their instincts. Whatever temporary aberration may occur, a return to mutual standards of right will certainly follow. Formal alliance between the two is out of the question, but a cordial recognition of the similarity of character and ideas will give birth to sympathy, which in turn will facilitate a cooperation beneficial to both; for, if sentimentality is weak, sentiment is strong.

STEPHEN B. LUCE, "THE BENEFITS OF WAR" *NORTH AMERICAN REVIEW* (DECEMBER 1891)

Second only to Mahan, Rear Admiral Stephen B. Luce (1827–1917) was the preeminent American naval officer of his era. In this essay, he urges Americans to shed their antipathy for war.

War is one of the great agencies by which human progress is effected.

Scourge though it be, and much as its practice is to be deplored, we must still recognize war as the operation of the economic laws of nature for the government of the human family. It stimulates national growth, solves otherwise insoluble problems of domestic and political economy, and purges a nation of its humors. . . .

War is the malady of nations; the disease is terrible while it lasts, but purifying in its results. It tries a nation and chastens it, as sickness or adversity tries and chastens the individual. There is a wisdom that comes only of suffering, whether to the family or to the aggregation of families—the nation. Man is perfected through suffering.

What is true of the average individual is true of the mass of individuals—the people.

Some of the richest contributions to literature, art, and science have been the offsprings of indigence. Want brings out the natural gifts that affluence stifles. So, in the economy of nature, or the providence of God, war is sent, not necessarily for the punishment of national sins, nor yet for national aggrandizement; but, rather, for the forming of national character, the shaping of a people's destiny, and the spreading of civilization.

It is only through long years of severe trials and tribulations that many men and women have been schooled to ultimate success. So nations, before achieving greatness, have had to struggle through periods of bitter strife before the various factions, with their conflicting interests, have been formed into one homogeneous mass.

As adversity and opposition toughen the mental and moral fibre and temper the spirit of man, so riches and easily-acquired success enervate the strongest character and unfit it for protracted effort. It is the same with nations. War arouses all the latent energies of a people, stimulates them to the highest exertion, and develops their mental and material resources. . . .

But for war the civilization we now enjoy would have been impossible. The swath cut by the reaper's sickle through fields of ripened grain is not more marked than the way cut by the sword for the path of human progress. . . .

From the "blue Cyclades" to the slopes of the Pacific, war has made possible the slow, but certain, development of the great law of human progress, and of the principles of democracy. The operation of this law is not to be arrested on the hither shores of the Pacific; nor is history to be turned back. The course of empire still holds its accustomed way. With the United States, as the dominant power of the western world, lies the obligation of contributing her share to the further extension of civilization, to the spreading of the gospel, and conveying to less favored nations the most enlightened views of civil government. Peaceful commerce is one of the forces by which this end may be attained; and the Pacific and its further shores the field of its operations. This splendid work our people are now content to leave to England and those most effective missionaries, her military and mercantile marines. The time will come, however, when the nation, in its manhood, will "put away childish things," assume its own high responsibilities, and organize its forces for practical use.

We are far from maintaining that war is the only agency through which the present advanced state of civilization has been reached. Christianity has been, and must continue to be, an indispensable factor. But the sword has ever preceded the banner of the cross. Indeed, Christianity, as we shall see, has often had to work its own way through the instrumentality of the sword.

Commerce is another great factor. By it civilization is carried over wide seas to distant lands; but commerce owes its extension and protection to the military arm of the people it represents.

Wars have sometimes been precipitated in spite of all human efforts to prevent them. As in the presence of the convulsions of nature man feels his utter nothingness, so in the great political and religious movements which have marked certain epochs in history man has found himself impotent to either control or guide the march of events. It is then that he acknowledges that human affairs are directed by a power above and beyond this world, for the ultimate good of his race. . . .

Our own Civil War furnishes as notable an example as may be found in history of the operation of this law of strife by which human progress is effected. War was the only means of solving the great political problem of the abolition of slavery, and the phenomenal progress, not of the South alone, but of the whole country, during the past twenty-five years, bears abundant testimony to the quickening influences of that momentous struggle.

Heaven forbid that we should even seem to be an advocate of war. We are not an advocate of war, nor of pestilence, nor of famine. On the contrary, we join with the church in praying for deliverance from them. But this is not a question of what one could wish: it is a question of a great fundamental truth. . . .

Strife in one form or another in the organic world seems to be the law of existence. "Life," the scientist tells us, is but "the sum of all the forces that resist death." Suspend the struggle, well called the battle of life, for a brief space, and death claims the victory. The struggle begins at birth, and ends in one unvarying way at the grave. . . .

By the very law of our nature, it thus appears, the wellspring of war is in the human heart. When the apostle of universal peace can change human nature itself, then may he hope to put an end to war. The utmost that we can now reasonably hope for is to lessen the frequency and the evils of war. . . .

The proper spirit in which to consider a great evil is to look it in the face, examine into its origin, and seek the causes which lead to its production. If these causes lie in the operation of the laws of nature, which cannot be influenced by human action, then we must endeavor to modify the effects and ameliorate, as far as lies in our power, the conditions to which they give rise.

Man cannot control the meteorological laws which manifest themselves in cyclones; but he can build ships and houses strong enough to withstand their violence. Medical science cannot conquer death, but it has done much to alleviate suffering; and statistics show that the average duration of human life has been increased through increased knowledge of the laws of hygiene. Moral science cannot boast of a like achievement. . . .

Questions in medical science are submitted to rigorous investigation according to scientific methods. Questions in moral science are too often treated from a sentimental standpoint, or quietly ignored. Even in this enlightened age we seek to eradicate the "great social evil" by shutting our eyes to it. There is a widespread disposition to treat war in the same way—by shutting the public eye to it. What progress had pathology made by that method?

It is the popular and very proper thing to say that the progressive spirit of the age is leaving the barbarism of war behind, and that as civilization advances it will learn less of war. Arbitration is now the sovereign panacea for that national ill. But, as a matter of fact, war has never been so carefully and so systematically studied as at the present time. The genius of invention has never been so prolific as now in devising and improving implements of war. That man is honored and enriched who contrives means of destroying the greatest number of human beings in the shortest space of time. As the conduct of war becomes more scientific, and the art becomes refined, and the implements more destructive, the recurrence of war is lessened, the duration shortened, and the loss of human life diminished. This is the direction the spirit of the age is taking—a direction in the interests of humanity.

These humane conditions, however, involve an advanced stage of preparation. As a science war should be sedulously cultivated by the few qualified to undertake it; as an art it should be constantly practised by the entire body set apart for that purpose, and with the implements actually to be used in war. It is to this state of preparation that we owe the peace of Europe today. The mere presence of the American army on our southern frontier in 1866 was sufficient to cause the collapse of Louis Napoleon's scheme for a Mexican empire. By a perfect state of preparation a collision of arms was avoided and the shedding of blood spared. To be unprepared is wicked. It invites aggression and a useless effusion of blood. . . .

There is a certain class of international questions for which arbitration is admirably suited; there is another class for which it is not suited at all—for which it is totally inadmissible. It is the lamb that advocates arbitration, even though the life and honor of the fold be involved, while the wolf maintains a lofty indifference to all such methods of proceeding. . . .

Arbitration was inadmissible in 1860-61, when so sorely needed. War, which had been in the course of preparation for thirty years preceding its outbreak, was the only solution of the great problem. It had to be.

Arbitration fails miserably when most needed, and what wonder? The high contracting parties and their umpires are all men of like passions, having no court of last resort but the battlefield.

Every Christian, whatever may be his private convictions, must hope and pray for the success of the Universal Peace Association and the sufficiency of arbitration in all international disputes. But no American, be he Christian or not, should forget the moral effect on negotiations of the propinquity of an adequate force. . . .

The United States are known of all the world to be wanting in the disposition to utilize their abundant resources for military purposes—not with a view to conquest, but even for the defences suggested by the most ordinary prudence. Ready as they are to wage a commercial warfare, our people close their eyes to the possibilities of an actual collision of arms.

There are false prophets who proclaim that war is to be abolished and that preparation for war is a useless extravagance; who offer a cheap nostrum for a dreadful disease. Out of that fearful concatenation of evils set forth in the solemn litany of the Holy Catholic Church of America, wherein we are taught to supplicate deliverance from sin; from the crafts and assaults of the devil; from plague, pestilence, and famine; from battle and murder, and from sudden death, they select battle alone for extirpation. Why should they not include sin as well? Why not include the whole dreadful catalogue? Why not form an association for the suppression of all inordinate and sinful affections?

The truth is that war is an ordinance of God. The flaming sword that guards the way to sinless Eden will continue to prevail, until man enters once more into that peace which passeth all understanding, when the lust of the eye and the pride of life shall no more be known. But mortal man cannot yet discern the coming of that day.

Meanwhile let practical America recognize the truth that war is a calamity that may overtake the most peaceful nation, and that insurance against war by preparation for it is, of all methods, the most business-like, the most humane, and the most in accordance with the teachings of the Christian religion.

Frederick Jackson Turner, "The Significance of the Frontier in American History" (1893)

With this essay, Frederick Jackson Turner (1861–1932) achieved a level of prominence rarely enjoyed by academic historians. His "frontier thesis" not only provides an overarching interpretation of the entire American experience, but suggests that the United States will inevitably seek new frontiers to tame.

In a recent bulletin of the Superintendent of the Census for 1890 appear these significant words: "Up to and including 1880 the country had a frontier of settlement, but at present the unsettled area has been so broken into by isolated bodies of settlement that there can hardly be said to be a frontier line. In the discussion of its extent, its westward movement, etc., it can not, therefore, any longer have a place in the census reports." This brief official statement marks the closing of a great historic movement. Up to our own day American history has been in a large degree the history of the colonization of the Great West. The existence of an area of free land, its continuous recession, and the advance of American settlement westward, explain American development.

Behind institutions, behind constitutional forms and modifications, lie the vital forces that call these organs into life and shape them to meet changing conditions. The peculiarity of American institutions is, the fact that they have been compelled to adapt themselves to the changes of an expanding people—to the changes involved in crossing a continent, in winning a wilderness, and in developing at each area of this progress out of the primitive economic and political conditions of the frontier into the complexity of city life. Said Calhoun in 1817, "We are great, and rapidly—I was about to say fearfully—growing!" So saying, he touched the distinguishing feature of American life.

All peoples show development; the germ theory of politics has been sufficiently emphasized. In the case of most nations, however, the development has occurred in a limited area; and if the nation has expanded, it has met other growing peoples whom it has conquered. But in the case of the United States we have a different phenomenon. Limiting our attention to the Atlantic coast, we have the familiar phenomenon of the evolution of institutions in a limited area, such as the rise of representative government; into complex organs; the progress from primitive industrial society, without division of labor, up to manufacturing civilization. But we have in addition to this a recurrence of the process of evolution in each western area reached in the process of expansion. Thus American development has exhibited not merely advance along a single line, but a return to primitive conditions on a continually advancing frontier line, and a new development for that area.

American social development has been continually beginning over again on the frontier. This perennial rebirth, this fluidity of American life, this expansion westward with its new opportunities, its continuous touch with the simplicity of primitive society, furnish the forces dominating American character. The true point of view in the history of this nation is not the Atlantic coast, it is the Great West. . . .

In this advance, the frontier is the outer edge of the wave— the meeting point between savagery and civilization. Much has been written about the frontier from the point of view of border warfare and the chase, but as a field for the serious study of the economist and the historian it has been neglected.

The American frontier is sharply distinguished from the European frontier—a fortified boundary line running through dense populations. The most significant thing about the American frontier is, that it lies at the hither edge of free land. In the census reports it is treated as the margin of that settlement which has a density of two or more to the square mile. The term is an elastic one, and for our purposes does not need sharp definition. We shall consider the whole frontier belt including the Indian country and the outer margin of the "settled area" of the census reports. . . .

In the settlement of America we have to observe how European life entered the continent, and how America modified and developed that life and reacted on Europe. Our early history is the study of European germs developing in an American environment. Too exclusive attention has been paid by institutional students to the Germanic origins, too little to the American factors. The frontier is the line of most rapid and effective Americanization. . . .

The fact is, that here is a new product that is American. At first, the frontier was the Atlantic coast. It was the frontier of Europe in a very real sense. Moving westward, the frontier became more and more American. As successive terminal moraines result from successive glaciations, so each frontier leaves its traces behind it, and when it becomes a settled area the region still partakes of the frontier characteristics. Thus the advance of the frontier has meant a steady movement away from the influence of Europe, a steady growth of independence on American lines. And to study this advance, the men who grew up under these conditions, and the political, economic, and social results of it, is to study the really American part of our history. . . .

In these successive frontiers we find natural boundary lines which have served to mark and to affect the characteristics of the frontiers, namely: the "fall line;" the Alleghany Mountains; the Mississippi; the Missouri where its direction approximates north and south; the line of the arid lands, approximately the ninety-ninth meridian; and the Rocky Mountains. The fall line marked the frontier of the seventeenth century; the Alleghanies that of the eighteenth; the Mississippi that of the first quarter of the nineteenth; the Missouri that of the middle of this century (omitting the California movement); and the belt of the Rocky Mountains and the arid tract, the present frontier. Each was won by a series of Indian wars.

At the Atlantic frontier one can study the germs of processes repeated at each successive frontier. We have the complex European life sharply precipitated by the wilderness into the simplicity of primitive conditions. The first frontier had to meet its Indian question, its question of the disposition of the public domain, of the means of intercourse with older settlements, of the extension of political organization, of religious and educational activity. And the settlement of these and similar questions for one frontier served as a guide for the next. . . . . Each tier of new States has found in the older ones material for its constitutions. Each frontier has made similar contributions to American character. . . . .

The United States lies like a huge page in the history of society. Line by line as we read this continental page from West to East we find the record of social evolution. It begins with the Indian and the hunter; it goes on to tell of the disintegration of savagery by the entrance of the trader, the pathfinder of civilization; we read the annals of the pastoral stage in ranch life; the exploitation of the soil by the raising of unrotated crops of corn and wheat in sparsely settled farming communities; the intensive culture of the denser farm settlement; and finally the manufacturing organization with city and factory system. . . .

The maps of the census reports show an uneven advance of the farmer's frontier, with tongues of settlement pushed forward and with indentations of wilderness. In part this is due to Indian resistance, in part to the location of river valleys and passes, in part to the unequal force of the centers of frontier attraction. Among the important centers of attraction may be mentioned the following: fertile and favorably situated soils, salt springs, mines, and army posts.

The frontier army post, serving to protect the settlers from the Indians, has also acted as a wedge to open the Indian country, and has been a nucleus for settlement. In this connection mention should also be made of the government military and exploring expeditions in determining the lines of settlement. But all the more important expeditions were greatly indebted to the earliest pathmakers, the Indian guides, the traders and trappers, and the French voyageurs, who were inevitable parts of governmental expeditions from the days of Lewis and Clark. Each expedition was an epitome of the previous factors in western advance. . . .

From the time the mountains rose between the pioneer and the seaboard, a new order of Americanism arose. The West and the East began to get out of touch of each other. The settlements from the sea to the mountains kept connection with the rear and had a certain solidarity. But the over-mountain men grew more and more independent. The East took a narrow view of American advance, and nearly lost these men. Kentucky and Tennessee history bears abundant witness to the truth of this statement. The East began to try to hedge and limit westward expansion. Though Webster could declare that there were no Alleghanies in his politics, yet in politics in general they were a very solid factor. . . .

The farmer's advance came in a distinct series of waves. . . . First comes the pioneer, who depends for the subsistence of his family chiefly upon the natural growth of vegetation, called the "range," and the proceeds of hunting. His implements of agriculture are rude, chiefly of his own make, and his efforts directed mainly to a crop of corn and a "truck patch." The last is a rude garden for growing cabbage, beans, corn for roasting ears, cucumbers, and potatoes. A log cabin, and, occasionally, a stable and corn-crib, and a field of a dozen acres, the timber girdled or "deadened," and fenced, are enough for his occupancy. It is quite immaterial whether he ever becomes the owner of the soil. He is the occupant for the time being, pays no rent, and feels as independent as the " lord of the manor." With a horse, cow, and one or two breeders of swine, he strikes into the woods with his family, and becomes the founder of a new county, or perhaps state. He builds his cabin, gathers around him a few other families of similar tastes and habits, and occupies till the range is somewhat subdued, and hunting a little precarious, or, which is more frequently the case, till the neighbors crowd around, roads, bridges, and fields annoy him, and he lacks elbow room. . . .

The next class of emigrants purchase the lands, add field to field, clear out the roads, throw rough bridges over the streams, put up hewn log houses with glass windows and brick or stone chimneys, occasionally plant orchards, build mills, schoolhouses, court-houses, etc., and exhibit the picture and forms of plain, frugal, civilized life.

Another wave rolls on. The men of capital and enterprise come. The settler is ready to sell out and take the advantage of the rise in property, push farther into the interior and become, himself, a man of capital and enterprise in turn. The small village rises to a spacious town or city; substantial edifices of brick, extensive fields, orchards, gardens, colleges, and churches are seen. Broadcloths, silks, leghorns, crepes, and all the refinements, luxuries, elegancies, frivolities, and fashions are in vogue. Thus wave after wave is rolling westward; the real Eldorado is still farther on. . . .

Having now roughly outlined the various kinds of frontiers, and their modes of advance, chiefly from the point of view of the frontier itself, we may next inquire what were the influences on the East and on the Old World. A rapid enumeration of some of the more noteworthy effects is all that I have time for.

First, we note that the frontier promoted the formation of a composite nationality for the American people. The coast was preponderantly English, but the later tides of continental immigration flowed across to the free lands. . . .

In the crucible of the frontier the immigrants were Americanized, liberated, and fused into a mixed race, English in neither nationality nor characteristics. The process has gone on from the early days to our own. . . .

The legislation which most developed the powers of the national government, and played the largest part in its activity, was conditioned on the frontier. Writers have discussed the subjects of tariff, land, and internal improvement, as subsidiary to the slavery question. But when American history comes to be rightly viewed it will be seen that the slavery question is an incident. . . .

It was this nationalizing tendency of the West that transformed the democracy of Jefferson into the national republicanism of Monroe and the democracy of Andrew Jackson. The West of the War of 1812, the West of Clay, and Benton and Harrison, and Andrew Jackson, shut off by the Middle States and the mountains from the coast sections, had a solidarity of its own with national tendencies. On the tide of the Father of Waters, North and South met and mingled into a nation. Interstate migration went steadily on—a process of crossfertilization of ideas and institutions. The fierce struggle of the sections over slavery on the western frontier does not diminish the truth of this statement; it proves the truth of it. Slavery was a sectional trait that would not down, but in the West it could not remain sectional. It was the greatest of frontiersmen who declared: "I believe this Government can not endure permanently half slave and half free. It will become all of one thing or all of the other." Nothing works for nationalism like intercourse within the nation. Mobility of population is death to localism, and the western frontier worked irresistibly in unsettling population. The effect reached back from the frontier and affected profoundly the Atlantic coast and even the Old World.

But the most important effect of the frontier has been in the promotion of democracy here and in Europe. As has been indicated, the frontier is productive of individualism. Complex society is precipitated by the wilderness into a kind of primitive organization based on the family. The tendency is anti-social. It produces antipathy to control, and particularly to any direct control. The tax-gatherer is viewed as a representative of oppression. . . .

The frontier individualism has from the beginning promoted democracy. The frontier States that came into the Union in the first quarter of a century of its existence came in with democratic suffrage provisions, and had reactive effects of the highest importance upon the older States whose peoples were being attracted there. An extension of the franchise became essential. It was *western* New York that forced an extension of suffrage in the constitutional convention of that State in 1821; and it was *western* Virginia that compelled the tide-water region to put a more liberal suffrage provision in the constitution framed in 1830, and to give to the frontier region a more nearly proportionate representation with the tidewater aristocracy. The rise of democracy as an effective force in the nation came in with western preponderance under Jackson and William Henry Harrison, and it meant the triumph of the frontier—with all of its good and with all of its evil elements. . . .

So long as free land exists, the opportunity for a competency exists, and economic power secures political power. But the democracy born of free land, strong in selfishness and individualism, intolerant of administrative experience and education, and pressing individual liberty beyond its proper bounds, has its dangers as well as its benefits. Individualism in America has allowed a laxity in regard to governmental affairs which has rendered possible the spoils system and all the manifest evils that follow from the lack of a highly developed civic spirit. In this connection may be noted also the influence of frontier conditions in permitting lax business honor, inflated paper currency and wild-cat banking. . . . . . A primitive society can hardly be expected to show the intelligent appreciation of the complexity of business interests in a developed society. The continual recurrence of these areas of paper-money agitation is another evidence that the frontier can be isolated and studied as a factor in American history of the highest importance. . . .

From the conditions of frontier life came intellectual traits of profound importance. The works of travelers along each frontier from colonial days onward describe certain common traits, and these traits have, while softening down, still persisted as survivals in the place of their origin, even when a higher social organization succeeded. The result is that to the frontier the American intellect owes its striking characteristics. That coarseness and strength combined with acuteness and inquisitiveness; that practical, inventive turn of mind, quick to find expedients; that masterful grasp of material things, lacking in the artistic but powerful to effect great ends; that restless, nervous energy; that dominant individualism, working for good and for evil, and withal that buoyancy and exuberance which comes with freedom—these are traits of the frontier, or traits called out elsewhere because of the existence of the frontier.

Since the days when the fleet of Columbus sailed into the waters of the New World, America has been another name for opportunity, and the people of the United States have taken their tone from the incessant expansion which has not only been open but has even been forced upon them. He would be a rash prophet who should assert that the expansive character of American life has now entirely ceased. Movement has been its dominant fact, and, unless this training has no effect upon a people, the American energy will continually demand a wider field for its exercise. . . .

ALBERT J. BEVERIDGE, "THE MARCH OF THE FLAG" (1898)

In 1898, the United States went to war with Spain, with liberating Cuba from Spanish rule the issue nominally at hand. In short order, the conflict presented US policymakers with opportunities to acquire far-flung overseas possessions. In this florid speech, Senator Albert Beveridge (1862–1927), a Republican from Indiana, explains why "God's chosen people" are called to seize those opportunities.

Fellow-citizens—It is a noble land that God has given us; a land that can feed and clothe the world; a land whose coast lines would inclose half the countries of Europe; a land set like a sentinel between the two imperial oceans of the globe; a greater England with a nobler destiny. It is a mighty people that He has planted on this soil; a people sprung from the most masterful blood of history; a people perpetually revitalized by the virile workingfolk of all the earth; a people imperial by virtue of their power, by right of their institutions, by authority of their heaven-directed purposes, the propagandists and not the misers of liberty. It is a glorious history our God has bestowed upon His chosen people; a history whose keynote was struck by Liberty Bell; a history heroic with faith in our mission and our future; a history of statesmen, who flung the boundaries of the Republic out into unexplored lands and savage wildernesses; a history of soldiers, who carried the flag across blazing deserts and through the ranks of hostile mountains, even to the gates of sunset; a history of a multiplying people, who overrun a continent in half a century; a history divinely logical, in the process of whose tremendous reasoning we find ourselves to-day.

Therefore, in this campaign the question is larger than a party question. It is an American question. It is a world question. Shall the American people continue their resistless march toward the commercial supremacy of the world? Shall free institutions broaden their blessed reign as the children of liberty wax in strength until the empire of our principles is established over the hearts of all mankind? Have we no mission to perform—no duty to discharge to our fellow-man? Has the Almighty Father endowed us with gifts beyond our deserts, and marked us as the people of His peculiar favor, merely to rot in our own selfishness, as men and nations must who take cowardice for their companion and self for their Deity—as China has, as India has, as Egypt has? Shall we be as the man who had one talent and hid it, or as he who had ten talents and used them until they grew to riches? And shall we reap the reward that waits on the discharge of our high duty as the sovereign power of earth; shall we occupy new markets for what our farmers raise, new markets for what our factories make, new markets for what our merchants sell—aye, and, please God, new markets for what our ships shall carry? Shall we avail ourselves of new sources of supply of what we do not raise or make, so that what are luxuries to-day will be necessities to-morrow? Shall we conduct the mightiest commerce of history with the best money known to man, or shall we use the pauper money of Mexico, China and the Chicago platform? Shall we be worthy of our mighty past of progress, brushing aside, as we have always done, the spider webs of technicality, and march ever onward upon the highway of development, to the doing of real deeds, the achievement of real things, and the winning of real victories?

In a sentence, shall the American people indorse at the polls the American administration of William McKinley, which, under the guidance of Divine Providence, has started the Republic on its noblest career of prosperity, duty and glory; or shall the American people rebuke that administration, reverse the wheels of history, halt the career of the flag and turn to that purposeless horde of criticism and carping that is assailing the government at Washington. . . .

What are the great facts of this administration? Not a failure of revenue, not a perpetual battle between the executive and legislative departments of government; not a rescue from dishonor by European syndicates at the price of tens of millions in cash and national humiliation unspeakable. But a war has marked it, the most holy ever waged by one nation against another; a war for civilization; a war for a permanent peace; a war which, under God, although we knew it not in the beginning, has swung open to the Republic the portals of the commerce of the world. . . .

William McKinley meant it to be a war of victory. William McKinley meant that the record should be made up before the grim judgment was pronounced; and then—then, when the day was full, when ships were manned and coasts defended, and powder purchased, and all was ready for battle—then, our soldier-President hurled the navy and army of the Republic upon the hosts of Spain and smote them West and East like the avenging hand of fate. History will tell our children the result—Manila, Santiago, Dewey, Sampson, Schley, and peace—peoples freed, new lands acquired, the geography of the earth remade by liberty, henceforth the master map-maker of the world. . . .

William McKinley is continuing the policy that Jefferson began, Monroe continued, Seward advanced, Grant promoted, Harrison championed, and the growth of the Republic has demanded. Hawaii is ours; Porto Rico is to be ours; at the prayer of the people Cuba will finally be ours; in the islands of the east, even to the gates of Asia, coaling stations are to be ours; at the very least the flag of a liberal government is to float over the Philippines, and it will be the stars and stripes of glory. And the burning question of this campaign is, whether the American people will accept the gifts of events; whether they will rise, as lifts their soaring destiny; whether they will proceed upon the lines of national development surveyed by the statesmen of our past; or whether, for the first time, the American people doubt their mission, question fate, prove apostate to the spirit of their race, and halt the ceaseless march of free institutions?

The opposition tells us that we ought not to govern a people without their consent. I answer, the rule of liberty that all just government derives its authority from the consent of the governed, applies only to those who are capable of self-government. We govern the Indians without their consent; we govern our territories without their consent; we govern our children without their consent. I answer, would not the natives of the Philippines prefer the just, humane, civilizing government of this Republic to the savage, bloody rule of pillage and extortion from which we have rescued them? Do not the blazing fires of joy and the ringing bells of gladness in Porto Rico prove the welcome of our flag? And, regardless of this formula of words made only for enlightened, self-governing peoples, do we owe no duty to the world? Shall we turn these peoples back to the reeking hands from which we have taken them? Shall we abandon them to their fate with the wolves of conquest all about them? Shall we save them from those nations, to give them a self-rule of tragedy? It would be like giving a razor to a babe and telling it to shave itself. It would be like giving a typewriter to an Eskimo and telling him to publish one of the great dailies of the world.

They ask us how we will govern these new possessions. I answer, out of local conditions and the necessities of the case methods of government will grow. If England can govern foreign lands so can America. If Germany can govern foreign lands so can America. If they can supervise protectorates so can America. Why is it more difficult to administer Hawaii than New Mexico or California? Both had a savage and an alien population; both were more remote from the seat of government when they came under our dominion than Hawaii is to-day. Will you say by your vote that American ability to govern has decayed, that you are an infidel to American vigor and practical sense? Or that we are of the ruling race of the world; that ours is the blood of government; ours the heart of dominion; ours the brain and the genius of administration? We do but what our fathers did—but pitch the tents of liberty farther westward, farther southward; we only continue the march of the flag.

The march of the flag! In 1789 the flag of the Republic waved over 4,000,000 souls in thirteen States, and this a savage territory which stretched to the Mississippi, to Canada, to the Floridas. The timid minds of that day said that no new territory was needed, and, for the hour, they were right. But under the lead of Jefferson we acquired the territory which sweeps from the Mississippi to the mountains, from Texas to the British possessions, and the march of the flag began. The infidels to the gospel of liberty raved, but the flag swept on. The title to that noble land out of which Oregon, Washington, Idaho and Montana have been carved was uncertain. Jefferson obeyed the Anglo-Saxon impulse within him and another empire was added to the Republic and the march of the flag went on. Those who deny the power of free institutions to expand urged every argument, and more, that we hear to-day, but the march of the flag went on. A screen of land from New Orleans to Florida shut us from the gulf, and over this and the Everglade Peninsula waved the saffron flag of Spain. Andrew Jackson seized both, the American people stood at his back, and under Monroe the Floridas came under the dominion of the republic, and the march of the flag went on. The Cassandras prophesied every prophecy of despair we hear to-day, but the march of the flag went on. Then Texas responded to the bugle calls of liberty and the march of the flag went on. And at last we waged war with Mexico and the flag swept over the Southwest, over peerless California, past the Gate of Gold to Oregon on the north, and from ocean to ocean its folds of glory blazed. And now, obeying the same voice that Jefferson, Jackson, Seward heard and obeyed, Grant and Harrison heard and obeyed, William McKinley plants the flag over the islands of the sea, and the march of the flag goes on.

Distance and oceans are no longer arguments. The fact that all the territory our fathers bought and seized is contiguous is no longer argument. In 1819 Florida was further from New York than Porto Rico is from Chicago to-day; Texas further from Washington in 1845 than Hawaii is from Boston in 1898; California more inaccessible in 1847 than the Philippines are now. Gibraltar is further from London than Havana is from Washington; Melbourne is further from Liverpool than Manila is from San Francisco. The ocean does not separate us from the lands of our duty and desire—the ocean to join us, a river never to be dredged, a canal never to be repaired. Steam joins us; electricity joins us—the very elements are in league with our destiny. Cuba not contiguous! Porto Rico not contiguous! Hawaii and the Philippines not contiguous! Our navy will make them contiguous. Dewey and Sampson and Schley have made them contiguous and American speed, American guns, American heart and brain and nerve will keep them contiguous forever.

But there is a difference. We did not need the western Mississippi Valley when we acquired it, nor Florida, nor Texas, nor California, nor the royal provinces of the far Northwest. We had no emigrants to people this vast wilderness, no money to develop it, even no highways to cover it. No trade awaited us in its savage fastnesses. Our productions were not greater than our internal trade. There was not one reason for the land lust of our statesmen from Jefferson to Harrison, other than the prophet and the Saxon within them. But, to-day, we are raising more than we can consume. To-day, we are making more than we can use. Therefore, we must find new markets for our produce, new occupation for our capital, new work for our labor. And so, while we did not need the territory taken during the past century at the time it was acquired, we do need what we have taken in 1898, and we need it now. Think of the thousands of Americans who will pour into Hawaii and Porto Rico when the Republic's laws cover those islands with justice and safety. Think of the tens of thousands of Americans who will invade the Philippines when a liberal government shall establish order and equity there. Think of the hundreds of thousands of Americans who will build a soap-and-water, common school civilization of energy and industry in Cuba, when a government of law replaces the double reign of anarchy and tyranny. Think of the prosperous millions that empress of islands will support when, obedient to the law of political gravitation, her people ask for the highest honor liberty can bestow—the sacred order of the stars and stripes, the citizenship of the great Republic!

What does all this mean for every one of us? First of all, it means opportunity for all the glorious young manhood of the republic. It means that the resources and the commerce of these immensely rich dominions will be increased as much as American energy is greater than Spanish sloth; for Americans, henceforth, will monopolize those resources and that commerce. In Cuba, alone, there are 15,000,000 acres of forest unacquainted with the ax. There are exhaustless mines of iron. There are priceless deposits of manganese. There are millions of acres yet unexplored. The resources of Porto Rico have only been trifled with. The riches of the Philippines have hardly been touched by the finger tips of modern methods. And they produce what we cannot, and they consume what we produce—the very predestination of reciprocity. And William McKinley intends that their trade shall be ours. It means an opportunity for the rich man to do something with his money, besides hoarding it or lending it. It means occupation for every workingman in the country at wages which the development of new resources, the launching of new enterprises, the monopoly of new markets always brings. Cuba is as large as Pennsylvania, and is the richest spot on all the globe. Hawaii is as large as New Jersey; Porto Rico half as large as Hawaii; the Philippines larger than all New England, New York, New Jersey and Delaware. The trade of these islands, developed as we will develop it, will set every reaper in this Republic singing, every spindle whirling, every furnace spouting the flames of industry. . . .

The commercial empire of the Republic! That is the greatest fact of the future. And that is why these islands involve considerations larger than their own commerce. The commercial supremacy of the Republic means that this Nation is to be the sovereign factor in the peace of the world. For the conflicts of the future are to be conflicts of trade—struggles for markets—commercial wars for existence. And the golden rule of peace is impregnability of position and invincibility of preparation. . . . . Within two decades the bulk of Oriental commerce will be ours—the richest commerce in the world. In the light of that golden future our chain of new-won stations rise like ocean sentinels from the night of waters—Porto Rico, a nobler Gibraltar; the Isthmian canal, a greater Suez; Hawaii, the Ladrones, the Philippines, commanding the Pacific! Ah! as our commerce spreads, the flag of liberty will circle the globe and the highways of the ocean-carrying trade of all mankind be guarded by the guns of the Republic. Shall this future of the race be left with those who, under God, began this career of sacred duty and immortal glory; or, shall we risk it to those who would build a dam in the current of destiny's large designs. We are enlisted in the cause of American supremacy, which will never end until American commerce has made the conquest of the world; until American citizenship has become the lord of civilization, and the stars and stripes the flag of flags throughout the world. . . .

Fellow-Americans, we are God's chosen people. Yonder at Bunker Hill and Yorktown His providence was above us. At New Orleans and on ensanguined seas His hand sustained us. Abraham Lincoln was his minister; and his was the altar of freedom, the boys in blue set on a hundred smoking battlefields. His power directed Dewey in the East, and He delivered the Spanish fleet into our hands on the eve of Liberty's natal day as He delivered the elder Armada into the hands of our English sires two centuries ago. His great purposes are revealed in the progress of the flag, which surpasses the intentions of Congresses and Cabinets, and leads us, like a holier pillar of cloud by day and pillar of fire by night, into situations unforeseen by finite wisdom and duties unexpected by the unprophetic heart of selfishness. The American people cannot use a dishonest medium of exchange; it is ours to set the world its example of right and honor. We cannot fly from our world duties; it is ours to execute the purpose of a fate that has driven us to be greater than our small intentions. We cannot retreat from any soil where Providence has unfurled our banner; it is ours to save that soil for liberty and civilization. For liberty and civilization and God's promises fulfilled, the flag must henceforth be the symbol and the sign to all mankind.

WILLIAM GRAHAM SUMNER, "ON EMPIRE AND THE PHILIPPINES" (1898)

In the wake of America's war with Spain, whether or not to annex the Philippines, a vast former Spanish colony thousands of miles west of San Francisco, became a hotly debated issue. William Graham Sumner (1840–1910), a professor at Yale and founder of modern sociology, opposed annexation. Imperialism engenders hatred and resistance, he argues. Americans are better served allowing others to work out their own destiny.

There is not a civilized nation that does not talk about its civilizing mission just as grandly as we do. The English, who really have more to boast of it in this respect than anybody else, talk least about it, but the Phariseeism with which they correct and instruct other people has made them hated all over the globe. The French believe themselves the guardians of the highest and purest culture, and that the eyes of all mankind are fixed on Paris, whence they expect oracles of thought and taste. The Germans regard themselves as charged with a mission, especially to us Americans, to save us from egoism and materialism. The Russians, in their books and newspapers, talk about the civilizing mission of Russia in language that might be translated from some of the finest paragraphs of our imperialistic newspapers.

The first principle of Mohammedanism is that we Christians are dogs and infidels, fit only to be enslaved or butchered by Moslems. It is a corollary that wherever Mohammedanism extends it carries, in the belief of its votaries, the highest blessings, and that the whole human race would be enormously elevated if Mohammedanism should supplant Christianity everywhere.

To come, last, to Spain, the Spaniards have, for centuries, considered themselves the most zealous and self-sacrificing Christians, especially charged by the Almighty, on this account, to spread the true religion and civilization over the globe. They think themselves free and noble, leaders in refinement and the sentiments of personal honor, and they despise us as sordid money-grabbers and heretics. I could bring you passages from peninsular authors of the first rank about the grand role of Spain and Portugal in spreading freedom and truth.

Now each nation laughs at all the others when it observes these manifestations of national vanity. You may rely upon it that they are all ridiculous by virtue of these pretensions, including ourselves. The point is that each of them repudiates the standards of the others, and the outlying nations, which are to be civilized, hate all the standards of civilized men.

We assume that what we like and practice, and what we think better, must come as a welcome blessing to Spanish-Americans and Filipinos. This is grossly and obviously untrue. They hate our ways. They are hostile to our ideas. Our religion, language, institutions, and manners offend them. They like their own ways, and if we appear amongst them as rulers, there will be social discord in all the great departments of social interest. The most important thing which we shall inherit from the Spaniards will be the task of suppressing rebellions.

If the United States takes out of the hands of Spain her mission, on the ground that Spain is not executing it well, and if this nation in its turn attempts to be schoolmistress to others, it will shrivel up into the same vanity and self-conceit of which Spain now presents an example. To read our current literature one would think that we were already well on the way to it.

Now, the great reason why all these enterprises which begin by saying to somebody else, "We know what is good for you better than you know yourself and we are going to make you do it," are false and wrong is that they violate liberty; or, to turn the same statement into other words, the reason why liberty, of which we Americans talk so much, is a good thing is that it means leaving people to live out their own lives in their own way, while we do the same.

If we believe in liberty, as an American principle, why do we not stand by it? Why are we going to throw it away to enter upon a Spanish policy of dominion and regulation?

RUDYARD KIPLING, "THE WHITE MAN'S BURDEN," *NEW YORK SUN* (FEBRUARY 10, 1899)

The British writer Rudyard Kipling (1865–1936) made a career out of promoting imperialism, which he depicted as a paternalistic enterprise. Here he instructs Americans that they are duty-bound to share in the responsibility of governing lesser breeds.

Take up the White Man's burden—
Send forth the best ye breed—
Go bind your sons to exile
To serve your captives' need;
To wait in heavy harness,
On fluttered folk and wild—
Your new-caught, sullen peoples,
Half-devil and half-child.

Take up the White Man's burden—
In patience to abide,
To veil the threat of terror
And check the show of pride;
By open speech and simple,
An hundred times made plain
To seek another's profit,
And work another's gain.
Take up the White Man's burden—
The savage wars of peace—
Fill full the mouth of Famine
And bid the sickness cease;
And when your goal is nearest
The end for others sought,
Watch sloth and heathen Folly
Bring all your hopes to nought.

Take up the White Man's burden—
No tawdry rule of kings,
But toil of serf and sweeper—
The tale of common things.

The ports ye shall not enter,
The roads ye shall not tread,
Go mark them with your living,
And mark them with your dead.

Take up the White Man's burden—
And reap his old reward:
The blame of those ye better,
The hate of those ye guard—
The cry of hosts ye humour
(Ah, slowly!) toward the light: —
"Why brought he us from bondage,
Our loved Egyptian night?"

Take up the White Man's burden—
Ye dare not stoop to less—
Nor call too loud on Freedom
To cloke your weariness;
By all ye cry or whisper,
By all ye leave or do,
The silent, sullen peoples
Shall weigh your gods and you.
Take up the White Man's burden—
Have done with childish days—
The lightly proferred laurel,
The easy, ungrudged praise.
Comes now, to search your manhood
Through all the thankless years
Cold, edged with dear-bought wisdom,
The judgment of your peers!

FINLEY PETER DUNNE, "EXPANSION," *MR. DOOLEY IN THE HEARTS OF HIS COUNTRYMEN* (1899)

A newspaperman who specialized in political satire, Finely Peter Dunne (1867–1936) would today qualify as politically incorrect. To comment on events of the day, he employed the fictitious Mr. Dooley, an ill-educated but opinionated Irish immigrant now tending bar in Chicago. In this column, Mr. Dooley offers his own take on the motives behind the proposed US annexation of the Philippines.

"Whin we plant what Hogan calls th' starry banner iv Freedom in th' Ph'lippeens," said Mr. Dooley, "an' give th' sacred blessin' iv liberty to the poor, down-trodden people iv thim unfortunate isles—dam thim!—we'll larn thim a lesson."

"Sure," said Mr. Hennessy, sadly, "we have a thing or two to larn oursilves."

"But it isn't f'r thim to larn us," said Mr. Dooley. 'Tis not f'r thim wretched an' degraded crathers, without a mind or a shirt iv their own, f'r to give lessons in politeness an' liberty to a nation that mannyfacthers more dhressed beef than anny other imperyal nation in th' wurruld. We say to thim: 'Naygurs,' we say, 'poor, dissolute, uncovered wretches,' says we, 'whin th' crool hand iv Spain forged man'cles f'r ye'er limbs, as Hogan says, who was it crossed th' say an' shtruck off th' comealongs? We did,—by dad, we did. An' now, ye mis'rable, childish-minded apes, we propose f'r to larn ye th' uses iv liberty. In ivry city in this unfair land we will erect school-houses an' packin' houses an' houses iv correction; an' we'll larn ye our language, because 'tis aisier to larn ye ours than to larn oursilves yours. An' we'll give ye clothes, if ye pay f'r thim; an', if ye don't, ye can go without. An', whin ye're hungry, ye can go to th' morgue—we mane th' resth'rant—an' ate a good square meal iv ar-rmy beef. An' we'll sind th' gr-reat Gin'ral Eagan over f'r to larn ye etiquette, an' Andhrew Carnegie to larn ye pathriteism with blow-holes into it, an' Gin'ral Alger to larn ye to hould onto a job; an', whin ye've become edycated an' have all th' blessin's iv civilization that we don't want, that 'll count ye one. We can't give ye anny votes, because we haven't more thin enough to go round now; but we'll threat ye th' way a father shud threat his childher if we have to break ivry bone in ye'er bodies. So come to our ar-rms,' says we.

"But, glory be, 'tis more like a rasslin' match than a father's embrace. Up gets this little monkey iv an' Aggynaldoo, an' says he, 'Not for us,' he says. 'We thank ye kindly; but we believe,' he says, 'in pathronizin' home industhries,' he says. 'An,' he says, 'I have on hand,' he says, 'an' f'r sale,' he says, 'a very superyor brand iv home-made liberty, like ye'er mother used to make,' he says. 'Tis a long way fr'm ye'er plant to here,' he says, 'an' be th' time a cargo iv liberty,' he says, 'got out here an' was handled be th' middlemen,' he says, 'it might spoil,' he says. 'We don't want anny col' storage or embalmed liberty,' he says. 'What we want an' what th' ol' reliable house iv Aggynaldoo,' he says, 'supplies to th' thrade,' he says, 'is fr-esh liberty r-right off th' far-rm,' he says. 'I can't do annything with ye'er proposition,' he says. 'I can't give up,' he says, 'th' rights f'r which f'r five years I've fought an' bled ivry wan I cud reach,' he says. 'Onless,' he says, 'ye'd feel like buyin' out th' whole business,' he says. 'I'm a pathrite,' he says; 'but I'm no bigot,' he says.

"An' there it stands, Hinnissy, with th' indulgent parent kneelin' on th' stomach iv his adopted child, while a dillygation fr'm Boston bastes him with an umbrella. There it stands, an' how will it come out I dinnaw. I'm not much iv an expansionist mesilf. F'r th' las' tin years I've been thryin' to decide whether 'twud be good policy an' thrue to me thraditions to make this here bar two or three feet longer, an' manny's th' night I've laid awake tryin' to puzzle it out. But I don't know what to do with th' Ph'lippeens anny more thin I did las' summer, befure I heerd tell iv thim. We can't give thim to anny wan without makin' th' wan that gets thim feel th' way Doherty felt to Clancy whin Clancy med a frindly call an' give

Finley Peter Dunne, "Expansion," *Mr. Dooley in the Hearts of His Countrymen*. Boston: Small, Maynard and Company (1899).

Doherty's childher th' measles. We can't sell thim, we can't ate thim, an' we can't throw thim into th' alley whin no wan is lookin'. An' 'twud be a disgrace f'r to lave befure we've pounded these frindless an' ongrateful people into insinsibility. So I suppose, Hinnissy, we'll have to stay an' do th' best we can, an' lave Andhrew Carnegie secede fr'm th' Union. They'se wan consolation; an' that is, if th' American people can govern thimsilves, they can govern annything that walks."

"An' what 'd ye do with Aggy—what-d'ye-call-him?" asked Mr. Hennessy.

"Well," Mr. Dooley replied, with brightening eyes, "I know what they'd do with him in this ward. They'd give that pathrite what he asks, an' thin they'd throw him down an' take it away fr'm him."

JANE ADDAMS, "DEMOCRACY OR MILITARISM" (1899)

Like Mr. Dooley, Jane Addams (1860–1935) was also a Chicagoan, albeit considerably more genteel in manner. A social reformer and tireless political activist, Addams included the Nobel Peace Prize among her many laurels. In this address, she warns that imperialism is at odds with America's true values.

None of us who has been reared and nurtured in America can be wholly without the democratic instinct. It is not a question with any of us of having it or not having it; it is merely a question of trusting it or not trusting it. For good or ill we suddenly find ourselves bound to an international situation.

The question practically reduces itself to this: Do we mean to democratize the situation? Are we going to trust our democracy, or are we going to weakly imitate the policy of other governments, which have never claimed a democratic basis?

The political code, as well as the moral law, has no meaning and becomes absolutely emptied of its contents if we take out of it all relation to the world and concrete cases, and it is exactly in such a time as this that we discover what we really believe. We may make a mistake in politics as well as in morals by forgetting that new conditions are ever demanding the evolution of a new morality, along old lines but in larger measure. Unless the present situation extends our nationalism into internationalism, unless it has thrust forward our patriotism into humanitarianism we cannot meet it.

We must also remember that peace has come to mean a larger thing. It is no longer merely absence of war, but the unfolding of life processes which are making for a common development. Peace is not merely something to hold congresses about and to discuss as an abstract dogma. It has come to be a rising tide of moral feeling, which is slowly engulfing all pride of conquest and making war impossible.

Under this new conception of peace it is perhaps natural that the first men to formulate it and give it international meaning should have been workingmen, who have always realized, however feebly and vaguely they may have expressed it, that it is they who in all ages have borne the heaviest burden of privation and suffering imposed on the world by the military spirit.

The first international organization founded not to promote a colorless peace, but to advance and develop the common life of all nations was founded in London in 1864 by workingmen and called simply "The International Association of Workingmen." They recognized that a supreme interest raised all workingmen above the prejudice of race, and united them by wider and deeper principles than those by which they were separated into nations. That as religion, science, art, had become international, so now at last labor took its position as an international interest. A few years later, at its third congress, held in Brussels in 1868, the internationals recommended in view of the Franco-German war, then threatening, that "the workers resist all war as systematic murder," and in case of war a universal strike be declared.

This is almost exactly what is now happening in Russia. The peasants are simply refusing to drill and fight and the czar gets credit for a peace manifesto the moral force of which comes from the humblest of his subjects. It is not, therefore, surprising that as long ago as last December, the organized workingmen of America recorded their protest against the adoption of an imperialistic policy.

In the annual convention of the American Federation of Labor, held that month in Kansas City, resolutions were adopted indorsing the declaration made by President Gompers in his opening address: "It has always been the hewers of wood and the carriers of water, the wealth producers, whose mission it has been not only to struggle for freedom, but to be ever vigilant to maintain the liberty of freedom achieved, and it behooves the representatives of the grand army of labor in convention assembled to give vent to the alarm we feel from the dangers threatening us and our entire people, to enter our solemn and emphatic protest against what we already feel; that, with the success of imperialism the decadence of our republic will have already set in."

There is a growing conviction among workingmen of all countries that, whatever may be accomplished by a national war, however high the supposed moral aim of such a war, there is one inevitable result—an increased standing army, the soldiers of which are non-producers and must be fed by the workers. The Russian peasants support an army of 1,000,000, the German peasants sow and reap for 500,000 more. The men in these armies spend their muscular force in drilling, their mental force in thoughts of warfare. The mere hours of idleness conduce mental and moral deterioration.

The appeal to the fighting instinct does not end in mere warfare, but arouses these brutal instincts latent in every human being. The countries with the large standing armies are likewise the countries with national hospitals for the treatment of diseases which should never exist, of large asylums for the care of children which should never have been born. These institutions, as well as the barracks, again increase the taxation, which rests, in the last analysis, upon producers, and, at the same time, withdraws so much of their product from the beneficent development of their national life. No one urges peaceful association with more fervor than the workingman. Organization is his

only hope, but it must be kept distinct from militarism, which can never be made a democratic instrument.

Let us not make the mistake of confusing moral issues sometimes involved in warfare with warfare itself. Let us not glorify the brutality. The same strenuous endeavor, the same heroic self-sacrifice, the same fine courage and readiness to meet death, may be displayed without the accompaniment of killing our fellow men. With all Kipling's insight he has, over and over, failed to distinguish between war and imperialism on the one hand and the advance of civilization on the other.

To "protect the weak" has always been the excuse of the ruler and tax-gatherer, the chief, the king, the baron; and now, at last, of "the white man." The form of government is not necessarily the function itself. Government is not something extraneous, consisting of men who wear gold lace and sit on high stools and write rows of figures in books.

We forget that an ideal government is merely an adjustment between men concerning their mutual relations towards those general matters which concern them all; that the office of an outside and alien people must always be to collect taxes and to hold a negative law and order. In its first attempt to restore mere order and quiet, the outside power inevitably breaks down the framework of the nascent government itself, the more virile and initiative forces are destroyed; new relations must in the end be established, not only with the handicap of smart animosity on the part of the conquered, but with the loss of the most able citizens among them.

Some of us were beginning to hope that we were getting away from the ideals set by the civil war, that we had made all the presidents we could from men who had distinguished themselves in that war, and were coming to seek another type of man. That we were ready to accept the peace ideal, to be proud of our title as a peace nation; to recognize that the man who cleans a city is greater than he who bombards it, and the man who irrigates a plain greater than he who lays it waste. Then came the Spanish war, with its gilt and lace and tinsel, and again the moral issues are confused with exhibitions of brutality.

For ten years I have lived in a neighborhood which is by no means criminal, and yet during last October and November we were startled by seven murders within a radius of ten blocks. A little investigation of details and motives, the accident of a personal acquaintance with two of the criminals, made it not in the least difficult to trace the murders back to the influence of war. Simple people who read of carnage and bloodshed easily receive its suggestions. Habits of self-control which have been but slowly and imperfectly acquired quickly break down under the stress.

Psychologists intimate that action is determined by the selection of this subject upon which the attention is habitually fixed. The newspapers, the theatrical posters, the street conversations for weeks had to do with war and bloodshed. The little children on the street played at war, day after day, killing Spaniards. The humane instinct, which keeps in abeyance the tendency to cruelty, the growing belief that the life of each human being—however hopeless or degraded, is still sacred—gives way, and the barbaric instinct asserts itself.

It is doubtless only during a time of war that the men and women of Chicago could tolerate whipping for children in our city prison, and it is only during such a time that the introduction in the legislature of a bill for the re-establishment of the whipping post could be possible. National events determine our ideals, as much as our ideals determine national events.

ANDREW CARNEGIE, "AMERICANISM VERSUS IMPERIALISM," NORTH AMERICAN REVIEW (JANUARY 1899)

The tycoon and philanthropist Andrew Carnegie (1835–1919) opposed both imperialism and militarism. Here he describes the links between the two. To claim the Philippines as an American colony was to head down the road to perdition.

For several grave reasons I regard possessions in the Far East as fraught with nothing but disaster to the Republic. Only one of these, however, can now he considered—the dangers of war and of the almost constant rumors and threats of war to which all nations interested in the Far East are subject. There is seldom a week which does not bring alarming reports of threatened hostilities, or of new alliances, or of changes of alliances, between the powers arming for the coming struggle. It is chiefly this Far Eastern question which keeps every shipyard, gunyard, and armor yard in the world busy night and day, Sunday and Saturday, forging engines of destruction. It is in that region the thunderbolt is expected; it is there the storm is to burst.

It is only four years since Japan defeated China and had ceded to it a portion of Chinese territory, the fruits of victory. Then appeared upon the scene a combination of France, Russia and Germany, which drove Japan out of China. Russia took part of the spoils for herself, and Germany later took territory near by. Japan got nothing. Britain, the most powerful of all, stood by neutral. Had she decided to defend Japan, the greatest war ever known would have been the probable result; the thunderbolt would have fallen. Were the question to be decided to-day, it is now considered probable that Britain would support Japan.

Germany obtained a concession in China, and Britain promptly appeared, demanding that Germany should maintain the "open door" in all her Chinese territory; the same demand was made on Russia. Both perforce consented. The Far East is a mine of dynamite, always liable to explode. . . .

I say, therefore, that no American statesman should place his country in any position which it could not defend, relying only upon its own strong right arm. Its arm at present is not much to depend upon; its 81 ships of war are too trifling to be taken into account; and as for its army—what are its 56,000 regulars? Its volunteers are being disbanded. Both its Navy and its Army are good for one thing only—for easy capture or destruction by either one of the stronger powers. It is the protection of Britain, and that alone, upon which we have to rely—in the Far East—a slender thread indeed. Upon the shifting sands of alliances we are to have our only foundation.

The writer is not of those who believe that the Republic cannot make herself strong enough to walk alone, and to hold her own, and to be an imperial power of herself, and by herself, and not the weak protege of a real imperial power. But, in order to make herself an imperial power she must do as imperial powers do—she must create a navy equal to the navy of any other power. She must have hundreds of thousands of regular troops to cooperate with the navy. . . .

Imperialism implies naval and military force behind; moral force, education, civilization, are not the backbone of Imperialism; these are the moral forces which make for the higher civilization, for Americanism—the foundation for Imperialism is brutal physical strength, fighting men with material forces, warships and artillery. . . .

For many years the United flag has floated from my summer home in my native land, the Stars and Stripes and the Union Jack sewn together—the first of that kind of flag ever seen. That flag will continue to fly there and the winds to blow the two from side to side in loving embrace. But I do not favor a formal alliance. . . . An alliance with Britain and Japan would make us a possible enemy of France. I would not make an alliance which involved that. I would make no alliance with any power under any circumstances that can be imagined; I would have the Republic remain the friend of all powers. That has been her policy from the beginning, and so it should remain. . . .

When a statesman has in his keeping the position and interests of his country, all speculation as to the future fruition of ideas of what should be or what will one day rule the world, and of the "good day coming" when the pen shall supersede the sword, and of all the noble hopes and aspirations for a better future, must be resolutely dismissed. It is not with things as they are to be in the future, but with things as they are in the present, that it is his serious duty to deal. The dream, in which no one perhaps indulges more than the writer, of the union of the English-speaking race, even that entrancing dream must be recognized as only a dream. The "Parliament of Man, the Federation of the World," we know is to come. The evolutionist has never any doubt about the realization of the highest ideals from the operation of that tendency

within us, not ourselves, which makes for righteousness. But he is no statesman—he is only a dreamer—who allows his hopes to stand against facts, and he who proposes that the United States, as she stands to-day, shall enter into the coming struggle in the Far East, depending upon any alliance that can be made with any or all of the powers, seems unsuited to shape the policy or deal with the destinies of the Republic.

Just consider her position, solid, compact, impregnable; if all the naval forces were to combine to attack her what would be her reply? She would fill her ports with mines, she would draw her ships of war behind them, ready to rush out as favorable opportunities might offer to attack. But she would do more than this in extremity; she would close her ports—a few loaded scows would do the business—and all the powers in the world would be impotent to injure her seriously. The fringe only would be troubled; the great empire within would scarcely feel the attack.

The injury she would inflict upon the principal powers by closing her ports would be much more serious than could be inflicted upon her; because non-exportation of food-stuffs and cotton would mean famine and distress to Britain and injure her to a greater degree than loss in battle. Even in France and in Germany the results of non-exportation would be more serious than the effects of ordinary war. It would only be a matter of a short time until the powers recognized how futile was their attempt to injure seriously this self-contained Republic, whose estate here lies secure within a ring fence. . . .

We should emerge from the embargo without serious injury. So much for the impregnability of the Republic. Today Fortune rains upon her. For the first time in her history, she has become the greatest exporting nation in the world, even the exports of Britain being less than hers. Her manufactures are invading all lands, commercial expansion proceeds by leaps and bounds; New York has become the financial centre of the world. It is London no more, but New York, which is today the financial centre. This, however, is not yet to be claimed as permanent, but it promises to become so ere long, unless the Republic becomes involved in European wars through Imperialism. Labor is in demand at the highest wages paid in the world; the Industrial supremacy of the world lies at our feet. Two questions are submitted to the decision of the American people: First—Shall we remain as we are, solid, compact, impregnable, republican, American; or. Second—Shall we creep under the protection, and become, as Bishop Potter says, "the catspaw" of Britain, in order that we may grasp the phantom of Imperialism?

If the latter be the choice, then it is submitted that we must first begin quietly to prepare ourselves for the new work which Imperialism imposes.

We need a large regular army of trained soldiers. There is no use trying to encounter regular armies with volunteers—we have found that out. Not that volunteers would not be superior to the class of men we shall get to enlist simply for pay in the regular army, if they would enlist there and be trained, but because they are not trained. Thirty-eight thousand more men are to be called for the regular army; but it is easy "to call spirits from the vasty deep"—they may not come. . . . . The President may not get the soldiers he desires, and whom he must have if he is not to make shipwreck of his Imperialism. There is very grave reason to doubt whether the army can be raised even to one hundred thousand men without a great advance in pay, perhaps not without conscription.

But surely before we appear in the arena in the Far East we must have a large regular army.

The second indispensable requirement is a navy corresponding, at least in some degree, to the navies of the other powers interested in the East. We can get this in twenty years, perhaps, if we push matters, but this means building twenty ships a year. The securing of men trained to man them will be as difficult a task as the building of the ships.

When we have armed ourselves thus, but not till then, shall we be in a position to take and hold territory in the Far East " by the sole power of our unlorded will," as we should hold it, or not hold it at all. To rush in now, without army or navy, trusting to the treacherous shifting foundation of anybody's "protection," or "neutrality," or "alliance," is to court defeat, and such humiliation as has rarely fallen to the lot of any nation, even the poorest and most madly or most foolishly governed. It is not good sense.

This ends the subject upon which I undertook to write, but there remains the practical question: What shall we do with the Philippines? These are not ours, unless the Senate approves the Treaty; but, assuming that it will, that question arises. . . .

If we insist "the slaves are ours because we bought them," and fail to tell them we come not as slave drivers, but as friends to assist them to Independence, we may have to "lick them" no doubt. It will say much for the Filipinos if they do rebel against "being bought and sold like cattle." It would be difficult to give a better proof of their fitness for self government.

Cuba is under the shield of the Monroe doctrine; no foreign interference is possible there. Place the Philippines under similar conditions until they have a stable government, when eight millions of people can be trusted to protect themselves. The truth is that none of the powers would risk the hostility of eight millions of people, who had tasted the hope of Independence. "Free and Independent" are magical words, never forgotten, and rarely unrealized.

Only one objection can be made to this policy. They are not fit to govern themselves. First, this has not been proved. This was said of every one of the sixteen Spanish Republics as they broke away from Spain; it was said even of Mexico within this generation; it was the belief of the British about ourselves. There is in the writer's opinion little force in the objection. . . .

The Filipinos are by no means in the lowest scale—far from it—nor are they much lower than the Cubans. If left to themselves they will make mistakes, but what nation does not? Riot and bloodshed may break out—in which nation are these absent? Certainly not in our own; but the inevitable result will be a government better suited to the people than any that our soldiers and their officers could ever give.

Thus only can the Republic stand true to its pledges, that the sword was drawn only in the cause of humanity and not for territorial aggrandizement, and true to the fundamental principles upon which she rests: "that government derives its just powers from the consent of the governed;" that the flag, wherever it floats, shall proclaim "the equality of the citizen," "one man's privilege every man's right"—"that all men are created equal," not that under its sway part only shall be citizens with rights and part only subjects without rights—freemen and serfs, not all freemen. Such is the issue between Americanism and Imperialism.

ALBERT J. BEVERIDGE, "IN SUPPORT OF AN AMERICAN EMPIRE" (1900)

Dismissing the arguments advanced by opponents of empire, Senator Beveridge enumerates for his colleagues the moral, material, and strategic factors that make it necessary for the United States to retain the Philippines. No true patriot will see otherwise, he insists.

Mr. President, the times call for candor. The Philippines are ours forever, "territory belonging to the United States," as the Constitution calls them. And just beyond the Philippines are China's illimitable markets. We will not retreat from either. We will not repudiate our duty in the archipelago. We will not abandon our opportunity in the Orient. We will not renounce our part in the mission of our race, trustee, under God, of the civilization of the world. And we will move forward to our work, not howling out regrets like slaves whipped to their burdens but with gratitude for a task worthy of our strength and thanksgiving to Almighty God that He has marked us as His chosen people, henceforth to lead in the regeneration of the world.

This island empire is the last land left in all the oceans. If it should prove a mistake to abandon it, the blunder once made would be irretrievable. If it proves a mistake to hold it, the error can be corrected when we will. Every other progressive nation stands ready to relieve us.

But to hold it will be no mistake. Our largest trade henceforth must be with Asia. The Pacific is our ocean. More and more Europe will manufacture the most it needs, secure from its colonies the most it consumes. Where shall we turn for consumers of our surplus? Geography answers the question. China is our natural customer. She is nearer to us than to England, Germany, or Russia, the commercial powers of the present and the future. They have moved nearer to China by securing permanent bases on her borders. The Philippines give us a base at the door of all the East.

Lines of navigation from our ports to the Orient and Australia, from the Isthmian Canal to Asia, from all Oriental ports to Australia converge at and separate from the Philippines. They are a self-supporting, dividend-paying fleet, permanently anchored at a spot selected by the strategy of Providence, commanding the Pacific. And the Pacific is the ocean of the commerce of the future. Most future wars will be conflicts for commerce. The power that rules the Pacific, therefore, is the power that rules the world. And, with the Philippines, that power is and will forever be the American Republic. . . .

Here, then, senators, is the situation. Two years ago there was no land in all the world which we could occupy for any purpose. Our commerce was daily turning toward the Orient, and geography and trade developments made necessary our commercial empire over the Pacific. And in that ocean we had no commercial, naval, or military base. Today, we have one of the three great ocean possessions of the globe, located at the most commanding commercial, naval, and military points in the Eastern seas, within hail of India, shoulder to shoulder with China, richer in its own resources than any equal body of land on the entire globe, and peopled by a race which civilization demands shall be improved. Shall we abandon it?

That man little knows the common people of the republic, little understands the instincts of our race who thinks we will not hold it fast and hold it forever, administering just government by simplest methods. We may trick up devices to shift our burden and lessen our opportunity; they will avail us nothing but delay. We may tangle conditions by applying academic arrangements of self-government to a crude situation; their failure will drive us to our duty in the end.

The military situation, past, present, and prospective, is no reason for abandonment. Our campaign has been as perfect as possible with the force at hand. We have been delayed, first, by a failure to comprehend the immensity of our acquisition; and, second, by insufficient force; and, third, by our efforts for peace. . . .

Those who complain do so in ignorance of the real situation. We attempted a great task with insufficient means; we became impatient that it was not finished before it could fairly be commenced; and I pray we may not add that other element of disaster, pausing in the work before it is thoroughly and forever done. That is the gravest mistake we could possibly make, and that is the only danger before us. Our Indian wars would have been shortened, the lives of soldiers and settlers saved, and the Indians themselves benefited had we made continuous and decisive war; and any other kind of war is criminal because ineffective. We acted toward the Indians as though we feared them, loved them, hated them—a mingling of foolish sentiment, inaccurate thought, and paralytic purpose. . . .

Mr. President, that must not be our plan. This war is like all other wars. It needs to be finished before it is stopped. I am prepared to vote either to make our work thorough or even now to abandon it. A lasting peace can be secured only by overwhelming forces in ceaseless action until universal and absolutely final defeat is inflicted on the enemy. To halt before every armed force, every guerrilla band opposing us is dispersed or exterminated will prolong hostilities and leave alive the seeds of perpetual insurrection.

Even then we should not treat. To treat at all is to admit that we are wrong. And any quiet so secured will be delusive and fleeting. And a false peace will betray us; a sham truce will curse us. It is not to serve the purposes of the hour, it is not to salve a present situation that peace should be established. It is for the tranquillity of the archipelago forever. It is for an orderly government for the Filipinos for all the future. It is to give this problem to posterity solved and settled, not vexed and involved. It is to establish the supremacy of the American republic over the Pacific and throughout the East till the end of time.

It has been charged that our conduct of the war has been cruel. Senators, it has been the reverse.

I have been in our hospitals and seen the Filipino wounded as carefully, tenderly cared for as our own. Within our lines they may plow and sow and reap and go about the affairs of peace with absolute liberty. And yet all this kindness was misunderstood, or rather not understood. Senators must remember that we are not dealing with Americans or Europeans. We are dealing with Orientals. We are dealing with Orientals who are Malays. We are dealing with Malays instructed in Spanish methods. They mistake kindness for weakness, forbearance for fear. It could not be otherwise unless you could erase hundreds of years of savagery, other hundreds of years of Orientalism, and still other hundreds of years of Spanish character and custom. . . .

Mr. President, reluctantly and only from a sense of duty am I forced to say that American opposition to the war has been the chief factor in prolonging it. Had Aguinaldo not understood that in America, even in the American Congress, even here in the Senate, he and his cause were supported; had he not known that it was proclaimed on the stump and in the press of a faction in the United States that every shot his misguided followers fired into the breasts of American soldiers was like the volleys fired by Washington's men against the soldiers of King George, his insurrection would have dissolved before it entirely crystallized.

The utterances of American opponents of the war are read to the ignorant soldiers of Aguinaldo and repeated in exaggerated form among the common people. Attempts have been made by wretches claiming American citizenship to ship arms and ammunition from Asiatic ports to the Filipinos, and these acts of infamy were coupled by the Malays with American assaults on our government at home. The Filipinos do not understand free speech, and therefore our tolerance of American assaults on the American President and the American government means to them that our President is in the minority or he would not permit what appears to them such treasonable criticism. . . .

All this has aided the enemy more than climate, arms, and battle. Senators, I have heard these reports myself; I have talked with the people; I have seen our mangled boys in the hospital and field; I have stood on the firing line and beheld our dead soldiers, their faces turned to the pitiless southern sky, and in sorrow rather than anger I say to those whose voices in America have cheered those misguided natives on to shoot our soldiers down, that the blood of those dead and wounded boys of ours is on their hands, and the flood of all the years can never wash that stain away. . . .

But, senators, it would be better to abandon this combined garden and Gibraltar of the Pacific, and count our blood and treasure already spent a profitable loss than to apply any academic arrangement of self-government to these children. They are not capable of self-government. How could they be? They are not of a self-governing race. They are Orientals, Malays, instructed by Spaniards in the latter's worst estate.

They know nothing of practical government except as they have witnessed the weak, corrupt, cruel, and capricious rule of Spain. What magic will anyone employ to dissolve in their minds and characters those impressions of governors and governed which three centuries of misrule has created? What alchemy will change the Oriental quality of their blood and set the self-governing currents of the American pouring through their Malay veins? How shall they, in the twinkling of an eye, be exalted to the heights of self-governing peoples which required a thousand years for us to reach, Anglo-Saxon though we are?

Let men beware how they employ the term "self-government." It is a sacred term. It is the watchword at the door of the inner temple of liberty, for liberty does not always mean self-government. Self-government is a method of liberty—the highest, simplest, best—and it is acquired only after centuries of study and struggle and experiment and instruction and all the elements of the progress of man. Self-government is no base and common thing to be bestowed on the merely audacious. It is the degree which crowns the graduate of liberty, not the name of liberty's infant class, who have not yet mastered the alphabet of freedom. Savage blood, Oriental blood, Malay blood, Spanish example—are these the elements of self-government?

We must act on the situation as it exists, not as we would wish it. I have talked with hundreds of these people, getting their views as to the practical workings of self-government. The great majority simply do not understand any participation in any government whatever. The most enlightened among them declare that self-government will succeed because the employers of labor will compel their employees to vote as their employer wills and that this will insure intelligent voting. I was assured that we could depend upon good men always being in office because the officials who constitute the government will nominate their successors, choose those among the people who will do the voting, and determine how and where elections will be held.

The most ardent advocate of self-government that I met was anxious that I should know that such a government would be tranquil because, as he said, if anyone criticized it, the government would shoot the offender. . . .

And so our government must be simple and strong. Simple and strong! The meaning of those two words must be written in every line of Philippine legislation, realized in every act of Philippine administration.

A Philippine office in our Department of State; an American governor-general in Manila, with power to meet daily emergencies; possibly an advisory council with no power except that of discussing measures with the governor-general, which council would be the germ for future legislatures, a school in practical government; American lieutenant governors in each province, with a like council about him if possible, an American resident in each district and a like council grouped about him. . . .

Better pure military occupation for years than government by any other quality of administration. Better abandon this priceless possession, admit ourselves incompetent to do our part in the world-redeeming work of our imperial race; better now haul down the flag of arduous deeds for civilization and run up the flag of reaction and decay than to apply academic notions of self-government to these children or attempt their government by any but the most perfect administrators our country can produce. . . .

Mr. President, self-government and internal development have been the dominant notes of our first century; administration and the development of other lands will be the dominant notes of our second century. And administration is as high and holy a function as self-government, just as the care of a trust estate is as sacred an obligation as the management of our own concerns. . . .

The Declaration of Independence does not forbid us to do our part in the regeneration of the world. If it did, the Declaration would be wrong, just as the Articles of Confederation, drafted by the very same men who signed the Declaration, was found to be wrong. The Declaration has no application to the present situation. It was written by self-governing men for self-governing men. It was written by men who, for a century and a half, had been experimenting in self-government on this continent, and whose ancestors for hundreds of years before had been gradually developing toward that high and holy estate.

The Declaration applies only to people capable of self-government. How dare any man prostitute this expression of the very elect of self-governing peoples to a race of Malay children of barbarism, schooled in Spanish methods and ideas? And you who say the Declaration applies to all men, how dare you deny its application to the American Indian? And if you deny it to the Indian at home, how dare you grant it to the Malay abroad?

The Declaration does not contemplate that all government must have the consent of the governed. It announces that man's "inalienable rights are life, liberty, and the pursuit of happiness; that to secure these rights governments are established among men deriving their just powers from the consent of the governed; that when any form of government becomes destructive of those rights, it is the right of the people to alter or abolish it." "Life, liberty, and the pursuit of happiness" are the important things; "consent of the governed" is one of the means to those ends. . . .

And so the Declaration contemplates all forms of government which secure the fundamental rights of life, liberty, and the pursuit of happiness. Self-government, when that will best secure these ends, as in the case of people capable of self-government; other appropriate forms when people are not capable of self-government. And so the authors of the Declaration themselves governed the Indian without his consent; the inhabitants of Louisiana without their consent; and ever since the sons of the makers of the Declaration have been governing not by theory but by practice, after the fashion of our governing race, now by one form, now by another, but always for the

purpose of securing the great eternal ends of life, liberty, and the pursuit of happiness, not in the savage but in the civilized meaning of those terms—life, according to orderly methods of civilized society; liberty regulated by law; pursuit of happiness limited by the pursuit of happiness by every other man. . . .

The ocean does not separate us from the field of our duty and endeavor—it joins us, an established highway needing no repair and landing us at any point desired. The seas do not separate the Philippine Islands from us or from each other. The seas are highways through the archipelago, which would cost hundreds of millions of dollars to construct if they were land instead of water. Land may separate men from their desire; the ocean, never. Russia has been centuries in crossing Siberian wastes; the Puritans cross the Atlantic in brief and flying weeks.

If the Boers must have traveled by land, they would never have reached the Transvaal; but they sailed on liberty's ocean; they walked on civilization's untaxed highway, the welcoming sea. Our ships habitually sailed round the Cape and anchored in California's harbors before a single trail had lined the desert with the whitening bones of those who made it. No! No! The ocean unites us; steam unites us; electricity unites us; all the elements of nature unite us to the region where duty and interest call us.

There is in the ocean no constitutional argument against the march of the flag, for the oceans, too, are ours. With more extended coastlines than any nation of history; with a commerce vaster than any other people ever dreamed of, and that commerce as yet only in its beginnings; with naval traditions equaling those of England or of Greece, and the work of our Navy only just begun; with the air of the ocean in our nostrils and the blood of a sailor ancestry in our veins; with the shores of all the continents calling us, the Great Republic before I die will be the acknowledged lord of the world's high seas. And over them the republic will hold dominion, by virtue of the strength God has given it, for the peace of the world and the betterment of man. . . .

The founders of the nation were not provincial. Theirs was the geography of the world. They were soldiers as well as landsmen, and they knew that where our ships should go our flag might follow.

They had the logic of progress, and they knew that the republic they were planting must, in obedience to the laws of our expanding race, necessarily develop into the greater republic which the world beholds today, and into the still mightier republic which the world will finally acknowledge as the arbiter, under God, of the destinies of mankind. And so our fathers wrote into the Constitution these words of growth, of expansion, of empire, if you will, unlimited by geography or climate or by anything but the vitality and possibilities of the American people: "Congress shall have power to dispose of and make all needful rules and regulations respecting the territory belonging to the United States." . . .

Mr. President, this question is deeper than any question of party politics; deeper than any question of the isolated policy of our country even; deeper even than any question of constitutional power. It is elemental. It is racial. God has not been preparing the English-speaking and Teutonic peoples for a thousand years for nothing but vain and idle self-contemplation and self-admiration. No! He has made us the master organizers of the world to establish system where chaos reigns. He has given us the spirit of progress to overwhelm the forces of reaction throughout the earth. He has made us adepts in government that we may administer government among savage and senile peoples. Were it not for such a force as this the world would relapse into barbarism and night. And of all our race He has marked the American people as His chosen nation to finally lead in the regeneration of the world. This is the divine mission of America, and it holds for us all the profit, all the glory, all the happiness possible to man. We are trustees of the world's progress, guardians of its righteous peace. The judgment of the Master is upon us: "Ye have been faithful over a few things; I will make you ruler over many things."

What shall history say of us? Shall it say that we renounced that holy trust, left the savage to his base condition, the wilderness to the reign of waste, deserted duty, abandoned glory, forget our sordid profit even, because we feared our strength and read the charter of our powers with the doubter's eye and the quibbler's mind? Shall it say that, called by events to captain and command the proudest, ablest, purest race of history in history's noblest work, we declined that great commission?

Our fathers would not have had it so. No! They founded no paralytic government, incapable of the simplest acts of administration. They planted no sluggard people, passive while the world's work calls them. They established no reactionary nation. They unfurled no retreating flag.

That flag has never paused in its onward march. Who dares halt it now—now, when history's largest events are carrying it forward; now, when we are at last one people, strong enough for any task, great enough for any glory destiny can bestow? How comes it that our first century closes with the process of consolidating the American people into a unit just accomplished, and quick upon the stroke of that great hour presses upon us our world opportunity, world duty, and world glory, which none but the people welded into an invisible nation can achieve or perform?

Blind indeed is he who sees not the hand of God in events so vast, so harmonious, so benign. Reactionary indeed is the mind that perceives not that this vital people is the strongest of the saving forces of the world; that our place, therefore, is at the head of the constructing and redeeming nations of the earth; and that to stand aside while events march on is a surrender of our interests, a betrayal of our duty as blind as it is base. Craven indeed is the heart that fears to perform a work so golden and so noble; that dares not win a glory so immortal.

Do you tell me that it will cost us money? When did Americans ever measure duty by financial standards? Do you tell me of the tremendous toil required to overcome the vast difficulties of our task? What mighty work for the world, for humanity, even for ourselves has ever been done with ease? Even our bread must we eat by the sweat of our faces. Why are we charged with power such as no people ever knew if we are not to use it in a work such as no people ever wrought? Who will dispute the divine meaning of the fable of the talents?

Do you remind me of the precious blood that must be shed, the lives that must be given, the broken hearts of loved ones for their slain? And this is indeed a heavier price than all combined. And, yet, as a nation, every historic duty we have done, every achievement we have accomplished has been by the sacrifice of our noblest sons. Every holy memory that glorifies the flag is of those heroes who have died that its onward march might not be stayed. It is the nation's dearest lives yielded for the flag that makes it dear to us; it is the nation's most precious blood poured out for it that makes it precious to us. That flag is woven of heroism and grief, of the bravery of men and women's tears, of righteousness and battle, of sacrifice and anguish, of triumph and of glory. It is these which make our flag a holy thing.

Who would tear from that sacred banner the glorious legends of a single battle where it has waved on land or sea? What son of a soldier of the flag whose father fell beneath it on any field would surrender that proud record for the heraldry of a king? In the cause of civilization, in the service of the republic anywhere on earth, Americans consider wounds the noblest decorations man can win, and count the giving of their lives a glad and precious duty.

Pray God that spirit never falls. Pray God the time may never come when Mammon and the love of ease shall so debase our blood that we will fear to shed it for the flag and its imperial destiny. Pray God the time may never come when American heroism is but a legend like the story of the Cid. American faith in our mission and our might a dream dissolved, and the glory of our mighty race departed.

And that time will never come. We will renew our youth at the fountain of new and glorious deeds. We will exalt our reverence for the flag by carrying it to a noble future as well as by remembering its ineffable past. Its immortality will not pass, because everywhere and always we will acknowledge and discharge the solemn responsibilities our sacred flag, in its deepest meaning, puts upon us. And so, senators, with reverent hearts, where dwells the fear of God, the American people move forward to the future of their hope and the doing of His work.

Mr. President and senators, adopt the resolution offered that peace may quickly come and that we may begin our saving, regenerating, and uplifting work. Adopt it, and this bloodshed will cease when these deluded children of our islands learn that this is the final word of the representatives of the American people in Congress assembled. Reject it, and the world, history, and the American people will know where to forever fix the awful responsibility for the consequences that will surely follow such failure to do our manifest duty. How dare we delay when our soldiers' blood is flowing?

MARK TWAIN, "THE BATTLE HYMN OF THE REPUBLIC, UPDATED" (1900)

In this grim parody of a famous patriotic song, Mark Twain (1835–1910) mocks the pretensions of American imperialists.

Mine eyes have seen the orgy of the launching
    of the Sword;
He is searching out the hoardings where the
    stranger's wealth is stored;
He hath loosed his fateful lightnings, and with
    woe and death has scored;
His lust is marching on.
I have seen him in the watch-fires of a hundred
    circling camps;
They have builded him an altar in the Eastern
    dews and damps;
I have read his doomful mission by the dim and
    flaring lamps—
His night is marching on.

I have read his bandit gospel writ in burnished
    rows of steel:
"As ye deal with my pretensions, so with you my
    wrath shall deal;
Let the faithless son of Freedom crush the patriot
    with his heel;
Lo, Greed is marching on!"

We have legalized the strumpet and are guarding
    her retreat;
Greed is seeking out commercial souls before his
    judgement seat;
O, be swift, ye clods, to answer him! be jubilant
    my feet!
Our god is marching on!

In a sordid slime harmonious Greed was born in
yonder ditch,
With a longing in his bosom—and for others'
goods an itch.

As Christ died to make men holy, let men die to
make us rich—
Our god is marching on.

WILLIAM JENNINGS BRYAN, "IMPERIALISM (FLAG OF AN EMPIRE)" (1900)

Today all but forgotten, William Jennings Bryan (1860–1925) was on three occasions the
Democratic Party's nominee for president. A better orator than candidate, he lost on all three
occasions. In 1898, Bryan had supported the war to liberate Cuba from Spanish rule. Two years
later, he explains why he opposes proposals to annex the Philippines.

Mr. Chairman, and Members of the Notification
Committee: I shall, at an early day, and in a more
formal manner accept the nomination which you
tender, and I shall at that time discuss the various
questions covered by the Democratic platform. It
may not be out of place, however, to submit a few
observations at this time upon the general character of the contest before us and upon the question
which is declared to be of paramount importance
in this campaign. . . .

For a time Republican leaders were inclined
to deny to opponents the right to criticise the
Philippine policy of the administration, but upon
investigation they found that both Lincoln and
Clay asserted and exercised the right to criticize a
President during the progress of the Mexican war.

Instead of meeting the issue boldly and submitting a clear and positive plan for dealing with the
Philippine question, the Republican convention
adopted a platform the larger part of which was
devoted to boasting and self-congratulation. . . .

But they shall not be permitted to evade the
stupendous and far-reaching issue which they
have deliberately brought into the arena of politics. When the president, supported by a practically unanimous vote of the House and Senate,
entered upon a war with Spain for the purpose of
aiding the struggling patriots of Cuba, the country, without regard to party, applauded.

Although the Democrats realized that the
administration would necessarily gain a political
advantage from the conduct of a war which in
the very nature of the case must soon end in a
complete victory, they vied with the Republicans

in the support which they gave to the president.
When the war was over and the Republican leaders began to suggest the propriety of a colonial
policy, opposition at once manifested itself. . . .

Lincoln embodied an argument in the question
when he asked, "Can aliens make treaties easier
than friends can make laws?" I believe that we are
now in a better position to wage a successful contest against imperialism than we would have been
had the treaty been rejected. With the treaty ratified a clean-cut issue is presented between a government by consent and a government by force,
and imperialists must bear the responsibility for all
that happens until the question is settled. . . .

When hostilities broke out at Manila
Republican speakers and Republican editors at
once sought to lay the blame upon those who
had delayed the ratification of the treaty, and, during the progress of the war, the same Republicans
have accused the opponents of imperialism of
giving encouragement to the Filipinos. This is a
cowardly evasion of responsibility.

If it is right for the United States to hold
the Philippine Islands permanently and imitate
European empires in the government of colonies,
the Republican Party ought to state its position
and defend it, but it must expect the subject races
to protest against such a policy and to resist to the
extent of their ability. . . .

Some one has said that a truth once spoken,
can never be recalled. It goes on and on, and no
one can set a limit to its ever-widening influence.
But if it were possible to obliterate every word
written or spoken in defense of the principles set

forth in the Declaration of Independence, a war of conquest would still leave its legacy of perpetual hatred, for it was God himself who placed in every human heart the love of liberty. He never made a race of people so low in the scale of civilization or intelligence that it would welcome a foreign master.

Those who would have this nation enter upon a career of empire must consider not only the effect of imperialism on the Filipinos, but they must also calculate its effects upon our own nation. We cannot repudiate the principle of self-government in the Philippines without weakening that principle here.

Lincoln said that the safety of this nation was not in its fleets, its armies, or its forts, but in the spirit which prizes liberty as the heritage of all men, in all lands, everywhere, and he warned his countrymen that they could not destroy this spirit without planting the seeds of despotism at their own doors.

Even now we are beginning to see the paralyzing influence of imperialism. Heretofore this nation has been prompt to express its sympathy with those who were fighting for civil liberty. While our sphere of activity has been limited to the western hemisphere, our sympathies have not been bounded by the seas. We have felt it due to ourselves and to the world, as well as to those who were struggling for the right to govern themselves, to proclaim the interest which our people have, from the date of their own independence, felt in every contest between human rights and arbitrary power. . . .

Our opponents, conscious of the weakness of their cause, seek to confuse imperialism with expansion, and have even dared to claim Jefferson as a supporter of their policy. Jefferson spoke so freely and used language with such precision that no one can be ignorant of his views. On one occasion he declared: "If there be one principle more deeply rooted than any other in the mind of every American, it is that we should have nothing to do with conquest." And again he said: "Conquest is not in our principles; it is inconsistent with our government."

The forcible annexation of territory to be governed by arbitrary power differs as much from the acquisition of territory to be built up into states as a monarchy differs from a democracy. The Democratic Party does not oppose expansion when expansion enlarges the area of the republic and incorporates land which can be settled by American citizens, or adds to our population people who are willing to become citizens and are capable of discharging their duties as such.

The acquisition of the Louisiana territory, Florida, Texas and other tracts which have been secured from time to time enlarged the republic and the constitution followed the flag into the new territory. It is now proposed to seize upon distant territory already more densely populated than our own country and to force upon the people a government for which there is no warrant in our constitution or our laws. . . .

A colonial policy means that we shall send to the Philippines a few traders, a few taskmasters and a few office-holders and an army large enough to support the authority of a small fraction of the people while they rule the natives.

If we have an imperial policy we must have a great standing army as its natural and necessary complement. The spirit which will justify the forcible annexation of the Philippine islands will justify the seizure of other islands and the domination of other people, and with wars of conquest we can expect a certain if not rapid, growth of our military establishment. . . .

A large standing army is not only a pecuniary burden to the people, and, if accompanied by compulsory service, a constant source of irritation, but it is ever a menace to a republican form of government.

The army is the personification of force, and militarism will inevitably change the ideals of the people and turn the thoughts of our young men from the arts of peace to the science of war. The government which relies for its defense upon its citizens is more likely to be just than one which has at call a large body of professional soldiers.

A small standing army and a well-equipped and well-disciplined state militia are sufficient at ordinary times, and in an emergency the nation should in the future as in the past place its dependence upon the volunteers who come from all occupations at their country's call and return to productive labor when their services are no longer required—men who fight when the country needs fighters and work when the country needs workers.

The Republican platform assumes that the Philippine islands will be retained under American sovereignty, and we have a right to demand of the Republican leaders a discussion of the future status of the Filipino. Is he to be a citizen or a subject? Are we to bring into the body politic eight or ten million Asiatics, so different from us in race and history that amalgamation is impossible? Are they to share with us in making the laws and shaping the destiny of this nation?. . . .

And what is the alternative? If the Filipino is not to be a citizen, shall we make him a subject? On that question the Democratic platform speaks with equal emphasis. It declares that the Filipino cannot be a subject without endangering our form of government. A republic can have no subjects. A subject is possible only in a government resting upon force; he is unknown in a government deriving its just powers from the consent of the governed. . . .

What is our title to the Philippine Islands? Do we hold them by treaty or by conquest? Did we buy them or did we take them? Did we purchase the people? If not, how did we secure title to them? Were they thrown in with the land? Will the Republicans say that inanimate earth has value but that when that earth is molded by the divine hand and stamped with the likeness of the Creator it becomes a fixture and passes with the soil? If governments derive their just powers from the consent of the governed, it is impossible to secure title to people, either by force or by purchase. . . .

Let us consider briefly the reasons which have been given in support of an imperialistic policy. Some say that it is our duty to hold the Philippine islands. But duty is not an argument; it is a conclusion. To ascertain what our duty is, in any emergency, we must apply well settled and generally accepted principles. It is our duty to avoid stealing, no matter whether the thing to be stolen is of great or little value. It is our duty to avoid killing a human being, no matter where the human being lives or to what race or class he belongs.

It is said that we have assumed before the world obligations which make it necessary for us to permanently maintain a government in the Philippine islands. I reply first, that the highest obligation of this nation is to be true to itself. No obligation to any particular nations, or to all the nations combined, can require the abandonment

of our theory of government, and the substitution of doctrines against which our whole national life has been a protest. And, second, that our obligation to the Filipinos, who inhabit the islands, is greater than any obligation which we can owe to foreigners who have a temporary residence in the Philippines or desire to trade there.

It is argued by some that the Filipinos are incapable of self-government and that therefore, we owe it to the world to take control of them. . . .

There are degrees of proficiency in the art of self-government, but it is a reflection upon the Creator to say that he denied to any people the capacity for self-government. Once admit that some people are capable of self-government and that others are not and that the capable people have a right to seize upon and govern the incapable, and you make force—brute force—the only foundation of government and invite the reign of a despot. I am not willing to believe that an all-wise and an all-loving God created the Filipinos and then left them thousands of years helpless until the islands attracted the attention of European nations.

Republicans ask, "Shall we haul down the flag that floats over our dead in the Philippines?" The same question might have been asked when the American flag floated over Chapultepec and waved over the dead who fell there; but the tourist who visits the City of Mexico finds there a national cemetery owned by the United States and cared for by an American citizen. Our flag still floats over our dead, but when the treaty with Mexico was signed American authority withdrew to the Rio Grande, and I venture the opinion that during the last fifty years the people of Mexico have made more progress under the stimulus of independence and self-government than they would have made under a carpet-bag government held in place by bayonets. The United States and Mexico, friendly republics, are each stronger and happier than they would have been had the former been cursed and the latter crushed by an imperialistic policy disguised as "benevolent assimilation."

"Can we not govern colonies?" we are asked. The question is not what we can do, but what we ought to do. This nation can do whatever it desires to do, but it must accept responsibility for what it does. If the constitution stands in the way, the people can amend the constitution. I repeat, the nation can do whatever it desires to do, but it cannot avoid the natural and legitimate results of its own conduct.

The young man upon reaching his majority can do what he pleases. He can disregard the teachings of his parents; he can trample upon all that he has been taught to consider sacred; he can disobey the laws of the state, the laws of society and the laws of God. He can stamp failure upon his life and make his very existence a curse to his fellow men and he can bring his father and mother in sorrow to the grave; but he cannot annul the sentence, "The wages of sin is death."

And so with this nation. It is of age and it can do what it pleases; it can spurn the traditions of the past; it can repudiate the principles upon which the nation rests; it can employ force instead of reason; it can substitute might for right; it can conquer weaker people; it can exploit their lands, appropriate their property and kill their people; but it cannot repeal the moral law or escape the punishment decreed for the violation of human rights. . . .

The principal arguments, however, advanced by those who enter upon a defense of imperialism are:

First—That we must improve the present opportunity to become a world power and enter into international politics.

Second—That our commercial interests in the Philippine islands and in the Orient make it necessary for us to hold the islands permanently.

Third—That the spread of the Christian religion will be facilitated by a colonial policy.

Fourth—That there is no honorable retreat from the position which the nation has taken.

The first argument is addressed to the nation's pride and the second to the nation's pocket-book. The third is intended for the church member and the fourth for the partisan.

It is a sufficient answer to the first argument to say that for more than a century this nation has been a world power. For ten decades it has been the most potent influence in the world. Not only has it been a world power, but it has done more to affect the politics of the human race than all the other nations of the world combined. Because our Declaration of Independence was promulgated others have been promulgated. Because the patriots of 1776 fought for liberty others have fought for it. Because our constitution was adopted other constitutions have been adopted.

The growth of the principle of self-government, planted on American soil, has been the overshadowing political fact of the nineteenth century. It has made this nation conspicuous among the nations and given it a place in history such as no other nation has ever enjoyed. Nothing has been able to check the onward march of this idea. I am not willing that this nation shall cast aside the omnipotent weapon of truth to seize again the weapons of physical warfare. I would not exchange the glory of this republic for the glory of all the empires that have risen and fallen since time began.

The permanent chairman of the last Republican national convention presented the pecuniary argument in all its baldness when he said: "We make no hypocritical pretense of being interested in the Philippines solely on account of others. While we regard the welfare of these people as a sacred trust, we regard the welfare of the American people first. We see our duty to ourselves as well as to others. We believe in trade expansion. By every legitimate means within the province of government and constitution we mean to stimulate the expansion of our trade and open new markets."

This is the commercial argument. It is based upon the theory that war can be rightly waged for pecuniary advantage, and that it is profitable to purchase trade by force and violence. . . .

It is not necessary to own people in order to trade with them. We carry on trade today with every part of the world, and our commerce has expanded more rapidly than the commerce of any European empire. We do not own Japan or China, but we trade with their people. We have not absorbed the republics of Central and South America, but we trade with them. It has not been necessary to have any political connections with Canada or the nations of Europe in order to trade with them. Trade cannot be permanently profitable unless it is voluntary.

When trade is secured by force, the cost of securing it and retaining it must be taken out of the profits and the profits are never large enough to cover the expense. Such a system would never be defended but for the fact that the expense is borne by all the people, while the profits are enjoyed by a few.

Imperialism would be profitable to the army contractors; it would be profitable to the ship owners, who would carry live soldiers to the Philippines and bring dead soldiers back; it would be profitable to those who would seize upon the franchises, and it would be profitable to the officials whose salaries would be fixed here and paid over there; but to the farmer, to the laboring man and to the vast majority of those engaged in other occupations it would bring expenditure without return and risk without reward. . . .

In addition to the evils which he and the farmer share in common, the laboring man will be the first to suffer if oriental subjects seek work in the United States; the first to suffer if American capital leaves our shores to employ oriental labor in the Philippines to supply the trade of China and Japan; the first to suffer from the violence which the military spirit arouses and the first to suffer when the methods of imperialism are applied to our own government. . . .

The pecuniary argument, though more effective with certain classes, is not likely to be used so often or presented with so much emphasis as the religious argument. If what has been termed the "gun-powder gospel" were urged against the Filipinos only it would be a sufficient answer to say that a majority of the Filipinos are now members of one branch of the Christian church; but the principle involved is one of much wider application and challenges serious consideration.

The religious argument varies in positiveness from a passive belief that Providence delivered the Filipinos into our hands for their good and our glory, to the exultation of the minister who said that we ought to "thrash the natives (Filipinos) until they understand who we are," and that "every bullet sent, every cannon shot and every flag waved means righteousness."

We cannot approve of this doctrine in one place unless we are willing to apply it everywhere. If there is poison in the blood of the hand it will ultimately reach the heart. It is equally true that forcible Christianity, if planted under the American flag in the far-away Orient, will sooner or later be transplanted upon American soil. . . .

The command "Go ye into all the world and preach the gospel to every creature" has no Gatling gun attachment. When Jesus visited a village of Samaria and the people refused to receive him, some of the disciples suggested that fire should be called down from heaven to avenge the insult; but the Master rebuked them and said: "Ye know not what manner of spirit ye are of; for the Son of Man is not come to destroy men's lives, but to save them." Suppose he had said "We will thrash them until they understand who we are," how different would have been the history of Christianity! Compare, if you will, the swaggering, bullying, brutal doctrine of imperialism with the golden rule and the commandment "Thou shalt love thy neighbor as thyself." . . .

The argument made by some that it was unfortunate for the nation that it had anything to do with the Philippine islands, but that the naval victory at Manila made the permanent acquisition of those islands necessary, is also unsound. We won a naval victory at Santiago, but that did not compel us to hold Cuba.

The shedding of American blood in the Philippine islands does not make it imperative that we should retain possession forever; American blood was shed at San Juan Hill and El Caney, and yet the president has promised the Cubans independence. The fact that the American flag floats over Manila does not compel us to exercise perpetual sovereignty over the islands; that flag waves over Havana today, but the president has promised to haul it down when the flag of the Cuban republic is ready to rise in its place. Better a thousand times that our flag in the Orient give way to a flag representing the idea of self-government than that the flag of this republic should become the flag of an empire.

When our opponents are unable to defend their position by argument they fall back upon the assertion that it is destiny, and insist that we must submit to it, no matter how much it violates our moral percepts and our principles of government. This is a complacent philosophy. It obliterates the distinction between right and wrong and makes individuals and nations the helpless victims of circumstance.

Destiny is the subterfuge of the invertebrate, who, lacking the courage to oppose error, seeks some plausible excuse for supporting it. Washington said that the destiny of the republican form of government was deeply, if not finally, staked on the experiment entrusted to the American people. How different Washington's definition of destiny from the Republican definition!

The Republicans say that this nation is in the hands of destiny; Washington believed that not only the destiny of our own nation but the destiny of the republican form of government throughout the world was entrusted to American hands. Washington was right. The destiny of this Republic is in the hands of its own people, and upon the success of the experiment here rests the hope of humanity. No exterior force can disturb this Republic, and no foreign influence should be permitted to change its course. What the future has in store for this nation no one has authority to declare, but each individual has his own idea of the nation's mission, and he owes it to his country as well as to himself to contribute as best he may to the fulfillment of that mission. . . .

I can conceive of a national destiny surpassing the glories of the present and the past— a destiny which meets the responsibilities of today and measures up to the possibilities of the future. Behold a republic, resting securely upon the foundation stones quarried by revolutionary patriots from the mountain of eternal truth—a republic applying in practice and proclaiming to the world the self-evident propositions that all men are created equal; that they are endowed with inalienable rights; that governments are instituted among men to secure these rights, and that governments derive their just powers from the consent of the governed. Behold a republic in which civil and religious liberty stimulates to earnest endeavor and in which the law restrains every hand uplifted for a neighbor's injury—a republic in which every citizen is a sovereign, but in which no one cares to wear a crown. Behold a republic standing erect while empires all around are bowed beneath the weight of their own armaments—a republic whose flag is loved while other flags are only feared. Behold a republic increasing in population, in wealth, in strength and in influence, solving the problems of civilization and hastening the coming of an universal brotherhood—a republic which shakes thrones and dissolves aristocracies by its silent example and gives light and inspiration to those who sit in darkness. Behold a republic gradually but surely becoming the supreme moral factor in the world's progress and the accepted arbiter of the world's disputes—a republic whose history, like the path of the just, "is as the shining light that shineth more and more unto the perfect day."

IV.

Rising Power

During the interval between America's war with Spain in 1898 and the outbreak of war in Europe in 1914, the United States took its first steps as a fledgling player on the world stage. Although popular enthusiasm for formal empire proved fleeting, experiments aimed at extending the reach of American power and influence were only just beginning.

While still keeping Europe at arm's length (except as a venue for trade and a source of capital), the United States now identified two regions of the world as critically important to its own well-being: East Asia and the Caribbean. East Asia mattered not only because the United States had assumed responsibility for governing and therefore defending the Philippines, but because senior figures in Washington and on Wall Street believed the United States had a vital interest in participating on an equal footing with other powers engaged in exploiting China. The allure surrounding China stemmed largely from its potential as a market for exports.

The Caribbean mattered because of the Panama Canal. Conniving in a fraudulent "revolution" that in 1903 created a nominally independent Republic of Panama, the United States secured on remarkably favorable terms an agreement to build and operate a canal through the isthmus. Construction began almost immediately. Although the canal itself would not open until 1914, securing the approaches to the canal now became a vital US interest. This in turn provided a rationale for a further bout of US military intervention and for the creation of an informal empire in the region. Rather than ruling directly, policymakers devised mechanisms that enabled the United States to exert indirect control. The documents below describe those mechanisms.

JOHN HAY, "FIRST OPEN DOOR NOTE" (1899)

At the turn of the twentieth century, as European powers and Japan competed with one another in taking advantage of a weak and vulnerable China, US officials were intent on ensuring that the United States should claim its share of the spoils. Secretary of State John Hay (1838–1905) issued a pair of diplomatic notes specifying American expectations—equal opportunity for all foreign powers engaged in exploiting the Chinese. This "open door" concept became an enduring motif of US policy.

At the time when the Government of the United States was informed by that of Germany that it had leased from His Majesty the Emperor of China the port of Kiao-chao and the adjacent territory in the province of Shantung, assurances were given to the ambassador of the United States at Berlin by the Imperial German minister for foreign affairs that the rights and privileges insured by treaties with China to citizens of the United States would not thereby suffer or be in anywise impaired within the area over which Germany had thus obtained control.

More recently, however, the British Government recognized by a formal agreement with Germany the exclusive right of the latter country to enjoy in said leased area and the contiguous "sphere of influence or interest" certain privileges, more especially those relating to railroads and mining enterprises; but as the exact nature and extent of the rights thus recognized have not been clearly defined, it is possible that serious conflicts of interest may at any time arise not only between British and German subjects within said area, but that the interests of our citizens may also be jeopardized thereby.

Earnestly desirous to remove any cause of irritation and to insure at the same time to the commerce of all nations in China the undoubted benefits which should accrue from a formal recognition by the various powers claiming "spheres of interest" that they shall enjoy perfect equality of treatment for their commerce and navigation within such "spheres," the Government of the United States would be pleased to see His German Majesty's Government give formal assurances, and lend its cooperation in securing like assurances from the other interested powers, that each, within its respective sphere of whatever influence—

First. Will in no way interfere with any treaty port or any vested interest within any so-called "sphere of interest" or leased territory it may have in China.

Second. That the Chinese treaty tariff of the time being shall apply to all merchandise landed or shipped to all such ports as are within said "sphere of interest" (unless they be "free ports"), no matter to what nationality it may belong, and that duties so leviable shall be collected by the Chinese Government.

Third. That it will levy no higher harbor dues on vessels of another nationality frequenting any port in such "sphere" than shall be levied on vessels of its own nationality, and no higher railroad charges over lines built, controlled, or operated within its "sphere" on merchandise belonging to citizens or subjects of other nationalities transported through such "sphere" than shall be levied on similar merchandise belonging to its own nationals transported over equal distances.

The liberal policy pursued by His Imperial German Majesty in declaring Kiao-chao a free port and in aiding the Chinese Government in the establishment there of a custom-house are so clearly in line with the proposition which this Government is anxious to see recognized that it entertains the strongest hope that Germany will give its acceptance and hearty support.

The recent ukase of His Majesty the Emperor of Russia declaring the port of Ta-lien-wan open during the whole of the lease under which it is held from China to the merchant ships of all nations, coupled with the categorical assurances made to this Government by His Imperial Majesty's representative at this capital at the time and since repeated to me by the present Russian ambassador, seem to insure the support of the Emperor to the proposed measure. Our ambassador at the Court of St. Petersburg has in consequence been instructed to submit it to the Russian Government and to request their early consideration of it. . . .

The commercial interests of Great Britain and Japan will be so clearly served by the desired declaration of intentions, and the views of the Governments of these countries as to the desirability of the adoption of measures insuring the benefits of equality of treatment of all foreign trade throughout China are so similar to those

entertained by the United States, that their acceptance of the propositions herein outlined and their cooperation in advocating their adoption by the other powers can be confidently expected. . . .

In view of the present favorable conditions, you are instructed to submit the above considerations to His Imperial German Majesty's Minister for Foreign Affairs, and to request his early consideration of the subject.

FIFTY-SIXTH CONGRESS, "THE PLATT AMENDMENT" (1901)

In 1898, a congressional action known as the Teller Amendment forswore any intention to "exercise sovereignty, jurisdiction, or control over" Cuba once the war with Spain ended, thereby affirming that the United States merely intended to liberate the island. By 1903, the administration of President Theodore Roosevelt was having second thoughts. At Roosevelt's behest, Congress passed legislation circumscribing the actual exercise of Cuban sovereignty. Known as the Platt Amendment, this legislation not only converted Cuba into an American protectorate but also offered a template for application elsewhere in the Caribbean.

That in fulfillment of the declaration contained in the joint resolution approved April twentieth, eighteen hundred and ninety-eight, entitled "For the recognition of the independence of the people of Cuba, demanding that the Government of Spain relinquish its authority and government in the island of Cuba, and withdraw its land and naval forces from Cuba and Cuban waters, and directing the President of the United States to use the land and naval forces of the United States to carry these resolutions into effect," the President is hereby authorized to "leave the government and control of the island of Cuba to its people" so soon as a government shall have been established in said island under a constitution which, either as a part thereof or in an ordinance appended thereto, shall define the future relations of the United States with Cuba, substantially as follows:

I. That the government of Cuba shall never enter into any treaty or other compact with any foreign power or powers which will impair or tend to impair the independence of Cuba, nor in any manner authorize or permit any foreign power or powers to obtain by colonization or for military or naval purposes or otherwise, lodgement in or control over any portion of said island.

II. That said government shall not assume or contract any public debt, to pay the interest upon which, and to make reasonable sinking fund provision for the ultimate discharge of which, the ordinary revenues of the island, after defraying the current expenses of government shall be inadequate.

III. That the government of Cuba consents that the United States may exercise the right to intervene for the preservation of Cuban independence, the maintenance of a government adequate for the protection of life, property, and individual liberty, and for discharging the obligations with respect to Cuba imposed by the treaty of Paris on the United States, now to be assumed and undertaken by the government of Cuba.

IV. That all Acts of the United States in Cuba during its military occupancy thereof are ratified and validated, and all lawful rights acquired thereunder shall be maintained and protected.

V. That the government of Cuba will execute, and as far as necessary extend, the plans already devised or other plans to be mutually agreed upon, for the sanitation of the cities of the island, to the end that a recurrence of epidemic and infectious diseases may be prevented, thereby assuring protection to the people and commerce of Cuba, as well as to the commerce of the southern ports of the United States and the people residing therein.

VI. That the Isle of Pines shall be omitted from the proposed constitutional boundaries of Cuba, the title thereto being left to future adjustment by treaty.

VII. That to enable the United States to maintain the independence of Cuba, and

to protect the people thereof, as well as for its own defense, the government of Cuba will sell or lease to the United States lands necessary for coaling or naval stations at certain specified points to be agreed upon with the President of the United States."

"VIII. That by way of further assurance the government of Cuba will embody the foregoing provisions in a permanent treaty with the United States."

THEODORE ROOSEVELT, "COROLLARY TO THE MONROE DOCTRINE" (1904)

As US president from 1901 to 1909, Theodore Roosevelt (1858–1919) did not hesitate to wield the "Big Stick" of America's growing power. Commencing construction of a canal through Panama—another American protectorate—Roosevelt came to see the maintenance of order in the Caribbean as a US priority. In his "corollary" to the Monroe Doctrine, he asserts the prerogative of policing that region.

In treating of our foreign policy and of the attitude that this great Nation should assume in the world at large, it is absolutely necessary to consider the Army and the Navy, and the Congress, through which the thought of the Nation finds its expression, should keep ever vividly in mind the fundamental fact that it is impossible to treat our foreign policy, whether this policy takes shape in the effort to secure justice for others or justice for ourselves, save as conditioned upon the attitude we are willing to take toward our Army, and especially toward our Navy. It is not merely unwise, it is contemptible, for a nation, as for an individual, to use high-sounding language to proclaim its purposes, or to take positions which are ridiculous if unsupported by potential force, and then to refuse to provide this force. If there is no intention of providing and keeping the force necessary to back up a strong attitude, then it is far better not to assume such an attitude.

The steady aim of this Nation, as of all enlightened nations, should be to strive to bring ever nearer the day when there shall prevail throughout the world the peace of justice. There are kinds of peace which are highly undesirable, which are in the long run as destructive as any war. Tyrants and oppressors have many times made a wilderness and called it peace. Many times peoples who were slothful or timid or shortsighted, who had been enervated by

ease or by luxury, or misled by false teachings, have shrunk in unmanly fashion from doing duty that was stern and that needed self-sacrifice, and have sought to hide from their own minds their shortcomings, their ignoble motives, by calling them love of peace. The peace of tyrannous terror, the peace of craven weakness, the peace of injustice, all these should be shunned as we shun unrighteous war. The goal to set before us as a nation, the goal which should be set before all mankind, is the attainment of the peace of justice, of the peace which comes when each nation is not merely safe-guarded in its own rights, but scrupulously recognizes and performs its duty toward others. Generally peace tells for righteousness; but if there is conflict between the two, then our fealty is due first to the cause of righteousness. Unrighteous wars are common, and unrighteous peace is rare; but both should be shunned. The right of freedom and the responsibility for the exercise of that right can not be divorced. One of our great poets has well and finely said that freedom is not a gift that tarries long in the hands of cowards. Neither does it tarry long in the hands of those too slothful, too dishonest, or too unintelligent to exercise it. The eternal vigilance which is the price of liberty must be exercised, sometimes to guard against outside foes; although of course far more often to guard against our own selfish or thoughtless shortcomings.

If these self-evident truths are kept before us, and only if they are so kept before us, we shall have a clear idea of what our foreign policy in its larger aspects should be. It is our duty to remember that a nation has no more right to do injustice to another nation, strong or weak, than an individual has to do injustice to another individual; that the same moral law applies in one case as in the other. But we must also remember that it is as much the duty of the Nation to guard its own rights and its own interests as it is the duty of the individual so to do. Within the Nation the individual has now delegated this right to the State, that is, to the representative of all the individuals, and it is a maxim of the law that for every wrong there is a remedy. But in international law we have not advanced by any means as far as we have advanced in municipal law. There is as yet no judicial way of enforcing a right in international law. When one nation wrongs another or wrongs many others, there is no tribunal before which the wrongdoer can be brought. Either it is necessary supinely to acquiesce in the wrong, and thus put a premium upon brutality and aggression, or else it is necessary for the aggrieved nation valiantly to stand up for its rights. Until some method is devised by which there shall be a degree of international control over offending nations, it would be a wicked thing for the most civilized powers, for those with most sense of international obligations and with keenest and most generous appreciation of the difference between right and wrong, to disarm. If the great civilized nations of the present day should completely disarm, the result would mean an immediate recrudescence of barbarism in one form or another. Under any circumstances a sufficient armament would have to be kept up to serve the purposes of international police; and until international cohesion and the sense of international duties and rights are far more advanced than at present, a nation desirous both of securing respect for itself and of doing good to others must have a force adequate for the work which it feels is allotted to it as its part of the general world duty. Therefore it follows that a self-respecting, just, and far-seeing nation should on the one hand endeavor by every means to aid in the development of the various movements which tend to provide substitutes for war, which tend to render nations in their actions toward one another, and indeed toward their own peoples, more responsive to the general sentiment of humane and civilized mankind; and on the other hand that it should keep prepared, while scrupulously avoiding wrongdoing itself, to repel any wrong, and in exceptional cases to take action which in a more advanced stage of international relations would come under the head of the exercise of the international police. A great free people owes it to itself and to all mankind not to sink into helplessness before the powers of evil.

We are in every way endeavoring to help on, with cordial good will, every movement which will tend to bring us into more friendly relations with the rest of mankind. In pursuance of this policy I shall shortly lay before the Senate treaties of arbitration with all powers which are willing to enter into these treaties with us. It is not possible at this period of the world's development to agree to arbitrate all matters, but there are many matters of possible difference between us and other nations which can be thus arbitrated. Furthermore, at the request of the Interparliamentary Union, an eminent body composed of practical statesmen from all countries, I have asked the Powers to join with this Government in a second Hague conference, at which it is hoped that the work already so happily begun at The Hague may be carried some steps further toward completion. This carries out the desire expressed by the first Hague conference itself.

It is not true that the United States feels any land hunger or entertains any projects as regards the other nations of the Western Hemisphere save such as are for their welfare. All that this country desires is to see the neighboring countries stable, orderly, and prosperous. Any country whose people conduct themselves well can count upon our hearty friendship. If a nation shows that it knows how to act with reasonable efficiency and decency in social and political matters, if it keeps order and pays its obligations, it need fear no interference from the United States. Chronic wrongdoing, or an impotence which results in a general loosening of the ties of civilized society, may in America, as elsewhere, ultimately require intervention by some civilized nation, and in the Western Hemisphere the adherence of the United States to the Monroe Doctrine may force the United States, however reluctantly, in flagrant cases of such wrongdoing or impotence, to the exercise of an international police power. If every country washed by the Caribbean Sea would show the progress in stable and just civilization which with the aid of the Platt Amendment Cuba has shown since our troops left the island, and which so many of the republics in both Americas are constantly and brilliantly showing, all question of interference by this Nation with their affairs would be at an end. Our interests and those of our southern neighbors are in reality identical. They have great natural riches, and if within their borders the reign of law and justice obtains, prosperity is sure to come to them. While they thus obey the primary laws of civilized society they may rest assured that they will be treated by us in a spirit of cordial and helpful sympathy. We would interfere with them only in the last resort, and then only if it became evident that their inability or unwillingness to do justice at home and abroad had violated the rights of the United States or had invited foreign aggression to the detriment of the entire body of American nations. It is a mere truism to say that every nation, whether in America or anywhere else, which desires to maintain its freedom, its independence, must ultimately realize that the right of such independence can not be separated from the responsibility of making good use of it.

In asserting the Monroe Doctrine, in taking such steps as we have taken in regard to Cuba, Venezuela, and Panama, and in endeavoring to circumscribe the theater of war in the Far East, and to secure the open door in China, we have acted in our own interest as well as in the interest of humanity at large. There are, however, cases in which, while our own interests are not greatly involved, strong appeal is made to our sympathies. Ordinarily it is very much wiser and more useful for us to concern ourselves with striving for our own moral and material betterment here at home than to concern ourselves with trying to better the condition of things in other nations. We have plenty of sins of our own to war against, and under ordinary circumstances we can do more for the general uplifting of humanity by striving with heart and soul to put a stop to civic corruption, to brutal lawlessness and violent race prejudices here at home than by passing resolutions and wrongdoing elsewhere. Nevertheless there are occasional crimes committed on so vast a scale and of such peculiar horror as to make us doubt whether it is not our manifest duty to endeavor at least to show our disapproval of the deed and our sympathy with those who have suffered by it. The cases must be extreme in which such a course is justifiable. There must be no effort made to remove the mote from our brother's eye if we refuse to remove the beam from our own. But in extreme cases action may be justifiable and proper. What form the action shall take must depend upon the circumstances of the case; that is, upon the degree of the atrocity and upon our power to remedy it. The cases in which we could interfere by force of arms as we interfered to put a stop to intolerable conditions in Cuba are necessarily very few. Yet it is not to be expected that a people like ours, which in spite of certain very obvious shortcomings, nevertheless as a whole shows by its consistent practice its belief in the principles of civil and religious liberty and of orderly freedom, a people among whom even the worst crime, like the crime of lynching, is never more than sporadic, so that individuals and not classes are molested in their fundamental rights—it is inevitable that such a nation should desire eagerly to give expression to its horror on an occasion like that of the massacre of the Jews in Kishenef, or when it witnesses such systematic and long-extended cruelty and oppression as the cruelty and oppression of which the Armenians have been the victims, and which have won for them the indignant pity of the civilized world.

HERBERT CROLY, *THE PROMISE OF AMERICAN LIFE* (1909)

Historians of the United States commonly refer to the first two decades of the twentieth century as the "progressive era." At home, progressives advocated government activism to alleviate the negative effects of industrialization. Abroad, they called for greater American assertiveness. In his influential book *The Promise of American Life,* Herbert Croly (1869–1930), one of the leading progressive thinkers of his day, spells out what that role should and should not include.

Herbert Croly, *The Promise of American Life* New York: The Macmillan Company (1909).

The fault in the vision of our national future possessed by the ordinary American does not consist in the expectation of some continuity of achievement. It consists rather in the expectation that the familiar benefits will continue to accumulate automatically. In his mind the ideal Promise is identified with the processes and conditions which hitherto have very much simplified its fulfillment, and he fails sufficiently to realize that the conditions and processes are one thing and the ideal Promise quite another. Moreover, these underlying social and economic conditions are themselves changing, in such wise that hereafter the ideal Promise, instead of being automatically fulfilled, may well be automatically stifled. For two generations and more the American people were, from the economic point of view, most happily situated. They were able, in a sense, to slide down hill into the valley of fulfillment. Economic conditions were such that, given a fair start, they could scarcely avoid reaching a desirable goal. But such is no longer the case. Economic conditions have been profoundly modified, and American political and social problems have been modified with them. The Promise of American life must depend less than it did upon the virgin wilderness and the Atlantic Ocean, for the virgin wilderness has disappeared, and the Atlantic Ocean has become merely a big channel. The same results can no longer be achieved by the same easy methods. Ugly obstacles have jumped into view, and ugly obstacles are peculiarly dangerous to a person who is sliding down hill. The man who is clambering up hill is in a much better position to evade or overcome them. Americans will possess a safer as well as a worthier vision of their national Promise as soon as they give it a house on a hilltop rather than in a valley. . . .

The transformation of the old sense of a glorious national destiny into the sense of a serious national purpose will inevitably tend to make the popular realization of the Promise of American life both more explicit and more serious. As long as Americans believed they were able to fulfill a noble national Promise merely by virtue of maintaining intact a set of political institutions and by the vigorous individual pursuit of private ends, their allegiance to their national fulfillment remained more a matter of words than of deeds; but now that they are being aroused from their patriotic slumber, the effect is inevitably to disentangle the national idea and to give it more dignity. The redemption of the national Promise has become a cause for which the good American

must fight, and the cause for which a man fights is a cause which he more than ever values. The American idea is no longer to be propagated merely by multiplying the children of the West and by granting ignorant aliens permission to vote. Like all sacred causes, it must be propagated by the Word and by that right arm of the Word, which is the Sword. . . .

The logic of a national democratic ideal and the responsibilities of a national career in the world involve a number of very definite consequences in respect to American foreign policy. They involve, in fact, a conception of the place of a democratic nation in relation to the other civilized nations, different from that which has hitherto prevailed in this country. Because of their geographical situation and their democratic institutions, Americans have claimed and still claim a large degree of national aloofness and independence; but such a claim could have been better defended several generations ago than it can today. Unquestionably the geographical situation of the United States must always have a decisive effect upon the nature of its policy in foreign affairs; and undoubtedly no course of action in respect to other nations can be national without serving the interests of democracy. But precisely because an American foreign policy must be candidly and vigorously national, it will gradually bring with it an increasingly complicated group of international ties and duties. The American nation, just in so far as it believes in its nationality and is ready to become more of a nation, must assume a more definite and a more responsible place in the international system. It will have an increasingly important and an increasingly specific part to play in the political affairs of the world; and, in spite of "old-fashioned democratic" scruples and prejudices, the will to play that part for all it is worth will constitute a beneficial and a necessary stimulus to the better realization of the Promise of our domestic life.

A genuinely national policy must, of course, be based upon a correct understanding of the national interest in relation to those of its neighbors and associates. That American policy did obtain such a foundation during the early years of American history is to be traced to the sound political judgment of Washington and Hamilton. Jefferson and the Republicans did their best for a while to persuade the American democracy to follow the dangerous course of the French democracy, and to base its international policy not upon the firm ground of national interest, but on the treacherous sands of international democratic propagandism. After a period of hesitation, the American people, with their usual good sense in the face of a practical emergency, rallied to the principles subsequently contained in Washington's Farewell Address; and the Jeffersonian Republicans, when they came into control of the Federal government, took over this conception of American national policy together with the rest of the Federalist outfit. But like the rest of the Federalist organization and ideas, the national foreign policy was emasculated by the expression it received at the hands of the Republicans. The conduct of American foreign affairs during the first fifteen years of the century are an illustration of the ills which may befall a democracy during a critical international period, when its foreign policy is managed by a party of anti-national patriots.

After 1815 the foreign policy of the United States was determined by a strict adherence to the principles enunciated in Washington's Farewell Address. The adherence was more in the letter than in the spirit, and the ordinary popular interpretation, which prevails until the present day, cannot be granted undivided approval; but so far as its immediate problems were concerned, American foreign policy did not, on the whole, go astray. The United States kept resolutely clear of European entanglements, and did not participate in international councils, except when the rights of neutrals were under discussion; and this persistent neutrality was precisely the course which was needed in order to confirm the international position of the country as well as to leave the road clear for its own national development. But certain consequences were at an early date deduced from a neutral policy which require more careful examination. During the presidency of Monroe the systematic isolation of the United States in respect to Europe was developed, so far as the two Americas were concerned, into a more positive doctrine. It was proclaimed that abstention on the part of the United States from European affairs should be accompanied by a corresponding abstention by the European Powers from aggressive action in the two Americas. What our government proposed to do was to divide sharply

the democratic political system of the Americas from the monarchical and aristocratic political system of Europe. The European system, based as it was upon royalist legitimacy and privileges, and denying as it did popular political rights, was declared to be inimical in spirit and in effect to the American democratic state.

The Monroe Doctrine has been accepted in this form ever since as an indisputable corollary of the Farewell Address. The American people and politicians cherish it as a priceless political heirloom. It is considered to be the equivalent of the Declaration of Independence in the field of foreign affairs; and it arouses an analogous volume and fury of conviction. Neither is this conviction merely the property of Fourth-of-July Americans. Our gravest publicists usually contribute to the Doctrine a no less emphatic adherence; and not very many years ago one of the most enlightened of American statesmen asserted that American foreign policy as a whole could be sufficiently summed up in the phrase, "The Monroe Doctrine and the Golden Rule." Does the Monroe Doctrine, as stated above, deserve such uncompromising adherence? Is it an adequate expression of the national interest of the American democracy in the field of foreign affairs? . . .

In seeking an answer to these questions we must return to the source of American foreign policy in the Farewell Address. That address contains the germ of a prudent and wise American national policy; but Hamilton, in preparing its phrasing, was guided chiefly by a consideration of the immediate needs and dangers of his country. The Jeffersonian Republicans in their enthusiasm for the French Revolution proposed for a while to bring about a permanent alliance between France and the United States, the object whereof should be the propagation of the democratic political faith. Both Washington and Hamilton saw clearly that such behavior would entangle the United States in all the vicissitudes and turmoil which might attend the development of European democracy; and their favorite policy of neutrality and isolation implied both that the national interest of the United States was not concerned in merely European complications, and that the American people, unlike those of France, did not propose to make their political principles an excuse for international aggression. The Monroe

Doctrine, as proclaimed in 1825, rounded out this negative policy with a more positive assertion of principles. It declared that the neutrality of the American democracy, so far as Europe was concerned, must be balanced by the non-intervention of European legitimacy and aristocracy in the affairs of the American continents. . . .

The Monroe Doctrine has, of course, no status in the accepted system of International Law. Its international standing is due almost entirely to its express proclamation as an essential part of the foreign policy of the United States, and it depends for its weight upon the ability of this country to compel its recognition by the use of latent or actual military force. Great Britain has, perhaps, tacitly accepted it, but no other European country has done so, and a number of them have expressly stated that it entails consequences against which they might sometime be obliged strenuously and forcibly to protest. No forcible protest has as yet been made, because no European country has had anything to gain from such a protest, comparable to the inevitable cost of a war with the United States. . . .

The Monroe Doctrine in its most popular form proclaims a rigid policy of continental isolation—of America for the Americans and of Europe for the Europeans. European nations may retain existing possessions in the Americas, but such possessions must not be increased. So far, so good. A European nation, which sought defiantly to increase its American possessions, in spite of the express declaration of the United States that such action would mean war, would deserve the war thereby incurred. . . .

But if the Monroe Doctrine could only be maintained by a war of this kind, or a succession of wars, it would defeat the very purpose which it is supposed to accomplish. It would embroil the United States and the two American continents in continual trouble with Europe; and it would either have to be abandoned or else would carry with it incessant and enormous expenditures for military and naval purposes. The United States would have to become a predominantly military power, armed to the teeth, to resist or forestall European attack; and our country would have to accept these consequences, for the express purpose of keeping the Americas unsullied by the complications of European politics. . . .

No one can believe more firmly than myself that the foreign policy of a democratic nation should seek by all practicable and inoffensive means the affirmation of democracy; but the challenge which the Monroe Doctrine in its popular form issues to Europe is neither an inoffensive nor a practicable means of affirmation. It is based usually upon the notion of an essential incompatibility between American and European political institutions; . . . . The emancipated and nationalized European states of to-day, so far from being essentially antagonistic to the American democratic nation, are constantly tending towards a condition which invites closer and more fruitful association with the United States; and any national doctrine which proclaims a rooted antagonism lies almost at right angles athwart the road of American democratic national achievement. . . .

The one way in which the foreign policy of the United States can make for democracy is by strengthening and encouraging those political forces which make for international peace. The one respect in which the political system, represented by the United States, is still antagonistic to the European political system is that the European nation, whatever its ultimate tendency, is actually organized for aggressive war, that the cherished purposes of some of its states cannot be realized without war, and that the forces which hope to benefit by war are stronger than the forces which hope to benefit by peace. That is the indubitable reason why the United States must remain aloof from the European system and must avoid scrupulously any entanglements in the complicated web of European international affairs. The policy of isolation is in this respect as wise to-day as it was in the time of its enunciation by Washington and Hamilton; and nobody seriously proposes to depart from it. On the other hand, the basis for this policy is wholly independent of the domestic institutions of the European nations. It derives from the fact that at any time those nations may go to war about questions in which the United States has no vital interest. The geographical situation of the United States emancipates her from these conflicts, and enables her to stand for the ultimate democratic interest in international peace. . . .

If the American system can be made to stand for peace, just as the European system stands at present for war, then the United States will have an unimpeachable reason in forbidding European intervention. European states would no longer have a legitimate ground for interference; it would be impossible for them to take any concerted action. The American nation would testify to its sincere democracy both by its negative attitude towards a militant European system and by its positive promotion of a peaceful international system in the two Americas. . . .

Possibly some of my readers will have inferred by this time that the establishment of a peaceable international system in the two Americas is only a sanctimonious paraphrase for a policy on the part of this country of political aggrandizement in the Western hemisphere. Such an inference would be wholly unjust. Before such a system can be established, the use of compulsion may on some occasions be necessary; but the United States acting individually, could rarely afford to employ forcible means. An essential condition of the realization of the proposed system would be the ability of American statesmen to convince the Latin-Americans of the disinterestedness of their country's intentions. . . .

The United States has already made an effective beginning in this great work, both by the pacification of Cuba and by the attempt to introduce a little order into the affairs of the turbulent Central American republics. The construction of the Panama Canal has given this country an exceptional interest in the prevalence of order and good government in the territory between Panama and Mexico; and in the near future our best opportunity for improving international political conditions in the Western hemisphere will be found in this comparatively limited but, from a selfish point of view, peculiarly important field. . . .

The most difficult task, however, connected with the establishment of a peaceful American international system is presented by Canada. In case such a system were constituted, Canada should most assuredly form a part of it. Yet she could not form a part of it without a radical alteration in her relations with Great Britain. Canada is tied to the British Imperial system, and her policy and destiny depends upon the policy and destiny of the British Empire. She is content with this situation, not merely because she is loyal to the mother country, but because she believes that

her association with Great Britain guarantees her independence in respect to the United States. Many Canadians cherish a profound conviction that the United States wishes nothing so much as the annexation of the Dominion; and the one thing in the world which they propose to prevent is a successful attack upon their independence. This is the natural attitude of a numerically weak people, divided by a long and indefensible frontier from a numerous and powerful neighbor; and while the people of this country have done nothing since the War of 1812 positively to provoke such suspicions, they have, on the other hand, done nothing to allay them. We have never attempted to secure the good will of the Canadians in any respect; and we have never done anything to establish better relations. Yet unless such better relations are established, the United States will lose an indispensable ally in the making of a satisfactory political system in the Western hemisphere while at the same time the American people will be in the sorry situation for a sincere democracy of having created only apprehension and enmity on the part of their nearest and most intelligent neighbors. . . .

The desirable result of the utmost possible commercial freedom between Canada and the United States would be to prepare the way for closer political association. By closer political association I do not mean the annexation of Canada to the United States. Such annexation might not be desirable even with the consent of Canada. What I do mean is some political recognition of the fact that the real interests of Canada in foreign affairs coincide with the interests of the United States rather than with the interests of Great Britain. . . .

A genuinely national foreign policy for the American democracy is not exhausted by the Monroe Doctrine. The United States already has certain colonial interests; and these interests may hereafter be extended. I do not propose at the present stage of this discussion to raise the question as to the legitimacy in principle of a colonial policy on the part of a democratic nation. The validity of colonial expansion even for a democracy is a manifest deduction from the foregoing political principles, always assuming that the people whose independence is thereby diminished are incapable of efficient national organization.

On the other hand, a democratic nation cannot righteously ignore an unusually high standard of obligation for the welfare of its colonial population. It would be distinctly recreant to its duty, in case it failed to provide for the economic prosperity of such a population, and for their educational discipline and social improvement. It by no means follows, however, that because there is no rigid objection on democratic principles to colonial expansion, there may not be the strongest practical objection on the score of national interest to the acquisition of any particular territory. A remote colony is, under existing international conditions, even more of a responsibility than it is a source of national power and efficiency; and it is always a grave question how far the assumption of any particular responsibility is worth while.

Without entering into any specific discussion, there can, I think, be little doubt that the United States was justified in assuming its existing responsibilities in respect to Cuba and its much more abundant responsibilities in respect to Porto Rico. Neither can it be fairly claimed that hitherto the United States has not dealt disinterestedly and in good faith with the people of these islands. On the other hand, our acquisition of the Philippines raises a series of much more doubtful questions. These islands have been so far merely an expensive obligation, from which little benefit has resulted to this country and a comparatively moderate benefit to the Filipinos. They have already cost an amount of money far beyond any chance of compensation, and an amount of American and Filipino blood, the shedding of which constitutes a grave responsibility. Their future defense against possible attack presents a military and naval problem of the utmost difficulty. In fact, they cannot be defended from Japan except by the maintenance of a fleet in Pacific waters at least as large as the Japanese fleet; and it does not look probable that the United States will be able to afford for another generation any such concentration of naval strength in the Pacific. But even though from the military point of view the Philippines may constitute a source of weakness and danger, their possession will have the political advantage of keeping the American people alive to their interests in the grave problems which will be raised in the Far East by the future development of China and Japan.

The future of China raises questions of American foreign policy second only in importance to the establishment of a stable American international organization; . . . Just what form the Chinese question will assume, after the industrial and the political awakening of China has resulted in a more effective military organization and in greater powers both of production and consumption, cannot be predicted with any certainty; but at present, it looks as if the maintenance of the traditional American policy with respect to China, viz., the territorial integrity and the free commercial development of that country, might require quite as considerable a concentration of naval strength in the Pacific as is required by the defense of the Philippines. It is easy enough to enunciate such a policy, just as it is easy to proclaim a Monroe Doctrine which no European Power has any sufficient immediate interest to dispute; but it is wholly improbable that China can be protected in its territorial integrity and its political independence without a great deal of diplomacy and more or less fighting. During the life of the coming generation there will be brought home clearly to the American people how much it will cost to assert its own essential interests in China; and the peculiar value of the Philippines as an American colony will consist largely in the fact that they will help American public opinion to realize more quickly than it otherwise would the complications and responsibilities created by Chinese political development and by Japanese ambition.

The existence and the resolute and intelligent facing of such responsibilities are an inevitable and a wholesome aspect of national discipline and experience. The American people have too easily evaded them in the past, but in the future they cannot be evaded; and it is better so. The irresponsible attitude of Americans in respect to their national domestic problems may in part be traced to freedom from equally grave international responsibilities. In truth, the work of internal reconstruction and amelioration, so far from being opposed to that of the vigorous assertion of a valid foreign policy, is really correlative and supplementary thereto; and it is entirely possible that hereafter the United States will be forced into the adoption of a really national domestic policy because of the dangers and duties incurred through her relations with foreign countries.

The increasingly strenuous nature of international competition and the constantly higher standards of international economic, technical, and political efficiency prescribe a constantly improving domestic political and economic organization. The geographical isolation which affords the United States its military security against foreign attack should not blind Americans to the merely comparative nature of their isolation. The growth of modern sea power and the vast sweep of modern national political interests have at once diminished their security, and multiplied the possible sources of contact between American and European interests. No matter how peaceably the United States is inclined, and no matter how advantageously it is situated, the American nation is none the less constantly threatened by political warfare, and constantly engaged in industrial warfare. The American people can no more afford than can a European people to neglect any necessary kind or source of efficiency. Sooner than ever before in the history of the world do a nation's sins and deficiencies find it out. Under modern conditions a country which takes its responsibilities lightly, and will not submit to the discipline necessary to political efficiency, does not gradually decline, as Spain did in the seventeenth century. It usually goes down with a crash. . . [A]nd if the Christian states of the West ever become so organized that their weaknesses are concealed until their consequences become irremediable, Western civilization itself will be on the road to decline. The Atlantic Ocean will, in the long run, fail to offer the United States any security from the application of the same searching standards. Its democratic institutions must be justified, not merely by the prosperity which they bestow upon its own citizens, but by its ability to meet the standards of efficiency imposed by other nations. Its standing as a nation is determined precisely by its ability to conquer and to hold a dignified and important place in the society of nations.

The inference inevitably is that the isolation which has meant so much to the United States, and still means so much, cannot persist in its present form. Its geographical position will always have a profound influence on the strategic situation of the United States in respect to the European Powers. It should always emancipate the United States from merely European complications. But,

while the American nation should never seek a positive place in an exclusively European system, Europe, the United States, Japan, and China must all eventually take their respective places in a world system. While such a system is still so remote that it merely shows dimly through the obscurity of the future, its manifest desirability brings with it certain definite but contingent obligations in addition to the general obligation of comprehensive and thorough-going national efficiency. It brings with it the obligation of interfering under certain possible circumstances in what may at first appear to be a purely European complication; and this specific obligation would be the result of the general obligation of a democratic nation to make its foreign policy serve the cause of international peace. Hitherto, the American preference and desire for peace has constituted the chief justification for its isolation. At some future time the same purpose, just in so far as it is sincere and rational, may demand intervention. The American responsibility in this respect is similar to that of any peace-preferring European Power. If it wants peace, it must be spiritually and physically prepared to fight for it. Peace will prevail in international relations, just as order prevails within a nation, because of the righteous use of superior force—because the power which makes for pacific organization is stronger than the power which makes for a warlike organization. It looks as if at some future time the power of the United States might well be sufficient, when thrown into the balance, to tip the scales in favor of a comparatively pacific settlement of international complications. Under such conditions a policy of neutrality would be a policy of irresponsibility and unwisdom.

The notion of American intervention in a European conflict, carrying with it either the chance or the necessity of war, would at present be received with pious horror by the great majority of Americans. Non-interference in European affairs is conceived, not as a policy dependent upon certain conditions, but as absolute law—derived from the sacred writings. If the issue should be raised in the near future, the American people would be certain to shirk it; and they would, perhaps, have some reason for a failure to understand their obligation, because the course of European political development has not as yet been such as to raise the question in a decisive form. . . . . But the point is that, whenever and however it is raised, the American national leaders should confront it with a sound, well-informed, and positive conception of the American national interest rather than a negative and ignorant conception. And there is at least a fair chance that such will be the case. The experience of the American people in foreign affairs is only beginning, and during the next few generations the growth of their traffic with Asia and Europe will afford them every reason and every opportunity to ponder seriously the great international problem of peace in its relation to the American national democratic interest.

The idea which is most likely to lead them astray is the idea which vitiates the Monroe Doctrine in its popular form—the idea of some essential incompatibility between Europeanism and Americanism. That idea has given a sort of religious sanctity to the national tradition of isolation; and it will survive its own utility because it flatters American democratic vanity. But if such an idea should prevent the American nation from contributing its influence to the establishment of a peaceful system in Europe, America, and Asia, such a refusal would be a decisive stop toward American democratic degeneracy. It would either mean that the American nation preferred its apparently safe and easy isolation to the dangers and complications which would inevitably attend the final establishment of a just system of public law; or else it would mean that the American people believed more in Americanism than they did in democracy. A decent guarantee of international peace would be precisely the political condition which would enable the European nations to release the springs of democracy; and the Americanism which was indifferent or suspicious of the spread of democracy in Europe would incur and deserve the enmity of the European peoples. Such an attitude would constitute a species of continental provincialism and chauvinism. Hence there is no shibboleth that patriotic Americans should fight more tenaciously and more fiercely than of America for the Americans, and Europe for the Europeans.

HOMER LEA, *THE VALOR OF IGNORANCE* (1909)

A paranoid fear of America being inundated and overrun by nonwhites forms a recurring theme of US history. In the late nineteenth and early twentieth century, some Americans worried that a "Yellow Peril" posed a proximate threat. An eccentric soldier-of-fortune with a gift for self-promotion, Homer Lea (1876–1912) took it upon himself to stoke such fears. Here he foresees a race war pitting the United States against Japan with "the supremacy of the Pacific" at stake.

There are certain conditions that tend to the preservation of peace, just as there are other phases of national life productive of war. While the sources and causes of international conflicts might belong to conditions both basic and necessary for the future development and existence of nations, yet there may be peace factors that more than counterbalance the provocations to war.

Conditions that prevent war, while numerous and peculiar to each combination of combatants, can be determined more or less accurately, and their potentiality measured against that of the causes of international conflict. . . .

Conditions potential enough to prevent war between two racially different nations, as Japan and the United States, can only exist when the causes of war, in either nation, are less imperative than the necessities of peace. Nations do not plunge into warfare without some comprehension of the possibilities of victory as weighed against, not only the disasters to be endured through defeat, but such losses as are incurred on account of the war per se.

We have shown that wars between great nations are resultant, not of passions, but of economic or political convergence. Man may, by his

Homer Lea, *The Valor of Ignorance*. New York: Harper and Brothers (1909).

passions, increase, or by forbearance decrease this convergence, but he cannot do away with war. . . .

Racially, there exists no relationship between the people of Japan and of the United States. And the perverse reluctance of man to forget his own tribal gods and fetishes postpones to such a remote time the assimilation of these two nations that it cannot now be considered. The ethical and sociological conditions extant in Japan, while antithetic to those existent in the United States, are nevertheless the product of two thousand years of Japanese development. To remake the Japanese racial character in order to conform with that of the Occident would require, even were it possible, a longer period of time than we can conceive. Such a racial change in Japan can no more take place than could the West alter its civilization to conform with that of the Orient. Both civilizations will, in due time, by natural but slow process, become so modified that it will be difficult to distinguish the outward forms of one from the other; but racial distinctions and antipathies will continue to remain even unto an unknown time.

A great race is like a rock in the wash of the sea, whereon, as birds of passage, transient civilizations momentarily pause in their flight ere they go on down into the dim twilight of a departed day. It is only the Undefined Sea, or the storms that come out of it, that batter, incrustate, erode, festoon, then swallow up this race-rock that seems in the eye of man made to endure forever.

No national ideals could be more antithetic than are the ethical and civic ideals of Japan to those existent in this Republic. One nation is a militant paternalism, where aught that belongs to man is first for the use of the state; the other an individualistic emporium where aught that belongs to man is for sale. In one is the complete subordination of the individual, in the other his supremacy.

When national religions differ, racial difference creates antagonism. Thus the Japanese, with their sword-girded gods and militant bonzes, are heathen in the eyes of this Republic, heathen in all the contemptuous, naked inferiority that that term in a Christian nation implies. This feeling will never decrease except with the deterioration of Christianity, since such a decadence is, as far as the Japanese are concerned, more probable than the Christianization of their country.

The ethical, sociological, or religious conditions as existent in Japan and this Republic have nothing in common, nor are their ways convergent or even parallel. Neither now nor at any time in the distant future will these nations coalesce to the extent that the sociological or religious phases of their national life will have a deterrent effect on war, or will alter in any way, other than to accentuate their racial ambitions, their perverse activities, their hates and their cries.

The only conditions that may have the power of preserving peace between Japan and the United States, or at least retarding hostilities, are to be found in the political relationship that these two nations bear to the world, and the economic interdependence they have with each other. Political conditions that have, in an international sense, a restraining influence upon the ambitions of a nation, and are instrumental in the prevention of war, are determined by the effect that such a war would have on these interests.

In a struggle between Japan and the United States for the supremacy of the Pacific, all nations have more or less interest in the outcome, but the interests of Japan and this Republic are so paramount that the aggregate interests of the remainder of the world are less than the interests of these two nations. . . .

At present, and for some time to come, there are only two powers, Japan and this Republic, that can, with geographical and political conditions favorable, enter into a war for the supremacy of the Pacific. Japan's interest and inherent advantage in this struggle is due to the fact that her entire empire is not only in this ocean, but in the strategic centre of it. . . .

Politically there are no conditions that can restrain Japan from entering into war with this nation. Strong in faith and in the Red Sun of her destiny, Japan began more than two decades ago her predetermined march to the Empire of the Pacific. One nation after another, by one means and another, she has removed them from her way. Nothing now remains but the overthrow of this Republic's power in the Pacific and nothing, as far as political restrictions are concerned, prevents her from entering upon this conquest: a war that shall bring greater glory to her samurai than they have gained heretofore, and new satrapies, more vast than any now within her realm, shall be given over to her princes and daimios. . . .

The belief most often expressed in this Republic concerning the impossibility of war between Japan and the United States is based on a fanciful and erroneous conception of the economic interdependency of these two nations. This belief has come about through a misconception on the part of the public as to the real significance of international trade and the laws that govern it. Because of this misconception commercialism has taken unto itself the habiliments of uncrowned monarchy a power that would scowl down from the alcove of kings. . . .

In modern wars, the interchange of commodities still remains governed by the law of supply and demand, much in the same manner as in peace, owing to the diversity of trade routes and complexity of international exchange. This condition of affairs is only affected by the destruction of the means of production or the relative impoverishment of the consumers or the naval command of the routes of trade emanating from the exporting country. . . .

The merchandise of individual and national consumption has, in these modern times, become so general to the whole of mankind that the world has become one vast emporium, and what in the time of war cannot be gotten directly from a nation can be secured indirectly through trans-shipments and devious routes of neutral trade. The delusion that the inter-commerce relationship between two nations is destroyed by war, and that economic interdependence is such that it prohibits war, should be put aside in the same manner as mankind has heretofore laid away some of his most cherished notions. . . .

Among nations, coalitions in a military sense are possible, since such combinations are brought about by governments, but in the struggle for commercial supremacy there can be no such alliances; this warfare is the endless conflict of multitudinous man, the tribal swarms of them and their spawn. . . .

It would be difficult to find in history an example more perfectly exemplifying the manner in which the struggle for commercial supremacy involves the competitors in warfare. In the national fabric of Japan and the United States, in their international and human relationship,

conditions potential of peace are not to be found. In their racially different characters, no harmonious similarity exists, only divergent and incompatible ideals; in their international politics, no restraining influence that might, at least, postpone into the indefinite future the probabilities of war. All political restraints have been removed; one after another pulled down and thrown aside by the relentless, predetermined policy of Japan. In their economic relationship conditions that might tend to the prevention of war not only do not exist, but in this economic struggle is to be found the near source of the approaching conflict. . . .

The value the Pacific possessions of this nation bear to Japan is that they determine her possible supremacy of Pacific littoral. These territories consist of Alaska in the North Pacific, Hawaii in the Central, Samoa in the South, and the Philippines in the East. . . . . In order to show how irresistible are the incentives that force Japan to the acquisition of this Republic's insular possessions, we will consider her position as a Pacific and World Power augmented by sovereignty over those territories, singly and as a whole. These possessions have two valuations to Japan their intrinsic wealth, and the value of their strategic position.

However rich they may be in natural resources, their strategic worth is infinitely greater. Intrinsically, the Philippines and Ladrones would more than double the territorial extent of Japan, as well as the empire's natural resources. This valuation, however great in itself, is insignificant in comparison to the strategic worth that these islands possess for Japan in their dominion over Asia and Asiatic hegemony. . . . . With the Philippines in possession of Japan, the dominion of European powers in Asia and the Pacific seas ends, and ends forever. . . .

Sovereignty over the Philippines is not only imperative to Japan in her overlordship of Asia and the Pacific, but is essential to the very preservation of her national existence. The Philippines, in the possession of a great power, forms on her most vulnerable flank a point of attack that is more dangerous than would be Korea in the hands of the same power. Possessed of the Philippines, Japan would complete her chain of island fortresses from the peninsula of Kamchatka to the Indian Ocean, by which she would bind in Asia from the West. With her castles put up on the mountain-tops of these seas, races of man could bay in vain. . . .

Nearly fifteen years ago the value of the Hawaiian Islands, and the necessity of their possession to any nation who would be sovereign over the Pacific, was recognized by Japan. When this Republic annexed the islands at that time, Japan alone protested and notified the American Government that she would not then, nor at any time in the future, acquiesce in the control of the Hawaiian Islands by this nation. Years have now passed, but the protest of Japan has never been withdrawn, nor have preparations ever ceased to bring about in due time its enforcement.

This Republic may forget, or after its conquests sleep, but in that Silent Pentagon where rests together the sceptre of the Mikado and the sword of the samurai there is no forgetfulness, and in their slumbers dreams. However great may be the singular value of each of the American Pacific possessions to the future development of Japan, it is in the strategic relationship each bears to the other, and their relation in the aggregate to Japanese maritime power, that is to be found their greatest value not the price of one, but a dozen wars. . . .

If, at the end of such a struggle, Japan should retain empire over the American Pacific provinces, we know of no war between single states so significant in its results and so basic for the formation of world empire under the hegemony of one nation. . . . . By such a war Japan would be placed in a naval and military position so invulnerable that no nation or coalition of them could attack her. Calmly, from this vast Gibraltar of the ocean, she could look down upon the world and smile at its rage and trepidation this island tribe that owns no heaven and annoys no god. Upon this foundation of one-third the world, Japan would begin the building of a new empire; and as the militant capacities of the nations in the West continued to deteriorate through Hague Conferences, the crumbling diseases of feminism, commercialism and socialism, one by one should they go into the great tumulus upon which, in due time, shall be raised the throne of the Three-Toed Dragon.

We know not nor how many years the Occident has been muttering to itself of a peril that it has called yellow. In the penumbra of its dreams it has seen indistinct shadows lightened, or rather made pallid, with uncertain consciousness, in which, sicklied over with fear, phantoms have rioted. These chimeras in the fear and dreaming of Western nations are what might be called probabilities, monstrous, terrifying, but for all that only phantoms, having their origin in truth, but transferred by that strange somnolence the public mind to the shadowiest of realms.

To this dim region belongs the Yellow Peril. Ever since the Occident entered into close contact with the Orient, politically as well as commercially, it has intuitively become cognizant of a peril. This intuition has been as correct as the reasons concerning its origin and consummation have been somnolently wrong. In this misplacement of the source of the Yellow Peril, the Occident has only repeated what has been done innumerable times before among all portions of mankind. When the dread of the Orient instinctively entered and permeated the consciousness of the West, the whole Occident asked: "Whence will it come?" The reply, based quite naturally on the old and popular misconception of what constitutes capacity to conquer, laid upon China the responsibility of the Yellow Peril because of its immensity.

The world never learns until too late what determines the militant qualities of a nation. True militancy belongs to primitive, homogeneous peoples, wherein political control is restricted to the fewest number of persons, or even to a single individual.

National militancy deteriorates in inverse ratio to the increasing complexity of social and political organisms, hence the larger a nation is and the more individualistic its inhabitants become through the multiplicity of avocations the less capable is a nation to be a conquering power. On account of this we invariably find that the conquesting period of a nation appears in the earliest portion of its career that is, when it first enters into the comity of nations. . . .

The mistake of the Occident is an old error. . . . Yet neither China nor India, neither the empires of Central Asia nor the kingdoms of Eastern Europe, could conceive, though this ill-defined fear brooded heavily over them, of any source of danger other than from those nations whose immensity they dreaded. Upon them fell no terror of certain snout-faced marauders who roamed with their herds over the deserts of Gobi. But with the suddenness of the terrible winds that sweep across Shamo these herders fell upon the world and wagged their cowtail banners in the faces of a hundred kings. In such a manner, in the immensity of China's shadow, four rocky islands have been overlooked.

It is difficult to make a just comparison between the naval and military capacity of one's own country and that of a nation which, through circumstances beyond the sphere of its control, has entered into a struggle for supremacy permitting of no consummation except through a conflict of arms. However sincere one's efforts may be to free himself from prejudice and exaggerated confidence in his country's prowess, yet so innumerable are the intricacies of modern warfare, and so limitless are the possibilities of self-deception, that, even in the sincerest efforts to be exact, one is apt to be unfair and his deductions unjust.

WILLIAM JAMES, "THE MORAL EQUIVALENT OF WAR" *MCCLURE'S MAGAZINE* (AUGUST 1910)

A professor of philosophy at Harvard and a committed pacifist, William James (1842–1910) nonetheless sensed that war fulfills a deep human need among its participants. In this famous essay, he argues that eliminating war will require devising alternative ways to satisfy that need.

The war against war is going to be no holiday excursion or camping party. The military feelings are too deeply grounded to abdicate their place among our ideals until better substitutes are offered than the glory and shame that come to nations as well as to individuals from the ups and downs of politics and the vicissitudes of trade. There is something highly paradoxical in the modern man's relation to war. Ask all our millions, north and south, whether they would vote now (were such a thing possible) to have our war for the Union expunged from history, and the record of a peaceful transition to the present time substituted for that of its marches and battles, and probably hardly a handful of eccentrics would say yes. Those ancestors, those efforts, those memories and legends, are the most ideal part of what we now own together, a sacred spiritual possession worth more than all the blood poured out. Yet ask those same people whether they would be willing, in cold blood, to start another civil war now to gain another similar possession, and not one man or woman would vote for the proposition. In modern eyes, precious though wars may be they must not be waged solely for the sake of the ideal harvest. Only when forced upon one, is a war now thought permissible.

It was not thus in ancient times. The earlier men were hunting men, and to hunt a neighboring tribe, kill the males, loot the village and possess the females, was the most profitable, as well as the most exciting, way of living. Thus were the more martial tribes selected, and in chiefs and peoples a pure pugnacity and love of glory came to mingle with the more fundamental appetite for plunder.

Modern war is so expensive that we feel trade to be a better avenue to plunder; but modern man inherits all the innate pugnacity and all the love of glory of his ancestors. Showing war's irrationality and horror is of no effect on him. The horrors make the fascination. War is the *strong* life; it is life *in extremis*; war taxes are the only ones men never hesitate to pay, as the budgets of all nations show us.

History is a bath of blood. The *Illiad* is one long recital of how Diomedes and Ajax, Sarpedon and Hector *killed*. No detail of the wounds they made is spared us, and the Greek mind fed upon the story. Greek history is a panorama of jingoism and imperialism—war for war's sake, all the citizen's being warriors. It is horrible reading—because of the irrationality of it all—save for the purpose of making "history"—and the history is that of the utter ruin of a civilization in intellectual respects perhaps the highest the earth has ever seen.

Those wars were purely piratical. Pride, gold, women, slaves, excitement were their only motives. In the Peloponesian war, for example, the

Athenians ask the inhabitants of Melos (the island where the "Venus de Milo" was found), hitherto neutral, to own their lordship. The envoys meet, and hold a debate which Thucydides gives in full, and which, for sweet reasonableness of form, would have satisfied Matthew Arnold. "The powerful exact what they can," said the Athenians, "and the weak grant what they must." When the Meleans say that sooner than be slaves they will appeal to the gods, the Athenians reply, "Of the gods we believe and of men we know that, by a law of their nature, wherever they can rule they will. This law was not made by us, and we are not the first to have acted upon it; we did but inherit it, and we know that you and all mankind, if you were as strong as we are, would do as we do. So much for the gods; we have told you why we expect to stand as high in their good opinion as you." Well, the Meleans still refused, and their town was taken. "The Athenians," Thucydides quietly says, "thereupon put to death all who were of military age and made slaves of the women and children. They then colonized the island, sending thither five hundred settlers of their own.

Alexander's career was piracy pure and simple, nothing but an orgy of power and plunder, made romantic by the character of the hero. There was no rational purpose in it, and the moment he died his generals and governors attacked one another. The cruelty of those times is incredible. When Rome finally conquered Greece, Paulus Aemilius, was told by the Roman Senate, to reward his soldiers for their toil by "giving" them the old kingdom of Epirus. They sacked seventy cities and carried off one hundred and fifty thousand inhabitants as slaves. How many they killed I know not; but in Etolia they killed all the senators, five hundred and fifty in number. Brutus was "the noblest Roman of them all," but to reanimate his soldiers on the eve of Philippi he similarly promises to give them the cities of Sparta and Thessalonica to ravage, if they win the fight.

Such was the gory nurse that trained soldiers to cohesiveness. We inherit the warlike type; and for most of the capacities of heroism that the human race is full of we have to thank this cruel history. Dead men tell no tales, and if there were any tribes of other type than this they have left no survivors. Our ancestors have bred pugnacity into our bone and marrow, and thousands of years of peace won't breed it out of us. The popular imagination fairly fattens on the thought of wars. Let public opinion once reach a certain fighting pitch, and no ruler can withstand it. In the Boer war both governments began with bluff, but they couldn't stay there; the military tension was too much for them. In 1898 our people had read the word "war" in letters three inches high for three months in every newspaper. The pliant politician, McKinley, was swept away by their eagerness, and our squalid war with Spain became a reality.

At the present day, civilized opinion is a curious mental mixture. The military instincts and ideals are as strong as ever, but they are confronted by reflective criticisms which sorely curb their ancient freedom. Innumerable writers are showing up the bestial side of military service. Pure loot and mastery seem no longer morally allowable motives, and pretexts must be found for attributing them solely to the enemy. England and we, our army and navy authorities repeat without ceasing, are solely for "peace." Germany and Japan it is who are bent on loot and glory. "Peace" in military mouths today is a synonym for "war expected." The word has become a pure provocative, and no government wishing peace sincerely should allow it ever to be printed in a newspaper. Every up-to-date dictionary should say that "peace" and "war" mean the same thing, now *in posse*, now *in actu*. It may even reasonably be said that the intensely sharp *preparation* for war by the nations is the *real war*, permanent, unceasing; and that the battles are only a sort of public verification of the mastery gained during the "peace"-interval.

It is plain that on this subject civilized man has developed a sort of double personality. If we take European nations, no legitimate interest of any one of them would seem to justify the tremendous destructions which a war to compass it would necessarily entail. It would seem that common sense and reason ought to find a way to reach agreement in every conflict of honest interests. I myself think it our bounden duty to believe in such international rationality as possible. But, as things stand, I see how desperately hard it is to bring the peace-party and the war-party together, and I believe that the difficulty is due to certain deficiencies in the program of pacifism which set the military imagination strongly, and to a certain extent justifiably, against it. In the whole discussion both sides are on imaginative and sentimental ground. It is but one utopia against another, and everything one says must be abstract and hypothetical. Subject to this criticism and caution, I will try to characterize in abstract strokes the opposite imaginative forces, and point out what to my own very fallible mind seems the best utopian hypothesis, the most promising line of conciliation.

In my remarks, pacifist though I am, I will refuse to speak of the bestial side of the war-*regime* (already done justice to by many writers) and consider only the higher aspects of militaristic sentiment. Patriotism no one thinks discreditable; nor does any one deny that war is the romance of history. But inordinate ambitions are the soul of any patriotism, and the possibility of violent death the soul of all romance. The militarily-patriotic and the romantic-minded everywhere, and especially the professional military class, refuse to admit for a moment that war may be a transitory phenomenon in social evolution. The notion of a sheep's paradise like that revolts, they say, our higher imagination. Where then would be the steeps of life? If war had ever stopped, we should have to re-invent it, on this view, to redeem life from flat degeneration.

Reflective apologists for war at the present day all take it religiously. It is a sort of sacrament. It's profits are to the vanquished as well as to the victor; and quite apart from any question of profit, it is an absolute good, we are told, for it is human nature at its highest dynamic. Its "horrors" are a cheap price to pay for rescue from the only alternative supposed, of a world of clerks and teachers, of co-education and zo-ophily, of "consumer's leagues" and "associated charities," of industrialism unlimited, and feminism unabashed. No scorn, no hardness, no valor any more! Fie upon such a cattleyard of a planet!

So far as the central essence of this feeling goes, no healthy minded person, it seems to me, can help to some degree parting of it. Militarism is the great preserver of our ideals of hardihood, and human life with no use for hardihood would be contemptible. Without risks or prizes for the darer, history would be insipid indeed; and there is a type of military character which every one feels that the race should never cease to breed, for everyone is sensitive to its superiority. The duty is incumbent on mankind, of keeping military character in stock—if keeping them, if not for use, then as ends in themselves and as pure pieces of perfection,—so that Roosevelt's weaklings and mollycoddles may not end by making everything else disappear from the face of nature.

This natural sort of feeling forms, I think, the innermost soul of army writings. Without any exception known to me, militarist authors take a highly mystical view of their subject, and regard war as a biological or sociological necessity, uncontrolled by ordinary psychological checks or motives. When the time of development is ripe the war must come, reason or no reason, for the justifications pleaded are invariably fictions. War is, in short, a permanent human *obligation*. General Homer Lea, in his recent book *The Valor of Ignorance*, plants himself squarely on this ground. Readiness for war is for him the essence of nationality, and ability in it the supreme measure of the health of nations.

Nations, General Lea says, are never stationary—they must necessarily expand or shrink, according to their vitality or decrepitude. Japan now is culminating; and by the fatal law in question it is impossible that her statesmen should not long since have entered, with extraordinary foresight, upon a vast policy of conquest—the game in which the first moves were her wars with China and Russia and her treaty with England, and of which the final objective is the capture of the Philippines, the Hawaiian Islands, Alaska, and whole of our Coast west of the Sierra passes. This will give Japan what her ineluctable vocation as a state absolutely forces her to claim, the possession of the entire Pacific Ocean; and to oppose these deep designs we Americans have, according to our author, nothing but our conceit, our ignorance, our commercialism, our corruption, and our feminism. General Lea makes a minute technical comparison of the military strength which we at present could oppose to the strength of Japan, and concludes that the Islands, Alaska, Oregon and Southern California, would fall almost without resistance, that San Francisco must surrender in a fortnight to a Japanese investment, that in three or four months the war would be over and our republic, unable to regain what it had heedlessly neglected to protect sufficiently, would then "disintegrate," until perhaps some Ceasar should arise to weld us again into a nation.

A dismal forecast indeed! Yet not unplausible, if the mentality of Japan's statesmen be of the Ceasarian type of which history shows us so many examples, and which is all that General Lea seems able to imagine. But there is no reason to think that women can no longer be the mother of Napoleonic or Alexandrian characters; and if these come in Japan and find their opportunity, just such surprises as *The Valor of Ignorance* paints may lurk in ambush for us. Ignorant as we still are of the innermost recesses of Japanese mentality, we may be foolhardy to disregard such possibilities.

Other militarists are more complex and more moral in their considerations. The *Philosophie des Krieges*, by S. R. Steinmetz is good example. War, according to this author, is an ordeal instituted by God, who weighs the nations in its balance. It is the essential form of the State, and the only function in which peoples can employ all their powers at once and convergently. No victory is possible save as the resultant of a totality of virtues, no defeat for which some vice or weakness is not responsible. Fidelity, cohesiveness, tenacity, heroism, conscience, education, inventiveness, economy, wealth, physical health and vigor—there isn't a moral or intellectual point of superiority that doesn't tell, when God holds his assizes and hurls the peoples upon one another. *Die Weltgeschichte ist das Weltgericht*; and Dr. Steinmetz does not believe that in the long run chance and luck play any part in apportioning the issues.

The virtues that prevail, it must be noted, are virtues anyhow, superiorities that count in peaceful as well as in military competition; but the strain is on them, being infinitely intenser in the latter case, makes war infinitely more searching as a trial. No ordeal is comparable to its winnowings. Its dread hammer is the welder of men into cohesive states, and nowhere but in such states can human nature adequately develop its capacity. The only alternative is "degeneration."

Dr. Steinmetz is a conscientious thinker, and his book, short as it is, takes much into account. Its upshot can, it seems to me, be summed up in Simon Patten's words, that mankind was nursed in pain and fear, and that the transition to a "pleasure economy" may be fatal to a being wielding no powers of defence against its degenerative influences. If we speak of the *fear of emancipation from the fear-regime*, we put the whole situation into a single phrase; fear regarding ourselves now taking the place of the ancient fear of the enemy.

Turn the fear over as I will in my mind, it all seems to lead back to two unwillingnesses of the imagination, one aesthetic, and the other moral; unwillingness, first, to envisage a future in which army-life, with its many elements of charm, shall be forever impossible, and in which the destinies of peoples shall nevermore be decided quickly, thrillingly, and tragically by force, but only gradually and insipidly by "evolution," and, secondly, unwillingness to see the supreme theatre of human strenuousness closed, and the splendid military aptitudes of men doomed to keep always in a state of latency and never show themselves in action. These insistent unwillingnesses, no less than other aesthetic and ethical insistencies, have, it seems to me, to be listened to and respected. One cannot meet them effectively by mere counter-insistency on war's expensiveness and horror. The horror makes the thrill; and when the question is of getting the extremest and supremest out of human nature, talk of expense sounds ignominious. The weakness of so much merely negative criticism is evident—pacifism makes no converts from the military party. The military party denies neither the bestiality nor the horror, nor the expense; it only says that these things tell but half the story. It only says that war is *worth* them; that, taking human nature as a whole, its wars are its best protection against its weaker and more cowardly self, and that mankind cannot *afford* to adopt a peace economy.

Pacifists ought to enter more deeply into the aesthetical and ethical point of view of their opponents. Do that first in any controversy, says J. J. Chapman, *then move the point*, and your opponent will follow. So long as antimilitarists propose no substitute for war's disciplinary function, no *moral equivalent* of war, analogous, as one might say, to the mechanical equivalent of heat, so long they fail to realize the full inwardness of the situation. And as a rule they do fail. The duties, penalties, and sanctions pictured in the utopias they paint are all too weak and tame to touch the military-minded. Tolstoi's pacifism is the only exception to this rule, for it is profoundly pessimistic as regards all this world's values, and makes the fear of the

Lord furnish the moral spur provided elsewhere by the fear of the enemy. But our socialistic peace-advocates all believe absolutely in this world's values; and instead of the fear of the Lord and the fear of the enemy, the only fear they reckon with is the fear of poverty if one be lazy. This weakness pervades all the socialistic literature with which I am acquainted. Even in Lowes Dickinson's exquisite dialogue, high wages and short hours are the only forces invoked for overcoming man's distaste for repulsive kinds of labor. Meanwhile men at large still live as they always have lived, under a pain-and-fear economy—for those of us who live in an ease-economy are but an island in the stormy ocean—and the whole atmosphere of present-day utopian literature tastes mawkish and dishwatery to people who still keep a sense for life's more bitter flavors. It suggests, in truth, ubiquitous inferiority.

Inferiority is always with us, and merciless scorn of it is the keynote of the military temper. "Dogs, would you live forever?" shouted Frederick the Great. "Yes," say our utopians, "let us live forever, and raise our level gradually." The best thing about our "inferiors" today is that they are as tough as nails, and physically and morally almost as insensitive. Utopians would see them soft and squeamish, while militarism would keep their callousness, but transfigure it into a meritorious characteristic, needed by "the service," and redeemed by that from the suspicion of inferiority. All the qualities of a man acquire dignity when he knows that the service of the collectivity that owns him needs him. If proud of the collectivity, his own pride rises in proportion. No collectivity is like an army for nourishing such pride; but it has to be confessed that the only sentiment which the image of pacific cosmopolitan industrialism is capable of arousing in countless worthy breasts is shame at the idea of belonging to *such* a collectivity. It is obvious that the United States of America as they exist today impress a mind like General Lea's as so much human blubber. Where is the sharpness and precipitousness, the contempt for life, whether one's own or another's? Where is the savage "yes" and "no," the unconditional duty? Where is the conscription? Where is the blood-tax? Where is anything that one feels honored by belonging to?

Having said thus much in preparation, I will now confess my own utopia. I devoutly believe in the reign of peace and in the gradual advent of some sort of socialistic equilibrium. The fatalistic view of the war function is to me nonsense, for I know that war-making is due to definite motives and subject to prudential checks and reasonable criticisms, just like any other form of enterprise. And when whole nations are the armies, and the science of destruction vies in intellectual refinement with the science of production, I see that war becomes absurd and impossible from its own monstrosity. Extravagant ambitions will have to be replaced by reasonable claims, and nations must make common cause against them. I see no reason why all this should not apply to yellow as well as to white countries, and I look forward to a future when acts of war shall be formally outlawed as between civilized peoples.

All these beliefs of mine put me firmly into the anti-military party. But I do not believe that peace either ought to be or will be permanent on this globe, unless the states, pacifically organized, preserve some of the old elements of army-discipline. A permanently successful peace-economy cannot be a simple pleasure-economy. In the more or less socialistic future toward which mankind seems drifting we must still subject ourselves collectively to those severities which answer to our real position upon this only partly hospitable globe. We must make new energies and hardihoods continue the manliness to which the military mind so faithfully clings. Martial virtues must be the enduring cement; intrepidity, contempt of softness, surrender of private interest, obedience to command, must still remain the rock upon which states are built—unless, indeed, we which for dangerous reactions against commonwealths, fit only for contempt, and liable to invite attack whenever a centre of crystallization for military-minded enterprise gets formed anywhere in their neighborhood.

The war-party is assuredly right in affirming and reaffirming that the martial virtues, although originally gain by the race through war, are absolute and permanent human goods. Patriotic pride and ambition in their military form are, after all, only specifications of a more general competitive passion. They are its first form, but that is no reason for supposing them to be its last form. Men are now proud of belonging to a conquering nation, and without a murmur they lay down their persons and their wealth, if by so doing they may fend off subjection. But who can be sure that *other aspects of one's country* may not, with time and education and suggestion enough, come to be regarded with similarly effective feelings of pride and shame? Why should men not some day feel that is it worth a blood-tax to belong to a collectivity superior in *any* respect? Why should they not blush with indignant shame if the community that owns them is vile in any way whatsoever? Individuals, daily more numerous, now feel this civic passion. It is only a question of blowing on the spark until the whole population gets incandescent, and on the ruins of the old morals of military honor, a stable system of morals of civic honor builds itself up. What the whole community comes to believe in grasps the individual as in a vise. The war-function has grasped us so far; but the constructive interests may some day seem no less imperative, and impose on the individual a hardly lighter burden.

Let me illustrate my idea more concretely. There is nothing to make one indignant in the mere fact that life is hard, that men should toil and suffer pain. The planetary conditions once for all are such, and we can stand it. But that so many men, by mere accidents of birth and opportunity, should have a life of *nothing else* but toil and pain and hardness and inferiority imposed upon them, should have *no* vacation, while others natively no more deserving never get any taste of this campaigning life at all,—*this* is capable of arousing indignation in reflective minds. It may end by seeming shameful to all of us that some of us have nothing but campaigning, and others nothing but unmanly ease. If now—and this is my idea—there were, instead of military conscription, a conscription of the whole youthful population to form for a certain number of years a part of the army enlisted against *Nature*, the injustice would tend to be evened out, and numerous other goods to the commonwealth would remain blind as the luxurious classes now are blind, to man's relations to the globe he lives on, and to the permanently sour and hard foundations of his higher life. To coal and iron mines, to freight trains, to fishing fleets in December, to dishwashing, clotheswashing, and windowwashing, to road-building and tunnel-making, to foundries and stoke-holes, and to the frames of skyscrapers, would our gilded youths be

drafted off, according to their choice, to get the childishness knocked out of them, and to come back into society with healthier sympathies and soberer ideas. They would have paid their blood-tax, done their own part in the immemorial human warfare against nature; they would tread the earth more proudly, the women would value them more highly, they would be better fathers and teachers of the following generation.

Such a conscription, with the state of public opinion that would have required it, and the many moral fruits it would bear, would preserve in the midst of a pacific civilization the manly virtues which the military party is so afraid of seeing disappear in peace. We should get toughness without callousness, authority with as little criminal cruelty as possible, and painful work done cheerily because the duty is temporary, and threatens not, as now, to degrade the whole remainder of one's life. I spoke of the "moral equivalent" of war. So far, war has been the only force that can discipline a whole community, and until and equivalent discipline is organized, I believe that war must have its way. But I have no serious doubt that the ordinary prides and shames of social man, once developed to a certain intensity, are capable of organizing such a moral equivalent as I have sketched, or some other just as effective for preserving manliness of type. It is but a question of time, of skilful propagandism, and of opinion-making men seizing historic opportunities.

The martial type of character can be bred without war. Strenuous honor and disinterestedness abound everywhere. Priests and medical men are in a fashion educated to it, and we should all feel some degree of its imperative if we were conscious of our work as an obligatory service to the state. We should be *owned*, as soldiers are by the army, and our pride would rise accordingly. We could be poor, then, without humiliation, as army officers now are. The only thing needed henceforward is to inflame the civic temper as part history has inflamed the military temper. H. G. Wells, as usual, sees the centre of the situation. "In many ways," he says, "military organization is the most peaceful of activities. When the contemporary man steps from the street, of clamorous insincere advertisement, push, adulteration, underselling and intermittent employment into the barrack-yard, he steps on to a higher social plane, into an atmosphere of service and cooperation and of infinitely more honorable emulations. Here at least men are not flung out of employment to degenerate because there is no immediate work for them to do. They are fed a drilled and training for better services. Here at least a man is supposed to win promotion by self-forgetfulness and not by self-seeking. And beside the feeble and irregular endowment of research by commercialism, its little shortsighted snatches at profit by innovation and scientific economy, see how remarkable is the steady and rapid development of method and appliances in naval and military affairs! Nothing is more striking than to compare the progress of civil conveniences which has been left almost entirely to the trader, to the progress in military apparatus during the last few decades. The house-appliances of today, for example, are little better than they were fifty years ago. A house of today is still almost as ill-ventilated, badly heated by wasteful fires, clumsily arranged and furnished as the house of 1858. Houses a couple of hundred years old are still satisfactory places of residence, so little have our standards risen. But the rifle or battleship of fifty years ago was beyond all comparison inferior to

those we now possess; in power, in speed, in convenience alike. No one has a use now for such superannuated things."

Wells adds that he thinks that the conceptions of order and discipline, the tradition of service and devotion, of physical fitness, unstinted exertion, and universal responsibility, which universal military duty is now teaching European nations, will remain a permanent acquisition when the last ammunition has been used in the fireworks that celebrate the final peace. I believe as he does. It would be simply preposterous if the only force that could work ideals of honor and standards of efficiency into English or American natures should be the fear of being killed by the Germans or the Japanese. Great indeed is Fear; but it is not, as our military enthusiasts believe and try to make us believe, the only stimulus known for awakening the higher ranges of men's spiritual energy. The amount of alteration in public opinion which my utopia postulates is vastly less than the difference between the mentality of those black warriors who pursued Stanley's party on the Congo with their cannibal war-cry of "Meat! Meat!" and that of the "general-staff" of any civilized nation. History has seen the latter interval bridged over; the former one can be bridged over much more easily.

WILLIAM HOWARD TAFT, "DOLLAR DIPLOMACY" (1912)

Theodore Roosevelt's hand-chosen successor as president was William Howard Taft (1857–1930). Their friendship did not survive Taft's generally undistinguished term in office. In lieu of the "Big Stick," Taft preferred what he called "dollar diplomacy." Here in his 1912 State of the Union Address he makes the case for government partnering with private investment firms to advance US interests while also turning a profit.

The foreign relations of the United States actually and potentially affect the state of the Union to a degree not widely realized and hardly surpassed by any other factor in the welfare of the whole nation. The position of the United States in the moral, intellectual, and material relations of the family of nations should be a matter of vital interest to every patriotic citizen. The national prosperity and power impose upon us duties which we cannot shirk if we are to be true to our ideals. The tremendous growth of the export trade of

the United States has already made that trade a very real factor in the industrial and commercial prosperity of the country. With the development of our industries, the foreign commerce of the United States must rapidly become a still more essential factor in its economic welfare.

Whether we have a farseeing and wise diplomacy and are not recklessly plunged into unnecessary wars, and whether our foreign policies are based upon an intelligent grasp of present-day world conditions and a clear view of the potentialities of the future, or are governed by a temporary and timid expediency or by narrow views befitting an infant nation, are questions in the alternative consideration of which must convince any thoughtful citizen that no department of national polity offers greater opportunity for promoting the interests of the whole people on the one hand, or greater chance on the other of permanent national injury, than that which deals with the foreign relations of the United States.

The fundamental foreign policies of the United States should be raised high above the conflict of partisanship and wholly dissociated from differences as to domestic policy. In its foreign affairs the United States should present to the world a united front. The intellectual, financial, and industrial interests of the country and the publicist, the wage earner, the farmer, and citizen of whatever occupation must cooperate in a spirit of high patriotism to promote that national solidarity which is indispensable to national efficiency and to the attainment of national ideals. . . .

The diplomacy of the present administration has sought to respond to modern ideas of commercial intercourse. This policy has been characterized as substituting dollars for bullets. It is one that appeals alike to idealistic humanitarian sentiments, to the dictates of sound policy and strategy, and to legitimate commercial aims. It is an effort frankly directed to the increase of American trade upon the axiomatic principle that the government of the United States shall extend all proper support to every legitimate and beneficial American enterprise abroad. . . .

In China the policy of encouraging financial investment to enable that country to help itself has had the result of giving new life and practical application to the open door policy. The consistent purpose of the present administration has been to encourage the use of American capital in the development of China by the promotion of those essential reforms to which China is pledged by treaties with the United States and other powers. . . .

In Central America the aim has been to help such countries as Nicaragua and Honduras to help themselves. They are the immediate beneficiaries. The national benefit to the United States is twofold. First, it is obvious that the Monroe Doctrine is more vital in the neighborhood of the Panama Canal and the zone of the Caribbean than anywhere else. There, too, the maintenance of that doctrine falls most heavily upon the United States. It is therefore essential that the countries within that sphere shall be removed from the jeopardy involved by heavy foreign debt and chaotic national finances and from the ever present danger of international complications due to disorder at home. . . .

The second advantage to the United States is one affecting chiefly all the Southern and Gulf ports and the business and industry of the South. The republics of Central America and the Caribbean possess great natural wealth. They need only a measure of stability and the means of financial regeneration to enter upon an era of peace and prosperity, bringing profit and happiness to themselves and at the same time creating conditions sure to lead to a flourishing interchange of trade with this country. . . .

I wish to congratulate the officers and men of the United States Navy and Marine Corps who took part in reestablishing order in Nicaragua upon their splendid conduct, and to record with sorrow the death of seven American Marines and Bluejackets. Since the reestablishment of peace and order, elections have been held amid conditions of quiet and tranquillity. Nearly all the American Marines have now been withdrawn. The country should soon be on the road to recovery. . . .

Congress should fully realize the conditions which obtain in the world as we find ourselves at the threshold of our middle age as a nation. We have emerged full grown as a peer in the great concourse of nations. We have passed through various formative periods. We have been self-centered in the struggle to develop our domestic resources and deal with our domestic questions. The nation is now too mature to continue in its foreign relations those temporary expedients natural to a people to whom domestic affairs are the sole concern.

In the past, our diplomacy has often consisted, in normal times, in a mere assertion of the right to international existence. We are now in a larger relation with broader rights of our own and obligations to others than ourselves. A number of great guiding principles were laid down early in the history of this government. The recent task of our diplomacy has been to adjust those principles to the conditions of today, to develop their corollaries, to find practical applications of the old principles expanded to meet new situations. Thus are being evolved bases upon which can rest the superstructure of policies which must grow with the destined progress of this nation.

The successful conduct of our foreign relations demands a broad and a modern view. We cannot meet new questions nor build for the future if we confine ourselves to outworn dogmas of the past and to the perspective appropriate at our emergence from colonial times and conditions. The opening of the Panama Canal will mark a new era in our international life and create new and worldwide conditions which, with their vast correlations and consequences, will obtain for hundreds of years to come. We must not wait for events to overtake us unawares. With continuity of purpose we must deal with the problems of our external relations by a diplomacy modern, resourceful, magnanimous, and fittingly expressive of the high ideals of a great nation.

V.

FATEFUL EMBRACE

When Europe went to war with itself in the summer of 1914, the initial US response, articulated by President Woodrow Wilson (1856–1924), was to steer clear of the conflict. Wilson called upon Americans to remain neutral in fact and in spirit. This position found favor with most Americans and was consistent with a well-established diplomatic tradition dating back to the administration of George Washington.

US policymakers assumed that the war would be a short one. So too did the warring Europeans. This proved to be a monumental miscalculation. Neither the Allies, led by France and Great Britain, nor the Central Powers, led by Germany, proved able to win. Waged with unprecedented ferocity and inflicting staggering casualties on both sides, the conflict settled into an intractable stalemate. US efforts to encourage a negotiated settlement went nowhere.

As the war dragged on, two factors played an especially notable role in undermining American neutrality. The first was German employment of the submarine, then something of a novelty, to sink unarmed merchant ships, to include American vessels engaged in trading with the Allies. The second factor was hardly less important: to sustain that lucrative trade, Wilson permitted banks in the United States to extend credit to the Allies, in effect mortgaging American economic prosperity to the Allied cause.

By early 1917, with a now nearly exhausted Germany announcing a policy of "unrestricted submarine warfare," Wilson concluded that the United States had no alternative but to enter the war on the side of the Allies. In urging Congress to declare war, he insisted that the moment had now arrived for the New World to come to the salvation of the Old and to create the basis for a permanent peace. Wilson himself offer a blueprint for such a peace based on "Fourteen Points" of his own devising. The most important of those points in Wilson's estimation envisioned the creation of a League of Nations to settle international disputes without resort to violence.

Critics denounced US entry into a European war as radical departure from the established tradition of American statecraft. Even so, Wilson got what he wanted. The Congress declared war and the United States set about raising up a great army to fight on the Western Front.

The results of US intervention, however, differed dramatically from those that Wilson had anticipated. Although the Allies ultimately prevailed, with US forces making a belated but not insignificant contribution to that victory, the president proved unable to persuade other Allied leaders to embrace his vision of a new international order. When the conference adjourned, little of his plan remained apart from the proposed League of Nations. The United States' entry into that League required the US Senate to ratify the treaty negotiated at Paris. Yet the Senate ignored Wilson's impassioned entreaties and rejected the treaty. The League came into existence, but without the United States.

Woodrow Wilson, "Speech in Philadelphia" (1915)

On May 7, 1915, a German submarine sunk the British liner *Lusitania,* killing 1,193, among them 128 Americans. Across the United States the event provoked outrage. Three days later, President Wilson made this speech, affirming his intention to remain neutral while also offering his own interpretation of American exceptionalism.

It warms my heart that you should give me such a reception; but it is not of myself that I wish to think tonight, but of those who have just become citizens of the United States.

This is the only country in the world which experiences this constant and repeated rebirth. Other countries depend upon the multiplication of their own native people. This country is constantly drinking strength out of new sources by the voluntary association with it of great bodies of strong men and forward-looking women out of other lands. And so by the gift of the free will of independent people it is being constantly renewed from generation to generation by the same process by which it was originally created. It is as if humanity had determined to see to it that this great Nation, founded for the benefit of humanity, should not lack for the allegiance of the people of the world.

You have just taken an oath of allegiance to the United States. Of allegiance to whom? Of allegiance to no one, unless it be God—certainly not of allegiance to those who temporarily represent this great Government. You have taken an oath of allegiance to a great ideal, to a great body of principles, to a great hope of the human race. You have said, "We are going to America not only to earn a living, not only to seek the things which it was more difficult to obtain where we were born, but to help forward the great enterprises of the human spirit—to let men know that everywhere in the world there are men who will cross strange oceans and go where a speech is spoken which is alien to them if they can but satisfy their quest for what their spirits crave; knowing that whatever the speech there is but one longing and utterance of the human heart, and that is for liberty and justice." And while you bring all countries with you, you come with a purpose of leaving all other countries behind you—bringing what is best of their spirit, but not looking over your shoulders and seeking to perpetuate what you intended to leave behind in them. I certainly would not be one even to suggest that a man cease to love the home of his birth and the nation of his origin—these things are very sacred and ought not to be put out of our hearts—but it is one thing to love the place where you were born and it is another thing to dedicate yourself to the place to which you go. You cannot dedicate yourself to America unless you become in every respect and with every purpose of your will thorough Americans. You cannot become thorough Americans if you think of yourselves in groups. America does not consist of groups. A man who thinks of himself as belonging to a particular national group in America has not yet become an American, and the man who goes among you to trade upon your nationality is no worthy son to live under the Stars and Stripes.

My urgent advice to you would be, not only always to think first of America, but always, also, to think first of humanity. You do not love humanity if you seek to divide humanity into jealous camps. Humanity can be welded together only by love, by sympathy, by justice, not by jealousy and hatred. I am sorry for the man who seeks to make personal capital out of the passions of his fellow-men. He has lost the touch and ideal of America, for America was created to unite mankind by those passions which lift and not by the passions which separate and debase. We came to America, either ourselves or in the persons of our ancestors, to better the ideals of men, to make them see finer things than they had seen before, to get rid of the things that divide and to make sure of the things that unite. It was but an historical accident no doubt that this great country was called the "United States"; yet I am very thankful that it has that word "United" in its title, and the man who seeks to divide man from man, group from group, interest from interest in this great Union is striking at its very heart.

It is a very interesting circumstance to me, in thinking of those of you who have just sworn allegiance to this great Government, that you were drawn across the ocean by some beckoning finger of hope, by some belief, by some vision of a new kind of justice, by some expectation of a better kind of life. No doubt you have been disappointed in some of us. Some of us are very disappointing. No doubt you have found that justice in the United States goes only with a pure heart and a right purpose as it does everywhere else in the world. No doubt what you found here did not seem touched for you, after all, with the complete beauty of the ideal which you had conceived beforehand. But remember this: If we had grown at all poor in the ideal, you brought some of it with you. A man does not go out to seek the thing that is not in him. A man does not hope for the thing that he does not believe in, and if some of us have forgotten what

America believed in, you, at any rate, imported in your own hearts a renewal of the belief. That is the reason that I, for one, make you welcome. If I have in any degree forgotten what America was intended for, I will thank God if you will remind me. I was born in America. You dreamed dreams of what America was to be, and I hope you brought the dreams with you. No man that does not see visions will ever realize any high hope or undertake any high enterprise. Just because you brought dreams with you, America is more likely to realize dreams such as you brought. You are enriching us if you came expecting us to be better than we are.

See, my friends, what that means. It means that Americans must have a consciousness different from the consciousness of every other nation in the world. I am not saying this with even the slightest thought of criticism of other nations. You know how it is with a family. A family gets centered on itself if it is not careful and is less interested in the neighbors than it is in its own members. So a nation that is not constantly renewed out of new sources is apt to have the narrowness and prejudice of a family; whereas, America must have this consciousness, that on all sides it touches elbows and touches hearts with all the nations of mankind. The example of America must be a special example. The example of America must be the example not merely of peace because it will not fight, but of peace because peace is the healing and elevating influence of the world and strife is not. There is such a thing as a man being too proud to fight. There is such a thing as a nation being so right that it does not need to convince others by force that it is right.

WOMAN'S PEACE PARTY, "PREAMBLE" (1915)

The outbreak of war in Europe gave impetus to an American peace movement. Founded in 1915 by Jane Addams, Carrie Chapman Catt (1859–1947), and Fanny Garrison Villard (1844–1928), the Woman's Peace Party insisted that women had a particular antipathy for war and should play a leading role in its abolition.

We, women of the United States, assembled on behalf of World Peace, grateful for the security of our own country, but sorrowing for the misery of all involved in the present struggle among warring nations, do hereby band ourselves together to demand that war be abolished.

Equally with men pacifists, we understand that planned-for, legalized, wholesale, human slaughter is today the sum of all villainies.

As women, we feel a particular moral passion of revolt against both the cruelty and the waste of war.

As women, we are especially the custodians of the life of the ages. We will no longer consent to its reckless destruction.

As women, we are particularly charged with the future of childhood and with the care of the helpless and the unfortunate. We will not longer endure without protest that added burden of maimed and invalid men and poverty stricken widows and orphans which war places upon us.

As women, we have builded [sic] by the patient drudgery of the past the basic foundation of the home and of peaceful industry. We will not longer endure without a protest that must be heard and heeded by men that hoary evil which in an hour destroys the social structures that centuries of toil have reared.

As women, we are called upon to start each generation onward toward a better humanity. We will not longer tolerate without determined opposition that denial of the sovereignty of reason and justice by which war and all that makes for war today render impotent the idealism of the race.

Therefore, as human beings and the mother half of humanity, we demand that our right to be consulted in the settlement of questions concerning not alone the life of individuals but of nations be recognized and respected.

We demand that women be given a share in deciding between war and peace in all the courts of high debate—within the home, the school, the church, the industrial order, and the state.

So protesting, and so demanding, we hereby form ourselves into a national organization to be called the Woman's Peace Party.

EMMA GOLDMAN, "PREPAREDNESS, THE ROAD TO UNIVERSAL SLAUGHTER" *MOTHER EARTH* (DECEMBER 1915)

Born to a Jewish family in what is today Lithuania, Emma Goldman (1864–1940) emigrated to the United States in 1885 and immersed herself in radical politics. Here she denounces what she sees as incipient militarism among those citing the stalemated European conflict as reason for the United States to gird itself for possible war.

Ever since the beginning of the European con-flagration, the whole human race almost has fallen into the deathly grip of the war anesthesis, overcome by the mad teaming fumes of a blood soaked chloroform, which has obscured its vision and paralyzed its heart. Indeed, with the exception of some savage tribes, who know nothing of Christian religion or of brotherly love, and who also know nothing of dreadnaughts, submarines, munition manufacture and war loans, the rest of the race is under this terrible narcosis. The human mind seems to be conscious of but one thing, murderous speculation. Our whole civilization, our entire culture is concentrated in the mad demand for the most perfected weapons of slaughter.

Ammunition! Ammunition! O, Lord, thou who rulest heaven and earth, thou God of love, of mercy and of justice, provide us with enough ammunition to destroy our enemy. Such is the prayer which is ascending daily to the Christian heaven. Just like cattle, panic-stricken in the face of fire, throw themselves into the very flames, so all of the European people have fallen over each other into the devouring flames of the furies of war, and America, pushed to the very brink by unscrupulous politicians, by ranting demagogues, and by military sharks, is preparing for the same terrible feat.

In the face of this approaching disaster, it behooves men and women not yet overcome by the war madness to raise their voice of protest, to call the attention of the people to the crime and outrage which are about to be perpetrated upon them.

America is essentially the melting pot. No national unit composing it is in a position to boast of superior race purity, particular historic mission, or higher culture. Yet the jingoes and war speculators are filling the air with the sentimental slogan of hypocritical nationalism, "America for Americans," "America first, last, and all the time." This cry has caught the popular fancy from one end of the country to another. In order to maintain America, military preparedness must be engaged in at once. A billion dollars of the people's sweat and blood is to be expended for dreadnaughts and submarines for the army and the navy, all to protect this precious America.

The pathos of it all is that the America which is to be protected by a huge military force is not the America of the people, but that of the privileged class; the class which robs and exploits the masses, and controls their lives from the cradle to the grave. No less pathetic is it that so few people realize that preparedness never leads to peace, but that it is indeed the road to universal slaughter.

With the cunning methods used by the scheming diplomats and military cliques of Germany to saddle the masses with Prussian militarism, the American military ring with its Roosevelts, its Garrisons, its Daniels, and lastly its Wilsons, are moving the very heavens to place the militaristic heel upon the necks of the American people, and, if successful, will hurl America into the storm of blood and tears now devastating the countries of Europe.

Forty years ago Germany proclaimed the slogan: "Germany above everything. Germany for the Germans, first, last and always. We want peace; therefore we must prepare for war. Only a well-armed and thoroughly prepared nation can maintain peace, can command respect, can be sure of its national integrity." And Germany continued to prepare, thereby forcing the other nations to do the same. The terrible European war is only the culminating fruition of the hydra-headed gospel, military preparedness.

Since the war began, miles of paper and oceans of ink have been used to prove the barbarity, the cruelty, the oppression of Prussian militarism. Conservatives and radicals alike are giving their support to the Allies for no other reason than to help crush that militarism, in the presence of which, they say, there can be no peace or progress in Europe. But though America grows fat on the manufacture of munitions and war loans to the Allies to help crush Prussians the same cry is now being raised in America which, if carried into national action, would build up and American militarism far more terrible than German or Prussian militarism could ever be, and that because nowhere in the world has capitalism become so brazen in its greed and nowhere is the state so ready to kneel at the feet of capital.

Like a plague, the mad spirit is sweeping the country, infesting the clearest heads and staunchest hearts with the deathly germ of militarism. National security leagues, with cannon as their emblem of protection, naval leagues with women in their lead have sprung up all over the country, women who boast of representing the gentler sex, women who in pain and danger bring forth life and yet are ready to dedicate it to the Moloch War. Americanization societies with well-known liberals as members, they who but yesterday decried the patriotic clap-trap of to-day, are now lending themselves to befog the minds of the people and to help build up the same destructive institutions in America which they are directly and indirectly helping to pull down in Germany—militarism, the destroyer of youth, the raper of women, the annihilator of the best in the race, the very mower of life.

Even Woodrow Wilson, who not so long ago indulged in the phrase "A nation too proud to fight," who in the beginning of the war ordered prayers for peace, who in his proclamations spoke of the necessity of watchful waiting, even he has been whipped into line. He has now joined his worthy colleagues in the jingo movement, echoing their clamor for preparedness and their howl of "America for Americans." The difference between Wilson and Roosevelt is this: Roosevelt, a born bully, uses the club; Wilson, the historian, the college professor, wears the smooth polished university mask, but underneath it he, like Roosevelt, has but one aim, to serve the big interests, to add to those who are growing phenomenally rich by the manufacture of military supplies.

Woodrow Wilson, in his address before the Daughters of the American Revolution, gave his case away when he said, "I would rather be beaten than ostracized." To stand out against the Bethlehem, du Pont, Baldwin, Remington, Winchester metallic cartridges and the rest of the armament ring means political ostracism and death. Wilson knows that, therefore he betrays his original position, goes back on the bombast of "too proud to fight" and howls as loudly as any other cheap politician for preparedness and national glory, the silly pledge the navy league women intend to impose upon every school child: "I pledge myself to do all in my power to further the interests of my country, to uphold its institutions and to maintain the honor of its name and its flag. As I owe everything in life to my country, I consecrate my heart, mind and body to its service and promise to work for its advancement and security in times of peace and to shrink from no sacrifices or privation in its cause should I be called upon to act in its defence for the freedom, peace and happiness of our people."

To uphold the institutions of our country— that's it—the institutions which protect and sustain a handful of people in the robbery and plunder of the masses, the institutions which drain the blood of the native as well as of the foreigner, and turn it into wealth and power; the institutions which rob the alien of whatever originality he brings with him and in return gives him cheap Americanism, whose glory consists in mediocrity and arrogance.

The very proclaimers of "America first" have long before this betrayed the fundamental principles of real Americanism, of the kind of Americanism that Jefferson had in mind when he said that the best government is that which governs least; the kind of America that David Thoreau worked for when he proclaimed that the best government is the one that doesn't govern at all; or the other truly great Americans who aimed to make of this country a haven of refuge, who hoped that all the disinherited and oppressed people in coming to these shores would give character, quality and meaning to the country. That is not the America of the politician and munition speculators. Their America is powerfully portrayed in the idea of a young New York Sculptor; a hard cruel hand with long, lean, merciless fingers, crushing in over the heart of the immigrant, squeezing out its blood in order to coin dollars out of it and give the foreigner instead blighted hopes and stulted aspirations.

No doubt Woodrow Wilson has reason to defend these institutions. But what an ideal to hold out to the young generation! How is a military drilled and trained people to defend freedom, peace and happiness? This is what Major General O'Ryan has to say of an efficiently trained generation: "The soldier must be so trained that he becomes a mere automation; he must be so trained that it will destroy his initiative; he must be so trained that he is turned into a machine. The soldier must be forced into the military noose; he must be jacked up; he must be ruled by his superiors with pistol in hand."

This was not said by a Prussian Junker; not by a German barbarian; not by Treitschke or Bernhardi, but by an American Major General. And he is right. You cannot conduct war with equals; you cannot have militarism with free born men; you must have slaves, automatons, machines, obedient disciplined creatures, who will move, act, shoot and kill at the command of their superiors. That is preparedness, and nothing else.

It has been reported that among the speakers before the Navy League was Samuel Gompers. If that is true, it signalizes the greatest outrage upon labor at the hands of its own leaders. Preparedness is not directed only against the external enemy; it aims much more at the internal enemy. It concerns that element of labor which has learned not to hope for anything from our institutions, that awakened part of the working people which has realized that the war of classes underlies all wars among nations, and that if war is justified at all it is the war against economic dependence and political slavery, the two dominant issues involved in the struggle of the classes.

Already militarism has been acting its bloody part in every economic conflict, with the approval and support of the state. Where was the protest of Washington when "our men, women and children" were killed in Ludlow? Where was that high sounding outraged protest contained in the note to Germany? Or is there any difference in killing "our men, women and children" in Ludlow or on the high seas? Yes, indeed. The men, women and children at Ludlow were working people, belonging to the disinherited of the earth, foreigners who had to be given a taste of the glories of Americanism, while the passengers of the Lusitania represented wealth and station—therein lies the difference.

Preparedness, therefore, will only add to the power of the privileged few and help them to subdue, to enslave and crush labor. Surely Gompers must know that, and if he joins the howl of the military clique, he must stand condemned as a traitor to the cause of labor.

Just as it is with all the other institutions in our confused life, which were supposedly created for the good of the people and have accomplished the very reverse, so it will be with preparedness. Supposedly, America is to prepare for peace; but in reality it will be the cause of war. It always has been thus—all through bloodstained history, and it will continue until nation will refuse to fight against nation, and until the people of the world will stop preparing for slaughter. Preparedness is like the seed of a poisonous plant; placed in the soil, it will bear poisonous fruit. The European mass destruction is the fruit of that poisonous seed. It is imperative that the American workers realize this before they are driven by the jingoes into the madness that is forever haunted by the spectre of danger and invasion; they must know that to prepare for peace means to invite war, means to unloose the furies of death over land and seas.

That which has driven the masses of Europe into the trenches and to the battlefields is not their inner longing for war; it must be traced to the cut-throat competition for military equipment, for more efficient armies, for larger warships, for more powerful cannon. You cannot build up a standing army and then throw it back into a box like tin soldiers. Armies equipped to the teeth with weapons, with highly developed instruments of murder and backed by their military interests, have their own dynamic functions. We have but to examine into the nature of militarism to realize the truism of this contention.

Militarism consumes the strongest and most productive elements of each nation. Militarism swallows the largest part of the national revenue. Almost nothing is spent on education, art, literature and science compared with the amount devoted to militarism in times of peace, while in times of war everything else is set at naught; all life stagnates, all effort is curtailed; the very sweat and blood of the masses are used to feed this insatiable monster—militarism. Under such circumstances, it must become more arrogant, more aggressive, more bloated with its own importance. If for no

other reason, it is out of surplus energy that militarism must act to remain alive; therefore it will seek an enemy or create one artificially. In this civilized purpose and method, militarism is sustained by the state, protected by the laws of the land, is fostered by the home and the school, and glorified by public opinion. In other words, the function of militarism is to kill. It cannot live except through murder.

But the most dominant factor of military preparedness and the one which inevitably leads to war, is the creation of group interests, which consciously and deliberately work for the increase of armament whose purposes are furthered by creating the war hysteria. This group interest embraces all those engaged in the manufacture and sale of munition and in military equipment for personal gain and profit. For instance, the family Krupp, which owns the largest cannon munition plant in the world; its sinister influence in Germany, and in fact in many other countries, extends to the press, the school, the church and to statesmen of highest rank. Shortly before the war, Carl Liebknecht, the one brave public man in Germany now, brought to the attention of the Reichstag that the family Krupp had in its employ officials of the highest military position, not only in Germany, but in France and in other countries. Everywhere its emissaries have been at work, systematically inciting national hatreds and antagonisms. The same investigation brought to light an international war supply trust who cares not a hang for patriotism, or for love of the people, but who uses both to incite war and to pocket millions of profits out of the terrible bargain.

It is not at all unlikely that the history of the present war will trace its origin to this international murder trust. But is it always necessary for one generation to wade through oceans of blood and heap up mountains of human sacrifice that the next generation may learn a grain of truth from it all? Can we of today not profit by the cause which led to the European war, can we not learn that it was preparedness, thorough and efficient preparedness on the part of Germany and the other countries for military aggrandizement and material gain; above all can we not realize that preparedness in America must and will lead to the same result, the same barbarity, the same senseless sacrifice of life? Is America to follow suit, is it to be turned over to the American Krupps, the American military cliques? It almost seems so when one hears the jingo howls of the press, the blood and thunder tirades of bully Roosevelt, the sentimental twaddle of our college-bred President.

The more reason for those who still have a spark of libertarianism and humanity left to cry out against this great crime, against the outrage now being prepared and imposed upon the American people. It is not enough to claim being neutral; a neutrality which sheds crocodile tears with one eye and keeps the other riveted upon the profits from war supplies and war loans, is not neutrality. It is a hypocritical cloak to cover, the countries' crimes. Nor is it enough to join the bourgeois pacifists, who proclaim peace among the nations, while helping to perpetuate the war among the classes, a war which in reality, is at the bottom of all other wars.

It is this war of the classes that we must concentrate upon, and in that connection the war against false values, against evil institutions, against all social atrocities. Those who appreciate the urgent need of cooperating in great struggles must oppose military preparedness imposed by the state and capitalism for the destruction of the masses. They must organize the preparedness of the masses for the overthrow of both capitalism and the state. Industrial and economic preparedness is what the workers need. That alone leads to revolution at the bottom as against mass destruction from on top. That alone leads to true internationalism of labor against Kaiserdom, Kingdom, diplomacies, military cliques and bureaucracy. That alone will give the people the means to take their children out of the slums, out of the sweat shops and the cotton mills. That alone will enable them to inculcate in the coming generation a new ideal of brotherhood, to rear them in play and song and beauty; to bring up men and women, not automatons. That alone will enable woman to become the real mother of the race, who will give to the world creative men, and not soldiers who destroy. That alone leads to economic and social freedom, and does away with all wars, all crimes, and all injustice.

WOODROW WILSON, "DEMOCRACY OF BUSINESS" (1916)

In a speech made to a gathering of sales executives, Wilson argues that the United States will promote world peace and advance the cause of liberty by prying open the world to commerce.

These are days of incalculable change, my fellow citizens. It is impossible for anybody to predict anything that is certain, in detail, with regard to the future either of this country or of the world in the large movements of business; but one thing is perfectly clear, and that is that the United States will play a new part, and that it will be a part of unprecedented opportunity and of greatly increased responsibility.

The United States has had a very singular history in respect of its business relationships with the rest of the world. I have always believed, and I think you have always believed, that there is more business genius in the United States than anywhere else in the world; and yet America has apparently been afraid of touching too intimately the great processes of international exchange. America, of all countries in the world, has been timid; has not until recently, has not until within the last two or three years, provided itself with the fundamental instrumentalities for playing a large part in the trade of the world. America, which ought to have had the broadest vision of any nation, has raised up an extraordinary number of provincial thinkers, men who thought provincially about business, men who thought that the United States was not ready to take her competitive part in the struggle for the peaceful conquest of the world. For anybody who reflects philosophically upon the history of this country, that is the most amazing fact about it.

But the time for provincial thinkers has gone by. We must play a great part in the world whether we choose it or not. Do you know the significance of this single fact, that within the last year or two we have, speaking in large terms, ceased to be a debtor nation and become a creditor nation? We have more of the surplus gold of the world than we ever had before, and our business hereafter is to be to lend and to help and to promote the great peaceful enterprises of the world. We have got to finance the world in some important degree, and those who finance the world must understand it and rule it with their spirits and with their minds. We can not cabin and confine ourselves any longer, and so I said that I came here to congratulate you upon the great role that lies ahead of you to play. This is a salesmanship congress and hereafter salesmanship will have to be closely related in its outlook and scope to statesmanship, to international statesmanship. It will have to be touched with an intimate comprehension of the conditions of business and enterprise throughout the round globe, because America will have to place her goods by running her intelligence ahead of her goods. No amount of mere push, no amount of mere hustling, or, to speak in the western language, no amount of mere rustling, no amount of mere active enterprise, will suffice.

There have been two ways of doing business in the world outside of the lands in which the great manufactures have been made. One has been to try to force the tastes of the manufacturing country on the country in which the markets were being sought, and the other way has been to study the tastes and needs of the countries where the markets were being sought and suit your goods to those tastes and needs: and the latter method has beaten the former method. . . . .

There is a great deal of cant talked, my fellow citizens, about service. I wish the word had not been surrounded with so much sickly sentimentality, because it is a good, robust, red-blooded word, and it is the key to everything that concerns the peace and prosperity of the world. You can not force yourself upon anybody who is not obliged to take you. The only way in which you can be sure of being accepted is by being sure that you have got something to offer that is worth taking, and the only way you can be sure of that is by being sure that you wish to adapt it to the use and the service of the people to whom you are trying to sell.

I was trying to expound in another place the other day the long way and the short way to get together. The long way is to fight. I hear some

gentlemen say that they want to help Mexico, and the way they propose to help her is to overwhelm her with force. That is the long way to help Mexico as well as the wrong way. After the fighting you have a nation full of justified suspicion and animated by well-founded hostility and hatred, and then will you help them? Then will you establish cordial business relationships with them? Then will you go in as neighbors and enjoy their confidence? On the contrary, you will have shut every door as if it were of steel against you. What makes Mexico suspicious of us is that she does not believe as yet that we want to serve her. She believes that we want to possess her, and she has justification for the belief in the way in which some of our fellow-citizens have tried to exploit her privileges and possessions. For my part, I will not serve the ambitions of these gentlemen, but I will try to serve all America, so far as intercourse with Mexico is concerned, by trying to serve Mexico herself. There are some things that are not debatable. Of course, we have to defend our border. That goes without saying. Of course, we must make good our own sovereignty, but we must respect the sovereignty of Mexico. I am one of those—I have sometimes suspected that there were not many of them—who believe, absolutely believe . . . that a people has a right to do anything they please with their own country and their own government. I am old-fashioned enough to believe that, and I am going to stand by that belief. (That is for the benefit of those gentlemen who wish to butt in.)

Now, I use that as an illustration, my fellow citizens. What do we all most desire when the present tragical confusion of the world's affairs is over? We desire permanent peace, do we not? Permanent peace can grow in only one soil. That is the soil of actual good will, and good will can not exist without mutual comprehension. . . . And so, not to compare like with unlike, in the relationship of nations with each other, many of our antagonisms are based upon misunderstandings, and as long as you do not understand a country you can not trade with it. As long as you can not take its point of view you can not commend your goods to its purchase. As long as you go to it with a supercilious air, for example, and patronize it, as we have tried to do in some less developed countries, and tell them that this is what they ought to want whether they want it or not, you can not do business with them. You have got to approach them just as you really ought to approach all matters of human relationship. . . .

This, then, my friends, is the simple message that I bring you. Lift your eyes to the horizons of business: do not look too close at the little processes with which you are concerned, but let your thoughts and your imaginations run abroad throughout the whole world. And with the inspiration of the thought that you are Americans and are meant to carry liberty and justice and the principles of humanity wherever you go, go out and sell goods that will make the world more comfortable, and more happy, and convert them to the principles of America.

WOODROW WILSON, "PEACE WITHOUT VICTORY" (1917)

In November 1916, running on the slogan "He Kept Us Out of War," Wilson narrowly won reelection to a second term. Convinced that it was now incumbent upon the United States to prescribe terms for ending the slaughter in Europe, Wilson on January 22, 1917 detailed his plan for peace. He spoke, by his own lights, on behalf of all humanity.

On the eighteenth of December last I addressed an identic note to the governments of the nations now at war requesting them to state, more definitely than they had yet been stated by either group of belligerents, the terms upon which they would deem it possible to make peace. I spoke on behalf of humanity and of the rights of all neutral nations like our own, many of whose most vital interests the war puts in constant jeopardy.

The Central Powers united in a reply which stated merely that they were ready to meet their antagonists in conference to discuss terms of peace.

The Entente Powers have replied much more definitely and have stated, in general terms, indeed, but with sufficient definiteness to imply details, the arrangements, guarantees, and acts of reparation which they deem to be the indispensable conditions of a satisfactory settlement.

We are that much nearer a definite discussion of the peace which shall end the present war. We are that much nearer the discussion of the international concert which must thereafter hold the world at peace.

In every discussion of the peace that must end this war it is taken for granted that that peace must be followed by some definite concert of power which will make it virtually impossible that any such catastrophe should ever overwhelm us again. Every lover of mankind, every sane and thoughtful man must take that for granted.

I have sought this opportunity to address you because I thought that I owed it to you, as the council associated with me in the final determination of our international obligations, to disclose to you without reserve the thought and purpose that have been taking form in my mind in regard to the duty of our Government in the days to come when it will be necessary to lay afresh and upon a new plan the foundations of peace among the nations.

It is inconceivable that the people of the United States should play no part in that great enterprise. To take part in such a service will be the opportunity for which they have sought to prepare themselves by the very principles and purposes of their polity and the approved practices of their Government ever since the days when they set up a new nation in the high and honorable hope that it might in all that it was and did show mankind the way to liberty.

They cannot in honor withhold the service to which they are now about to be challenged. They do not wish to withhold it. But they owe it to themselves and to the other nations of the world to state the conditions under which they will feel free to render it. That service is nothing less than this, to add their authority and their power to the authority and force of other nations to guarantee peace and justice throughout the world. Such a settlement cannot now be long postponed. It is right that before it comes this Government should frankly formulate the conditions upon which it would feel justified in asking our people to approve its formal and solemn adherence to a League for Peace. I am here to attempt to state those conditions.

The present war must first be ended; but we owe it to candor and to a just regard for the opinion of mankind to say that, so far as our participation in guarantees of future peace is concerned, it makes a great deal of difference in what way and upon what terms it is ended. The treaties and agreements which bring it to an end must embody terms which will create a peace that is worth guaranteeing and preserving, a peace that will win the approval of mankind, not merely a peace that will serve the several interests and immediate aims of the nations engaged.

We shall have no voice in determining what those terms shall be, but we shall, I feel sure, have a voice in determining whether they shall be made lasting or not by the guarantees of a universal covenant; and our judgment upon what is fundamental and essential as a condition precedent to permanency should be spoken now, not afterwards when it may be too late.

No covenant of cooperative peace that does not include the peoples of the New World can suffice to keep the future safe against war; and yet there is only one sort of peace that the peoples of America could join in guaranteeing.

The elements of that peace must be elements that engage the confidence and satisfy the principles of the American governments, elements consistent with their political faith and with the practical convictions which the peoples of America have once for all embraced and undertaken to defend.

I do not mean to say that any American government would throw any obstacle in the way of any terms of peace the governments now at war might agree upon, or seek to upset them when made, whatever they might be. I only take it for granted that mere terms of peace between the belligerents will not satisfy even the belligerents themselves.

Mere agreements may not make peace secure. It will be absolutely necessary that a force be created as a guarantor of the permanency of the settlement so much greater than the force of any nation now engaged or any alliance hitherto formed or projected that no nation, no probable combination of nations could face or withstand it.

If the peace presently to be made is to endure, it must be a peace made secure by the organized major force of mankind.

The terms of the immediate peace agreed upon will determine whether it is a peace for which such a guarantee can be secured. The question upon which the whole future peace and policy of the world depends is this:

Is the present war a struggle for a just and secure peace, or only for a new balance of power? If it be only a struggle for a new balance of power, who will guarantee, who can guarantee, the stable equilibrium of the new arrangement?

Only a tranquil Europe can be a stable Europe. There must be, not a balance of power, but a community of power; not organized rivalries, but an organized common peace.

Fortunately we have received very explicit assurances on this point. The statesmen of both of the groups of nations now arrayed against one another have said, in terms that could not be misinterpreted, that it was no part of the purpose they had in mind to crush their antagonists. But the implications of these assurances may not be equally clear to all—may not be the same on both sides of the water. I think it will be serviceable if I attempt to set forth what we understand them to be.

They imply, first of all, that it must be a peace without victory. It is not pleasant to say this. I beg that I may be permitted to put my own interpretation upon it and that it may be understood that no other interpretation was in my thought.

I am seeking only to face realities and to face them without soft concealments. Victory would mean peace forced upon the loser, a victor's terms imposed upon the vanquished. It would be accepted in humiliation, under duress, at an intolerable sacrifice, and would leave a sting, a resentment, a bitter memory upon which terms of peace would rest, not permanently, but only as upon quicksand.

Only a peace between equals can last. Only a peace the very principle of which is equality and a common participation in a common benefit. The right state of mind, the right feeling between nations, is as necessary for a lasting peace as is the just settlement of vexed questions of territory or of racial and national allegiance.

The equality of nations upon which peace must be founded if it is to last must be an equality of rights; the guarantees exchanged must neither recognize nor imply a difference between big nations and small, between those that are powerful and those that are weak.

Right must be based upon the common strength, not upon the individual strength, of the nations upon whose concert peace will depend.

Equality of territory or of resources there of course cannot be; nor any other sort of equality not gained in the ordinary peaceful and legitimate development of the peoples themselves. But no one asks or expects anything more than an equality of rights. Mankind is looking now for freedom of life, not for equipoises of power.

And there is a deeper thing involved than even equality of right among organized nations. No peace can last, or ought to last, which does not recognize and accept the principle that governments derive all their just powers from the consent of the governed, and that no right anywhere exists to hand peoples about from sovereignty to sovereignty as if they were property.

I take it for granted, for instance, if I may venture upon a single example, that statesmen everywhere are agreed that there should be a united, independent, and autonomous Poland, and that henceforth inviolable security of life, of worship, and of industrial and social development should be guaranteed to all peoples who have lived hitherto under the power of governments devoted to a faith and purpose hostile to their own.

I speak of this, not because of any desire to exalt an abstract political principle which has always been held very dear by those who have sought to build up liberty in America, but for the same reason that I have spoken of the other conditions of peace which seem to me clearly indispensable,—because I wish frankly to uncover realities.

Any peace which does not recognize and accept this principle will inevitably be upset. It will not rest upon the affections or the convictions of mankind. The ferment of spirit of whole populations will fight subtly and constantly against it, and all the world will sympathize. The world can be at peace only if its life is stable, and there can be no stability where the will is in rebellion, where there is not tranquillity of spirit and a sense of justice, of freedom, and of right.

So far as practicable, moreover, every great people now struggling towards a full development of its resources and of its powers should be assured a direct outlet to the great highways of the sea. Where this cannot be done by the cession of territory, it can no doubt be done by the neutralization of direct rights of way under the general guarantee which will assure the peace itself. With a right comity of arrangement no nation need be shut away from free access to the open paths of the world's commerce.

And the paths of the sea must alike in law and in fact be free. The freedom of the seas is the *sine qua non* of peace, equality, and cooperation.

No doubt a somewhat radical reconsideration of many of the rules of international practice hitherto thought to be established may be necessary in order to make the seas indeed free and common in practically all circumstances for the use of mankind, but the motive for such changes is convincing and compelling. There can be no trust or intimacy between the peoples of the world without them.

The free, constant, unthreatened intercourse of nations is an essential part of the process of peace and of development. It need not be difficult either to define or to secure the freedom of the seas if the governments of the world sincerely desire to come to an agreement concerning it.

It is a problem closely connected with the limitation of naval armaments and the cooperation of the navies of the world in keeping the seas at once free and safe. And the question of limiting naval armaments opens the wider and perhaps more difficult question of the limitation of armies and of all programs of military preparation.

Difficult and delicate as these questions are, they must be faced with the utmost candor and decided in a spirit of real accommodation if peace is to come with healing in its wings, and come to stay. Peace cannot be had without concession and sacrifice. There can be no sense of safety and equality among the nations if great preponderating armaments are henceforth to continue here and there to be built up and maintained.

The statesmen of the world must plan for peace and nations must adjust and accommodate their policy to it as they have planned for war and made ready for pitiless contest and rivalry. The question of armaments, whether on land or sea, is the most immediately and intensely practical question connected with the future fortunes of nations and of mankind.

I have spoken upon these great matters without reserve and with the utmost explicitness because it has seemed to me to be necessary if the world's yearning desire for peace was anywhere to find free voice and utterance. Perhaps I am the only person in high authority amongst all the peoples of the world who is at liberty to speak and hold nothing back.

I am speaking as an individual, and yet I am speaking also, of course, as the responsible head of a great government, and I feel confident that I have said what the people of the United States would wish me to say. May I not add that I hope and believe that I am in effect speaking for liberals and friends of humanity in every nation and of every program of liberty?

I would fain believe that I am speaking for the silent mass of mankind everywhere who have as yet had no place or opportunity to speak their real hearts out concerning the death and ruin they see to have come already upon the persons and the homes they hold most dear.

And in holding out the expectation that the people and Government of the United States will join the other civilized nations of the world in guaranteeing the permanence of peace upon such terms as I have named I speak with the greater boldness and confidence because it is clear to every man who can think that there is in this promise no breach in either our traditions or our policy as a nation, but a fulfilment, rather, of all that we have professed or striven for.

I am proposing, as it were, that the nations should with one accord adopt the doctrine of President Monroe as the doctrine of the world: that no nation should seek to extend its polity over any other nation or people, but that every people should be left free to determine its own polity, its own way of development, unhindered, unthreatened, unafraid, the little along with the great and powerful.

I am proposing that all nations henceforth avoid entangling alliances which would draw them into competitions of power, catch them in a net of intrigue and selfish rivalry, and disturb their own affairs with influences intruded from without. There is no entangling alliance in a concert of power. When all unite to act in the same sense and with the same purpose all act in the common interest and are free to live their own lives under a common protection.

I am proposing government by the consent of the governed; that freedom of the seas which in international conference after conference representatives of the United States have urged with the eloquence of those who are the convinced disciples of liberty; and that moderation of armaments which makes of armies and navies a power for order merely, not an instrument of aggression or of selfish violence.

These are American principles, American policies. We could stand for no others. And they are also the principles and policies of forward looking men and women everywhere, of every modern nation, of every enlightened community. They are the principles of mankind and must prevail.

WOODROW WILSON, "WAR MESSAGE" (1917)

Committed to victory, the belligerents were unpersuaded by Wilson's appeal. Instead, in February 1917, as part of a last desperate effort to defeat the Allies, Germany announced that it was resuming submarine attacks against neutral shipping. An intercepted telegram from the Germany foreign ministry promising to restore territories lost in the war of 1846–1848 if Mexico went to war against the United States was the last straw. In April, Wilson appeared before Congress to ask for a declaration of war against Germany.

I have called the Congress into extraordinary session because there are serious, very serious, choices of policy to be made, and made immediately, which it was neither right nor constitutionally permissible that I should assume the responsibility of making.

On the third of February last I officially laid before you the extraordinary announcement of the Imperial German Government that on and after the first day of February it was its purpose to put aside all restraints of law or of humanity and use its submarines to sink every vessel that sought to approach either the ports of Great Britain and Ireland or the western coasts of Europe or any of the ports controlled by the enemies of Germany within the Mediterranean. That had seemed to be the object of the German submarine warfare earlier in the war, but since April of last year the Imperial Government had somewhat restrained the commanders of its undersea craft in conformity with its promise then given to us that passenger boats should not be sunk and that due warning would be given to all other vessels which its submarines might seek to destroy when no resistance was offered or escape attempted, and care taken that their crews were given at least a fair chance to save their lives in their open boats. The precautions taken were meager and haphazard enough, as was proved in distressing instance after instance in the progress of the cruel and unmanly business, but a certain degree of restraint was observed. The new policy has swept every restriction aside. Vessels of every kind, whatever their flag, their character, their cargo, their destination, their errand, have been ruthlessly sent to the bottom: without warning and without thought of help or mercy for those on board, the vessels of friendly neutrals along with those of belligerents. Even hospital ships and ships carrying relief to the sorely bereaved and stricken people of Belgium, though the latter were provided with safe conduct through the proscribed areas by the German Government itself and were distinguished by unmistakable marks of identity, have been sunk with the same reckless lack of compassion or of principle.

I was for a little while unable to believe that such things would in fact be done by any government that had hitherto subscribed to the humane practices of civilized nations. International law had its origin in the attempt to set up some law which would be respected and observed upon the seas, where no nation had right of dominion and where lay the free highways of the world. . . .

This minimum of right the German Government has swept aside under the plea of retaliation and necessity and because it had no weapons which it could use at sea except these which it is impossible to employ as it is employing them without throwing to the winds all scruples of humanity or of respect for the understandings that were supposed to underlie the intercourse of the world. I am not now thinking of the loss of property involved, immense and serious as that is, but only of the wanton and wholesale destruction of the lives of noncombatants, men, women, and children, engaged in pursuits which have always, even in the darkest periods of modern history, been deemed innocent and legitimate. Property can be paid for; the lives of peaceful and innocent people cannot be. The present German submarine warfare against commerce is a warfare against mankind.

It is a war against all nations. American ships have been sunk, American lives taken, in ways which it has stirred us very deeply to learn of, but the ships and people of other neutral and friendly nations have been sunk and overwhelmed in the waters in the same way. There has been no discrimination. The challenge is to all mankind. Each nation must decide for itself how it will meet it. The choice we make for ourselves must be made with a moderation of counsel and a temperateness of judgment befitting our character and our motives as a nation. We must put excited feeling away. Our motive will not be revenge or the victorious assertion of the physical might of the nation, but only the vindication of right, of human right, of which we are only a single champion.

When I addressed the Congress on the twenty-sixth of February last I thought that it would suffice to assert our neutral rights with arms, our right to use the seas against unlawful interference, our right to keep our people safe against unlawful violence. But armed neutrality, it now appears, is impracticable. Because submarines are in effect outlaws when used as the German submarines have been used against merchant shipping, it is impossible to defend ships against their attacks as the law of nations has assumed that merchantmen would defend themselves against privateers or cruisers, visible craft giving chase upon the open sea. It is common prudence in such circumstances, grim necessity indeed, to endeavor to destroy them before they have shown their own intention. They must be dealt with upon sight, if dealt with at all. The German Government denies the right of neutrals to use arms at all within the areas of the sea which it has proscribed, even in the defense of rights which no modern publicist has ever before questioned their right to defend. The intimation is conveyed that the armed guards which we have placed on our merchant ships will be treated as beyond the pale of law and subject to be dealt with as pirates would be. Armed neutrality is ineffectual enough at best; in such circumstances and in the face of such pretensions it is worse than ineffectual: it is likely only to produce what it was meant to prevent; it is practically certain to draw us into the war without either the rights or the effectiveness of belligerents. There is one choice we cannot make, we are incapable of making: we will not choose the path of submission and suffer the most sacred rights of our Nation and our people to be ignored or violated. The wrongs against which we now array ourselves are no common wrongs; they cut to the very roots of human life.

With a profound sense of the solemn and even tragical character of the step I am taking and of the grave responsibilities which it involves, but in unhesitating obedience to what I deem my constitutional duty, I advise that the Congress declare the recent course of the Imperial German Government to be in fact nothing less than war against the government and people of the United States; that it formally accept the status of belligerent which has thus been thrust upon it, and that it take immediate steps not only to put the country in a more thorough state of defense but also to exert all its power and employ all its resources to bring the Government of the German Empire to terms and end the war.

What this will involve is clear. It will involve the utmost practicable cooperation in counsel and action with the governments now at war with Germany, and, as incident to that, the extension to those governments of the most liberal financial credit, in order that our resources may so far as possible be added to theirs. It will involve the organization and mobilization of all the material resources of the country to supply the materials of war and serve the incidental needs of the Nation in the most abundant and yet the most economical and efficient way possible. It will

involve the immediate full equipment of the navy in all respects but particularly in supplying it with the best means of dealing with the enemy's submarines. It will involve the immediate addition to the armed forces of the United States already provided for by law in case of war at least five hundred thousand men, who should, in my opinion, be chosen upon the principle of universal liability to service, and also the authorization of subsequent additional increments of equal force so soon as they may be needed and can be handled in training. It will involve also, of course, the granting of adequate credits to the Government, sustained, I hope, so far as they can equitably be sustained by the present generation, by well conceived taxation.

I say sustained so far as may be equitable by taxation because it seems to me that it would be most unwise to base the credits which will now be necessary entirely on money borrowed. It is our duty, I most respectfully urge, to protect our people so far as we may against the very serious hardships and evils which would be likely to arise out of the inflation which would be produced by vast loans.

In carrying out the measures by which these things are to be accomplished we should keep constantly in mind the wisdom of interfering as little as possible in our own preparation and in the equipment of our own military forces with the duty—for it will be a very practical duty—of supplying the nations already at war with Germany with the materials which they can obtain only from us or by our assistance. They are in the field and we should help them in every way to be effective there.

I shall take the liberty of suggesting, through the several executive departments of the Government, for the consideration of your committees, measures for the accomplishment of the several objects I have mentioned. I hope that it will be your pleasure to deal with them as having been framed after very careful thought by the branch of the Government upon which the responsibility of conducting the war and safeguarding the Nation will most directly fall.

While we do these things, these deeply momentous things, let us be very clear, and make very clear to all the world what our motives and our objects are. My own thought has not been driven from its habitual and normal course by the unhappy events of the last two months, and I do not believe that the thought of the Nation has been altered or clouded by them. I have exactly the same things in mind now that I had in mind when I addressed the Senate on the twenty-second of January last, the same that I had in mind when I addressed the Congress on the third of February and on the twenty-sixth of February. Our object now, as then, is to vindicate the principles of peace and justice in the life of the world as against selfish and autocratic power and to set up amongst the really free and self-governed peoples of the world such a concert of purpose and of action as will henceforth insure the observance of those principles.

Neutrality is no longer feasible or desirable where the peace of the world is involved and the freedom of its peoples, and the menace to that peace and freedom lies in the existence of autocratic governments backed by organized force which is controlled wholly by their will, not by the will of their people. We have seen the last of neutrality in such circumstances. We are at the beginning of an age in which it will be insisted that the same standards of conduct and of responsibility for wrong done shall be observed among nations and their governments that are observed among the individual citizens of civilized states.

We have no quarrel with the German people. We have no feeling towards them but one of sympathy and friendship. It was not upon their impulse that their government acted in entering this war. It was not with their previous knowledge or approval. It was a war determined upon as wars used to be determined upon in the old, unhappy days when peoples were nowhere consulted by their rulers and wars were provoked and waged in the interest of dynasties or of little groups of ambitious men who were accustomed to use their fellow men as pawns and tools. Self-governed nations do not fill their neighbor states with spies or set the course of intrigue to bring about some critical posture of affairs which will give them an opportunity to strike and make conquest. Such designs can be successfully worked out only under cover and where no one has the right to ask questions. Cunningly contrived plans of deception or aggression, carried, it may be, from generation to generation, can be worked out and kept from the

light only within the privacy of courts or behind the carefully guarded confidences of a narrow and privileged class. They are happily impossible where public opinion commands and insists upon full information concerning all the nation's affairs.

A steadfast concert for peace can never be maintained except by a partnership of democratic nations. No autocratic government could be trusted to keep faith within it or observe its covenants. It must be a league of honor, a partnership of opinion. Intrigue would eat its vitals away; the plottings of inner circles who could plan what they would and render account to no one would be a corruption seated at its very heart. Only free peoples can hold their purpose and their honor steady to a common end and prefer the interests of mankind to any narrow interest of their own.

Does not every American feel that assurance has been added to our hope for the future peace of the world by the wonderful and heartening things that have been happening within the last few weeks in Russia? Russia was known by those who knew it best to have been always in fact democratic at heart, in all the vital habits of her thought, in all the intimate relationships of her people that spoke their natural instinct, their habitual attitude towards life. The autocracy that crowned the summit of her political structure, long as it had stood and terrible as was the reality of its power, was not in fact Russian in origin, character, or purpose; and now it has been shaken off and the great, generous Russian people have been added in all their naive majesty and might to the forces that are fighting for freedom in the world, for justice, and for peace. Here is a fit partner for a League of Honor.

One of the things that has served to convince us that the Prussian autocracy was not and could never be our friend is that from the very outset of the present war it has filled our unsuspecting communities and even our offices of government with spies and set criminal intrigues everywhere afoot against our national unity of counsel, our peace within and without, our industries and our commerce. Indeed it is now evident that its spies were here even before the war began; and it is unhappily not a matter of conjecture but a fact proved in our courts of justice that the intrigues which have more than once come perilously near to disturbing the peace and dislocating the industries of the country have been carried on at the instigation, with the support, and even under the personal direction of official agents of the Imperial Government accredited to the Government of the United States. Even in checking these things and trying to extirpate them we have sought to put the most generous interpretation possible upon them because we knew that their source lay, not in any hostile feeling or purpose of the German people towards us (who were, no doubt, as ignorant of them as we ourselves were), but only in the selfish designs of a Government that did what it pleased and told its people nothing. But they have played their part in serving to convince us at last that that Government entertains no real friendship for us and means to act against our peace and security at its convenience. That it means to stir up enemies against us at our very doors the intercepted note to the German Minister at Mexico City is eloquent evidence.

We are accepting this challenge of hostile purpose because we know that in such a Government, following such methods, we can never have a friend; and that in the presence of its organized power, always lying in wait to accomplish we know not what purpose, there can be no assured security for the democratic Governments of the world. We are now about to accept gauge of battle with this natural foe to liberty and shall, if necessary, spend the whole force of the nation to check and nullify its pretensions and its power. We are glad, now that we see the facts with no veil of false pretense about them, to fight thus for the ultimate peace of the world and for the liberation of its peoples, the German peoples included: for the rights of nations great and small and the privilege of men everywhere to choose their way of life and of obedience. The world must be made safe for democracy. Its peace must be planted upon the tested foundations of political liberty. We have no selfish ends to serve. We desire no conquest, no dominion. We seek no indemnities for ourselves, no material compensation for the sacrifices we shall freely make. We are but one of the champions of the rights of mankind. We shall be satisfied when those rights have been made as secure as the faith and the freedom of nations can make them.

Just because we fight without rancor and without selfish object, seeking nothing for ourselves but what we shall wish to share with all free peoples, we shall, I feel confident, conduct our operations as belligerents without passion and ourselves observe with proud punctilio the principles of right and of fair play we profess to be fighting for.

I have said nothing of the Governments allied with the Imperial Government of Germany because they have not made war upon us or challenged us to defend our right and our honor. The Austro-Hungarian Government has, indeed, avowed its unqualified endorsement and acceptance of the reckless and lawless submarine warfare adopted now without disguise by the Imperial German Government, and it has therefore not been possible for this Government to receive Count Tarnowski, the Ambassador recently accredited to this Government by the Imperial and Royal Government of Austria-Hungary; but that Government has not actually engaged in warfare against citizens of the United States on the seas, and I take the liberty, for the present at least, of postponing a discussion of our relations with the authorities at Vienna. We enter this war only where we are clearly forced into it because there are no other means of defending our rights.

It will be all the easier for us to conduct ourselves as belligerents in a high spirit of right and fairness because we act without animus, not in enmity towards a people or with the desire to bring any injury or disadvantage upon them, but only in armed opposition to an irresponsible government which has thrown aside all considerations of humanity and of right and is running amuck. We are, let me say again, the sincere friends of the German people, and shall desire nothing so much as the early reestablishment of intimate relations of mutual advantage between us, however hard it may be for them, for the time being, to believe that this is spoken from our hearts. We have borne with their present Government through all these bitter months because of that friendship, exercising a patience and forbearance which would otherwise have been impossible. We shall, happily, still have an opportunity to prove that friendship in our daily attitude and actions towards the millions of men and women of German birth and native sympathy who live amongst us and share our life, and we shall be proud to prove it towards all who are in fact loyal to their neighbors and to the Government in the hour of test. They are, most of them, as true and loyal Americans as if they had never known any other fealty or allegiance. They will be prompt to stand with us in rebuking and restraining the few who may be of a different mind and purpose. If there should be disloyalty, it will be dealt with with a firm hand of stern repression; but, if it lifts its head at all, it will lift it only here and there and without countenance except from a lawless and malignant few.

It is a distressing and oppressive duty, Gentlemen of the Congress, which I have performed in thus addressing you. There are, it may be many months of fiery trial and sacrifice ahead of us. It is a fearful thing to lead this great peaceful people into war, into the most terrible and disastrous of all wars, civilization itself seeming to be in the balance. But the right is more precious than peace, and we shall fight for the things which we have always carried nearest our hearts—for democracy, for the right of those who submit to authority to have a voice in their own Governments, for the rights and liberties of small nations, for a universal dominion of right by such a concert of free peoples as shall bring peace and safety to all nations and make the world itself at last free. To such a task we can dedicate our lives and our fortunes, every thing that we are and everything that we have, with the pride of those who know that the day has come when America is privileged to spend her blood and her might for the principles that gave her birth and happiness and the peace which she has treasured. God helping her, she can do no other.

GEORGE NORRIS, "AGAINST ENTRY INTO WAR" (1917)

Congress acceded to Wilson's request, although not without opposition. Here Nebraska Senator George Norris (1861–1944), a progressive Republican, makes the case for staying out of war. Among other points, Norris argues that American neutrality has been a sham, its actions actually working to the benefit of Great Britain and France.

Mr. President, while I am most emphatically and sincerely opposed to taking any step that will force our country into the useless and senseless war now being waged in Europe, yet if this resolution passes I shall not permit my feeling of opposition to its passage to interfere in any way with my duty either as a Senator or as a citizen in bringing success and victory to American arms. I am bitterly opposed to my country entering the war, but if, notwithstanding my opposition, we do enter it, all of my energy and all of my power will be behind our flag in carrying it on to victory.

The resolution now before the Senate is a declaration of war. Before taking this momentous step, and while standing on the brink of this terrible vortex, we ought to pause and calmly and judiciously consider the terrible consequences of the step we are about to take. We ought to consider likewise the route we have recently traveled and ascertain whether we have reached our present position in a way that is compatible with the neutral position which we claimed to occupy at beginning and through the various stages of this unholy and unrighteous war.

No close student of recent history will deny that both Great Britain and Germany have, on numerous occasions since the beginning of the war, flagrantly violated in the most serious manner the rights of neutral vessels and neutral nations under existing international law as recognized up to the beginning of this war by the civilized world.

The reason given by the President in asking Congress to declare war against Germany is that the German government has declared certain war zones, within which, by the use of submarines, she sinks, without notice, American ships and destroys American lives. . . . The first war zone was declared by Great Britain. She gave us and the world notice of it on, the 4th day of November, 1914. The zone became effective Nov. 5, 1914. . . . This zone so declared by Great Britain covered the whole of the North Sea. . . .

The first German war zone was declared on the 4th day of February, 1915, just three months after the British war zone was declared. Germany gave fifteen days' notice of the establishment of her zone, which became effective on the 18th day of February, 1915. The German war zone covered the English Channel and the high seawaters around the British Isles. . . .

It is unnecessary to cite authority to show that both of these orders declaring military zones were illegal and contrary to international law. It is sufficient to say that our government has officially declared both of them to be illegal and has officially protested against both of them. The only difference is that in the case of Germany we have persisted in our protest, while in the case of England we have submitted.

What was our duty as a government and what were our rights when we were confronted with these extraordinary orders declaring these military zones? First, we could have defied both of them and could have gone to war against both of these nations for this violation of international law and interference with our neutral rights. Second, we had the technical right to defy one and to acquiesce in the other. Third, we could, while denouncing them both as illegal, have acquiesced in them both and thus remained neutral with both sides, although not agreeing with either as to the righteousness of their respective orders. We could have said to American shipowners that, while these orders are both contrary to international law and are both unjust, we do not believe that the provocation is sufficient to cause us to go to war for the defense of our rights as a neutral nation, and, therefore, American ships and American citizens will go into these zones at their own peril and risk.

Fourth, we might have declared an embargo against the shipping from American ports of any merchandise to either one of these governments that persisted in maintaining its military zone. We might have refused to permit the sailing of any ship from any American port to either of these military zones. In my judgment, if we had pursued this course, the zones would have been of short duration. England would have been compelled to take her mines out of the North Sea in order to get any supplies from our country. When her mines were taken out of the North

Sea then the German ports upon the North Sea would have been accessible to American shipping and Germany would have been compelled to cease her submarine warfare in order to get any supplies from our nation into German North Sea ports.

There are a great many American citizens who feel that we owe it as a duty to humanity to take part in the war. Many instances of cruelty and inhumanity can be found on both sides. Men are often biased in their judgment on account of their sympathy and their interests. To my mind, what we ought to have maintained from the beginning was the strictest neutrality. If we had done this, I do not believe we would have been on the verge of war at the present time. We had a right as a nation, if we desired, to cease at any time to be neutral. We had a technical right to respect the English war zone and to disregard the German war zone, but we could not do that and be neutral. I have no quarrel to find with the man who does not desire our country to remain neutral. While many such people are moved by selfish motives and hopes of gain, I have no doubt that in a great many instances, through what I believe to be a misunderstanding of the real condition, there are many honest, patriotic citizens who think we ought to engage in this war and who are behind the President in his demand that we should declare war against Germany. I think such people err in judgment and to a great extent have been misled as to the real history and the true facts by the almost unanimous demand of the great combination of wealth that has a direct financial interest in our participation in the war. . . .

We have loaned many hundreds of millions of dollars to the Allies in this controversy. While such action was legal and countenanced by international law, there is no doubt in my mind but the enormous amount of money loaned to the Allies in this country has been instrumental in bringing about a public sentiment in favor of our country taking a course that would make every bond worth a hundred cents on the dollar and making the payment of every debt certain and sure. Through this instrumentality and also through the instrumentality of others who have not only made millions out of the war in the manufacture of munitions, etc., and who would expect to make millions more if our country can be drawn into the catastrophe, a large number of the great newspapers and news agencies of the country have been controlled and enlisted in the greatest propaganda that the world has ever known to manufacture sentiment in favor of war.

It is now demanded that the American citizens shall be used as insurance policies to guarantee the safe delivery of munitions of war to belligerent nations. The enormous profits of munition manufacturers, stockbrokers, and bond dealers must be still further increased by our entrance into the war. This has brought us to the present moment, when Congress, urged by the President and backed by the artificial sentiment, is about to declare war and engulf our country in the greatest holocaust that the world has ever known.

In showing the position of the bondholder and the stockbroker, I desire to read an extract from a letter written by a member of the New York Stock Exchange to his customers. This writer says:

> Regarding the war as inevitable, Wall Street believes that it would be preferable to this uncertainty about the actual date of its commencement. Canada and Japan are at war and are more prosperous than ever before. The popular view is that stocks would have a quick, clear, sharp reaction immediately upon outbreak of hostilities, and that then they would enjoy an old fashioned bull market such as followed the outbreak of war with Spain in 1898. The advent of peace would force a readjustment of commodity prices and would probably mean a postponement of new enterprises. As peace negotiations would be long drawn out, the period of waiting and uncertainty for business would be long. If the United States does not go to war, it is nevertheless good opinion that the preparedness program will compensate in good measure for the loss of the stimulus of actual war.

Here we have the Wall Street view. Here we have the man representing the class of people who will be made prosperous should we become entangled in the present war, who have already made millions of dollars, and who will make many hundreds of millions more if we get into the war. Here we have the cold-blooded proposition that war brings prosperity to that class of people who are within the viewpoint of this writer.

He expresses the view, undoubtedly, of Wall Street, and of thousands of men elsewhere who see only dollars coming to them through the handling of stocks and bonds that will be necessary in case of war. "Canada and Japan," he says, "are at war, and are more prosperous than ever before."

To whom does war bring prosperity? Not to the soldier who for the munificent compensation of $16 per month shoulders his musket and goes into the trench, there to shed his blood and to die if necessary; not to the broken-hearted widow who waits for the return of the mangled body of her husband; not to the mother who weeps at the death of her brave boy; not to the little children who shiver with cold; not to the babe who suffers from hunger; nor to the millions of mothers and daughters who carry broken hearts to their graves. War brings no prosperity to the great mass of common and patriotic citizens. It increases the cost of living of those who toil and those who already must strain every effort to keep soul and body together. War brings prosperity to the stock gambler on Wall Street—to those who are already in possession of more wealth than can be realized or enjoyed. . . .

We are taking a step to-day that is fraught with untold danger. We are going into war upon the command of gold. We are going to run the risk of sacrificing millions of our countrymen's lives in order that other countrymen may coin their lifeblood into money. And even if we do not cross the Atlantic and go into the trenches, we are going to pile up a debt that the toiling masses that shall come many generations after us will have to pay. Unborn millions will bend their backs in toil in order to pay for the terrible step we are now about to take. We are about to do the bidding of wealth's terrible mandate. By our act we will make millions of our countrymen suffer, and the consequences of it may well be that millions of our brethren must shed their lifeblood, millions of broken-hearted women must weep, millions of children must suffer with cold, and millions of babes must die from hunger, and all because we want to preserve the commercial right of American citizens to deliver munitions of war to belligerent nations.

Robert LaFollette, "War with Germany" (1917)

Another impassioned opponent of U.S. intervention in 1917 was Robert LaFollette (1855–1925), a progressive Republican from Wisconsin. He argued to no avail. The final vote for war was 82 to 6 in the Senate and 373 to 50 in the House of Representatives.

Mr. President, I had supposed until recently that it was the duty of senators and representatives in Congress to vote and act according to their convictions on all public matters that came before them for consideration and decision. Quite another doctrine has recently been promulgated by certain newspapers, which unfortunately seems to have found considerable support elsewhere, and that is the doctrine of "standing back of the President" without inquiring whether the President is right or wrong.

For myself, I have never subscribed to that doctrine and never shall. I shall support the President in the measures he proposes when I believe them to be right. I shall oppose measures proposed by the President when I believe them to be wrong. The fact that the matter which the President submits for consideration is of the greatest importance is only an additional reason why we should be sure that we are right and not to be swerved from that conviction or intimidating in its expression by any influence of its power whatsoever.

If it is important for us to speak and vote our convictions in matters of internal policy, though we may unfortunately be in disagreement with the President, it is infinitely more important for us to speak and vote our convictions when the question is one of peace or war, certain to involve the lives and fortunes of many of our people and, it may be, the destiny of all of them and of the civilized world as well. If, unhappily, on such momentous questions the most patient research and conscientious consideration we could give to them leave us in disagreement with the President, I know of no course to take except to oppose, regretfully but not the less firmly, the demands of the Executive. . . .

It is unfortunately true that a portion of the irresponsible and war-crazed press, feeling secure in the authority of the President's condemnation of the senators who opposed the armed-ship bill, have published the most infamous and scurrilous libels on the honor of the senators who opposed that bill. It was particularly unfortunate that such malicious falsehoods should fill the public press of the country at a time when every consideration for our country required that a spirit of fairness should be observed in the discussions of the momentous questions under consideration. . . .

The poor, sir, who are the ones called upon to rot in the trenches, have no organized power, have no press to voice their will upon this question of peace or war; but, oh, Mr. President, at some time they will be heard. I hope and I believe they will be heard in an orderly and a peaceful way. I think they may be heard from before long. I think, sir, if we take this step, when the people today who are staggering under the burden of supporting families at the present prices of the necessaries of life find those prices multiplied, when they are raised 100 percent, or 200 percent, as they will be quickly, aye, sir, when beyond that those who pay taxes come to have their taxes doubled and again doubled to pay the interest on the nontaxable bonds held by [J. P.] Morgan and his combinations, which have been issued to meet this war, there will come an awakening; they will have their day and they will be heard. It will be as certain and as inevitable as the return of the tides, and as resistless, too. . . .

In his message of April 2, the President said: We have no quarrel with the German people—it was not upon their impulse that their government acted in entering this war; it was not with their previous knowledge or approval.

Again he says: We are, let me say again, sincere friends of the German people and shall desire nothing so much as the early re-establishment of intimate relations of mutual advantage between us. At least, the German people, then, are not outlaws.

What is the thing the President asks us to do to these German people of whom he speaks so highly and whose sincere friends he declares us to be? Here is what he declares we shall do in this war. We shall undertake, he says—

The utmost practicable cooperation in council and action with the governments now at war with Germany, and as an incident to that, the extension to those governments of the most liberal financial credits in order that our resources may so far as possible, be added to theirs.

"Practicable cooperation!" Practicable cooperation with England and her allies in starving to death the old men and women, the children, the sick and the maimed of Germany. The thing we are asked to do is the thing I have stated. It is idle to talk of a war upon a government only. We are leagued in this war, or it is the President's proposition that we shall be so leagued, with the hereditary enemies of Germany. Any war with Germany, or any other country for that matter, would be bad enough, but there are not words strong enough to voice my protest against the proposed combination with the Entente Allies.

When we cooperate with those governments we endorse their methods; we endorse the violations of international law by Great Britain; we endorse the shameful methods of warfare against which we have again and again protested in this war; we endorse her purpose to wreak upon the German people the animosities which for years her people have been taught to cherish against Germany; finally, when the end comes, whatever it may be, we find ourselves in cooperation with our ally, Great Britain and if we cannot resist now the pressure she is exerting to carry us into the war, how can we hope to resist, then, the thousand fold greater pressure she will exert to bend us to her purposes and compel compliance with her demands?

We do not know what they are. We do not know what is in the minds of those who have made the compact, but we are to subscribe to it. We are irrevocably, by our votes here, to marry ourselves to a non-divorceable proposition veiled from us now. Once enlisted, once in the copartnership, we will be carried through with the purposes, whatever they may be, of which we now know nothing.

Sir, if we are to enter upon this war in the manner the President demands, let us throw pretense to the winds, let us be honest, let us admit that this is a ruthless war against not only Germany's Army and her Navy but against her civilian population as well, and frankly state that the purpose of Germany's hereditary European enemies has become our purpose.

Again, the President says "we are about to accept the gage of battle with this natural foe of liberty and shall, if necessary, spend the whole force of the nation to check and nullify its pretensions and its power." That much, at least, is clear; that program is definite. The whole force and power of this nation, if necessary, is to be used to bring victory to the Entente Allies, and to us as their ally in this war. Remember, that not yet has the "whole force" of one of the warring nations been used.

Countless millions are suffering from want and privation; countless other millions are dead and rotting on foreign battlefields; countless other millions are crippled and maimed, blinded, and dismembered; upon all and upon their children's children for generations to come has been laid a burden of debt which must be worked out in poverty and suffering, but the "whole force" of no one of the warring nations has yet been expended; but our "whole force" shall be expended, so says the President. We are pledged by the President, so far as he can pledge us, to make this fair, free, and happy land of ours the same shambles and bottomless pit of horror that we see in Europe today.

Just a word of comment more upon one of the points in the President's address. He says that this is a war "for the things which we have always carried nearest to our hearts—for democracy, for the right of those who submit to authority to have a voice in their own government." In many places throughout the address is this exalted sentiment given expression.

It is a sentiment peculiarly calculated to appeal to American hearts and, when accompanied by acts consistent with it, is certain to receive our support; but in this same connection, and strangely enough, the President says that we have become convinced that the German government as it now exists—"Prussian autocracy" he calls it—can never again maintain friendly relations with us. His expression is that "Prussian autocracy was not and could never be our friend," and repeatedly throughout the address the suggestion is made that if the German people would overturn their government, it would probably be the way to peace. So true is this that the dispatches from London all hailed the message of the President as sounding the death knell of Germany's government.

But the President proposes alliance with Great Britain, which, however liberty-loving its people, is a hereditary monarchy, with a hereditary ruler, with a hereditary House of Lords, with a hered itary landed system, with a limited and restricted suffrage for one class and a multiplied suffrage power for another, and with grinding industrial conditions for all the wage workers. The President has not suggested that we make our support of Great Britain conditional to her granting home rule to Ireland, or Egypt, or India. We rejoice in the establishment of a democracy in Russia, but it will hardly be contended that if Russia was still an autocratic government, we would not be asked to enter this alliance with her just the same.

Italy and the lesser powers of Europe, Japan in the Orient; in fact, all the countries with whom we are to enter into alliance, except France and newly revolutionized Russia, are still of the old order—and it will be generally conceded that no one of them has done as much for its people in the solution of municipal problems and in securing social and industrial reforms as Germany.

Is it not a remarkable democracy which leagues itself with allies already far overmatching in strength the German nation and holds out to such beleaguered nation the hope of peace only at the price of giving up their government? I am not talking now of the merits or demerits of any government, but I am speaking of a profession of democracy that is linked in action with the most brutal and domineering use of autocratic power. Are the people of this country being so well-represented in this war movement that we need to go abroad to give other people control of their governments?

Will the President and the supporters of this war bill submit it to a vote of the people before the declaration of war goes into effect? Until we are willing to do that, it becomes us to offer as an excuse for our entry into the war the unsupported claim that this war was forced upon the German people by their government "without their previous knowledge or approval."

Who has registered the knowledge or approval of the American people of the course this Congress is called upon to take in declaring war upon Germany? Submit the question to the people, you who support it. You who support it dare not do it, for you know that by a vote of more than ten to one the American people as a body would register their declaration against it.

In the sense that this war is being forced upon our people without their knowing why and without their approval, and that wars are usually forced upon all peoples in the same way, there is some truth in the statement; but I venture to say that the response which the German people have made to the demands of this war shows that it has a degree of popular support which the war upon which we are entering has not and never will have among our people. The espionage bills, the conscription bills, and other forcible military measures which we understand are being ground out of the war machine in this country is the complete proof that those responsible for this war fear that it has no popular support and that armies sufficient to satisfy the demand of the Entente Allies cannot be recruited by voluntary enlistments. . . .

Now, I want to repeat: It was our absolutely right as a neutral to ship food to the people of Germany. That is a position that we have fought for through all of our history. . . .

In the first days of the war with Germany, Great Britain set aside, so far as her own conduct was concerned, all these rules of civilized naval warfare.

According to the Declaration of London, well as the rules of international law, there could have been no interference in trade between the United States and Holland or Scandinavia and other countries, except in the case of ships which could be proven to carry absolute contraband, like arms and ammunition, with ultimate German destination. There could have been no interference with the importation into Germany of any goods on the free list, such as cotton, rubber, and hides. There could have properly been no interference with our export to Germany of anything on the conditional contraband list, like flour, grain, and provisions, unless it could be proven by England that such shipments were intended for the use of the German Army. There could be no lawful interference with foodstuffs intended for the civilian population of Germany, and if those foodstuffs were shipped to other countries to be reshipped to Germany no question could be raised that they were not intended for the use of the civilian population.

It is well to recall at this point our rights as declared by the Declaration of London and as declared without the Declaration of London by settled principles of international law, for we have during the present war become so used to having Great Britain utterly disregard our rights on the high seas that we have really forgotten that we have any, as far as Great Britain and her allies are concerned.

Great Britain, by what she called her modifications of the Declaration of London, shifted goods from the free list to the conditional contraband and contraband lists, reversed the presumption of destination for civilian population, and abolished the principle that a blockade to exist at all must be effective.

It is not my purpose to go into detail into the violations of our neutrality by any of the belligerents. While Germany has again and again yielded to our protests, I do not recall a single instance in which a protest we have made to Great Britain has won for us the slightest consideration, except for a short time in the case of cotton. I will not stop to dwell upon the multitude of minor violations of our neutral rights, such as seizing our mails, violations of the neutral flag, seizing and appropriating our goods without the least warrant or authority in law, and impressing, seizing, and taking possession of our vessels and putting them into her own service. . . .

The only reason why we have not suffered the sacrifice of just as many ships and just as many lives from the violation of our rights by the war zone and the submarine mines of Great Britain as we have through the unlawful acts of Germany in making her war zone in violation of our neutral rights is simply because we have submitted to Great Britain's dictation. If our ships had been sent into her forbidden high-sea war zone as they have into the proscribed area Germany marked out on the high seas as a war zone, we would have had the same loss of life and property in the one case as in the other; but because we avoided doing that, in the case of England, and acquiesced in her violation of law, we have not only a legal but a moral responsibility for the position in which Germany has been placed by our collusion and cooperation with Great Britain. By suspending the rule with respect to neutral rights in Great Britain's case, we have been actively aiding her in starving the civil population of Germany. We have helped to drive Germany into a corner, her back to the wall, to fight with what weapons she can lay her hands on to prevent the starving of her women and children, her old men and babes.

The flimsy claim which has sometimes been put forth that possibly the havoc in the North Sea was caused by German mines is too absurd for consideration. . . .

I am talking now about principles. You cannot distinguish between the principles which allowed England to mine a large area of the Atlantic Ocean and the North Sea in order to shut in Germany, and the principle on which Germany by her submarines seeks to destroy all shipping which enters the war zone which she has laid out around the British Isles.

The English mines are intended to destroy without warning every ship that enters the war zone she has proscribed, killing or drowning every passenger that cannot find some means of escape. It is neither more nor less than that which Germany tries to do with her submarines in her war zone. We acquiesced in England's action without protest. It is proposed that we now go to war with Germany for identically the same action upon her part. . . .

I say again that when two nations are at war any neutral nation, in order to preserve its character as a neutral nation, must exact the same conduct from both warring nations; both must equally obey the principles of international law. If a neutral nation fails in that, then its rights upon the high seas—to adopt the President's phrase—are relative and not absolute. There can be no greater violation of our neutrality than the requirement that one of two belligerents shall adhere to the settled principles of law and that the other shall have the advantage of not doing so. The respect that German naval authorities were required to pay to the rights of our people upon the high seas would depend upon the question whether we had exacted the same rights from German's enemies. If we had not done so, we lost our character as a neutral nation and our people unfortunately had lost the protection that belongs to neutrals. Our responsibility was joint in the sense that we must exact the same conduct from both belligerents.

The failure to treat the belligerent nations of Europe alike, the failure to reject the unlawful "war zones" of both Germany and Great Britain is wholly accountable for our present dilemma. We should not seek to hide our blunder behind the smoke of battle to inflame the mind of our people by half-truths into the frenzy of war in order that they may never appreciate the real cause of it until it is too late. I do not believe that our national honor is served by such a course. The right way is the honorable way.

George M. Cohan, "Over There" (1917)

A popular songwriter and Broadway star, George M. Cohan (1878–1942) gives voice to expectations that upon their arrival in Europe "the Yanks" will sort matters out in short order.

Johnnie, get your gun
Get your gun, get your gun
Take it on the run
On the run, on the run
Hear them calling, you and me
Every son of liberty
Hurry right away
No delay, go today
Make your daddy glad
To have had such a lad
Tell your sweetheart not to pine
To be proud her boy's in line

Over there, over there
Send the word, send the word over there
That the Yanks are coming
The Yanks are coming
The drums rum-tumming
Everywhere
So prepare, say a prayer
Send the word, send the word to beware
We'll be over, we're coming over
And we won't come back till it's over
Over there

Woodrow Wilson, "Address on Flag Day" (1917)

President Wilson explains what Americans are fighting for and warns against anyone daring to oppose him.

We meet to celebrate Flag Day because this flag which we honour and under which we serve is the emblem of our unity, our power, our thought and purpose as a nation. It has no other character than that which we give it from generation to generation. The choices are ours. It floats in majestic silence above the hosts that execute those choices, whether in peace or in war. And yet, though silent, it speaks to us—speaks to us of the past, of the men and women who went before us and of the records they wrote upon it. We celebrate the day of its birth; and from its birth until now it has witnessed a great history, has floated on high the symbol of great, events, of a great plan of life worked out by a great people. We are about to carry it into battle, to lift it where it will draw the fire of our enemies. We are about to bid thousands, hundreds of thousands, it may be millions, of our men, the young, the strong, the capable men of the nation, to go forth and die beneath it on fields of blood far away, —for what? For some unaccustomed thing? For something for which it has never sought the fire before? American armies were never before sent across the seas. Why are they sent now? For some new purpose, for which this great flag has never been carried before, or for some old, familiar, heroic purpose for which it has seen men, its own men, die on every battlefield upon which Americans have borne arms since the Revolution?

These are questions which must be answered. We are Americans. We in our turn serve America, and can serve her with no private purpose. We must use her flag as she has always used it. We are accountable at the bar of history and must plead in utter frankness what purpose it is we seek to serve.

It is plain enough how we were forced into the war. The extraordinary insults and aggressions of the Imperial German Government left us no self-respecting choice but to take up arms in defense of our rights as a free people and of our honour as a sovereign government. The military masters of Germany denied us the right to be neutral. They filled our unsuspecting communities with vicious spies and conspirators and sought to corrupt the opinion of our people in their own behalf. When they found that they could not do that, their agents diligently spread sedition amongst us and sought to draw our own citizens from their allegiance. . . . They sought by violence to destroy our industries and arrest our commerce. They tried to incite Mexico to take up arms against us and to draw Japan into a hostile alliance with her. . . . They impudently denied us the use of the high seas and repeatedly executed their threat that they would send to their death any of our people who ventured to approach the coasts of Europe. And many of our own people were corrupted. Men began to look upon their own neighbours with suspicion and to wonder in their hot resentment and surprise whether there was any community in which hostile intrigue did not lurk. What great nation in such circumstances would not have taken up arms? Much as we had desired peace, it was denied us, and not of our own choice. This flag under which we serve would have been dishonoured had we withheld our hand.

But that is only part of the story. We know now as clearly as we knew before we were ourselves engaged that we are not the enemies of the German people and that they are not our enemies. They did not originate or desire this hideous war or wish that we should be drawn into it; and we are vaguely conscious that we are fighting their cause, as they will some day see it, as well as our own. They are themselves in the grip of the same sinister power that has now at last stretched

its ugly talons out and drawn blood from us. The whole world is at war because the whole world is in the grip of that power and is trying out the great battle which shall determine whether it is to be brought under its mastery or fling itself free.

The war was begun by the military masters of Germany, who proved to be also the masters of Austria-Hungary. These men have never regarded nations as peoples, men, women, and children of like blood and frame as themselves, for whom governments existed and in whom governments had their life. They have regarded them merely as serviceable organizations which they could by force or intrigue bend or corrupt to their own purpose. . . .

Their plan was to throw a broad belt of German military power and political control across the very centre of Europe and beyond the Mediterranean into the heart of Asia; and Austria-Hungary was to be as much their tool and pawn as Servia or Bulgaria or Turkey or the ponderous states of the East. Austria-Hungary, indeed, was to become part of the central German Empire, absorbed and dominated by the same forces and influences that had originally cemented the German states themselves. The dream had its heart at Berlin. It could have had a heart nowhere else! It rejected the idea of solidarity of race entirely. The choice of peoples played no part in it at all. It contemplated binding together racial and political units which could be kept together only by force—Czechs, Magyars, Croats, Serbs, Roumanians, Turks, Armenians—the proud states of Bohemia and Hungary, the stout little commonwealths of the Balkans, the indomitable Turks, the subtle peoples of the East . . .

The military masters under whom Germany is bleeding see very clearly to what point Fate has brought them. If they fall back or are forced back an inch, their power both abroad and at home will fall to pieces like a house of cards. . . .

Do you not now understand the new intrigue, the intrigue for peace, and why the masters of Germany do not hesitate to use any agency that promises to effect their purpose, the deceit of the nations? Their present particular aim is to deceive all those who throughout the world stand for the rights of peoples and the self-government of nations; for they see what immense strength the forces of justice and of liberalism are gathering out of this war. . . .

The sinister intrigue is being no less actively conducted in this country than in Russia and in every country in Europe to which the agents and dupes of the Imperial German Government can get access. That government has many spokesmen here, in places high and low. . . .

But they will make no headway. The false betray themselves always in every accent. It is only friends and partisans of the German Government whom we have already identified who utter these thinly disguised disloyalties. The facts are patent to all the world, and nowhere are they more plainly seen than in the United States, where we are accustomed to deal with facts and not with sophistries; and the great fact that stands out above all the rest is that this is a Peoples' War, a war for freedom and justice and self-government amongst all the nations of the world, a war to make the world safe for the peoples who live upon it and have made it their own, the German people themselves included; and that with us rests the choice to break through all these hypocrisies and patent cheats and masks of brute force and help set the world free, or else stand aside and let it be dominated a long age through by sheer weight, of arms and the arbitrary choices of self-constituted masters, by the nation which can maintain the biggest armies and the most irresistible armaments—a power to which the world has afforded no parallel and in the face of which political freedom must wither and perish.

For us there is but one choice. We have made it. Woe be to the man or group of men that seeks to stand in our way in this day of high resolution when every principle we hold dearest is to be vindicated and made secure for the salvation of the nations. We are ready to plead at the bar of history, and our flag shall wear a new lustre. Once more we shall make good with our lives and fortunes the great faith to which we were born, and a new glory shall shine in the face of our people.

RANDOLPH BOURNE, "THE STATE" (1918)

One of those who did dare to oppose the war was the journalist Randolph Bourne (1886–1918). This essay, unfinished when he died in the influenza epidemic of 1918, has since become an antiwar manifesto, especially cherished by libertarians.

To most Americans of the classes which consider themselves significant the war brought a sense of the sanctity of the State which, if they had had time to think about it, would have seemed a sudden and surprising alteration in their habits of thought. In times of peace, we usually ignore the State in favour of partisan political controversies, or personal struggles for office, or the pursuit of party policies. It is the Government rather than the State with which the politically minded are concerned. The State is reduced to a shadowy emblem which comes to consciousness only on occasions of patriotic holiday.

Government is obviously composed of common and unsanctified men, and is thus a legitimate object of criticism and even contempt. If your own party is in power, things may be assumed to be moving safely enough; but if the opposition is in, then clearly all safety and honor have fled the State. Yet you do not put it to yourself in quite that way. What you think is only that there are rascals to be turned out of a very practical machinery of offices and functions which you take for granted. When we say that Americans are lawless, we usually mean that they are less conscious than other peoples of the august majesty of the institution of the State as it stands behind the objective government of men and laws which we see. In a republic the men who hold office are indistinguishable from the mass. Very few of them possess the slightest personal dignity with which they could endow their political role; even if they ever thought of such a thing. And they have no class distinction to give them glamour. In a republic the Government is obeyed grumblingly, because it has no bedazzlements or sanctities to gild it. If you are a good old-fashioned democrat, you rejoice at this fact, you glory in the plainness of a system where every citizen has become a king. If you are more sophisticated you bemoan the passing of dignity and honor from affairs of State. But in practice, the democrat does not in the least treat his elected citizen with the respect due to a king, nor does the sophisticated citizen pay tribute to the dignity even when he finds it. The republican State has almost no trappings to appeal to the common man's emotions. What it has are of military origin, and in an unmilitary era such as we have passed through since the Civil War, even military trappings have been scarcely seen. In such an era the sense of the State almost fades out of the consciousness of men.

With the shock of war, however, the State comes into its own again. The Government, with no mandate from the people, without consultation of the people, conducts all the negotiations, the backing and filling, the menaces and explanations, which slowly bring it into collision with some other Government, and gently and irresistibly slides the country into war. For the benefit of proud and haughty citizens, it is fortified with a list of the intolerable insults which have been hurled toward us by the other nations; for the benefit of the liberal and beneficent, it has a convincing set of moral purposes which our going to war will achieve; for the ambitious and aggressive classes, it can gently whisper of a bigger role in the destiny of the world. The result is that, even in those countries where the business of declaring war is theoretically in the hands of representatives of the people, no legislature has ever been known to decline the request of an Executive, which has conducted all foreign affairs in utter privacy and irresponsibility, that it order the nation into battle. Good democrats are wont to feel the crucial difference between a State in which the popular Parliament or Congress declares war, and the State in which an absolute monarch or ruling class declares war. But, put to the stern pragmatic test, the difference is not striking. In the freest of republics as well as in the most tyrannical of empires, all foreign policy, the diplomatic negotiations which produce or forestall war, are equally the private property of the Executive part of the Government, and are equally exposed to no check

whatever from popular bodies, or the people voting as a mass themselves.

The moment war is declared, however, the mass of the people, through some spiritual alchemy, become convinced that they have willed and executed the deed themselves. They then, with the exception of a few malcontents, proceed to allow themselves to be regimented, coerced, deranged in all the environments of their lives, and turned into a solid manufactory of destruction toward whatever other people may have, in the appointed scheme of things, come within the range of the Government's disapprobation. The citizen throws off his contempt and indifference to Government, identifies himself with its purposes, revives all his military memories and symbols, and the State once more walks, an august presence, through the imaginations of men. Patriotism becomes the dominant feeling, and produces immediately that intense and hopeless confusion between the relations which the individual bears and should bear toward the society of which he is a part.

The patriot loses all sense of the distinction between State, nation, and government. In our quieter moments, the Nation or Country forms the basic idea of society. We think vaguely of a loose population spreading over a certain geographical portion of the earth's surface, speaking a common language, and living in a homogeneous civilization. Our idea of Country concerns itself with the non-political aspects of a people, its ways of living, its personal traits, its literature and art, its characteristic attitudes toward life. We are Americans because we live in a certain bounded territory, because our ancestors have carried on a great enterprise of pioneering and colonization, because we live in certain kinds of communities which have a certain look and express their aspirations in certain ways. . . . We may be intensely proud of and congenial to our particular network of civilization, or we may detest most of its qualities and rage at its defects. This does not alter the fact that we are inextricably bound up in it. The Country, as an inescapable group into which we are born, and which makes us its particular kind of a citizen of the world, seems to be a fundamental fact of our consciousness, an irreducible minimum of social feeling.

Now this feeling for country is essentially non-competitive; we think of our own people merely as living on the earth's surface along with other groups, pleasant or objectionable as they may be, but fundamentally as sharing the earth with them. In our simple conception of country there is no more feeling of rivalry with other peoples than there is in our feeling for our family. Our interest turns within rather than without, is intensive and not belligerent. . . . Country is a concept of peace, of tolerance, of living and letting live. But State is essentially a concept of power, of competition: it signifies a group in its aggressive aspects. And we have the misfortune of being born not only into a country but into a State, and as we grow up we learn to mingle the two feelings into a hopeless confusion.

The State is the country acting as a political unit, it is the group acting as a repository of force, determiner of law, arbiter of justice. International politics is a power politics because it is a relation of States and that is what States infallibly and calamitously are, huge aggregations of human and industrial force that may be hurled against each other in war. When a country acts as a whole in relation to another country, or in imposing laws on its own inhabitants, or in coercing or punishing individuals or minorities, it is acting as a State. The history of America as a country is quite different from that of America as a State. In one case it is the drama of the pioneering conquest of the land, of the growth of wealth and the ways in which it was used, of the enterprise of education, and the carrying out of spiritual ideals, of the struggle of economic classes. But as a State, its history is that of playing a part in the world, making war, obstructing international trade, preventing itself from being split to pieces, punishing those citizens whom society agrees are offensive, and collecting money to pay for all.

Government on the other hand is synonymous with neither State nor Nation. It is the machinery by which the nation, organized as a State, carries out its State functions. Government is a framework of the administration of laws, and the carrying out of the public force. Government is the idea of the State put into practical operation in the hands of definite, concrete, fallible men. It is the visible sign of the invisible grace. It is the word made flesh. And it has necessarily the limitations inherent in all practicality. Government is the only form in which we can envisage the State, but it is by no means identical with it. That the State is a mystical conception is something that must never be forgotten. Its glamor and its significance linger behind the framework of Government and direct its activities.

Wartime brings the ideal of the State out into very clear relief, and reveals attitudes and tendencies that were hidden. In times of peace the sense of the State flags in a republic that is not militarized. For war is essentially the health of the State. The ideal of the State is that within its territory its power and influence should be universal. As the Church is the medium for the spiritual salvation of man, so the State is thought of as the medium for his political salvation. Its idealism is a rich blood flowing to all the members of the body politic. And it is precisely in war that the urgency for union seems greatest, and the necessity for universality seems most unquestioned. The State is the organization of the herd to act offensively or defensively against another herd similarly organized. The more terrifying the occasion for defense, the closer will become the organization and the more coercive the influence upon each member of the herd. War sends the current of purpose and activity flowing down to the lowest levels of the herd, and to its remote branches. All the activities of society are linked together as fast as possible to this central purpose of making a military offensive or military defense, and the State becomes what in peacetimes it has vainly struggled to become—the inexorable arbiter and determinant of men's businesses and attitudes and opinions. . . .

The classes which are able to play an active and not merely a passive role in the organization for war get a tremendous liberation of activity and energy. Individuals are jolted out of their old routine, many of them are given new positions of responsibility, new techniques must be learnt. Wearing home times are broken and women who would have remained attached with infantile bonds are liberated for service overseas. A vast sense of rejuvenescence pervades the significant classes, a sense of new importance in the world. Old national ideals are taken out, re-adapted to the purpose and used as the universal touchstones, or molds into which all thought is poured. Every individual citizen who in peacetimes had no living fragment of the State becomes an active amateur agent of the Government in reporting spies and disloyalists, in raising Government funds, or in propagating such measures as are considered necessary by officialdom. Minority opinion, which in times of peace was only irritating and could not be dealt with by law unless it was conjoined with actual crime, becomes with the outbreak of war, a case for outlawry. Criticism of the State, objections to war, lukewarm opinions concerning the necessity or the beauty of conscription, are made subject to ferocious penalties, far exceeding [in] severity those affixed to actual pragmatic crimes. Public opinion, as expressed in the newspapers, and the pulpits and the schools, becomes one solid block. Loyalty, or rather war orthodoxy, becomes the sole test for all professions, techniques, occupations. . . .

War is the health of the State. It automatically sets in motion throughout society those irresistible forces for uniformity, for passionate cooperation with the Government in coercing into obedience the minority groups and individuals which lack the larger herd sense. The machinery of government sets and enforces the drastic penalties. The minorities are either intimidated into silence, or brought slowly around by subtle process of persuasion which may seem to them really to be converting them. Of course, the ideal of perfect loyalty, perfect uniformity is never really attained. The classes upon whom the amateur work of coercion falls are unwearied in their zeal, but often their agitation, instead of converting merely serves to stiffen their resistance. Minorities are rendered sullen, and some intellectual opinion bitter and satirical. But in general, the nation in wartime attains a uniformity of feeling, a hierarchy of values culminating at the undisputed apex of the State ideal, which could not possibly be produced through any other agency than war. Other values such as artistic creation, knowledge, reason, beauty, the enhancement of life, are instantly and almost unanimously sacrificed, and the significant classes who have constituted themselves the amateur agents of the State, are engaged not only in sacrificing these values for themselves but in coercing all other persons into sacrificing them.

War—or at least modern war waged by a democratic republic against a powerful enemy—seems to achieve for a nation almost all that the most inflamed political idealist could desire. Citizens are no longer indifferent to their Government, but each cell of the body politic is brimming with life and activity. We are at last on the way to full realization of that collective community in which each individual somehow contains the virtue of the whole. In a nation at war, every citizen identifies himself with the whole and feels immensely strengthened in that identification. The purpose and desire of the collective community live in each person who throws himself whole-heartedly into the cause of war. The impeding distinction between society and the individual is almost blotted out. At war, the individual becomes almost identical with his society. He achieves a superb self-assurance, an intuition of the rightness of all his ideas and emotions, so that in the suppression of opponents or heretics he is invincibly strong; he feels behind him all the power of the collective community. The individual as social being in war seems to have achieved almost his apotheosis. . . .

For just as in modern societies the sex-instinct is enormously over-supplied for the requirements of human propagation, so the gregarious impulse is enormously over-supplied for the work of protection which it is called upon to perform. It would be quite enough if we were gregarious enough to enjoy the companionship of others, to be able to cooperate with them, and to feel a slight malaise at solitude. . . .

Joining as it does to these very vigorous tendencies of the individual—the pleasure in power and the pleasure of obedience—this gregarious impulse becomes irresistible in society. War stimulates it to the highest possible degree, sending the influence of its mysterious herd-current with its inflations of power and obedience to the farthest reaches of the society, to every individual and little group that can possibly be affected. And it is these impulses which the State—the organization of the entire herd, the entire collectivity—is founded on and makes use of.

There is, of course, in the feeling towards the State a large element of pure filial mysticism. The sense of insecurity, the desire for protection, sends one's desire back to the father and mother, with whom is associated the earliest feelings of protection. It is not for nothing that one's State is still thought of as Father or Motherland, that one's relation towards it is conceived in terms of family affection. The war has shown that nowhere under the shock of danger have these primitive childlike attitudes failed to assert themselves again, as much in this country as anywhere. If we have not the intense Father-sense of the German who worships his Vaterland, at least in Uncle Sam we have a symbol of protecting, kindly authority, and in the many Mother-posters of the Red Cross, we see how easily in the more tender functions of war service, the ruling organization is conceived in family terms. A people at war have become in the most literal sense obedient, respectful, trustful children again, full of that naive faith in the all-wisdom and all-power of the adult who takes care of them, imposes his mild but necessary rule upon them and in whom they lose their responsibility and anxieties. . . .

The members of the working-classes, that portion at least which does not identify itself with the significant classes and seek to imitate it and rise to it, are notoriously less affected by the symbolism of the State, or, in other words, are less patriotic than the significant classes. For theirs is neither the power nor the glory. The State in wartime does not offer them the opportunity to regress, for, never having acquired social adulthood, they cannot lose it. If they have been drilled and regimented, as by the industrial regime of the last century, they go out docilely enough to do battle for their State, but they are almost entirely without that filial sense and even without that herd-intellect sense which operates so powerfully among their betters. They live habitually in an industrial serfdom, by which though nominally free, they are in practice as a class bound to a system of a machine-production, the implements of which they do not own, and in the distribution of whose product they have not the slightest voice, except what they can occasionally exert by a veiled intimidation which draws slightly more of the product in their direction. From such serfdom, military conscription is not so great a change. But into the military enterprise they go, not with those hurrahs of the significant classes whose instincts war so powerfully feeds, but with the same apathy with which they enter and continue in the industrial enterprise.

From this point of view, war can be called almost an upper-class sport. The novel interests and excitements it provides, the inflations of power, the satisfaction it gives to those very tenacious human impulses—gregariousness and parent-regression—endow it with all the qualities of a luxurious collective game which is felt intensely just in proportion to the sense of significant rule the person has in the class-division of society. A country at war—particularly our own country at war—does not act as a purely homogenous herd. The significant classes have all the herd-feeling in all its primitive intensity, so that this feeling does not flow freely without impediment throughout the entire nation. . . .

This herd-feeling, this newly awakened consciousness of the State, demands universality. The leaders of the significant classes, who feel most intensely this State-compulsion, demand a one hundred per cent Americanism, among one hundred per cent of the population. The State is a jealous God and will brook no rivals. Its sovereignty must pervade everyone and all feeling must be run into the stereotyped forms of romantic patriotic militarism which is the traditional expression of the State herd-feeling.

Thus arises conflict within the State. War becomes almost a sport between the hunters and the hunted. The pursuit of enemies within outweighs in psychic attractiveness the assault on the enemy without. The whole terrific force of the State is brought to bear against the heretics. The nation boils with a slow insistent fever. A white terrorism is carried on by the Government against all pacifists, Socialists, enemy aliens, and a milder unofficial persecution against all persons or movements that can be imagined as connected with the enemy. War, which should be the health of the State, unifies all the bourgeois elements and the common people, and outlaws the rest. . . .

But the emotions that play around the defense of the State do not take into consideration the pragmatic results. A nation at war, led by its significant classes, is engaged in liberating certain of its impulses which have had all too little exercise in the past. It is getting certain satisfactions and the actual conduct of the war or the condition of the country are really incidental to the enjoyment of new forms of virtue and power and aggressiveness. If it could be shown conclusively that the persecution of slightly disaffected elements actually increased enormously the difficulties of production and the organization of the war technique, it would be found that public policy would scarcely change. The significant classes must have their pleasure in hunting down and chastising everything that they feel instinctively to be not imbued with the current State-enthusiasm, though the State itself be actually impeded in its efforts to carry out those objects for which they are passionately contending. . . . On our entrance into the war there were many persons who predicted exactly this derangement of values, who feared lest democracy suffer more at home from an America at war than could be gained for democracy abroad. That fear has been amply justified. The question whether the American nation would act like an enlightened democracy going to war for the sake of high ideals, or like a State-obsessed herd, has been decisively answered. The record is written and cannot be erased. History will decide whether the terrorization of opinion, and the regimentation of life was justified under the most idealistic of democratic administrations. It will see that when the American nation had ostensibly a chance to conduct a gallant war, with scrupulous regard to the safety of democratic values at home, it chose rather to adopt all the most obnoxious and coercive techniques of the enemy and of the other countries at war, and to rival in intimidation and ferocity of punishment the worst governmental systems of the age. . . .

We cannot crusade against war without crusading implicitly against the State. And we cannot expect, or take measures to ensure, that this war is a war to end war, unless at the same time we take measures to end the State in its traditional form. The State is not the nation, and the State can be modified and even abolished in its present form, without harming the nation. On the contrary, with the passing of the dominance of the State, the genuine life-enhancing forces of the nation will be liberated. If the State's chief function is war, then the State must suck out of the nation a large part of its energy for purely sterile purposes of defense and aggression. It devotes to waste or to actual destruction as much as it can of the vitality of the nation. . . .

In this great herd-machinery, dissent is like sand in the bearings. The State ideal is primarily a sort of blind animal push towards military unity. Any interference with that unity turns the whole vast impulse towards crushing it. Dissent is speedily outlawed, and the Government, backed by the significant classes and those who in every locality, however small, identify themselves with them, proceeds against the outlaws, regardless of their value to other institutions of the nation, or of the effect that their persecution may have on public opinion. The herd becomes divided into the hunters and the hunted, and war-enterprise becomes not only a technical game but a sport as well. . . .

However representative of the people Parliaments and Congresses may be in all that concerns the internal administration of a country's political affairs, in international relations it has never been possible to maintain that the popular body acted except as a wholly mechanical ratifier of the Executive's will. The formality by which Parliaments and Congresses declare war is the merest technicality. Before such a declaration can take place, the country will have been brought to the very brink of war by the foreign policy of the Executive. A long series of steps on the downward path, each one more fatally committing the unsuspecting country to a warlike course of action will have been taken without either the people or its representatives being consulted or expressing its feeling. When the declaration of war is finally demanded by the Executive, the Parliament or Congress could not refuse it without reversing the course of history, without repudiating what has been representing itself in the eyes of the other states as the symbol and interpreter of the nation's will and animus. . . . That is why the referendum which was advocated by some people as a test of American sentiment in entering the war was considered even by thoughtful democrats to be something subtly improper. The die had been cast. Popular whim could derange and bungle monstrously the majestic march of State policy in its new crusade for the peace of the world. . . .

War is the health of the State. Only when the State is at war does the modern society function with that unity of sentiment, simple uncritical patriotic devotion, cooperation of services, which have always been the ideal of the State lover. . . .

It is in foreign policy that the State acts most concentratedly as the organized herd, acts with fullest sense of aggressive-power, acts with freest arbitrariness. In foreign policy, the State is most itself. States, with reference to each other, may be said to be in a continual state of latent war. The armed truce, a phrase so familiar before 1914, was an accurate description of the normal relation of States when they are not at war. Indeed, it is not too much to say that the normal relation of States is war. Diplomacy is a disguised war, in which States seek to gain by barter and intrigue, by the cleverness of wits, the objectives which they would have to gain more clumsily by means of war. Diplomacy is used while the States are recuperating from conflicts in which they have exhausted themselves. It is the wheedling and the bargaining of the worn-out bullies as they rise from the ground and slowly restore their strength to begin fighting again. If diplomacy had been a moral equivalent for war, a higher stage in human progress, an inestimable means of making words prevail instead of blows, militarism would have broken down and given place to it. But since it is a mere temporary substitute, a mere appearance of war's energy under another form, a surrogate effect is almost exactly proportioned to the armed force behind it. When it fails, the recourse is immediate to the military technique whose thinly veiled arm it has been. . . .

Society and its institutions are, to the individual who enters it, as much naturalistic phenomena as is the weather itself. There is, therefore, no natural sanctity in the State any more than there is in the weather. We may bow down before it, just as our ancestors bowed before the sun and moon, but it is only because something in us unregenerate finds satisfaction in such an attitude, not because there is anything inherently reverential in the institution worshiped. Once the State has begun to function, and a large class finds its interest and its expression of power in maintaining the State, this ruling class may compel obedience from any uninterested minority. The State thus becomes an instrument by which the power of the whole herd is wielded for the benefit of a class. The rulers soon learn to capitalize the reverence which the State produces in the majority, and turn it into a general resistance toward a lessening of their privileges. The sanctity of the State becomes identified with the sanctity of the ruling class, and the latter are permitted to remain in power under the impression that in obeying and serving them, we are obeying and serving society, the nation, the great collectivity of all of us.

Eugene V. Debs, "Canton, Ohio Anti-War Speech" (1918)

This antiwar speech by Eugene Debs (1855–1926) landed the socialist leader in prison, convicted in federal court of sedition. President Wilson called Debs a "traitor to his country."

I realize that, in speaking to you this afternoon, there are certain limitations placed upon the right of free speech. I must be exceedingly careful, prudent, as to what I say, and even more careful and prudent as to how I say it. I may not be able to say all I think; but I am not going to say anything that I do not think. I would rather a thousand times be a free soul in jail than to be a sycophant and coward in the streets. . . .

Are we opposed to Prussian militarism? Why, we have been fighting it since the day the Socialist movement was born; and we are going to continue to fight it, day and night, until it is wiped

from the face of the earth. Between us there is no truce—no compromise. . . .

You remember that, at the close of Theodore Roosevelt's second term as President, he went over to Africa to make war on some of his ancestors. You remember that, at the close of his expedition, he visited the capitals of Europe; and that he was wined and dined, dignified and glorified by all the Kaisers and Czars and Emperors of the Old World. He visited Potsdam while the Kaiser was there; and, according to the accounts published in the American newspapers, he and the Kaiser were soon on the most familiar terms. They were hilariously intimate with each other, and slapped each other on the back. After Roosevelt had reviewed the Kaiser's troops, according to the same accounts, he became enthusiastic over the Kaiser's legions and said: "If I had that kind of an army, I could conquer the world." He knew the Kaiser then just as well as he knows him now. He knew that he was the Kaiser, the Beast of Berlin. And yet, he permitted himself to be entertained by that Beast of Berlin; had his feet under the mahogany of the Beast of Berlin; was cheek by jowl with the Beast of Berlin. . . .

"Birds of a feather flock together." . . .

If Theodore Roosevelt is the great champion of democracy—the arch foe of autocracy, what business had he as the guest of honor of the Prussian Kaiser? And when he met the Kaiser, and did honor to the Kaiser, under the terms imputed to him, wasn't it pretty strong proof that he himself was a Kaiser at heart? Now, after being the guest of Emperor Wilhelm, the Beast of Berlin, he comes back to this country, and wants you to send ten million men over there to kill the Kaiser; to murder his former friend and pal. Rather queer, isn't it? And yet, he is the patriot, and we are the traitors. . . .

A little more history along the same line. In 1902 Prince Henry paid a visit to this country. Do you remember him? I do, exceedingly well. Prince Henry is the brother of Emperor Wilhelm. Prince Henry is another Beast of Berlin, an autocrat, an aristocrat, a Junker of Junkers—very much despised by our American patriots. He came over here in 1902 as the representative of Kaiser Wilhelm; he was received by Congress and by several state legislatures . . .

All of our plutocracy, all of the wealthy representatives living along Fifth Avenue—all, all of them—threw their palace doors wide open and received Prince Henry with open arms. But they were not satisfied with this; they got down and grovelled in the dust at his feet. Our plutocracy—women and men alike—vied with each other to lick the boots of Prince Henry, the brother and representative of the "Beast of Berlin." And still our plutocracy, our Junkers, would have us believe that all the Junkers are confined to Germany. It is precisely because we refuse to believe this that they brand us as disloyalists. They want our eyes focused on the Junkers in Berlin so that we will not see those within our own borders.

I hate, I loathe, I despise Junkers and junkerdom. I have no earthly use for the Junkers of Germany, and not one particle more use for the Junkers in the United States.

They tell us that we live in a great free republic; that our institutions are democratic; that we are a free and self-governing people. This is too much, even for a joke. But it is not a subject for levity; it is an exceedingly serious matter.

To whom do the Wall Street Junkers in our country marry their daughters? After they have wrung their countless millions from your sweat, your agony and your life's blood, in a time of war as in a time of peace, they invest these untold millions in the purchase of titles of broken-down aristocrats, such as princes, dukes, counts and other parasites and no-accounts. Would they be satisfied to wed their daughters to honest workingmen? To real democrats? Oh, no! They scour the markets of Europe for vampires who are titled and nothing else. And they swap their millions for the titles, so that matrimony with them becomes literally a matter of money.

These are the gentry who are today wrapped up in the American flag, who shout their claim from the housetops that they are the only patriots, and who have their magnifying glasses in hand, scanning the country for evidence of disloyalty, eager to apply the brand of treason to the men who dare to even whisper their opposition to Junker rule in the United Sates. No wonder Sam Johnson declared that "patriotism is the last refuge of the scoundrel." He must have had this Wall Street gentry in mind, or at least their prototypes, for in every age it has been the tyrant, the oppressor and the exploiter who has wrapped himself in the cloak of patriotism, or religion, or both to deceive and overawe the people.

They would have you believe that the Socialist Party consists in the main of disloyalists and traitors. It is true in a sense not at all to their discredit. We frankly admit that we are disloyalists and traitors to the real traitors of this nation. . . .

Every solitary one of these aristocratic conspirators and would-be murderers claims to be an arch-patriot; every one of them insists that the war is being waged to make the world safe for democracy. What humbug! What rot! What false pretense! These autocrats, these tyrants, these red-handed robbers and murderers, the "patriots," while the men who have the courage to stand face to face with them, speak the truth, and fight for their exploited victims—they are the disloyalists and traitors. If this be true, I want to take my place side by side with the traitors in this fight. . . .

Who appoints our federal judges? The people? In all the history of the country, the working class have never named a federal judge. There are 121 of these judges and every solitary one holds his position, his tenure, through the influence and power of corporate capital. The corporations and trusts dictate their appointment. And when they go to the bench, they go, not to serve, the people, but to serve the interests that place them and keep them where they are. . . .

And this in a country that boasts of fighting to make the world safe for democracy! The history of this country is being written in the blood of the childhood the industrial lords have murdered.

These are not palatable truths to them. They do not like to hear them; and what is more they do not want you to hear them. And that is why they brand us as undesirable citizens, and as disloyalists and traitors. If we were actual traitors—traitors to the people and to their welfare and progress, we would be regarded as eminently respectable citizens of the republic; we would hold high office, have princely incomes, and ride in limousines; and we would be pointed out as the elect who have succeeded in life in honorable pursuit, and worthy of emulation by the youth of the land. It is precisely because we are disloyal to the traitors that we are loyal to the people of this nation. . . .

The Man of Galilee, the Carpenter, the workingman who became the revolutionary agitator of his day soon found himself to be an undesirable citizen in the eyes of the ruling knaves and they had him crucified. . . .

How stupid and shortsighted the ruling class really is! Cupidity is stone blind. It has no vision. The greedy, profit-seeking exploiter cannot see beyond the end of his nose. He can see a chance for an "opening"; he is cunning enough to know what graft is and where it is, and how it can be secured, but vision he has none—not the slightest. He knows nothing of the great throbbing world that spreads out in all directions. . . .

Socialism is a growing idea; an expanding philosophy. It is spreading over the entire face of the earth: It is as vain to resist it as it would be to arrest the sunrise on the morrow. It is coming, coming, coming all along the line. . . .

Yes, my comrades, my heart is attuned to yours. Aye, all our hearts now throb as one great heart responsive to the battle cry of the social revolution. Here, in this alert and inspiring assemblage our hearts are with the Bolsheviki of Russia. Those heroic men and women, those unconquerable comrades have by their incomparable valor and sacrifice added fresh luster to the fame of the international movement. Those Russian comrades of ours have made greater sacrifices, have suffered more, and have shed more heroic blood than any like number of men and women anywhere on earth; they have laid the foundation of the first real democracy that ever drew the breath of life in this world. And the very first act of the triumphant Russian revolution was to proclaim a state of peace with all mankind, coupled with a fervent moral appeal, not to kings, not to emperors, rulers or diplomats but to the people of all nations. Here we have the very breath of democracy, the quintessence of the dawning freedom. The Russian revolution proclaimed its glorious triumph in its ringing and inspiring appeal to the peoples of all the earth. In a humane and fraternal spirit new Russia, emancipated at last from the curse of the centuries, called upon all nations engaged in the frightful war, the Central Powers as well as the Allies, to send representatives to a conference to lay down terms of peace that should be just and lasting. Here was the supreme opportunity to strike the blow to make the world safe for democracy. Was there any response to that noble appeal that in some day to come will be written in letters of gold in the history of the world? Was there any response whatever to that appeal for universal peace? No, not the slightest attention was paid to it by the Christian nations engaged in the terrible slaughter.

It has been charged that Lenin and Trotsky and the leaders of the revolution were treacherous, that they made a traitorous peace with Germany. Let us consider that proposition briefly. At the time of the revolution Russia had been three years in the war. Under the Czar she had lost more than four million of her ill-clad, poorly-equipped, half-starved soldiers, slain outright or disabled on the field of battle. She was absolutely bankrupt. Her soldiers were mainly without arms. This was what was bequeathed to the revolution by the Czar and his regime; and for this condition Lenin and Trotsky were not responsible, nor the Bolsheviki. For this appalling state of affairs the Czar and his rotten bureaucracy were solely responsible. When the Bolsheviki came into power and went through the archives they found and exposed the secret treaties—the treaties that were made between the Czar and the French government, the British government and the Italian government, proposing, after the victory was achieved, to dismember the German Empire and destroy the Central Powers. . . .

The master class has always declared the wars; the subject class has always fought the battles. The master class has had all to gain and nothing to lose, while the subject class has had nothing to gain and all to lose—especially their lives.

They have always taught and trained you to believe it to be your patriotic duty to go to war and to have yourselves slaughtered at their command. But in all the history of the world you, the people, have never had a voice in declaring war, and strange as it certainly appears, no war by any nation in any age has ever been declared by the people. . . .

The truth alone will make the people free. And for this reason the truth must not be permitted to reach the people. The truth has always been dangerous to the rule of the rogue, the exploiter, the robber. So the truth must be ruthlessly suppressed. That is why they are trying to destroy the Socialist movement; and every time they strike a blow they add a thousand new voices to the hosts proclaiming that socialism is the hope of humanity and has come to emancipate the people from their final form of servitude. . . .

In the Republican and Democratic parties you of the common herd are not expected to think. That is not only unnecessary but might lead you astray. That is what the "intellectual" leaders are for. They do the thinking and you do the voting. They ride in carriages at the front where the band plays and you tramp in the mud, bringing up the rear with great enthusiasm.

The capitalist system affects to have great regard and reward for intellect, and the capitalists give themselves full credit for having superior brains. When we have ventured to say that the time would come when the working class would rule they have bluntly answered "Never!

it requires brains to rule." The workers of course have none. And they certainly try hard to prove it by proudly supporting the political parties of their masters under whose administration they are kept in poverty and servitude. . . .

They are continually talking about your patriotic duty. It is not their but your patriotic duty that they are concerned about. There is a decided difference. Their patriotic duty never takes them to the firing line or chucks them into the trenches.

In passing I suggest that we stop a moment to think about the term "landlord." "LANDLORD!" Lord of the Land! The lord of the land is indeed a superpatriot. This lord who practically owns the earth tells you that we are fighting this war to make the world safe for democracy—he who shuts out all humanity from his private domain; he who profiteers at the expense of the people who have been slain and mutilated by multiplied thousands, under pretense of being the great American patriot. It is he, this identical patriot who is in fact the archenemy of the people; it is he that you need to wipe from power. It is he who is a far greater menace to your liberty and your well-being than the Prussian Junkers on the other side of the Atlantic ocean. . . .

War makes possible all such crimes and outrages. And war comes in spite of the people. When Wall Street says war the press says war and the pulpit promptly follows with its Amen. In every age the pulpit has been on the side of the rulers and not on the side of the people. . . .

And now for all of us to do our duty! The clarion call is ringing in our ears and we cannot falter without being convicted of treason to ourselves and to our great cause.

Do not worry over the charge of treason to your masters, but be concerned about the treason that involves yourselves. Be true to yourself and you cannot be a traitor to any good cause on earth.

Yes, in good time we are going to sweep into power in this nation and throughout the world. We are going to destroy all enslaving and degrading capitalist institutions and re-create them as free and humanizing institutions. The world is daily changing before our eyes. The sun of capitalism is setting; the sun of socialism is rising. It is our duty to build the new nation and the free republic. . . .

In due time the hour will strike and this great cause triumphant—the greatest in history—will proclaim the emancipation of the working class and the brotherhood of all mankind.

WOODROW WILSON, "LEAGUE OF NATIONS SPEECH" (1919)

When the Armistice ended hostilities in November 1918, Wilson himself led the American delegation to the ensuing Paris Peace Conference, expecting that he would dictate the terms of the settlement. Negotiations with allied leaders proved difficult, however. Forced to give way on many points, Wilson did preserve the idea of a League of Nations that he hoped would prevent all future wars. Here he urges Senators to ratify the resulting Versailles Treaty.

Gentlemen of the Senate: The treaty of peace with Germany was signed at Versailles on the twenty-eighth of June. I avail myself of the earliest opportunity to lay the treaty before you for ratification and to inform you with regard to the work of the conference by which that treaty was formulated.

The treaty constitutes nothing less than a world settlement. It would not be possible for me either to summarize or to construe its manifold provisions in an address which must of necessity be something less than a treatise. My services and all the information I possess will be at your disposal and at the disposal of your Committee on Foreign Relations at any time, either informally or in session, as you may prefer; and I hope that you will not hesitate to make use of them. I shall at this time, prior to your own study of the document, attempt only a general characterization of its scope and purpose.

In one sense, no doubt, there is no need that I should report to you what was attempted and done at Paris. You have been daily cognizant of what was going on there—of the problems with which the Peace Conference had to deal and of the difficulty of laying down straight lines of settlement anywhere on a field on which the old lines of international relationship and the new alike, followed so intricate a pattern and were for the most part cut so deep by historical circumstances which dominated action even where it would have been best to ignore or reverse them. The cross currents of politics and of interest must have been evident to you. . . .

The United States entered the war upon a different footing from every other nation except our associates on this side the sea. We entered it, not because our material interests were directly threatened or because any special treaty obligations to which we were parties had been involved, but only because we saw the supremacy, and even the validity, of right everywhere put in jeopardy and free government likely to be everywhere imperiled by the intolerable aggression of a power which respected neither right nor obligation and whose very system of government flouted the rights of the citizen as against the autocratic authority of his governors. And in the settlement of the peace we have sought no special reparation for ourselves, but only the restoration of right and the assurance of liberty everywhere that the effects of the settlement were to be felt. We entered the war as the disinterested champions of right and we interested ourselves in the terms of the peace in no other capacity.

The hopes of the nations allied against the Central Powers were at a very low ebb when our soldiers began to pour across the sea. There was everywhere amongst them, except in their stoutest spirits, a sombre foreboding of disaster. The war ended in November, eight months ago, but you have only to recall what was feared in midsummer last, four short months before the armistice, to realize what it was that our timely aid accomplished alike for their morale and their physical safety. . . .

Anxious men and women, leading spirits of France, attended the celebration of the Fourth of July last year in Paris out of generous courtesy, with no heart for festivity, little zest for hope. But they came away with something new at their hearts; they have themselves told us so. The mere sight of our men, of their vigour, of the confidence that showed itself in every movement of their stalwart figures and every turn of their swinging march, in their steady comprehending eyes and easy discipline, in the indomitable air that added spirit to everything they did, made everyone who saw them that memorable day realize that something had happened that was much more than a mere incident in the fighting, something very different from the mere arrival of fresh troops. A great moral force had flung itself into the struggle. The fine physical force of those spirited men spoke of something more than bodily vigor. They carried the great ideals of a free people at their hearts and with that vision were unconquerable. Their very presence, brought reassurance; their fighting made victory certain.

They were recognized as crusaders, and as their thousands swelled to millions their strength was seen to mean salvation. And they were fit men to carry such a hope and make good the assurance it forecast. Finer men never went into battle; and their officers were worthy of them. This is not the occasion upon which to utter a eulogy of the armies America sent to France, but perhaps, since I am speaking of their mission, I may speak also of the pride I shared with every American who saw or dealt with them there. They were the sort of men America would wish to be represented by, the sort of men every American would wish to claim as fellow-countrymen and comrades in a great cause. They were terrible in battle, and gentle and helpful out of it, remembering the mothers and the sisters, the wives and the little children at home. They were free men under arms, not forgetting their ideals of duty in the midst of tasks of violence. I am proud to have had the privilege of being associated with them and of calling myself their leader.

But I speak now of what they meant to the men by whose sides they fought and to the people with whom they mingled with such utter simplicity, as friends who asked only to be of service. They were for all the visible embodiment of America. What they did made America and all that she stood for a living reality in the thoughts not only of the people of France but also of tens of millions of men and women throughout all the toiling nations of a world standing everywhere in peril of its freedom and of the loss of everything it held dear, in deadly fear that its bonds were never to be loosed, its hopes forever to be mocked and disappointed.

And the compulsion of what they stood for was upon us who represented America at the peace table. It was our duty to see to it that every decision we took part in contributed, so far as we were able to influence it, to quiet the fears and realize the hopes of the peoples who had been living in that shadow, the nations that had come by our assistance to their freedom. It was our duty to do everything that it was within our power to do to make the triumph of freedom and of right a lasting triumph in the assurance of which men might everywhere live without fear.

Old entanglements of every kind stood in the way—promises which governments had made to one another in the days when might and right were confused and the power of the victor was without restraint. Engagements which contemplated any dispositions of territory, any extensions of sovereignty that might seem to be to the interest of those who had the power to insist upon them, had been entered into without thought of what the peoples concerned might wish or profit by; and these could not always be honorably brushed aside. It was not easy to graft the new order of ideas on the old, and some of the fruits of the grafting may, I fear, for a time be bitter. But, with very few exceptions, the men who sat with us at the peace table desired as sincerely as we did to get away from the bad influences, the illegitimate purposes, the demoralizing ambitions, the international counsels and expedients out of which the sinister designs of Germany had sprung as a natural growth.

It had been our privilege to formulate the principles which were accepted as the basis of the peace, but they had been accepted, not because we had come in to hasten and assure the victory and insisted upon them, but because they were readily acceded to as the principles to which honorable and enlightened minds everywhere had been bred. They spoke the conscience of the world as well as the conscience of America, and I am happy to pay my tribute of respect and gratitude to the able, forward-looking men with whom it was my privilege to co-operate. . . .

The atmosphere in which the Conference worked seemed created, not by the ambitions of strong governments, but by the hopes and aspirations of small nations and of peoples hitherto under bondage to the power that victory had shattered and destroyed. Two great empires had been forced into political bankruptcy, and we were the receivers. Our task was not only to make peace with the Central Empires and remedy the wrongs their armies had done. The Central Empires had lived in open violation of many of the very rights for which the war had been fought, dominating alien peoples over whom they had no natural right to rule, enforcing, not obedience, but veritable bondage, exploiting those who were weak for the benefit of those who were masters and overlords only by force of arms. There could be no peace until the whole order of central Europe was set right. . . .

The Turkish Empire, moreover, had fallen apart, as the Austro-Hungarian had. It had never had any real unity. It had been held together only by pitiless, inhuman force. Its peoples cried aloud for release, for succor from unspeakable distress, for all that the new day of hope seemed at last to bring within its dawn. Peoples hitherto in utter darkness were to be led out into the same light and given at last a helping hand. Undeveloped peoples and peoples ready for recognition but not yet ready to assume the full responsibilities of statehood were to be given adequate guarantees of friendly protection, guidance, and assistance.

And out of the execution of these great enterprises of liberty sprang opportunities to attempt what statesmen had never found the way before to do; an opportunity to throw safeguards about the rights of racial, national, and religious minorities by solemn international covenant; an opportunity to limit and regulate military establishments where they were most likely to be mischievous; an opportunity to effect a complete and systematic internationalization of waterways and railways which were necessary to the free economic life of more than one nation and to clear many of the normal channels of commerce of unfair obstructions of law or of privilege; and the very welcome opportunity to secure for labor the concerted protection of definite international pledges of principle and practice.

These were not tasks which the Conference looked about it to find and went out of its way to perform. They were inseparable from the settlements of peace. They were thrust upon it by circumstances which could not be overlooked. The war had created them. In all quarters of the world old established relationships had been disturbed or broken and affairs were at loose ends, needing to be mended or united again, but could not be made what they were before. They had to be set right by applying some uniform principle of justice or enlightened expediency. And they could not be adjusted by merely prescribing in a treaty what should be done. New states were to be set up which could not hope to live through their first period of weakness without assured support by the great nations that had consented to their creation and won for them their independence. Ill-governed colonies could not be put in the hands of governments which were to act as trustees for their people and not as their masters if there was to be no common authority among the nations to which they were to be responsible in the execution of their trust. Future international conventions with regard to the control of waterways, with regard to illicit traffic of many kinds, in arms or in deadly drugs, or with regard to the adjustment of many varying international administrative arrangements could not be assured if the treaty were to provide no permanent common international agency, if its execution in such matters were to be left to the slow and uncertain processes of cooperation by ordinary methods of negotiation. . . . A league of free nations had become a practical necessity. Examine the treaty of peace and you will find that everywhere throughout its manifold provisions its framers have felt obliged to turn to the League of Nations as an indispensable instrumentality for the maintenance of the new order it has been their purpose to set up in the world—the world of civilized men.

That there should be a league of nations to steady the counsels and maintain the peaceful understandings of the world, to make, not treaties alone, but the accepted principles of international law as well, the actual rule of conduct among the governments of the world, had been one of the agreements accepted from the first as the basis of peace with the Central Powers. The statesmen of all the belligerent countries were agreed that such a league must be created to sustain the settlements that were to be effected. . . .

The fact that the Covenant of the League was the first substantive part of the treaty to be worked out and agreed upon, while all else was in solution, helped to make the formulation of the rest easier. The Conference was, after all, not to be ephemeral. The concert of nations was to continue under a definite Covenant which had been agreed upon and which all were convinced was workable. They could go forward with confidence to make arrangements intended to be permanent. . . .

It was universally recognized that all the peoples of the world demanded of the Conference that it should create such a continuing concert of free nations as would make wars of aggression and spoilation such as this that has just ended forever impossible. A cry had gone out from every home in every stricken land from which sons and brothers and fathers had gone forth to the great sacrifice that such a sacrifice should never again be exacted. It was manifest why it had been exacted. It had been exacted because one nation desired dominion and other nations had known no means of defense except armaments and alliances. War had lain at the heart of every arrangement of the Europe—of every arrangement of the world—that preceded the war. Restive peoples had been told that fleets and armies, which they toiled to sustain, meant peace; and they now knew that they had been lied to: that fleets and armies had been maintained to promote national ambitions and meant war. They knew that no old policy meant anything else but force, force—always force. And they knew that it was intolerable. Every true heart in the world, and every enlightened judgment demanded that, at whatever cost of independent action, every government that took thought for its people or for justice or for ordered freedom should lend itself to a new purpose and utterly destroy the old order of international politics. Statesmen might see difficulties, but the people could see none and could brook no denial. A war in which they had been bled white to beat the terror that lay concealed in every Balance of Power must not end in a mere victory of arms and a new balance. The monster that had resorted to arms must be put in chains that could not be broken. The united power of free nations must put a stop to aggression, and the world must be given peace. If there was not the will or the intelligence to

accomplish that now, there must be another and a final war and the world must be swept clean of every power that could renew the terror. The League of Nations was not merely an instrument to adjust and remedy old wrongs under a new treaty of peace; it was the only hope for mankind. Again and again had the demon of war been cast out of the house of the peoples and the house swept clean by a treaty of peace; only to prepare a time when he would enter in again with spirits worse than himself. The house must now be given a tenant who could hold it against all such. Convenient, indeed indispensable, as statesmen found the newly planned League of Nations to be for the execution of present plans of peace and reparation, they saw it in a new aspect before their work was finished. They saw it as the main object of the peace, as the only thing that could complete it or make it worth while. They saw it as the hope of the world, and that hope they did not dare to disappoint. Shall we or any other free people hesitate to accept this great duty? Dare we reject it and break the heart of the world?

And so the result of the Conference of Peace, so far as Germany is concerned, stands complete. The difficulties encountered were very many. Sometimes they seemed insuperable. It was impossible to accommodate the interests of so great a body of nations,—interests which directly or indirectly affected almost every nation in the world,—without many minor compromises. The treaty, as a result, is not exactly what we would have written. It is probably not what any one of the national delegations would have written. But results were worked out which on the whole bear test. I think that it will be found that the compromises which were accepted as inevitable nowhere cut to the heart of any principle. The work of the Conference squares, as a whole, with the principles agreed upon as the basis of the peace as well as with the practical possibilities of the international situations which had to be faced and dealt with as facts. . . .

The role which America was to play in the Conference seemed determined, as I have said, before my colleagues and I got to Paris— determined by the universal expectations of the nations whose representatives, drawn from all quarters of the globe, we were to deal with. It was universally recognized that America had entered the war to promote no private or peculiar interest of her own but only as the champion of rights which she was glad to share with free men and lovers of justice everywhere. We had formulated the principles upon which the settlement was to be made—the principles upon which the armistice had been agreed to and the parleys of peace undertaken—and no one doubted that our desire was to see the treaty of peace formulated along the actual lines of those principles—and desired nothing else. We were welcomed as disinterested friends. We were resorted to as arbiters in many a difficult matter. It was recognized that our material aid would be indispensable in the days to come, when industry and credit would have to be brought back to their normal operation again and communities beaten to the ground assisted to their feet once more, and it was taken for granted, I am proud to say, that we would play the helpful friend in these things as in all others without prejudice or favor. We were generously accepted as the unaffected champions of what was right. . . .

And that confidence, it seems to me, is the measure of our opportunity and of our duty in the days to come, in which the new hope of the peoples of the world is to be fulfilled or disappointed. The fact that America is the friend of the nations, whether they be rivals or associates, is no new fact; it is only the discovery of it by the rest of the world that is new.

America may be said to have just reached her majority as a world power. It was almost exactly twenty-one years ago that the results of the war with Spain put us unexpectedly in possession of rich islands on the other side of the world and brought us into association with other governments in the control of the West Indies. It was regarded as a sinister and ominous thing by the statesmen of more than one European chancellory that we should have extended our power beyond the confines of our continental dominions. They were accustomed to think of new neighbors as a new menace, of rivals as watchful enemies. There were persons amongst us at home who looked with deep disapproval and avowed anxiety on such extensions of our national authority over distant islands and over peoples whom they feared we might exploit, not serve and assist. But we have not exploited them. We have been their friends and have sought to serve them. And our dominion has been a menace to no other nation. . . . . . They know that there is no ground for fear in receiving us as their mentors and guides. Our isolation was ended twenty years ago; and now, fear of us is ended also, our counsel and association sought after and desired. There can be no question of our ceasing to be a world power. The only question is whether we can refuse the moral leadership that is offered us, whether we shall accept or reject the confidence of the world.

The war and the Conference of Peace now sitting in Paris seem to me to have answered that question. Our participation in the war established our position among the nations and nothing but our own mistaken action can alter it. It was not an accident or a matter of sudden choice that we are no longer isolated and devoted to a policy which has only our own interest and advantage for its object. It was our duty to go in, if we were indeed the champions of liberty and of right. We answered to the call of duty in a way so spirited, so utterly without thought of what we spent of blood or treasure, so effective, so worthy of the admiration of true men everywhere, so wrought out of the stuff of all that was heroic, that the whole world saw at last, in the flesh, in noble action, a great ideal asserted and vindicated, by a nation they had deemed material and now found to be compact of the spiritual forces that must free men of every nation from every unworthy bondage. It is thus that a new role and a new responsibility have come to this great nation that we honor and which we would all wish to lift to yet higher levels of service and achievement.

The stage is set, the destiny disclosed. It has come about by no plan of our conceiving, but by the hand of God who led us into this way. We cannot turn back. We can only go forward, with lifted eyes and freshened spirit, to follow the vision. It was of this that we dreamed at our birth. America shall in truth show the way. The light streams upon the path ahead, and nowhere else.

WOODROW WILSON, "PUEBLO, COLORADO SPEECH" (1919)

Meeting resistance from a Republican-controlled Senate, Wilson appealed directly to the people and embarked upon a cross-country speaking campaign. At Pueblo, however, the president fell ill. Canceling further stops, he returned to Washington.

I have gained a renewed impression as I have crossed the continent this time of the homogeneity of this great people to whom we belong. They come from many stocks, but they are all of one kind. They come from many origins, but they are all shot through with the same principles and desire the same righteous and honest things. I have received a more inspiring impression this time of the public opinion of the United States than it was ever my privilege to receive before. . . .

But there have been unpleasant impressions as well as pleasant impressions, my fellow citizens, as I have crossed the continent. I have perceived more and more that men have been busy creating an absolutely false impression of what the treaty of peace and the covenant of the league of nations contain and mean. I find, moreover, that there is an organized propaganda against the league of nations and against the treaty proceeding from exactly the same sources that the organized propaganda proceeded from which threatened this country here and there with disloyalty. And I want to say—I cannot say it too often—any man who carries a hyphen about with him carries a dagger that he is ready to plunge into the vitals of this Republic whenever he gets ready. If I can catch any man with a hyphen in this great contest, I will know that I have caught an enemy of the Republic. My fellow citizens, it is only certain bodies of foreign sympathies, certain bodies of sympathy with foreign nations that are organized against this great document which the American representatives have brought back from Paris. Therefore, in order to clear away the mists, in order to remove the impressions, in order to check the falsehoods that have clustered around this great subject, I want to tell you a few very simple things about the treaty and the covenant.

Do not think of this treaty of peace as merely a settlement with Germany. It is that. It is a very severe settlement with Germany, but there is not anything in it that she did not earn. Indeed, she earned more than she can ever be able to pay for, and the punishment exacted of her is not a punishment greater than she can bear, and it is absolutely necessary in order that no other nation may ever plot such a thing against humanity and civilization. But the treaty is so much more than that. It is not merely a settlement with Germany; it is a readjustment of those great injustices which underlie the whole structure of European and Asiatic society. This is only the first of several treaties. They are all constructed upon the same plan. . . . . What are those lines? They are based upon the purpose to see that every government dealt with in this great settlement is put in the hands of the people and taken out of the hands of coteries and of sovereigns who had no right to rule over the people. It is a people's treaty, that accomplishes by a great sweep of practical justice the liberation of men who never could have liberated themselves, and the power of the most powerful nations has been devoted not to their aggrandizement but to the liberation of people whom they could have put under their control if they had chosen to do so. Not one foot of territory is demanded by the conquerors, not one single item of submission to their authority is demanded by them. The men who sat around that table in Paris knew that the time had come when the people were no longer going to consent to live under masters, but were going to live the lives that they chose themselves, to live under such governments as they chose to erect. That is the fundamental principle of this great settlement. . . .

Unless you get the united, concerted purpose and power of the great Governments of the world behind this settlement, it will fall down like a house of cards. There is only one power to put behind the liberation of mankind, and that is the power of mankind. It is the power of the united moral forces of the world, and in the covenant of the league of nations, the moral forces of the world are mobilized. For what purpose? Reflect, my fellow citizens, that the membership of this great league is going to include all the great fighting nations of the world, as well as the weak ones. It is not for the present going to include Germany, but for the time being Germany is not a great fighting country. All the nations that have power that can be mobilized are going to be members of this League, including the United States. And what do they unite for? They enter into a solemn promise to one another that they will never use their power against one another for aggression; that they never will impair the territorial integrity of a neighbor; that they never will interfere with the political independence of a neighbor; that they will abide by the principle that great populations are entitled to determine their own destiny and that they will not interfere with that destiny; and that no matter what differences arise amongst them they will never resort to war without first having done one or other of two things—either submitted the matter of controversy to arbitration, in which case they agree to abide by the result without question, or submitted it to the consideration of the council of the league of nations, laying before that council all the documents, all the facts, agreeing that the council can publish the documents and the facts to the whole world, agreeing that there shall be six months allowed for the mature consideration of those facts by the council, and agreeing that at the expiration of these six months, even if they are not then ready to accept the advice of the council with regard to the settlement of the dispute, they will still not go to war for another three months. In other words, they consent, no matter what happens, to submit every matter of difference between them to the judgment of mankind, and just so certainly as they do that, my fellow citizens, war will be in the far background, war will be pushed out of that foreground of terror in which it has kept the world for generation after generation, and men will know that there will be a calm time of deliberate counsel. . . .

But you say, "We have heard that we might be at a disadvantage in the league of nations." Well, whoever told you that either was deliberately falsifying or he had not read the covenant of the league of nations. I leave him the choice. I want to give you a very simple account of the organization of the league of nations and let you judge for yourselves. It is a very simple organization. The power of the league, or rather the activities of the league, lie in two bodies. There is the council, which consists of one representative from each of the principal allied and associated powers—that is to say, the United States, Great Britain, France, Italy, and Japan, along with four other representatives of the smaller powers chosen out of the general body of the membership of the league. The council is the source of every active policy of the league, and no active policy of the league can be adopted without a unanimous vote of the council. That is explicitly stated in the covenant itself. Does it not evidently follow that the league of nations can adopt no policy whatever without the consent of the United States? The affirmative vote of the representative of the United States is necessary in every case. . . .

Look at it in another aspect. The assembly is the talking body. The assembly was created in order that anybody that purposed anything wrong would be subjected to the awkward circumstance that everybody could talk about it. This is the great assembly in which all the things that are likely to disturb the peace of the world or the good understanding between nations are to be exposed to the general view. . . .

When you come to the heart of the covenant, my fellow citizens, you will find it in article 10, and I am very much interested to know that the other things have been blown away like bubbles. There is nothing in the other contentions with regard to the league of nations, but there is something in article 10 that you ought to realize and ought to accept or reject. Article 10 is the heart of the whole matter. What is article 10? I never am certain that I can from memory give a literal repetition of its language, but I am sure that I can give an exact interpretation of its meaning. Article 10 provides that every member of the league covenants to respect and preserve the territorial integrity and existing political independence of every other member of the league as against external aggression. Not against internal disturbance. There was not a man at that table who did not admit the sacredness of the right of self-determination, the sacredness of the right of any body of people to say that they would not continue to live under the Government they were then living under, and under article 11 of the covenant, they are given a place to say whether they will live under it or not. For following article 10 is article 11, which makes it the right of any member of the league at any time to call attention to anything, anywhere, that is likely to disturb the peace of the world or the good understanding between nations upon which the peace of the world depends. . . .

But, you will say, "What is the second sentence of article 10? That is what gives very disturbing thoughts." The second sentence is that the council of the league shall advise what steps, if any, are necessary to carry out the guaranty of the first sentence, namely, that the members will respect and preserve the territorial integrity and political independence of the other members. I do not know any other meaning for the word "advise" except "advise." The council advises, and it cannot advise without the vote of the United States. Why gentlemen should fear that the Congress of the United States would be advised to do something that it did not want to do I frankly cannot imagine, because they cannot even be advised to do anything unless their own representative has participated in the advice. It may be that that will impair somewhat the vigor of the league, but, nevertheless, the fact is so, that we are not obliged to take any advice except our own, which to any man who wants to go his own course is a very satisfactory state of affairs. Every man regards his own advice as best, and I dare say every man mixes his own advice with some thought of his own interest. Whether we use it wisely or unwisely, we can use the vote of the United States to make impossible drawing the United States into any enterprise that she does not care to be drawn into.

Yet article 10 strikes at the taproot of war. Article 10 is a statement that the very things that have always been sought in imperialistic wars are henceforth forgone by every ambitious nation in the world. I would have felt very lonely, my fellow countrymen, and I would have felt very much disturbed if, sitting at the peace table in Paris, I had supposed that I was expounding my own ideas. Whether you believe it or not, I know the relative size of my own ideas; I know how they stand related in bulk and proportion to the moral judgments of my fellow countrymen, and I proposed nothing whatever at the peace table at Paris that I had not sufficiently certain knowledge embodied the moral judgment of the citizens of the United States. I had gone over there with, so to say, explicit instructions. Don't you remember that we laid down 14 points which should contain the principles of the settlement? They were not my points. In every one of them I was conscientiously trying to read the thought of the people of the United States, and after I uttered those points, I had every assurance given me that could be given me that they did speak the moral judgment of the United States and not my single judgment. Then, when it came to that critical period just a little less than a year ago, when it was evident that the war was coming to its critical end, all the nations engaged in the war accepted those 14 principles explicitly as the basis of the armistice and the basis of the peace. In those circumstances I crossed the ocean under bond to my own people and to the other governments with which I was dealing. The whole specification of the method of settlement was written down and accepted beforehand, and we were architects building on those specifications. It reassures me and fortifies my position to find how, before I went over men whose judgment the United States has often trusted were of exactly the same opinion that I went abroad to express. . . .

Now, the other specification is in the covenant. The covenant in another portion guarantees to the members the independent control of their domestic question. There is not a leg for these gentlemen to stand on when they say that the interests of the United States are not safeguarded in the very points where we are most sensitive. You do not need to be told again that the covenant expressly says that nothing in this covenant shall be construed as affecting the validity of the Monroe doctrine, for example. You could not be more explicit than that. . . .

I am dwelling upon these points, my fellow citizens, in spite of the fact that I dare say to most of you they are perfectly well known, because in order to meet the present situation we have got to know what we are dealing with. We are not dealing with the kind of document which this is represented by some gentlemen to be; and inasmuch as we are dealing with a document simon-pure in respect of the very principles we have professed and lived up to, we have got to do one or other of two things—we have got to adopt it or reject it. There is no middle course. You can not go in on a special-privilege basis of your own. I take it that you are too proud to ask to be exempted from responsibilities which the other members of the league will carry. We go in upon equal terms or we do not go in at all; and if we do not go in, my fellow citizens, think of the tragedy of that result—the only sufficient guaranty of the peace of the world withheld! Ourselves drawn apart with that dangerous pride which means that we shall be ready to take care of ourselves, and that means that we shall maintain great standing armies and an irresistible navy; that means we shall have the organization of a military nation; that means we shall have a general staff, with the kind of power that the general staff of Germany had; to mobilize this great manhood of the Nation when it pleases, all the energy of our young men drawn into the thought and preparation for war. What of our pledges to the men that lie dead in France? We said that they went over there, not to prove the prowess of America or her readiness for another war, but to see to it that there never was such a war again. It always seems to make it difficult for me to say anything, my fellow citizens, when I think of my clients in this case. My clients are the children; my clients are the next generation. They do not know what promises and bonds I undertook when I ordered the armies of the United States to the soil of France, but I know, and I intend to redeem my pledges to the children; they shall not be sent upon a similar errand.

Again and again, my fellow citizens, mothers who lost their sons in France have come to me and, taking my hand, have shed tears upon it not only, but they have added, "God bless you, Mr. President!" Why, my fellow citizens, should they pray God to bless me? I advised the Congress of the United States to create the situation that led to the death of their sons. I ordered their sons oversea. I consented to their sons being put in the most difficult parts of the battle line, where death was certain, as in the impenetrable difficulties of the forest of Argonne. Why should they weep upon my hand and call down the blessings of God upon me? Because they believe that their boys died for something that vastly transcends any of the immediate and palpable objects of the war. They believe, and they rightly believe, that their sons saved the liberty of the world. They believe that wrapped up with the liberty of the world is the continuous protection of that liberty by the concerted powers of all civilized people. They believe that this sacrifice was made in order that other sons should not be called upon for a similar gift—the gift of life, the gift of all that died—and if we did not see this thing through, if we fulfilled the dearest present wish of Germany and now dissociated ourselves from those alongside whom we fought in the war, would not something of the halo go away from the gun over the mantelpiece, or the sword? Would not the old uniform lose something of its significance? These men were crusaders. They were not going forth to prove the might of the United States. They were going forth to prove the might of justice and right, and all the world accepted them as crusaders, and their transcendent achievement has made all the world believe in America as it believes in no other nation organized in the modern world. There seems to me to stand between us and the rejection or qualification of this treaty the serried ranks of those boys in khaki, not only those boys who came home, but those dear ghosts that still deploy upon the fields of France.

My friends, on last Decoration Day, I went to a beautiful hillside near Paris, where was located the cemetery of Suresnes, a cemetery given over to the burial of the American dead. Behind me on the slopes was rank upon rank of living American soldiers, and lying before me upon the levels of the plain was rank upon rank of departed American soldiers. Right by the side of the stand where I spoke there was a little group of French women who had adopted those graves, had made themselves mothers of those dear ghosts by putting flowers every day upon those graves, taking them as their own sons, their own beloved, because they had died in the same cause—France was free and the world was free because America had come! I wish that some men in public life who are now opposing the settlement for which these men died could visit such a spot as that. I wish that the thought that comes out of those graves could penetrate their consciousness. I wish that they could feel the moral obligation that rests upon us not to go back on those boys, but to see the thing through, to see it through to the end and make good their redemption of the world. For nothing less depends upon this decision, nothing less than the liberation and salvation of the world.

HENRY CABOT LODGE, "OPPOSING THE LEAGUE OF NATIONS" (1919)

The patrician Lodge (1850–1924) was a prolific historian, close friend of Theodore Roosevelt, and longtime US senator from Massachusetts. Like TR, he loathed Wilson. At the time of the fight over the League of Nations, Lodge chaired the Senate Foreign Relations Committee. Here he details his strong reservations about the proposed US entry into the League.

The independence of the United States is not only more precious to ourselves but to the world than any single possession. Look at the United States today. We have made mistakes in the past. We have had shortcomings. We shall make mistakes in the future and fall short of our own best hopes. But none the less is there any country today on the face of the earth which can compare with this in ordered liberty, in peace, and in the largest freedom?

I feel that I can say this without being accused of undue boastfulness, for it is the simple fact, and in making this treaty and taking on these obligations all that we do is in a spirit of unselfishness and in a desire for the good of mankind. But it is well to remember that we are dealing with nations every one of which has a direct individual interest to serve, and there is grave danger in an unshared idealism.

Contrast the United States with any country on the face of the earth today and ask yourself whether the situation of the United States is not the best to be found. I will go as far as anyone in world service, but the first step to world service is the maintenance of the United States. . . .

You may call me selfish if you will, conservative or reactionary, or use any other harsh adjective you see fit to apply, but an American I was born, an American I have remained all my life. I can never be anything else but an American, and I must think of the United States first, and when I think of the United States first in an arrangement like this I am thinking of what is best for the world, for if the United States fails, the best hopes of mankind fail with it.

I have never had but one allegiance—I cannot divide it now. I have loved but one flag and I cannot share that devotion and give affection to the mongrel banner invented for a league. Internationalism, illustrated by the Bolshevik and by the men to whom all countries are alike provided they can make money out of them, is to me repulsive.

National I must remain, and in that way I like all other Americans can render the amplest service to the world. The United States is the world's best hope, but if you fetter her in the interests and quarrels of other nations, if you tangle her in the intrigues of Europe, you will destroy her power for good and endanger her very existence. Leave her to march freely through the centuries to come as in the years that have gone.

Strong, generous, and confident, she has nobly served mankind. Beware how you trifle with your marvelous inheritance, this great land of ordered liberty, for if we stumble and fall freedom and civilization everywhere will go down in ruin.

We are told that we shall 'break the heart of the world' if we do not take this league just as it stands. I fear that the hearts of the vast majority of mankind would beat on strongly and steadily and without any quickening if the league were to perish altogether. If it should be effectively and beneficently changed the people who would lie awake in sorrow for a single night could be easily gathered in one not very large room but those who would draw a long breath of relief would reach to millions.

We hear much of visions and I trust we shall continue to have visions and dream dreams of a fairer future for the race. But visions are one thing and visionaries are another, and the mechanical appliances of the rhetorician designed to give a picture of a present which does not exist and of a future which no man can predict are as unreal and short-lived as the steam or canvas clouds, the angels suspended on wires and the artificial lights of the stage.

They pass with the moment of effect and are shabby and tawdry in the daylight. Let us at least be real. Washington's entire honesty of mind and his fearless look into the face of all facts are qualities which can never go out of fashion and which we should all do well to imitate.

Ideals have been thrust upon us as an argument for the league until the healthy mind which rejects cant revolts from them. Are ideals confined to this deformed experiment upon a noble purpose, tainted, as it is, with bargains and tied to a peace treaty which might have been disposed of long ago to the great benefit of the world if it had not been compelled to carry this rider on its back? 'Post equitem sedet atra cura,' Horace tells us, but no blacker care ever sat behind any rider than we shall find in this covenant of doubtful and disputed interpretation as it now perches upon the treaty of peace.

No doubt many excellent and patriotic people see a coming fulfillment of noble ideals in the words 'league for peace.' We all respect and share these aspirations and desires, but some of us see no hope, but rather defeat, for them in this murky covenant. For we, too, have our ideals, even if we differ from those who have tried to establish a monopoly of idealism.

Our first ideal is our country, and we see her in the future, as in the past, giving service to all her people and to the world. Our ideal of the future is that she should continue to render that service of her own free will. She has great problems of her own to solve, very grim and perilous problems, and a right solution, if we can attain to it, would largely benefit mankind.

We would have our country strong to resist a peril from the West, as she has flung back the German menace from the East. We would not have our politics distracted and embittered by the dissensions of other lands. We would not have our country's vigour exhausted or her moral force abated, by everlasting meddling and muddling in every quarrel, great and small, which afflicts the world.

Our ideal is to make her ever stronger and better and finer, because in that way alone, as we believe, can she be of the greatest service to the world's peace and to the welfare of mankind.

William E. Borah, "The League of Nations" (1919)

Another influential critic of the League of Nations was William Borah (1865–1940), Republican US Senator from Idaho. Unlike Lodge and others who may have endorsed the League in some modified form, Borah was adamant in his opposition, earning Wilson's enmity as leader of the "irreconcilables." In the end, he prevailed and the Senate rejected the Versailles Treaty.

When the league shall have been formed, we shall be a member of what is known as the council of the league. Our accredited representative will sit in judgment with the accredited representatives of the other members of the league to pass upon the concerns not only of our country but of all Europe and all Asia and the entire world. Our accredited representatives will be members of the assembly. They will sit there to represent the judgment of these 110,000,000 people—more then—just as we are accredited here to represent our constituencies. We can not send our representatives to sit in council with the representatives of the other great nations of the world with mental reservations as to what we shall do in case their judgment shall not be satisfactory to us. If we go to the council or to the assembly with any other purpose than that of complying in good faith and in absolute integrity with all upon which the council or the assembly may pass, we shall soon return to our country with our self-respect forfeited and the public opinion of the world condemnatory.

Why need you gentlemen across the aisle worry about a reservation here or there when we are sitting in the council and in the assembly and bound by every obligation in morals, which the President said was supreme above that of law, to comply with the judgment which our representatives and the other representatives finally form? Shall we go there, Mr. President, to sit in judgment, and in case that judgment works for peace join with our allies, but in case it works for war withdraw our cooperation? How long would we stand as we now stand a great Republic commanding the respect and holding the leadership of the world, if we should adopt any such course?. . . .

We have said, Mr. President, that we would not send our troops abroad without the consent of Congress. Pass by now for a moment the legal proposition. If we create executive functions, the Executive will perform those functions without the authority of Congress. Pass that question by and go to the other question. Our members of the council are there. Our members of the assembly are there. Article 11 is complete, and it authorizes the league, a member of which is our representative, to deal with matters of peace and war, and the league through its council and its assembly deals with the matter, and our accredited representative joins with the others in deciding upon a certain course, which involves a question of sending troops. What will the Congress of the United States do? What right will it have left, except the bare technical right to refuse, which as a moral proposition it will not dare to exercise? Have we not been told day by day for the last nine months that the Senate of the United States, a coordinate part of the treaty-making power, should accept this league as it was written because the wise men sitting at Versailles had so written it, and has not every possible influence and every source of power in public opinion been organized and directed against the Senate to compel it to do that thing? How much stronger will be the moral compulsion upon the Congress of the United States when we ourselves have indorsed the proposition of sending our accredited representatives there to vote for us?

Ah, but you say that there must be unanimous consent, and that there is vast protection in unanimous consent.

I do not wish to speak disparagingly; but has not every division and dismemberment of every nation which has suffered dismemberment taken place by unanimous consent for the last 300 years? Did not Prussia and Austria and Russia by unanimous consent divide Poland? Did not the United States and Great Britain and Japan and Italy and France divide China and give Shantung to Japan? Was that not a unanimous decision? Close the

doors upon the diplomats of Europe, let them sit in secret, give them the material to trade on, and there always will be unanimous consent. . . .

Mr. President, if you have enough territory, if you have enough material, if you have enough subject peoples to trade upon and divide, there will be no difficulty about unanimous consent.

Do our Democratic friends ever expect any man to sit as a member of the council or as a member of the Assembly equal in intellectual power and in standing before the world with that of our representative at Versailles? Do you expect a man to sit in the council who will have made more pledges, and I shall assume made them in sincerity, for self-determination and for the rights of small peoples, than had been made by our accredited representative? And yet, what became of it? The unanimous consent was obtained nevertheless.

But take another view of it. We are sending to the council one man. That one man represents 110,000,000 people.

Here, sitting in the Senate, we have two from every State in the Union, and over in the other House we have Representatives in accordance with population, and the responsibility is spread out in accordance with our obligations to our constituency. But now we are transferring to one man the stupendous power of representing the sentiment and convictions of 110,000,000 people in tremendous questions which may involve the peace or may involve the war of the world. . . .

What is the result of all this? We are in the midst of all of the affairs of Europe. We have entangled ourselves with all European concerns. We have joined in alliance with all the European nations which have thus far joined the league, and all nations which may be admitted to the league. We are sitting there dabbling in their affairs and intermeddling in their concerns. In other words, Mr. President—and this comes to the question which is fundamental with me—we have forfeited and surrendered, once and for all, the great policy of "no entangling alliances" upon which the strength of this Republic has been founded for 150 years.

My friends of reservations, tell me where is the reservation in these articles which protects us against entangling alliances with Europe?

Those who are differing over reservations, tell me what one of them protects the doctrine laid down by the Father of his Country. That fundamental proposition is surrendered, and we are a part of the European turmoils and conflicts from the time we enter this league. . . .

Lloyd-George is reported to have said just a few days before the conference met at Versailles that Great Britain could give up much, and would be willing to sacrifice much, to have America withdraw from that policy. That was one of the great objects of the entire conference at Versailles, so far as the foreign representatives were concerned. Clemenceau and Lloyd-George and others like them were willing to make any reasonable sacrifice which would draw America away from her isolation and into the internal affairs and concerns of Europe. This league of nations, with or without reservations, whatever else it does or does not do, does surrender and sacrifice that policy; and once having surrendered and become a part of the European concerns, where, my friends, are you going to stop?

You have put in here a reservation upon the Monroe doctrine. I think that, in so far as language could protect the Monroe doctrine, it has been protected. But as a practical proposition, as a working proposition, tell me candidly, as men familiar with the history of your country and of other countries, do you think that you can intermeddle in European affairs; and, secondly, never to permit Europe to [interfere in our affairs].

We can not protect the Monroe doctrine unless we protect the basic principle upon which it rests, and that is the Washington policy. I do not care how earnestly you may endeavor to do so, as a practical working proposition your league will come to the United States. . . .

Mr. President, there is another and even a more commanding reason why I shall record my vote against this treaty. It imperils what I conceive to be the underlying, the very first principles of this Republic. It is in conflict with the right of our people to govern themselves free from all restraint, legal or moral, of foreign powers. . . .

Sir, since the debate opened months ago those of us who have stood against this proposition have been taunted many times with being little Americans. Leave us the word American, keep that in your presumptuous impeachment, and no

taunt can disturb us, no gibe discompose our purposes. Call us little Americans if you will, but leave us the consolation and the pride which the term American, however modified, still imparts. . . . We have sought nothing save the tranquillity of our own people and the honor and independence of our own Republic. No foreign flattery, no possible world glory and power have disturbed our poise or come between us and our, devotion to the traditions which have made us a people or the policies which have made us a Nation, unselfish and commanding. If we have erred we have erred out of too much love for those things which from childhood you and we together have been taught to revere—yes, to defend even at the cost of limb and life. If we have erred it is because we have placed too high an estimate upon the wisdom of Washington and Jefferson, too exalted an opinion upon the patriotism of the sainted Lincoln. . . .

Senators, even in an hour so big with expectancy we should not close our eyes to the fact that democracy is something more, vastly more, than a mere form of government by which society is restrained into free and orderly life. It is a moral entity, a spiritual force, as well. And these are things which live only and alone in the atmosphere of liberty. The foundation upon which democracy rests is faith in the moral instincts of the people. Its ballot boxes, the franchise, its laws, and constitutions are but the outward manifestations of the deeper and more essential thing—a continuing trust in the moral purposes of the average man and woman. When this is lost or forfeited your outward forms, however democratic in terms, are a mockery. Force may find expression through institutions democratic in structure equal with the simple and more direct processes of a single supreme ruler. These distinguishing virtues of a real republic you can not commingle with the discordant and destructive forces of the Old World and still preserve them. You can not yoke a government whose fundamental maxim is that of liberty to a government whose first law is that of force and hope to preserve the former. These things are in eternal war, and one must ultimately destroy the other. You may still keep for a time the outward form, you may still delude yourself, as others have done in the past, with appearances and symbols, but when you shall have committed this Republic to a scheme of world control based upon force, upon the combined military force of the four great nations of the world, you will have soon destroyed the atmosphere of freedom, of confidence in the self-governing capacity of the masses, in which alone a democracy may thrive. We may become one of the four dictators of the world, but we shall no longer be master of our own spirit. And what shall it profit us as a Nation if we shall go forth to the domination of the earth and share with others the glory of world control and lose that fine sense of confidence in the people, the soul of democracy?

Look upon the scene as it is now presented. Behold the task we are to assume, and then contemplate the method by which we are to deal with this task. Is the method such as to address itself to a Government "conceived in liberty and dedicated to the proposition that all men are created equal"? When this league, this combination, is formed four great powers representing the dominant people will rule one-half of the inhabitants of the globe as subject peoples—rule by force, and we shall be a party to the rule of force. There is no other way by which you can keep people in subjection. You must either give them independence, recognize their rights as nations to live their own life and to set up their own form of government, or you must deny them these things by force. That is the scheme, the method proposed by the league. It proposes no other. We will in time become inured to its inhuman precepts and its soulless methods strange as this doctrine now seems to a free people. If we stay with our contract, we will come in time to declare with our associates that force—force, the creed of the Prussian military oligarchy—is after all the true foundation upon which must rest all stable governments. Korea, despoiled and bleeding at every pore; India, sweltering in ignorance and burdened with inhuman taxes after more than one hundred years of dominant rule; Egypt, trapped and robbed of her birthright; Ireland, with 700 years of sacrifice for independence—this is the task, this is the atmosphere, and this is the creed in and under which we are to keep alive our belief in the moral purposes and self-governing capacity of the people, a belief without which the Republic must disintegrate and die. The maxim of liberty will soon give way to the rule of blood and iron. We have been pleading here for our Constitution.

Conform this league, it has been said, to the technical terms of our charter, and all will be well. But I declare to you that we must go further and conform to those sentiments and passions for justice and freedom which are essential to the existence of democracy. . . .

Sir, we are told that this treaty means peace. Even so, I would not pay the price. Would you purchase peace at the cost of any part of our independence? We could have had peace in 1776—the price was high, but we could have had it. James Otis, Sam Adams, Hancock, and Warren were surrounded by those who urged peace and British rule. All through that long and trying struggle, particularly when the clouds of adversity lowered upon the cause, there was a cry of peace—let us have peace. We could have had peace in 1860; Lincoln was counseled by men of great influence and accredited wisdom to let our brothers— and, thank Heaven, they are brothers— depart in peace. But the tender, loving Lincoln, bending under the fearful weight of impending civil war, an apostle of peace, refused to pay the price, and a reunited country will praise his name forevermore—bless it because he refused peace at the price of national honor and national integrity. Peace upon any other basis than national independence, peace purchased at the cost of any part of our national integrity, is fit only for slaves, and even when purchased at such a price it is a delusion, for it can not last.

But your treaty does not mean peace—far, very far, from it. If we are to judge the future by the past it means war. Is there any guaranty of peace other than the guaranty which comes of the control of the war-making power by the people? Yet what great rule of democracy does the treaty leave unassailed? The people in whose keeping alone you can safely lodge the power of peace or war nowhere, at no time and in no place, have any voice in this scheme for world peace. Autocracy which has bathed the world in blood for centuries reigns supreme. Democracy is everywhere excluded. This, you say, means peace.

Can you hope for peace when love of country is disregarded in your scheme, when the spirit of nationality is rejected, even scoffed at? Yet what law of that moving and mysterious force does your treaty not deny? With a ruthlessness unparalleled your treaty in a dozen instances runs counter to the divine law of nationality. Peoples who speak the same language, kneel at the same ancestral tombs, moved by the same traditions, animated by a common hope, are torn asunder, broken in pieces, divided, and parceled out to antagonistic nations. And this you call justice. This, you cry, means peace. Peoples who have dreamed of independence, struggled and been patient, sacrificed and been hopeful, peoples who were told that through this peace conference they should realize the aspirations of centuries, have again had their hopes dashed to earth. One of the most striking and commanding figures in this war, soldier and statesmen, turned away from the peace table at Versailles declaring to the world, "The promise of the new life, the victory of the great humane ideals for which the peoples have shed their blood and their treasure without stint, the fulfillment of their aspirations toward a new international order and a fairer and better world, are not written into the treaty." No, your treaty means injustice. It means slavery. It means war. And to all this you ask this Republic to become a party. You ask it to abandon the creed under which it has grown to power and accept the creed of autocracy, the creed of repression and force.

VI.

INTERWAR

Erroneously enshrined as a period of abject "isolationism," the period between the two world wars saw considerable US activism and even greater debate regarding the threats to America's security and well-being.

By the early 1920s, most Americans had concluded that US entry into the European War of 1914–1918 had been a mistake. More than 116,000 American soldiers had died during that conflict, with little to show for their sacrifices. Identifying the culprits to blame for this misadventure became a major preoccupation, with President Wilson, British propagandists, Wall Street bankers, and arms manufacturers, among others, fingered as responsible. That the war had been fought to "make the world safe for democracy" became something of a bad joke.

Yet once having inserted itself into European politics, the United States could not easily disengage. Whether Americans cared to admit it or not, their nation had now become a world power with interests and commitments extending far beyond the continental United States. Furthermore, new dangers demanding US attention had appeared on the global scene. The Bolshevik Revolution of 1917 had transformed the Russian Empire into the enormous Union of Soviet Socialist Republics, which declared itself an avowed enemy of capitalism. In the East, Japan had emerged as a rising power with imperial ambitions of its own. At home, a postwar "Red Scare" and racist fears of a "Yellow Peril" magnified the perceived threat posed by the USSR and Imperial Japan.

In the face of these developments, Washington pursued an active diplomatic course, albeit one limited by the US refusal to join the League of Nations and by its relative military weakness. The onset of the Great Depression in the fall of 1929 curbed Washington's appetite even for diplomacy. Responding to the unprecedented economic crisis at home became the overriding priority and would remain so for the next decade.

UNITED STATES SENATE, "REPORT OF THE OVERMAN COMMITTEE" (1919)

The Bolshevik Revolution of 1917 that created the Soviet Union spurred fear of a "Red" threat to the United States. A special Senate committee convened to investigate this threat spelled out the implications.

[T]he word "Bolshevism" has now become merely a generic term, and in America is nothing more than a slogan of the elements of unrest and discontent. By reason of their ignorance as to what Bolshevism means, almost every dissatisfied element, from the radical anarchist to the theoretical idealist, has seized upon it as approaching something of a Utopian nature. . . .

The word Bolshevism has been so promiscuously applied to various political and social programs that we feel that it is of paramount importance that the delusions and misconceptions as to what it really is, as it exists today in Russia, should be, as far as possible, removed and that the people of the United States should be thoroughly informed as to just what this much-discussed institution really is, both in theory and in practice. . . .

The Bolsheviki have inaugurated a reign of terror unparalleled in the history of modern civilization, in many of its aspects rivaling even the inhuman savagery of the Turk and the terrors of the French Revolution. . . . In Bolshevik Russia every instrument available for the exercise of force and power is in the possession of government, and those opposed to the government are completely suppressed and absolutely powerless. . . .

The Government is founded upon class hatred; its avowed purpose is the extermination of all elements of society that are opposed to or are capable of opposing the Bolshevist party. "Merciless suppression" and "extermination" of all classes except the present governing class are familiar slogans of the Bolsheviki and confiscation is adopted as the essential instrument in the government formula. . . .

In practice, the Government has classified all those people who fail to sympathize with and support the existing dictatorship as the bourgeoisie and has proclaimed the doctrine that their refusal to bow to the edict of the dictatorship should be answered by "violence toward the bourgeoisie". . . .

Every activity of the Bolshevik government indicates clearly the antipathy of the Bolsheviki toward Christianity and the Christian religion. Its program is a direct challenge to that religion. The Christian church and Bolshevism cannot both survive the program that is being developed by the Russian dictatorship and which it is undertaking to extend throughout the world. . . .

The features which constitute the features of Bolshevism as it exists today in Russia and is presented to the rest of the world as a panacea for all ills may be summarized as follows:

(1) The repudiation of democracy and the establishment of a dictatorship;
(2) The confiscation of all land and the improvements thereon;
(3) The confiscation of all forests and natural resources;
(4) The confiscation of all live stock and agricultural implements;
(5) The confiscation of all banks and banking institutions . . . ;
(6) The confiscation of all factories, mills, mines, and industrial institutions . . . ;
(7) The confiscation of all churches and all church property . . . ;
(8) The confiscation of all newspapers and periodicals . . . ; . . .
(14) The establishment of universal compulsory military service regardless of religious scruples or conscientious objection;
(15) The establishment of universal compulsory labor; . . .
(18) The establishment, through marriage and divorce laws, of a method for the legalization of prostitution. . . .

United States Senate, "Report of the Overman Committee" (1919) [as printed in *New York Times*, June 1919].

(27) The denial of the existence of any "inalienable" rights in the individual citizen;

(29) The inauguration of a reign of fear, terrorism, and violence.

This is the program that the revolutionary elements and the so-called "Parlor Bolshevik" would have this country accept as a substitute for the Government of the United States. . . .

The activities of the Bolsheviki constitute a complete repudiation of modern civilization and the promulgation of the doctrine that the best attainment of the most backward member of society shall be the level at which mankind shall find its final and victorious goal. . . . To carry this message to the uttermost parts of the earth, they have appropriated enormous sums of money, and, incidentally, their process of equalization in Russia was promoted by the starvation which the funds thus expended might have been utilized to alleviate. Their messengers and their friends have afflicted this country, and their new civilization has been represented as Utopian in its nature. Many well-disposed persons have been deceived into the belief that they were promoting a social welfare movement in advocating it. . . . Yet while these people who have been popularly called "parlor Bolshevists" are contributing to these Bolshevik agents, these same agents are appealing to the hatred and lowest instincts of the more ignorant elements of the population, reinforced by the criminally inclined, to whom the doctrine of confiscation furnishes a version of legalized robbery, and a means of livelihood without physical or mental effort, to rise en masse and destroy our civilization. . . .

It is significant, however, that in the United States only a portion of the so-called radical revolutionary groups and organizations accept in its entirety the doctrine of the Bolsheviki. They have, however, all seized upon Bolshevism as a rallying cry and are undertaking to unite all of these elements under that banner for the purpose of accomplishing the initial step in their common formula, to wit, the overthrow of existing governmental institutions and the complete demoralization of modern society. With this accomplished, each group hopes that it can muster sufficient strength to maintain a supremacy in the new social order and invoke the policies of its particular creed. Most of these groups accept the common ground that forcible, as distinguished from political, action should be used as the instrument to secure the overthrow of the present government and in so doing defy and repudiate the democratic form of government which guarantees under our Constitution the rule of the majority. . . .

The radical revolutionary elements in this country and the Bolshevik government of Russia have, therefore, found a common cause in support of which they can unite their forces. They are both fanning the flame of discontent and endeavoring to incite revolution. Numerous newspapers are openly advocating revolution. Literature and circular matter demanding a resort to violence are being widely circulated. Bombs and high explosives have been used in many parts of the country in an attempt to inaugurate a reign of terror and to accomplish the assassination of public officials. The demonstration of the consequences of this movement in Russia, no matter how graphic the description, is a distant, faraway picture to the average citizen of the United States. While entertaining and perhaps amusing him, much as the novel in modern fiction does, it fails to impress him as an actual existing institution, in a world growing smaller and smaller through the accomplishments in transportation and communication, that must be considered and met as an actuality. To understand and realize its real consequences, it must be brought home to the citizen and applied to the life and institutions which he knows. . . .

The nation having engaged in the greatest war in history, with the purpose of saving the world for democracy, now emerges from that struggle confronted with the paramount duty of saving democracy for the world . . .

MADISON GRANT, "INTRODUCTION" TO LOTHROP STODDARD, *RISING TIDE OF COLOR* (1921)

During the period between the world wars, fear of white America being inundated and overrun by people of color competed with fear of Bolshevism. Madison Grant (1865–1937) was a leader in the movement to preserve white supremacy, both through the systematic implementation of eugenics and by limiting immigration of people viewed as undesirable.

In our present era of convulsive changes, a prophet must be bold, indeed, to predict anything more definite than a mere trend in events, but the study of the past is the one safe guide in forecasting the future. . . .

Viewed in the light of geography and zoology, Europe west of Russia is but a peninsula of Asia with the southern shores of the Mediterranean Sea included. True Africa, or rather Ethiopia, lies south of the Sahara Desert and has virtually no connection with the North except along the valley of the Nile.

This Eurasiatic continent has been, perhaps since the origin of life itself, the most active centre of evolution and radiation of the higher forms. . . .

The impulse that inaugurated the development of mankind seems to have had its basic cause in the stress of changing climatic conditions in central Asia at the close of the Pliocene, and the human inhabitants of Eurasia have ever since exhibited in a superlative degree the energy developed at that time. This energy, however, has not been equally shared by the various species of man, either extinct or living, and the survivors of the earlier races are, for the most part, to be found on the other continents and islands or in the extreme outlying regions of Eurasia itself.

In other words those groups of mankind which at an early period found refuge in the Americas, in Australia, in Ethiopia, or in the islands of the sea, represent to a large extent stages in man's physical and cultural development, from which the more energized inhabitants of Eurasia have long since emerged. In some cases, as in Mexico and Peru, the outlying races developed in their isolation a limited culture of their own, but, for the most part, they have exhibited, and continue to this day to exhibit, a lack of capacity for sustained evolution from within as well as a lack of capacity to adjust themselves of their own initiative to the rapid changes which modern times impose upon them from without.

In Eurasia itself this same inequality of potential capacity is found, but in a lesser degree, and consequently, in the progress of humanity, there has been constant friction between those who push forward and those who are unable to keep pace with changing conditions. . . .

Without attempting a scientific classification of the inhabitants of Eurasia, it is sufficient to describe the three main races. The first are the yellow-skinned, straight black-haired, black-eyed, round-skulled Mongols and Mongoloids massed in central and eastern Asia north of the Himalayan system.

To the west of them, and merged with them, lie the Alpines, also characterized by dark, but not straight hair, dark eyes, relatively short stature, and round skulls. These Alpines are thrust like a wedge into Europe between the Nordics and the Mediterraneans, with a tip that reaches the Atlantic Ocean. Those of western Europe are derived from one or more very ancient waves of round-skulled invaders from the East, who probably came by way of Asia Minor and the Balkans, but they have been so long in their present homes that they retain little except their brachycephalic skull-shape to connect them with the Asiatic Mongols.

South of the Himalayas and westward in a narrow belt to the Atlantic, and on both sides of the Inland Sea, lies the Mediterranean race, more or less swarthy-skinned, black-haired, dark-eyed, and long-skulled. On the northwest, grouped around the Baltic and North Seas, lies the great Nordic race. It is characterized by a fair white skin, wavy hair with a range of color from dark brown to flaxen, light eyes, tall stature, and long skulls.

Madison Grant, "Introduction" to Lothrop Stoddard, *Rising Tide of Color,* New York: Charles Scribner's Sons (1921).

These races show other physical characters which are definite but difficult to describe, such as texture of skin and cast of features, especially of the nose. The contrast of mental and spiritual endowments is equally definite, but even more elusive of definition.

It is with the action and interaction of these three groups, together with internal civil wars, that recorded history deals. . . .

So we find, thrust westward from the Heartland, a race touching the Atlantic at Brittany, thoroughly Asiatic and Mongoloid in the east, very imperfectly Nordicized in the centre, and thoroughly Nordicized culturally in the far west of Europe, where it has become, and must be accepted as, an integral part of the White World. . . .

By the time of Charlemagne the White Man's world was reduced to Scandinavia, Germany west of the Elbe, the British Isles, the Low Countries, and northern France and Italy, with outlying groups in southern France and Spain. This was the lowest ebb for the Nordics and it was the crowning glory of Charlemagne's career that he not only turned back the flood, but began the organization of a series of more or less Nordicized marches or barrier states from the Baltic to the Adriatic, which have served as ramparts against Asiatic pressure from his day to ours. West of this line the feudal states of mediaeval Europe developed into western Christendom, the nucleus of the civilized world of to-day. . . .

Never again did Asia push so far west, but the danger was not finally removed until Charlemagne and his successors had organized the Western Empire. . . .

Christendom, however, had sore trials ahead when the successors of Jenghiz Khan destroyed Moscovy and Poland and devastated eastern Europe. . . .

Some conception of the almost unbelievable horrors that western Europe escaped at this time may be gathered from the fate of the countries which fell before the irresistible rush of the Mongols, whose sole descernible motive seems to have been blood lust. The destruction wrought in China, central Asia, and Persia is almost beyond conception. In twelve years, in China and the neighboring states, Jenghiz Khan and his lieutenants slaughtered more than 18,500,000 human beings. . . .

Almost in modern times these same Mongoloid invaders, entering by way of Asia Minor, and calling themselves Turks, after destroying the Eastern Empire, the Balkan States, and Hungary, again met the Nordic chivalry of western Europe under the walls of Vienna, in 1683, and again the Asiatics went down in rout.

On these four separate occasions the Nordic race and it alone saved modern civilization. The half-Nordicized lands to the south and to the east collapsed under the invasions.

Unnumbered Nordic tribes, nameless and unsung, have been massacred, or submerged, or driven from their lands. The survivors had been pushed ever westward until their backs were against the Northern Ocean. There the Nordics came to bay the tide was turned. Few stop to reflect that it was more than sixty years after the first American legislature sat at Jamestown, Virginia, that Asia finally abandoned the conquest of Europe.

One of the chief results of forcing the Nordic race back to the seacoast was the creation of maritime power and its development to a degree never before known even in the days of the Phoenicians and Carthaginians. With the recession of the Turkish flood, modern Europe emerges and inaugurates a counterattack on Asia which has placed virtually the entire world under European domination.

While in the mediaeval conflicts between Europe and Asia the latter was the aggressor, the case was otherwise in the early wars between the Nordic and the Mediterranean peoples. Here for three thousand years the Nordics were the aggressors, and, although these wars were terribly destructive to their numbers, they were the medium through which classic civilization was introduced into Nordic lands. As to the ethnic consequences, northern barbarians poured over the passes of the Balkans, Alpines, and Pyrenees into the sunny lands of the south only to slowly vanish in the languid environment which lacked the stimulus of fierce strife with hostile nature and savage rivals.

Nevertheless, long before the opening of the Christian era the Alpines of western Europe were thoroughly Nordicized, and in the centuries that followed, the old Nordic element in Spain, Italy, and France has been again and again strongly reinforced, so that these lands are now an integral part of the White World.

In recent centuries Russia was again superficially Nordicized with a top dressing of Nordic nobility, chiefly coming from the Baltic provinces. Along with this process there was everywhere in Europe a resurgence among the submerged and forgotten Alpines and among the Mediterranean elements of the British Isles, while Bolshevism in Russia means the elimination of the Nordic aristocracy and the dominance of the half-Asiatic Slavic peasantry.

All wars thus far discussed have been race wars of Europe against Asia, or of the Nordics against Mediterraneans. The wars against the Mongols were necessary and vital; there was no alternative except to fight to the finish. But the wars of northern Europe against the south, from the racial point of view, were not only useless but destructive. Bad as they were, however, they left untouched to a large extent the broodland of the race in the north and west. . . .

From that time on all the wars of Europe, other than those against the Asiatics and Saracens, were essentially civil wars fought between peoples or leaders of Nordic blood.

Mediaeval Europe was one long welter of Nordic immolation until the Wars of the Roses in England, the Hundred Years' War in the Lowlands, the religious, revolutionary, and Napoleonic wars in France, and the ghastly Thirty Years' War in Germany dangerously depleted the ruling Nordic race and paved the way for the emergence from obscurity of the servile races which for ages had been dominated by them. . . .

The backbone of western civilization is racially Nordic, the Alpines and Mediterraneans being effective precisely to the extent in which they have been Nordicized and vitalized.

If this great race, with its capacity for leadership and fighting, should ultimately pass, with it would pass that which we call civilization. It would be succeeded by an unstable and bastardized population, where worth and merit would have no inherent right to leadership and among which a new and darker age would blot out our racial inheritance.

Such a catastrophe cannot threaten if the Nordic race will gather itself together in time, shake off the shackles of an inveterate altruism, discard the vain phantom of internationalism, and reassert the pride of race and the right of merit to rule.

The Nordic race has been driven from many of its lands, but still grasps firmly the control of the world, and it is certainly not at a greater numerical disadvantage than often before in contrast to the teeming population of eastern Asia.

It has repeatedly been confronted with crises where the accident of battle, or the genius of a leader, saved a well-nigh hopeless day. It has survived defeat, it has survived the greater danger of victory, and, if it takes warning in time, it may face the future with assurance. Fight it must, but let that fight be not a civil war against its own blood kindred but against the dangerous foreign races, whether they advance sword in hand or in the more insidious guise of beggars at our gates, pleading for admittance to share our prosperity. If we continue to allow them to enter they will in time drive us out of our own land by mere force of breeding.

The great hope of the future here in America lies in the realization of the working class that competition of the Nordic with the alien is fatal, whether the latter be the lowly immigrant from southern or eastern Europe or whether he be the more obviously dangerous Oriental against whose standards of living the white man cannot compete. In this country we must look to such of our people our farmers and artisans as are still of American blood to recognize and meet this danger.

Our present condition is the result of following the leadership of idealists and philanthropic doctrinaires, aided and abetted by the perfectly understandable demand of our captains of industry for cheap labor.

To-day the need for statesmanship is great, and greater still is the need for thorough knowledge of history. All over the world the first has been lacking, and in the passions of the Great War the lessons of the past have been forgotten both here and in Europe.

The establishment of a chain of Alpine states from the Baltic to the Adriatic, as a sequel to the war, all of them organized at the expense of the Nordic ruling classes, may bring Europe back to the days when Charlemagne, marching from the Rhine to the Elbe, found the valley of that river inhabited by heathen Wends. Beyond lay Asia, and his successors spent a thousand years pushing eastward the frontiers of Europe.

Now that Asia, in the guise of Bolshevism with Semitic leadership and Chinese execution-ers, is organizing an assault upon western Europe, the new states, Slavic-Alpine in race, with little Nordic blood may prove to be not frontier guards of western Europe but vanguards of Asia in central Europe. None of the earlier Alpine states have held firm against Asia, and it is more than doubtful whether Poland, Bohemia, Rumania, Hungary, and Jugo-Slavia can face the danger successfully, now that they have been deprived of the Nordic ruling classes through democratic institutions.

Democratic ideals among an homogeneous population of Nordic blood, as in England or America, is one thing, but it is quite another for the white man to share his blood with, or intrust his ideals to brown, yellow, black, or red men.

This is suicide pure and simple, and the first victim of this amazing folly will be the white man himself.

CHARLES EVANS HUGHES, "THE CONFERENCE ON LIMITATION OF ARMAMENT" (1921)

After the war of 1914–1918, arms limitation as an approach to preventing future wars enjoyed widespread popularity. In November 1921, the United States convened in Washington an international conference aimed at preventing a naval arms race that could potentially lead to another great power war. Here are the remarks by Secretary of State Charles Evans Hughes (1862–1948) that opened the conference. The conference resulted in three major agreements, each ratified by the U.S. Senate: A Five Power Treaty limiting the size of the world's biggest navies; a Four Power Treaty committing the United States, Great Britain, Japan, and France to maintaining the status quo in the Pacific; and a Nine Power Treaty committing the signatories to respecting the policy of the Open Door regarding China.

The world looks to this Conference to relieve humanity of the crushing burden created by competition in armament, and it is the view of the American Government that we should meet that expectation without any unnecessary delay. It is therefore proposed that the Conference should proceed at once to consider the question of the limitation of armament. . . .

The proposal to limit armament by an agreement of the Powers is not a new one, and we are admonished by the futility of earlier efforts. . . .

In view, however, of the resolution which had been adopted at the First Hague Conference the delegates of the United States were instructed that the subject of limitation of armament "should be regarded as unfinished business, and that the Second Conference should ascertain and give full consideration to the results of such examination as the Governments may have given to the possibility of an agreement pursuant to the wish expressed by the First Conference." But by reason of the obstacles which the subject had encountered, the Second Peace Conference at The Hague, although it made notable progress in provision for the peaceful settlement of controversies, was unable to deal with limitation of armament. . . .

Although the effect was clearly perceived, the race in preparation of armament, wholly unaffected by these futile suggestions, went on until it fittingly culminated in the greatest war of history; and we are now suffering from the unparalleled loss of life, the destruction of hopes, the economic dislocations and the widespread impoverishment which measure the cost of the victory over the brutal pretensions of military force.

But if we are warned by the inadequacy of earlier endeavors for limitation of armament, we cannot fail to recognize the extraordinary opportunity now presented. We not only have the lessons of the past to guide us, not only do we have the reaction from the disillusioning experiences of war, but we must meet the challenge of imperative economic demands. What was convenient or highly desirable before is now a matter of vital necessity. If there is to be economic rehabilitation, if the longings for reasonable progress are not to be denied, if we are to be spared the uprisings of peoples made desperate in the desire to shake off burdens no longer endurable, competition in armament must stop. The present opportunity not only derives its advantage from a general appreciation of this fact, but the power to deal with the exigency now rests with a small group of nations, represented here, who have every reason to desire peace and to promote amity. The astounding ambition which lay athwart the promise of the Second Hague Conference no longer menaces the world, and the great opportunity of liberty-loving and peace-preserving democracies has come. Is it not plain that the time has passed for mere resolutions that the responsible Powers should examine the question of limitation of armament? We can no longer content ourselves with investigations, with statistics, with reports, with the circumlocution of inquiry. The essential facts are sufficiently known. The time has come, and this Conference has been called, not for general resolutions or mutual advice, but for action. We meet with full understanding that the aspirations of mankind are not to be defeated either by plausible suggestions of postponement or by impracticable counsels of perfection. Power and responsibility are here and the world awaits a practicable program which shall at once be put into execution.

I am confident that I shall have your approval in suggesting that in this matter, as well as in others before the Conference, it is desirable to follow the course of procedure which has the best promise of achievement rather than one which would facilitate division; and thus, constantly aiming to agree so far as possible, we shall, with each point of agreement, make it easier to proceed to others.

The question, in relation to armament, which may be regarded as of primary importance at this time, and with which we can deal most promptly and effectively, is the limitation of naval armament. There are certain general considerations which may be deemed pertinent to this subject.

The first is that the core of the difficulty is to be found in the competition in naval programs, and that, in order appropriately to limit naval armament, competition in its production must be abandoned. Competition will not be remedied by resolves with respect to the method of its continuance. One program inevitably leads to another, and if competition continues, its regulation is impracticable. There is only one adequate way out and that is to end it now.

It is apparent that this cannot be accomplished without serious sacrifices. Enormous sums have been expended upon ships under construction and building programs which are now under way can not be given up without heavy loss. Yet if the present construction of capital ships goes forward other ships will inevitably be built to rival them and this will lead to still others. Thus the race will continue so long as ability to continue lasts. The effort to escape sacrifices is futile. We must face them or yield our purpose.

It is also clear that no one of the naval Powers should be expected to make these sacrifices alone. The only hope of limitation of naval armament is by agreement among the nations concerned, and this agreement should be entirely fair and reasonable in the extent of the sacrifices required of each of the Powers. In considering the basis of such an agreement, and the commensurate sacrifices to be required, it is necessary to have regard to the existing naval strength of the great naval Powers, including the extent of construction already effected in the case of ships in process. This follows from the fact that one nation is as free to compete as another, and each may find grounds for its action. What one may do another may demand the opportunity to rival, and we remain in the thrall of competitive effort. I may add that the American delegates are advised by their naval experts that the tonnage of capital ships may fairly be taken to measure the relative strength of navies, as the provision for auxiliary combatant craft should sustain a reasonable relation to the capital ship tonnage allowed.

It would also seem to be a vital part of a plan for the limitation of naval armament that there should be a naval holiday. It is proposed that for a period of not less than 10 years there should be no further construction of capital ships.

I am happy to say that I am at liberty to go beyond these general propositions and, on behalf of the American delegation acting under the instructions of the President of the United States, to submit to you a concrete proposition for an agreement for the limitation of naval armament.

It should be added that this proposal immediately concerns the British Empire, Japan, and the United States. . . . In making the present proposal the United States is most solicitous to deal with the question upon an entirely reasonable and practicable basis, to the end that the just interests of all shall be adequately guarded and that national security and defense shall be maintained. Four general principles have been applied:

(1) That all capital-ship building programs, either actual or projected, should be abandoned;
(2) That further reduction should be made through the scrapping of certain of the older ships;
(3) That in general regard should be had to the existing naval strength of the Powers concerned;
(4) That the capital ship tonnage should be used as the measurement of strength for navies and a proportionate allowance of auxiliary combatant craft prescribed.

The principal features of the proposed agreement are as follows:

CAPITAL SHIPS

United States —
The United States is now completing its program of 1916 calling for 10 new battleships and 6 battle cruisers. One battleship has been completed. The others are in various stages of construction; in some cases from 60 to over 80 per cent of the construction has been done. On these 15 capital ships now being built over $330,000,000 have been spent. Still, the United States is willing in the interest of an immediate limitation of naval armament to scrap all these ships. The United States proposes, if this plan is accepted —

(1) To scrap all capital ships now under construction. This includes 6 battle cruisers and 7 battleships on the ways and in course of building, and 2 battleships launched. The total number of new capital ships thus to be scrapped is 15. The total tonnage of the new capital ships when completed would be 618,000 tons.
(2) To scrap all of the older battleships up to, but not including, the DELAWARE and NORTH DAKOTA. The number of these old battleships to be scrapped is 15. Their total tonnage is 227,740 tons. Thus the number of capital ships to be scrapped by the United States, if this plan is accepted, is 30, with an aggregate tonnage (including that of ships in construction, if completed) of 845,740 tons.

Great Britain —
The plan contemplates that Great Britain and Japan shall take action which is fairly commensurate with this action on the part of the United States. It is proposed that Great Britain —

(1) Shall stop further construction of the 4 new Hoods, the new capital ships not laid down but upon which money has been spent. These 4 ships, if completed, would have tonnage displacement of 172,000 tons.
(2) Shall, in addition, scrap her pre-dreadnaughts, second line battleships, and first line battleships up to, but not including, the King George V class. These, with certain pre-dreadnaughts which it is understood have already been scrapped, would amount to 19 capital ships and a tonnage reduction of 411,375 tons. The total tonnage of ships thus to be scrapped by Great Britain (including the tonnage of the 4 Hoods, if completed) would be 583,375 tons.

Japan —
It is proposed that Japan

(1) Shall abandon her program of ships not yet laid down, viz, the Kii, Owari, No. 7 and No. 8 battleships, and Nos. 5, 6, 7, and 8, battle cruisers. It should be observed that this does not involve the stopping of construction, as the construction of none of these ships has been begun.
(2) Shall scrap 3 capital ships (the Mutsu launched, the Tosa, and Kago in course of building) and 4 battle cruisers (the Amagi and Akagi in course of building, and the Atoga and Takao not yet laid down, but for which certain material has been assembled). The total number of new capital ships to be scrapped under this paragraph is seven. The total tonnage of these new capital ships when completed would be 289,100 tons.
(3) Shall scrap all predreadnaughts and battleships of the second line. This would include the scrapping of all ships up to but not including the Settsu; that is, the scrapping of 10 older ships, with a total tonnage of 159,828 tons.

The total reduction of tonnage on vessels existing, laid down, or for which material has been assembled (taking the tonnage of the new ships when completed), would be 448,928 tons. Thus, under this plan there would be immediately destroyed, of the navies of the three Powers, 66 capital fighting ships, built and building, with a total tonnage of 1,878,043. It is proposed that it should be agreed by the United States, Great Britain, and Japan that their navies, with respect to capital ships, within three months after the making of the agreement shall consist of certain ships designated in the proposal and numbering for the United States 18, for Great Britain 22, for Japan 10. The tonnage of these ships would be as follows: Of the United States, 500,650; of Great Britain, 604,450; of Japan, 299,700. In reaching this result, the age factor in the case of the respective navies has received appropriate consideration.

Replacement—
With respect to replacement, the United States proposes:

(1) That it be agreed that the first replacement tonnage shall not be laid down until 10 years from the date of the agreement;
(2) That replacement be limited by an agreed maximum of capital ship tonnage as follows:
    For the United States . . . . . . 500,000 tons.
    For Great Britain . . . . 500,000 tons.
    For Japan . . . . 300,000 tons.

(3) That subject to the 10-year limitation above fixed and the maximum standard, capital ships may be replaced when they are 20 years old by new capital ship construction;
(4) That no capital ship shall be built in replacement with a tonnage displacement of more than 35,000 tons.

I have sketched the proposal only in outline, leaving the technical details to be supplied by the formal proposition which is ready for submission to the delegates.

The plan includes provision for the limitation of auxiliary combatant craft. This term embraces three classes, that is (1) auxiliary surface combatant craft, such as cruisers (exclusive of battle cruisers), flotilla leaders, destroyers, and various surface types; (2) submarines; and (3) airplane carriers.

I shall not attempt to review the proposals for these various classes, as they bear a definite relation to the provisions for capital fighting ships.

With the acceptance of this plan the burden of meeting the demands of competition in naval armament will be lifted. Enormous sums will be released to aid the progress of civilization. At the same time the proper demands of national defense will be adequately met and the nations will have ample opportunity during the naval holiday of 10 years to consider their future course. Preparation for offensive naval war will stop now.

KELLOGG–BRIAND PACT (1928)

Later that decade, the prospect of nations jointly renouncing war altogether captured popular attention. Enthusiasm for this shortcut to permanent peace culminated in a solemn international agreement, eventually signed by sixty-two nations. The lead American negotiator for this compact was Secretary of State Frank B. Kellogg (1856–1937). The U.S. Senate ratified the Kellogg-Briand Pact by a vote of 85 to 1.

Deeply sensible of their solemn duty to promote the welfare of mankind;

Persuaded that the time has come when a frank renunciation of war as an instrument of national policy should be made to the end that the peaceful and friendly relations now existing between their peoples may be perpetuated;

Convinced that all changes in their relations with one another should be sought only by pacific means and be the result of a peaceful and orderly process, and that any signatory Power which shall hereafter seek to promote its national interests by resort to war should be denied the benefits furnished by this Treaty;

Hopeful that, encouraged by their example, all the other nations of the world will join in this humane endeavor and by adhering to the present Treaty as soon as it comes into force bring their peoples within the scope of its beneficent provisions, thus uniting the civilized nations of the world in a common renunciation of war as an instrument of their national policy;. . . .

ARTICLE I

The High Contracting Parties solemnly declare in the names of their respective peoples that they condemn recourse to war for the solution of international controversies, and renounce it, as an instrument of national policy in their relations with one another.

ARTICLE II

The High Contracting Parties agree that the settlement or solution of all disputes or conflicts of whatever nature or of whatever origin they may be, which may arise among them, shall never be sought except by pacific means.

ARTICLE III

The present Treaty shall be ratified by the High Contracting Parties named in the Preamble in accordance with their respective constitutional requirements, and shall take effect as between them as soon as all their several instruments of ratification shall have been deposited at Washington.

This Treaty shall, when it has come into effect as prescribed in the preceding paragraph, remain open as long as may be necessary for adherence by all the other Powers of the world. . . .

It shall be the duty of the Government of the United States to furnish each Government named in the Preamble and every Government subsequently adhering to this Treaty with a certified copy of the Treaty and of every instrument of ratification or adherence. It shall also be the duty of the Government of the United States telegraphically to notify such Governments immediately upon the deposit with it of each instrument of ratification or adherence.

HENRY L. STIMSON, "LETTER TO SENATOR BORAH" (1932)

The Kellogg-Briand Pact did not live up to its expectations. In 1931, Imperial Japan embarked upon a program of conquest in East Asia, the Japanese army's invasion and subsequent occupation of Manchuria violating the US policy of the Open Door. Secretary of State Henry L. Stimson (1867–1950) condemned Japanese aggression. In what became known as the Stimson Doctrine, he stated that the United States would refuse to recognize any action at odds with the Open Door. In a letter to Senator Borah, then chairing the Senate Foreign Relations Committee, Stimson explains the basis for his response.

You have asked my opinion whether, as has been sometimes recently suggested, present conditions in China have in any way indicated that the so-called Nine Power Treaty has become inapplicable or ineffective or rightly in need of modifications, and if so, what I considered should be the policy of this Government.

This Treaty, as you of course know, forms the legal basis upon which now rests the "Open Door" policy towards China. That policy enunciated by John Hay in 1899, brought to an end the struggle among various powers for so-called spheres of interest in China which was threatening the dismemberment of that empire. To accomplish this Mr. Hay invoked two principles (1) equality of commercial opportunity among all nations in dealing with China, and (2) as necessary to that equality the preservation of China's territorial and administrative integrity. These principles were not new in the foreign policy of America. They had been the principles upon which it rested in its dealing with other nations for many years. In the case of China they were invoked to save a situation which not only threatened the future development and sovereignty of that great Asiatic people, but also threatened to create dangerous and constantly increasing rivalries between the other nations of the world. War had already taken place between Japan and China. At the close of that war three other nations intervened to prevent Japan from obtaining some of the results of that war claimed by her. Other nations sought and had obtained spheres of interest. Partly as a result of these actions a serious uprising had broken out in China which endangered the legations of all of the powers at Peking. While the attack on those legations was in progress, Mr. Hay made an announcement in respect to this policy and the principle upon which the powers should act in the settlement of the rebellion. He said:

> The policy of the Government of the United States is to seek a solution which may bring about permanent safety and peace to China, preserve Chinese territorial and administrative entity, protect all rights guaranteed to friendly powers by treaty and international law, and safeguard for the world the principle of equal and impartial trade with all parts of the Chinese Empire.

He was successful in obtaining the assent of the other powers to the policy thus announced. . . .

For twenty years thereafter the Open Door policy rested upon the informal commitments thus made by the various powers. But in the winter of 1921 to 1922, at a conference participated in by all of the principal powers which had interests in the Pacific, the policy was crystallized into the so-called Nine Power Treaty, which gave definition and precision to the principles upon which the policy rested. . . .

This Treaty thus represents a carefully developed and matured international policy intended, on the one hand, to assure to all of the contracting parties their rights and interests in and with regard to China, and on the other hand, to assure to the people of China the fullest opportunity to develop without molestation their sovereignty and independence according to the modern and enlightened standards believed to maintain among the peoples of the earth. At the time this Treaty was signed, it was known that China was engaged in an attempt to develop the free institutions of a self-governing republic after her recent revolution from an autocratic form of government;

that she would require many years of both economic and political effort to that end; and that her progress would necessarily be slow. The Treaty was thus a covenant of self-denial among the signatory powers in deliberate renunciation of any policy of aggression which might tend to interfere with that development. It was believed—and the whole history of the development of the "Open Door" policy reveals that faith—that only by such a process, under the protection of such an agreement, could the fullest interests not only of China but of all nations which have intercourse with her best be served.

In its report to the President announcing this Treaty, the American Delegation, headed by the then Secretary of State, Mr. Charles E. Hughes, said:

> It is believed that through this Treaty the "Open Door" in China has at last been made a fact.

During the course of the discussions which resulted in the Treaty, the Chairman of the British delegation, Lord Balfour, had stated that:

> The British Empire delegation understood that there was no representative of any power around the table who thought that the old practice of "spheres of interest" was either advocated by any government or would be tolerable to this conference. So far as the British Government was concerned, they had, in the most formal manner, publicly announced that they regarded this practice as utterly inappropriate to the existing situation.

At the same time the representative of Japan, Baron Shidehara, announced the position of his government as follows:

> No one denies to China her sacred right to govern herself. No one stands in the way of China to work out her own great national destiny. . . .

It must be remembered also that this Treaty was one of several treaties and agreements entered into at the Washington Conference by the various powers concerned, all of which were interrelated and interdependent. No one of these treaties can be disregarded without disturbing the general understanding and equilibrium which were intended to be accomplished and effected by the group of agreements arrived at in their entirety. The Washington Conference was essentially a disarmament conference, aimed to promote the possibility of peace in the world not only through the cessation of competition in naval armament but also by the solution of various other disturbing problems which threatened the peace of the world, particularly in the Far East. These problems were all interrelated. The willingness of the American government to surrender its then commanding lead in battleship construction and to leave its positions at Guam and in the Philippines without further fortification, was predicated upon, among other things, the self-denying covenants contained in the Nine Power Treaty, which assured the nations of the world not only of equal opportunity for their Eastern trade but also against the military aggrandizement of any other power at the expense of China. One cannot discuss the possibility of modifying or abrogating those provisions of the Nine Power Treaty without considering at the same time the other promises upon which they were really dependent.

Six years later the policy of self-denial against aggression by a stronger against a weaker power, upon which the Nine Power Treaty had been based, received a powerful reinforcement by the execution by substantially all the nations of the world of the Pact of Paris, the so-called Kellogg-Briand Pact. These two treaties represent independent but harmonious steps taken for the purpose of aligning the conscience and public opinion of the world in favor of a system of orderly development by the law of nations including the settlement of all controversies by methods of justice and peace instead of by arbitrary force. The program for the protection of China from outside aggression is an essential part of any such development. The signatories and adherents of the Nine Power Treaty rightly felt that the orderly and peaceful welfare of the 400,000,000 people inhabiting China was necessary to the peaceful welfare of the entire world and that no program for the welfare of the world as a whole could afford to neglect the welfare and protection of China.

The recent events which have taken place in China, especially the hostilities which having been begun in Manchuria have latterly been extended to Shanghai, far from indicating the advisability of any modification of the treaties we have been discussing, have tended to bring home the vital importance of the faithful observance of the covenants therein to all of the nations interested in the Far East. It is not necessary in that connection to inquire into the causes of the controversy or attempt to apportion the blame between the two nations which are unhappily involved; for regardless of cause or responsibility, it is clear beyond peradventure that a situation has developed which cannot, under any circumstances, be reconciled with the obligations of the covenants of these two treaties, and that if the treaties had been faithfully observed such a situation could not have arisen. The signatories of the Nine Power Treaty and of the Kellogg-Briand Pact who are not parties to that conflict are not likely to see any reason for modifying the terms of those treaties. To them the real value of the faithful performance of the treaties has been brought sharply home by the perils and losses to which their nationals have been subjected in Shanghai.

That is the view of this Government. We see no reason for abandoning the enlightened principles which are embodied in these treaties. We believe that this situation would have been avoided had these covenants been faithfully observed, and no evidence has come to us to indicate that a due compliance with them would have interfered with the adequate protection of the legitimate rights in China of the signatories of those treaties and their nationals.

On January 7th last, upon the instruction of the President, this Government formally notified Japan and China that it would not recognize any situation, treaty or agreement entered into by those governments in violation of the covenants of these treaties, which affected the rights of our Government or its citizens in China. . . .

In the past our Government, as one of the leading powers on the Pacific Ocean, has rested its policy upon an abiding faith in the future of the people of China and upon the ultimate success in dealing with them of the principles of fair play, patience, and mutual goodwill. We appreciate the immensity of the task which lies before her statesmen in the development of her country and its government. The delays in her progress, the instability of her attempts to secure a responsible government, were foreseen by Messrs. Hay and Hughes and their contemporaries and were the very obstacles which the policy of the Open Door was designed to meet. We concur with those statesmen, representing all nations in the Washington Conference who decided that China was entitled to the time necessary to accomplish her development. We are prepared to make that our policy for the future. . . .

H. C. ENGELBRECHT AND F. C. HANIGHEN, *MERCHANTS OF DEATH* (1934)

By the 1930s, with U.S. participation in the World War of 1914–1918 now widely seen as a horrendous error and with the Great Depression causing widespread distress at home, Americans were in no mood for further involvement in foreign wars, regardless of what expansionist powers on the other side of the planet might be plotting. Wilson's depiction of the US intervention as an expression of American idealism was no longer persuasive. Alternative—and more nefarious— explanations for the persistence of war gained credence. Here is one example.

One may be horrified by the activities of an industry which thrives on the greatest of human curses; still it is well to acknowledge that the arms industry did not create the war system. On the contrary, the war system created the arms industry. And our civilization which, however reluctantly, recognizes war as the final arbiter in international disputes, is also responsible for the existence of the arms maker. . . .

The arms industry is undeniably a menace to peace, but it is an industry to which our present civilization clings and for which it is responsible. It is an evidence of the superficiality of many peace advocates that they should denounce the arms industry and accept the present state of civilization which fosters it. . . .

The root of the trouble, therefore, goes far deeper than the arms industry. It lies in the prevailing temper of peoples toward nationalism, militarism, and war, in the civilization which forms this temper and prevents any drastic and radical change. Only when this underlying basis of the war system is altered, will war and its concomitant, the arms industry, pass out of existence.

While critics of the arms makers are thus frequently lacking in a thorough understanding of the problems involved, the apologists of the arms makers, who defend the purely commercial and nonpolitical nature of the traffic in arms, are far from profound. The fact is that the armament maker is the right-hand man of all war and navy departments, and, as such, he is a supremely important political figure. His sales to his home government are political acts, as much as, perhaps even more so, than the transactions of a tax collector. His international traffic is an act of international politics and is so recognized in solemn international treaties.

The reason this aspect has never been emphasized is that most nations are extremely anxious to continue the free and uninterrupted commerce in armaments, because they do not and cannot manufacture the arms they deem necessary for their national safety. From this the curious paradox arises that an embargo on arms is everywhere considered an act of international politics, while the international sale of arms, even in war time, is merely business. . . .

The world at present apparently wants both the war system and peace; it believes that "national safety" lies in preparedness, and it denounces the arms industry. This is not merely confused thinking, but a striking reflection of the contradictory forces at work in our social and political life. Thus it happens that so-called friends of peace frequently uphold the institution of armies and navies to preserve "national security," support "defensive wars," and advocate military training in colleges.

H. C. Engelbrecht and F. C. Hanighen, *Merchants of Death,* New York: Dodd Mead (1934).

On the other hand, arms makers sometimes make dramatic gestures for peace. Nobel, the Dynamite King, established the world's most famous peace prize; Andrew Carnegie endowed a peace foundation and wrote pamphlets on the danger of armaments; Charles Schwab declared that he would gladly scrap all his armor plants if it would bring peace to the world; and Du Pont recently informed its stockholders that it was gratified that the world was rebelling against war.

Out of this background of conflicting forces the arms maker has risen and grown powerful, until today he is one of the most dangerous factors in world affairs—a hindrance to peace, a promoter of war. He has reached this position not through any deliberate plotting or planning of his own, but simply as a result of the historic forces of the nineteenth century. Granting the nineteenth century with its amazing development of science and invention, its industrial and commercial evolution, its concentration of economic wealth, its close international ties, its spread and intensification of nationalism, its international political conflicts, the modern armament maker with all his evils was inevitable. If the arms industry is a cancer on the body of modern civilization, it is not an extraneous growth; it is the result of the unhealthy condition of the body itself. . . .

Fifteen years have elapsed since the "war to end all wars." Yet the arms industry has moved forward with growing momentum as if the pacific resolutions of the various peoples and governments had never existed. All these technical improvements, all the international mergers, the cooperation between governments and the industry bear an uncomfortable resemblance to the situation during the epoch preceding 1914. Is this present situation necessarily a preparation for another world struggle and what, if any, are the solutions to these problems?. . . .

No fundamental political attitudes have been changed by the World War. The nations continue their reliance on "mass murder" as a means of settling vexing problems. Armies and navies and air forces have increased, military budgets mount every year, new and more frightful weapons make their appearance every month. None of the basic causes of war have been removed and the League of Nations, the Kellogg Pact, and other agencies and methods designed to bring about a peaceful settlement of international disputes have shown a distressing ineptitude in dealing with pressing world problems. Every modern war threatens to involve half the world, bring disaster to world economy, and blot out civilization. The question is urgent then: What will be done about the armament industry?

The future may very well bring fiercer and more destructive wars and increased business for the arms makers. Certainly one great current of world affairs is flowing strongly in that direction. The business of the arms industry is steadily increasing—it was the only industry which flourished in spite of the world depression—and governments are everywhere drawing closer the ties which bind them in a virtual partnership with the merchants of death.

If wars continue, it is not at all fantastic to predict that the arms merchants will grow increasingly important. Already the stage in national affairs has been reached where the largest item in national budgets is for past and future wars. Already war appears as the greatest and most important activity of government. The economic consequences of this new nationalistic militarism will soon be apparent in the arms industry.

The arms merchants will supply to the government its most vital necessities and inevitably they will grow constantly more important in the councils of state. . . .

It would almost seem as though governments exist merely to prepare for war. This "industrial mobilization" is the education and preparation of industries in peace time for their tasks in war. The World War has taught governments that modern war involves the entire economic life of the nation. . . .

This system of industrial mobilization is a long step toward placing war in the center of our economic life, or to put it another way, to make the arms industry the hub of our industrial machine. An alliance of governments with war industries threatens to make the arms makers supreme in economic life and after that in government.

A world dominated economically and politically by the armament industry will eventually result, if wars continue unabated. . . .

The international sale of arms, then, has far deeper roots than the "conscienceless greed" of the arms makers. If all private arms makers decided to discontinue their international traffic tomorrow, a world-wide protest of governments would not permit them to do it. As long as war is a possibility, nations will demand arms. The world economic situation makes it difficult or impossible for most, if not all, of them to manufacture all types of armaments which they demand. Hence it is laid down and affirmed in solemn international treaties that arms must at all times be sold freely, even in times of war. The rules of contraband may interrupt this traffic in war times, but in times of peace and under normal conditions the "obligation to sell" is clearly established. . . .

There remains then but one real way out, disarmament. The various futile conferences on disarmament have not been in vain if they have opened the eyes of the peace forces to the real problem which confronts them. Disarmament has not been achieved because of the international political situation. International politics in turn are determined by our whole civilization. Our civilization has permitted and even fostered war-making forces, such as nationalism and chauvinism, economic rivalry and competitive capitalism, imperialism and colonialism, political and territorial disputes, race hatred and pressure of population. The traditional way of establishing an equilibrium between these rival forces has been and is violence, armed warfare.

Disarmament is thus a problem of our civilization. It will never be achieved unless these war-making forces are crushed or eliminated. The problem of disarmament is therefore the problem of building a new civilization. All attempts at dealing with disarmament by itself, without consideration of the deeper issues involved, are doomed to failure. Minor agreements may be reached, limited to a short period of time, but the world will never cease being an armed camp until the basic elements of our present civilization have been changed.

The same holds true of the armament industry. A world which recognizes and expects war cannot get along without an enterprising, progressive, and up-to-date arms industry. All attempts to attack the problem of the arms makers in isolation—by nationalization or by international control—are almost certain to fail.

The arms industry is plainly a perfectly natural product of our present civilization. More than that, it is an essential element in the chaos and anarchy which characterize our international politics. To eliminate it requires the creation of a world which can get along without war by settling its differences and disputes by peaceful means. And that involves remaking our entire civilization.

Meanwhile those interested in creating a war-less world need not be idle and await the dawn of a new day. They can support every move made for the peaceful settlement of international disputes; they can help to reduce the exorbitant budgets of war and navy departments; they can work for regional limitation of armaments and back all treaties which tend to avoid competition in arms; they can oppose nationalism and chauvinism wherever they show themselves, in the press, in the schools, on the lecture platform; they can strive to bring order into the chaotic economic and political conditions of the world.

The skies are again overcast with lowering war clouds and the Four Horsemen are again getting ready to ride, leaving destruction, suffering and death in their path. Wars are man-made, and peace, when it comes, will also be man-made. Surely the challenge of war and of the armament maker is one that no intelligent or civilized being can evade.

SMEDLEY BUTLER, *WAR IS A RACKET* (1935)

As a Marine officer, Major General Smedley Butler (1881–1940) participated in almost every US military campaign, large or small, beginning with the war against Spain in 1898 and extending over the next quarter century. During his career, he was twice awarded the Medal of Honor. As a serving officer, Butler was colorful, cantankerous, and opinionated. Upon his retirement, he became a vociferous critic of US military policy, as evidence by the pamphlet for which he is best remembered.

War is a racket. It always has been.

It is possibly the oldest, easily the most profitable, surely the most vicious. It is the only one international in scope. It is the only one in which the profits are reckoned in dollars and the losses in lives.

A racket is best described, I believe, as something that is not what it seems to the majority of the people. Only a small "inside" group knows what it is about. It is conducted for the benefit of the very few, at the expense of the very many. Out of war a few people make huge fortunes.

In the World War a mere handful garnered the profits of the conflict. At least 21,000 new millionaires and billionaires were made in the United States during the World War. That many admitted their huge blood gains in their income tax returns. How many other war millionaires falsified their tax returns no one knows.

How many of these war millionaires shouldered a rifle? How many of them dug a trench? How many of them knew what it meant to go hungry in a rat-infested dug-out? How many of them spent sleepless, frightened nights, ducking shells and shrapnel and machine gun bullets? How many of them parried a bayonet thrust of an enemy? How many of them were wounded or killed in battle?

Out of war nations acquire additional territory, if they are victorious. They just take it. This newly acquired territory promptly is exploited by the few—the selfsame few who wrung dollars out of blood in the war. The general public shoulders the bill.

And what is this bill?

This bill renders a horrible accounting. Newly placed gravestones. Mangled bodies. Shattered minds. Broken hearts and homes. Economic instability. Depression and all its attendant miseries. Back-breaking taxation for generations and generations.

For a great many years, as a soldier, I had a suspicion that war was a racket; not until I retired to civil life did I fully realize it. Now that I see the international war clouds gathering, as they are today, I must face it and speak out. . . .

There are 40,000,000 men under arms in the world today, and our statesmen and diplomats have the temerity to say that war is not in the making.

Hell's bells! Are these 40,000,000 men being trained to be dancers?

Not in Italy, to be sure. Premier Mussolini knows what they are being trained for. . . .

His well-trained army, his great fleet of planes, and even his navy are ready for war—anxious for it, apparently. . . .

Herr Hitler, with his rearming Germany and his constant demands for more and more arms, is an equal if not greater menace to peace. France only recently increased the term of military service for its youth from a year to eighteen months.

Yes, all over, nations are camping in their arms. The mad dogs of Europe are on the loose. In the Orient the maneuvering is more adroit. Back in 1904, when Russia and Japan fought, we kicked out our old friends the Russians and backed Japan. Then our very generous international bankers were financing Japan. Now the trend is to poison us against the Japanese. What does the "open door" policy to China mean to us? Our trade with China is about $90,000,000 a year. Or the Philippine Islands? We have spent about $600,000,000 in the Philippines in thirty-five years and we (our bankers and industrialists and speculators) have private investments there of less than $200,000,000.

Smedley Butler, *War Is a Racket,* New York: Round Table Press (1935).

Then, to save that China trade of about $90,000,000, or to protect these private investments of less than $200,000,000 in the Philippines, we would be all stirred up to hate Japan and go to war—a war that might well cost us tens of billions of dollars, hundreds of thousands of lives of Americans, and many more hundreds of thousands of physically maimed and mentally unbalanced men.

Of course, for this loss, there would be a compensating profit—fortunes would be made. Millions and billions of dollars would be piled up. By a few. Munitions makers. Bankers. Ship builders. Manufacturers. Meat packers. Speculators. They would fare well.

Yes, they are getting ready for another war. Why shouldn't they? It pays high dividends.

But what does it profit the men who are killed? What does it profit their mothers and sisters, their wives and their sweethearts? What does it profit their children?

What does it profit anyone except the very few to whom war means huge profits?

Yes, and what does it profit the nation?

Take our own case. Until 1898 we didn't own a bit of territory outside the mainland of North America. At that time our national debt was a little more than $1,000,000,000. Then we became "internationally minded." We forgot, or shunted aside, the advice of the Father of our country. We forgot George Washington's warning about "entangling alliances." We went to war. We acquired outside territory. At the end of the World War period, as a direct result of our fiddling in international affairs, our national debt had jumped to over $25,000,000,000. Our total favorable trade balance during the twenty-five-year period was about $24,000,000,000. Therefore, on a purely bookkeeping basis, we ran a little behind year for year, and that foreign trade might well have been ours without the wars.

It would have been far cheaper (not to say safer) for the average American who pays the bills to stay out of foreign entanglements. For a very few this racket, like bootlegging and other underworld rackets, brings fancy profits, but the cost of operations is always transferred to the people—who do not profit.

WHO MAKES THE PROFITS?

The World War, rather our brief participation in it, has cost the United States some $52,000,000,000. Figure it out. That means $400 to every American man, woman, and child. And we haven't paid the debt yet. We are paying it, our children will pay it, and our children's children probably still will be paying the cost of that war.

The normal profits of a business concern in the United States are six, eight, ten, and sometimes twelve percent. But war-time profits—ah! that is another matter—twenty, sixty, one hundred, three hundred, and even eighteen hundred per cent—the sky is the limit. All that traffic will bear. Uncle Sam has the money. Let's get it.

Of course, it isn't put that crudely in war time. It is dressed into speeches about patriotism, love of country, and "we must all put our shoulders to the wheel," but the profits jump and leap and skyrocket—and are safely pocketed. . . .

Take our friends the du Ponts, the powder people—didn't one of them testify before a Senate committee recently that their powder won the war? Or saved the world for democracy? Or something? How did they do in the war? They were a patriotic corporation. Well, the average earnings of the du Ponts for the period 1910 to 1914 were $6,000,000 a year. It wasn't much, but the du Ponts managed to get along on it. Now let's look at their average yearly profit during the war years, 1914 to 1918. Fifty-eight million dollars a year profit we find! Nearly ten times that of normal times, and the profits of normal times were pretty good. An increase in profits of more than 950 per cent.

Take one of our little steel companies that patriotically shunted aside the making of rails and girders and bridges to manufacture war materials. Well, their 1910-1914 yearly earnings averaged

$6,000,000. Then came the war. And, like loyal citizens, Bethlehem Steel promptly turned to munitions making. Did their profits jump—or did they let Uncle Sam in for a bargain? Well, their 1914-1918 average was $49,000,000 a year!

Or, let's take United States Steel. The normal earnings during the five-year period prior to the war were $105,000,000 a year. Not bad. Then along came the war and up went the profits. The average yearly profit for the period 1914-1918 was $240,000,000. Not bad. . . .

And let us not forget the bankers who financed the great war. If anyone had the cream of the profits it was the bankers. Being partnerships rather than incorporated organizations, they do not have to report to stockholders. And their profits were as secret as they were immense. How the bankers made their millions and their billions I do not know, because those little secrets never become public—even before a Senate investigatory body. . . .

Airplane and engine manufacturers felt they, too, should get their just profits out of this war. Why not? Everybody else was getting theirs. So $1,000,000,000—count them if you live long enough—was spent by Uncle Sam in building airplane engines that never left the ground! Not one plane, or motor, out of the billion dollars worth ordered, ever got into a battle in France. Just the same the manufacturers made their little profit of 30, 100, or perhaps 300 per cent. . . .

The shipbuilders felt they should come in on some of it, too. They built a lot of ships that made a lot of profit. More than $3,000,000,000 worth. Some of the ships were all right. But $635,000,000 worth of them were made of wood and wouldn't float! The seams opened up—and they sank. We paid for them, though. And somebody pocketed the profits.

It has been estimated by statisticians and economists and researchers that the war cost your Uncle Sam $52,000,000,000. Of this sum, $39,000,000,000 was expended in the actual war itself. This expenditure yielded $16,000,000,000 in profits. That is how the 21,000 billionaires and millionaires got that way. This $16,000,000,000 profits is not to be sneezed at. It is quite a tidy sum. And it went to a very few. . . .

Who Pays The Bills?

Who provides the profits—these nice little profits of 20, 100, 300, 1,500 and 1,800 per cent? We all pay them—in taxation. . . .

But the soldier pays the biggest part of the bill.

If you don't believe this, visit the American cemeteries on the battlefields abroad. Or visit any of the veteran's hospitals in the United States. On a tour of the country, in the midst of which I am at the time of this writing, I have visited eighteen government hospitals for veterans. In them are a total of about 50,000 destroyed men—men who were the pick of the nation eighteen years ago. . . .

Boys with a normal viewpoint were taken out of the fields and offices and factories and classrooms and put into the ranks. There they were remolded; they were made over; they were made to "about face"; to regard murder as the order of the day. They were put shoulder to shoulder and, through mass psychology, they were entirely changed. We used them for a couple of years and trained them to think nothing at all of killing or of being killed.

Then, suddenly, we discharged them and told them to make another "about face"! This time they had to do their own readjustment, sans mass psychology, sans officers' aid and advice and sans nation-wide propaganda. We didn't need them any more. So we scattered them about without any "three-minute" or "Liberty Loan" speeches or parades. Many, too many, of these fine young boys are eventually destroyed, mentally, because they could not make that final "about face" alone.

In the government hospital in Marion, Indiana, 1,800 of these boys are in pens! Five hundred of them in a barracks with steel bars and wires all around outside the buildings and on the porches.

These already have been mentally destroyed. These boys don't even look like human beings. Oh, the looks on their faces! Physically, they are in good shape; mentally, they are gone. . . .

That's a part of the bill. So much for the dead—they have paid their part of the war profits. So much for the mentally and physically wounded—they are paying now their share of the war profits. But the others paid, too—they paid with heartbreaks when they tore themselves away from their firesides and their families to don the uniform of Uncle Sam—on which a profit had been made. They paid another part in the training camps where they were regimented and drilled while others took their jobs and their places in the lives of their communities. The paid for it in the trenches where they shot and were shot; where they were hungry for days at a time; where they slept in the mud and the cold and in the rain—with the moans and shrieks of the dying for a horrible lullaby. . . .

In the World War, we used propaganda to make the boys accept conscription. They were made to feel ashamed if they didn't join the army.

So vicious was this war propaganda that even God was brought into it. With few exceptions our clergymen joined in the clamor to kill, kill, kill. To kill the Germans. God is on our side . . . it is His will that the Germans be killed.

And in Germany, the good pastors called upon the Germans to kill the allies . . . to please the same God. That was a part of the general propaganda, built up to make people war conscious and murder conscious.

Beautiful ideals were painted for our boys who were sent out to die. This was the "war to end all wars." This was the "war to make the world safe for democracy." No one mentioned to them, as they marched away, that their going and their dying would mean huge war profits. No one told these American soldiers that they might be shot down by bullets made by their own brothers here. No one told them that the ships on which they were going to cross might be torpedoed by submarines built with United States patents. They were just told it was to be a "glorious adventure." Thus, having stuffed patriotism down their throats, it was decided to make them help pay for the war, too. So, we gave them the large salary of $30 a month.

All they had to do for this munificent sum was to leave their dear ones behind, give up their jobs, lie in swampy trenches, eat canned willy (when they could get it) and kill and kill and kill . . . and be killed. . . .

Yes, the soldier pays the greater part of the bill. His family pays too. They pay it in the same heart-break that he does. As he suffers, they suffer. At nights, as he lay in the trenches and watched shrapnel burst about him, they lay home in their beds and tossed sleeplessly—his father, his mother, his wife, his sisters, his brothers, his sons, and his daughters. . . .

And even now the families of the wounded men and of the mentally broken and those who never were able to readjust themselves are still suffering and still paying. . . .

Well, it's a racket, all right.

A few profit—and the many pay. But there is a way to stop it. You can't end it by disarmament conferences. You can't eliminate it by peace parleys at Geneva. Well-meaning but impractical groups can't wipe it out by resolutions. It can be smashed effectively only by taking the profit out of war.

The only way to smash this racket is to conscript capital and industry and labor before the nation's manhood can be conscripted. One month before the Government can conscript the young men of the nation—it must conscript capital and industry and labor. Let the officers and the directors and the high-powered executives of our armament factories and our munitions makers and our shipbuilders and our airplane builders and the manufacturers of all the other things that provide profit in war time as well as the bankers and the speculators, be conscripted—to get $30 a month, the same wage as the lads in the trenches get.

Let the workers in these plants get the same wages—all the workers, all presidents, all executives, all directors, all managers, all bankers—yes, and all generals and all admirals and all officers and all politicians and all government office holders—everyone in the nation be restricted to a total monthly income not to exceed that paid to the soldier in the trenches! . . .

Another step necessary in this fight to smash the war racket is the limited plebiscite to determine whether a war should be declared. A plebiscite not of all the voters but merely of those who would be called upon to do the fighting and dying. There wouldn't be very much sense in having a 76-year-old president of a munitions factory or the flat-footed head of an international banking firm or the cross-eyed manager of a uniform manufacturing plant—all of whom see visions of tremendous profits in the event of war—voting on whether the nation should go to war or not. They never would be called upon to shoulder arms—to sleep in a trench and to be shot. Only those who would be called upon to risk their lives for their country should have the privilege of voting to determine whether the nation should go to war.

There is ample precedent for restricting the voting to those affected. Many of our states have restrictions on those permitted to vote. In most, it is necessary to be able to read and write before you may vote. In some, you must own property. It would be a simple matter each year for the men coming of military age to register in their communities as they did in the draft during the World War and be examined physically. Those who could pass and who would therefore be called upon to bear arms in the event of war would be eligible to vote in a limited plebiscite. They should be the ones to have the power to decide—and not a Congress few of whose members are within the age limit and fewer still of whom are in physical condition to bear arms. Only those who must suffer should have the right to vote.

A third step in this business of smashing the war racket is to make certain that our military forces are truly forces for defense only.

At each session of Congress the question of further naval appropriations comes up. The swivel-chair admirals of Washington (and there are always a lot of them) are very adroit lobbyists. And they are smart. They don't shout that "We need a lot of battleships to war on this nation or that nation." Oh no. First of all, they let it be known that America is menaced by a great naval power. Almost any day, these admirals will tell you, the great fleet of this supposed enemy will strike suddenly and annihilate 125,000,000 people. Just like that. Then they begin to cry for a larger navy. For what? To fight the enemy? Oh my, no. Oh, no. For defense purposes only.

Then, incidentally, they announce maneuvers in the Pacific. For defense. Uh, huh. The Pacific is a great big ocean. We have a tremendous coastline on the Pacific. Will the maneuvers be off the coast, two or three hundred miles? Oh, no. The maneuvers will be two thousand, yes, perhaps even thirty-five hundred miles, off the coast.

The Japanese, a proud people, of course will be pleased beyond expression to see the United States fleet so close to Nippon's shores. Even as pleased as would be the residents of California were they to dimly discern through the morning mist, the Japanese fleet playing at war games off Los Angeles.

The ships of our navy, it can be seen, should be specifically limited, by law, to within 200 miles of our coastline. Had that been the law in 1898 the Maine would never have gone to Havana Harbor. She never would have been blown up. There would have been no war with Spain with its attendant loss of life. Two hundred miles is ample, in the opinion of experts, for defense purposes. Our nation cannot start an offensive war if its ships can't go further than 200 miles from the coastline. Planes might be permitted to go as far as 500 miles from the coast for purposes of reconnaissance. And the army should never leave the territorial limits of our nation. . . .

I am not a fool as to believe that war is a thing of the past. I know the people do not want war, but there is no use in saying we cannot be pushed into another war.

Looking back, Woodrow Wilson was re-elected president in 1916 on a platform that he had "kept us out of war" and on the implied promise that he would "keep us out of war." Yet five months later he asked Congress to declare war on Germany.

In that five-month interval the people had not been asked whether they had changed their minds. The 4,000,000 young men who put on uniforms and marched or sailed away were not asked whether they wanted to go forth to suffer and die.

Then what caused our government to change its mind so suddenly?

Money.

An allied commission, it may be recalled, came over shortly before the war declaration and called on the President. The President summoned a group of advisers. The head of the commission spoke. Stripped of its diplomatic language, this is what he told the President and his group: "There is no use kidding ourselves any longer. The cause of the allies is lost.

We now owe you (American bankers, American munitions makers, American manufacturers, American speculators, American exporters) five or six billion dollars.

"If we lose (and without the help of the United States we must lose) we, England, France and Italy, cannot pay back this money . . . and Germany won't.

"So . . ."

Had secrecy been outlawed as far as war negotiations were concerned, and had the press been invited to be present at that conference, or had radio been available to broadcast the proceedings, America never would have entered the World War. But this conference, like all war discussions, was shrouded in utmost secrecy. When our boys were sent off to war they were told it was a "war to make the world safe for democracy" and a "war to end all wars."

Well, eighteen years after, the world has less of democracy than it had then. Besides, what business is it of ours whether Russia or Germany or England or France or Italy or Austria live under democracies or monarchies? Whether they are Fascists or Communists? Our problem is to preserve our own democracy.

And very little, if anything, has been accomplished to assure us that the World War was really the war to end all wars.

Yes, we have had disarmament conferences and limitations of arms conferences. They don't mean a thing. . . .

The professional soldiers and sailors don't want to disarm. No admiral wants to be without a ship. No general wants to be without a command. Both mean men without jobs. They are not for disarmament. They cannot be for limitations of arms. And at all these conferences, lurking in the background but all-powerful, just the same, are the sinister agents of those who profit by war. They see to it that these conferences do not disarm or seriously limit armaments.

The chief aim of any power at any of these conferences has not been to achieve disarmament to prevent war but rather to get more armament for itself and less for any potential foe.

There is only one way to disarm with any semblance of practicability. That is for all nations to get together and scrap every ship, every gun, every rifle, every tank, every war plane. Even this, if it were possible, would not be enough. . . .

Secretly each nation is studying and perfecting newer and ghastlier means of annihilating its foes wholesale. Yes, ships will continue to be built, for the shipbuilders must make their profits. And guns still will be manufactured and powder and rifles will be made, for the munitions makers must make their huge profits. . . .

But victory or defeat will be determined by the skill and ingenuity of our scientists. If we put them to work making poison gas and more and more fiendish mechanical and explosive instruments of destruction, they will have no time for the constructive job of building greater prosperity for all peoples. By putting them to this useful job, we can all make more money out of peace than we can out of war—even the munitions makers.

So . . . I say, TO HELL WITH WAR!

FRANKLIN D. ROOSEVELT, "CHATAUQUA SPEECH" (1936)

Elected to the presidency in 1932 while promising to end the Great Depression, Franklin Roosevelt made little effort to push back against the anti-interventionist sentiments prevailing across much of the country. Here he is, speaking five years after Japan has embarked upon a course of imperial expansion in Asia, three years after Adolf Hitler has come to power in Germany, and just months after the eruption of civil war in Spain gives evidence of fascism being on the march in Europe. The United States pursues a course of isolationism, FDR insists, only in isolating itself from the folly of war.

Many who have visited me in Washington in the past few months may have been surprised when

I have told them that personally and because of my own daily contacts with all manner of difficult situations I am more concerned and less cheerful about international world conditions than about our immediate domestic prospects.

I say this to you not as a confirmed pessimist but as one who still hopes that envy, hatred and malice among Nations have reached their peak and will be succeeded by a new tide of peace and good-will. I say this as one who has participated in many of the decisions of peace and war before, during and after the World War; one who has traveled much; and one who has spent a goodly portion of every twenty-four hours in the study of foreign relations.

Long before I returned to Washington as President of the United States, I had made up my mind that pending what might be called a more opportune moment on other continents, the United States could best serve the cause of a peaceful humanity by setting an example. That was why on the 4th of March, 1933, I made the following declaration:

> "In the field of world policy I would dedicate this Nation to the policy of the good neighbor— the neighbor who resolutely respects himself and, because he does so, respects the rights of others— the neighbor who respects his obligations and respects the sanctity of his agreements in and with a world of neighbors."

This declaration represents my purpose; but it represents more than a purpose, for it stands for a practice. To a measurable degree it has succeeded; the whole world now knows that the United States cherishes no predatory ambitions. We are strong; but less powerful Nations know that they need not fear our strength. We seek no conquest; we stand for peace.

In the whole of the Western Hemisphere our good-neighbor policy has produced results that are especially heartening.

The noblest monument to peace and to neighborly economic and social friendship in all the world is not a monument in bronze or stone, but the boundary which unites the United States and Canada—3,000 miles of friendship with no barbed wire, no gun or soldier, and no passport on the whole frontier.

Mutual trust made that frontier. To extend the same sort of mutual trust throughout the Americas was our aim.

The American Republics to the south of us have been ready always to cooperate with the United States on a basis of equality and mutual respect, but before we inaugurated the good-neighbor policy there were among them resentment and fear, because certain Administrations in Washington had slighted their national pride and their sovereign rights.

In pursuance of the good-neighbor policy, and because in my younger days I had learned many lessons in the hard school of experience, I stated that the United States was opposed definitely to armed intervention.

We have negotiated a Pan-American convention embodying the principle of non-intervention. We have abandoned the Platt Amendment which gave us the right to intervene in the internal affairs of the Republic of Cuba. We have withdrawn American marines from Haiti. We have signed a new treaty which places our relations with Panama on a mutually satisfactory basis. We have undertaken a series of trade agreements with other American countries to our mutual commercial profit. . . .

Throughout the Americas the spirit of the good neighbor is a practical and living fact. The twenty-one American Republics are not only living together in friendship and in peace; they are united in the determination so to remain. . . .

Peace, like charity, begins at home; that is why we have begun at home. But peace in the Western world is not all that we seek.

It is our hope that knowledge of the practical application of the good-neighbor policy in this hemisphere will be borne home to our neighbors across the seas. For ourselves we are on good terms with them—terms in most cases of straightforward friendship, of peaceful understanding.

But, of necessity, we are deeply concerned about tendencies of recent years among many of the Nations of other continents. It is a bitter experience to us when the spirit of agreements to which we are a party is not lived up to. It is an even more bitter experience for the whole company of Nations to witness not only the spirit but the letter of international agreements violated with impunity and without regard to the simple principles of honor. Permanent friendships between Nations as between men can be sustained only by scrupulous respect for the pledged word.

In spite of all this we have sought steadfastly to assist international movements to prevent war. We cooperated to the bitter end—and it was a bitter end—in the work of the General Disarmament Conference. When it failed we sought a separate treaty to deal with the manufacture of arms and the international traffic in arms. That proposal also came to nothing. We participated—again to the bitter end—in a conference to continue naval limitations, and when it became evident that no general treaty could be signed because of the objections of other Nations, we concluded with Great Britain and France a conditional treaty of qualitative limitation which, much to my regret, already shows signs of ineffectiveness.

We shun political commitments which might entangle us in foreign wars; we avoid connection with the political activities of the League of Nations; but I am glad to say that we have cooperated whole-heartedly in the social and humanitarian work at Geneva. Thus we are a part of the world effort to control traffic in narcotics, to improve international health, to help child welfare, to eliminate double taxation and to better working conditions and laboring hours throughout the world.

We are not isolationists except in so far as we seek to isolate ourselves completely from war. Yet we must remember that so long as war exists on earth there will be some danger that even the Nation which most ardently desires peace may be drawn into war.

I have seen war. I have seen war on land and sea. I have seen blood running from the wounded. I have seen men coughing out their gassed lungs. I have seen the dead in the mud. I have seen cities destroyed. I have seen two hundred limping, exhausted men come out of line—the survivors of a regiment of one thousand that went forward forty-eight hours before. I have seen children starving. I have seen the agony of mothers and wives. I hate war.

I have passed unnumbered hours, I shall pass unnumbered hours, thinking and planning how war may be kept from this Nation.

I wish I could keep war from all Nations; but that is beyond my power. I can at least make certain that no act of the United States helps to produce or to promote war. I can at least make clear that the conscience of America revolts against war and that any Nation which provokes war forfeits the sympathy of the people of the United States.

Many causes produce war. There are ancient hatreds, turbulent frontiers, the "legacy of old forgotten, far-off things, and battles long ago." There are new-born fanaticisms, convictions on the part of certain peoples that they have become the unique depositories of ultimate truth and right.

A dark old world was devastated by wars between conflicting religions. A dark modern world faces wars between conflicting economic and political fanaticisms in which are intertwined race hatreds. To bring it home, it is as if within the territorial limits of the United States, forty-eight Nations with forty-eight forms of government, forty-eight customs barriers, forty-eight languages, and forty-eight eternal and different verities, were spending their time and their substance in a frenzy of effort to make themselves strong enough to conquer their neighbors or strong enough to defend themselves against their neighbors.

In one field, that of economic barriers, the American policy may be, I hope, of some assistance in discouraging the economic source of war and therefore a contribution toward the peace of the world. The trade agreements which we are making are not only finding outlets for the products of American fields and American factories but are also pointing the way to the elimination of embargoes, quotas and other devices which place such pressure on Nations not possessing great natural resources that to them the price of peace seems less terrible than the price of war.

We do not maintain that a more liberal international trade will stop war; but we fear that without a more liberal international trade, war is a natural sequence.

The Congress of the United States has given me certain authority to provide safeguards of American neutrality in case of war.

The President of the United States, who, under our Constitution, is vested with primary authority to conduct our international relations, thus has been given new weapons with which to maintain our neutrality. . . .

It is clear that our present policy and the measures passed by the Congress would, in the event of a war on some other continent, reduce war profits which would otherwise accrue to American citizens. Industrial and agricultural production for a war market may give immense fortunes to a few men; for the Nation as a whole it produces disaster. It was the prospect of war profits that made our farmers in the West plow up prairie land that should never have been plowed, but should have been left for grazing cattle. Today we are reaping the harvest of those war profits in the dust storms which have devastated those war-plowed areas.

It was the prospect of war profits that caused the extension of monopoly and unjustified expansion of industry and a price level so high that the normal relationship between debtor and creditor was destroyed.

Nevertheless, if war should break out again in another continent, let us not blink the fact that we would find in this country thousands of Americans who, seeking immediate riches—fools' gold—would attempt to break down or evade our neutrality.

They would tell you—and, unfortunately, their views would get wide publicity—that if they could produce and ship this and that and the other article to belligerent Nations, the unemployed of America would all find work. They would tell you that if they could extend credit to warring Nations that credit would be used in the United States to build homes and factories and pay our debts. They would tell you

that America once more would capture the trade of the world.

It would be hard to resist that clamor; it would be hard for many Americans, I fear, to look beyond—to realize the inevitable penalties, the inevitable day of reckoning, that come from a false prosperity. To resist the clamor of that greed, if war should come, would require the unswerving support of all Americans who love peace.

If we face the choice of profits or peace, the Nation will answer—must answer—"We choose peace." It is the duty of all of us to encourage such a body of public opinion in this country that the answer will be clear and for all practical purposes unanimous. . . .

We can keep out of war if those who watch and decide have a sufficiently detailed understanding of international affairs to make certain that the small decisions of each day do not lead toward war and if, at the same time, they possess the courage to say "no" to those who selfishly or unwisely would let us go to war.

Of all the Nations of the world today we are in many ways most singularly blessed. Our closest neighbors are good neighbors. If there are remoter Nations that wish us not good but ill, they know that we are strong; they know that we can and will defend ourselves and defend our neighborhood.

We seek to dominate no other Nation. We ask no territorial expansion. We oppose imperialism. We desire reduction in world armaments.

We believe in democracy; we believe in freedom; we believe in peace. We offer to every Nation of the world the handclasp of the good neighbor. Let those who wish our friendship look us in the eye and take our hand.

VII.

THE SUMMONS

In September 1939 Germany invaded Poland. France and Great Britain responded by declaring war on Adolf Hitler's Third Reich. The outbreak of another European war triggered intense debate among Americans about how the United States should respond. It took the Japanese attack on Pearl Harbor to settle that debate.

Very few Americans sympathized with Nazi Germany (or with Imperial Japan, which had launched a war of aggression against China in 1937). With memories of the previous world war still fresh, however, large numbers were reluctant to be drawn into a distant conflict that did not, in their view, directly threaten the well-being of the United States. This was by no means a minority view. During the 1930s, Congress had passed and President Roosevelt had signed into law a series of "Neutrality Acts" intended to prevent the United States ever again taking the path that it had followed in 1917.

The course of events in Europe—most notably the spring 1940 collapse of France in the face of a Nazi onslaught, leaving Britain isolated and alone—led Roosevelt to conclude that the United States could not allow Hitler to have a free hand. Careful never to get too far ahead of public opinion, the president initiated a step-by-step process of offering aid to Britain while preparing the United States for war. By no means did this shift in FDR's own views eliminate popular opposition to US intervention. The controversy, ultimately an argument about what role the United States was destined to play in global affairs, continued unabated until December 1941.

CHARLES A. BEARD, "GIDDY MINDS AND FOREIGN QUARRELS," HARPER'S (SEPTEMBER 1939)

The most prominent American historian of the first half of the twentieth century, Charles Beard (1874–1948) had supported US entry into World War I before subsequently deciding that intervention had been a mistake. During the 1930s, he argued against any commitment of US military forces beyond the confines of the Western Hemisphere.

Only in relatively recent times has wholesale interference with foreign quarrels and disturbances become a major concern of the intelligentsia, the press, and professional politicians in the United States.

But frenetic preoccupation with foreign quarrels has now reached the proportion of a heavy industry in this country. All our universities have funds and endowments for teaching what is called "international relations," and since about 1918 a large part of this instruction has been stripped of all scientific pretensions and has been little more than propaganda for the League of Nations, collective security, collaboration with Great Britain and France, or some kind of regularized intervention of the United States Government everywhere, except perhaps at Amritsar and in Syria . . .

In fact, advocacy of American interventionism and adventurism abroad has become a huge vested interest. The daily press and the radio, thriving on hourly sensations, do their best to inflame readers, listeners, and lookers with a passion for putting down the wicked abroad . . .

The era of universal American jitters over foreign affairs of no vital interest to the United States was opened in full blast about 1890 by four of the most powerful agitators that ever afflicted any nation: Alfred Thayer Mahan, Theodore Roosevelt, Henry Cabot Lodge, and Albert J. Beveridge. These were the chief manufacturers of the new doctrine correctly characterized as "imperialism for America". . . .

The heady ideology put forth to sustain the imperialist policy may be summarized as follows: America has grown up, has acquired man's stature and put on long pants; the frontier has passed; the continent has been rounded out; America must put aside childish things, become a great big world power, follow the example of Great Britain, France, and Germany, build a monster navy, grab colonies, sea bases and trading posts throughout the world, plunge into every big dispute among European powers, and carry "civilization" to "backward" races. . . .

By one of the ironies of history, it fell to the lost of [Woodrow] Wilson, whom Theodore Roosevelt hated like poison, to mount the world stage and outdo Roosevelt in using the power of the United States to put the whole world aright. Roosevelt had lunged and plunged here and there. . . . Wilson's ambitions were without limit. He proposed to make the world safe for the American brand of democracy and transform backward places into mandated trusts for civilization.

The lines of the Wilsonian creed of interventionism and adventurism are in substance: Imperialism is bad (well, partly); every nation must have a nice constitutional government, more or less like ours; if any government dislikes the settlement made at Versailles it must put up its guns and sit down with its well-armed neighbors for a "friendly" conference; trade barriers must be lowered and that will make everybody round the globe prosperous (almost, if not entirely); backwards people are to be kept in order but otherwise treated nicely, as wards; the old history, full of troubles, is to be closed; brethren, and presumably sisters, are to dwell together in unity; everything in the world is to be managed as decorously as a Baptist convention . . . ; if not, we propose to fight disturbers everywhere (well, nearly everywhere). . . .

Some of our fellow citizens of course do not believe that America can deny or refuse to accept the obligation of directing world destiny. Mr. Walter Lippmann is among them. "Our foreign policy," he has recently said in a tone of contempt, "is regulated finally by an attempt to neutralize the fact that America has preponderant power and decisive influence in the affairs of the world . . . What Rome was to the ancient world, what Great

Britain has been to the modern world, America is to be to the world of to-morrow. . . ."

That sounds big but the test of facts bursts the bubble. Rome conquered, ruled, and robbed other peoples from the frontiers of Scotland to the sands of Arabia, from the Rhine to the Sahara, and then crumbled to ruins. Does anyone in his right mind really believe that the United States can or ought to play that role in the future, or anything akin to it? Well, what has Great Britain been to the modern world? Many fine and good things, no doubt. But in terms of foreign policy, Britain swept the Spanish, the Dutch, the French, and the Germans from the surface of the seven seas. During the past three hundred years Britain has waged numerous wars on the Continent to maintain, among other things, the balance of power. Britain has wrested colonies from the Spanish, the Dutch, the French, and the Germans, has conquered, ruled, and dictated to a large part of the globe. Does anyone believe that the United States can or ought to do all these things, or anything akin to them? . . .

American people are resolutely taking stock of their past follies. Forty years ago bright young men of tongue and pen told them they had an opportunity and responsibility to go forth and, after the manner of Rome and Britain, conquer, rule, and civilize backward peoples. And the same bright boys told them that all of this would "pay," that it would find outlets for their "surpluses" of manufactures and farm produce. It did not. Twenty-two years ago American people

were told that they were to make the world safe for democracy. They nobly responded. Before they got through they heard about the secret treaties by which the Allies divided the loot. They saw the Treaty of Versailles which distributed the spoils and made an impossible "peace." What did they get out of the adventure? Wounds and death. . . .

Those Americans who refuse to plunge blindly into the maelstrom of European and Asiatic politics are not defeatist or neurotic. They are giving evidence of sanity, not cowardice; of adult thinking as distinguished from infantilism. Experience had educated them and made them all the more determined to concentrate their energies on the making of a civilization within the circle of their continental domain. They do not propose to withdraw from the world, but they propose to deal with the world as it is and not as romantic propagandists picture it. They propose to deal with it in American terms, this is, in terms of national interest and security on this continent. Like their ancestors who made a revolution, built the Republic, and made it stick, they intend to preserve and defend the Republic, and under its shelter carry forward the work of employing their talents and resources in enriching American life. They know that this task for call for all the enlightened statesmanship, the constructive energy, and imaginative intelligence that the nation can command. America is not to be Rome or Britain. It is to be America.

CHARLES LINDBERGH, "NEUTRALITY AND WAR" (1939)

A 1927 transatlantic solo flight in a single-engine aircraft won Charles Lindbergh (1902–1974) lasting renown. By the late 1930s, Lindbergh had become de facto leader of the "America First" movement aiming to prevent US involvement in any future European wars. Here, with Nazi Germany having recently launched that war, he makes the case for American neutrality and outlines the principles that he believes should guide US defense policy.

Tonight, I speak again to the people of this country who are opposed to the United States entering the war which is now going on in Europe. We are faced with the need of deciding on a policy of American neutrality. The future of our nation and of our civilization rests upon the wisdom and

foresight we use. Much as peace is to be desired, we should realize that behind a successful policy of neutrality must stand a policy of war. It is essential to define clearly those principles and circumstances for which a nation will fight. Let us give no one the impression that America's love for peace means that she is afraid of war, of that we are not fully capable and willing to defend all that is vital to us. National life and influence depend upon national strength, both in character and in arms. A neutrality built on pacifism alone will eventually fail.

Before we can intelligently enact regulations for the control of our armaments, our credit, and our ships, we must draw a sharp dividing line between neutrality and war; there must be no gradual encroachment on the defenses of our nation. Up to this line we may adjust our affairs to gain the advantages of peace, but beyond it must lie all the armed might of America, coiled in readiness to spring if once this bond is cut. Let us make clear to all countries where this line lies. It must be both within our intent and our capabilities. There must be no question of trading or bluff in this hemisphere. Let us give no promises we cannot keep, make no meaningless assurances to an Ethiopia, a Czechoslovakia, or a Poland. The policy we decide upon should be as clear cut as our shorelines, and as easily defended as our continent.

This western hemisphere is our domain. It is our right to trade freely within it. From Alaska to Labrador, from the Hawaiian Islands to Bermuda, from Canada to South America, we must allow no invading army to set foot. These are the outposts of the United States. They form the essential outline of our geographical defense. We must be ready to wage war with all the resources of our nation if they are ever seriously threatened. Their defense is the mission of our army, our navy, and our air corps the minimum requirement of our military strength. Around these places should lie our line between neutrality and war. Let there be no compromise about our right to defend or trade within this area. If it is challenged by any nation, the answer must be war. Our policy of neutrality should have this as its foundation.

We must protect our sister American nations from foreign invasion, both for their welfare and our own. But, in turn, they have a duty to us. They should not place us in the position of having to defend them in America while they engage in wars abroad. Can we rightfully permit any country in America to give bases to foreign warships, or to send its army abroad to fight while it remains secure in our protection at home? We desire the utmost friendship with the people of Canada. If their country is ever attacked, our Navy will be defending their seas, our soldiers will fight on their battlefields, our fliers will die in their skies. But have they the right to draw this hemisphere into a European war simply because they prefer the Crown of England to American independence?

Sooner or later we must demand the freedom of this continent and its surrounding islands from the dictates of European power. American history clearly indicates this need. As long as European powers maintain their influence in our hemisphere, we are likely to find ourselves involved in their troubles. And they will lose no opportunity to involve us.

Our congress is now assembled to decide upon the best policy for this country to maintain during the war which is going on in Europe. The legislation under discussion involves three major issues—the embargo of arms, the restriction of shipping, and the allowance of credit. The action we take in regard to these issues will be an important indication to ourselves, and to the nations of Europe, whether or not we are likely to enter the conflict eventually as we did in the last war. The entire world is watching us. The action we take in America may either stop or precipitate this war.

Let us take up these issues, one at a time, and examine them. First, the embargo of arms: It is argued that the repeal of this embargo would assist democracy in Europe, that it would let us make a profit for ourselves from the sale of munitions abroad, and, at the same time, help to build up our own arms industry.

I do not believe that repealing the arms embargo would assist democracy in Europe—because I do not believe this is a war for democracy. This is a war over the balance of power in Europe, a war brought about by the desire for strength on the part of Germany and the fear of strength on the part of England and France. The munitions the armies obtain, the longer the war goes on, and the more devastated Europe becomes, the less hope there is for democracy. That is a lesson we should have learned from participation in the last war. If democratic principles had been applied in Europe after that war, if the "democracies" of Europe had been willing to make some sacrifice to help democracy in Europe while it was fighting for its life, if England and France had offered a hand to the struggling republic of Germany, there would be no war today.

If we repeal the arms embargo with the idea of assisting one of the warring sides to overcome the other, then why mislead ourselves by talk of neutrality? Those who advance this argument should admit openly that repeal is a step toward war. The next step would the extension of credit, and the next step would be the sending of American troops.

To those who argue that we could make a profit and build up our own industry by selling munitions abroad, I reply that we in America have not yet reached a point where we wish to capitalize on the destruction and death of war. I do not believe that the material welfare of this country need, or that our spiritual welfare could withstand, such a policy. If our industry depends upon a commerce of arms for its strength, then our industrial system should be changed.

It is impossible for me to understand how America can contribute civilization and humanity by sending offensive instruments of destruction to European battlefields. This would not only implicate us in the war, but it would make us partly responsible for its devastation. The fallacy of helping to defend a political ideology, even though it be somewhat similar to our own, was clearly demonstrated to us in the last war. Through our help that war was won, but neither the democracy nor the justice for which we fought grew in the peace that followed our victory.

Our bond with Europe is a bond of race and not of political ideology. We had to fight a European army to establish democracy in this country. It is the European race we must preserve; political progress will follow. Racial strength is vital, politics a luxury. If the white race is ever seriously threatened, it may then be time for us to take our part in its protection, to fight side by side with the English, French, and Germans, but not with one against the other for our mutual destruction.

Let us not dissipate our strength, or help Europe to dissipate hers, in these wars of politics and possession. For the benefit of western civilization, we should continue our embargo on offensive armaments. As far as purely defensive arms are concerned, I, for one, am in favor of supplying European countries with as much as we can

spare of the material that falls within this category. There are technicians who will argue that offensive and defensive arms cannot be separated completely. That is true, but it is no more difficult to make a list of defensive weapons than it is to separate munitions of war from semi-manufactured articles, and we are faced with that problem today. No one says that we should sell opium because it is difficult to make a list of narcotics. I would as soon see our country traffic in opium as in bombs. There are certain borderline cases, but there are plenty of clear cut examples: for instance, the bombing plane and the anti-aircraft cannon. I do not want to see American bombers dropping bombs which will kill and mutilate European children, even if they are not flown by American pilots. But I am perfectly willing to see American anti-aircraft guns shooting American shells at invading bombers over any European country. And I believe that most of you who are listening tonight will agree with me.

The second major issue for which we must create a policy concerns the restrictions to be placed on our shipping. Naval blockades have long been accepted as an element of warfare. They began on the surface of the sea, followed the submarine beneath it, and now reach up into the sky with aircraft. The laws and customs which were developed during the surface era were not satisfactory to the submarine. Now, aircraft bring up new and unknown factors for consideration. It is simple enough for a battleship to identify the merchantman she captures. It is a more difficult problem for a submarine if that merchantman may carry cannon; it is safer to fire a torpedo than to come up and ask. For bombing planes flying at high altitudes and through conditions of poor visibility, identification of a surface vessel will be more difficult still.

In modern naval blockades and warfare, torpedoes will be fired and bombs dropped on probabilities rather than on certainties of identification. The only safe course for neutral shipping at this time is to stay away from the warring countries and dangerous waters of Europe.

The third issue to be decided relates to the extension of credit. Here again we may draw from our experience in the last war. After that war was over, we found ourselves in the position of having financed a large portion of European countries.

And when the time came to pay us back, these countries simply refused to do so. They not only refused to pay the wartime loans we made, but they refused to pay back what we loaned them after the war was over. As is so frequently the case, we found that loaning money eventually created animosity instead of gratitude. European countries felt insulted when we asked to be repaid. They called us "Uncle Shylock." They were horror struck at the idea of turning over to us any of their islands in America to compensate for their debts, or for our help in winning their war. They seized all the German colonies and carved up Europe to suit their fancy. These were the "fruits of war." They took our money and they took our soldiers. But there was not the offer of one Caribbean island in return for the debts they "could not afford to pay."

The extension of Credit to a belligerent country is a long step toward war, and it would leave us close to the edge. If American industry loans money to a belligerent country, many interests will feel that it is more important for that country to win than for our own to avoid the war. It is unfortunate but true that there are interests in America who would rather lose American lives than their own dollars. We should give them no opportunity.

I believe that we should adopt as our program of American neutrality—as our contribution to western civilization—the following policy:

1 An embargo on offensive weapons and munitions.
2 The unrestricted sale of purely defensive armaments.
3 The prohibition of American shipping from the belligerent countries of Europe and their danger zones.
4 The refusal of credit to belligerent nations or their agents.

Whether or not this program is adopted depends upon the support of those of us who believe in it. The United States of America is a democracy. The policy of our country is still controlled by our people. It is time for us to take action. There has never been a greater test for the democratic principle of government.

Several weeks have passed since I received the honor of your invitation to speak in Chicago.

At that time it was essential to create strong and immediate opposition to the trend toward war which was taking place in this country. The agitation for our entry in the war was increasing with alarming rapidity. Hysteria had mounted to the point where anti-parachute corps were being formed to defend American cities against air attacks from Europe. Greenland, with its Arctic climate, its mountainous terrain, and its ice-filled seas was called an easy stepping-stone for German bombing planes invading America. Cartoons showed the Atlantic Ocean reduced to the width of the English Channel. American safety was said to depend upon the success of European armies. Foreign propaganda was in full swing, and it seemed in many ways that we were approaching the greatest crisis in the history of our country.

But events move swiftly in this modern world, and the true character of a nation lies beneath such surface foam. When the danger of foreign war was fully realized by our people, the underlying tradition of American independence arose, and in recent weeks its voice has thundered through the weaker cries for war.

We have by no means escaped the foreign entanglements and favoritisms that Washington warned us against when he passed the guidance of our nation's destiny to the hands of future generations. We have participated deeply in the intrigues of Europe, and not always in an open "democratic" way. There are still interests in this country and abroad who will do their utmost to draw us into the war. Against these interests we must be continuously on guard. But American opinion is now definitely and overwhelmingly against our involvement. Both political parties have declared against our entry into the war. People are beginning to realize that the problems of Europe cannot be solved by the interference of America. We have at last started to build and to plan for the defense of our own continent. By these acts, our eyes are turned once more in the direction of security and peace, for if our own military forces are strong, no foreign nation can invade us, and, if we do not interfere with their affairs, none will desire to.

Since we have decided against entering the war in Europe, it is time for us to consider the relationship we will have with Europe after this war is over. It is only by using the utmost intelligence in establishing and maintaining this relationship that we can keep America out of war in the future. . . .

From 1936 to 1939, as I travelled through European countries, I saw the phenomenal military strength of Germany growing like a giant at the side of an aged, and complacent England. France was awake to her danger, but far too occupied with personal ambitions, industrial troubles, and internal politics to make more than a feeble effort to rearm. In England there was organization without spirit. In France there was spirit without organization. In Germany there were both.

I realized that I was witnessing a clash between the heirs of another war. A generation had passed since the Treaty of Versailles. The sons of victory and the sons of defeat were about to meet on the battlefields of their fathers. As I travelled first among those who had won, and then among those who had lost, the words of a French philosopher kept running through my mind: "Man thrives on adversity."

The underlying issue was clear. It was not the support of "democracy," or the so-called democratic nations would have given more assistance to the struggling republic of post-war Germany. It was not a crusade for Christianity, or the Christian nations of the west would have carried their battle flags to the confiscated churches of Russia. It was not the preservation of small and helpless nations, or sanctions would have been followed by troops in Abyssinia, and England would not have refused to cooperate with the United States in Manchuria. The issue was one of the oldest and best known among men. It concerned the division of territory and wealth between nations. It has caused conflict in Europe since European history began.

The longer I lived in Europe, the more I felt that no outside influence could solve the problems of European nations, or bring them lasting peace. They must work out their destiny, as we must work out ours. I am convinced that the better acquainted we in America become with the background of European conflicts, the less we will desire to take part in them. But here I would like to make this point clear: while I advocate the non-interference by America in the internal affairs of Europe, I believe it is of the utmost importance for us to cooperate with Europe in our relationships with the other peoples of the earth. It is only by cooperation that we can maintain the supremacy of our western civilization and the right of our commerce to proceed unmolested throughout the world. Neither they nor we are strong enough to police the earth against the opposition of the other.

In the past, we have dealt with a Europe dominated by England and France. In the future we may have to deal with a Europe dominated by Germany. But whether England or Germany wins this war, Western civilization will still depend upon two great centers, one in each hemisphere. With all the aids of modern science, neither of these centers is in a position to attack the other successfully as long as the defenses of both are reasonably strong. A war between us could easily last for generations, and bring all civilization tumbling down, as has happened more than once before. An agreement between us could maintain civilization and peace throughout the world as far into the future as we can see.

But we are often told that if Germany wins this war, cooperation will be impossible, and treaties no more than scraps of paper. I reply that cooperation is never impossible when there is sufficient gain on both sides, and that treaties are seldom torn apart when they do not cover a weak nation. I would be among the last to advocate depending upon treaties for our national safety. I believe that we should rearm fully for the defense of America, and that we should never make the type of treaty that would lay us open to invasion if it were broken. But if we refuse to consider treaties with the dominant nation of Europe, regardless of who that may be, we remove all possibility of peace.

Nothing is to be gained by shouting names and pointing the finger of blame across the ocean. Our grandstand advice to England, and our criticism of her campaigns, have been neither wanted nor helpful. Our accusations of aggression and barbarism on the part of Germany, simply bring back echoes of hypocrisy and Versailles. Our hasty condemnation of a French government, struggling desperately to save a defeated nation from complete collapse, can do nothing but add to famine, hatred, and chaos.

If we desire to keep America out of war, we must take the lead in offering a plan for peace. That plan should be based upon the welfare of America. It should be backed by an impregnable system of defense. It should incorporate terms of mutual advantage. But it should not involve the internal affairs of Europe; they never were, and never will be, carried on according to our desires.

Let us offer Europe a plan for the progress and protection of the western civilization of which they and we each form a part. But whatever their reply may be, let us carry on the American destiny of which our forefathers dreamed as they cut their farm lands from the virgin forests. What would they think of the claim that our frontiers lie in Europe? Let us guard the independence that the soldiers of our Revolution won against overwhelming odds. What, I ask you, would those soldiers say if they could hear this nation, grown a hundred and thirty million strong, being told that only the British fleet protects us from invasion?

Our nation was born of courage and hardship. It grew on the fearless spirit of the pioneer. Now that it has become one of the greatest powers on earth, ours must not be the generation that kneels in fear of future hardships, or of invasion by a Europe already torn by war.

I do not believe we will ever accept a philosophy of calamity, weakness, and fear. I have faith in an American army, an American navy, an American air force and, most important of all, the American character, which in normal times, lies quietly beneath the surface of this nation.

FRANKLIN D. ROOSEVELT, "FIRESIDE CHAT" (1940)

A string of German military successes culminating in the fall of France in the spring of 1940 led President Franklin Roosevelt to revise his assessment of the threat posed by Nazi Germany. Through incremental shifts in policy, FDR aligned the United States with Great Britain and committed the United States to ensuring the survival of that country. In doing so, Roosevelt both followed and attempted to prod American public opinion as this radio address suggests.

This is not a fireside chat on war. It is a talk on national security; because the nub of the whole purpose of your President is to keep you now, and your children later, and your grandchildren much later, out of a last-ditch war for the preservation of American independence and all the things that American independence means to you and to me and to ours.

Tonight, in the presence of a world crisis, my mind goes back eight years to a night in the midst of a domestic crisis. It was a time when the wheels of American industry were grinding to a full stop, when the whole banking system of our country had ceased to function.

I well remember that while I sat in my study in the White House, preparing to talk with the people of the United States, I had before my eyes the picture of all those Americans with whom I was talking. I saw the workmen in the mills, the mines, the factories; the girl behind the counter; the small shopkeeper; the farmer doing his spring plowing; the widows and the old men wondering about their life's savings.

I tried to convey to the great mass of American people what the banking crisis meant to them in their daily lives.

Tonight, I want to do the same thing, with the same people, in this new crisis which faces America. We met the issue of 1933 with courage and realism.

We face this new crisis—this new threat to the security of our nation—with the same courage and realism.

Never before since Jamestown and Plymouth Rock has our American civilization been in such danger as now.

For, on September 27, 1940, by an agreement signed in Berlin, three powerful nations, two in Europe and one in Asia, joined themselves together in the threat that if the United States of America interfered with or blocked the expansion program of these three nations—a program aimed at world control—they would unite in ultimate action against the United States.

The Nazi masters of Germany have made it clear that they intend not only to dominate all life and thought in their own country, but also to enslave the whole of Europe, and then to use the resources of Europe to dominate the rest of the world.

It was only three weeks ago their leader stated this: "There are two worlds that stand opposed to each other." And then in defiant reply to his opponents, he said this: "Others are correct when they say: With this world we cannot ever reconcile ourselves. . . . I can beat any other power in the world." So said the leader of the Nazis.

In other words, the Axis not merely admits but proclaims that there can be no ultimate peace between their philosophy of government and our philosophy of government.

In view of the nature of this undeniable threat, it can be asserted, properly and categorically, that the United States has no right or reason to encourage talk of peace, until the day shall come when there is a clear intention on the part of the aggressor nations to abandon all thought of dominating or conquering the world.

At this moment, the forces of the states that are leagued against all peoples who live in freedom, are being held away from our shores. The Germans and the Italians are being blocked on the other side of the Atlantic by the British, and by the Greeks, and by thousands of soldiers and sailors who were able to escape from subjugated countries. In Asia, the Japanese are being engaged by the Chinese nation in another great defense. In the Pacific Ocean is our fleet.

Some of our people like to believe that wars in Europe and in Asia are of no concern to us. But it is a matter of most vital concern to us that European and Asiatic war-makers should not gain control of the oceans which lead to this hemisphere.

One hundred and seventeen years ago the Monroe Doctrine was conceived by our Government as a measure of defense in the face of a threat against this hemisphere by an alliance in Continental Europe. Thereafter, we stood on guard in the Atlantic, with the British as neighbors. There was no treaty. There was no "unwritten agreement."

And yet, there was the feeling, proven correct by history, that we as neighbors could settle any disputes in peaceful fashion. The fact is that during the whole of this time the Western Hemisphere has remained free from aggression from Europe or from Asia.

Does anyone seriously believe that we need to fear attack anywhere in the Americas while a free Britain remains our most powerful naval neighbor in the Atlantic? Does anyone seriously believe, on the other hand, that we could rest easy if the Axis powers were our neighbors there?

If Great Britain goes down, the Axis powers will control the continents of Europe, Asia, Africa, Australasia, and the high seas—and they will be in a position to bring enormous military and naval resources against this hemisphere. It is no exaggeration to say that all of us, in all the Americas, would be living at the point of a gun—a gun loaded with explosive bullets, economic as well as military.

We should enter upon a new and terrible era in which the whole world, our hemisphere included, would be run by threats of brute force. To survive in such a world, we would have to convert ourselves permanently into a militaristic power on the basis of war economy.

Some of us like to believe that even if Great Britain falls, we are still safe, because of the broad expanse of the Atlantic and of the Pacific.

But the width of those oceans is not what it was in the days of clipper ships. At one point between Africa and Brazil the distance is less than from Washington to Denver, Colorado, five hours for the latest type of bomber. And at the North end of the Pacific Ocean America and Asia almost touch each other.

Even today we have planes that could fly from the British Isles to New England and back again without refueling. And remember that the range of the modern bomber is ever being increased.

During the past week many people in all parts of the nation have told me what they wanted me to say tonight. Almost all of them expressed a courageous desire to hear the plain truth about the gravity of the situation. One telegram, however, expressed the attitude of the small minority who want to see no evil and hear no evil, even though they know in their hearts that evil exists. That telegram begged me not to tell again of the ease with which our American cities could be bombed by any hostile power which had gained bases in this Western Hemisphere. The gist of that telegram was: "Please, Mr. President, don't frighten us by telling us the facts."

Frankly and definitely there is danger ahead—danger against which we must prepare. But we well know that we cannot escape danger, or the fear of danger, by crawling into bed and pulling the covers over our heads.

Some nations of Europe were bound by solemn non-intervention pacts with Germany. Other nations were assured by Germany that they need never fear invasion. Non-intervention pact or not, the fact remains that they were attacked, overrun and thrown into the modern form of slavery at an hour's notice, or even without any notice at all. As an exiled leader of one of these nations said to me the other day—"The notice was a minus quantity. It was given to my Government two hours after German troops had poured into my country in a hundred places."

The fate of these nations tells us what it means to live at the point of a Nazi gun.

The Nazis have justified such actions by various pious frauds. One of these frauds is the claim that they are occupying a nation for the purpose of "restoring order." Another is that they are occupying or controlling a nation on the excuse that they are "protecting it" against the aggression of somebody else.

For example, Germany has said that she was occupying Belgium to save the Belgians from the British. Would she then hesitate to say to any South American country, "We are occupying you to protect you from aggression by the United States"?

Belgium today is being used as an invasion base against Britain, now fighting for its life. Any South American country, in Nazi hands, would always constitute a jumping-off place for German attack on any one of the other Republics of this hemisphere.

Analyze for yourselves the future of two other places even nearer to Germany if the Nazis won. Could Ireland hold out? Would Irish freedom be permitted as an amazing pet exception in an unfree world? Or the Islands of the Azores which still fly the flag of Portugal after five centuries? You and I think of Hawaii as an outpost of defense in the Pacific. And yet, the Azores are closer to our shores in the Atlantic than Hawaii is on the other side.

There are those who say that the Axis powers would never have any desire to attack the Western Hemisphere. That is the same dangerous form of wishful thinking which has destroyed the powers of resistance of so many conquered peoples.

The plain facts are that the Nazis have proclaimed, time and again, that all other races are their inferiors and therefore subject to their orders. And most important of all, the vast resources and wealth of this American Hemisphere constitute the most tempting loot in all the round world.

Let us no longer blind ourselves to the undeniable fact that the evil forces which have crushed and undermined and corrupted so many others are already within our own gates. Your Government knows much about them and every day is ferreting them out.

Their secret emissaries are active in our own and in neighboring countries. They seek to stir up suspicion and dissension to cause internal strife. They try to turn capital against labor, and vice versa. They try to reawaken long slumbering racial and religious enmities which should have no place in this country. They are active in every group that promotes intolerance. They exploit for their own ends our natural abhorrence of war. These trouble-breeders have but one purpose. It is to divide our people into hostile groups and to destroy our unity and shatter our will to defend ourselves.

There are also American citizens, many of them in high places, who, unwittingly in most cases, are aiding and abetting the work of these agents. I do not charge these American citizens with being foreign agents. But I do charge them with doing exactly the kind of work that the dictators want done in the United States.

These people not only believe that we can save our own skins by shutting our eyes to the fate of other nations. Some of them go much further than that. They say that we can and should become the friends and even the partners of the Axis powers. Some of them even suggest that we should imitate the methods of the dictatorships. Americans never can and never will do that.

The experience of the past two years has proven beyond doubt that no nation can appease the Nazis. No man can tame a tiger into a kitten by stroking it. There can be no appeasement with ruthlessness. There can be no reasoning with an incendiary bomb. We know now that a nation can have peace with the Nazis only at the price of total surrender.

Even the people of Italy have been forced to become accomplices of the Nazis; but at this moment they do not know how soon they will be embraced to death by their allies.

The American appeasers ignore the warning to be found in the fate of Austria, Czechoslovakia, Poland, Norway, Belgium, the Netherlands, Denmark, and France. They tell you that the Axis powers are going to win anyway; that all this bloodshed in the world could be saved; that the United States might just as well throw its influence into the scale of a dictated peace, and get the best out of it that we can.

They call it a "negotiated peace." Nonsense! Is it a negotiated peace if a gang of outlaws surrounds your community and on threat of extermination makes you pay tribute to save your own skins?

Such a dictated peace would be no peace at all. It would be only another armistice, leading to the most gigantic armament race and the most devastating trade wars in all history. And in these contests the Americas would offer the only real resistance to the Axis powers.

With all their vaunted efficiency, with all their parade of pious purpose in this war, there are still in their background the concentration camp and the servants of God in chains.

The history of recent years proves that shootings and chains and concentration camps are not simply the transient tools but the very altars of modern dictatorships. They may talk of a "new order" in the world, but what they have in mind is only a revival of the oldest and the worst tyranny. In that there is no liberty, no religion, no hope.

The proposed "new order" is the very opposite of a United States of Europe or a United States of Asia. It is not a Government based upon the consent of the governed. It is not a union of ordinary, self-respecting men and women to protect themselves and their freedom and their dignity from oppression. It is an unholy alliance of power and pelf to dominate and enslave the human race.

The British people and their allies today are conducting an active war against this unholy alliance. Our own future security is greatly dependent on the outcome of that fight. Our ability to "keep out of war" is going to be affected by that outcome.

Thinking in terms of today and tomorrow, I make the direct statement to the American people that there is far less chance of the United States getting into war, if we do all we can now to support the nations defending themselves against attack by the Axis than if we acquiesce in their defeat, submit tamely to an Axis victory, and wait our turn to be the object of attack in another war later on.

If we are to be completely honest with ourselves, we must admit that there is risk in any course we may take. But I deeply believe that the great majority of our people agree that the course that I advocate involves the least risk now and the greatest hope for world peace in the future.

The people of Europe who are defending themselves do not ask us to do their fighting. They ask us for the implements of war, the planes, the tanks, the guns, the freighters which will enable them to fight for their liberty and for our security. Emphatically we must get these weapons to them in sufficient volume and quickly enough, so that we and our children will be saved the agony and suffering of war which others have had to endure.

Let not the defeatists tell us that it is too late. It will never be earlier. Tomorrow will be later than today. Certain facts are self-evident.

In a military sense Great Britain and the British Empire are today the spearhead of resistance to world conquest. They are putting up a fight which will live forever in the story of human gallantry.

There is no demand for sending an American Expeditionary Force outside our own borders. There is no intention by any member of your Government to send such a force. You can, therefore, nail any talk about sending armies to Europe as deliberate untruth.

Our national policy is not directed toward war. Its sole purpose is to keep war away from our country and our people. Democracy's fight against world conquest is being greatly aided, and must be more greatly aided, by the rearmament of the United States and by sending every ounce and every ton of munitions and supplies that we can possibly spare to help the defenders who are in the front lines. It is no more unneutral for us to do that than it is for Sweden, Russia and other nations near Germany, to send steel and ore and oil and other war materials into Germany every day in the week.

We are planning our own defense with the utmost urgency; and in its vast scale we must integrate the war needs of Britain and the other free nations which are resisting aggression.

This is not a matter of sentiment or of controversial personal opinion. It is a matter of realistic, practical military policy, based on the advice of our military experts who are in close touch with existing warfare. These military and naval experts and the members of the Congress and the Administration have a single-minded purpose—the defense of the United States.

This nation is making a great effort to produce everything that is necessary in this emergency—and with all possible speed. This great effort requires great sacrifice.

I would ask no one to defend a democracy which in turn would not defend everyone in the nation against want and privation. The strength of this nation shall not be diluted by the failure of the Government to protect the economic well-being of its citizens.

If our capacity to produce is limited by machines, it must ever be remembered that these machines are operated by the skill and the stamina of the workers. As the Government is determined to protect the rights of the workers, so the nation has a right to expect that the men who man the machines will discharge their full responsibilities to the urgent needs of defense.

The worker possesses the same human dignity and is entitled to the same security of position as the engineer or the manager or the owner. For the workers provide the human power that turns out the destroyers, the airplanes and the tanks.

The nation expects our defense industries to continue operation without interruption by strikes or lock-outs. It expects and insists that management and workers will reconcile their differences by voluntary or legal means, to continue to produce the supplies that are so sorely needed.

And on the economic side of our great defense program, we are, as you know, bending every effort to maintain stability of prices and with that the stability of the cost of living.

Nine days ago I announced the setting up of a more effective organization to direct our gigantic efforts to increase the production of munitions. The appropriation of vast sums of money and a well coordinated executive direction of our defense efforts are not in themselves enough. Guns, planes, ships and many other things have to be built in the factories and arsenals of America. They have to be produced by workers and managers and engineers with the aid of machines which in turn have to be built by hundreds of thousands of workers throughout the land.

In this great work there has been splendid cooperation between the Government and industry and labor; and I am very thankful.

American industrial genius, unmatched throughout the world in the solution of production problems, has been called upon to bring its resources and its talents into action. Manufacturers of watches, farm implements, linotypes, cash registers, automobiles, sewing machines, lawn mowers and locomotives are now making fuses, bomb packing crates, telescope mounts, shells, pistols and tanks.

But all our present efforts are not enough. We must have more ships, more guns, more planes—more of everything. This can only be accomplished if we discard the notion of "business as usual." This job cannot be done merely by superimposing on the existing productive facilities the added requirements of the nation for defense.

Our defense efforts must not be blocked by those who fear the future consequences of surplus plant capacity. The possible consequences of failure of our defense efforts now are much more to be feared.

After the present needs of our defenses are past, a proper handling of the country's peace-time needs will require all the new productive capacity—if not more.

No pessimistic policy about the future of America shall delay the immediate expansion of those industries essential to defense. We need them.

I want to make it clear that it is the purpose of the nation to build now with all possible speed every machine, every arsenal, every factory that we need to manufacture our defense material. We have the men, the skill, the wealth, and above all, the will.

I am confident that if and when production of consumer or luxury goods in certain industries requires the use of machines and raw materials that are essential for defense purposes, then such production must yield, and will gladly yield, to our primary and compelling purpose.

I appeal to the owners of plants—to the managers—to the workers—to our own Government employees—to put every ounce of effort into producing these munitions swiftly and without stint. With this appeal I give you the pledge that all of us who are officers of your Government will devote ourselves to the same whole-hearted extent to the great task that lies ahead.

As planes and ships and guns and shells are produced, your Government, with its defense experts, can then determine how best to use them to defend this hemisphere. The decision as to how much shall be sent abroad and how much shall remain at home must be made on the basis of our over-all military necessities.

We must be the great arsenal of democracy. For us this is an emergency as serious as war itself. We must apply ourselves to our task with the same resolution, the same sense of urgency, the same spirit of patriotism and sacrifice as we would show were we at war.

We have furnished the British great material support and we will furnish far more in the future.

There will be no "bottlenecks" in our determination to aid Great Britain. No dictator, no combination of dictators, will weaken that determination by threats of how they will construe that determination.

The British have received invaluable military support from the heroic Greek army, and from the forces of all the governments in exile. Their strength is growing. It is the strength of men and women who value their freedom more highly than they value their lives.

I believe that the Axis powers are not going to win this war. I base that belief on the latest and best information.

We have no excuse for defeatism. We have every good reason for hope—hope for peace, hope for the defense of our civilization and for the building of a better civilization in the future.

I have the profound conviction that the American people are now determined to put forth a mightier effort than they have ever yet made to increase our production of all the implements of defense, to meet the threat to our democratic faith.

As President of the United States I call for that national effort. I call for it in the name of this nation which we love and honor and which we are privileged and proud to serve. I call upon our people with absolute confidence that our common cause will greatly succeed.

"Step by Step—The War," *Social Justice* (September 2, 1940)

Among Roosevelt's most impassioned critics was a Catholic priest Charles E. Coughlin, whose weekly radio show "The Hour of Power" attracted an audience in the tens of millions. To promote his views, which in addition to being anti-interventionist were also anticommunist, anti–Wall Street, and anti-Semitic, Coughlin published the magazine *Social Justice*. Here is an excerpt from that publication, warning that the United States was being dragged into a misbegotten war.

"Alarmist!"

The was the name applied to all patriots who opposed the type of *Neutrality Bill* proposed by the New Deal last year.

Father Coughlin, among others, was loud in proclaiming that it would lead to war—and step by step.

The *Neutrality Bill*—even as written by the New Deal—has been emasculated.

In the beginning, American ships were not allowed to proceed into belligerent waters.

Now, American ships are being directed to proceed not only through belligerent waters

but through mine-strewn areas which our Government knows to be mine-strewn.

We are solicitous about evacuating refugee children from Europe.

Bunk!

That is the advertised propaganda being fed to our people.

We have not enough ships to rescue more than a handful of children.

And for every child rescued from the port of Petsamo, 10,000 will be left un-rescued—and unfed; for the law is that our ships going to Europe may not carry food or clothing or medicine. Their hulls must be filled with water—salt water at that.

But more alarming than all this is the fact that our State Department, having been advised by the German State Department of a certain mine-strewn area south of Iceland and north of Scotland, officially instructs the captain of the *American Legion*—a rescue ship—to proceed practically through the mine-strewn area, thereby not only jeopardizing the lives of the passengers on the *American Legion,* but also the last remnants of international peace.

Why?

Because *this Government wants war with Germany without declaring war on Germany.*

The so-called alarmists, last year, said something about incidents created to hurtle us into war.

If the *American Legion* will not prove to be an incident, rest assured one will be found even if it has to be manufactured.

Social Justice Magazine is no pessimist in its prognostications. Nevertheless, being realists, we feel morally certain that this country will be engaged in war up to the hilt before many moons will have waned.

Possibly, some of you are too young to remember the impassioned appeals for war and the hysterical desires created thereby in the hearts of the people "to make the world safe for democracy" back in 1917.

Possibly, most of you forgot what happened following 1919:

The boys returning from abroad had only one job to perform—the job of tramping the pavements in the army of the unemployed.

The "democracy" for which they fought produced Lenin and his Russian revolution.

The pledges proffered to us by Great Britain were not fulfilled.

Nothing better can be expected following this war, into which we are about to be high-balled by the New Deal Administration.

As we see it, we will not be militaristically engaged in this present phase of the war.

We are preparing for the big showdown some years hence.

The *Neutrality Bill* was the first step.

God knows what will be the last step in the days to come.

COMMITTEE TO DEFEND AMERICA BY AIDING THE ALLIES, "STATEMENT OF POLICY" (1941)

Opposing the America First movement was the Committee to Defend America by Aiding the Allies. Its name notwithstanding, this was not a committee but a mass organization founded in May 1940 under the leadership of the journalist William Allen White (1968–1944). By January 1941, the Committee had organized some 700 local chapters nationwide and claimed a membership exceeding 5,000,000. Here, as it appeared in leading American newspapers, is the Committee's plan of action.

The Committee to Defend America by Aiding the Allies is committed to an Allied success because America and the American way of life will be gravely imperiled by an Axis victory. By the passage of the Lend-Lease Bill, the American people have committed themselves to full material aid to the Allies. This policy must now be supported by a united nation. The Committee will support the following measures to make this policy effective.

I. The full mobilization of American economic life for greater production with whatever sacrifices are necessary on the part of business, labor, agriculture and the consumer. . . .

Use by the American government of whatever means are necessary to insure prompt delivery of war materials to the Allies, including . . . convoy of ships with American naval vessels if need be.

Our slogan will be "Deliver the goods to Britain now."

II. Congressional revision of legislation in order to permit the recruiting of Americans who wish to serve voluntarily in the armed or civilian forces of those nations whose defense is necessary for American security.

III. Freezing of all foreign assets in the United States under the license system to prevent further withdrawal of Axis balances and to control Nazi activities in the Western Hemisphere.

IV. A firm policy in the Pacific, including (1) increase of American naval strength in the Far East; (2) increased aid to China; (3) extension of embargoes on war materials to Japan; (4) clear indication of our determination to prevent the conquest of Singapore and the Dutch East Indies. . . .

V. Strenuous efforts to combat Nazi and totalitarian propaganda in the Americas. . . .

We are convinced that that course which we advocate involves the lesser danger of war and contributes to a constructive peace.

Eventual victory for the forces of democracy must be translated into the institutions and machinery for durable peace with American participation. Public opinion must be mobilized now so that America will play an effective part in the organization of a lasting peace and will this time see the job through.

We take this position because should Britain fall:

(1) All the exits from and entrances to the Atlantic would immediately fall into hostile hands. This in the past has meant invasion of our country. It might mean invasion again.

(2) A large part of South America, conscious of our inability to defend it, would almost at once come within the orbit of the Nazi regime. . . .

(3) All of the Orient . . . would fall under the domination of the aggressor nations.

(4) We would be barred from the external world . . . except on such terms as the Nazis might dictate. We would be encircled in the South; restricted in the Atlantic; and hemmed in in the Pacific.

(5) It is doubtful whether we could build our war forces rapidly enough in this sort of a world either to insure our own integrity or to enforce our own terms externally. The forces of despotism would control all of Europe, all of Africa, and most of Asia. They would, therefore, control every essential resource, natural and otherwise, to organize military domination of the world. . . .

We believe, and without reservation, that our only chance of establishing a peaceful world in which we might live in freedom and tranquility and preserve our institutions is to insure Allied victory.

CHARLES LINDBERGH, "DES MOINES SPEECH" (1941)

As Great Britain's position became ever more precarious, Charles Lindbergh and "America Firsters" became ever more determined to keep the United States out of the war. Lindbergh's own accusations against those taking the opposite view became more pointed.

It is now two years since this latest European war began. From that day in September, 1939, until the present moment, there has been an over-increasing effort to force the United States into the conflict.

That effort has been carried on by foreign interests, and by a small minority of our own people; but it has been so successful that, today, our country stands on the verge of war.

At this time, as the war is about to enter its third winter, it seems appropriate to review the circumstances that have led us to our present position. Why are we on the verge of war? Was it necessary for us to become so deeply involved? Who is responsible for changing our national policy from one of neutrality and independence to one of entanglement in European affairs?

Personally, I believe there is no better argument against our intervention than a study of the causes and developments of the present war. I have often said that if the true facts and issues were placed before the American people, there would be no danger of our involvement.

Here, I would like to point out to you a fundamental difference between the groups who advocate foreign war, and those who believe in an independent destiny for America.

If you will look back over the record, you will find that those of us who oppose intervention have constantly tried to clarify facts and issues; while the interventionists have tried to hide facts and confuse issues. . . .

The subterfuge and propaganda that exists in our country is obvious on every side. Tonight, I shall try to pierce through a portion of it, to the naked facts which lie beneath.

When this war started in Europe, it was clear that the American people were solidly opposed to entering it. Why shouldn't we be? We had the best defensive position in the world; we had a tradition of independence from Europe; and the one time we did take part in a European war left European problems unsolved, and debts to America unpaid.

National polls showed that when England and France declared war on Germany, in 1939, less than 10 percent of our population favored a similar course for America. But there were various groups of people, here and abroad, whose interests and beliefs necessitated the involvement of the United States in the war. I shall point out some of these groups tonight, and outline their methods of procedure. In doing this, I must speak with the utmost frankness, for in order to counteract their efforts, we must know exactly who they are.

The three most important groups who have been pressing this country toward war are the British, the Jewish and the Roosevelt administration.

Behind these groups, but of lesser importance, are a number of capitalists, Anglophiles, and intellectuals who believe that the future of mankind depends upon the domination of the British empire. Add to these the Communistic groups who were opposed to intervention until a few weeks ago, and I believe I have named the major war agitators in this country.

I am speaking here only of war agitators, not of those sincere but misguided men and women who, confused by misinformation and frightened by propaganda, follow the lead of the war agitators.

As I have said, these war agitators comprise only a small minority of our people; but they control a tremendous influence. Against the determination of the American people to stay out of war, they have marshaled the power of their propaganda, their money, their patronage.

Let us consider these groups, one at a time.

First, the British: It is obvious and perfectly understandable that Great Britain wants the United States in the war on her side. England is now in a desperate position. Her population is not large enough and her armies are not strong enough to invade the continent of Europe and win the war she declared against Germany.

Her geographical position is such that she cannot win the war by the use of aviation alone, regardless of how many planes we send her. Even if America entered the war, it is improbable that the Allied armies could invade Europe and overwhelm the Axis powers. But one thing is certain. If England can draw this country into the war, she can shift to our shoulders a large portion of the responsibility for waging it and for paying its cost.

As you all know, we were left with the debts of the last European war; and unless we are more cautious in the future than we have been in the past, we will be left with the debts of the present case. If it were not for her hope that she can make us responsible for the war financially, as well as militarily, I believe England would have negotiated a peace in Europe many months ago, and be better off for doing so.

England has devoted, and will continue to devote every effort to get us into the war. We know that she spent huge sums of money in this country during the last war in order to involve us. Englishmen have written books about the cleverness of its use.

We know that England is spending great sums of money for propaganda in America during the present war. If we were Englishmen, we would do the same. But our interest is first in America; and as Americans, it is essential for us to realize the effort that British interests are making to draw us into their war.

The second major group I mentioned is the Jewish.

It is not difficult to understand why Jewish people desire the overthrow of Nazi Germany. The persecution they suffered in Germany would be sufficient to make bitter enemies of any race.

No person with a sense of the dignity of mankind can condone the persecution of the Jewish race in Germany. But no person of honesty and vision can look on their pro-war policy here today without seeing the dangers involved in such a policy both for us and for them. Instead of agitating for war, the Jewish groups in this country should be opposing it in every possible way for they will be among the first to feel its consequences.

Tolerance is a virtue that depends upon peace and strength. History shows that it cannot survive war and devastations. A few far-sighted Jewish people realize this and stand opposed to intervention. But the majority still do not.

Their greatest danger to this country lies in their large ownership and influence in our motion pictures, our press, our radio and our government.

I am not attacking either the Jewish or the British people. Both races, I admire. But I am saying that the leaders of both the British and the Jewish races, for reasons which are as understandable from their viewpoint as they are inadvisable from ours, for reasons which are not American, wish to involve us in the war.

We cannot blame them for looking out for what they believe to be their own interests, but we also must look out for ours. We cannot allow the natural passions and prejudices of other peoples to lead our country to destruction.

The Roosevelt administration is the third powerful group which has been carrying this country toward war. Its members have used the war emergency to obtain a third presidential term for the first time in American history. They have used the war to add unlimited billions to a debt which was already the highest we have ever known. And they have just used the war to justify the restriction of congressional power, and the assumption of dictatorial procedures on the part of the president and his appointees.

The power of the Roosevelt administration depends upon the maintenance of a war-time emergency. The prestige of the Roosevelt administration depends upon the success of Great Britain to whom the president attached his political future at a time when most people thought that England and France would easily win the war. The danger of the Roosevelt administration lies in its subterfuge. While its members have promised us peace, they have led us to war heedless of the platform upon which they were elected. . . .

When hostilities commenced in Europe, in 1939, it was realized by these groups that the American people had no intention of entering the war. They knew it would be worse than useless to ask us for a declaration of war at that time. But they believed that this country could be entered into the war in very much the same way we were entered into the last one.

They planned: first, to prepare the United States for foreign war under the guise of American defense; second, to involve us in the war, step by step, without our realization; third, to create a series of incidents which would force us into the actual conflict. These plans were of course, to be covered and assisted by the full power of their propaganda.

Our theaters soon became filled with plays portraying the glory of war. Newsreels lost all semblance of objectivity. Newspapers and magazines began to lose advertising if they carried anti-war articles. A smear campaign was instituted against individuals who opposed intervention. The terms "fifth columnist," "traitor," "Nazi," "anti-Semitic" were thrown ceaselessly at any one who dared to suggest that it was not to the best interests of the United States to enter the war. Men lost their jobs if they were frankly anti-war. Many others dared no longer speak.

Before long, lecture halls that were open to the advocates of war were closed to speakers who opposed it. A fear campaign was inaugurated. We were told that aviation, which has held the British fleet off the continent of Europe, made America more vulnerable than ever before to invasion. Propaganda was in full swing.

There was no difficulty in obtaining billions of dollars for arms under the guise of defending America. Our people stood united on a program of defense. Congress passed appropriation after appropriation for guns and planes and battleships, with the approval of the overwhelming majority of our citizens. That a large portion of these appropriations was to be used to build arms for

Europe, we did not learn until later. That was another step.

To use a specific example; in 1939, we were told that we should increase our air corps to a total of 5,000 planes. Congress passed the necessary legislation. A few months later, the administration told us that the United States should have at least 50,000 planes for our national safety. But almost as fast as fighting planes were turned out from our factories, they were sent abroad, although our own air corps was in the utmost need of new equipment; so that today, two years after the start of war, the American army has a few hundred thoroughly modern bombers and fighters—less in fact, than Germany is able to produce in a single month.

Ever since its inception, our arms program has been laid out for the purpose of carrying on the war in Europe, far more than for the purpose of building an adequate defense for America.

Now at the same time we were being prepared for a foreign war, it was necessary, as I have said, to involve us in the war. This was accomplished under that now famous phrase "steps short of war."

England and France would win if the United States would only repeal its arms embargo and sell munitions for cash, we were told. And then . . . began a refrain that marked every step we took toward war for many months—"the best way to defend America and keep out of war," we were told, was "by aiding the Allies."

First, we agreed to sell arms to Europe; next, we agreed to loan arms to Europe; then we agreed to patrol the ocean for Europe; then we occupied a European island in the war zone. Now, we have reached the verge of war.

The war groups have succeeded in the first two of their three major steps into war. The greatest armament program in our history is under way.

We have become involved in the war from practically every standpoint except actual shooting. Only the creation of sufficient "incidents" yet remains; and you see the first of these already taking place. . . .

Our system of democracy and representative government is on test today as it has never been before. We are on the verge of a war in which the only victor would be chaos and prostration.

We are on the verge of a war for which we are still unprepared, and for which no one has offered a feasible plan for victory—a war which cannot be won without sending our soldiers across the ocean to force a landing on a hostile coast against armies stronger than our own.

We are on the verge of war, but it is not yet too late to stay out. It is not too late to show that no amount of money, or propaganda, or patronage can force a free and independent people into war against its will. It is not yet too late to retrieve and to maintain the independent American destiny that our forefathers established in this new world. . . .

FRANKLIN D. ROOSEVELT, "THE FOUR FREEDOMS" (1941)

Although elected to an unprecedented third term in November 1940, President Roosevelt still hesitated to come out in favor of direct military intervention against Nazi Germany. Instead, he focused on building up US forces to defend the Western hemisphere, even while depicting the danger facing America in dire terms.

I address you, the Members of the Seventy-seventh Congress, at a moment unprecedented in the history of the Union. I use the word "unprecedented," because at no previous time has American security been as seriously threatened from without as it is today.

Since the permanent formation of our Government under the Constitution, in 1789, most of the periods of crisis in our history have related to our domestic affairs. Fortunately, only one of these—the four-year War Between the States—ever threatened our national unity. Today, thank God, one hundred and thirty million Americans, in forty-eight States, have forgotten points of the compass in our national unity.

It is true that prior to 1914 the United States often had been disturbed by events in other Continents. We had even engaged in two wars with European nations and in a number of undeclared wars in the West Indies, in the Mediterranean and in the Pacific for the maintenance of American rights and for the principles of peaceful commerce. But in no case had a serious threat been raised against our national safety or our continued independence.

What I seek to convey is the historic truth that the United States as a nation has at all times maintained clear, definite opposition, to any attempt to lock us in behind an ancient Chinese wall while the procession of civilization went past. Today, thinking of our children and of their children, we oppose enforced isolation for ourselves or for any other part of the Americas. . . .

That determination of ours, extending over all these years, was proved, for example, during the quarter century of wars following the French Revolution.

While the Napoleonic struggles did threaten interests of the United States because of the French foothold in the West Indies and in Louisiana, and while we engaged in the War of 1812 to vindicate our right to peaceful trade, it is nevertheless clear that neither France nor Great Britain, nor any other nation, was aiming at domination of the whole world.

In like fashion from 1815 to 1914—ninety-nine years—no single war in Europe or in Asia constituted a real threat against our future or against the future of any other American nation.

Except in the Maximilian interlude in Mexico, no foreign power sought to establish itself in this Hemisphere; and the strength of the British fleet in the Atlantic has been a friendly strength. It is still a friendly strength.

Even when the World War broke out in 1914, it seemed to contain only small threat of danger to our own American future. But, as time went on, the American people began to visualize what the downfall of democratic nations might mean to our own democracy.

We need not overemphasize imperfections in the Peace of Versailles. We need not harp on failure of the democracies to deal with problems of world reconstruction. We should remember that the Peace of 1919 was far less unjust than the kind of "pacification" which began even before Munich, and which is being carried on under the new order of tyranny that seeks to spread over every continent today. The American people have unalterably set their faces against that tyranny.

Every realist knows that the democratic way of life is at this moment being directly assailed in every part of the world—assailed either by arms, or by secret spreading of poisonous propaganda by those who seek to destroy unity and promote discord in nations that are still at peace.

During sixteen long months this assault has blotted out the whole pattern of democratic life in an appalling number of independent nations, great and small. The assailants are still on the march, threatening other nations, great and small.

Therefore, as your President, performing my constitutional duty to "give to the Congress information of the state of the Union," I find it, unhappily, necessary to report that the future and the safety of our country and of our democracy are overwhelmingly involved in events far beyond our borders.

Armed defense of democratic existence is now being gallantly waged in four continents. If that defense fails, all the population and all the resources of Europe, Asia, Africa and Australasia will be dominated by the conquerors. Let us remember that the total of those populations and their resources in those four continents greatly exceeds the sum total of the population and the resources of the whole of the Western Hemisphere—many times over.

In times like these it is immature—and incidentally, untrue—for anybody to brag that an unprepared America, single-handed, and with one hand tied behind its back, can hold off the whole world.

No realistic American can expect from a dictator's peace international generosity, or return of true independence, or world disarmament, or freedom of expression, or freedom of religion—or even good business.

Such a peace would bring no security for us or for our neighbors. "Those, who would give up essential liberty to purchase a little temporary safety, deserve neither liberty nor safety."

As a nation, we may take pride in the fact that we are softhearted; but we cannot afford to be soft-headed.

We must always be wary of those who with sounding brass and a tinkling cymbal preach the "ism" of appeasement.

We must especially beware of that small group of selfish men who would clip the wings of the American eagle in order to feather their own nests.

I have recently pointed out how quickly the tempo of modern warfare could bring into our very midst the physical attack which we must eventually expect if the dictator nations win this war.

There is much loose talk of our immunity from immediate and direct invasion from across the seas. Obviously, as long as the British Navy retains its power, no such danger exists. Even if there were no British Navy, it is not probable that any enemy would be stupid enough to attack us by landing troops in the United States from across thousands of miles of ocean, until it had acquired strategic bases from which to operate.

But we learn much from the lessons of the past years in Europe—particularly the lesson of Norway, whose essential seaports were captured by treachery and surprise built up over a series of years.

The first phase of the invasion of this Hemisphere would not be the landing of regular troops. The necessary strategic points would be occupied by secret agents and their dupes—and great numbers of them are already here, and in Latin America.

As long as the aggressor nations maintain the offensive, they—not we—will choose the time and the place and the method of their attack.

That is why the future of all the American Republics is today in serious danger.

That is why this Annual Message to the Congress is unique in our history.

That is why every member of the Executive Branch of the Government and every member of the Congress faces great responsibility and great accountability.

The need of the moment is that our actions and our policy should be devoted primarily—almost exclusively—to meeting this foreign peril. For all our domestic problems are now a part of the great emergency.

Just as our national policy in internal affairs has been based upon a decent respect for the rights and the dignity of all our fellow men within our gates, so our national policy in foreign affairs has been based on a decent respect for the rights and dignity of all nations, large and small. And the justice of morality must and will win in the end.

Our national policy is this:

First, by an impressive expression of the public will and without regard to partisanship, we are committed to all-inclusive national defense.

Second, by an impressive expression of the public will and without regard to partisanship, we are committed to full support of all those resolute peoples, everywhere, who are resisting aggression and are thereby keeping war away from our Hemisphere. By this support, we express our determination that the democratic cause shall prevail; and we strengthen the defense and the security of our own nation.

Third, by an impressive expression of the public will and without regard to partisanship, we are committed to the proposition that principles of morality and considerations for our own security will never permit us to acquiesce in a peace dictated by aggressors and sponsored by appeasers. We know that enduring peace cannot be bought at the cost of other people's freedom.

In the recent national election there was no substantial difference between the two great parties in respect to that national policy. No issue was fought out on this line before the American electorate. Today it is abundantly evident that American citizens everywhere are demanding and supporting speedy and complete action in recognition of obvious danger.

Therefore, the immediate need is a swift and driving increase in our armament production.

Leaders of industry and labor have responded to our summons. Goals of speed have been set. In some cases these goals are being reached ahead of time; in some cases we are on schedule; in other cases there are slight but not serious delays; and in some cases—and I am sorry to say very important cases—we are all concerned by the slowness of the accomplishment of our plans.

The Army and Navy, however, have made substantial progress during the past year. Actual experience is improving and speeding up our methods of production with every passing day. And today's best is not good enough for tomorrow.

I am not satisfied with the progress thus far made. The men in charge of the program represent the best in training, in ability, and in patriotism. They are not satisfied with the progress thus far made. None of us will be satisfied until the job is done.

No matter whether the original goal was set too high or too low, our objective is quicker and better results. To give you two illustrations:

We are behind schedule in turning out finished airplanes; we are working day and night to solve the innumerable problems and to catch up.

We are ahead of schedule in building warships but we are working to get even further ahead of that schedule.

To change a whole nation from a basis of peacetime production of implements of peace to a basis of wartime production of implements of war is no small task. And the greatest difficulty comes at the beginning of the program, when new tools, new plant facilities, new assembly lines, and new ship ways must first be constructed before the actual materiel begins to flow steadily and speedily from them.

The Congress, of course, must rightly keep itself informed at all times of the progress of the program. However, there is certain information, as the Congress itself will readily recognize, which, in the interests of our own security and those of the nations that we are supporting, must of needs be kept in confidence.

New circumstances are constantly begetting new needs for our safety. I shall ask this Congress for greatly increased new appropriations and authorizations to carry on what we have begun.

I also ask this Congress for authority and for funds sufficient to manufacture additional munitions and war supplies of many kinds, to be turned over to those nations which are now in actual war with aggressor nations.

Our most useful and immediate role is to act as an arsenal for them as well as for ourselves. They do not need man power, but they do need billions of dollars worth of the weapons of defense.

The time is near when they will not be able to pay for them all in ready cash. We cannot, and

we will not, tell them that they must surrender, merely because of present inability to pay for the weapons which we know they must have.

I do not recommend that we make them a loan of dollars with which to pay for these weapons—a loan to be repaid in dollars.

I recommend that we make it possible for those nations to continue to obtain war materials in the United States, fitting their orders into our own program. Nearly all their materiel would, if the time ever came, be useful for our own defense.

Taking counsel of expert military and naval authorities, considering what is best for our own security, we are free to decide how much should be kept here and how much should be sent abroad to our friends who by their determined and heroic resistance are giving us time in which to make ready our own defense.

For what we send abroad, we shall be repaid within a reasonable time following the close of hostilities, in similar materials, or, at our option, in other goods of many kinds, which they can produce and which we need.

Let us say to the democracies: "We Americans are vitally concerned in your defense of freedom. We are putting forth our energies, our resources and our organizing powers to give you the strength to regain and maintain a free world. We shall send you, in ever-increasing numbers, ships, planes, tanks, guns. This is our purpose and our pledge."

In fulfillment of this purpose we will not be intimidated by the threats of dictators that they will regard as a breach of international law or as an act of war our aid to the democracies which dare to resist their aggression. Such aid is not an act of war, even if a dictator should unilaterally proclaim it so to be.

When the dictators, if the dictators, are ready to make war upon us, they will not wait for an act of war on our part. They did not wait for Norway or Belgium or the Netherlands to commit an act of war.

Their only interest is in a new one-way international law, which lacks mutuality in its observance, and, therefore, becomes an instrument of oppression.

The happiness of future generations of Americans may well depend upon how effective and how immediate we can make our aid felt. No one can tell the exact character of the emergency

234 IDEAS AND AMERICAN FOREIGN POLICY

situations that we may be called upon to meet. The Nation's hands must not be tied when the Nation's life is in danger.

We must all prepare to make the sacrifices that the emergency—almost as serious as war itself—demands. Whatever stands in the way of speed and efficiency in defense preparations must give way to the national need.

A free nation has the right to expect full cooperation from all groups. A free nation has the right to look to the leaders of business, of labor, and of agriculture to take the lead in stimulating effort, not among other groups but within their own groups.

The best way of dealing with the few slackers or trouble makers in our midst is, first, to shame them by patriotic example, and, if that fails, to use the sovereignty of Government to save Government.

As men do not live by bread alone, they do not fight by armaments alone. Those who man our defenses, and those behind them who build our defenses, must have the stamina and the courage which come from unshakable belief in the manner of life which they are defending. The mighty action that we are calling for cannot be based on a disregard of all things worth fighting for.

The Nation takes great satisfaction and much strength from the things which have been done to make its people conscious of their individual stake in the preservation of democratic life in America. Those things have toughened the fibre of our people, have renewed their faith and strengthened their devotion to the institutions we make ready to protect.

Certainly this is no time for any of us to stop thinking about the social and economic problems which are the root cause of the social revolution which is today a supreme factor in the world.

For there is nothing mysterious about the foundations of a healthy and strong democracy. The basic things expected by our people of their political and economic systems are simple. They are:

Equality of opportunity for youth and for others.

Jobs for those who can work.

Security for those who need it.

The ending of special privilege for the few.

The preservation of civil liberties for all.

The enjoyment of the fruits of scientific progress in a wider and constantly rising standard of living.

These are the simple, basic things that must never be lost sight of in the turmoil and unbelievable complexity of our modern world. The inner and abiding strength of our economic and political systems is dependent upon the degree to which they fulfill these expectations. . . .

I have called for personal sacrifice. I am assured of the willingness of almost all Americans to respond to that call.

A part of the sacrifice means the payment of more money in taxes. In my Budget Message I shall recommend that a greater portion of this great defense program be paid for from taxation than we are paying today. No person should try, or be allowed, to get rich out of this program; and the principle of tax payments in accordance with ability to pay should be constantly before our eyes to guide our legislation.

If the Congress maintains these principles, the voters, putting patriotism ahead of pocketbooks, will give you their applause.

In the future days, which we seek to make secure, we look forward to a world founded upon four essential human freedoms.

The first is freedom of speech and expression—everywhere in the world.

The second is freedom of every person to worship God in his own way—everywhere in the world.

The third is freedom from want—which, translated into world terms, means economic understandings which will secure to every nation a healthy peacetime life for its inhabitants—everywhere in the world.

The fourth is freedom from fear—which, translated into world terms, means a world-wide reduction of armaments to such a point and in such a thorough fashion that no nation will be in a position to commit an act of physical aggression against any neighbor—anywhere in the world.

That is no vision of a distant millennium. It is a definite basis for a kind of world attainable in our own time and generation. That kind of world is the very antithesis of the so-called new order of tyranny which the dictators seek to create with the crash of a bomb.

To that new order we oppose the greater conception—the moral order. A good society is able to face schemes of world domination and foreign revolutions alike without fear.

Since the beginning of our American history, we have been engaged in change—in a perpetual peaceful revolution—a revolution which goes on steadily, quietly adjusting itself to changing conditions—without the concentration camp or the quick-lime in the ditch. The world order which we seek is the cooperation of free countries, working together in a friendly, civilized society.

This nation has placed its destiny in the hands and heads and hearts of its millions of free men and women; and its faith in freedom under the guidance of God. Freedom means the supremacy of human rights everywhere. Our support goes to those who struggle to gain those rights or keep them. Our strength is our unity of purpose. To that high concept there can be no end save victory.

Henry Luce, "The American Century," *Life* (February 17, 1941)

As founder and publisher of the weekly magazines *Time* and *Life,* Henry Luce (1898–1967) had at hand his own bully pulpit, which he used without hesitation to promote his views. Luce loathed Roosevelt and the New Deal, but he favored coming to Britain's rescue. Here, in an editorial appearing in *Life* in February 1941, he makes the case not only for intervention, but for the United States assuming the mantle of world leadership.

We Americans are unhappy. We are not happy about America. We are not happy about ourselves in relation to America. We are nervous—or gloomy—or apathetic. As we look out at the rest of the world we are confused; we don't know what to do. "Aid to Britain short of war" is typical of halfway hopes and halfway measures. As we look toward the future—our own future and the future of other nations—we are filled with foreboding. The future doesn't seem to hold anything for us except conflict, disruption, war.

There is a striking contrast between our state of mind and that of the British people. On Sept. 3, 1939, the first day of the war in England, Winston Churchill had this to say: "Outside the storms of war may blow and the land may be lashed with the fury of its gales, but in our hearts this Sunday morning there is Peace." Since Mr. Churchill spoke those words the German Luftwaffe has made havoc of British cities, driven the population underground, frightened children from their sleep, and imposed upon everyone a nervous strain as great as any that people have ever endured. . . .

Yet close observers agree that when Mr. Churchill spoke of peace in the hearts of the British people he was not indulging in idle oratory. The British people are profoundly calm. There seems to be a complete absence of nervousness. It seems as if all the neuroses of modern life had vanished from England. . . . The British are calm in their spirit not because they have nothing to worry about but because they are fighting for their lives. They have made that decision. And they have no further choice. All their mistakes of the past 20 years, all the stupidities and failures that they have shared with the rest of the democratic world, are now of the past. They can forget them because they are faced with a supreme task—defending, yard by yard, their island home. With us it is different. We do not have to face any attack tomorrow or the next day. Yet we are faced with something almost as difficult. We are faced with great decisions. We know how lucky we are compared to all the rest of mankind. At least two-thirds of us are just plain rich compared to all the rest of the human family—rich in food, rich in clothes, rich in entertainment and amusement, rich in leisure, rich. And yet we also know that the sickness of the world is also our sickness. We, too, have miserably failed to solve the problems of our epoch. And nowhere in the world have man's failures been so little excusable as in the United States of America. Nowhere has the contrast been so great between the reasonable hopes of our age and the actual facts of failure and frustration. And so now all our failures and mistakes hover like birds of ill omen over the White House, over the Capitol dome and over this printed page. Naturally, we have no peace. But, even beyond this necessity for living with our own misdeeds, there is another reason why there is no peace in our hearts. It is that we have not been honest with ourselves. In this whole matter of War and Peace especially, we have been at various times and in various ways false to ourselves, false to each other, false to the facts of history and false to the future.

In this self-deceit our political leaders of all shades of opinion are deeply implicated. Yet we cannot shove the blame off on them. If our leaders have deceived us it is mainly because we ourselves have insisted on being deceived. Their deceitfulness has resulted from our own moral and intellectual confusion. In this confusion, our educators and churchmen and scientists are deeply implicated. Journalists, too, of course, are implicated. But if Americans are confused it is not for lack of accurate and pertinent information. The American people are by far the best informed people in the history of the world. The trouble is not with the facts. The trouble is that clear and honest inferences have not been drawn from the facts. The day-to-day present is clear. The issues of tomorrow are befogged. There is one fundamental issue which faces America as it faces no other nation. It is an issue peculiar to America and peculiar to America in the 20th Century—now. It is deeper even than the immediate issue of War. If America meets it correctly, then, despite hosts of dangers and difficulties, we can look forward and move forward to a future worthy of men, with peace in our hearts. If we dodge the issue, we shall flounder for ten or 20 or 30 bitter years in a chartless and meaningless series of disasters. The purpose of this article is to state that issue, and its solution, as candidly and as completely as possible. But first of all let us be completely candid about where we are and how we got there. . . .

Where are we? We are in the war. All this talk about whether this or that might or might not get us into the war is wasted effort. We are, for a fact, in the war. If there's one place we Americans did not want to be, it was in the war. We didn't want much to be in any kind of war but, if there was one kind of war we most of all didn't want to be in, it was a European war. Yet, we're in a war, as

vicious and bad a war as ever struck this planet, and, along with being worldwide, a European war. Of course, we are not technically at war, we are not painfully at war, and we may never have to experience the full hell that war can be. Nevertheless the simple statement stands: we are in the war. The irony is that Hitler knows it—and most Americans don't. . . . Perhaps the best way to show ourselves that we are in the war is to consider how we can get out of it. Practically, there's only one way to get out of it and that is by a German victory over England. If England should surrender soon, Germany and America would not start fighting the next day. So we would be out of the war. For a while. Except that Japan might then attack the South Seas and the Philippines. We could abandon the Philippines, abandon Australia and New Zealand, withdraw to Hawaii. And wait. We would be out of the war. We say we don't want to be in the war. We also say we want England to win. We want Hitler stopped—more than we want to stay out of the war. So, at the moment, we're in. . . .

Now that we are in this war, how did we get in? We got in on the basis of defense. Even that very word, defense, has been full of deceit and self-deceit. To the average American the plain meaning of the word defense is defense of the American territory. Is our national policy today limited to the defense of the American homeland by whatever means may seem wise? It is not. We are not in a war to defend American territory. We are in a war to defend and even to promote, encourage and incite so-called democratic principles throughout the world. The average American begins to realize now that that's the kind of war he's in. And he's halfway for it. But he wonders how he ever got there, since a year ago he had not the slightest intention of getting into any such thing. Well, he can see now how he got there. He got there via "defense."

Behind the doubts in the American mind there were and are two different picture-patterns. One of them stressing the appalling consequences of the fall of England leads us to a war of intervention. As a plain matter of the defense of American territory is that picture necessarily true? It is not necessarily true. For the other picture is roughly this: while it would be much better for us if Hitler were severely checked, nevertheless regardless of what happens in Europe it would be entirely possible for us to organize a defense of the northern part of the Western Hemisphere so that this country could not be successfully attacked. . . .

We are in this war. We can see how we got into it in terms of defense. Now why do we object so strongly to being in it? There are lots of reasons. First, there is the profound and almost universal aversion to all war—to killing and being killed. But the reason which needs closest inspection, since it is one peculiar to this war and never felt about any previous war, is the fear that if we get into this war, it will be the end of our constitutional democracy. We are all acquainted with the fearful forecast—that some form of dictatorship is required to fight a modern war, that we will certainly go bankrupt, that in the process of war and its aftermath our economy will be largely socialized, that the politicians now in office will seize complete power and never yield it up, and that what with the whole trend toward collectivism, we shall end up in such a total national socialism that any faint semblances of our constitutional American democracy will be totally unrecognizable. We start into this war with huge Government debt, a vast bureaucracy and a whole generation of young people trained to look to the Government as the source of all life. The Party in power is the one which for long years has been most sympathetic to all manner of socialist doctrines and collectivist trends. The President of the United States has continually reached for more and more power, and he owes his continuation in office today largely to the coming of the war. Thus, the fear that the United States will be driven to a national socialism, as a result of cataclysmic circumstances and contrary to the free will of the American people, is an entirely justifiable fear. . . .

So there's the mess—to date. Much more could be said in amplification, in qualification, and in argument. But, however elaborately they might be stated, the sum of the facts about our present position brings us to this point—that the paramount question of this immediate moment is not whether we get into war but how do we win it?

If we are in a war, then it is no little advantage to be aware of the fact. And once we admit to ourselves we are in a war, there is no shadow of doubt that we Americans will be determined to win it—cost what it may in life or treasure. Whether or not we declare war, whether or not we send expeditionary forces abroad, whether or not we go bankrupt in the process—all these tremendous considerations are matters of strategy and management and are secondary to the overwhelming importance of winning the war. . . .

Having now, with candor, examined our position, it is time to consider, to better purpose than would have been possible before, the larger issue which confronts us. Stated most simply, and in general terms, that issue is: What are we fighting for? Each of us stands ready to give our life, our wealth, and all our hope of personal happiness, to make sure that America shall not lose any war she is engaged in. But we would like to know what war we are trying to win—and what we are supposed to win when we win it.

This questioning reflects our truest instincts as Americans. But more than that. Our urgent desire to give this war its proper name has a desperate practical importance. If we know what we are fighting for, then we can drive confidently toward a victorious conclusion and, what's more, have at least an even chance of establishing a workable Peace. Furthermore—and this is an extraordinary and profoundly historical fact which deserves to be examined in detail—America and only America can effectively state the war aims of this war.

Almost every expert will agree that Britain cannot win complete victory—cannot even, in the common saying, "stop Hitler"—without American help. Therefore, even if Britain should from time to time announce war aims, the American people are continually in the position of effectively approving or not approving those aims. On the contrary, if America were to announce war aims, Great Britain would almost certainly accept them. And the entire world including Adolf Hitler would accept them as the gauge of this battle. Americans have a feeling that in any collaboration with Great Britain we are somehow playing Britain's game and not our own. Whatever sense there may have been in this notion in the past, today it is an ignorant and foolish conception of the situation. In any sort of partnership with the British Empire, Great Britain is perfectly willing that the United States of America should assume the role of senior partner. This has been true for a long time. Among serious Englishmen, the chief complaint against America (and incidentally their best alibi for themselves) has really amounted to this—that America has refused to rise to the opportunities of leadership in the world. . . .

The big, important point to be made here is simply that the complete opportunity of leadership is ours. Like most great creative opportunities, it is an opportunity enveloped in stupendous difficulties and dangers. If we don't want it, if we refuse to take it, the responsibility of refusal is also ours, and ours alone. Admittedly, the future of the world cannot be settled all in one piece. It is stupid to try to blueprint the future as you blueprint an engine or as you draw up a constitution for a sorority. But if our trouble is that we don't know what we are fighting for, then it's up to us to figure it out. Don't expect some other country to tell us. Stop this Nazi propaganda about fighting somebody else's war. We fight no wars except our wars. "Arsenal of Democracy?" We may prove to be that. But today we must be the arsenal of America and of the friends and allies of America. Friends and allies of America? Who are they, and for what? This is for us to tell them. . . .

[S]hall we use some big words like Democracy and Freedom and Justice? Yes, we can use the big words. The President has already used them. And perhaps we had better get used to using them again. Maybe they do mean something—about the future as well as the past. Some amongst us are likely to be dying for them—on the fields and in the skies of battle. Either that, or the words themselves and what they mean die with us—in our beds. But is there nothing between the absurd sound of distant cities and the brassy trumpeting of majestic words? . . . . Is there not something a little more practically satisfying that we can get our teeth into? Is there no sort of understandable program? A program which would be clearly good for America, which would make sense for America—and which at the same time might have the blessing of the Goddess of Democracy . . . ? Is there none such? There is. And so we now come squarely and closely face to face with the issue which Americans hate most to face. It is that old, old issue with those old, old battered labels—the issue of Isolationism versus Internationalism. We detest both words. We spit them at each other with the fury of hissing geese. We duck and dodge them. Let us face that issue squarely now. If we face it squarely now—and if in facing it we take

full and fearless account of the realities of our age—then we shall open the way, not necessarily to peace in our daily lives but to peace in our hearts. . . . In the field of national policy, the fundamental trouble with America has been, and is, that whereas their nation became in the 20th Century the most powerful and the most vital nation in the world, nevertheless Americans were unable to accommodate themselves spiritually and practically to that fact. Hence they have failed to play their part as a world power—a failure which has had disastrous consequences for themselves and for all mankind. And the cure is this: to accept wholeheartedly our duty and our opportunity as the most powerful and vital nation in the world and in consequence to exert upon the world the full impact of our influence, for such purposes as we see fit and by such means as we see fit. "For such purposes as we see fit" leaves entirely open the question of what our purposes may be or how we may appropriately achieve them. . . .

America cannot be responsible for the good behavior of the entire world. But America is responsible, to herself as well as to history, for the world environment in which she lives. Nothing can so vitally affect America's environment as America's own influence upon it, and therefore if America's environment is unfavorable to the growth of American life, then America has nobody to blame so deeply as she must blame herself. In its failure to grasp this relationship between America and America's environment lies the moral and practical bankruptcy of any and all forms of isolationism. It is most unfortunate that this virus of isolationist sterility has so deeply infected an influential section of the Republican Party. For until the Republican Party can develop a vital philosophy and program for America's initiative and activity as a world power, it will continue to cut itself off from any useful participation in this hour of history. And its participation is deeply needed for the shaping of the future of America and of the world. But politically speaking, it is an equally serious fact that for seven years Franklin Roosevelt was, for all practical purposes, a complete isolationist. He was more of an isolationist than Herbert Hoover or Calvin Coolidge. The fact that Franklin Roosevelt has recently emerged as an emergency world leader should not obscure the fact that for seven years his policies ran absolutely counter to any possibility of effective American leadership in international co-operation. There is of course a justification which can be made for the President's first two terms. It can be said, with reason, that great social reforms were necessary in order to bring democracy up-to-date in the greatest of democracies. But the fact is that Franklin Roosevelt failed to make American democracy work successfully on a narrow, materialistic and nationalistic basis. And under Franklin Roosevelt we ourselves have failed to make democracy work successfully. Our only chance now to make it work is in terms of a vital international economy and in terms of an international moral order. This objective is Franklin Roosevelt's great opportunity to justify his first two terms and to go down in history as the greatest rather than the last of American Presidents. Our job is to help in every way we can, for our sakes and our children's sakes, to ensure that Franklin Roosevelt shall be justly hailed as America's greatest President. Without our help he cannot be our greatest President. With our help he can and will be. Under him and with his leadership we can make isolationism as dead an issue as slavery, and we can make a truly American internationalism something as natural to us in our time as the airplane or the radio. In 1919 we had a golden opportunity, an opportunity unprecedented in all history, to assume the leadership of the world—a golden opportunity handed to us on the proverbial silver platter. We did not understand that opportunity. Wilson mishandled it. We rejected it. The opportunity persisted. We bungled it in the 1920's and in the confusions of the 1930's we killed it. To lead the world would never have been an easy task. To revive the hope of that lost opportunity makes the task now infinitely harder than it would have been before. Nevertheless, with the help of all of us, Roosevelt must succeed where Wilson failed. . . . Consider the 20th Century. It is not only in the sense that we happen to live in it but ours also because it is America's first century as a dominant power in the world. So far, this century of ours has been a profound and tragic disappointment. No other century has been so big with promise for human progress and happiness. And in no one century have so many men and women and children suffered such pain and anguish and bitter death. It is a baffling and

difficult and paradoxical century. No doubt all centuries were paradoxical to those who had to cope with them. But, like everything else, our paradoxes today are bigger and better than ever. Yes, better as well as bigger—inherently better. We have poverty and starvation—but only in the midst of plenty. We have the biggest wars in the midst of the most widespread, the deepest and the most articulate hatred of war in all history. We have tyrannies and dictatorships—but only when democratic idealism, once regarded as the dubious eccentricity of a colonial nation, is the faith of a huge majority of the people of the world. And ours is also a revolutionary century. The paradoxes make it inevitably revolutionary. Revolutionary, of course, in science and in industry. And also revolutionary, as a corollary in politics and the structure of society. But to say that a revolution is in progress is not to say that the men with either the craziest ideas or the angriest ideas or the most plausible ideas are going to come out on top. The Revolution of 1776 was won and established by men most of whom appear to have been both gentlemen and men of common sense. Clearly a revolutionary epoch signifies great changes, great adjustments. And this is only one reason why it is really so foolish for people to worry about our "constitutional democracy" without worrying or, better, thinking hard about the world revolution. For only as we go out to meet and solve for our time the problems of the world revolution, can we know how to re-establish our constitutional democracy for another 50 or 100 years. This 20th Century is baffling, difficult, paradoxical, revolutionary. But by now, at the cost of much pain and many hopes deferred, we know a good deal about it. And we ought to accommodate our outlook to this knowledge so dearly bought. For example, any true conception of our world of the 20th Century must surely include a vivid awareness of at least these four propositions.

First: our world of 2,000,000,000 human beings is for the first time in history one world, fundamentally indivisible.

Second: modern man hates war and feels intuitively that, in its present scale and frequency, it may even be fatal to his species.

Third: our world, again for the first time in human history, is capable of producing all the material needs of the entire human family.

Fourth: the world of the 20th Century, if it is to come to life in any nobility of health and vigor, must be to a significant degree an American Century.

As to the first and second: in postulating the indivisibility of the contemporary world, one does not necessarily imagine that anything like a world state—a parliament of men—must be brought about in this century. Nor need we assume that war can be abolished. All that it is necessary to feel—and to feel deeply—is that terrific forces of magnetic attraction and repulsion will operate as between every large group of human beings on this planet. Large sections of the human family may be effectively organized into opposition to each other. Tyrannies may require a large amount of living space. But Freedom requires and will require far greater living space than Tyranny. Peace cannot endure unless it prevails over a very large part of the world. Justice will come near to losing all meaning in the minds of men unless Justice can have approximately the same fundamental meanings in many lands and among many peoples.

As to the third point—the promise of adequate production for all mankind, the "more abundant life"—be it noted that this is characteristically an American promise. It is a promise easily made, here and elsewhere, by demagogues and proponents of all manner of slick schemes and "planned economies." What we must insist on is that the abundant life is predicated on Freedom—on the Freedom which has created its possibility—on a vision of Freedom under Law. Without Freedom, there will be no abundant life. With Freedom, there can be. And finally there is the belief—shared let us remember by most men living—that the 20th Century must be to a significant degree an American Century. This knowledge calls us to action now. . . .

What can we say and foresee about an American Century? It is meaningless merely to say that we reject isolationism and accept the logic of internationalism. What internationalism? . . .

Ours cannot come out of the vision of any one man. It must be the product of the imaginations of many men. It must be a sharing with all peoples of our Bill of Rights, our Declaration of Independence, our Constitution, our magnificent industrial products, our technical skills. It must be an internationalism of the people, by the people and for the people. In general, the issues which the American people champion revolve around their determination to make the society of men safe for the freedom, growth and increasing satisfaction of all individual men. Beside that resolve, the sneers, groans, catcalls, teeth-grinding, hisses and roars of the Nazi Propaganda Ministry are of small moment. Once we cease to distract ourselves with lifeless arguments about isolationism, we shall be amazed to discover that there is already an immense American internationalism. American jazz, Hollywood movies, American slang, American machines and patented products, are in fact the only things that every community in the world, from Zanzibar to Hamburg, recognizes in common. Blindly, unintentionally, accidentally and really in spite of ourselves, we are already a world power in all the trivial ways—in very human ways. But there is a great deal more than that. America is already the intellectual, scientific and artistic capital of the world. . . .

America's worldwide experience in commerce is also far greater than most of us realize. Most important of all, we have that indefinable, unmistakable sign of leadership: prestige. And unlike the prestige of Rome or Genghis Khan or 19th Century England, American prestige throughout the world is faith in the good intentions as well as in the ultimate intelligence and ultimate strength of the whole American people. We have lost some of that prestige in the last few years. But most of it is still there. No narrow definition can be given to the American internationalism of the 20th Century. It will take shape, as all civilizations take shape, by the living of it, by work and effort, by trial and error, by enterprise and adventure and experience. And by imagination! As America enters dynamically upon the world scene, we need most of all to seek and to bring forth a vision of America as a world power which is authentically American and which can inspire us to live and work and fight with vigor and enthusiasm. And as we come now to the great test, it may yet turn out that in all our trials and tribulations of spirit during the first part of this century we as a people have been painfully apprehending the meaning of our time and now in this moment of testing there may come clear at last the vision which will guide us to the authentic creation of the 20th Century—our Century. Consider four areas of life and thought in which we may seek to realize such a vision: First, the economic. It is for America and for America alone to determine whether a system of free economic enterprise—an economic order compatible with freedom and progress—shall or shall not prevail in this century. We know perfectly well that there is not the slightest chance of anything faintly resembling a free economic system prevailing in this country if it prevails nowhere else. What then does America have to decide? Some few decisions are quite simple. For example: we have to decide whether or not we shall have for ourselves and our friends freedom of the seas—the right to go with our ships and our ocean-going airplanes where we wish, when we wish and as we wish. The vision of America as the principal guarantor of the freedom of the seas, the vision of America as the dynamic leader of world trade, has within it the possibilities of such enormous human progress as to stagger the imagination. Let us not be staggered by it. Let us rise to its tremendous possibilities.

Our thinking of world trade today is on ridiculously small terms. For example, we think of Asia as being worth only a few hundred millions a year to us. Actually, in the decades to come Asia will be worth to us exactly zero—or else it will be worth to us four, five, ten billions of dollars a year. And the latter are the terms we must think in, or else confess a pitiful impotence. Closely akin to the purely economic area and yet quite different from it, there is the picture of an America which will send out through the world its technical and artistic skills. Engineers, scientists, doctors, movie men, makers of entertainment, developers of airlines, builders of roads, teachers, educators. Throughout the world, these skills, this training, this leadership is needed and will be eagerly welcomed, if only we have the imagination to see it and the sincerity and good will to create the world of the 20th Century. But now there is a third thing which our vision must immediately be concerned with. We must undertake now to be the Good Samaritan of the entire world. It is the manifest duty of this country to undertake to feed all the people of the world who as a result of this worldwide collapse of civilization are hungry and destitute—all of them, that is, whom we can from time to time reach consistently with a very tough attitude toward all hostile governments. For every dollar we spend on armaments, we should spend at least a dime in a gigantic effort to feed the world—and all the world should know that we have dedicated ourselves to this task. Every farmer in America should be encouraged to produce all the crops he can, and all that we cannot eat—and perhaps some of us could eat less—should forthwith be dispatched to the four quarters of the globe as a free gift, administered by a humanitarian army of Americans, to every man, woman and child on this earth who is really hungry. But all this is not enough. All this will fail and none of it will happen unless our vision of America as a world power includes a passionate devotion to great American ideals. We have some things in this country which are infinitely precious and especially American—a love of freedom, a feeling for the equality of opportunity, a tradition of self-reliance and independence and also of co-operation. In addition to ideals and notions which are especially American, we are the inheritors of all the great principles of Western civilization—above all Justice, the love of Truth, the ideal of Charity. . . .

For the moment it may be enough to be the sanctuary of these ideals. But not for long. It now becomes our time to be the powerhouse from which the ideals spread throughout the world and do their mysterious work of lifting the life of mankind from the level of the beasts to what the Psalmist called a little lower than the angels. America as the dynamic center of ever-widening spheres of enterprise, America as the training center of the skillful servants of mankind, America as the Good Samaritan, really believing again that it is more blessed to give than to receive, and America as the powerhouse of the ideals of Freedom and Justice—out of these elements surely can be fashioned a vision of the 20th Century to which we can and will devote ourselves in joy and gladness and vigor and enthusiasm.

Other nations can survive simply because they have endured so long—sometimes with more and sometimes with less significance. But this nation, conceived in adventure and dedicated to the progress of man—this nation cannot truly endure unless there courses strongly through its veins from Maine to California the blood of purposes and enterprise and high resolve. Throughout the 17th Century and the 18th Century and the 19th Century, this continent teemed with manifold projects and magnificent purposes. Above them all and weaving them all together into the most exciting flag of all the world and of all history was the triumphal purpose of freedom. It is in this spirit that all of us are called, each to his own measure of capacity, and each in the widest horizon of his vision, to create the first great American Century.

WALTER LIPPMANN, *U. S. FOREIGN POLICY: SHIELD OF THE REPUBLIC* (1943)

After Pearl Harbor, winning the war against Germany, Italy, and Japan took precedence over all other considerations. Yet influential Americans, not wishing to repeat the disappointments that had followed the previous world war, also took up the question of what should come next. Here Walter Lippmann, the most respected journalist of his day, prescribes principles that should govern postwar U.S. policy. The old habit of keeping Europe at a distance, he believes, must now end.

As the climax of the war finds the people of the United States approaching a national election, we must face the fact that for nearly fifty years the nation has not had a settled and generally accepted foreign policy. This is a danger to the Republic. For when a people is divided within itself about the conduct of its foreign relations, it is unable to agree on the determination of its true interest. It is unable to prepare adequately for war or to safeguard successfully its peace. Thus its course in foreign affairs depends, in Hamilton's words, not on reflection and choice but on accident and force.

The country, as I shall try to demonstrate, had a secure foreign policy toward the great powers from the decade after the War of 1812 to the end of the war with Spain in 1898. In that long period it was true that politics stopped at the water's edge, and that the people were not seriously divided on our relations with the Old World. But in the election of 1900 the nation became divided over the consequences of the war with Spain, and never since then has it been possible for any President of the United States to rely upon the united support of the nation in the conduct of foreign affairs.

The consequences have been grave. The war with Spain left the United States with commitments in the Pacific 7000 miles west of California. The lack of a settled foreign policy made it impossible for the United States to liquidate the commitment by withdrawing from the Far Pacific or to fulfill the commitment by assuring the defense of the Philippines. The outbreak of the first World War in Europe precipitated an internal controversy in the United States about America's rights and its interests, its duties and its obligations. As a result of that division of opinion the country was unable to prepare for that war even when American participation had become probable, and it was unable to consolidate the victory which it helped to win. During the twenty years that followed there was unending domestic controversy over foreign policy. The made the American government as ineffective in preventing the second World War as it was in preparing for it. Now, under the spell cast by the coming elections of 1944, the country again finds itself unable to think clearly and to decide firmly what policy it will follow in the settlement of the war.

The spectacle of this great nation which does not know its own mind is as humiliating as it is dangerous. It casts doubt upon the capacity of the people to govern themselves. For nowhere else on earth, and never before in all history, has any people had conditions so favorable as they are in the United States to proving their capacity for self-government. It will be a profound humiliation, therefore, if once again we fail to form a national policy, and the acids of this failure will be with us for ages to come, corroding our self-confidence and our self-respect. Our failure now to form a national policy will, though we defeat our enemies, leave us dangerously exposed to deadly conflict at home and to unmanageable perils from abroad. For the return from a state of total war

Walter Lippmann, *U. S. Foreign Policy: Shield of the Republic,* Boston: Little, Brown and Company (1943).

to a state of peace which no one trusts will raise catastrophic issues in our midst. Rent by domestic controversy, for want of a settled foreign policy we shall act not upon reflection and choice but under the impulse of accidents and the impact of force. . . . .

An objective study of our foreign relations in the past fifty years will, I believe, show that our national failure to form a foreign policy is due to an historic circumstance. For about eighty years— from the promulgation of the Monroe Doctrine to the end of the war with Spain—there was no need for the American people to form a foreign policy. In that long period the very nature of foreign policy, of what it consists and how it is formed, was forgotten. Thus, when events compelled us once again to attend to foreign relations, we had lost the art of shaping a policy, and could not find a policy because we no longer knew what we needed.

This is why good and patriotic Americans have differed so sharply and so long without reaching a common view. They have forgotten the compelling and, once seen, the self-evident common principle of all foreign policy—the principle that alone can force decisions, can settle controversy, and can induce agreement. This is the principle that in foreign relations, as in all other relations, a policy has been formed only when commitments and power have been brought into balance. This is the forgotten principle which must be recovered and restored to the first place in American thought if the nation is to achieve the foreign policy which it so desperately wants.

Without the controlling principle that the nation must maintain its objective and its power in equilibrium, its purposes within its means and its means equal to its purposes, its commitments related to its resources and its resources adequate to its commitments, it is impossible to think at all about foreign affairs. . . .

No one would seriously suppose that he had a fiscal policy if he did not consider together expenditure and revenue, outgo and income, liabilities and assets. But in foreign relations we have habitually in our minds divorced the discussion of our war aims, our peace aims, our ideals, our interests, our commitments, from the discussion of our armaments, our strategic position, our potential allies and our probable enemies. For what settles practical controversy is the knowledge that ends and means have to be balanced: an agreement has eventually to be reached when men admit that they must pay for what they want and that they must want only what they are willing to pay for. If they do not want to come to such an agreement, they will never except by accident agree. For they will lack a yardstick by which to measure their ideals and their interests, or their ways and means of protecting and promoting them.

If we survey . . . our own course since the war with Spain, we shall find that there has been no serious and sustained conviction that American commitments and interests and ideals must be covered by our armaments, our strategic frontiers, and our alliances. In fact we shall find that we have been guilty of a blinding prejudice—that concern with our frontiers, our armaments, and with alliances, is immoral and reactionary.

Yet now that the Philippines have been lost, now that we have been attacked by a combination of exceedingly dangerous enemies, we must see how awful is the price we must pay because in our foreign relations for nearly a half-century the United States has been insolvent. This is the time of the reckoning. We are liquidating in sweat and blood and tears, and at our mortal peril, the fact that we made commitments, asserted rights, and proclaimed ideals while we left our frontiers unguarded, our armaments unprepared, and our alliances unformed and unsustained. . . . .

The habits of a century have fostered prejudices and illusions that vitiate our capacity to think effectively about foreign relations. The elementary means by which all foreign policy must be conducted are the armed forces of the nation, the arrangement of its strategic position, and the choice of its alliances. In the American ideology of our times these things had come to be regarded as militaristic, imperialistic, reactionary, and archaic; the proper concern of right-minded men was held to be peace, disarmament, and a choice between non-intervention and collective security.

We not only ignored the development of the means to achieve our ends: we chose as the ends of our efforts a set of ideals which were incompatible with all the means of achieving any ideals. The ideal of peace diverted our attention from the idea of national security. The ideal of disarmament caused us to be inadequately armed. The apparently opposed ideals of non-intervention on the one hand, and of collective security on the other, had at bottom the same practical result in that they inhibited us from forming our necessary alliances. Thus for nearly half a century after our vast commitments in the Pacific had been superimposed upon our immense commitment in the Western Hemisphere, we have had to conduct our pre-war diplomacy verbally—by promises, threats, and exhortations; we have had to wage war three times without being prepared to fight; and we have twice made peace without knowing what we wanted.

These spendthrift habits have led us to the bankruptcy of a total war in which we have suffered humiliating initial disasters at the hands of the Japanese; and our very independence was for a time in jeopardy. The habits of mind of Americans of our generation are quite alien to those of the Founders of the Republic. Washington, Hamilton, Jefferson, Madison, Monroe, entertained none of the basic illusions and prejudices which have dominated the later generations of Americans. They did not regard peace as more important than national security. . . .

The fundamental subject of foreign policy is how a nation stands in relation to the principal military powers. For only the great powers can wage great wars. Only a great power can resist a great power. Only a great power can defeat a great power. And therefore the relationship of this nation with the other great powers is the paramount—not by any means the sole, but the paramount—concern of the maker of foreign policy. Unless this relationship is such that the combination against him is not stronger than the combination to which he belongs, his foreign policy is not solvent: his commitments exceed his means, and he is leading his people into grave trouble.

Therefore, no great power can be indifferent to any of the other great powers. It must take a position in regard to all of them. No great power can stand alone against all the others. For none can be great enough for that. If its object is to win a war it has chosen to wage, or to not lose a war imposed upon it, a great power must have allies among the great powers. And if its object is, as ours must be, to preserve the peace, then it

must form a combination of indisputably preponderant power with other great states which also desire peace.

Thus the statesman, who means to maintain peace, can no more ignore the order of power than an engineer can ignore the mechanics of physical force. He should not, to be sure, frivolously "play power politics." But he must with cold calculation organize and regulate the politics of power. If he does not do that, and do it correctly, the result must be a cycle of disastrous wars followed by peace settlements which breed more wars. . . .

This nation cannot, as Lincoln said, escape history. It can, however, at fearful cost misread its own history. It can imagine, until it is smitten by the hard realities of life, that by some special dispensation of Providence or some peculiarity of geography, it can be a great power without being involved in the order of the great powers.

Yet though this illusion is passing, there remains the practical question of how in fact to form an American foreign policy which fits the realities of the American position. In answering it we cannot afford to deceive ourselves and, therefore, we must begin by recognizing the uncomfortable fact that our commitments in the outer world are tremendously extended and that our position for fulfilling them is extremely vulnerable. . . .

If this estimate of our real position seems at first incredible, let us remember that it seems incredible only because we have talked about our isolation but have never been so foolish or unlucky as to be in fact isolated. We were extricated in 1823 from the threat of true isolation by the statesmanship of Canning and Monroe. Their construction lasted until 1917 when we averted the threat of true isolation by Wilson's intervention. In 1940 we were so near to true isolation that for a whole appallingly dangerous year the issue hung precariously upon the valor and skill of the people of Britain, and upon the historic campaign which President Roosevelt waged to arouse this country in time to its awful peril.

The security which Monroe had been able to achieve by diplomacy, Wilson and Roosevelt were unable to accomplish without engaging in war. But in all three instances the United States was faced with the problem of averting the threat of military isolation. The fact that Monroe averted it by diplomacy, and, indeed, by secret diplomacy, and that Wilson and Roosevelt averted it by joining an alliance which was already in the field, has prevented many Americans from perceiving the realities of our position. They do not believe that the consequences of isolation would be so fatal as they would in fact be because, thus far in our history, we have always in the nick of time found adequate allies.

But our luck might not hold. Our improvisations at the eleventh hour might the next time be too little and too late. Thus we must safeguard the future by founding our foreign policy on the undeniable necessity of forming dependable alliances in the Old World.

VIII.

CRUSADE

World War II ended in 1945 in the complete defeat of the Axis Powers. The Grand Alliance forged to oppose Nazi Germany came undone once Hitler's regime collapsed. A rivalry pitting the Soviet Union against the United States or more broadly between a communist bloc and a group of nations that rejected communism became the defining issue in international politics. The result was a Cold War destined to dominate international politics for four decades.

Between 1941 and 1945, the existence of Nazi Germany as a common threat led to the partial suspension of the hostility and mistrust that had characterized US–Soviet relations since 1917. When the threat disappeared, hostility and mistrust almost immediately returned. By the spring of 1947, senior US officials considered the Soviets adversaries rather than allies, with Soviet ideological and geopolitical ambitions seen as endangering not only the United States, but any nation opposed to communism. Washington responded by committing itself to defending and rebuilding critical parts of this "Free World." Western Europe, devastated and demoralized by war, and the western precincts of a now divided and occupied Germany received priority attention.

The outbreak of armed conflict on the divided Korean peninsula during the summer of 1950 globalized the Cold War. In response to an attack by communist North Korea into South Korea, US forces intervened to defend the anticommunist South. Within months, a US-led counteroffensive into North Korean territory induced the People's Republic of China to enter the fight. What began as a small-scale "police action," launched without Congressional authority, now seemingly carried the risk of Third World War, potentially involving the use of nuclear weapons. To avert that prospect, the United States limited the scope of further military action, the Korean conflict settling into a standoff that many Americans found deeply unsatisfactory. A major crisis in civil–military relations was one result.

Korea prompted the United States to embark upon a major rearmament program, expanding both its conventional and nuclear capabilities. The US commitment to maintaining very large, very lethal, and deployable combat forces dates from this decision. Waging the Cold War now became the centerpiece of US national security policy.

HARRY S TRUMAN, "THE TRUMAN DOCTRINE" (1947)

On the eve of victory over Nazi Germany, Franklin Roosevelt had died. Vice President Harry Truman (1884–1972) succeeded Roosevelt and wasted no time putting his imprint on US policy. In this speech to members of Congress in the spring of 1947, Truman prescribes the basic azimuth of America's Cold War strategy.

The gravity of the situation which confronts the world today necessitates my appearance before a joint session of the Congress. The foreign policy and the national security of this country are involved.

One aspect of the present situation, which I wish to present to you at this time for your consideration and decision, concerns Greece and Turkey.

The United States has received from the Greek Government an urgent appeal for financial and economic assistance. Preliminary reports from the American Economic Mission now in Greece and reports from the American Ambassador in Greece corroborate the statement of the Greek Government that assistance is imperative if Greece is to survive as a free nation.

I do not believe that the American people and the Congress wish to turn a deaf ear to the appeal of the Greek Government.

Greece is not a rich country. Lack of sufficient natural resources has always forced the Greek people to work hard to make both ends meet. Since 1940, this industrious and peace loving country has suffered invasion, four years of cruel enemy occupation, and bitter internal strife.

When forces of liberation entered Greece they found that the retreating Germans had destroyed virtually all the railways, roads, port facilities, communications, and merchant marine. More than a thousand villages had been burned. Eighty-five per cent of the children were tubercular. Livestock, poultry, and draft animals had almost disappeared. Inflation had wiped out practically all savings.

As a result of these tragic conditions, a militant minority, exploiting human want and misery, was able to create political chaos which, until now, has made economic recovery impossible.

Greece is today without funds to finance the importation of those goods which are essential to bare subsistence. Under these circumstances the people of Greece cannot make progress in solving their problems of reconstruction. Greece is in desperate need of financial and economic assistance to enable it to resume purchases of food, clothing, fuel and seeds. These are indispensable for the subsistence of its people and are obtainable only from abroad. Greece must have help to import the goods necessary to restore internal order and security, so essential for economic and political recovery.

The Greek Government has also asked for the assistance of experienced American administrators, economists and technicians to insure that the financial and other aid given to Greece shall be used effectively in creating a stable and self-sustaining economy and in improving its public administration.

The very existence of the Greek state is today threatened by the terrorist activities of several thousand armed men, led by Communists, who defy the government's authority at a number of points, particularly along the northern boundaries. . . .

Meanwhile, the Greek Government is unable to cope with the situation. The Greek army is small and poorly equipped. It needs supplies and equipment if it is to restore the authority of the government throughout Greek territory. Greece must have assistance if it is to become a self-supporting and self-respecting democracy.

The United States must supply that assistance. We have already extended to Greece certain types of relief and economic aid but these are inadequate.

There is no other country to which democratic Greece can turn.

No other nation is willing and able to provide the necessary support for a democratic Greek government.

The British Government, which has been helping Greece, can give no further financial or economic aid after March 31. Great Britain finds itself under the necessity of reducing or liquidating its commitments in several parts of the world, including Greece. . . .

It is of the utmost importance that we supervise the use of any funds made available to Greece; in such a manner that each dollar spent will count toward making Greece self-supporting, and will help to build an economy in which a healthy democracy can flourish.

No government is perfect. One of the chief virtues of a democracy, however, is that its defects are always visible and under democratic processes can be pointed out and corrected. The Government of Greece is not perfect. . . .

The Greek Government has been operating in an atmosphere of chaos and extremism. It has made mistakes. The extension of aid by this country does not mean that the United States condones everything that the Greek Government has done or will do. We have condemned in the past, and we condemn now, extremist measures of the right or the left. We have in the past advised tolerance, and we advise tolerance now.

Greece's neighbor, Turkey, also deserves our attention.

The future of Turkey as an independent and economically sound state is clearly no less important to the freedom-loving peoples of the world than the future of Greece. The circumstances in which Turkey finds itself today are considerably different from those of Greece. . . .

Nevertheless, Turkey now needs our support.

Since the war Turkey has sought financial assistance from Great Britain and the United States for the purpose of effecting that modernization necessary for the maintenance of its national integrity.

That integrity is essential to the preservation of order in the Middle East.

The British government has informed us that, owing to its own difficulties can no longer extend financial or economic aid to Turkey.

As in the case of Greece, if Turkey is to have the assistance it needs, the United States must supply it. We are the only country able to provide that help. . . .

One of the primary objectives of the foreign policy of the United States is the creation of conditions in which we and other nations will be able to work out a way of life free from coercion. This was a fundamental issue in the war with Germany and Japan. Our victory was won over countries which sought to impose their will, and their way of life, upon other nations.

To ensure the peaceful development of nations, free from coercion, the United States has taken a leading part in establishing the United Nations. The United Nations is designed to make possible lasting freedom and independence for all its members. We shall not realize our objectives, however, unless we are willing to help free peoples to maintain their free institutions and their national integrity against aggressive movements that seek to impose upon them totalitarian regimes. This is no more than a frank recognition that totalitarian regimes imposed on free peoples, by direct or indirect aggression, undermine the foundations of international peace and hence the security of the United States. . . .

At the present moment in world history nearly every nation must choose between alternative ways of life. The choice is too often not a free one.

One way of life is based upon the will of the majority, and is distinguished by free institutions, representative government, free elections, guarantees of individual liberty, freedom of speech and religion, and freedom from political oppression.

The second way of life is based upon the will of a minority forcibly imposed upon the majority. It relies upon terror and oppression, a controlled press and radio; fixed elections, and the suppression of personal freedoms.

I believe that it must be the policy of the United States to support free peoples who are resisting attempted subjugation by armed minorities or by outside pressures.

I believe that we must assist free peoples to work out their own destinies in their own way.

I believe that our help should be primarily through economic and financial aid which is essential to economic stability and orderly political processes.

The world is not static, and the status quo is not sacred. But we cannot allow changes in the status quo in violation of the Charter of the United Nations by such methods as coercion, or by such subterfuges as political infiltration. In helping free and independent nations to maintain their freedom, the United States will be giving effect to the principles of the Charter of the United Nations.

It is necessary only to glance at a map to realize that the survival and integrity of the Greek nation are of grave importance in a much wider situation. If Greece should fall under the control of an armed minority, the effect upon its neighbor, Turkey, would be immediate and serious. Confusion and disorder might well spread throughout the entire Middle East.

Moreover, the disappearance of Greece as an independent state would have a profound effect upon those countries in Europe whose peoples are struggling against great difficulties to maintain their freedoms and their independence while they repair the damages of war.

It would be an unspeakable tragedy if these countries, which have struggled so long against overwhelming odds, should lose that victory for which they sacrificed so much. Collapse of free institutions and loss of independence would be disastrous not only for them but for the world. Discouragement and possibly failure would

quickly be the lot of neighboring peoples striving to maintain their freedom and independence.

Should we fail to aid Greece and Turkey in this fateful hour, the effect will be far reaching to the West as well as to the East.

We must take immediate and resolute action.

I therefore ask the Congress to provide authority for assistance to Greece and Turkey in the amount of $400,000,000 for the period ending June 30, 1948. . . .

In addition to funds, I ask the Congress to authorize the detail of American civilian and military personnel to Greece and Turkey, at the request of those countries, to assist in the tasks of reconstruction, and for the purpose of supervising the use of such financial and material assistance as may be furnished. I recommend that authority also be provided for the instruction and training of selected Greek and Turkish personnel. . . .

This is a serious course upon which we embark. . . .

The seeds of totalitarian regimes are nurtured by misery and want. They spread and grow in the evil soil of poverty and strife. They reach their full growth when the hope of a people for a better life has died. We must keep that hope alive.

The free peoples of the world look to us for support in maintaining their freedoms.

If we falter in our leadership, we may endanger the peace of the world—and we shall surely endanger the welfare of our own nation. . . .

X [GEORGE F. KENNAN], "THE SOURCES OF SOVIET CONDUCT," *FOREIGN AFFAIRS* (JULY 1947)

A career Foreign Service officer, George Kennan (1904–2005) emerged after World War II as the preeminent American interpreter of Soviet behavior. In this essay, published anonymously in the journal *Foreign Affairs,* Kennan offers his views on what makes the Soviet Union tick and describes the rationale for the policy of containment that the Truman administration had already begun to put in place.

Part I

The political personality of Soviet power as we know it today is the product of ideology and circumstances: ideology inherited by the present

Soviet leaders from the movement in which they had their political origin, and circumstances of the power which they now have exercised for nearly three decades in Russia. There can be few tasks of psychological analysis more difficult than to try to trace the interaction of these two forces and the relative role of each in the determination of official Soviet conduct. yet the attempt must be made if that conduct is to be understood and effectively countered.

It is difficult to summarize the set of ideological concepts with which the Soviet leaders came into power. Marxian ideology, in its Russian-Communist projection, has always been in process of subtle evolution. The materials on which it bases itself are extensive and complex. But the outstanding features of Communist thought as it existed in 1916 may perhaps be summarized as follows: (a) that the central factor in the life of man, the factor which determines the character of public life and the "physiognomy of society," is the system by which material goods are produced and exchanged; (b) that the capitalist system of production is a nefarious one which inevitable leads to the exploitation of the working class by the capital-owning class and is incapable of developing adequately the economic resources of society or of distributing fairly the material good produced by human labor; (c) that capitalism contains the seeds of its own destruction and must, in view of the inability of the capital-owning class to adjust itself to economic change, result eventually and inescapably in a revolutionary transfer of power to the working class; and (d) that imperialism, the final phase of capitalism, leads directly to war and revolution.

The rest may be outlined in Lenin's own words: "Unevenness of economic and political development is the inflexible law of capitalism. It follows from this that the victory of Socialism may come originally in a few capitalist countries or even in a single capitalist country. The victorious proletariat of that country, having expropriated the capitalists and having organized Socialist production at home, would rise against the remaining capitalist world, drawing to itself in the process the oppressed classes of other countries." It must be noted that there was no assumption that capitalism would perish without proletarian revolution. A final push was needed from a revolutionary proletariat movement in order to tip over the tottering structure. But it was regarded as inevitable that sooner of later that push be given.

For 50 years prior to the outbreak of the Revolution, this pattern of thought had exercised great fascination for the members of the Russian revolutionary movement. Frustrated, discontented, hopeless of finding self-expression—or too impatient to seek it—in the confining limits of the Tsarist political system, yet lacking wide popular support or their choice of bloody revolution as a means of social betterment, these revolutionists found in Marxist theory a highly convenient rationalization for their own instinctive desires. It afforded pseudo-scientific justification for their impatience, for their categoric denial of all value in the Tsarist system, for their yearning for power and revenge and for their inclination to cut corners in the pursuit of it. It is therefore no wonder that they had come to believe implicitly in the truth and soundness of the Marxist-Leninist teachings, so congenial to their own impulses and emotions. Their sincerity need not be impugned. This is a phenomenon as old as human nature itself. It is has never been more aptly described than by Edward Gibbon, who wrote in *The Decline and Fall of the Roman Empire*: "From enthusiasm to imposture the step is perilous and slippery; the demon of Socrates affords a memorable instance of how a wise man may deceive himself, how a good man may deceive others, how the conscience may slumber in a mixed and middle state between self-illusion and voluntary fraud." And it was with this set of conceptions that the members of the Bolshevik Party entered into power.

Now it must be noted that through all the years of preparation for revolution, the attention of these men, as indeed of Marx himself, had been centered less on the future form which Socialism would take than on the necessary overthrow of rival power which, in their view, had to precede the introduction of Socialism. Their views, therefore, on the positive program to be put into effect, once power was attained, were for the most part nebulous, visionary and impractical. Beyond the nationalization of industry and the expropriation of large private capital holdings there was no agreed program. The treatment of the peasantry, which, according to the Marxist formulation was not of the proletariat, had always been a vague spot in the pattern of Communist thought: and it remained an object of controversy and vacillation for the first ten years of Communist power.

The circumstances of the immediate post-revolution period—the existence in Russia of civil war and foreign intervention, together with the obvious fact that the Communists represented only a tiny minority of the Russian people—made the establishment of dictatorial power a necessity. The experiment with "war Communism" and the abrupt attempt to eliminate private production and trade had unfortunate economic consequences and caused further bitterness against the new revolutionary regime. While the temporary relaxation of the effort to communize Russia, represented by the New Economic Policy, alleviated some of this economic distress and thereby served its purpose, it also made it evident that the "capitalistic sector of society" was still prepared to profit at once from any relaxation of governmental pressure, and would, if permitted to continue to exist, always constitute a powerful opposing element to the Soviet regime and a serious rival for influence in the country. Somewhat the same situation prevailed with respect to the individual peasant who, in his own small way, was also a private producer.

Lenin, had he lived, might have proved a great enough man to reconcile these conflicting forces to the ultimate benefit of Russian society, though this is questionable. But be that as it may, Stalin, and those whom he led in the struggle for succession to Lenin's position of leadership, were not the men to tolerate rival political forces in the sphere of power which they coveted. Their sense of insecurity was too great. Their particular brand of fanaticism, unmodified by any of the Anglo-Saxon traditions of compromise, was too fierce and too jealous to envisage any permanent sharing of power. From the Russian-Asiatic world out of which they had emerged they carried with them a skepticism as to the possibilities of permanent and peaceful coexistence of rival forces. Easily persuaded of their own doctrinaire "rightness," they insisted on the submission or destruction of all competing power. Outside the Communist Party, Russian society was to have no rigidity. There were to be no forms of collective human activity or association which would not be dominated by the Party. No other force in Russian society was to be permitted to achieve vitality or integrity. Only the Party was to have structure. All else was to be an amorphous mass.

And within the Party the same principle was to apply. The mass of Party members might go through the motions of election, deliberation, decision and action; but in these motions they were to be animated not by their own individual wills but by the awesome breath of the Party leadership and the overbrooding presence of "the word."

Let it be stressed again that subjectively these men probably did not seek absolutism for its own sake. They doubtless believed—and found it easy to believe—that they alone knew what was good for society and that they would accomplish that good once their power was secure and unchallengeable. But in seeking that security of their own rule they were prepared to recognize no restrictions, either of God or man, on the character of their methods. And until such time as that security might be achieved, they placed far down on their scale of operational priorities the comforts and happiness of the peoples entrusted to their care.

Now the outstanding circumstance concerning the Soviet regime is that down to the present day this process of political consolidation has never been completed and the men in the Kremlin have continued to be predominantly absorbed with the struggle to secure and make absolute the power which they seized in November 1917. They have endeavored to secure it primarily against forces at home, within Soviet society itself. But they have also endeavored to secure it against the outside world. For ideology, as we have seen, taught them that the outside world was hostile and that it was their duty eventually to overthrow the political forces beyond their borders. Then powerful hands of Russian history and tradition reached up to sustain them in this feeling. Finally, their own aggressive intransigence with respect to the outside world began to find its own reaction; and they were soon forced, to use another Gibbonesque phrase, "to chastise the contumacy" which they themselves had provoked. It is an undeniable privilege of every man to prove himself right in the thesis that the world is his enemy; for if he reiterates it frequently enough and makes it the background of his conduct he is bound eventually to be right.

Now it lies in the nature of the mental world of the Soviet leaders, as well as in the character of their ideology, that no opposition to them can be officially recognized as having any merit or justification whatsoever. Such opposition can flow, in theory, only from the hostile and incorrigible forces of dying capitalism. As long as remnants of capitalism were officially recognized as existing in Russia, it was possible to place on them, as an internal element, part of the blame for the maintenance of a dictatorial form of society. But as these remnants were liquidated, little by little, this justification fell away, and when it was indicated officially that they had been finally destroyed, it disappeared altogether. And this fact created one of the most basic of the compulsions which came to act upon the Soviet regime: since capitalism no longer existed in Russia and since it could not be admitted that there could be serious or widespread opposition to the Kremlin springing spontaneously from the liberated masses under its authority, it became necessary to justify the retention of the dictatorship by stressing the menace of capitalism abroad.

This began at an early date. In 1924 Stalin specifically defended the retention of the "organs of suppression," meaning, among others, the army and the secret police, on the ground that "as long as there is a capitalistic encirclement there will be danger of intervention with all the consequences that flow from that danger." In accordance with that theory, and from that time on, all internal opposition forces in Russia have consistently been portrayed as the agents of foreign forces of reaction antagonistic to Soviet power.

By the same token, tremendous emphasis has been placed on the original Communist thesis of a basic antagonism between the capitalist and Socialist worlds. It is clear, from many indications, that this emphasis is not founded in reality. The real facts concerning it have been confused by the existence abroad of genuine resentment provoked by Soviet philosophy and tactics and occasionally by the existence of great centers of military power, notably the Nazi regime in Germany and the Japanese Government of the late 1930s, which indeed have aggressive designs against the Soviet Union. But there is ample evidence that the stress laid in Moscow on the menace confronting Soviet society from the world outside its borders is founded not in the realities of foreign antagonism but in the necessity of explaining away the maintenance of dictatorial authority at home.

Now the maintenance of this pattern of Soviet power, namely, the pursuit of unlimited authority domestically, accompanied by the cultivation of the semi-myth of implacable foreign hostility, has gone far to shape the actual machinery of Soviet power as we know it today. Internal organs of administration which did not serve this purpose withered on the vine. Organs which did serve this purpose became vastly swollen. The security of Soviet power came to rest on the iron discipline of the Party, on the severity and ubiquity of the secret police, and on the uncompromising economic monopolism of the state. The "organs of suppression," in which the Soviet leaders had sought security from rival forces, became in large measures the masters of those whom they were designed to serve. Today the major part of the structure of Soviet power is committed to the perfection of the dictatorship and to the maintenance of the concept of Russia as in a state of siege, with the enemy lowering beyond the walls. And the millions of human beings who form that part of the structure of power must defend at all costs this concept of Russia's position, for without it they are themselves superfluous.

As things stand today, the rulers can no longer dream of parting with these organs of suppression. The quest for absolute power, pursued now for nearly three decades with a ruthlessness unparalleled (in scope at least) in modern times, has again produced internally, as it did externally, its own reaction. The excesses of the police apparatus have fanned the potential opposition to the regime into something far greater and more dangerous than it could have been before those excesses began.

But least of all can the rulers dispense with the fiction by which the maintenance of dictatorial power has been defended. For this fiction has been canonized in Soviet philosophy by the excesses already committed in its name; and it is now anchored in the Soviet structure of thought by bonds far greater than those of mere ideology.

Part II

So much for the historical background. What does it spell in terms of the political personality of Soviet power as we know it today?

Of the original ideology, nothing has been officially junked. Belief is maintained in the basic badness of capitalism, in the inevitability of its destruction, in the obligation of the proletariat to assist in that destruction and to take power into its own hands. But stress has come to be laid primarily on those concepts which relate most specifically to the Soviet regime itself: to its position as the sole truly Socialist regime in a dark and misguided world, and to the relationships of power within it.

The first of these concepts is that of the innate antagonism between capitalism and Socialism. We have seen how deeply that concept has become imbedded in foundations of Soviet power. It has profound implications for Russia's conduct as a member of international society. It means that there can never be on Moscow's side an sincere assumption of a community of aims between the Soviet Union and powers which are regarded as capitalist. It must inevitably be assumed in Moscow that the aims of the capitalist world are antagonistic to the Soviet regime, and therefore to the interests of the peoples it controls. If the Soviet government occasionally sets it signature to documents which would indicate the contrary, this is to regarded as a tactical maneuver permissible in dealing with the enemy (who is without honor) and should be taken in the spirit of *caveat emptor*. Basically, the antagonism remains. It is postulated. And from it flow many of the phenomena which we find disturbing in the Kremlin's conduct of foreign policy: the secretiveness, the lack of frankness, the duplicity, the wary suspiciousness, and the basic unfriendliness of purpose. These phenomena are there to stay, for the foreseeable future. There can be variations of degree and of emphasis. When there is something the Russians want from us, one or the other of these features of their policy may be thrust temporarily into the background; and when that happens there will always be Americans who will leap forward with gleeful announcements that "the Russians have changed," and some who will even try to take credit for having brought about such "changes." But we should not be misled by tactical maneuvers. These characteristics of Soviet policy, like the postulate from which they flow, are basic to the internal nature of Soviet power, and will be with us, whether in the foreground or the background, until the internal nature of Soviet power is changed.

This means we are going to continue for long time to find the Russians difficult to deal with. It does not mean that they should be considered as embarked upon a do-or-die program to overthrow our society by a given date. The theory of the inevitability of the eventual fall of capitalism has

the fortunate connotation that there is no hurry about it. The forces of progress can take their time in preparing the final *coup de grâce*. Meanwhile, what is vital is that the "Socialist fatherland"— that oasis of power which has already been won for Socialism in the person of the Soviet Union— should be cherished and defended by all good Communists at home and abroad, its fortunes promoted, its enemies badgered and confounded. The promotion of premature, "adventuristic" revolutionary projects abroad which might embarrass Soviet power in any way would be an inexcusable, even a counter-revolutionary act. The cause of Socialism is the support and promotion of Soviet power, as defined in Moscow.

This brings us to the second of the concepts important to contemporary Soviet outlook. That is the infallibility of the Kremlin. The Soviet concept of power, which permits no focal points of organization outside the Party itself, requires that the Party leadership remain in theory the sole repository of truth. For if truth were to be found elsewhere, there would be justification for its expression in organized activity. But it is precisely that which the Kremlin cannot and will not permit.

The leadership of the Communist Party is therefore always right, and has been always right ever since in 1929 Stalin formalized his personal power by announcing that decisions of the Politburo were being taken unanimously.

On the principle of infallibility there rests the iron discipline of the Communist Party. In fact, the two concepts are mutually self-supporting. Perfect discipline requires recognition of infallibility. Infallibility requires the observance of discipline. And the two go far to determine the behaviorism of the entire Soviet apparatus of power. But their effect cannot be understood unless a third factor be taken into account: namely, the fact that the leadership is at liberty to put forward for tactical purposes any particular thesis which it finds useful to the cause at any particular moment and to require the faithful and unquestioning acceptance of that thesis by the members of the movement as a whole. This means that truth is not a constant but is actually created, for all intents and purposes, by the Soviet leaders themselves. It may vary from week to week, from month to month. It is nothing absolute and immutable—nothing which flows from objective reality. It is only the most recent manifestation of the wisdom of those in whom the ultimate wisdom is supposed to reside, because they represent the logic of history. The accumulative effect of these factors is to give to the whole subordinate apparatus of Soviet power an unshakable stubbornness and steadfastness in its orientation. This orientation can be changed at will by the Kremlin but by no other power. Once a given party line has been laid down on a given issue of current policy, the whole Soviet governmental machine, including the mechanism of diplomacy, moves inexorably along the prescribed path, like a persistent toy automobile wound up and headed in a given direction, stopping only when it meets with some unanswerable force. The individuals who are the components of this machine are unamenable to argument or reason, which comes to them from outside sources. Their whole training has taught them to mistrust and discount the glib persuasiveness of the outside world. Like the white dog before the phonograph, they hear only the "master's voice." And if they are to be called off from the purposes last dictated to them, it is the master who must call them off. Thus the foreign representative cannot hope that his words will make any impression on them. The most that he can hope is that they will be transmitted to those at the top, who are capable of changing the party line. But even those are not likely to be swayed by any normal logic in the words of the bourgeois representative. Since there can be no appeal to common purposes, there can be no appeal to common mental approaches. For this reason, facts speak louder than words to the ears of the Kremlin; and words carry the greatest weight when they have the ring of reflecting, or being backed up by, facts of unchallengeable validity.

But we have seen that the Kremlin is under no ideological compulsion to accomplish its purposes in a hurry. Like the Church, it is dealing in ideological concepts which are of long-term validity, and it can afford to be patient. It has no right to risk the existing achievements of the revolution for the sake of vain baubles of the future. The very teachings of Lenin himself require great caution and flexibility in the pursuit of Communist purposes. Again, these precepts are fortified by the lessons of Russian history: of centuries of obscure battles between nomadic forces over the stretches of a vast unfortified plain. Here caution, circumspection, flexibility and deception are the valuable qualities; and their value finds a natural appreciation in the Russian or the oriental mind. Thus the Kremlin has no compunction about retreating in the face of superior forces. And being under the compulsion of no timetable, it does not get panicky under the necessity for such retreat. Its political action is a fluid stream which moves constantly, wherever it is permitted to move, toward a given goal. Its main concern is to make sure that it has filled every nook and cranny available to it in the basin of world power. But if it finds unassailable barriers in its path, it accepts these philosophically and accommodates itself to them. The main thing is that there should always be pressure, unceasing constant pressure, toward the desired goal. There is no trace of any feeling in Soviet psychology that that goal must be reached at any given time.

These considerations make Soviet diplomacy at once easier and more difficult to deal with than the diplomacy of individual aggressive leaders like Napoleon and Hitler. On the one hand it is more sensitive to contrary force, more ready to yield on individual sectors of the diplomatic front when that force is felt to be too strong, and thus more rational in the logic and rhetoric of power. On the other hand it cannot be easily defeated or discouraged by a single victory on the part of its opponents. And the patient persistence by which it is animated means that it can be effectively countered not by sporadic acts which represent the momentary whims of democratic opinion but only by intelligent long-range policies on the part of Russia's adversaries—policies no less steady in their purpose, and no less variegated and resourceful in their application, than those of the Soviet Union itself.

In these circumstances it is clear that the main element of any United States policy toward the Soviet Union must be that of long-term, patient but firm and vigilant containment of Russian expansive tendencies. It is important to note, however, that such a policy has nothing to do with outward histrionics: with threats or blustering or superfluous gestures of outward "toughness." While the Kremlin is basically flexible in its reaction to political realities, it is by no means unamenable to considerations of prestige. Like almost

any other government, it can be placed by tact-
less and threatening gestures in a position where it
cannot afford to yield even though this might be
dictated by its sense of realism. The Russian leaders are keen judges of human psychology, and as
such they are highly conscious that loss of temper
and of self-control is never a source of strength
in political affairs. They are quick to exploit such
evidences of weakness. For these reasons it is a *sine
qua non* of successful dealing with Russia that the
foreign government in question should remain at
all times cool and collected and that its demands
on Russian policy should be put forward in such a
manner as to leave the way open for a compliance
not too detrimental to Russian prestige.

Part III

In the light of the above, it will be clearly seen that
the Soviet pressure against the free institutions of
the western world is something that can be contained by the adroit and vigilant application of
counter-force at a series of constantly shifting
geographical and political points, corresponding
to the shifts and maneuvers of Soviet policy, but
which cannot be charmed or talked out of existence. The Russians look forward to a duel of infinite duration, and they see that already they have
scored great successes. It must be borne in mind
that there was a time when the Communist Party
represented far more of a minority in the sphere
of Russian national life than Soviet power today
represents in the world community.

But if the ideology convinces the rulers of
Russia that truth is on their side and they can
therefore afford to wait, those of us on whom
that ideology has no claim are free to examine objectively the validity of that premise. The
Soviet thesis not only implies complete lack of
control by the west over its own economic destiny, it likewise assumes Russian unity, discipline
and patience over an infinite period. Let us bring
this apocalyptic vision down to earth, and suppose that the western world finds the strength
and resourcefulness to contain Soviet power over
a period of ten to fifteen years. What does that
spell for Russia itself?

The Soviet leaders, taking advantage of the
contributions of modern techniques to the arts of
despotism, have solved the question of obedience

within the confines of their power. Few challenge
their authority; and even those who do are unable
to make that challenge valid as against the organs
of suppression of the state.

The Kremlin has also proved able to accomplish its purpose of building up Russia, regardless
of the interests of the inhabitants, and industrial
foundation of heavy metallurgy, which is, to be
sure, not yet complete but which is nevertheless
continuing to grow and is approaching those of
the other major industrial countries. All of this,
however, both the maintenance of internal political security and the building of heavy industry, has
been carried out at a terrible cost in human life
and in human hopes and energies. It has necessitated the use of forced labor on a scale unprecedented in modern times under conditions of
peace. It has involved the neglect or abuse of other
phases of Soviet economic life, particularly agriculture, consumers' goods production, housing
and transportation.

To all that, the war has added its tremendous
toll of destruction, death and human exhaustion. In consequence of this, we have in Russia
today a population which is physically and spiritually tired. The mass of the people are disillu-
sioned, skeptical and no longer as accessible as
they once were to the magical attraction which
Soviet power still radiates to its followers abroad.
The avidity with which people seized upon the
slight respite accorded to the Church for tactical
reasons during the war was eloquent testimony
to the fact that their capacity for faith and devotion found little expression in the purposes of the
regime.

In these circumstances, there are limits to the
physical and nervous strength of people themselves. These limits are absolute ones, and are
binding even for the cruelest dictatorship, because
beyond them people cannot be driven. The forced
labor camps and the other agencies of constraint
provide temporary means of compelling people
to work longer hours than their own volition
or mere economic pressure would dictate; but if
people survive them at all they become old before
their time and must be considered as human casualties to the demands of dictatorship. In either case
their best powers are no longer available to society and can no longer be enlisted in the service
of the state.

Here only the younger generations can help. The younger generation, despite all vicissitudes and sufferings, is numerous and vigorous; and the Russians are a talented people. But it still remains to be seen what will be the effects on mature performance of the abnormal emotional strains of childhood which Soviet dictatorship created and which were enormously increased by the war. Such things as normal security and placidity of home environment have practically ceased to exist in the Soviet Union outside of the most remote farms and villages. And observers are not yet sure whether that is not going to leave its mark on the over-all capacity of the generation now coming into maturity.

In addition to this, we have the fact that Soviet economic development, while it can list certain formidable achievements, has been precariously spotty and uneven. Russian Communists who speak of the "uneven development of capitalism" should blush at the contemplation of their own national economy. Here certain branches of economic life, such as the metallurgical and machine industries, have been pushed out of all proportion to other sectors of economy. Here is a nation striving to become in a short period one of the great industrial nations of the world while it still has no highway network worthy of the name and only a relatively primitive network of railways. Much has been done to increase efficiency of labor and to teach primitive peasants something about the operation of machines. But maintenance is still a crying deficiency of all Soviet economy. Construction is hasty and poor in quality. Depreciation must be enormous. And in vast sectors of economic life it has not yet been possible to instill into labor anything like that general culture of production and technical self-respect which characterizes the skilled worker of the west.

It is difficult to see how these deficiencies can be corrected at an early date by a tired and dispirited population working largely under the shadow of fear and compulsion. And as long as they are not overcome, Russia will remain economically a vulnerable, and in a certain sense an impotent, nation, capable of exporting its enthusiasms and of radiating the strange charm of its primitive political vitality but unable to back up those articles of export by the real evidences of material power and prosperity.

Meanwhile, a great uncertainty hangs over the political life of the Soviet Union. That is the uncertainty involved in the transfer of power from one individual or group of individuals to others.

This is, of course, outstandingly the problem of the personal position of Stalin. We must remember that his succession to Lenin's pinnacle of pre-eminence in the Communist movement was the only such transfer of individual authority which the Soviet Union has experienced. That transfer took 12 years to consolidate. It cost the lives of millions of people and shook the state to its foundations. The attendant tremors were felt all through the international revolutionary movement, to the disadvantage of the Kremlin itself.

It is always possible that another transfer of pre-eminent power may take place quietly and inconspicuously, with no repercussions anywhere. But again, it is possible that the questions involved may unleash, to use some of Lenin's words, one of those "incredibly swift transitions" from "delicate deceit" to "wild violence" which characterize Russian history, and may shake Soviet power to its foundations.

But this is not only a question of Stalin himself. There has been, since 1938, a dangerous congealment of political life in the higher circles of Soviet power. The All-Union Congress of Soviets, in theory the supreme body of the Party, is supposed to meet not less often than once in three years. It will soon be eight full years since its last meeting. During this period membership in the Party has numerically doubled. Party mortality during the war was enormous; and today well over half of the Party members are persons who have entered since the last Party congress was held. Meanwhile, the same small group of men has carried on at the top through an amazing series of national vicissitudes. Surely there is some reason why the experiences of the war brought basic political changes to every one of the great governments of the west. Surely the causes of that phenomenon are basic enough to be present somewhere in the obscurity of Soviet political life, as well. And yet no recognition has been given to these causes in Russia.

It must be surmised from this that even within so highly disciplined an organization as the Communist Party there must be a growing divergence in age, outlook and interest between the great mass of Party members, only so recently recruited into the movement, and the little self-perpetuating clique of men at the top, whom most of these Party members have never met, with whom they have never conversed, and with whom they can have no political intimacy.

Who can say whether, in these circumstances, the eventual rejuvenation of the higher spheres of authority (which can only be a matter of time) can take place smoothly and peacefully, or whether rivals in the quest for higher power will not eventually reach down into these politically immature and inexperienced masses in order to find support for their respective claims? If this were ever to happen, strange consequences could flow for the Communist Party: for the membership at large has been exercised only in the practices of iron discipline and obedience and not in the arts of compromise and accommodation. And if disunity were ever to seize and paralyze the Party, the chaos and weakness of Russian society would be revealed in forms beyond description. For we have seen that Soviet power is only concealing an amorphous mass of human beings among whom no independent organizational structure is tolerated. In Russia there is not even such a thing as local government. The present generation of Russians have never known spontaneity of collective action. If, consequently, anything were ever to occur to disrupt the unity and efficacy of the Party as a political instrument, Soviet Russia might be changed overnight from one of the strongest to one of the weakest and most pitiable of national societies.

Thus the future of Soviet power may not be by any means as secure as Russian capacity for self-delusion would make it appear to the men of the Kremlin. That they can quietly and easily turn it over to others remains to be proved. Meanwhile, the hardships of their rule and the vicissitudes of international life have taken a heavy toll of the strength and hopes of the great people on whom their power rests. It is curious to note that the ideological power of Soviet authority is strongest today in areas beyond the frontiers of Russia, beyond the reach of its police power. This phenomenon brings to mind a comparison used by Thomas Mann in his great novel *Buddenbrooks*. Observing that human institutions often show the greatest outward brilliance at a moment when inner decay is in reality farthest advanced, he compared one of those stars whose light shines most brightly on this world when in reality it has long since ceased to exist. And who can say with assurance that the strong light still cast by the Kremlin on the dissatisfied peoples of the western world is not the powerful afterglow of a constellation which is in actuality on the wane? This cannot be proved. And it cannot be disproved. But the possibility remains (and in the opinion of this writer it is a strong one) that Soviet power, like the capitalist world of its conception, bears within it the seeds of its own decay, and that the sprouting of these seeds is well advanced.

Part IV

It is clear that the United States cannot expect in the foreseeable future to enjoy political intimacy with the Soviet regime. It must continue to regard the Soviet Union as a rival, not a partner, in the political arena. It must continue to expect that Soviet policies will reflect no abstract love of peace and stability, no real faith in the possibility of a permanent happy coexistence of the Socialist and capitalist worlds, but rather a cautious, persistent pressure toward the disruption and, weakening of all rival influence and rival power.

Balanced against this are the facts that Russia, as opposed to the western world in general, is still by far the weaker party, that Soviet policy is highly flexible, and that Soviet society may well contain deficiencies which will eventually weaken its own total potential. This would of itself warrant the United States entering with reasonable confidence upon a policy of firm containment, designed to confront the Russians with unalterable counter-force at every point where they show signs of encroaching upon the interests of a peaceful and stable world.

But in actuality the possibilities for American policy are by no means limited to holding the line and hoping for the best. It is entirely possible for the United States to influence by its actions the internal developments, both within Russia and throughout the international Communist movement, by which Russian policy is largely determined. This is not only a question of the modest measure of informational activity which this government can conduct in the Soviet Union and elsewhere, although that, too, is important. It is rather a question of the degree to which the

United States can create among the peoples of the world generally the impression of a country which knows what it wants, which is coping successfully with the problem of its internal life and with the responsibilities of a World Power, and which has a spiritual vitality capable of holding its own among the major ideological currents of the time. To the extent that such an impression can be created and maintained, the aims of Russian Communism must appear sterile and quixotic, the hopes and enthusiasm of Moscow's supporters must wane, and added strain must be imposed on the Kremlin's foreign policies. For the palsied decrepitude of the capitalist world is the keystone of Communist philosophy. Even the failure of the United States to experience the early economic depression which the ravens of the Red Square have been predicting with such complacent confidence since hostilities ceased would have deep and important repercussions throughout the Communist world.

By the same token, exhibitions of indecision, disunity and internal disintegration within this country have an exhilarating effect on the whole Communist movement. At each evidence of these tendencies, a thrill of hope and excitement goes through the Communist world; a new jauntiness can be noted in the Moscow tread; new groups of foreign supporters climb on to what they can only view as the band wagon of international politics; and Russian pressure increases all along the line in international affairs.

It would be an exaggeration to say that American behavior unassisted and alone could exercise a power of life and death over the Communist movement and bring about the early fall of Soviet power in Russia. But the United States has it in its power to increase enormously the strains under which Soviet policy must operate, to force upon the Kremlin a far greater degree of moderation and circumspection than it has had to observe in recent years, and in this way to promote tendencies which must eventually find their outlet in either the breakup or the gradual mellowing of Soviet power. For no mystical, Messianic movement—and particularly not that of the Kremlin—can face frustration indefinitely without eventually adjusting itself in one way or another to the logic of that state of affairs.

Thus the decision will really fall in large measure in this country itself. The issue of Soviet-American relations is in essence a test of the overall worth of the United States as a nation among nations. To avoid destruction the United States need only measure up to its own best traditions and prove itself worthy of preservation as a great nation.

Surely, there was never a fairer test of national quality than this. In the light of these circumstances, the thoughtful observer of Russian-American relations will find no cause for complaint in the Kremlin's challenge to American society. He will rather experience a certain gratitude to a Providence which, by providing the American people with this implacable challenge, has made their entire security as a nation dependent on their pulling themselves together and accepting the responsibilities of moral and political leadership that history plainly intended them to bear.

ELEANOR ROOSEVELT, "STATEMENT TO THE UNITED NATIONS' GENERAL ASSEMBLY ON THE UNIVERSAL DECLARATION OF HUMAN RIGHTS" (1948)

As a former First Lady and formidable political figure in her own right, Eleanor Roosevelt (1884–1962) served after World War II as head of the United Nations Human Rights Commission and played a key role in drafting and subsequently promoting the UN's Universal Declaration of Human Rights.

The long and meticulous study and debate of which this universal Declaration of Human Rights is the product means that it reflects the composite views of the many men and governments who have contributed to its formulation. Not every man nor every government can have what he wants in a document of this kind. There are of course particular provisions in the declaration before us with which we are not fully satisfied. I have no doubt this is true of other delegations, but taken as a whole the Delegation of the United States believes that this is a good document—even a great document—and we propose to give it our full support. . . .

Certain provisions of the declaration are stated in such broad terms as to be acceptable only because of the limitations in article 29 providing for limitation on the exercise of the rights for the purpose of meeting the requirements of morality, public order, and the general welfare. An example of this is the provision that everyone has the right of equal access to the public service in his country. The basic principle of equality and of non-discrimination as to public employment is sound, but it cannot be accepted without limitations. My Government, for example, would consider that this is unquestionably subject to limitation in the interest of public order and the general welfare. It would not consider that the exclusion from public employment of persons holding subversive political beliefs and not loyal to the basic principles and practices of the constitution and laws of the country would in any way infringe upon this right.

Likewise, my Government has made it clear in the course of the development of the declaration that it does not consider that the economic and social and cultural rights stated in the declaration imply an obligation on governments to assure the enjoyment of these rights by direct governmental action. This was made quite clear in the Human Rights Commission text of article 23 which served as a so-called "umbrella" article to the articles on economic and social rights. We consider that the principle has not been affected by the fact that this article no longer contains a reference to the articles which follow it. This in no way affects our whole-hearted support for the basic principles of economic, social, and cultural rights set forth in these articles.

In giving our approval to the declaration today, it is of primary importance that we keep clearly in mind the basic character of the document. It is not a treaty; it is not an international agreement. It is not and does not purport to be a statement of law or of legal obligation. It is a declaration of basic principles of human rights and freedoms, to be stamped with the approval of the General Assembly by formal vote of its members, and to serve as a common standard of achievement for all peoples of all nations.

We stand today at the threshold of a great event both in the life of the United Nations and in the life of mankind, that is the approval by the General Assembly of the Universal Declaration of Human Rights recommended by the Third Committee. This declaration may well become the international Magna Carta of all men everywhere. We hope its proclamation by the General Assembly will be an event comparable to the proclamation of the Declaration of the Rights of Man by the French people in 1789, the adoption of the Bill of Rights by the people of the United States, and the adoption of comparable declarations at different times in other countries.

At a time when there are so many issues on which we find it difficult to reach a common basis of agreement, it is a significant fact that 58 states have found such a large measure of agreement in the complex field of human rights. This must be taken as testimony of our common aspiration first voiced in the Charter of the United Nations to lift men everywhere to a higher standard of life and to a greater enjoyment of freedom. Man's desire for peace lies behind this declaration. The realization that the flagrant violation of human rights by Nazi and Fascist countries sowed the seeds of the last world war has supplied the impetus for the work which brings us to the moment of achievement here today.

HENRY A. WALLACE, "MY COMMITMENTS" (1948)

Henry A. Wallace (1888–1965) served under President Franklin Roosevelt as agriculture secretary, vice president, and then commerce secretary, continuing to hold the latter post under Truman. In September 1946, President Truman fired Wallace, who publicly spoke against the anti-Soviet turn in US policy. Wallace soon became the most prominent left-wing critic of that policy. In 1948, he ran for the presidency as the candidate of a reconstituted Progressive Party. Charged with being a communist dupe, Wallace won less than 3% of votes cast. Here, in addressing the Progressive Party convention, he castigates the bipartisan Cold War foreign policy consensus and calls for reviving the liberal domestic reforms of Roosevelt's New Deal.

Four years and four days ago, as Vice President of the United States and head of the Iowa delegation to the Democratic convention, I rose to second the nomination of Franklin Roosevelt, and said: "The future belongs to those who go down the line unswervingly for the liberal principles of both political democracy and economic democracy regardless of race, color or religion. . . . Roosevelt can and will lead the United States, in cooperation with the rest of the world, toward that type of peace which will prevent World War 3."

That was four years ago. Do you remember that summer of casualty lists, and the wreckage still smoldering on the beaches of Normandy? A time of dying and destruction and, yet, something more.

For in that time, you remember, every one of us held a dream. At the lathe, in the fields in early morning, at the kitchen window, sweating out a barrage in the line, everyone of us dreamed of a time when the sound of peace would come back to the land, and there would be no more fear, and men would begin to build again.

And in that dark time, you remember, Franklin Roosevelt looked beyond the horizon and gave us a vision of peace, an economic bill of rights; the right to work, for every man willing. The right of every family to a decent home. The right to protection from the fears of old age and sickness. The right to a good education. All the rights which spell security for every man, woman and child, from the cradle to the grave.

It was the dream that all of us had, and Roosevelt put it into words, and we loved him for it.

Two years later the war was over, and Franklin Roosevelt was dead.

And what followed was the great betrayal.

Instead of the dream, we have inherited disillusion.

Instead of the promised years of harvest, the years of the locust are upon us. . . .

Into the Government came the ghosts of the great depression, the banking house boys and the oil-well diplomats.

In marched the generals—and out went the men who had built the TVA and the Grand Coulee, the men who had planned social security and built Federal housing, the men who had dug the farmer out of the dust bowl and the workman out of the sweatshop.

A time of comings and goings . . . the shadows of the past coming in fast—and the lights going out, slowly—the exodus of the torchbearers of the New Deal. . . .

You have read your papers. In the two years since the people who planned for living were eased out of Washington, and the ghosts who plan for destruction were invited in—in those two short years during which the Department of State has been subtly annexed to the Pentagon, and the hand of military has come to guide the pen of the diplomat—we have ricocheted from crisis to crisis.

The "get tough policy" has spawned its inevitable bread—the "get tougher policy."

And what harvest do we have of all our hoping, what fruits of the hard-won victory? Not peace—but the sword; not an economic bill of rights—but a mounting bill of wrongs.

Not life—but tens of thousands of deaths, on unnecessary battlefields in Greece—in Palestine—in China.

One world, yes—frozen in one fear. . . .

We who are met here tonight—who are met here at a time of crisis—are talking to the people of the United States and the world on behalf of the everlasting principles of the founding fathers of our country. . . .

One hundred and fifty years ago Thomas Jefferson took leadership in forming a new party—a successful new party, which overcame the odds of a hostile press, of wealth and vested interests arrayed against it, and of a Government which sought to undermine the new movement by jailing its leaders.

The party Jefferson founded 150 years ago was buried here in Philadelphia last week. It could not survive the Pauleys, the Hagues, the Crumps, the racists and bigots, the generals, the admirals, the Wall Street alumni. A party founded by a Jefferson died in the arms of a Truman.

But the spirit which animated that party in the days of Jefferson has been captured anew. It has been captured by those who have met here this week-end with a firm resolve to keep our tradition of freedom that we may fulfill the promises of an abundant, peaceful life for all men.

Four score and seven years ago, the successful candidate of another new party took office in Washington.

Lincoln, with the Emancipation Proclamation fulfilled the promise of the new party which he led to victory. He headed a government of the people, by the people, and for the people. In the generations which followed his party became a party of the corporations, by the corporations, and for the corporations. . . .

But we here tonight—we of the Progressive party—we here dedicate ourselves to the complete fulfillment of Lincoln's promise; we consecrate ourselves to a second emancipation; an emancipation that will achieve for the Negro and all Americans of every race, creed, and national origin a full, free, and complete citizenship everywhere in these United States.

We ally ourselves against those who turn to nightmares the peoples' dreams of peace and equality.

We ally ourselves to stand against the kings of privilege who own the old parties—the corrupted parties, the parties whose founders rebelled in times past, even as we do today, against those whose private greed jeopardizes the general welfare.

We stand against their cold war and their red smear, under cover of which they steal our resources, strike terror into our hearts, and attempt to control our thoughts and dominate the life of man everywhere in the world.

We stand together to stop the disasters—economic, political, and military, which their policies must breed.

Only those who take the spirit of Jefferson and Lincoln and apply it to the present world situation can bring the peace and security which will end fear and unleash creative force beyond the power of man to imagine.

It was in the spirit of Jefferson and Lincoln that Roosevelt challenged the money changers in his first inaugural address fifteen years ago: It was in the spirit of Jefferson and Lincoln that he told the Wall Street crowd in 1940 that they had met their master. In the spirit of Jefferson and Lincoln he outlined the Four Freedoms and the economic bill of rights. . . .

Franklin Roosevelt did not fear; he reveled in the names hurled by those who feared the shape of his vision. We of the new party—the Progressive party—shall cherish the adjectives and mound of hate thrown at us. They are a measure of the fear in the temples of the money changers and the clubs of the military. The base metal of vituperation cannot withstand the attack of truth. . . .

There are some who say they agree with our objectives, but we are ahead of our times. But we are the land of pioneers and trail blazers. Though we have reached the end of the old trails to the West, a new wilderness rises before us. The wilderness of poverty and sickness and fear.

Once again America has need of frontiersmen. A new frontier awaits us—no longer west of the Pacific—but forward across the wilderness of poverty and sickness, and fear. We move, as the Pilgrim ships moved, as the Conestoga wagons moved, not ahead of our time, but in the very tide. And always before us, the bright star, the dream of the promised land, of what this nation might be.

But the American dream is no Utopian vision. We do not plan rocket ships for week-end trips to Mars. The dream is the hard and simple truth of what can be done. . . .

We can build new schools to rescue our children from the fire-traps where they now crowd two at a desk. We can end the murderous tyranny of sickness, and disease. The dream is nothing but the facts. The facts are that we spend $20,000,000,000 a year for cold war. The facts are that world health authorities, given one-tenth of this sum, could, in one year, with $2,000,000,000, wipe from the face of the earth tuberculosis, typhoid; malaria and cholera!

The cold war has already brought death to millions of Americans. . . .

Within the past month other men, candidates of the graveyard parties, have stood in this city, have flexed their muscles, and have declared their intention to continue the cold war whose heaviest tolls have been taken here at home. Both have said that "partisan politics must stop at the water's edge." They have declared their agreement. It is an agreement which would doom the nation and the world.

It is the policies which operate beyond the water's edge; the policies which demand heavy arms, and draft acts, and the waste of resources and skills in producing for disaster—it is those policies which determine the real wages for American workers, prices for American consumers, and the life-span of all the people of the world.

Yes, other candidates have stood before the American people to declare that they have made no commitments to obtain their nominations. But they have committed themselves; they have committed themselves to the policies of the big brass and big gold; to the policies of militarization and imperialism; to the policies which cast a shroud over the life-giving, life-saving course Franklin Roosevelt had charted for this post-war world.

I tell you frankly that in obtaining the nomination of the Progressive party—a nomination I accept with pride—I have made commitments. I have made them in every section of this land. I have made them in great halls and sports arenas, in huge open air meetings and in small gatherings. I have made commitments in the basement of a Negro church and in union halls and on picket lines. I have made commitments. I have made them freely. I shall abide by them. I repeat them with pride:

I am committed to the policy of placing human rights above property rights.

I am committed to using the power of our democracy to control rigorously and, wherever necessary, to remove from private to public hands, the power of huge corporate monopolies and international big business.

I am committed to peaceful negotiations with the Soviet Government. I am committed to do everything I can through the new party to save the lives of those who are now to be drafted through the establishment of peace without sacrificing any American principle or public interest. . . .

I am committed to using the power and prestige of the United States to help the peoples of the world, not their exploiters and rulers; to help the suffering, frustrated people in the colonial areas of the world even as we help other civilizations which have felt the full destructive force of war.

I am committed to planning as carefully and thoroughly for production for peace as the militarists and bankers plan and plot for war. For many of today's 60 million jobs are cold war jobs, unstable jobs, suicide jobs. I am committed to making 60 million—and more—jobs of producing for peace—house building jobs, school building jobs, the jobs of building dams and power plants and highways and clinics.

I am committed to a program of progressive capitalism—a program which will protect from the tentacles of monopolists the initiative and creative and productive powers of truly independent enterprise. . . .

I am pledged to fight the murderers who block, impede and stifle legislation and appropriations which would eliminate segregation and provide health and education facilities to bridge the gap of ten years life expectancy between a Negro child and a white child born this day.

I am pledged to licking inflation by stopping the cold war, the ruthless profiteering of monopolies, and the waste of resources which could give us an abundance of the goods of peace.

I am committed to helping lift the heavy hand of fear from our elder citizens, whose minds and bodies have served to build this America and whose reward must be the economic security which will enable them to spend their days with the peace of mind that comes from work well done and appreciated. And I am committed to those programs—principally the program for peace, which will lift from our young people the dread of war and drafts and unemployment and which will replace these fears with hope born of security and the equal opportunity to develop fully their individual talents and careers. . . .

I am committed to stopping the creation of fear; to using all my powers to prevent the fearmakers from clogging the minds of the people with the "red issue." The American people want and deserve fewer red issues and more red meat. Millions know and millions more must see that it is not the Kremlin, not the Communists who have sent milk to 24 cents a quart and meat to $1.30 a pound; that it is the red issue not the reds who did this to us. . . .

And I am committed and do renounce the support of those who practice hate and preach prejudice; of those who would limit the civil rights of others; of those who would restrict the use of the ballot; of those who advocate force and violence; and I am committed to accept and do accept the support of those who favor the program of peace I have outlined here; the support of all those who truly believe in democracy.

ARTHUR M. SCHLESINGER, JR., *THE VITAL CENTER: THE POLITICS OF FREEDOM* (1949)

By the late 1940s, resistance to the Soviet Union and communism more generally had emerged as central themes of US policy. Yet the Cold War did not command unanimous support. Some Americans on the left balked at the Truman administration's depiction of the communist threat. Some on the right worried that opposition to communism abroad would drag the United States into needless wars. A Pulitzer Prize–winning historian active in liberal Democratic circles, Arthur Schlesinger (1917–2007) waded into this disagreement, aiming to discredit both left and right while promoting a muscular liberalism as the only acceptable basis for policy.

I was born in 1917. I heard Franklin Roosevelt's first inaugural address as a boy at school, fifteen years old. Since that March day in 1933, one has been able to feel that liberal ideas had access to power in the United States, that liberal purposes, in general, were dominating our national policy. For one's own generation, then, American liberalism has had a positive and confident ring. It has stood for responsibility and for achievement, not for frustration and sentimentalism; it has been the instrument of social change, not of private neurosis. During most of my political consciousness this has been a New Deal country. I expect that it will continue to be a New Deal country.

The experience of growing up under the New Deal meant too that Communism shone for few of one's generation with the same unearthly radiance that it apparently shone for other young men a decade earlier. It was partly the fact that we did not need so desperately to believe in the Soviet utopia. Franklin Roosevelt was showing that democracy was capable of taking care of its own; the New Deal was filling the vacuum of faith which we had inherited from the cynicism and complacency of the twenties, and from the breadlines of the early thirties. Partly too the Soviet Union itself was no longer the bright dream of the twenties—the land of hope encircled by capitalist aggressors and traduced by newspapermen sending lies out of Riga. What we saw in the Russia of the thirties was a land where industrialization was underwritten by mass starvation, where delusions of political infallibility led to the brutal extermination of dissent, and where the execution of heroes of the revolution testified to some deep inner contradiction in the system. This conclusion was not, for most of us, a process of disillusionment for which we had to pay the psychological price of a new extremism. We were simply the children of a new atmosphere: history had spared us any emotional involvement in the Soviet mirage.

The degeneration of the Soviet Union taught us a useful lesson, however. It broke the bubble of the false optimism of the nineteenth century. Official liberalism had long been almost inextricably identified with a picture of man as perfectible, as endowed with sufficient wisdom and selflessness to endure power and to use it infallibly for the general good. The Soviet experience, on top of the rise of fascism, reminded my generation rather forcibly that man was, indeed, imperfect, and that the corruptions of power could unleash great evil in the world. We discovered a new dimension of experience—the dimension of anxiety, guilt and corruption. . . .

Mid-twentieth-century liberalism, I believe, has thus been fundamentally reshaped by the hope

Arthur M. Schlesinger, Jr., *The Vital Center: The Politics of Freedom*. Boston: Houghton Mifflin Company (1949).

of the New Deal, by the exposure of the Soviet Union, and by the deepening of our knowledge of man. The consequence of this historical re-education has been an unconditional rejection of totalitarianism and a reassertion of the ultimate integrity of the individual. This awakening con-stitutes the unique experience and fundamental faith of contemporary liberalism.

This faith has been and will continue to be under attack from the far right and the far left. In this book I have deliberately given more space to the problem of protecting the liberal faith from Communism than from reaction, not because reaction is the lesser threat, but because it is the enemy we know, whose features are clearly delineated for us, against whom our efforts have always been oriented. It is perhaps our very absorption in this age-old foe which has made us fatally slow to recognize the danger on what we carelessly thought was our left—forgetting in our enthusiasm that the totalitarian left and the totalitarian right meet at last on the murky grounds of tyranny and terror. I am persuaded that the restoration of business to political power in this country would have the calamitous results that have generally accompanied business con-trol of the government; that this time we might be delivered through the incompetence of the right into the hands of the totalitarians of the left. But I am persuaded too that liberals have values in common with most members of the business community—in particular, a belief in free society—which they do not have in com-mon with the totalitarians.

The experience with Communism has had one singularly healthy effect: it has made us reclaim democratic ideas which a decade ago we tended to regret and even to abandon. The defense of these ideas against both right and left will be a continuous and exacting commitment. But there lies in that commitment the possibility of recharging the faith in democracy with some of its old passion and principle. I am certain that history has equipped modern American liberalism with the ideas and the knowledge to construct a society where men will be both free and happy. Whether we have the moral vigor to do the job depends on ourselves. . . .

Optimism gave the progressives a soft and shallow concept on of human nature. With the

aggressive and sinister impulses eliminated from the equation, the problem of social change assumed too simple a form. The corruptions of power—the desire to exercise it, the desire to increase it, the desire for prostration before it—had no place in the progressive calculations. As a result, progressivism became politically inade-quate: it could neither persuade nor control the emotions of man. And it became intellectually inadequate: it could not anticipate nor explain the tragic movements of history in the twentieth century. Ideologies which exploited the darker passions captured men by appeals unknown to the armory of progressivism.

Doughface progressivism—the faith of the present-day fellow traveler—may be defined briefly as progressivism kept alive by main force in face of all the lessons of modern history. It is this final fatuity of progressivism which has turned it into, if not an accomplice of totalitarianism, at least an accessory before the fact. For its persistent and sentimental optimism has endowed Doughface progressivism with what in the middle of the twentieth century are fatal weaknesses: a weakness for impotence, because progressivism believes that history will make up for human error; a weak-ness for rhetoric, because it believes that man can be reformed by argument; a weakness for eco-nomic fetishism, because it believes that the good in man will be liberated by a change in economic institutions; a weakness for political myth, because Doughface optimism requires somewhere an act of faith in order to survive the contradictions of history.

The weakness of impotence is related to a fear of responsibility—a fear, that is, of making con-crete decisions and being held to account for con-crete consequences. Problems are much simpler when viewed from the office of a liberal weekly than when viewed in terms of what will actu-ally happen when certain ideologically attractive steps are taken. Too often the Doughface really does not want power or responsibility. For him the more subtle sensations of the perfect syllo-gism, the lost cause, the permanent minority, where he can be safe from the exacting job of trying to work out wise policies in an imperfect world. Politics becomes, not a means of getting things done, but an outlet for private grievances and frustrations. The progressive once disciplined by the responsibilities of power is often the most useful of all public servants; but he, alas, ceases to be a progressive and is regarded by all true Doughfaces as a cynical New Dealer or a tired Social Democrat.

Having renounced power, the Doughface seeks compensation in emotion. The pretext for progressive rhetoric is, of course, the idea that man, the creature of reason and benevolence, has only to understand the truth in order to act upon it. But the function of progressive rhetoric is another matter; it is, in [Dwight] Macdonald's phrase, to accomplish "in fantasy what cannot be accomplished in reality." Because politics is for the Doughface a means of accommodating himself to a world he does not like but does not really want to change, he can find ample gratification in words. They appease his twinges of guilt without committing him to very drastic action. Thus the expiatory role of resolutions in progressive meetings. A telegram of protest to a foreign chancellery gives the satisfaction of a job well done and a night's rest well earned. The Doughfaces differ from Mr. Churchill: dreams, they find, are better than facts. Progressive dreams are tinged with a brave purity, a rich sentiment and a noble defiance. But, like most dreams, they are notable for the distortion of facts by desire.

The progressive attitude toward history is sufficiently revealing. The responsible conservative, we have seen, finds in history a profound sense of national continuity which overrides his contemporary fears and trepidations. The Doughface, less humble in his approach, is like the neanderthal conservative, looking at history long and wistfully until it reassembles itself in patterns which support his current vagaries. Mr. [Henry] Wallace and his followers, for example, have proclaimed repeatedly that they are doing no more on behalf of the Russian Revolution than Thomas Jefferson did on behalf of the French: it is their support of social change that exposes them to the same reactionary persecutions as those which harried Jefferson in the nineties. It is quite true that Jefferson was an enthusiast for the French Revolution. But he was too intelligent a man and too profound a believer in human freedom to let his enthusiasm survive the transformation of the Revolution into an aggressive military despotism. Napoleon, Jefferson observed, was "the Attila of the age . . . the ruthless destroyer of ten millions of the human race, whose

thirst for blood appeared unquenchable, the great oppressor of the rights and liberties of the world a cold-blooded, calculating, unprincipled usurper, without a virtue." Mr. Wallace, who restrained his passion for Soviet Russia in its revolutionary days and opposed its recognition as late as 1933, became a great enthusiast for the Soviet Union only after it was embarked on its Napoleonic phase.

In life one must make a choice and accept the consequences; in Doughface fantasy, one can denounce a decision without accepting the consequences of the alternative. Ask a progressive what he thinks of the Mexican War, or of our national policy toward the Indians, and he will probably say that these outbursts of American imperialism are black marks on our history. Ask him whether he then regrets that California, Texas and the West are today part of the United States. And was there perhaps some way of taking lands from the Indians or from Mexico without violating rights in the process? Pushed to it, the progressive probably thinks that there is some solution hidden in the back of his fantasy; but ordinarily he never has to push the question that far back, because he never dreams of facing a question in terms of responsibility for the decision. For him it is sufficient to dissociate himself from the Mexican War so long as he is not required to dissociate himself from the fruits of victory.

Or take the question of the "robber barons." The phrase itself suggests the attitude of disfavor with which the progressive regards the industrialists of the second half of the nineteenth century. The robber baron, of course, used to sally forth from his castle and steal the goods of innocent travelers. His was a thoroughly nonproductive form of economic enterprise. Does even the most unregenerate Doughface consider this to be analogous to the achievements of Andrew Carnegie or John D. Rockefeller? And, to save the nation from the "robber barons," would the Doughface reduce our industrial capacity to the point where it was when the "robber barons" came on the scene? Or has he some other formula for industrialization in a single generation? The fact is, of course, that this nation paid a heavy price for industrialization—a price in political and moral decadence, in the wasteful use of economic resources, in the centralization of economic power. But the price we paid, though perhaps exorbitant, was infinitely less in human terms than the price paid by the people of Russia; and it is not clear that the managers who charged more have done the better job. . . .

The belief that man is perfectible commits the progressive to the endless task of explaining why, in spite of history and in spite of rhetoric, he does not always behave that way. One favorite Doughface answer, borrowed from the Communists, is that contemporary man has been corrupted by the system of private ownership; let us change all this, they say, and our problems will be solved. . . .

But is private ownership the root of all evil? Private property, Reinhold Niebuhr has reminded us, is "not the cause but the instrument of human egotism." It is only one embodiment of the will to power. "By abolishing private property," as Freud puts it, "one deprives the human love of aggression of one of its instruments, a strong one undoubtedly, but assuredly not the strongest." Some social arrangements pander more than others to the human love of aggression; but aggression underlies all social arrangements, whether capitalist or Communist, and it remains a question whether aggression is more checked and controlled by Russian totalitarianism than by American pluralism. In any case, the root remains man.

At the bottom of the set of Doughface illusions is a need for faith. As the gap has widened between the sentimental abstractions of Doughface fantasy and the cruel complexities of life, the need has increased for mythology to take up the slack. One myth, to which the Doughface has clung in the face of experience with the imperturbable ardor of an early Christian, is the mystique of the proletariat. This myth, given its classical form by Marx, himself so characteristically a bourgeois intellectual, states that the action of the working class will overthrow capitalist tyranny and establish by temporary dictatorship a classless society. Its appeal lies partly in the progressive intellectual's sense of guilt over living pleasantly by his skills instead of unpleasantly by his hands, partly in the intellectual's somewhat feminine fascination with the rude and muscular power of the proletariat, partly in the intellectual's desire to compensate for his own sense of alienation by immersing himself in the broad maternal expanse of the masses. Worship of the proletariat becomes a perfect fulfillment for the frustrations of the progressive.

At one time perhaps there was prima facie support for the myth. Before capitalism raised mass living standards, the working classes had a genuinely revolutionary potential. This was visible in Britain and America in the early days of the nineteenth century and in France as late as the Paris Commune. In countries like Spain and Yugoslavia, where industrialization and its benefits have been delayed, the revolutionary potential existed well into the twentieth century. But, contrary to Marx's prediction of increasing proletarian misery, capitalism, once it has had the chance, has vastly increased the wealth and freedom of the ordinary worker. It has reduced the size of the working class and deradicalized the worker.

As a result, workers as a mass have decreasingly the impulses attributed to them by Marxism. They too often believe in patriotism or religion, or read comic strips, go to movies, play slot machines and patronize taxi dance halls. In one way or another, they try to cure their discontent by narcotics rather than by surgery. The general strike is in principle the most potent weapon in the world, but it always remains potent in principle. The last great moment for the general strike was perhaps 1914, when syndicalist agitation had at least kept alive mass revolutionary emotions. But, even had Jaures survived and led the call, the working classes would probably have succumbed to the bugle, the flag and the military parade. Marx recognized that many workers were not Marxists and so invented a classification called the Lumpenproletariat in which were dumped those who did not live up to theory. Lenin recognized this too and so invented a disciplined party which announced itself as the only true representative of the proletariat, reducing non-Communist workers to political non-existence.

Progressives defending their belief in the proletariat sometimes cite the trade-union movement. Yet the trade union has, in fact, surely been the culminating agency in the deradicalization of the masses. As an institution, it is as clearly indigenous to the capitalist system as the corporation itself, and has no real meaning apart from that system. Thus trade unions, while giving the working masses a sense of having an organization of their own, insure that the goals of this organization are compatible with capitalism. And, as unions become more powerful, they increase their vested interests in the existing order. Labor leadership acquires satisfactions in terms of prestige and power. Only acute mass disaffection could radicalize the union leadership; and, up to this point, at least, the increase in capitalist productivity has enabled the labor movement to bring the rank-and-file steady benefits in the shape of higher wages, reduced hours and better working conditions.

What operational meaning, indeed, does the conception of the proletariat as an agency of change have? Can it mean anything more than the proletariat as a pool of discontent from which leaders can draw recruits for a variety of programs? The technical necessity for organization, as Robert Michel showed long ago, sets in motion an inevitable tendency toward oligarchy. The leadership after a time is bound to have separate interests from the rank-and-file. A working-class organization will soon stand, not for the working class, but for the working class plus the organization's own instincts for survival plus the special bureaucratic interests of the organization's top leadership. No loopholes have yet been discovered in the iron law of oligarchy.

For these various reasons, the mystique of the working class has faded somewhat since the First War. In its place has arisen a new mystique, more radiant and palpable, and exercising the same fascinations of power and guilt: the mystique of the USSR. Each success of the Soviet Union has conferred new delights on those possessed of the need for prostration and frightened of the responsibilities of decision. In a world which makes very little sense, these emotions are natural enough. But surrender to them destroys the capacity for clear intellectual leadership which ought to be the progressive's function in the world. In an exact sense, Soviet Russia has become the opiate of the progressives.

"The facts of life do not penetrate to the sphere in which our beliefs are cherished," writes Proust; "as it was not they that engendered those beliefs, so they are powerless to destroy them; they can aim at them continual blows of contradiction and disproof without weakening them; and an avalanche of miseries and maladies coming, one after another, without interruption into the bosom of a family, will not make it lose faith in either the clemency of its God or the capacity of its physician." The Soviet Union can do very little any more to disenchant its believers; it has done about everything in the book already. I remember in the summer of 1939 asking a fellow traveler what the USSR could possibly do which would make him lose faith. He said, "Sign a pact with Hitler." But two months later he had absorbed the pact with Hitler; and so the hunger to believe, the anxiety and the guilt, continue to triumph over the evidence.

Conservatism in its crisis of despair turns to fascism: so progressivism in its crisis of despair turns to Communism. Each in a sober mood has a great contribution to make to free society: the conservative in his emphasis on law and liberty, the progressive in his emphasis on mass welfare. But neither is capable of saving free society. Both, faced by problems they cannot understand and fear to meet, tend to compound their own failure by delivering free society to its totalitarian foe.

NSC 68: "UNITED STATES OBJECTIVES AND PROGRAMS FOR NATIONAL SECURITY" (1950)

President Truman initially resisted pressures to create a large "peacetime" military establishment as a part of US Cold War strategy. As long as the United States retained a monopoly in nuclear weapons, the logic of maintaining relatively modest conventional forces prevailed. In August 1949, however, the Soviets detonated a nuclear device, ending the American monopoly. In October, communist revolutionaries seized power in China, hitherto seen as a member of the "Free World." These twin setbacks prompted a full-scale reevaluation of US national security strategy. Although that evaluation, conducted under the leadership of State Department official Paul Nitze (1907–2004) affirmed the basic logic of containment, it argued for greatly expanding US military capabilities. President Truman hesitated to endorse the conclusions of this study known as NSC-68. The onset of the Korean War in the summer of 1950 prompted him to approve it.

ANALYSIS

I. Background of the Present Crisis

Within the past thirty-five years the world has experienced two global wars of tremendous violence. It has witnessed two revolutions—the Russian and the Chinese—of extreme scope and intensity. It has also seen the collapse of five empires—the Ottoman, the Austro-Hungarian, German, Italian, and Japanese—and the drastic decline of two major imperial systems, the British and the French. During the span of one generation, the international distribution of power has been fundamentally altered. For several centuries it had proved impossible for any one nation to gain such preponderant strength that a coalition of other nations could not in time face it with greater strength. The international scene was marked by recurring periods of violence and war, but a system of sovereign and independent states was maintained, over which no state was able to achieve hegemony.

Two complex sets of factors have now basically altered this historic distribution of power. First, the defeat of Germany and Japan and the decline of the British and French Empires have interacted with the development of the United States and the Soviet Union in such a way that power increasingly gravitated to these two centers. Second, the Soviet Union, unlike previous aspirants to hegemony, is animated by a new fanatic faith, antithetical to our own, and seeks to impose its absolute authority over the rest of the world. Conflict has, therefore, become endemic and is waged, on the part of the Soviet Union, by violent or non-violent methods in accordance with the dictates of expediency. With the development of increasingly terrifying weapons of mass destruction, every individual faces the ever-present possibility of annihilation should the conflict enter the phase of total war.

On the one hand, the people of the world yearn for relief from the anxiety arising from the risk of atomic war. On the other hand, any substantial further extension of the area under the domination of the Kremlin would raise the possibility that no coalition adequate to confront the Kremlin with greater strength could be assembled. It is in this context that this Republic and its citizens in the ascendancy of their strength stand in their deepest peril.

The issues that face us are momentous, involving the fulfillment or destruction not only of this Republic but of civilization itself. They are issues which will not await our deliberations. With conscience and resolution this Government and the people it represents must now take new and fateful decisions.

II. Fundamental Purpose of the United States

The fundamental purpose of the United States is laid down in the Preamble to the Constitution: ". . . to form a more perfect Union, establish justice, insure domestic Tranquility, provide for the common defence, promote the general Welfare, and secure the Blessings of Liberty to ourselves and our Posterity." In essence, the fundamental purpose is to assure the integrity and vitality of our free society, which is founded upon the dignity and worth of the individual. . . .

III. Fundamental Design of the Kremlin

The fundamental design of those who control the Soviet Union and the international communist movement is to retain and solidify their absolute power, first in the Soviet Union and second in the areas now under their control. In the minds of the Soviet leaders, however, achievement of this design requires the dynamic extension of their authority and the ultimate elimination of any effective opposition to their authority.

The design, therefore, calls for the complete subversion or forcible destruction of the machinery of government and structure of society in the countries of the non-Soviet world and their replacement by an apparatus and structure subservient to and controlled from the Kremlin. To that end Soviet efforts are now directed toward the domination of the Eurasian land mass. The United States, as the principal center of power in the non-Soviet world and the bulwark of opposition to Soviet expansion, is the principal enemy whose integrity and vitality must be subverted or destroyed by one means or another if the Kremlin is to achieve its fundamental design.

IV. The Underlying Conflict in the Realm of ideas and Values between the U.S. Purpose and the Kremlin Design

A. Nature of conflict

The Kremlin regards the United States as the only major threat to the conflict between idea of slavery under the grim oligarchy of the Kremlin, which has come to a crisis with the polarization of power described in Section I, and the exclusive posses-sion of atomic weapons by the two protagonists. The idea of freedom, moreover, is peculiarly and intolerably subversive of the idea of slavery. But the converse is not true. The implacable purpose of the slave state to eliminate the challenge of freedom has placed the two great powers at opposite poles. It is this fact which gives the present polarization of power the quality of crisis.

The free society values the individual as an end in himself, requiring of him only that measure of self-discipline and self-restraint which make the rights of each individual compatible with the rights of every other individual. The freedom of the individual has as its counterpart, therefore, the negative responsibility of the individual not to exercise his freedom in ways inconsistent with the freedom of other individuals and the positive responsibility to make constructive use of his free-dom in the building of a just society.

From this idea of freedom with responsibil-ity derives the marvelous diversity, the deep tol-erance, the lawfulness of the free society. This is the explanation of the strength of free men. It constitutes the integrity and the vitality of a free and democratic system. The free society attempts to create and maintain an environment in which every individual has the opportunity to realize his creative powers. It also explains why the free soci-ety tolerates those within it who would use their freedom to destroy it. By the same token, in rela-tions between nations, the prime reliance of the free society is on the strength and appeal of its idea, and it feels no compulsion sooner or later to bring all societies into conformity with it.

For the free society does not fear, it welcomes, diversity. It derives its strength from its hospitality even to antipathetic ideas. It is a market for free trade in ideas, secure in its faith that free men will take the best wares, and grow to a fuller and bet-ter realization of their powers in exercising their choice.

The idea of freedom is the most contagious idea in history, more contagious than the idea of submission to authority. For the breadth of free-dom cannot be tolerated in a society which has come under the domination of an individual or group of individuals with a will to absolute power. Where the despot holds absolute power—the absolute power of the absolutely powerful will—all

other wills must be subjugated in an act of willing submission, a degradation willed by the individ-ual upon himself under the compulsion of a per-verted faith. It is the first article of this faith that he finds and can only find the meaning of his exist-ence in serving the ends of the system. The system becomes God, and submission to the will of God becomes submission to the will of the system. It is not enough to yield outwardly to the system—even Gandhian non-violence is not acceptable—for the spirit of resistance and the devotion to a higher authority might then remain, and the indi-vidual would not be wholly submissive.

The same compulsion which demands total power over all men within the Soviet state with-out a single exception, demands total power over all Communist Parties and all states under Soviet domination. Thus Stalin has said that the theory and tactics of Leninism as expounded by the Bolshevik party are mandatory for the proletarian parties of all countries. A true internationalist is defined as one who unhesitatingly upholds the position of the Soviet Union and in the satellite states true patriot-ism is love of the Soviet Union. By the same token the "peace policy" of the Soviet Union, described at a Party Congress as "a more advantageous form of fighting capitalism," is a device to divide and immobilize the non-Communist world, and the peace the Soviet Union seeks is the peace of total conformity to Soviet policy.

The antipathy of slavery to freedom explains the iron curtain, the isolation, the autarchy of the society whose end is absolute power. The exist-ence and persistence of the idea of freedom is a permanent and continuous threat to the founda-tion of the slave society; and it therefore regards as intolerable the long continued existence of freedom in the world. What is new, what makes the continuing crisis, is the polarization of power which now inescapably confronts the slave society with the free.

The assault on free institutions is world-wide now, and in the context of the present polariza-tion of power a defeat of free institutions any-where is a defeat everywhere. . . .

Thus unwillingly our free society finds itself mortally challenged by the Soviet system. No other value system is so wholly irreconcilable with ours, so implacable in its purpose to destroy ours, so capable of turning to its own uses the most dangerous and divisive trends in our own society, no other so skillfully and powerfully evokes the elements of irrationality in human nature everywhere, and no other has the support of a great and growing center of military power.

B. Objectives

The objectives of a free society are determined by its fundamental values and by the necessity for maintaining the material environment in which they flourish. Logically and in fact, therefore, the Kremlin's challenge to the United States is directed not only to our values but to our physical capacity to protect their environment. It is a challenge which encompasses both peace and war and our objectives in peace and war must take account of it.

1. Thus we must make ourselves strong, both in the way in which we affirm our values in the conduct of our national life, and in the development of our military and economic strength.
2. We must lead in building a successfully functioning political and economic system in the free world. It is only by practical affirmation, abroad as well as at home, of our essential values, that we can preserve our own integrity, in which lies the real frustration of the Kremlin design.
3. But beyond thus affirming our values our policy and actions must be such as to foster a fundamental change in the nature of the Soviet system, a change toward which the frustration of the design is the first and perhaps the most important step. Clearly it will not only be less costly but more effective if this change occurs to a maximum extent as a result of internal forces in Soviet society.

In a shrinking world, which now faces the threat of atomic warfare, it is not an adequate objective merely to seek to check the Kremlin design, for the absence of order among nations is becoming less and less tolerable. This fact imposes on us, in our own interests, the responsibility of world leadership. It demands that we make the attempt, and accept the risks inherent in it, to bring about order and justice by means consistent with the principles of freedom and democracy. We should limit our requirement of the Soviet Union to its participation with other nations on the basis

of equality and respect for the rights of others. Subject to this requirement, we must with our allies and the former subject peoples seek to create a world society based on the principle of consent. . . .

C. Means

The free society is limited in its choice of means to achieve its ends.

Compulsion is the negation of freedom, except when it is used to enforce the rights common to all. The resort to force, internally or externally, is therefore a last resort for a free society. . . .

The resort to force, to compulsion, to the imposition of its will is therefore a difficult and dangerous act for a free society, which is warranted only in the face of even greater dangers. The necessity of the act must be clear and compelling; the act must commend itself to the overwhelming majority as an inescapable exception to the basic idea of freedom; or the regenerative capacity of free men after the act has been performed will be endangered.

The Kremlin is able to select whatever means are expedient in seeking to carry out its fundamental design. Thus it can make the best of several possible worlds, conducting the struggle on those levels where it considers it profitable and enjoying the benefits of a pseudo-peace on those levels where it is not ready for a contest. At the ideological or psychological level, in the struggle for men's minds, the conflict is worldwide. At the political and economic level, within states and in the relations between states, the struggle for power is being intensified. And at the military level, the Kremlin has thus far been careful not to commit a technical breach of the peace, although using its vast forces to intimidate its neighbors, and to support an aggressive foreign policy, and not hesitating through its agents to resort to arms in favorable circumstances. The attempt to carry out its fundamental design is being pressed, therefore, with all means which are believed expedient in the present situation, and the Kremlin has inextricably engaged us in the conflict between its design and our purpose.

We have no such freedom of choice, and least of all in the use of force. Resort to war is not only a last resort for a free society, but it is also an act which cannot definitively end the fundamental conflict in the realm of ideas. The idea of slavery can only be overcome by the timely and persistent demonstration of the superiority of the idea of freedom. Military victory alone would only partially and perhaps only temporarily affect the fundamental conflict, for although the ability of the Kremlin to threaten our security might be for a time destroyed, the resurgence of totalitarian forces and the re-establishment of the Soviet system or its equivalent would not be long delayed unless great progress were made in the fundamental conflict.

Practical and ideological considerations therefore both impel us to the conclusion that we have no choice but to demonstrate the superiority of the idea of freedom by its constructive application, and to attempt to change the world situation by means short of war in such a way as to frustrate the Kremlin design and hasten the decay of the Soviet system.

For us the role of military power is to serve the national purpose by deterring an attack upon us while we seek by other means to create an environment in which our free society can flourish, and by fighting, if necessary, to defend the integrity and vitality of our free society and to defeat any aggressor. The Kremlin uses Soviet military power to back up and serve the Kremlin design. It does not hesitate to use military force aggressively if that course is expedient in the achievement of its design. The differences between our fundamental purpose and the Kremlin design, therefore, are reflected in our respective attitudes toward and use of military force.

Our free society, confronted by a threat to its basic values, naturally will take such action, including the use of military force, as may be required to protect those values. The integrity of our system will not be jeopardized by any measures, covert or overt, violent or non-violent, which serve the purposes of frustrating the Kremlin design, nor does the necessity for conducting ourselves so as to affirm our values in actions as well as words forbid such measures, provided only they are appropriately calculated to that end and are not so excessive or misdirected as to make us enemies of the people instead of the evil men who have enslaved them.

But if war comes, what is the role of force? Unless we so use it that the Russian people can perceive that our effort is directed against the regime and its power for aggression, and not against their own interests, we will unite the regime and the people in the kind of last ditch fight in which no underlying problems are solved, new ones are created, and where our basic principles are obscured and compromised. If we do not in the application of force demonstrate the nature of our objectives we will, in fact, have compromised from the outset our fundamental purpose. . . .

V. Soviet Intentions and Capabilities
A. Political and psychological

The Kremlin's design for world domination begins at home. The first concern of a despotic oligarchy is that the local base of its power and authority be secure. . . .

Being a totalitarian dictatorship, the Kremlin's objectives in these policies is the total subjective submission of the peoples now under its control. The concentration camp is the prototype of the society which these policies are designed to achieve, a society in which the personality of the individual is so broken and perverted that he participates affirmatively in his own degradation.

The Kremlin's policy toward areas not under its control is the elimination of resistance to its will and the extension of its influence and control. It is driven to follow this policy because it cannot, for the reasons set forth in Chapter IV, tolerate the existence of free societies; to the Kremlin the most mild and inoffensive free society is an affront, a challenge and a subversive influence. Given the nature of the Kremlin, and the evidence at hand, it seems clear that the ends toward which this policy is directed are the same as those where its control has already been established.

The means employed by the Kremlin in pursuit of this policy are limited only by considerations of expediency. Doctrine is not a limiting factor; rather it dictates the employment of violence, subversion, and deceit, and rejects moral considerations. In any event, the Kremlin's conviction of its own infallibility has made its devotion to theory so subjective that past or present pronouncements as to doctrine offer no reliable guide to future actions. The only apparent restraints on resort to war are, therefore, calculations of practicality.

With particular reference to the United States, the Kremlin's strategic and tactical policy is affected by its estimate that we are not only the greatest immediate obstacle which stands between it and world domination, we are also the only power which could release forces in the free and Soviet worlds which could destroy it. The Kremlin's policy toward us is consequently animated by a peculiarly virulent blend of hatred and fear. Its strategy has been one of attempting to undermine the complex of forces, in this country and in the rest of the free world, on which our power is based. In this it has both adhered to doctrine and followed the sound principle of seeking maximum results with minimum risks and commitments. The present application of this strategy is a new form of expression for traditional Russian caution. However, there is no justification in Soviet theory or practice for predicting that, should the Kremlin become convinced that it could cause our downfall by one conclusive blow, it would not seek that solution.

In considering the capabilities of the Soviet world, it is of prime importance to remember that, in contrast to ours, they are being drawn upon close to the maximum possible extent. Also in contrast to us, the Soviet world can do more with less—it has a lower standard of living, its economy requires less to keep it functioning, and its military machine operates effectively with less elaborate equipment and organization.

The capabilities of the Soviet world are being exploited to the full because the Kremlin is inescapably militant. It is inescapably militant because it possesses and is possessed by a world-wide revolutionary movement, because it is the inheritor of Russian imperialism, and because it is a totalitarian dictatorship. Persistent crisis, conflict, and expansion are the essence of the Kremlin's militancy. This dynamism serves to intensify all Soviet capabilities.

Two enormous organizations, the Communist Party and the secret police, are an outstanding source of strength to the Kremlin. In the Party, it has an apparatus designed to impose at home an ideological uniformity among its people and to act abroad as an instrument of propaganda, subversion and espionage. In its police apparatus, it has a domestic repressive instrument guaranteeing under present circumstances the continued security of the Kremlin. The demonstrated capabilities of these two basic organizations, operating openly or in disguise, in mass or through single agents, is unparalleled in history. The party, the police and the conspicuous might of the Soviet military machine together tend to create an overall impression of irresistible Soviet power among many peoples of the free world.

The ideological pretensions of the Kremlin are another great source of strength. Its identification of the Soviet system with communism, its peace campaigns and its championing of colonial peoples may be viewed with apathy, if not cynicism, by the oppressed totalitariat of the Soviet world, but in the free world these ideas find favorable responses in vulnerable segments of society. . . .

Finally, there is a category of capabilities, strictly speaking neither institutional nor ideological, which should be taken into consideration. The extraordinary flexibility of Soviet tactics is certainly a strength. It derives from the utterly amoral and opportunistic conduct of Soviet policy. Combining this quality with the elements of secrecy, the Kremlin possesses a formidable capacity to act with the widest tactical latitude, with stealth, and with speed.

The greatest vulnerability of the Kremlin lies in the basic nature of its relations with the Soviet people.

That relationship is characterized by universal suspicion, fear, and denunciation. It is a relationship in which the Kremlin relies, not only for its power but its very survival, on intricately devised mechanisms of coercion. The Soviet monolith is held together by the iron curtain around it and the iron bars within it, not by any force of natural cohesion. These artificial mechanisms of unity have never been intelligently challenged by a strong outside force. The full measure of their vulnerability is therefore not yet evident.

The Kremlin's relations with its satellites and their peoples is likewise a vulnerability. Nationalism still remains the most potent emotional-political force. The well-known ills of colonialism are compounded, however, by the excessive demands of the Kremlin that its satellites accept not only the imperial authority of Moscow but that they believe in and proclaim the ideological primacy and infallibility of the Kremlin.

These excessive requirements can be made good only through extreme coercion. The result is that if a satellite feels able to effect its independence of the Kremlin, as Tito was able to do, it is likely to break away.

In short, Soviet ideas and practices run counter to the best and potentially the strongest instincts of men, and deny their most fundamental aspirations. Against an adversary which effectively affirmed the constructive and hopeful instincts of men and was capable of fulfilling their fundamental aspirations, the Soviet system might prove to be fatally weak. . . .

The Kremlin is, of course, aware of these weaknesses. It must know that in the present world situation they are of secondary significance. So long as the Kremlin retains the initiative, so long as it can keep on the offensive unchallenged by clearly superior counter-force—spiritual as well as material—its vulnerabilities are largely inoperative and even concealed by its successes. The Kremlin has not yet been given real reason to fear and be diverted by the rot within its system.

B. Economic

The Kremlin has no economic intentions unrelated to its overall policies. Economics in the Soviet world is not an end in itself. The Kremlin's policy, in so far as it has to do with economics, is to utilize economic processes to contribute to the overall strength, particularly the war-making capacity of the Soviet system. The material welfare of the totalitariat is severely subordinated to the interest of the system. . . .

The USSR today is on a near maximum production basis. No matter what efforts Moscow might make, only a relatively slight change in the rate of increase in overall production could be brought about. In the U.S., on the other hand, a very rapid absolute expansion could be realized. The fact remains, however, that so long as the Soviet Union is virtually mobilized, and the United States has scarcely begun to summon up its forces, the greater capabilities of the U.S. are to that extent inoperative in the struggle for power. Moreover, as the Soviet attainment of an atomic capability has demonstrated, the totalitarian state, at least in time of peace, can focus its efforts on any given project far more readily than the democratic state. . . .

C. Military

The Soviet Union is developing the military capacity to support its design for world domination. The Soviet Union actually possesses armed forces far in excess of those necessary to defend its national territory. These armed forces are probably not yet considered by the Soviet Union to be sufficient to initiate a war which would involve the United States. This excessive strength, coupled now with an atomic capability, provides the Soviet Union with great coercive power for use in time of peace in furtherance of its objectives and serves as a deterrent to the victims of its aggression from taking any action in opposition to its tactics which would risk war.

Should a major war occur in 1950 the Soviet Union and its satellites are considered by the Joint Chiefs of Staff to be in a sufficiently advanced state of preparation immediately to undertake and carry out the following campaigns.

a. To overrun Western Europe, with the possible exception of the Iberian and Scandinavian Peninsulas; to drive toward the oil-bearing areas of the Near and Middle East; and to consolidate Communist gains in the Far East;

b. To launch air attacks against the British Isles and air and sea attacks against the lines of communications of the Western Powers in the Atlantic and the Pacific;

c. To attack selected targets with atomic weapons, now including the likelihood of such attacks against targets in Alaska, Canada, and the United States. Alternatively, this capability, coupled with other actions open to the Soviet Union, might deny the United Kingdom as an effective base of operations for allied forces. It also should be possible for the Soviet Union to prevent any allied "Normandy" type amphibious operations intended to force a reentry into the continent of Europe. . . .

The Soviet Union now has aircraft able to deliver the atomic bomb. Our Intelligence estimates assign to the Soviet Union an atomic bomber capability already in excess of that needed to deliver available bombs. We have at present no evaluated estimate regarding the Soviet accuracy of delivery on target. It is believed that the Soviets cannot deliver their bombs on target with a degree of accuracy comparable to ours, but a planning estimate might well place it at 40-60 percent of bombs sorted. For planning purposes, therefore, the date the Soviets possess an atomic stockpile of 200 bombs would be a critical date for the United States, for the delivery of 100 atomic bombs on targets in the United States would seriously damage this country.

At the time the Soviet Union has a substantial atomic stockpile and if it is assumed that it will strike a strong surprise blow and if it is assumed further that its atomic attacks will be met with no more effective defense opposition than the United States and its allies have programmed, results of those attacks could include:

a. Laying waste to the British Isles and thus depriving the Western Powers of their use as a base;
b. Destruction of the vital centers and of the communications of Western Europe, thus precluding effective defense by the Western Powers; and
c. Delivering devastating attacks on certain vital centers of the United States and Canada.

The possession by the Soviet Union of a thermonuclear capability in addition to this substantial atomic stockpile would result in tremendously increased damage.

During this decade, the defensive capabilities of the Soviet Union will probably be strengthened, particularly by the development and use of modem aircraft, aircraft warning and communications devices, and defensive guided missiles.

VI. U.S. Intentions and Capabilities—Actual and Potential

A. Political and psychological

Our overall policy at the present time may be described as one designed to foster a world environment in which the American system can survive and flourish. It therefore rejects the concept of isolation and affirms the necessity of our positive participation in the world community.

This broad intention embraces two subsidiary policies. One is a policy which we would probably pursue even if there were no Soviet threat. It is a policy of attempting to develop a healthy international community. The other is the policy of "containing" the Soviet system. These two policies are closely interrelated and interact on one

another. Nevertheless, the distinction between them is basically valid and contributes to a clearer understanding of what we are trying to do.

The policy of striving to develop a healthy international community is the long-term constructive effort which we are engaged in. It was this policy which gave rise to our vigorous sponsorship of the United Nations. It is of course the principal reason for our long continuing endeavors to create and now develop the Inter-American system. It, as much as containment, underlay our efforts to rehabilitate Western Europe. Most of our international economic activities can likewise be explained in terms of this policy. . . .

As for the policy of "containment," it is one which seeks by all means short of war to (1) block further expansion of Soviet power, (2) expose the falsities of Soviet pretensions, (3) induce a retraction of the Kremlin's control and influence, and (4) in general, so foster the seeds of destruction within the Soviet system that the Kremlin is brought at least to the point of modifying its behavior to conform to generally accepted international standards.

It was and continues to be cardinal in this policy that we possess superior overall power in ourselves or in dependable combination with other likeminded nations. One of the most important ingredients of power is military strength. In the concept of "containment," the maintenance of a strong military posture is deemed to be essential for two reasons: (1) as an ultimate guarantee of our national security and (2) as an indispensable backdrop to the conduct of the policy of "containment." Without superior aggregate military strength, in being and readily mobilizable, a policy of "containment"—which is in effect a policy of calculated and gradual coercion—is no more than a policy of bluff. . . .

In "containment" it is desirable to exert pressure in a fashion which will avoid so far as possible directly challenging Soviet prestige, to keep open the possibility for the USSR to retreat before pressure with a minimum loss of face and to secure political advantage from the failure of the Kremlin to yield or take advantage of the openings we leave it.

We have failed to implement adequately these two fundamental aspects of "containment." In the face of obviously mounting Soviet military strength ours has declined relatively. Partly as a byproduct of this, but also for other reasons, we now find ourselves at a diplomatic impasse with the Soviet Union, with the Kremlin growing bolder, with both of us holding on grimly to what we have, and with ourselves facing difficult decisions. . . .

The vast majority of Americans are confident that the system of values which animates our society—the principles of freedom, tolerance, the importance of the individual, and the supremacy of reason over will—are valid and more vital than the ideology which is the fuel of Soviet dynamism. Translated into terms relevant to the lives of other peoples—our system of values can become perhaps a powerful appeal to millions who now seek or find in authoritarianism a refuge from anxieties, bafflement, and insecurity.

Essentially, our democracy also possesses a unique degree of unity. Our society is fundamentally more cohesive than the Soviet system, the solidarity of which is artificially created through force, fear, and favor. This means that expressions of national consensus in our society are soundly and solidly based. It means that the possibility of revolution in this country is fundamentally less than that in the Soviet system.

These capabilities within us constitute a great potential force in our international relations. The potential within us of bearing witness to the values by which we live holds promise for a dynamic manifestation to the rest of the world of the vitality of our system. The essential tolerance of our world outlook, our generous and constructive impulses, and the absence of covetousness in our international relations are assets of potentially enormous influence. . . .

The democratic way is harder than the authoritarian way because, in seeking to protect and fulfill the individual, it demands of him understanding, judgment, and positive participation in the increasingly complex and exacting problems of the modern world. It demands that he exercise discrimination: that while pursuing through free inquiry the search for truth he knows when he should commit an act of faith; that he distinguish between the necessity for tolerance and the necessity for just suppression. A free society is vulnerable in that it is easy for people to lapse into excesses—the excesses of a permanently open mind wishfully waiting for evidence that evil design may become noble purpose, the excess of faith becoming prejudice, the excess of tolerance degenerating into indulgence of conspiracy and the excess of resorting to suppression when more moderate measures are not only more appropriate but more effective.

In coping with dictatorial governments acting in secrecy and with speed, we are also vulnerable in that the democratic process necessarily operates in the open and at a deliberate tempo. Weaknesses in our situation are readily apparent and subject to immediate exploitation. This Government therefore cannot afford in the face of the totalitarian challenge to operate on a narrow margin of strength. A democracy can compensate for its natural vulnerability only if it maintains clearly superior overall power in its most inclusive sense.

The very virtues of our system likewise handicap us in certain respects in our relations with our allies. While it is a general source of strength to us that our relations with our allies are conducted on a basis of persuasion and consent rather than compulsion and capitulation, it is also evident that dissent among us can become a vulnerability. Sometimes the dissent has its principal roots abroad in situations about which we can do nothing. Sometimes it arises largely out of certain weaknesses within ourselves, about which we can do something—our native impetuosity and a tendency to expect too much from people widely divergent from us.

The full capabilities of the rest of the free world are a potential increment to our own capabilities. It may even be said that the capabilities of the Soviet world, specifically the capabilities of the masses who have nothing to lose but their Soviet chains, are a potential which can be enlisted on our side.

Like our own capabilities, those of the rest of the free world exceed the capabilities of the Soviet system. Like our own they are far from being effectively mobilized and employed in the struggle against the Kremlin design. This is so because the rest of the free world lacks a sense of unity, confidence, and common purpose. This is true in even the most homogeneous and advanced segment of the free world—Western Europe.

As we ourselves demonstrate power, confidence, and a sense of moral and political direction, so those same qualities will be evoked in Western Europe. In such a situation, we may also anticipate a general improvement in the political tone in Latin America, Asia, and Africa and the real beginnings of awakening among the Soviet totalitariat.

In the absence of affirmative decision on our part, the rest of the free world is almost certain to become demoralized. Our friends will become more than a liability to us; they can eventually become a positive increment to Soviet power.

In sum, the capabilities of our allies are, in an important sense, a function of our own. An affirmative decision to summon up the potential within ourselves would evoke the potential strength within others and add it to our own.

B. Economic

1. *Capabilities.* In contrast to the war economy of the Soviet world . . . , the American economy (and the economy of the free world as a whole) is at present directed to the provision of rising standards of living. The military budget of the United States represents 6 to 7 percent of its gross national product (as against 13.8 percent for the Soviet Union). Our North Atlantic Treaty allies devoted 4.8 percent of their national product to military purposes in 1949.

This difference in emphasis between the two economies means that the readiness of the free world to support a war effort is tending to decline relative to that of the Soviet Union. There is little direct investment in production facilities for military end-products and in dispersal. There are relatively few men receiving military training and a relatively low rate of production of weapons. However, given time to convert to a war effort, the capabilities of the United States economy and also of the Western European economy would be tremendous. In the light of Soviet military capabilities, a question which may be of decisive importance in the event of war is the question whether there will be time to mobilize our superior human and material resources for a war effort. . . .

The capability of the American economy to support a build-up of economic and military strength at home and to assist a build-up abroad is limited not, as in the case of the Soviet Union, so much by the ability to produce as by the decision on the proper allocation of resources to this and other purposes. Even Western Europe could afford to assign a substantially larger proportion of its resources to defense, if the necessary foundation in public understanding and will could be laid, and if the assistance needed to meet its dollar deficit were provided. . . .

The Soviet Union is now allocating nearly 40 percent of its gross available resources to military purposes and investment, much of which is in war-supporting industries. It is estimated that even in an emergency the Soviet Union could not increase this proportion to much more than 50 percent, or by one-fourth. The United States, on the other hand, is allocating only about 20 percent of its resources to defense and investment (or 22 percent including foreign assistance), and little of its investment outlays are directed to war-supporting industries. In an emergency the United States could allocate more than 50 percent of its resources to military purposes and foreign assistance, or five to six times as much as at present. . . .

2. *Intentions.* Foreign economic policy is a major instrument in the conduct of United States foreign relations. It is an instrument which can powerfully influence the world environment in ways favorable to the security and welfare of this country. It is also an instrument which, if unwisely formulated and employed, can do actual harm to our national interests. It is an instrument uniquely suited to our capabilities, provided we have the tenacity of purpose and the understanding requisite to a realization of its potentials. Finally, it is an instrument peculiarly appropriate to the cold war.

The preceding analysis has indicated that an essential element in a program to frustrate the Kremlin design is the development of a successfully functioning system among the free nations. It is clear that economic conditions are among the fundamental determinants of the will and the strength to resist subversion and aggression.

United States foreign economic policy has been designed to assist in the building of such a system and such conditions in the free world. . . .

In both their short and long term aspects, these policies and programs are directed to the strengthening of the free world and therefore to the frustration of the Kremlin design. Despite certain inadequacies and inconsistencies, which are now being studied in connection with the problem of the United States balance of payments, the United States has generally pursued a foreign economic policy which has powerfully supported its overall objectives. The question must nevertheless be asked whether current and currently projected programs will adequately support this policy in the future, in terms both of need and urgency. . . .

Several conclusions seem to emerge. First, the Soviet Union is widening the gap between its preparedness for war and the unpreparedness of the free world for war. It is devoting a far greater *proportion* of its resources to military purposes than are the free nations and, in significant components of military power, a greater *absolute* quantity of resources. Second, the Communist success in China, taken with the politico-economic situation in the rest of South and South-East Asia, provides a springboard for a further incursion in this troubled area. Although Communist China faces serious economic problems which may impose some strains on the Soviet economy, it is probable that the social and economic problems faced by the free nations in this area present more than offsetting opportunities for Communist expansion. Third, the Soviet Union holds positions in Europe which, if it maneuvers skillfully, could be used to do great damage to the Western European economy and to the maintenance of the Western orientation of certain countries, particularly Germany and Austria. Fourth, despite (and in part because of) the Titoist defection, the Soviet Union has accelerated its efforts to integrate satellite economy with its own and to increase the degree of autarchy within the areas under its control.

Fifth, meanwhile, Western Europe, with American (and Canadian) assistance, has achieved a record level of production. However, it faces the prospect of a rapid tapering off of American assistance without the possibility of achieving, by its own efforts, a satisfactory equilibrium with the dollar area. It has also made very little progress toward "economic integration," which would in the long run tend to improve its productivity and to provide an economic environment conducive to political stability. . . .

Sixth, throughout Asia the stability of the present moderate governments, which are more in sympathy with our purposes than any probable successor regimes would be, is doubtful. The problem is only in part an economic one. Assistance in economic development is important as a means of holding out to the peoples of Asia some prospect of improvement in standards of living under their present governments. But probably more important are a strengthening of central institutions, an improvement in administration, and generally a development of an economic and social structure within which the peoples of Asia can make more effective use of their great human and material resources.

Seventh, and perhaps most important, there are indications of a let-down of United States efforts under the pressure of the domestic budgetary situation, disillusion resulting from excessively optimistic expectations about the duration and results of our assistance programs, and doubts about the wisdom of continuing to strengthen the free nations as against preparedness measures in light of the intensity of the cold war.

Eighth, there are grounds for predicting that the United States and other free nations will within a period of a few years at most experience a decline in economic activity of serious proportions unless more positive governmental programs are developed than are now available.

In short, as we look into the future, the programs now planned will not meet the requirements of the free nations. The difficulty does not lie so much in the inadequacy or misdirection of policy as in the inadequacy of planned programs, in terms of timing or impact, to achieve our objectives. . . .

C. Military

The United States now possesses the greatest military potential of any single nation in the world. The military weaknesses of the United States vis-à-vis the Soviet Union, however, include its numerical inferiority in forces in being and in total manpower. Coupled with the inferiority of forces in being, the United States also lacks tenable positions from which to employ its forces in event of war and munitions power in being and readily available.

It is true that the United States armed forces are now stronger than ever before in other times of apparent peace; it is also true that there exists a sharp disparity between our actual military strength and our commitments. The relationship of our strength to our present commitments, however, is not alone the governing factor. The world situation, as well as commitments, should govern; hence, our military strength more properly should be related to the world situation confronting us. When our military strength is related to the world situation and balanced against the likely exigencies of such a situation, it is clear that our military strength is becoming dangerously inadequate. . . .

VII. *Present Risks*
A. **General**

It is apparent from the preceding sections that the integrity and vitality of our system is in greater jeopardy than ever before in our history. Even if there were no Soviet Union we would face the great problem of the free society, accentuated many fold in this industrial age, of reconciling order, security, the need for participation, with the requirement of freedom. We would face the fact that in a shrinking world the absence of order among nations is becoming less and less tolerable. . . .

B. **Specific**

It is quite clear from Soviet theory and practice that the Kremlin seeks to bring the free world under its dominion by the methods of the cold war. The preferred technique is to subvert by infiltration and intimidation. Every institution of our society is an instrument which it is sought to stultify and turn against our purposes. Those that touch most closely our material and moral strength are obviously the prime targets, labor unions, civic enterprises, schools, churches, and all media for influencing opinion. The effort is not so much to make them serve obvious Soviet ends as to prevent them from serving our ends, and thus to make them sources of confusion in our economy, our culture, and our body politic. The doubts and diversities that in terms of our values are part of the merit of a free system, the weaknesses and the problems that are peculiar to it, the rights and privileges that free men enjoy, and the disorganization and destruction left in the wake of the last attack on our freedoms, all are but opportunities for the Kremlin to do its evil work. . . .

Since everything that gives us or others respect for our institutions is a suitable object for attack, it also fits the Kremlin's design that where, with impunity, we can be insulted and made to suffer indignity the opportunity shall not be missed, particularly in any context which can be used to cast dishonor on our country, our system, our motives, or our methods. Thus the means by which we sought to restore our own economic health in the '30's, and now seek to restore that of the free world, come equally under attack. The military aid by which we sought to help the free world was frantically denounced by the Communists in the early days of the last war, and of course our present efforts to develop adequate military strength for ourselves and our allies are equally denounced.

At the same time the Soviet Union is seeking to create overwhelming military force, in order to back up infiltration with intimidation. In the only terms in which it understands strength, it is seeking to demonstrate to the free world that force and the will to use it are on the side of the Kremlin, that those who lack it are decadent and doomed. In local incidents it threatens and encroaches both for the sake of local gains and to increase anxiety and defeatism in all the free world.

The possession of atomic weapons at each of the opposite poles of power, and the inability (for different reasons) of either side to place any trust in the other, puts a premium on a surprise attack against us. It equally puts a premium on a more violent and ruthless prosecution of its design by cold war, especially if the Kremlin is sufficiently objective to realize the improbability of our prosecuting a preventive war. It also puts a premium on piecemeal aggression against others, counting on our unwillingness to engage in atomic war unless we are directly attacked. We run all these risks and the added risk of being confused and immobilized by our inability to weigh and choose, and pursue a firm course based on a rational assessment of each.

The risk that we may thereby be prevented or too long delayed in taking all needful measures to maintain the integrity and vitality of our system is great. The risk that our allies will lose their determination is greater. And the risk that in this manner a descending spiral of too little and too late, of doubt and recrimination, may present us with ever narrower and more desperate alternatives, is the greatest risk of all. . . .

The risk of having no better choice than to capitulate or precipitate a global war at any of a number of pressure points is bad enough in itself, but it is multiplied by the weakness it imparts to our position in the cold war. Instead of appearing strong and resolute we are continually at the verge of appearing and being alternately irresolute and desperate; yet it is the cold war which we must win, because both the Kremlin design, and our fundamental purpose give it the first priority. . . .

But there are risks in making ourselves strong. A large measure of sacrifice and discipline will be demanded of the American people. They will be asked to give up some of the benefits which they have come to associate with their freedoms. Nothing could be more important than that they fully understand the reasons for this. . . .

VIII. *Atomic Armaments*
A. Military evaluation of U.S. and USSR atomic capabilities

1. The United States now has an atomic capability, including both numbers and deliverability, estimated to be adequate, if effectively utilized, to deliver a serious blow against the war-making capacity of the USSR. It is doubted whether such a blow, even if it resulted in the complete destruction of the contemplated target systems, would cause the USSR to sue for terms or prevent Soviet forces from occupying Western Europe against such ground resistance as could presently be mobilized. . . .

2. As the atomic capability of the USSR increases, it will have an increased ability to hit at our atomic bases and installations and thus seriously hamper the ability of the United States to carry out an attack such as that outlined above. . . .

It is estimated that, within the next four years, the USSR will attain the capability of seriously damaging vital centers of the United States, provided it strikes a surprise blow and provided further that the blow is opposed by no more effective opposition than we now have programmed. Such a blow could so seriously damage the United States as to greatly reduce its superiority in economic potential.

Effective opposition to this Soviet capability will require among other measures greatly increased air warning systems, air defenses, and vigorous development and implementation of a civilian defense program which has been thoroughly integrated with the military defense systems.

In time the atomic capability of the USSR can be expected to grow to a point where, given surprise and no more effective opposition than we now have programmed, the possibility of a decisive initial attack cannot be excluded.

3. In the initial phases of an atomic war, the advantages of initiative and surprise would be very great. A police state living behind an iron curtain has an enormous advantage in maintaining the necessary security and centralization of decision required to capitalize on this advantage.

4. For the moment our atomic retaliatory capability is probably adequate to deter the Kremlin from a deliberate direct military attack against ourselves or other free peoples. However, when it calculates that it has a sufficient atomic capability to make a surprise attack on us, nullifying our atomic superiority and creating a military situation decisively in its favor, the Kremlin might be tempted to strike swiftly and with stealth. The existence of two large atomic capabilities in such a relationship might well act, therefore, not as a deterrent, but as an incitement to war. . . .

B. Stockpiling and use of atomic weapons

1. From the foregoing analysis it appears that it would be to the long-term advantage of the United States if atomic weapons were to be effectively eliminated from national peacetime armaments; the additional objectives which must be secured if there is to be a reasonable prospect of such effective elimination of atomic weapons. . . . In the absence of such elimination and the securing of these objectives, it would appear that we have no alternative but to increase our atomic capability as rapidly as other considerations make appropriate. In either case, it appears to be imperative to increase as rapidly as possible our general air, ground, and sea strength and that of our allies to a point where we are militarily not so heavily dependent on atomic weapons.

2. [I]t is important that the United States employ military force only if the necessity for its use is clear and compelling and commends itself

to the overwhelming majority of our people. The United States cannot therefore engage in war except as a reaction to aggression of so clear and compelling a nature as to bring the overwhelming majority of our people to accept the use of military force. In the event war comes, our use of force must be to compel the acceptance of our objectives and must be congruent to the range of tasks which we may encounter.

In the event of a general war with the USSR, it must be anticipated that atomic weapons will be used by each side in the manner it deems best suited to accomplish its objectives. In view of our vulnerability to Soviet atomic attack, it has been argued that we might wish to hold our atomic weapons only for retaliation against prior use by the USSR. To be able to do so and still have hope of achieving our objectives, the non-atomic military capabilities of ourselves and our allies would have to be fully developed and the political weaknesses of the Soviet Union fully exploited. In the event of war, however, we could not be sure that we could move toward the attainment of these objectives without the USSR's resorting sooner or later to the use of its atomic weapons. Only if we had overwhelming atomic superiority and obtained command of the air might the USSR be deterred from employing its atomic weapons as we progressed toward the attainment of our objectives.

In the event the USSR develops by 1954 the atomic capability which we now anticipate, it is hardly conceivable that, if war comes, the Soviet leaders would refrain from the use of atomic weapons unless they felt fully confident of attaining their objectives by other means.

In the event we use atomic weapons either in retaliation for their prior use by the USSR or because there is no alternative method by which we can attain our objectives, it is imperative that the strategic and tactical targets against which they are used be appropriate and the manner in which they are used be consistent with those objectives.

It appears to follow from the above that we should produce and stockpile thermonuclear weapons in the event they prove feasible and would add significantly to our net capability. Not enough is yet known of their potentialities to warrant a judgment at this time regarding their use in war to attain our objectives.

3. It has been suggested that we announce that we will not use atomic weapons except in retaliation against the prior use of such weapons by an aggressor. It has been argued that such a declaration would decrease the danger of an atomic attack against the United States and its allies.

In our present situation of relative unpreparedness in conventional weapons, such a declaration would be interpreted by the USSR as an admission of great weakness and by our allies as a clear indication that we intended to abandon them. . . .

Unless we are prepared to abandon our objectives, we cannot make such a declaration in good faith until we are confident that we will be in a position to attain our objectives without war, or, in the event of war, without recourse to the use of atomic weapons for strategic or tactical purposes. . . .

IX. Possible Courses of Action
Introduction. Four possible courses of action by the United States in the present situation can be distinguished. . . .

A. The first course—continuation of current policies, with current and currently projected programs for carrying out these policies

1. *Military aspects.* On the basis of current programs, the United States has a large potential military capability but an actual capability which, though improving, is declining relative to the USSR, particularly in light of its probable fission bomb capability and possible thermonuclear bomb capability. The same holds true for the free world as a whole relative to the Soviet world as a whole. If war breaks out in 1950 or in the next few years, the United States and its allies, apart from a powerful atomic blow, will be compelled to conduct delaying actions, while building up their strength for a general offensive. A frank evaluation of the requirements, to defend the United States and its vital interests and to support a vigorous initiative in the cold war, on

the one hand, and of present capabilities, on the other, indicates that there is a sharp and growing disparity between them. . . .

From the military point of view, the actual and potential capabilities of the United States, given a continuation of current and projected programs, will become less and less effective as a war deterrent. Improvement of the state of readiness will become more and more important not only to inhibit the launching of war by the Soviet Union but also to support a national policy designed to reverse the present ominous trends in international relations. A building up of the military capabilities of the United States and the free world is a pre-condition to the achievement of the objectives outlined in this report and to the protection of the United States against disaster. . . .

2. *Political aspects.* The Soviet Union is pursuing the initiative in the conflict with the free world. Its atomic capabilities, together with its successes in the Far East, have led to an increasing confidence on its part and to an increasing nervousness in Western Europe and the rest of the free world. We cannot be sure, of course, how vigorously the Soviet Union will pursue its initiative, nor can we be sure of the strength or weakness of the other free countries in reacting to it. There are, however, ominous signs of further deterioration in the Far East. There are also some indications that a decline in morale and confidence in Western Europe may be expected. In particular, the situation in Germany is unsettled. . . .

Politically, recognition of the military implications of a continuation of present trends will mean that the United States and especially other free countries will tend to shift to the defensive, or to follow a dangerous policy of bluff, because the maintenance of a firm initiative in the cold war is closely related to aggregate strength in being and readily available.

This is largely a problem of the incongruity of the current actual capabilities of the free world and the threat to it, for the free world has an economic and military potential far superior to the potential of the Soviet Union and its satellites. The shadow of Soviet force falls darkly on Western Europe and Asia and supports a policy of encroachment. The free world lacks adequate means—in the form of forces in being—to thwart such expansion locally. . . .

3. *Economic and social aspects.* [T]he present foreign economic policies and programs of the United States will not produce a solution to the problem of international economic equilibrium, notably the problem of the dollar gap, and will not create an economic base conducive to political stability in many important free countries.

The European Recovery Program has been successful in assisting the restoration and expansion of production in Western Europe and has been a major factor in checking the dry rot of Communism in Western Europe. However, little progress has been made toward the resumption by Western Europe of a position of influence in world affairs commensurate with its potential strength. Progress in this direction will require integrated political, economic, and military policies and programs, which are supported by the United States and the Western European countries and which will probably require a deeper participation by the United States than has been contemplated. . . .

In short, by continuing along its present course the free world will not succeed in making effective use of its vastly superior political, economic, and military potential to build a tolerable state of order among nations. On the contrary, the political, economic, and military situation of the free world is already unsatisfactory and will become less favorable unless we act to reverse present trends. . . .

B. The second course—isolation

Continuation of present trends, it has been shown above, will lead progressively to the withdrawal of the United States from most of its present commitments in Europe and Asia and to our isolation in the Western Hemisphere and its approaches. This would result not from a conscious decision but from a failure to take the actions necessary to bring our capabilities into line with our commitments and thus to a withdrawal under pressure. . . .

There are some who advocate a deliberate decision to isolate ourselves. Superficially, this has some attractiveness as a course of action, for it appears to bring our commitments and capabilities into harmony by reducing the former and by concentrating our present, or perhaps even reduced, military expenditures on the defense of the United States.

This argument overlooks the relativity of capabilities. With the United States in an isolated position, we would have to face the probability that the Soviet Union would quickly dominate most of Eurasia, probably without meeting armed resistance. It would thus acquire a potential far superior to our own, and would promptly proceed to develop this potential with the purpose of eliminating our power, which would, even in isolation, remain as a challenge to it and as an obstacle to the imposition of its kind of order in the world. There is no way to make ourselves inoffensive to the Kremlin except by complete submission to its will. Therefore isolation would in the end condemn us to capitulate or to fight alone and on the defensive, with drastically limited offensive and retaliatory capabilities in comparison with the Soviet Union. . . .

The argument also overlooks the imponderable, but nevertheless drastic, effects on our belief in ourselves and in our way of life of a deliberate decision to isolate ourselves. As the Soviet Union came to dominate free countries, it is clear that many Americans would feel a deep sense of responsibility and guilt for having abandoned their former friends and allies. As the Soviet Union mobilized the resources of Eurasia, increased its relative military capabilities, and heightened its threat to our security, some would be tempted to accept "peace" on its terms, while many would seek to defend the United States by creating a regimented system which would permit the assignment of a tremendous part of our resources to defense. Under such a state of affairs our national morale would be corrupted and the integrity and vitality of our system subverted.

Under this course of action, there would be no negotiation, unless on the Kremlin's terms, for we would have given up everything of importance.

It is possible that at some point in the course of isolation, many Americans would come to favor a surprise attack on the Soviet Union and the area under its control, in a desperate attempt to alter decisively the balance of power by an overwhelming blow with modern weapons of mass destruction. It appears unlikely that the Soviet Union would wait for such an attack before launching one of its own. But even if it did and even if our attack were successful, it is clear that the United States would face appalling tasks in establishing a tolerable state of order among nations after such a war and after Soviet occupation of all or most of Eurasia for some years. These tasks appear so enormous and success so unlikely that reason dictates an attempt to achieve our objectives by other means.

C. The third course—war

Some Americans favor a deliberate decision to go to war against the Soviet Union in the near future. It goes without saying that the idea of "preventive" war—in the sense of a military attack not provoked by a military attack upon us or our allies—is generally unacceptable to Americans. Its supporters argue that since the Soviet Union is in fact at war with the free world now and that since the failure of the Soviet Union to use all-out military force is explainable on grounds of expediency, we are at war and should conduct ourselves accordingly. Some further argue that the free world is probably unable, except under the crisis of war, to mobilize and direct its resources to the checking and rolling back of the Kremlin's drive for world dominion. This is a powerful argument in the light of history, but the considerations against war are so compelling that the free world must demonstrate that this argument is wrong. The case for war is premised on the assumption that the United States could launch and sustain an attack of sufficient impact to gain a decisive advantage for the free world in a long war and perhaps to win an early decision.

The ability of the United States to launch effective offensive operations is now limited to attack with atomic weapons. A powerful blow could be delivered upon the Soviet Union, but it is estimated that these operations alone would not force or induce the Kremlin to capitulate and that the Kremlin would still be able to use the forces under its control to dominate most or all of Eurasia. This would probably mean a long and difficult struggle during which the free institutions of Western Europe and many freedom-loving people would be destroyed and the regenerative capacity of Western Europe dealt a crippling blow.

Apart from this, however, a surprise attack upon the Soviet Union, despite the provocativeness of recent Soviet behavior, would be repugnant to many Americans. Although the American people would probably rally in support of the war effort, the shock of responsibility for a surprise attack would be morally corrosive. Many would doubt that it was a "just war" and that all reasonable possibilities for a peaceful settlement had been explored in good faith. Many more, proportionately, would hold such views in other countries, particularly in Western Europe and particularly after Soviet occupation, if only because the Soviet Union would liquidate articulate opponents. It would, therefore, be difficult after such a war to create a satisfactory international order among nations. Victory in such a war would have brought us little if at all closer to victory in the fundamental ideological conflict. . . .

D. The remaining course of action—a rapid build-up of political, economic, and military strength in the free world

A more rapid build-up of political, economic, and military strength and thereby of confidence in the free world than is now contemplated is the only course which is consistent with progress toward achieving our fundamental purpose. The frustration of the Kremlin design requires the free world to develop a successfully functioning political and economic system and a vigorous political offensive against the Soviet Union. These, in turn, require an adequate military shield under which they can develop. . . .

1. *Military aspects.* It has been indicated in Chapter VI that U.S. military capabilities are strategically more defensive in nature than offensive and are more potential than actual. It is evident, from an analysis of the past and of the trend of weapon development, that there is now and will be in the future no absolute defense. The history of war also indicates that a favorable decision can only be achieved through offensive action. Even a defensive strategy, if it is to be successful, calls not only for defensive forces to hold vital positions while mobilizing and preparing for the offensive, but also for offensive forces to attack the enemy and keep him off balance. . . .

Forces of this size and character are necessary not only for protection against disaster but also to support our foreign policy. In fact, it can be argued that larger forces in being and readily available are necessary to inhibit a would-be aggressor than to provide the nucleus of strength and the mobilization base on which the tremendous forces required for victory can be built. . . .

Moreover, the United States and the other free countries do not now have the forces in being and readily available to defeat local Soviet moves with local action, but must accept reverses or make these local moves the occasion for war— for which we are not prepared. This situation makes for great uneasiness among our allies, particularly in Western Europe, for whom total war means, initially, Soviet occupation. Thus, unless our combined strength is rapidly increased, our allies will tend to become increasingly reluctant to support a firm foreign policy on our part and increasingly anxious to seek other solutions, even though they are aware that appeasement means defeat. An important advantage in adopting the fourth course of action lies in its psychological impact—the revival of confidence and hope in the future. . . .

2. *Political and economic aspects.* The immediate objectives—to the achievement of which such a build-up of strength is a necessary though not a sufficient condition—are a renewed initiative in the cold war and a situation to which the Kremlin would find it expedient to accommodate itself, first by relaxing tensions and pressures and then by gradual withdrawal. The United States cannot alone provide the resources required for such a build-up of strength. The other free countries must carry their part of the burden, but their ability and determination to do it will depend on the action the United States takes to develop its own strength and on the adequacy of its foreign political and economic policies. . . .

At the same time, we should take dynamic steps to reduce the power and influence of the Kremlin inside the Soviet Union and other areas under its control. The objective would be the establishment of friendly regimes not under Kremlin domination. Such action is essential to engage the Kremlin's attention, keep it off balance, and force an increased expenditure of Soviet resources in counteraction. In other words, it would be the current Soviet cold war technique used against the Soviet Union.

A program for rapidly building up strength and improving political and economic conditions will place heavy demands on our courage and intelligence; it will be costly; it will be dangerous. But half-measures will be more costly and more dangerous, for they will be inadequate to prevent and may actually invite war. Budgetary considerations will need to be subordinated to the stark fact that our very independence as a nation may be at stake. . . .

The United States is currently devoting about 22 percent of its gross national product ($255 billion in 1949) to military expenditures (6 percent), foreign assistance (2 percent), and investment (14 percent), little of which is in war-supporting industries. . . . In an emergency the United States could devote upward of 50 percent of its gross national product to these purposes (as it did during the last war), an increase of several times present expenditures for direct and indirect military purposes and foreign assistance.

From the point of view of the economy as a whole, the program might not result in a real decrease in the standard of living, for the economic effects of the program might be to increase the gross national product by more than the amount being absorbed for additional military and foreign assistance purposes. One of the most significant lessons of our World War II experience was that the American economy, when it operates at a level approaching full efficiency, can provide enormous resources for purposes other than civilian consumption while simultaneously providing a high standard of living. . . .

The threat to the free world involved in the development of the Soviet Union's atomic and other capabilities will rise steadily and rather rapidly. For the time being, the United States possesses a marked atomic superiority over the Soviet Union which, together with the potential capabilities of the United States and other free countries in other forces and weapons, inhibits aggressive Soviet action. This provides an opportunity for the United States, in cooperation with other free countries, to launch a build-up of strength which

will support a firm policy directed to the frustration of the Kremlin design. The immediate goal of our efforts to build a successfully functioning political and economic system in the free world backed by adequate military strength is to postpone and avert the disastrous situation which, in light of the Soviet Union's probable fission bomb capability and possible thermonuclear bomb capability, might arise in 1954 on a continuation of our present programs. By acting promptly and vigorously in such a way that this date is, so to speak, pushed into the future, we would permit time for the process of accommodation, withdrawal and frustration to produce the necessary changes in the Soviet system. Time is short, however, and the risks of war attendant upon a decision to build up strength will steadily increase the longer we defer it.

Conclusions and Recommendations

Conclusions

. . . A continuation of present trends would result in a serious decline in the strength of the free world relative to the Soviet Union and its satellites. This unfavorable trend arises from the inadequacy of current programs and plans rather than from any error in our objectives and aims. These trends lead in the direction of isolation, not by deliberate decision but by lack of the necessary basis for a vigorous initiative in the conflict with the Soviet Union.

Our position as the center of power in the free world places a heavy responsibility upon the United States for leadership. We must organize and enlist the energies and resources of the free world in a positive program for peace which will frustrate the Kremlin design for world domination by creating a situation in the free world to which the Kremlin will be compelled to adjust. Without such a cooperative effort, led by the United States, we will have to make gradual withdrawals under pressure until we discover one day that we have sacrificed positions of vital interest.

It is imperative that this trend be reversed by a much more rapid and concerted build-up of the actual strength of both the United States and the other nations of the free world. The analysis shows that this will be costly and will involve significant domestic financial and economic adjustments.

The execution of such a build-up, however, requires that the United States have an affirmative program beyond the solely defensive one of countering the threat posed by the Soviet Union. This program must light the path to peace and order among nations in a system based on freedom and justice, as contemplated in the Charter of the United Nations. Further, it must envisage the political and economic measures with which and the military shield behind which the free world can work to frustrate the Kremlin design by the strategy of the cold war; for every consideration of devotion to our fundamental values and to our national security demands that we achieve our objectives by the strategy of the cold war, building up our military strength in order that it may not have to be used. The only sure victory lies in the frustration of the Kremlin design by the steady development of the moral and material strength of the free world and its projection into the Soviet world in such a way as to bring about an internal change in the Soviet system. Such a positive program—harmonious with our fundamental national purpose and our objectives—is necessary if we are to regain and retain the initiative and to win and hold the necessary popular support and cooperation in the United States and the rest of the free world. . . .

In summary, we must, by means of a rapid and sustained build-up of the political, economic, and military strength of the free world, and by means of an affirmative program intended to wrest the initiative from the Soviet Union, confront it with convincing evidence of the determination and ability of the free world to frustrate the Kremlin design of a world dominated by its will. Such evidence is the only means short of war which eventually may force the Kremlin to abandon its present course of action and to negotiate acceptable agreements on issues of major importance.

The whole success of the proposed program hangs ultimately on recognition by this Government, the American people, and all free peoples, that the cold war is in fact a real war in which the survival of the free world is at stake. Essential prerequisites to success are consultations with Congressional leaders designed to make the program the object of non-partisan legislative support, and a presentation to the public of a full explanation of the facts and implications of the present international situation. The prosecution of the program will require of us all the ingenuity, sacrifice, and unity demanded by the vital importance of the issue and the tenacity to persevere until our national objectives have been attained.

DOUGLAS MACARTHUR, "FAREWELL ADDRESS TO CONGRESS" (1951)

The Korean War was unlike any previous large-scale armed conflict in American history. Prior to World War II, Korea had been a Japanese colony. Plans to create a unified, independent Korea after the war fell victim to the Cold War. By 1950, a Democratic People's Republic of Korea, aligned with the Soviet Union, controlled the peninsula north of the 38th Parallel. An anticommunist Republic of Korea (ROK) controlled everything to the south. Neither entity accepted the other's legitimacy. Both were intent on unifying the country on its own terms. In June 1950, the Soviet-equipped North Korean army invaded South Korea and quickly put ROK forces to flight. Although the United States was not formally committed to defend South Korea, President Truman ordered US forces to intervene, citing a United Nations Security Council resolution as his authority to do so. Truman neither asked for nor received a Congressional declaration of war. After difficult months of fighting, US and allies forces operating under the overall command of General Douglas MacArthur succeeded in restoring the territorial integrity of South Korea. MacArthur then received permission to continue attacking northward, with the aim of unifying the peninsula. This ill-advised action induced the People's Republic of China to send "volunteers" to defend North Korea. Caught by surprise, MacArthur's forces were soon retreating southward in disorder. The imperious MacArthur now pressed publicly for expanding the war into China proper, using nuclear weapons, if need be, to achieve victory in what he depicted as the decisive theater of the Cold War. Faced with this direct challenge to civilian control and determined to avoid any further escalation of hostilities, Truman relieved MacArthur of command in April 1951. Upon his return to the United States, the general received a hero's welcome and made this report to Congress.

I stand on this rostrum with a sense of deep humility and great pride—humility in the wake of those great American architects of our history who have stood here before me; pride in the reflection that this forum of legislative debate represents human liberty in the purest form yet devised. Here are centered the hopes and aspirations and faith of the entire human race. I do not stand here as advocate for any partisan cause, for the issues are fundamental and reach quite beyond the realm of partisan consideration. They must be resolved on the highest plane of national interest if our course is to prove sound and our future protected. I trust, therefore, that you will do me the justice of receiving that which I have to say as solely expressing the considered viewpoint of a fellow American.

I address you with neither rancor nor bitterness in the fading twilight of life, with but one purpose in mind: to serve my country. The issues are global and so interlocked that to consider the problems of one sector, oblivious to those of another, is but to court disaster for the whole. While Asia is commonly referred to as the Gateway to Europe, it is no less true that Europe is the Gateway to Asia, and the broad influence of the one cannot fail to have its impact upon the other. There are those who claim our strength is inadequate to protect on both fronts, that we cannot divide our effort. I can think of no greater expression of defeatism. If a potential enemy can divide his strength on two fronts, it is for us to counter his effort. The Communist threat is a global one. Its successful advance in one sector threatens the destruction of every other sector. You can not appease or otherwise surrender to communism in Asia without simultaneously undermining our efforts to halt its advance in Europe.

Beyond pointing out these general truisms, I shall confine my discussion to the general areas of Asia. Before one may objectively assess the situation now existing there, he must comprehend something of Asia's past and the revolutionary changes which have marked her course up to the present. Long exploited by the so-called colonial powers, with little opportunity to achieve any degree of social justice, individual dignity, or a higher standard of life such as guided our own noble administration in the Philippines, the peoples of Asia found their opportunity in the war just past to throw off the shackles of colonialism and now see the dawn of new opportunity, a heretofore unfelt dignity, and the self-respect of political freedom.

Mustering half of the earth's population, and 60 percent of its natural resources these peoples are rapidly consolidating a new force, both moral and material, with which to raise the living standard and erect adaptations of the design of modern progress to their own distinct cultural environments. Whether one adheres to the concept of colonization or not, this is the direction of Asian progress and it may not be stopped. It is a corollary to the shift of the world economic frontiers as the whole epicenter of world affairs rotates back toward the area whence it started.

In this situation, it becomes vital that our own country orient its policies in consonance with this basic evolutionary condition rather than pursue a course blind to the reality that the colonial era is now past and the Asian peoples covet the right to shape their own free destiny. What they seek now is friendly guidance, understanding, and support—not imperious direction—the dignity of equality and not the shame of subjugation. Their pre-war standard of life, pitifully low, is infinitely lower now in the devastation left in war's wake. World ideologies play little part in Asian thinking and are little understood. What the peoples strive for is the opportunity for a little more food in their stomachs, a little better clothing on their backs, a little firmer roof over their heads, and the realization of the normal nationalist urge for political freedom. These political-social conditions have but an indirect bearing upon our own national security, but do form a backdrop to contemporary planning which must be thoughtfully considered if we are to avoid the pitfalls of unrealism.

Of more direct and immediate bearing upon our national security are the changes wrought in the strategic potential of the Pacific Ocean in the course of the past war. Prior thereto the western strategic frontier of the United States lay on the littoral line of the Americas, with an exposed island salient extending out through Hawaii, Midway, and Guam to the Philippines. That salient proved not an outpost of strength but an avenue of weakness along which the enemy could and did attack.

The Pacific was a potential area of advance for any predatory force intent upon striking at the bordering land areas. All this was changed by our

Pacific victory. Our strategic frontier then shifted to embrace the entire Pacific Ocean, which became a vast moat to protect us as long as we held it. Indeed, it acts as a protective shield for all of the Americas and all free lands of the Pacific Ocean area. We control it to the shores of Asia by a chain of islands extending in an arc from the Aleutians to the Mariannas held by us and our free allies. From this island chain we can dominate with sea and air power every Asiatic port from Vladivostok to Singapore . . . and prevent any hostile movement into the Pacific. . . .

Under such conditions, the Pacific no longer represents menacing avenues of approach for a prospective invader. It assumes, instead, the friendly aspect of a peaceful lake. Our line of defense is a natural one and can be maintained with a minimum of military effort and expense. It envisions no attack against anyone, nor does it provide the bastions essential for offensive operations, but properly maintained, would be an invincible defense against aggression. The holding of this littoral defense line in the western Pacific is entirely dependent upon holding all segments thereof; for any major breach of that line by an unfriendly power would render vulnerable to determined attack every other major segment.

This is a military estimate as to which I have yet to find a military leader who will take exception. For that reason, I have strongly recommended in the past, as a matter of military urgency, that under no circumstances must Formosa fall under Communist control. Such an eventuality would at once threaten the freedom of the Philippines and the loss of Japan and might well force our western frontier back to the coast of California, Oregon and Washington.

To understand the changes which now appear upon the Chinese mainland, one must understand the changes in Chinese character and culture over the past 50 years. China, up to 50 years ago, was completely non-homogenous, being compartmented into groups divided against each other. The war-making tendency was almost non-existent, as they still followed the tenets of the Confucian ideal of pacifist culture. At the turn of the century, under the regime of Chang Tso Lin, efforts toward greater homogeneity produced the start of a nationalist urge. This was further and more successfully developed under the leadership of Chiang Kai-Shek, but has been brought to its greatest fruition under the present regime to the point that it has now taken on the character of a united nationalism of increasingly dominant, aggressive tendencies.

Through these past 50 years the Chinese people have thus become militarized in their concepts and in their ideals. They now constitute excellent soldiers, with competent staffs and commanders. This has produced a new and dominant power in Asia, which, for its own purposes, is allied with Soviet Russia but which in its own concepts and methods has become aggressively imperialistic, with a lust for expansion and increased power normal to this type of imperialism.

There is little of the ideological concept either one way or another in the Chinese make-up. The standard of living is so low and the capital accumulation has been so thoroughly dissipated by war that the masses are desperate and eager to follow any leadership which seems to promise the alleviation of local stringencies.

I have from the beginning believed that the Chinese Communists' support of the North Koreans was the dominant one. Their interests are, at present, parallel with those of the Soviet. But I believe that the aggressiveness recently displayed not only in Korea but also in Indo-China and Tibet and pointing potentially toward the South reflects predominantly the same lust for the expansion of power which has animated every would-be conqueror since the beginning of time.

The Japanese people, since the war, have undergone the greatest reformation recorded in modern history. With a commendable will, eagerness to learn, and marked capacity to understand, they have, from the ashes left in war's wake, erected in Japan an edifice dedicated to the supremacy of individual liberty and personal dignity; and in the ensuing process there has been created a truly representative government committed to the advance of political morality, freedom of economic enterprise, and social justice.

Politically, economically, and socially Japan is now abreast of many free nations of the earth and will not again fail the universal trust. That it may be counted upon to wield a profoundly beneficial influence over the course of events in Asia is attested by the magnificent manner in which the Japanese people have met the recent challenge of war, unrest, and confusion surrounding them from the outside and checked communism within their own frontiers without the slightest slackening in their forward progress. . . . . I know of no nation more serene, orderly, and industrious, nor in which higher hopes can be entertained for future constructive service in the advance of the human race.

Of our former ward, the Philippines, we can look forward in confidence that the existing unrest will be corrected and a strong and healthy nation will grow in the longer aftermath of war's terrible destructiveness. We must be patient and understanding and never fail them—as in our hour of need, they did not fail us. A Christian nation, the Philippines stand as a mighty bulwark of Christianity in the Far East, and its capacity for high moral leadership in Asia is unlimited.

On Formosa, the government of the Republic of China has had the opportunity to refute by action much of the malicious gossip which so undermined the strength of its leadership on the Chinese mainland. The Formosan people are receiving a just and enlightened administration with majority representation on the organs of government, and politically, economically, and socially they appear to be advancing along sound and constructive lines.

With this brief insight into the surrounding areas, I now turn to the Korean conflict. While I was not consulted prior to the President's decision to intervene in support of the Republic of Korea, that decision from a military standpoint, proved a sound one, as we . . . as we hurled back the invader and decimated his forces. Our victory was complete, and our objectives within reach, when Red China intervened with numerically superior ground forces.

This created a new war and an entirely new situation, a situation not contemplated when our forces were committed against the North Korean invaders; a situation which called for new decisions in the diplomatic sphere to permit the realistic adjustment of military strategy.

Such decisions have not been forthcoming.

While no man in his right mind would advocate sending our ground forces into continental China, and such was never given a thought, the new situation did urgently demand a drastic revision of strategic planning if our political aim was to defeat this new enemy as we had defeated the old.

Apart from the military need, as I saw it, to neutralize the sanctuary protection given the enemy north of the Yalu, I felt that military necessity in the conduct of the war made necessary: first, the intensification of our economic blockade against China; two, the imposition of a naval blockade against the China coast; three, removal of restrictions on air reconnaissance of China's coastal areas and of Manchuria; four, removal of restrictions on the forces of the Republic of China on Formosa, with logistical support to contribute to their effective operations against the common enemy.

For entertaining these views, all professionally designed to support our forces committed to Korea and bring hostilities to an end with the least possible delay and at a saving of countless American and allied lives, I have been severely criticized in lay circles, principally abroad, despite my understanding that from a military standpoint the above views have been fully shared in the past by practically every military leader concerned with the Korean campaign, including our own Joint Chiefs of Staff.

I called for reinforcements but was informed that reinforcements were not available. I made clear that if not permitted to destroy the enemy built-up bases north of the Yalu, if not permitted to utilize the friendly Chinese Force of some 600,000 men on Formosa, if not permitted to blockade the China coast to prevent the Chinese Reds from getting succor from without, and if there were to be no hope of major reinforcements, the position of the command from the military standpoint forbade victory.

We could hold in Korea by constant maneuver and in an approximate area where our supply line advantages were in balance with the supply line disadvantages of the enemy, but we could hope at best for only an indecisive campaign with its terrible and constant attrition upon our forces if the enemy utilized its full military potential. I have constantly called for the new political decisions essential to a solution.

Efforts have been made to distort my position. It has been said, in effect, that I was a warmonger.

Nothing could be further from the truth. I know war as few other men now living know it, and nothing to me is more revolting. I have long advocated its complete abolition, as its very destructiveness on both friend and foe has rendered it useless as a means of settling international disputes. Indeed, on the second day of September, nineteen hundred and forty-five, just following the surrender of the Japanese nation on the Battleship Missouri, I formally cautioned as follows:

Men since the beginning of time have sought peace. Various methods through the ages have been attempted to devise an international process to prevent or settle disputes between nations. From the very start workable methods were found in so far as individual citizens were concerned, but the mechanics of an instrumentality of larger international scope have never been successful. Military alliances, balances of power, Leagues of Nations, all in turn failed, leaving the only path to be by way of the crucible of war. The utter destructiveness of war now blocks out this alternative. We have had our last chance. If we will not devise some greater and more equitable system, Armageddon will be at our door. The problem basically is theological and involves a spiritual recrudescence and improvement of human character that will synchronize with our almost matchless advances in science, art, literature, and all material and cultural developments of the past 2000 years. It must be of the spirit if we are to save the flesh.

But once war is forced upon us, there is no other alternative than to apply every available means to bring it to a swift end.

War's very object is victory, not prolonged indecision.

In war there is no substitute for victory.

There are some who, for varying reasons, would appease Red China. They are blind to history's clear lesson, for history teaches with unmistakable emphasis that appeasement but begets new and bloodier war. It points to no single instance where this end has justified that means, where appeasement has led to more than a sham peace. Like blackmail, it lays the basis for new and successively greater demands until, as in blackmail, violence becomes the only other alternative.

"Why," my soldiers asked of me, "surrender military advantages to an enemy in the field?" I could not answer.

Some may say: to avoid spread of the conflict into an all-out war with China; others, to avoid Soviet intervention. Neither explanation seems valid, for China is already engaging with the maximum power it can commit, and the Soviet will not necessarily mesh its actions with our moves. Like a cobra, any new enemy will more likely strike whenever it feels that the relativity in military or other potential is in its favor on a world-wide basis.

The tragedy of Korea is further heightened by the fact that its military action is confined to its territorial limits. It condemns that nation, which it is our purpose to save, to suffer the devastating impact of full naval and air bombardment while the enemy's sanctuaries are fully protected from such attack and devastation.

Of the nations of the world, Korea alone, up to now, is the sole one which has risked its all against communism. The magnificence of the courage and fortitude of the Korean people defies description.

They have chosen to risk death rather than slavery. Their last words to me were: "Don't scuttle the Pacific!"

I have just left your fighting sons in Korea. They have met all tests there, and I can report to you without reservation that they are splendid in every way.

It was my constant effort to preserve them and end this savage conflict honorably and with the least loss of time and a minimum sacrifice of life. Its growing bloodshed has caused me the deepest anguish and anxiety.

Those gallant men will remain often in my thoughts and in my prayers always.

I am closing my 52 years of military service. When I joined the Army, even before the turn of the century, it was the fulfillment of all of my boyish hopes and dreams. The world has turned over many times since I took the oath on the plain at West Point, and the hopes and dreams have long since vanished, but I still remember the refrain of one of the most popular barrack ballads of that day which proclaimed most proudly that "old soldiers never die; they just fade away."

And like the old soldier of that ballad, I now close my military career and just fade away, an old soldier who tried to do his duty as God gave him the light to see that duty.

Good Bye.

Reinhold Niebuhr, *The Irony of American History* (1952)

As moral theologian and commentator on contemporary affairs, Reinhold Niebuhr (1892–1971) was a commanding presence on the American intellectual scene from the 1930s to the 1960s. On matters related to America's role in the world, Niebuhr was a proponent of "Christian realism," a perspective combining a recognition of the imperative to confront evil with a sense of modesty about America's own motives and capacity to make things right. Niebuhr both acknowledged the existence of American exceptionalism and also warned against it. Here he reflects on the predicament facing the United States during the formative stage of the Cold War.

Whether our nation interprets its spiritual heritage through Massachusetts or Virginia, we came into existence with the sense of being a "separated" nation, which God was using to make a new beginning for mankind. We had renounced the evils of European feudalism. We had escaped from the evils of European religious bigotry. We had found broad spaces for the satisfaction of human desires in place of the crowded Europe. Whether, as in the case of the New England theocrats, our forefathers thought of our "experiment" as primarily the creation of a new and purer church, or, as in the case of Jefferson and his coterie, they thought primarily of a new political community, they believed in either case that we had been called out by God to create a new humanity. We were God's "American Israel." Our pretensions of innocency therefore heightened the whole concept of a virtuous humanity which characterizes the culture of our era; and involve us in the ironic incongruity between our illusions and the realities which we experience. We find it almost as difficult as the communists to believe that anyone could think ill of us, since we are as persuaded as they that our society is so essentially virtuous that only malice could prompt criticism of any of our actions. . . .

In any event, nature's God had a very special purpose in founding this new community. The purpose was to make a new beginning in a corrupt world. Two facts about America impressed the Jeffersonians. The one was that we had broken with tyranny. The other was that the wide economic opportunities of the new continent would prevent the emergence of those social vices which

characterized the social life of an overcrowded Continent of Europe. . . .

Every nation has its own form of spiritual pride. These examples of American self-appreciation could be matched by similar sentiments in other nations. But every nation also has its peculiar version. Our version is that our nation turned its back upon the vices of Europe and made a new beginning.

The Jeffersonian conception of virtue, had it not overstated the innocency of American social life, would have been a tolerable prophecy of some respects of our social history which have distinguished us from Europe. For it can hardly be denied that the fluidity of our class structure, derived from the opulence of economic opportunities, saved us from the acrimony of the class struggle, which Marx could prompt in Europe but not in America. When the frontier ceased to provide for the expansion of opportunities, our superior technology created ever new frontiers for the ambitious and adventurous. In one sense the opulence of American life has served to perpetuate Jeffersonian illusions about human nature. For we have thus far sought to solve all our problems by the expansion of our economy. This expansion cannot go on forever and ultimately we must face some vexatious issues of social justice in terms which will not differ too greatly from those which the wisest nations of Europe have been forced to use. . . .

Our foreign policy reveals even more marked contradictions between our early illusions of innocency and the hard realities of the present day than do our domestic policies. We lived for a century not only in the illusion but in the reality of innocency in our foreign relations. We lacked the power in the first instance to become involved in the guilt of its use. As we gradually achieved power, through the economic consequences of

Reinhold Niebuhr, *The Irony of American History.* New York: Charles Scribner's Sons (1952).

our richly stored continent, the continental unity of our economy, and the technical efficiency of our business and industrial enterprise, we sought for a time to preserve innocency by disavowing the responsibilities of power. We were, of course, never as innocent as we pretended to be, even as a child is not as innocent as is implied in the use of the child as the symbol of innocency. The surge of our infant strength over a continent, which claimed Oregon, California, Florida, and Texas against any sovereignty which may have stood in our way, was not innocent. It was the expression of a will-to-power of a new community in which the land-hunger of hardy pioneers and settlers furnished the force of imperial expansion. The organs of government, whether political or military, played only a secondary role. From those early days to the present moment we have frequently been honestly deceived because our power availed itself of covert rather than overt instruments. One of the most prolific causes of delusion about power in a commercial society is that economic power is more covert than political or military power.

We believed, until the outbreak of the First World War, that there was a generic difference between us and the other nations of the world. This was proved by the difference between their power rivalries and our alleged contentment with our lot. The same President of the United States who ultimately interpreted the First World War as a crusade to "make the world safe for democracy" reacted to its first alarms with the reassuring judgment that the conflict represented trade rivalries with which we need not be concerned. We were drawn into the war by considerations of national interest, which we hardly dared confess to ourselves. Our European critics may, however, overshoot the mark if they insist that the slogan of making "the world safe for democracy" was merely an expression of that moral cant which we seem to have inherited from the British, only to express it with less subtlety than they. For the fact is that every nation is caught in the moral paradox of refusing to go to war unless it can be proved that the national interest is imperiled, and of continuing in the war only by proving that something much more than the national interest is at stake. Our nation is not the only community of mankind which is tempted to hypocrisy. . . .

More significant than our actions and interpretations in the First World War was our mood after its conclusion. Our "realists" feared that our sense of responsibility toward a nascent world community had exceeded the canons of a prudent self-interest. Our idealists, of the thirties, sought to preserve our innocence by neutrality. The main force of isolationism came from the "realists," as the slogan "America First" signifies. But the abortive effort to defy the forces of history which were creating a potential world community and increasing the power of America beyond that of any other nation, was supported by pacifist idealists, Christian and secular, and by other visionaries who desired to preserve our innocency. They had a dim and dark understanding of the fact that power cannot be yielded without guilt, since it is never transcendent over interest, even when it tries to subject itself to universal standards and places itself under the control of a nascent world-wide community. They did not understand that the disavowal of the responsibilities of power can involve an individual or nation in even more grievous guilt.

There are two ways of denying our responsibilities to our fellowmen. The one is the way of imperialism, expressed in seeking to dominate them by our power. The other is the way of isolationism, expressed in seeking to withdraw from our responsibilities to them. Geographic circumstances and the myths of our youth rendered us more susceptible to the latter than the former temptation. This has given our national life a unique color, which is not without some moral advantages. No powerful nation in history has ever been more reluctant to acknowledge the position it has achieved in the world than we. The moral advantage lies in the fact that we do not have a strong lust for power, though we are quickly acquiring the pride of power which always accompanies its possession. Our lack of the lust for power makes the fulminations of our foes against us singularly inept. On the other hand, we have been so deluded by the concept of our innocency that we are ill prepared to deal with the temptations of power which now assail us . . .

Except in moments of aberration we do not think of ourselves as the potential masters, but as the tutors of mankind in its pilgrimage to perfection. . . .

[T]he tragic dilemmas and the pathetic uncertainties and frustrations of contemporary history offer ironic refutations of the dreams of happiness and virtue of a liberal age and, especially, of the American hopes. Escape from our ironic situation obviously demands that we moderate our conception of the ability of men and of nations to discern the future; and of the power even of great nations to bring a tortuous historical process to, what seems to them, a logical and proper conclusion.

The difficulty of our own powerful nation in coming to terms with the frustrations of history, and our impatience with a situation which requires great exertions without the promise of certain success, is quite obviously symbolic of the whole perplexity of modern culture. The perplexity arises from the fact that men have been preoccupied with man's capacity to master historical forces and have forgotten that the same man, including the collective man embodied in powerful nations, is also a creature of these historical forces. . . .

We have enough discernment as creators of history to know that there is a certain "logic" in its course. We know that recently the development of an inchoate world community requires that it acquire global political organs for the better integration of its life. But if we imagine that we can easily transmute this logic into historical reality we will prove ourselves blind to the limitations of man as creature of history . . .

The tendency of a liberal culture to regard the highest human possibilities as capable of human attainment, and to interpret all tragic and contradictory elements in the pattern of history as merely provisional, has immersed the spirit of our age in a sentimentality which so uncritically identifies idealism with prudence that it can find no place in its scheme of things for heroic action or heroic patience. . . .

The fact that the European nations, more accustomed to the tragic vicissitudes of history, still have a measure of misgiving about our leadership in the world community is due to their fear that our "technocratic" tendency to equate the mastery of nature with the mastery of history could tempt us to lose patience with the tortuous path of history. We might be driven to hysteria by its inevitable frustrations. We might be tempted to bring the whole of modern history to a tragic conclusion by one final and mighty effort to overcome its frustrations. The political term for such an effort is "preventive war." It is not an immediate temptation; but it could become so in the next decade or two.

A democracy cannot, of course, engage in an explicit preventive war. But military leadership can heighten crises to the point where war becomes unavoidable.

The power of such a temptation to a nation, long accustomed to expanding possibilities and only recently subjected to frustration, is enhanced by the spiritual aberrations which arise in a situation of extreme enmity. The certainty of the foe's continued intransigence seems to be the only fixed fact in an uncertain future. Nations find it even more difficult than individuals to preserve sanity when confronted with a resolute and unscrupulous foe. Hatred disturbs all residual serenity of spirit and vindictiveness muddies every pool of sanity. In the present situation even the sanest of our statesmen have found it convenient to conform their policies to the public temper of fear and hatred which the most vulgar of our politicians have generated or exploited. Our foreign policy is thus threatened with a kind of apoplectic rigidity and inflexibility. Constant proof is required that the foe is hated with sufficient vigor. Unfortunately the only persuasive proof seems to be the disavowal of precisely those discriminate judgments which are so necessary for an effective conflict with the evil, which we are supposed to abhor. There is no simple triumph over this spirit of fear and hatred. It is certainly an achievement beyond the resources of a simple idealism. For naïve idealists are always so preoccupied with their own virtues that they have no residual awareness of the common characteristics in all human foibles and frailties and could not bear to be reminded that there is a hidden kinship between the vices of even the most vicious and the virtues of even the most upright. . . .

We cannot expect even the wisest of nations to escape every peril of moral and spiritual complacency; for nations have always been constitutionally self-righteous. But it will make a difference whether the culture in which the policies of nations are formed is only as deep and as high as the nation's highest ideals; or whether there is a dimension in the culture from the standpoint of which the element of vanity in all human ambitions and achievements is discerned. But this is a height that can be grasped only by faith; for everything that is related in terms of simple rational coherence with the ideals of a culture or a nation will prove in the end to be a simple justification of its most cherished values. The God before whom "the nations are as a drop in the bucket and are counted as small dust in the balances" is known by faith and not by reason. The realm of mystery and meaning which encloses and finally makes sense out of the baffling configurations of history is not identical with any scheme of rational intelligibility. The faith which appropriates the meaning in the mystery inevitably involves an experience of repentance for the false meanings which the pride of nations and cultures introduces into the pattern. Such repentance is the true source of charity; and we are more desperately in need of genuine charity than of more technocratic skills.

W. W. ROSTOW, *THE STAGES OF ECONOMIC GROWTH: A NON-COMMUNIST MANIFESTO* (1960)

Walt Whitman Rostow (1916–2003) was a noted American economist who during the 1960s served as a senior national security official in the administrations of Presidents John F. Kennedy and Lyndon Baines Johnson. Here is an excerpt from the work that gained him entrée into the policy world, a theory attributing to the United States an ability to rapidly modernize underdeveloped societies.

It is possible to identify all societies, in their economic dimensions, as lying within one of five categories: the traditional society, the preconditions for take-off, the take-off, the drive to maturity, and the age of high mass-consumption.

First, the traditional society. A traditional society is one whose structure is developed within limited production functions, based on pre-Newtonian science and technology, and on pre-Newtonian attitudes towards the physical world. Newton is here used as a symbol for that watershed in history when men came widely to believe that the external world was subject to a few knowable laws, and was systematically capable of productive manipulation.

The conception of the traditional society is, however, in no sense static; and it would not exclude increases in output. Acreage could be expanded; some ad hoc technical innovations, often highly productive innovations, could be introduced in trade, industry and agriculture; productivity could rise with, for example, the improvement of irrigation works or the discovery and diffusion of a new crop. But the central fact about the traditional society was that a ceiling existed on the level of attainable output per head. This ceiling resulted from the fact that the potentialities which flow from modern science and technology were either not available or not regularly and systematically applied.

Both in the longer past and in recent times the story of traditional societies was thus a story of endless change. The area and volume of trade within them and between them fluctuated, for example, with the degree of political and social turbulence, the efficiency of central rule, the upkeep of the roads. Population—and, within limits, the level of life—rose and fell not only with the sequence of the harvests, but with the incidence of war and of plague. Varying degrees of manufacture developed; but, as in agriculture, the level of productivity was limited by the inaccessibility of modern science, its applications, and its frame of mind.

Generally speaking, these societies, because of the limitation on productivity, had to devote a very high proportion of their resources to agriculture; and flowing from the agricultural system

W. W. Rostow, *The Stages of Economic Growth: A Non-Communist Manifesto*. Cambridge: Cambridge University Press (1960).

there was an hierarchical social structure, with relatively narrow scope—but some scope—for vertical mobility. Family and clan connexions played a large role in social organization. The value system of these societies was generally geared to what might be called a long-run fatalism; that is, the assumption that the range of possibilities open to one's grandchildren would be just about what it had been for one's grandparents. But this long-run fatalism by no means excluded the short-run option that, within a considerable range, it was possible and legitimate for the individual to strive to improve his lot, within his lifetime. . . .

Although central political rule—in one form or another—often existed in traditional societies, transcending the relatively self-sufficient regions, the centre of gravity of political power generally lay in the regions, in the hands of those who owned or controlled the land. The landowner maintained fluctuating but usually profound influence over such central political power as existed, backed by its entourage of civil servants and soldiers, imbued with attitudes and controlled by interests transcending the regions. . . .

The second stage of growth embraces societies in the process of transition; that is, the period when the preconditions for take-off are developed; for it takes time to transform a traditional society in the ways necessary for it to exploit the fruits of modern science, to fend off diminishing returns, and thus to enjoy the blessings and choices opened up by the march of compound interest.

The preconditions for take-off were initially developed, in a clearly marked way, in Western Europe of the late seventeenth and early eighteenth centuries as the insights of modern science began to be translated into new production functions in both agriculture and industry, in a setting given dynamism by the lateral expansion of world markets and the international competition for them. But all that lies behind the break-up of the Middle Ages is relevant to the creation of the preconditions for take-off in Western Europe. Among the Western European states, Britain, favoured by geography, natural resources, trading possibilities, social and political structure, was the first to develop fully the preconditions for take-off.

The more general case in modern history, however, saw the stage of preconditions arise not endogenously but from some external intrusion by more advanced societies. These invasions—literal or figurative—shocked the traditional society and began or hastened its undoing; but they also set in motion ideas and sentiments which initiated the process by which a modern alternative to the traditional society was constructed out of the old culture.

The idea spreads not merely that economic progress is possible, but that economic progress is a necessary condition for some other purpose, judged to be good: be it national dignity, private profit, the general welfare, or a better life for the children. Education, for some at least, broadens and changes to suit the needs of modern economic activity. New types of enterprising men come forward—in the private economy, in government, or both—willing to mobilize savings and to take risks in pursuit of profit or modernization. Banks and other institutions for mobilizing capital appear. Investment increases, notably in transport, communications, and in raw materials in which other nations may have an economic interest. The scope of commerce, internal and external, widens. And, here and there, modern manufacturing enterprise appears, using the new methods. But all this activity proceeds at a limited pace within an economy and a society still mainly characterized by traditional low-productivity methods, by the old social structure and values, and by the regionally based political institutions that developed in conjunction with them. . . .

Although the period of transition—between the traditional society and the take-off—saw major changes in both the economy itself and in the balance of social values, a decisive feature was often political. Politically, the building of an effective centralized national state—on the basis of coalitions touched with a new nationalism, in opposition to the traditional landed regional interests, the colonial power, or both, was a decisive aspect of the preconditions period; and it was, almost universally, a necessary condition for take-off. . . .

We come now to the great watershed in the life of modern societies: the third stage in this sequence, the take-off. The take-off is the interval when the old blocks and resistances to steady growth are finally overcome. The forces making for economic progress, which yielded limited bursts and enclaves of modern activity, expand and come to dominate the society. Growth becomes its normal condition. Compound interest becomes built, as it were, into its habits and institutional structure.

In Britain and the well-endowed parts of the world populated substantially from Britain (the United States, Canada etc.) the proximate stimulus for take-off was mainly (but not wholly) technological. In the more general case, the take-off awaited not only the build-up of social overhead capital and a surge of technological development in industry and agriculture, but also the emergence to political power of a group prepared to regard the modernization of the economy as serious, high-order political business. . . .

During the take-off new industries expand rapidly, yielding profits a large proportion of which are reinvested in new plant; and these new industries, in turn, stimulate, through their rapidly expanding requirement for factory workers, the services to support them, and for other manufactured goods, a further expansion in urban areas and in other modern industrial plants. The whole process of expansion in the modern sector yields an increase of income in the hands of those who not only save at high rates but place their savings at the disposal of those engaged in modern sector activities. The new class of entrepreneurs expands; and it directs the enlarging flows of investment in the private sector. The economy exploits hitherto unused natural resources and methods of production.

New techniques spread in agriculture as well as industry, as agriculture is commercialized, and increasing numbers of farmers are prepared to accept the new methods and the deep changes they bring to ways of life. The revolutionary changes in agricultural productivity are an essential condition for successful take-off; for modernization of a society increases radically its bill for agricultural products. In a decade or two both the basic structure of the economy and the social and political structure of the society are transformed in such a way that a steady rate of growth can be, thereafter, regularly sustained. . . .

After take-off there follows a long interval of sustained if fluctuating progress, as the now regularly growing economy drives to extend modern technology over the whole front of its economic activity. Some 10-20% of the national income is steadily invested, permitting output regularly to outstrip the increase in population. The make-up of the economy changes unceasingly as technique improves, new industries accelerate, older industries level off. The economy finds its place in the international economy: goods formerly imported are produced at home; new import requirements develop, and new export commodities to match them. The society makes such terms as it will with the requirements of modern efficient production, balancing off the new against the older values and institutions, or revising the latter in such ways as to support rather than to retard the growth process.

Some sixty years after take-off begins (say, forty years after the end of take-off) what may be called maturity is generally attained. The economy, focused during the take-off around a relatively narrow complex of industry and technology, has extended its range into more refined and technologically often more complex processes; for example, there may be a shift in focus from the coal, iron, and heavy engineering industries of the railway phase to machine-tools, chemicals, and electrical equipment. . . .

Formally, we can define maturity as the stage in which an economy demonstrates the capacity to move beyond the original industries which powered its take-off and to absorb and to apply efficiently over a very wide range of its resources—if not the whole range—the most advanced fruits of (then) modern technology. This is the stage in which an economy demonstrates that it has the technological and entrepreneurial skills to produce not everything, but anything that it chooses to produce. . . .

We come now to the age of high mass-consumption, where, in time, the leading sectors shift towards durable consumers' goods and services: a phase from which Americans are beginning to emerge; whose not unequivocal joys Western Europe and Japan are beginning energetically to probe; and with which Soviet society is engaged in an uneasy flirtation.

As societies achieved maturity in the twentieth century two things happened: real income per head rose to a point where a large number of persons gained a command over consumption which transcended basic food, shelter, and clothing; and the structure of the working force changed in ways which increased not only the proportion of urban to total population, but also the proportion of the population working in offices or in skilled factory jobs—aware of and anxious to acquire the consumption fruits of a mature economy.

In addition to these economic changes, the society ceased to accept the further extension of modern technology as an overriding objective. It is in this post-maturity stage, for example, that, through the political process, Western societies have chosen to allocate increased resources to social welfare and security. The emergence of the welfare state is one manifestation of a society's moving beyond technical maturity; but it is also at this stage that resources tend increasingly to be directed to the production of consumers' durables and to the diffusion of services on a mass basis, if consumers' sovereignty reigns. . . .

For the United States, the turning point was, perhaps, Henry Ford's moving assembly line of 1913–14; but it was in the 1920's, and again in the post-war decade, 1946-56, that this stage of growth was pressed to, virtually, its logical conclusion. In the 1950's Western Europe and Japan appear to have fully entered this phase, accounting substantially for a momentum in their economies quite unexpected in the immediate post-war years. The Soviet Union is technically ready for this stage, and, by every sign, its citizens hunger for it; but Communist leaders face difficult political and social problems of adjustment if this stage is launched. . . .

These stages are not merely descriptive. They are not merely a way of generalizing certain factual observations about the sequence of development of modern societies. They have an inner logic and continuity. They have an analytic bone-structure, rooted in a dynamic theory of production. . . .

Within the framework set by forces determining the total level of output, sectoral optimum positions are determined on the side of demand, by the levels of income and of population, and by the character of tastes; on the side of supply, by the state of technology and the quality of entrepreneurship, as the latter determines the proportion of technically available and potentially profitable innovations actually incorporated in the capital stock. . . .

Nevertheless, the economic history of growing societies takes a part of its rude shape from the effort of societies to approximate the optimum sectoral paths. At any period of time, the rate of growth in the sectors will vary greatly; and it is possible to isolate empirically certain leading sectors, at early stages of their evolution, whose rapid rate of expansion plays an essential direct and indirect role in maintaining the overall momentum of the economy. . . .

The course of birth-rates, for example, represents one form of welfare choice made by societies, as income has changed; and population curves reflect (in addition to changing death-rates) how the calculus about family size was made in the various stages; from the usual (but not universal) decline in birth-rates, during or soon after the take-off, as urbanization took hold and progress became a palpable possibility, to the recent rise, as Americans (and others in societies marked by high mass-consumption) have appeared to seek in larger families values beyond those afforded by economic security and by an ample supply of durable consumers' goods and services.

And there are other decisions as well that societies have made as the choices open to them have been altered by the unfolding process of economic growth; and these broad collective decisions, determined by many factors—deep in history, culture, and the active political process—outside the market-place, have interplayed with the dynamics of market demand, risk-taking, technology and entrepreneurship, to determine the specific content of the stages of growth for each society. . . .

When independent modern nationhood is achieved, how should the national energies be disposed: in external aggression, to right old wrongs or to exploit newly created or perceived possibilities for enlarged national power; in completing and refining the political victory of the new national government over old regional interests; or in modernizing the economy?

Once growth is under way, with the take-off, to what extent should the requirements of diffusing modern technology and maximizing the rate of growth be moderated by the desire to increase consumption per capita and to increase welfare?

When technological maturity is reached, and the nation has at its command a modernized and differentiated industrial machine, to what ends should it be put, and in what proportions: to increase social security, through the welfare state; to expand mass-consumption into the range of durable consumers' goods and services; to increase the nation's stature and power on the world scene; or to increase leisure?

And then the question beyond, where history offers us only fragments: what to do when the increase in real income itself loses its charm? Babies, boredom, three-day week-ends, the moon, or the creation of new inner, human frontiers in substitution for the imperatives of scarcity?

In surveying now the broad contours of each stage-of-growth, we are examining, then, not merely the sectoral structure of economies, as they transformed themselves for growth, and grew; we are also examining a succession of strategic choices made by various societies concerning the disposition of their resources. . . .

JOHN F. KENNEDY, "INAUGURAL ADDRESS" (1961)

In his Inaugural Address, President John F. Kennedy (1917–1963) summons Americans to redouble their efforts undertaken on behalf of freedom. Waging the Cold War is to take precedence over all other national priorities.

We observe today not a victory of party but a celebration of freedom—symbolizing an end as well as a beginning—signifying renewal as well as change. For I have sworn before you and Almighty God the same solemn oath our forebears prescribed nearly a century and three quarters ago.

The world is very different now. For man holds in his mortal hands the power to abolish all forms of human poverty and all forms of human life. And yet the same revolutionary beliefs for which our forebears fought are still at issue around the globe—the belief that the rights of man come not from the generosity of the state but from the hand of God.

We dare not forget today that we are the heirs of that first revolution. Let the word go forth from this time and place, to friend and foe alike, that the torch has been passed to a new generation of Americans—born in this century, tempered by war, disciplined by a hard and bitter peace, proud of our ancient heritage—and unwilling to witness or permit the slow undoing of those human rights to which this nation has always been committed, and to which we are committed today at home and around the world.

Let every nation know, whether it wishes us well or ill, that we shall pay any price, bear any burden, meet any hardship, support any friend, oppose any foe to assure the survival and the success of liberty.

This much we pledge—and more.

To those old allies whose cultural and spiritual origins we share, we pledge the loyalty of faithful friends. United, there is little we cannot do in a host of cooperative ventures. Divided, there is little we can do—for we dare not meet a powerful challenge at odds and split asunder.

To those new states whom we welcome to the ranks of the free, we pledge our word that one form of colonial control shall not have passed away merely to be replaced by a far more iron tyranny. We shall not always expect to find them supporting our view. But we shall always hope to find them strongly supporting their own freedom-and to remember that, in the past, those who foolishly sought power by riding the back of the tiger ended up inside.

To those peoples in the huts and villages of half the globe struggling to break the bonds of mass misery, we pledge our best efforts to help them help themselves, for whatever period is required—not because the communists may be doing it, not because we seek their votes, but because it is right. If a free society cannot help the many who are poor, it cannot save the few who are rich.

To our sister republics south of our border, we offer a special pledge—to convert our good words into good deeds—in a new alliance for progress—to assist free men and free governments in casting off the chains of poverty. But this peaceful revolution of hope cannot become the prey of hostile powers. Let all our neighbors know that we shall join with them to oppose aggression or subversion anywhere in the Americas. And let every other power know that this Hemisphere intends to remain the master of its own house.

To that world assembly of sovereign states, the United Nations, our last best hope in an age where the instruments of war have far outpaced the instruments of peace, we renew our pledge of support—to prevent it from becoming merely a forum for invective—to strengthen its shield of the new and the weak—and to enlarge the area in which its writ may run.

Finally, to those nations who would make themselves our adversary, we offer not a pledge but a request: that both sides begin anew the quest for peace, before the dark powers of destruction unleashed by science engulf all humanity in planned or accidental self-destruction.

We dare not tempt them with weakness. For only when our arms are sufficient beyond doubt can we be certain beyond doubt that they will never be employed.

But neither can two great and powerful groups of nations take comfort from our present course—both sides overburdened by the cost of modern weapons, both rightly alarmed by the steady spread of the deadly atom, yet both racing to alter that uncertain balance of terror that stays the hand of mankind's final war.

So let us begin anew—remembering on both sides that civility is not a sign of weakness, and sincerity is always subject to proof. Let us never negotiate out of fear. But let us never fear to negotiate.

Let both sides explore what problems unite us instead of belaboring those problems which divide us.

Let both sides, for the first time, formulate serious and precise proposals for the inspection and control of arms—and bring the absolute power to destroy other nations under the absolute control of all nations.

Let both sides seek to invoke the wonders of science instead of its terrors. Together let us explore the stars, conquer the deserts, eradicate disease, tap the ocean depths and encourage the arts and commerce.

Let both sides unite to heed in all corners of the earth the command of Isaiah—to "undo the heavy burdens . . . (and) let the oppressed go free."

And if a beach-head of cooperation may push back the jungle of suspicion, let both sides join in creating a new endeavor, not a new balance of power, but a new world of law, where the strong are just and the weak secure and the peace preserved.

All this will not be finished in the first one hundred days. Nor will it be finished in the first one thousand days, nor in the life of this Administration, nor even perhaps in our lifetime on this planet. But let us begin.

In your hands, my fellow citizens, more than mine, will rest the final success or failure of our course. Since this country was founded, each generation of Americans has been summoned to give testimony to its national loyalty. The graves of young Americans who answered the call to service surround the globe.

Now the trumpet summons us again—not as a call to bear arms, though arms we need—not as a call to battle, though embattled we are—but a call to bear the burden of a long twilight struggle, year in and year out, "rejoicing in hope, patient in tribulation"—a struggle against the common enemies of man: tyranny, poverty, disease and war itself.

Can we forge against these enemies a grand and global alliance, North and South, East and West, that can assure a more fruitful life for all mankind? Will you join in that historic effort?

In the long history of the world, only a few generations have been granted the role of defending freedom in its hour of maximum danger. I do not shrink from this responsibility—I welcome it. I do not believe that any of us would exchange places with any other people or any other generation. The energy, the faith, the devotion which we bring to this endeavor will light our country and all who serve it—and the glow from that fire can truly light the world.

And so, my fellow Americans: ask not what your country can do for you—ask what you can do for your country.

My fellow citizens of the world: ask not what America will do for you, but what together we can do for the freedom of man.

Finally, whether you are citizens of America or citizens of the world, ask of us here the same high standards of strength and sacrifice which we ask of you. With a good conscience our only sure reward, with history the final judge of our deeds, let us go forth to lead the land we love, asking His blessing and His help, but knowing that here on earth God's work must truly be our own.

LYNDON BAINES JOHNSON, "PEACE WITHOUT CONQUEST" (1965)

Kennedy's assassination in November 1963 vaulted Lyndon Johnson (1908–1973) into the presidency. Among the problems that LBJ inherited upon taking office was the war in South Vietnam. For years, the United States had been attempting to create a secure and viable government in a territory besieged by an internal insurgency with support from communist North Vietnam. Kennedy had greatly escalated levels of US military support, without positive effect. After winning the presidency in his own right in November 1964, Johnson concluded that preventing the Republic of Vietnam from collapse required the commitment of large numbers of US combat troops into the south combined with sustained bombing of the north. This decision prompted widespread protest within the United States, eventually resulting in a massive antiwar movement. Here Johnson attempts to place the Vietnam War in the broader context of US history and to justify his decision to "Americanize" the conflict.

Tonight Americans and Asians are dying for a world where each people may choose its own path to change.

This is the principle for which our ancestors fought in the valleys of Pennsylvania. It is the principle for which our sons fight tonight in the jungles of Viet-Nam.

Viet-Nam is far away from this quiet campus. We have no territory there, nor do we seek any. The war is dirty and brutal and difficult. And some 400 young men, born into an America that is bursting with opportunity and promise, have ended their lives on Viet-Nam's steaming soil.

Why must we take this painful road?

Why must this Nation hazard its ease, and its interest, and its power for the sake of a people so far away?

We fight because we must fight if we are to live in a world where every country can shape its own destiny. And only in such a world will our own freedom be finally secure.

This kind of world will never be built by bombs or bullets. Yet the infirmities of man are such that force must often precede reason, and the waste of war, the works of peace.

We wish that this were not so. But we must deal with the world as it is, if it is ever to be as we wish.

The world as it is in Asia is not a serene or peaceful place.

The first reality is that North Viet-Nam has attacked the independent nation of South Viet-Nam. Its object is total conquest.

Of course, some of the people of South Viet-Nam are participating in attack on their own government. But trained men and supplies, orders and arms, flow in a constant stream from north to south.

This support is the heartbeat of the war.

And it is a war of unparalleled brutality. Simple farmers are the targets of assassination and kidnapping. Women and children are strangled in the night because their men are loyal to their government. And helpless villages are ravaged by sneak attacks. Large-scale raids are conducted on towns, and terror strikes in the heart of cities.

The confused nature of this conflict cannot mask the fact that it is the new face of an old enemy.

Over this war—and all Asia—is another reality: the deepening shadow of Communist China. The rulers in Hanoi are urged on by Peking. This is a regime which has destroyed freedom in Tibet, which has attacked India, and has been condemned by the United Nations for aggression in Korea. It is a nation which is helping the forces of violence in almost every continent. The contest in Viet-Nam is part of a wider pattern of aggressive purposes.

Why are these realities our concern? Why are we in South Viet-Nam?

We are there because we have a promise to keep. Since 1954 every American President has offered support to the people of South Viet-Nam. We have helped to build, and we have helped to defend. Thus, over many years, we have made a national pledge to help South Viet-Nam defend its independence.

And I intend to keep that promise.

To dishonor that pledge, to abandon this small and brave nation to its enemies, and to the terror that must follow, would be an unforgivable wrong.

We are also there to strengthen world order. Around the globe, from Berlin to Thailand, are people whose well-being rests, in part, on the belief that they can count on us if they are attacked. To leave Viet-Nam to its fate would shake the confidence of all these people in the value of an American commitment and in the value of America's word. The result would be increased unrest and instability, and even wider war.

We are also there because there are great stakes in the balance. Let no one think for a moment that retreat from Viet-Nam would bring an end to conflict. The battle would be renewed in one country and then another. The central lesson of our time is that the appetite of aggression is never satisfied. To withdraw from one battlefield means only to prepare for the next. We must say in southeast Asia—as we did in Europe—in the words of the Bible: "Hitherto shalt thou come, but no further."

There are those who say that all our effort there will be futile—that China's power is such that it is bound to dominate all southeast Asia. But there is no end to that argument until all of the nations of Asia are swallowed up.

There are those who wonder why we have a responsibility there. Well, we have it there for the same reason that we have a responsibility for the defense of Europe. World War II was fought in both Europe and Asia, and when it ended we found ourselves with continued responsibility for the defense of freedom.

Our objective is the independence of South Viet-Nam, and its freedom from attack. We want nothing for ourselves—only that the people of South Viet-Nam be allowed to guide their own country in their own way.

We will do everything necessary to reach that objective. And we will do only what is absolutely necessary.

In recent months attacks on South Viet-Nam were stepped up. Thus, it became necessary for us to increase our response and to make attacks by air. This is not a change of purpose. It is a change in what we believe that purpose requires.

We do this in order to slow down aggression.

We do this to increase the confidence of the brave people of South Viet-Nam who have bravely borne this brutal battle for so many years with so many casualties.

And we do this to convince the leaders of North Viet-Nam—and all who seek to share their conquest—of a very simple fact: We will not be defeated. We will not grow tired.

We will not withdraw, either openly or under the cloak of a meaningless agreement.

We know that air attacks alone will not accomplish all of these purposes. But it is our best and prayerful judgment that they are a necessary part of the surest road to peace.

We hope that peace will come swiftly. But that is in the hands of others besides ourselves. And we must be prepared for a long continued conflict. It will require patience as well as bravery, the will to endure as well as the will to resist.

I wish it were possible to convince others with words of what we now find it necessary to say with guns and planes: Armed hostility is futile. Our resources are equal to any challenge. Because we fight for values and we fight for principles, rather than territory or colonies, our patience and our determination are unending.

Once this is clear, then it should also be clear that the only path for reasonable men is the path of peaceful settlement.

Such peace demands an independent South Viet-Nam—securely guaranteed and able to shape its own relationships to all others—free from outside interference—tied to no alliance—a military base for no other country.

These are the essentials of any final settlement.

We will never be second in the search for such a peaceful settlement in Viet-Nam.

There may be many ways to this kind of peace: in discussion or negotiation with the governments concerned; in large groups or in small ones; in the reaffirmation of old agreements or their strengthening with new ones.

We have stated this position over and over again, fifty times and more, to friend and foe alike. And we remain ready, with this purpose, for unconditional discussions.

And until that bright and necessary day of peace we will try to keep conflict from spreading. We have no desire to see thousands die in battle—Asians or Americans. We have no desire to devastate that which the people of North Viet-Nam have built with toil and sacrifice. We will use our power with restraint and with all the wisdom that we can command.

But we will use it.

This war, like most wars, is filled with terrible irony. For what do the people of North Viet-Nam want? They want what their neighbors also desire: food for their hunger; health for their bodies; a chance to learn; progress for their country; and an end to the bondage of material misery. And they would find all these things far more readily in peaceful association with others than in the endless course of battle.

These countries of southeast Asia are homes for millions of impoverished people. Each day these people rise at dawn and struggle through until the night to wrestle existence from the soil. They are often wracked by disease, plagued by hunger, and death comes at the early age of 40.

Stability and peace do not come easily in such a land. Neither independence nor human dignity will ever be won, though, by arms alone. It also requires the work of peace. The American people have helped generously in times past in these works. Now there must be a much more massive effort to improve the life of man in that conflict-torn corner of our world.

The first step is for the countries of southeast Asia to associate themselves in a greatly expanded cooperative effort for development. We would hope that North Viet-Nam would take its place in the common effort just as soon as peaceful cooperation is possible.

The United Nations is already actively engaged in development in this area. As far back as 1961 I conferred with our authorities in Viet-Nam in connection with their work there. And I would hope tonight that the Secretary General of the United Nations could use the prestige of his great office, and his deep knowledge of Asia, to initiate, as soon as possible, with the countries of that area, a plan for cooperation in increased development.

For our part I will ask the Congress to join in a billion dollar American investment in this effort as soon as it is underway.

And I would hope that all other industrialized countries, including the Soviet Union, will join in this effort to replace despair with hope, and terror with progress.

The task is nothing less than to enrich the hopes and the existence of more than a hundred million people. And there is much to be done.

The vast Mekong River can provide food and water and power on a scale to dwarf even our own TVA.

The wonders of modern medicine can be spread through villages where thousands die every year from lack of care.

Schools can be established to train people in the skills that are needed to manage the process of development.

And these objectives, and more, are within the reach of a cooperative and determined effort.

I also intend to expand and speed up a program to make available our farm surpluses to assist in feeding and clothing the needy in Asia. We should not allow people to go hungry and wear rags while our own warehouses overflow with an abundance of wheat and corn, rice and cotton.

So I will very shortly name a special team of outstanding, patriotic, distinguished Americans to inaugurate our participation in these programs. . . .

This will be a disorderly planet for a long time. In Asia, as elsewhere, the forces of the modern world are shaking old ways and uprooting ancient civilizations. There will be turbulence and struggle and even violence. Great social change—as we see in our own country now—does not always come without conflict.

We must also expect that nations will on occasion be in dispute with us. It may be because we are rich, or powerful; or because we have made some mistakes; or because they honestly fear our intentions. However, no nation need ever fear that we desire their land, or to impose our will, or to dictate their institutions.

But we will always oppose the effort of one nation to conquer another nation.

We will do this because our own security is at stake.

But there is more to it than that. For our generation has a dream. It is a very old dream. But we have the power and now we have the opportunity to make that dream come true.

For centuries nations have struggled among each other. But we dream of a world where disputes are settled by law and reason. And we will try to make it so.

For most of history men have hated and killed one another in battle. But we dream of an end to war. And we will try to make it so.

For all existence most men have lived in pov-erty, threatened by hunger. But we dream of a world where all are fed and charged with hope. And we will help to make it so.

The ordinary men and women of North Viet-Nam and South Viet-Nam—of China and India—of Russia and America—are brave people. They are filled with the same proportions of hate and fear, of love and hope. Most of them want the same things for themselves and their families. Most of them do not want their sons to ever die in battle, or to see their homes, or the homes of others, destroyed.

Well, this can be their world yet. Man now has the knowledge—always before denied—to make this planet serve the real needs of the people who live on it.

I know this will not be easy. I know how difficult it is for reason to guide passion, and love to master hate. The complexities of this world do not bow easily to pure and consistent answers.

But the simple truths are there just the same. We must all try to follow them as best we can.

We often say how impressive power is. But I do not find it impressive at all. The guns and the bombs, the rockets and the warships, are all sym-bols of human failure. They are necessary symbols. They protect what we cherish. But they are wit-ness to human folly.

A dam built across a great river is impressive.

In the countryside where I was born, and where I live, I have seen the night illuminated, and the kitchens warmed, and the homes heated, where once the cheerless night and the ceaseless cold held sway. And all this happened because electric-ity came to our area along the humming wires of the REA. Electrification of the countryside—yes, that, too, is impressive.

A rich harvest in a hungry land is impressive.

The sight of healthy children in a classroom is impressive.

These—not mighty arms—are the achieve-ments which the American Nation believes to be impressive.

And, if we are steadfast, the time may come when all other nations will also find it so.

Every night before I turn out the lights to sleep I ask myself this question: Have I done everything that I can do to unite this country? Have I done everything I can to help unite the world, to try to bring peace and hope to all the peoples of the world? Have I done enough?

Ask yourselves that question in your homes—and in this hall tonight. Have we, each of us, all done all we could? Have we done enough?

We may well be living in the time foretold many years ago when it was said: "I call heaven and earth to record this day against you, that I have set before you life and death, blessing and cursing: therefore choose life, that both thou and thy seed may live."

This generation of the world must choose: destroy or build, kill or aid, hate or understand.

We can do all these things on a scale never dreamed of before.

Well, we will choose life. In so doing we will prevail over the enemies within man, and over the natural enemies of all mankind.

IX.

CHALLENGING THE CONSENSUS

Within a decade after World War II, waging the Cold War took precedence over all other considerations in American politics. Before long, however, challenges to this foreign policy consensus began to emerge. Among the sources of those challenges none was more important than the Vietnam War, which beginning in the mid-1960s produced widespread division and unrest. The resulting antiwar movement merged with other expressions of popular protest related to issues such as race, culture, inequality, free speech, abuses of power by an increasingly unaccountable state, and the excessive militarization of US policy.

By the time US forces finally withdrew from the Vietnam War in early 1973, the foreign policy consensus had been largely broken. Confidence in the efficacy of US military power and in the wisdom of the foreign policy establishment was reaching a low ebb. Policymakers understood that the "lessons" of Vietnam demanded that they avoid any recurrence of such a disaster. Yet with the US economy suffering, American prestige badly damaged, and the Soviet Union perceived to be flexing its muscles, defining an alternative to that consensus proved a daunting proposition. The way ahead appeared cloudy.

GRAHAM GREENE, *THE QUIET AMERICAN* (1955)

Graham Greene (1904–1991) was a British writer of a decidedly anti-American bent. Even before US military intervention in Vietnam, he accurately anticipated the snares awaiting the United States in that country. Greene's novel *The Quiet American* is set a decade earlier in the 1950s, when the French were fighting to retain their colonies in Indochina. Greene's protagonists are Fowler, a cynical British journalist, and Alden Pyle, an American intelligence operative. Inspired by the work of the fictional journalist York Harding, Pyle is engaged in a conspiracy that will enable the United States to displace France and thereby determine the destiny of Vietnam. Here Fowler and Pyle are stranded in countryside controlled by communist insurgents. Sharing a watchtower with two Vietnamese soldiers that the French have pressed into service to defend their empire, they discuss the merits of the war. America's intentions seem innocent and well-intentioned. Yet as Fowler observes in an aside, "innocence is like a dumb leper who has lost his bell, wandering the world, meaning no harm."

Now that we had settled on the floor, the Vietnamese relaxed a little. I felt some sympathy for them: it wasn't an easy job for a couple of ill-trained men to sit up here night after night, never sure of when the Viets might creep up on the road through the fields of paddy. I said to Pyle, 'Do you think they know they are fighting for democracy? We ought to have York Harding here to explain it to them.'

'You always laugh at York,' said Pyle.

'I laugh at anyone who spends so much time writing about what doesn't exist—mental concepts.'

'They exist for him. Haven't you got any mental concepts? God, for instance?'

'I've no reason to believe in a God. Do you?'

'Yes. I'm a Unitarian.'

'How many hundred millions Gods to people believe in? Why, even a Roman Catholic believes in quite a different God when he's scared or happy or hungry.'

'Maybe, if there is a God, he'd be so vast he'd look different to everyone.'

'Like the great Buddha in Bangkok,' I said. 'You can't see all of him at once. Anyway *he* keeps still.'

'I guess you're just trying to be tough,' Pyle said. 'There's something you must believe in. Nobody can go on living without some belief.'

'Oh, I'm not a Berkeleian. I believe my back's against this wall. I believe there's a sten gun over there.'

'I didn't mean that.'

'I believe what I report, which is more than most of your correspondents do.'

'Cigarette?'

'I don't smoke—except opium. Give one to the guards. We'd better stay friends with them.' Pyle got up and lit their cigarettes and came back. I said, 'I wish cigarettes had a symbolic significance like salt.'

'Don't you trust them?'

'No French officer,' I said, 'would care to spend the night alone with two scared guards in one of these towers. Why, even a platoon have been known to hand over their officers. Sometimes the Viets have a better success with a megaphone than a bazooka. I don't blame them. They don't believe in anything either. You and your like are trying to make a war with the help of people who just aren't interested.'

'They don't want Communism.'

'They want enough rice,' I said. 'They don't want to be shot at. They want one day to be much the same as another. They don't want our white skins around telling them what they want.'

'If Indo-China goes . . . '

'I know the record, Siam goes. Malaya goes. Indonesia goes. What does "go" mean? If I believed in your God and another life, I'd be my future harp against your golden crown that in five hundred years there may be no New York or London, but they'll be growing paddy in these fields, they'll be carrying their produce to market on long poles wearing their pointed hats. The small boys will be sitting on the buffaloes. I like the buffaloes, they don't like our smell, the smell of Europeans. And remember—from a buffalo's point of view you are a European too.'

Graham Greene, *The Quiet American.* New York: The Viking Press (1955).

'They'll be forced to believe what they are told, they won't be allowed to think for themselves.'

'Thought's a luxury. Do you think the peasant sits and thinks of God and Democracy when he gets inside his mud hut at night?'

'You talk as if the whole country were peasant. What about the educated? Are they going to be happy?'

'Oh no,' I said, 'we've brought them up in *our* ideas. We've taught them dangerous games, and that's why we are waiting here, hoping we don't get our throats cut. We deserve to have them cut. I wish your friend York was here too. I wonder how he'd relish it.'

'York Harding's a very courageous man. Why, in Korea . . . '

'He wasn't an enlisted man, was he? He had a return ticket. With a return ticket courage becomes an intellectual exercise, like a monk's flagellation. How much can I stick? Those poor devils can't catch a plane home. Hi,' I called to them, 'what are your names?' I thought that knowledge somehow would bring them into the circle of our conversation. They didn't answer: just lowered back at us behind the stumps of their cigarettes. 'They think we are French,' I said.

'That's just it,' Pyle said. 'You shouldn't be against York, you should be against the French. Their colonialism.'

'Isms and ocracies. Give me facts. A rubber planter beats his labourer—all right, I'm against him. He hasn't been instructed to do it by the Minister of the Colonies. In France I expect he'd beat his wife. I've seen a priest, so poor he hasn't a change of trousers, working fifteen hours a day from hut to hut in a cholera epidemic, eating nothing but rice and salt fish, saying his Mass with an old cup—a wooden platter. I don't believe in God and yet I'm for that priest. Why don't you can that colonialism?'

'It *is* colonialism. York says it's often the good administrators who make it hard to change a bad system.'

'Anyway the French are dying every day—that's not a mental concept. They aren't leading these people with half-lies like your politicians—and ours. I've been in India, Pyle, and I know the harm liberals do. We haven't a liberal party any more—liberalism's infected all the other parties. We are all either liberal conservatives or liberal socialists: we all have a good conscience. I'd rather be an exploiter who fights for what he exploits, and dies with it. Look at the history of Burma. We go and invade the country: the local tribes support us: we are victorious: but like you Americans we weren't colonialists in those days. Oh no, we made peace with the king and we handed him back his province and left our allies to be crucified and sawn in two. They were innocent. They thought we'd stay. But we were liberals and we didn't want a bad conscience.'

. . . .

'So you think we've lost?'

'That's not the point,' I said. 'I've no particular desire to see you win. I'd like those two poor buggers there to be happy—that's all. I wish they didn't have to sit in the dark at night scared.'

'You have to fight for liberty.'

'I haven't seen any Americans fighting around here. And as for liberty, I don't know what it means. Ask them.' I called across the floor in French to them. '*La liberté—qu'est ce que c'est la liberté?*' They sucked in the rice and stared back and said nothing.

Pyle said, 'Do you want everybody to be made in the same mould? You're arguing for the sake of arguing. You're an intellectual. You stand for the importance of the individual as much as I do—or York.'

'Why have we only just discovered it?' I said. 'Forty years ago no one talked that way.'

'It wasn't threatened then.'

'Ours wasn't threatened, oh no, but who cared about the individuality of the man in the paddy field—and who does now? The only man to treat him as a man is the political commissar. He'll sit in his hut and ask his name and listen to his complaints; he'll give up an hour a day to teaching him—it doesn't matter what, he's being treated like a man, like someone of value. Don't go on in the East with that parrot cry about a threat to the individual soul. Here you'd find yourself on the wrong side—it's they who stand for the individual and we just stand for Private 23987, unit in the global strategy.'

'You don't mean half of what you are saying,' Pyle said uneasily.

'Probably three quarters. I've been here a long time. You know, it's lucky I'm not *engagé*, there are things I'd be tempted to do—because here in the East—well, I don't like Ike. I like—well, these two. This is their country.'

C. WRIGHT MILLS, *THE POWER ELITE* (1956)

A sociologist who spent most of his career teaching at Columbia University, C. Wright Mills (1916–1962) was among the first to explain how preoccupations with national security were warping American democracy.

The powers of ordinary men are circumscribed by the everyday worlds in which they live, yet even in these rounds of job, family, and neighborhood they often seem driven by forces they can neither understand nor govern. "Great changes" are beyond their control, but affect their conduct and outlook none the less. The very framework of modern society confines them to projects not their own, but from every side, such changes now press upon the men and women of the mass society, who accordingly feel that they are without purpose in an epoch in which they are without power.

But not all men are in this sense ordinary. As the means of information and of power are centralized, some men come to occupy positions in American society from which they can look down upon, so to speak, and by their decisions mightily affect, the everyday worlds of ordinary men and women. . . .

The power elite is composed of men whose positions enable them to transcend the ordinary environments of ordinary men and women; they are in positions to make decisions having major consequences. Whether they do or do not make such decisions is less important than the fact that they do occupy such pivotal positions: their failure to act, their failure to make decisions, is itself an act that is often of greater consequence than the decisions they do make. For they are in command of the major hierarchies and organizations of modern society. They rule the big corporations. They run the machinery of state and claim its prerogatives. They direct the military establishment. They occupy the strategic command posts of the social structure, in which are now centered the effective means of the power and the wealth and the celebrity which they enjoy.

The power elite are not solitary rulers. Advisers and consultants, spokesmen and opinion-makers are often the captains of their higher thought and decision. Immediately below the elite are the professional politicians of the middle levels of power, in the Congress and in the pressure groups, as well as among the new and old upper classes of town and city and region. Mingling with them . . . are those professional celebrities who live by being continually displayed but are never, so long as they remain celebrities, displayed enough. . . . More or less unattached, as critics of morality and technicians of power, as spokesmen of God and creators of mass sensibility, such celebrities and consultants are part of the immediate scene in which the drama of the elite is enacted. But that drama itself is centered on the command posts of the major institutional hierarchies. . . .

Within American society, major national power now resides in the economic, the political, and the military domains. Other institutions seem off to the side of modern history, and, on occasion, duly subordinated to these. No family is as directly powerful in national affairs as any major corporation; no church is as directly powerful in the external biographies of young men in America today as the military establishment; no college is as powerful in the shaping of momentous events as the National Security Council. Religious, educational, and family institutions are not autonomous centers of national power; on the contrary, these decentralized areas are increasingly shaped by the big three, in which developments of decisive and immediate consequence now occur.

Families and churches and schools adapt to modern life; governments and armies and corporations shape it; and, as they do so, they turn these lesser institutions into means for their ends. . . .

Within each of the big three, the typical institutional unit has become enlarged, has become administrative, and, in the power of its decisions, has become centralized. Behind these developments there is a fabulous technology, for as institutions, they have incorporated this technology and guide it, even as it shapes and paces their developments.

C. Wright Mills, *The Power Elite*. New York: Oxford University Press (1956).

The economy—once a great scatter of small productive units in autonomous balance—has become dominated by two or three hundred giant corporations, administratively and politically interrelated, which together hold the keys to economic decisions.

The political order, once a decentralized set of several dozen states with a weak spinal cord, has become a centralized, executive establishment whch has taken up into itself many powers previously scattered, and now enters into each and every crany of the social structure.

The military order, once a slim establishment in a context of distrust fed by state militia, has become the largest and most expensive feature of government, and although well versed in smiling public relations, now has all the grim and clumsy efficiency of a sprawling bureaucratic domain. . . .

At the pinnacle of each of the three enlarged and centralized domains, there have arisen those higher circles which make up the economic, the political, and the military elites. At the top of the economy, among the corporate rich, there are the chief executives; at the top of the political order, the members of the political directorate; at the top of the military establishment, the elite of soldier-statesmen clustered in and around the Joint Chiefs of Staff and the upper echelon. As each of these domains has coincided with the others, as decisions tend to become total in their consequences, the leading men in each of the three domains—the warlords, the corporate chieftains, the political directorate—tend to come together, to form the power elite of America. . . .

The American government is not, in any simple way nor as a structural fact, a committee of "the ruling class." It is a network of "committees," and other men from other hierarchies besides the corporate rich sit in these committees. Of these, the professional politician himself is the most complicated, but the high military, the warlords of Washington, are the newest. . . .

All over the world, the warlord is returning. All over the world, reality is defined in his terms. And in America, too, into the political vacuum the warlords have marched. Alongside the corporate executives and the politicians, the generals and admirals—those uneasy cousins within the American elite—have gained and have been given increased power to make and to influence decisions of the gravest consequence. . . .

Like other nations, the United States was born in violence, but it was born at a time when warfare did not seem to be a dominating feature of human society. And it was born in a place which could not easily be reached by the machines of war, was not easily open to the devastation of war, not subject to the anxiety of those who live in military neighborhoods. In the time and place of its earlier period, the United States was well-situated to erect and to maintain a civilian government, and to hold well subordinated such militarist ambition as might prevail. . . .

A country whose people have been most centrally preoccupied by the individual acquisition of wealth would not be expected to favor subsidizing an organized body of men who, economically speaking, are parasitical. A country whose middle class cherished freedom and personal initiative would not be likely to esteem disciplined soldiers who all too often seemed to be tyrannically used in the support of less free governments. Economic forces and political climate, therefore, have historically favored the civilian devaluation of the military as an at-times necessary evil but always a burden. . . .

In the middle of the twentieth century, the influence of such peaceful and civilian values as exist in the United States—and with them the effective distrust and subordination of professional military men—must be balanced by the unprecedented situation which the American elite defines as the situation of the nation. . . .

The terms in which they have defined international reality are predominantly military. As a result, in the higher circles there has been a replacement of diplomacy in any historically recognized sense by calculations of war potential and the military seriousness of war threats. . . .

These definitions of reality and proposed orientations to it have led to a further feature of America's international posture: for the first time in American history, men in authority are talking about an "emergency" without a foreseeable end. During modern times, and especially in the United States, men had come to look upon history as a peaceful continuum interrupted by war. But now, the American elite does not have any real image of peace—other than as an uneasy interlude existing precariously by virtue of the balance of mutual fright. The only seriously accepted plan for "peace" is the fully loaded pistol. In short, war or a high state of war preparedness is felt to be the normal and seemingly permanent condition of the United States. . . .

This means, for one thing, that there is no free and wide debate of military policy or of policies of military relevance. But that, of course, is in line with the professional soldier's training for command and obedience, and with his ethos, which is certainly not that of a debating society in which decisions are put to a vote. It is also in line with the tendency in a mass society for manipulation to replace explicitly debated authority, as well as with the fact of total war in which the distinction between soldier and civilian is obliterated.

The military manipulation of civilian opinion and the military invasion of the civilian mind are now important ways in which the power of the warlords is steadily exerted.

The extent of the military publicity, and the absence of opposition to it, also means that it is not merely this proposal or that point of view that is being pushed. In the absence of contrasting views, the very highest form of propaganda warfare can be fought: the propaganda for a definition of reality within which only certain limited viewpoints are possible. What is being promulgated and reinforced in the military metaphysics—the cast of mind that defines international reality as basically military. The publicists of the military ascendency need not really work to indoctrinate with this metaphysics those who count: they have already accepted it.

WILLIAM APPLEMAN WILLIAMS, *THE TRAGEDY OF AMERICAN DIPLOMACY* (1959)

A graduate of the U.S. Naval Academy, World War II veteran, and influential diplomatic historian, William Appleman Williams (1921–1990) directly challenged the postwar consensus. His revised understanding of the "Open Door" formed the point of departure for a radical reinterpretation of US foreign policy.

The United States has more to offer the world, materially and spiritually, than the Soviet Union; hence the object of abandoning our clichés and reconsidering our assumptions is to return to the essence of America's contribution to mankind and to devise new programs and policies which will honor rather than distort those ideas and ideals. The rigor of the analysis and the vigor of the criticism are but means to achieve that goal.

Such a re-exmination of American foreign policy must be based upon a searching review of the way America has defined its own problems and objectives, and its relationship with the rest of the world. The reason for this is simple: realism goes nowhere unless it starts at home. Combined with a fresh look at Soviet behavior, such an understanding of American policy should help in

William Appleman Williams, *The Tragedy of American Diplomacy.* Cleveland: World Publishing Company (1959).

the effort to outline new programs and policies designed to bring America's ideals and practical objectives closer to realization. For in the most fundamental sense, the present crisis in American diplomacy is defined by the conflict within and between America's ideals and practice.

At the outset it is important to get a clear picture of the dilemma. In the realm of ideas and ideals, American policy is guided by three conceptions. One is the warm, generous, humanitarian impulse to help other people solve their problems. A second is the principle of self-determination applied at the international level, which asserts the right of every society to establish its own goals and objectives, and to realize them internally through the means it decides are appropriate. These two ideas can be reconciled; indeed, they complement each other to an extensive degree. But the third idea entertained by many Americans is one which insists that other people cannot *really* solve their problems and improve their lives unless they go about it the same way as the United States. . . .

The over-all result is that America's humanitarian urge to assist other peoples is undercut—even subverted—by the way it goes about helping them. Other societies come to feel that American policy causes them to lose their economic as well as their political right to self-determination. Feeling that they are being harmed rather than helped, they are inclined to resort to political and economic measures in retaliation, which only intensify a problem that is very complex to begin with. Hence it seems wise to start any analysis of the crisis of American diplomacy by trying to understand how the contradiction in its policy developed. . . .

A good starting point for such an effort is provided by Joseph A. Schumpter, an exceptionally brilliant and perceptive political economist, who once remarked that the American Dream was to become "a world unto itself." In theory, at any rate, that objective could be attained by one of two methods. America could concentrate on its position as leader of the Western Hemisphere and by careful planning and effort continue its development as a powerful and largely self-contained democratic and liberal empire. Only a few Americans have seriously entertained, developed, and advocated that approach. The other way of make America "a world unto itself" would be to Americanize a sizable potion of the world beyond the Western Hemisphere. Though never undertaken in a concerted effort through a resort to force, that general approach has nevertheless characterized American foreign policy, since the crucial decade of the 1890's, when Americans reacted to the threat of economic stagnation and the fear of social upheaval by turning abroad for new frontiers.

The enthusiastic support given by a majority of Americans to such leaders as Presidents Theodore Roosevelt and Woodrow Wilson, who emphasized the need and virtue of such ideological and economic expansion, serves to illustrate that attitude and outlook. Confident in America's role as the civilizing agent of the world, and also convinced that it had to expand economically, Roosevelt dismissed such struggles as those of the Boers in South Africa with the sweeping judgment that they were "battling on the wrong side of the fight for civilization and will have to go under." Wilson uttered so many classic expressions of his "moral imperialism" that it is more illuminating to recall his persistent concern for America's economic expansion. "There is nothing in which I am more interested," he assured the corporation leaders of the country in 1914, "than the fullest development of the trade of this country and its righteous conquest of foreign markets."

At the end of World War II, moreover, most American leaders were strongly inclined to deal with the problems of the postwar era by relying on the traditional approach of Roosevelt and Wilson. The great majority of them defined "internationalism" and "collective security" in terms of a system organized and led by the United States in opposition to the Soviet Union and exercising extensive authority in other areas of the world. Under their guidance, American power in the form of a monopoly of the atom bomb, and an economy temporarily more powerful than that of the rest of the world combined, was deployed to thwart the evil designs of Russia and to rehabilitate the rest of the world for the beneficent application of American leadership. Most Americans concluded that the program was necessary and just. They agreed with Secretary of State James Byrnes, who remarked in July, 1945, that the problem was "not to make the world safe for democracy, but to make the world safe for the United States." It was simply assumed that the two things were the same.

The rest of the world was assured that it had nothing to fear; its tomorrows would be even better versions of America's yesterdays. As President Harry S. Truman explained, the future itself was America's new frontier: "All we need to do is to undertake the proper development of vast areas and virtually unlimited resources in many parts of the world." Skeptics who fretted over the morality of the economics of the program were answered by Secretary of State Dean Acheson. Overseas aid and investment, he explained, would solve the persistent practical problem of building a viable system at home. As for morality, nothing could be more just: "We are willing to help people who believe the way we do, to continue to live the way they want to live."

. . . .

Though ridiculed and condemned by many experts and commentators (who nonetheless followed its essentials in their own policy recommendations and actions), the Open Door Policy worked brilliantly for a half-century. Its strategy and tactics enabled the United States to establish a new and persuasive empire during the era when the colonial empires of the eighteenth and nineteenth centuries were dying and being given the *coup de grâce* by the twentieth-century revolutions in economics, politics, color, and anticolonial nationalism. The very success of the Open Door Policy enabled America to exercise varying degrees of economic, political, and military influence and authority in the very countries that were driving the British, French, and Dutch back to Europe. Such power also carried with it the spirit of American idealism and the vision of a better life for foreign peoples. And in many specific cases these ideals had been realized to some extent in the process of American expansion.

But the triumph of the Open Door Policy was subject to the same process of cause and consequence—of change—which carried it to victory in fifty years. These results were inherent in the conception of the world which originally produced the policy and which translated it into concrete programs and actions. Central to the failure in success was the fact that the Open Door Policy defined America as an alien power in the eyes and the experience of most of the rest of the world. The Open Door Policy did not cease being a program of imperial expansion simply because it spurned territorial and administrative colonialism in favor of an empire of economics, ideology, and bases.

Attracted by its anticolonial character, foreign peoples initially welcomed it as a policy of assistance and friendship with no strings of absentee ownership attached. But within a generation they sense that its minimum objective was to stabilize and freeze the *status quo* of Western supremacy and that its optimum goal was to institutionalize American expansion. At the end of a half-century they were rebelling against the subordination of their own cultural, political, and economic life that was implicit in, and was practiced under, the policy of open-door expansion. . . .

Considerable intellectual and emotional discipline and courage are required if Americans are to change—not merely revise—their conception of themselves and the world. Yet is wiser to employ such courage and discipline for living than for dying. There is, indeed, no courage or discipline in following failure down the trail to disaster. . . .

Applied to the issue of America's conception of itself and the world, that insight suggests that the first step is to deny the validity of the crucial assumptions which provide the foundations for that *Weltanschauung*. Thus a radically different concept replaces the accepted thesis that America's freedom and prosperity depend upon the continued expansion of its economic and ideological system through the policy of the open door. Instead, it appears that America's political and economic well-being depend upon the rational and equitable use of its human and material resources at home and in interdependent cooperation with *all* other peoples of the world. America can neither take its place in nor makes its contribution to the world community until it believes and demonstrates that it can sustain prosperity and democracy without recourse to open-door imperial expansion.

The issue of the mid-twentieth century is how to sustain democracy and prosperity without imperial expansion. . . .

Having structured a creative response to the issue of democracy and prosperity at home, the United States could again devote a greater share of its attention and energy to the world scene. Its revamped foreign policy would be geared to helping other peoples achieve their own aspirations in their own way. The essence of such a foreign policy would be an open door for revolutions.

DWIGHT D. EISENHOWER, "FAREWELL ADDRESS TO THE NATION" (1961)

Just prior to leaving office as the nation's 34th president, Dwight D. Eisenhower (1890–1969) issued his own warning about the dangers posed by allowing national security to eclipse all other considerations. Eisenhower was anything but a radical. Yet in referencing the potential dangers of a "military-industrial complex," he was echoing the concerns expressed by C. Wright Mills a few years earlier.

Three days from now, after half a century in the service of our country, I shall lay down the responsibilities of office as, in traditional and solemn ceremony, the authority of the Presidency is vested in my successor.

This evening I come to you with a message of leave-taking and farewell, and to share a few final thoughts with you, my countrymen. . . .

We now stand ten years past the midpoint of a century that has witnessed four major wars among great nations. Three of these involved our own country. Despite these holocausts America is today the strongest, the most influential and most productive nation in the world. Understandably proud of this pre-eminence, we yet realize that America's leadership and prestige depend, not merely upon our unmatched material progress, riches and military strength, but on how we use our power in the interests of world peace and human betterment.

Throughout America's adventure in free government, our basic purposes have been to keep the peace; to foster progress in human achievement, and to enhance liberty, dignity and integrity among people and among nations. To strive for less would be unworthy of a free and religious people. Any failure traceable to arrogance, or our lack of comprehension or readiness to sacrifice would inflict upon us grievous hurt both at home and abroad.

Progress toward these noble goals is persistently threatened by the conflict now engulfing the world. It commands our whole attention, absorbs our very beings. We face a hostile ideology—global in scope, atheistic in character, ruthless in purpose, and insidious in method. Unhappily the danger it poses promises to be of indefinite duration. To meet it successfully, there is called for, not so much the emotional and transitory sacrifices of crisis, but rather those which enable us to carry forward steadily, surely, and without complaint the burdens of a prolonged and complex struggle—with liberty the stake. Only thus shall we remain, despite every provocation, on our charted course toward permanent peace and human betterment.

Crises there will continue to be. In meeting them, whether foreign or domestic, great or small, there is a recurring temptation to feel that some spectacular and costly action could become the miraculous solution to all current difficulties. A huge increase in newer elements of our defense; development of unrealistic programs to cure every ill in agriculture; a dramatic expansion in basic and applied research—these and many other possibilities, each possibly promising in itself, may be suggested as the only way to the road we wish to travel.

But each proposal must be weighed in the light of a broader consideration: the need to maintain balance in and among national programs—balance between the private and the public economy, balance between cost and hoped for advantage—balance between the clearly necessary and the comfortably desirable; balance between our essential requirements as a nation and the duties imposed by the nation upon the individual; balance between actions of the moment and the national welfare of the future. Good judgment seeks balance and progress; lack of it eventually finds imbalance and frustration.

The record of many decades stands as proof that our people and their government have, in the main, understood these truths and have responded to them well, in the face of stress and threat. But threats, new in kind or degree, constantly arise. I mention two only.

A vital element in keeping the peace is our military establishment. Our arms must be mighty, ready for instant action, so that no potential aggressor may be tempted to risk his own destruction.

Our military organization today bears little relation to that known by any of my predecessors in peacetime, or indeed by the fighting men of World War II or Korea.

Until the latest of our world conflicts, the United States had no armaments industry. American makers of plowshares could, with time and as required, make swords as well. But now we can no longer risk emergency improvisation of national defense; we have been compelled to create a permanent armaments industry of vast proportions. Added to this, three and a half million men and women are directly engaged in the defense establishment. We annually spend on military security more than the net income of all United States corporations.

This conjunction of an immense military establishment and a large arms industry is new in the American experience. The total influence-economic, political, even spiritual—is felt in every city, every State house, every office of the Federal government. We recognize the imperative need for this development. Yet we must not fail to comprehend its grave implications. Our toil, resources and livelihood are all involved; so is the very structure of our society.

In the councils of government, we must guard against the acquisition of unwarranted influence, whether sought or unsought, by the military-industrial complex. The potential for the disastrous rise of misplaced power exists and will persist.

We must never let the weight of this combination endanger our liberties or democratic processes. We should take nothing for granted. Only an alert and knowledgeable citizenry can compel the proper meshing of the huge industrial and military machinery of defense with our peaceful methods and goals, so that security and liberty may prosper together.

Akin to, and largely responsible for the sweeping changes in our industrial-military posture, has been the technological revolution during recent decades.

In this revolution, research has become central; it also becomes more formalized, complex, and costly. A steadily increasing share is conducted for, by, or at the direction of, the Federal government.

Today, the solitary inventor, tinkering in his shop, has been overshadowed by task forces of scientists in laboratories and testing fields. In the same fashion, the free university, historically the fountainhead of free ideas and scientific discovery, has experienced a revolution in the conduct of research. Partly because of the huge costs involved, a government contract becomes virtually a substitute for intellectual curiosity. For every old blackboard there are now hundreds of new electronic computers.

The prospect of domination of the nation's scholars by Federal employment, project allocations, and the power of money is ever present—and is gravely to be regarded.

Yet, in holding scientific research and discovery in respect, as we should, we must also be alert to the equal and opposite danger that public policy could itself become the captive of a scientific-technological elite.

It is the task of statesmanship to mold, to balance, and to integrate these and other forces, new and old, within the principles of our democratic system—ever aiming toward the supreme goals of our free society.

Another factor in maintaining balance involves the element of time. As we peer into society's future, we—you and I, and our government—must avoid the impulse to live only for today, plundering, for our own ease and convenience, the precious resources of tomorrow. We cannot mortgage the material assets of our grandchildren without risking the loss also of their political and spiritual heritage. We want democracy to survive for all generations to come, not to become the insolvent phantom of tomorrow.

Down the long lane of the history yet to be written America knows that this world of ours, ever growing smaller, must avoid becoming a community of dreadful fear and hate, and be, instead, a proud confederation of mutual trust and respect.

Such a confederation must be one of equals. The weakest must come to the conference table with the same confidence as do we, protected as we are by our moral, economic, and military strength. That table, though scarred by many past frustrations, cannot be abandoned for the certain agony of the battlefield.

Disarmament, with mutual honor and confidence, is a continuing imperative. Together we must learn how to compose differences, not with arms, but with intellect and decent purpose. Because this need is so sharp and apparent I confess that I lay down my official responsibilities in this field with a definite sense of disappointment. As one who has witnessed the horror and the lingering sadness of war—as one who knows that another war could utterly destroy this civilization which has been so slowly and painfully built over thousands of years—I wish I could say tonight that a lasting peace is in sight.

Happily, I can say that war has been avoided. Steady progress toward our ultimate goal has been made. But, so much remains to be done. . . .

STUDENTS FOR A DEMOCRATIC SOCIETY, "THE PORT HURON STATEMENT" (1962)

The decade of the 1960s saw the revival of American political radicalism, fueled by concerns related to race, war, inequality, consumerism, and fears of nuclear extinction. At the forefront of protest were college students. This document, largely drafted by Tom Hayden (1929–2016), then a student at the University of Michigan, provides insight into the worldview and ambitions that helped shape the protest movements of the Sixties.

We are people of this generation, bred in at least modest comfort, housed now in universities, looking uncomfortably to the world we inherit.

When we were kids the United States was the wealthiest and strongest country in the world: the only one with the atom bomb, the least scarred by modern war, an initiator of the United Nations that we thought would distribute Western influence throughout the world. Freedom and equality for each individual, government of, by, and for the people—these American values we found good, principles by which we could live as men. Many of us began maturing in complacency.

As we grew, however, our comfort was penetrated by events too troubling to dismiss. First, the permeating and victimizing fact of human degradation, symbolized by the Southern struggle against racial bigotry, compelled most of us from silence to activism. Second, the enclosing fact of the Cold War, symbolized by the presence of the Bomb, brought awareness that we ourselves, and our friends, and millions of abstract "others" we knew more directly because of our common peril, might die at any time. We might deliberately ignore, or avoid, or fail to feel all other human problems, but not these two, for these were too immediate and crushing in their impact, too challenging in the demand that we as individuals take the responsibility for encounter and resolution.

While these and other problems either directly oppressed us or rankled our consciences and became our own subjective concerns, we began to see complicated and disturbing paradoxes in our surrounding America. The declaration "all men are created equal . . ." rang hollow before the facts of Negro life in the South and the big cities of the North. The proclaimed peaceful intentions of the United States contradicted its economic and military investments in the Cold War status quo.

We witnessed, and continue to witness, other paradoxes. With nuclear energy whole cities can easily be powered, yet the dominant nation states seem more likely to unleash destruction greater than that incurred in all wars of human history. Although our own technology is destroying old and creating new forms of social organization, men still tolerate meaningless work and idleness. While two-thirds of mankind suffers undernourishment, our own upper classes revel amidst superfluous abundance. Although world population is expected to double in forty years, the nations still tolerate anarchy as a major principle of international conduct and uncontrolled exploitation governs the sapping of the earth's physical resources. Although mankind desperately needs revolutionary leadership, America rests in national stalemate, its goals ambiguous and tradition-bound instead of informed and clear, its democratic system apathetic and manipulated rather than "of, by, and for the people."

Not only did tarnish appear on our image of American virtue, not only did disillusion occur when the hypocrisy of American ideals was discovered, but we began to sense that what we had originally seen as the American Golden Age was actually the decline of an era. The worldwide outbreak of revolution against colonialism and imperialism, the entrenchment of totalitarian states, the menace of war, overpopulation, international disorder, super-technology—these trends were testing the tenacity of our own commitment to democracy and freedom and our abilities to visualize their application to a world in upheaval.

Our work is guided by the sense that we may be the last generation in the experiment with living. But we are a minority—the vast majority of our people regard the temporary equilibriums of our society and world as eternally-functional parts. In this is perhaps the outstanding paradox: we ourselves are imbued with urgency, yet the message of our society is that there is no viable alternative to the present. Beneath the reassuring tones of the politicians, beneath the common opinion that America will "muddle through," beneath the stagnation of those who have closed their minds to the future, is the pervading feeling that there simply are no alternatives, that our times have witnessed the exhaustion not only of Utopias, but of any new departures as well. Feeling the press of complexity upon the emptiness of life, people are fearful of the thought that at any moment things might thrust out of control. They fear change itself, since change might smash whatever invisible framework seems to hold back chaos for them now. For most Americans, all crusades are suspect, threatening. The fact that each individual sees apathy in his fellows perpetuates the common reluctance to organize for change. The dominant institutions are complex enough to blunt the minds of their potential critics, and entrenched enough to swiftly dissipate or entirely repel the energies of protest and reform, thus limiting human expectancies. Then, too, we are a materially improved society, and by our own improvements we seem to have weakened the case for further change.

Some would have us believe that Americans feel contentment amidst prosperity—but might it not better be called a glaze above deeply felt anxieties about their role in the new world? And if these anxieties produce a developed indifference to human affairs, do they not as well produce a yearning to believe there is an alternative to the present, that something can be done to change circumstances in the school, the workplaces, the bureaucracies, the government? It is to this latter yearning, at once the spark and engine of change, that we direct our present appeal. The search for truly democratic alternatives to the present, and a commitment to social experimentation with them, is a worthy and fulfilling human enterprise, one which moves us and, we hope, others today. On such a basis do we offer this document of our convictions and analysis: as an effort in understanding and changing the conditions of humanity in the late twentieth century, an effort rooted in the ancient, still unfulfilled conception of man attaining determining influence over his circumstances of life. . . .

We regard men as infinitely precious and possessed of unfulfilled capacities for reason, freedom, and love. In affirming these principles we are aware of countering perhaps the dominant conceptions of man in the twentieth century: that he is a thing to be manipulated, and that he is inherently incapable of directing his own affairs. We oppose the depersonalization that reduces human beings to the status of things—if anything, the brutalities of the twentieth century teach that means and ends are intimately related, that vague appeals to "posterity" cannot justify the mutilations of the present. We oppose, too, the doctrine of human incompetence because it rests essentially on the modern fact that men have been "competently" manipulated into incompetence—we see little reason why men cannot meet with increasing skill the complexities and responsibilities of their situation, if society is organized not for minority, but for majority, participation in decision-making. . . .

Human relationships should involve fraternity and honesty. Human interdependence is contemporary fact; human brotherhood must be willed however, as a condition of future survival and as the most appropriate form of social relations. Personal links between man and man are needed, especially to go beyond the partial and fragmentary bonds of function that bind men only as worker to worker, employer to employee, teacher to student, American to Russian.

Loneliness, estrangement, isolation describe the vast distance between man and man today. These dominant tendencies cannot be overcome by better personnel management, nor by improved gadgets, but only when a love of man overcomes the idolatrous worship of things by man. . . .

In social change or interchange, we find violence to be abhorrent because it requires generally the transformation of the target, be it a human being or a community of people, into a depersonalized object of hate. It is imperative that the means of violence be abolished and the institutions—local, national, international—that encourage nonviolence as a condition of conflict be developed. . . .

The desperation of people threatened by forces about which they know little and of which they can say less; the cheerful emptiness of people "giving up" all hope of changing things; the faceless ones polled by Gallup who listed "international affairs" fourteenth on their list of "problems" but who also expected thermonuclear war in the next few years: in these and other forms, Americans are in withdrawal from public life, from any collective effort at directing their own affairs.

Some regard this national doldrums as a sign of healthy approval of the established order—but is it approval by consent or manipulated acquiescence? Others declare that the people are withdrawn because compelling issues are fast disappearing—perhaps there are fewer breadlines in America, but is Jim Crow gone, is there enough work and work more fulfilling, is world war a diminishing threat, and what of the revolutionary new peoples? Still others think the national quietude is a necessary consequence of the need for elites to resolve complex and specialized problems of modern industrial society—but, then, why should business elites help decide foreign policy, and who controls the elites anyway, and are they solving mankind's problems? Others, finally, shrug knowingly and announce that full democracy never worked anywhere in the past—but why lump qualitatively different civilizations together, and how can a social order work well if its best thinkers are skeptics, and is man really doomed forever to the domination of today?

There are no convincing apologies for the contemporary malaise. While the world tumbles toward the final war, while men in other nations are trying desperately to alter events, while the very future qua future is uncertain—America is without community, impulse, without the inner momentum necessary for an age when societies cannot successfully perpetuate themselves by their military weapons, when democracy must be viable because of its quality of life, not its quantity of rockets. . . .

The American political system is not the democratic model of which its glorifiers speak. In actuality it frustrates democracy by confusing the individual citizen, paralyzing policy discussion, and consolidating the irresponsible power of military and business interests.

A crucial feature of the political apparatus in America is that greater differences are harbored within each major party than the differences existing between them. . . .

What emerges from the party contradictions and insulation of privately held power is the organized political stalemate: calcification dominates flexibility as the principle of parliamentary organization, frustration is the expectancy of legislators intending liberal reform, and Congress becomes less and less central to national decision-making, especially in the area of foreign policy. In this context, confusion and blurring is built into the formulation of issues, long-range priorities are not discussed in the rational manner needed for policymaking, the politics of personality and "image" become a more important mechanism than the construction of issues in a way that affords each voter a challenging and real option. The American voter is buffeted from all directions by pseudo-problems, by the structurally-initiated sense that nothing political is subject to human mastery. Worried by his mundane problems which never get solved, but constrained by the common belief that politics is an agonizingly slow accommodation of views, he quits all pretense of bothering.

A most alarming fact is that few, if any, politicians are calling for changes in these conditions. . . . . While in practice they rig public opinion to suit their own interests, in word and ritual they enshrine "the sovereign public" and call for more and more letters. Their speeches and campaign actions are banal, based on a degrading conception of what people want to hear. They respond not to dialogue, but to pressure: and knowing this, the ordinary citizen sees even greater inclination to shun the political sphere. The politicians is usually a trumpeter to "citizenship" and "service to the nation," but since he is unwilling to seriously rearrange power relationships, his trumpetings only increase apathy by creating no outlets. Much of the time the call to "service" is justified not in idealistic terms, but in the crasser terms of "defending the free world from communism"—thus making future idealistic impulses harder to justify in anything but Cold War terms.

In such a setting of status quo politics, where most if not all government activity is rationalized in Cold War anti-communist terms, it is somewhat natural that discontented, super-patriotic groups would emerge through political channels and explain their ultra-conservatism as the best means of Victory over Communism. . . . Their political views are defined generally as the opposite of the supposed views of communists: complete individual freedom in the economic sphere, non-participation by the government in the machinery of production. But actually "anticommunism" becomes an umbrella by which to protest liberalism, internationalism, welfarism, the active civil rights and labor movements. . . .

We live amidst a national celebration of economic prosperity while poverty and deprivation remain an unbreakable way of life for millions in the "affluent society," including many of our own generation. We hear glib reference to the "welfare state," "free enterprise," and "shareholder's democracy" while military defense is the main item of "public" spending and obvious oligopoly and other forms of minority rule defy real individual initiative or popular control. Work, too, is often unfulfilling and victimizing, accepted as a channel to status or plenty, if not a way to pay the bills, rarely as a means of understanding and controlling self and events. In work and leisure the individual is regulated as part of the system, a consuming unit, bombarded by hardsell soft-sell, lies and semi-true appeals and his basest drives. He is always told what he is supposed to enjoy while being told, too, that he is a "free" man because of "free enterprise." . . .

The most spectacular and important creation of the authoritarian and oligopolistic structure of economic decision-making in America is the institution called "the military-industrial complex" by former President Eisenhower, the powerful congruence of interest and structure among military and business elites which affects so much of our development and destiny. Not only is ours the first generation to live with the possibility of world-wide cataclysm—it is the first to experience the actual social preparation for cataclysm, the general militarization of American society. . . .

Business and politics, when significantly militarized, affect the whole living condition of each American citizen. Worker and family depend on the Cold War for life. Half of all research and development is concentrated on military ends. The press mimics conventional cold war opinion in its editorials. In less than a full generation, most Americans accept the military-industrial structure as "the way things are." War is still pictured as one more kind of diplomacy, perhaps a gloriously satisfying kind.

Our saturation and atomic bombings of Germany and Japan are little more than memories of past "policy necessities" that preceded the wonderful economic boom of 1946. The facts that our once-revolutionary 20,000 ton Hiroshima Bomb is now paled by 50 megaton weapons, that our lifetime has included the creation of intercontinental ballistic missiles, that "greater" weapons are to follow, that weapons refinement is more rapid than the development of weapons of defense, that soon a dozen or more nations will have the Bomb, that one simple miscalculation could incinerate mankind: these orienting facts are but remotely felt. . . .

Past senselessness permits present brutality; present brutality is prelude to future deeds of still greater inhumanity; that is the moral history of the twentieth century, from the First World War to the present. A half-century of accelerating destruction has flattened out the individual's ability to make moral distinction, it has made people understandably give up, it has forced private worry and public silence.

To a decisive extent, the means of defense, the military technology itself, determines the political and social character of the state being defended—that is, defense mechanism themselves in the nuclear age alter the character of the system that creates them for protection. So it has been with American, as her democratic institutions and habits have shriveled in almost direct proportion to the growth of her armaments. Decisions about military strategy, including the monstrous decision to go to war, are more and more the property of the military and the industrial arms race machine, with the politicians assuming a ratifying role instead of a determining one. This is increasingly a fact not just because of the installation of the permanent military, but because of constant revolutions in military technology. The new technologies allegedly require military expertise, scientific comprehension, and the mantle of secrecy. As Congress relies more and more on the Joint Chiefs of Staff, the existing chasm between people and decision-makers becomes irreconcilably wide, and more alienating in its effects.

A necessary part of the military effort is propaganda: to "sell" the need for congressional appropriations, to conceal various business scandals, and to convince the American people that the arms race is important enough to sacrifice civil liberties and social welfare. So confusion prevails about the national needs, while the three major services and the industrial allies jockey for power—the Air Force tending to support bombers and missilery, the Navy, Polaris and carriers, the Army, conventional ground forces and invulnerable nuclear arsenals, and all three feigning unity and support of the policy of weapons and agglomeration called the "mix." Strategies are advocated on the basis of power and profit, usually more so than on the basis of national military needs. In the meantime, Congressional investigating committees—most notably the House Un-American Activities Committee and the Senate Judiciary Committee—attempt to curb the little dissent that finds its way into off-beat magazines. A huge militant anticommunist brigade throws in its support, patriotically willing to do anything to achieve "total victory" in the Cold War; the government advocates peaceful confrontation with international Communism, then utterly pillories and outlaws the tiny American Communist Party. University professors withdraw prudently from public issues; the very style of social science writing becomes more qualified. Needs in housing, education, minority rights, health care, land redevelopment, hourly wages, all are subordinated—though a political tear is shed gratuitously—to the primary objective of the "military and economic strength of the Free World."

What are the governing policies which supposedly justify all this human sacrifice and waste? With few exceptions they have reflected the quandaries and confusion, stagnation and anxiety, of a stalemated nation in a turbulent world. They have shown a slowness, sometimes a sheer inability to react to a sequence of new problems.

Of these problems, two of the newest are foremost: the existence of poised nuclear weapons and the revolutions against the former colonial powers. In the both areas, the Soviet Union and the various national communist movements have aggravated international relations in inhuman and undesirable ways, but hardly so much as to blame only communism for the present menacing situation.

The accumulation of nuclear arsenals, the threat of accidental war, the possibility of limited war becoming illimitable holocaust, the impossibility of achieving final arms superiority or invulnerability, the approaching nativity of a cluster of infant atomic powers; all of these events are tending to undermine traditional concepts of power relations among nations. War can no longer be considered as an effective instrument of foreign policy, a means of strengthening alliances, adjusting the balance of power, maintaining national sovereignty, or preserving human values. War is no longer simply a forceful extension of foreign policy; it can obtain no constructive ends in the modern world. Soviet or American "megatonnage" is sufficient to destroy all existing social structures as well as value systems. Missiles have (figuratively) thumbed their nosecones at national boundaries. But America, like other countries, still operates by means of national defense and deterrence systems. These are seen to be useful so long as they are never fully used: unless we as a national entity can convince Russia that we are willing to commit the most heinous action in human history, we will be forced to commit it.

Deterrence advocates, all of them prepared at least to threaten mass extermination, advance arguments of several kinds. At one pole are the minority of open partisans of preventive war—who falsely assume the inevitability of violent conflict and assert the lunatic efficacy of striking the first blow, assuming that it will be easier to "recover" after thermonuclear war than to recover now from the grip of the Cold War. Somewhat more reluctant to advocate initiating a war, but perhaps more disturbing for their numbers within the Kennedy Administration, are the many advocates of the "counterforce" theory of aiming strategic nuclear weapons at military installations—though this might "save" more lives than a preventive war, it would require drastic, provocative and perhaps impossible social change to separate many cities from weapons sites, it would be impossible to ensure the immunity of cities after one or two counterforce nuclear "exchanges," it would generate a perpetual arms race for less vulnerability and greater weapons power and mobility, it would make outer space a region subject to militarization, and accelerate the suspicions and arms build-ups which are incentives to precipitate nuclear action. Others would support fighting "limited wars" which use conventional (all but atomic) weapons, backed by deterrents so mighty that both sides would fear to use them—although underestimating the implications of numerous new atomic powers on the world stage, the extreme difficulty of anchoring international order with weapons of only transient invulner-ability, the potential tendency for a "losing side" to push limited protracted fighting on the soil of underdeveloped countries. Still other deterrence artists propose limited, clearly defensive and retal-iatory, nuclear capacity, always potent enough to deter an opponent's aggressive designs—the best of deterrence stratagems, but inadequate when it rests on the equation of an arms "stalemate" with international stability.

All the deterrence theories suffer in several common ways. They allow insufficient attention to preserving, extending, and enriching demo-cratic values, such matters being subordinate rather than governing in the process of conducting for-eign policy. Second, they inadequately realize the inherent instabilities of the continuing arms race and balance of fear. Third, they operationally tend to eclipse interest and action towards disarma-ment by solidifying economic, political and even moral investments in continuation of tensions. Fourth, they offer a disinterested and even patri-otic rationale for the boondoggling, belligerence, and privilege of military and economic elites. Finally, deterrence stratagems invariably understate or dismiss the relatedness of various dangers; they inevitably lend tolerability to the idea of war by neglecting the dynamic interaction of problems—such as the menace of accidental war, the proba-ble future tensions surrounding the emergence of ex-colonial nations, the imminence of several new nations joining the "Nuclear Club," the destabi-lizing potential of technological breakthrough by either arms race contestant, the threat of Chinese atomic might, the fact that "recovery" after World War III would involve not only human survivors but, as well, a huge and fragile social structure and culture which would be decimated perhaps irrep-arably by total war.

Such a harsh critique of what we are doing as a nation by no means implies that sole blame for the Cold War rests on the United States. Both sides have behaved irresponsibly—the Russians by an exaggerated lack of trust, and by much dependence on aggressive military strategists rather than on proponents of nonviolent conflict

and coexistence. But we do contend, as Americans concerned with the conduct of our representative institutions, that our government has blamed the Cold War stalemate on nearly everything but its own hesitations, its own anachronistic dependence on weapons. To be sure, there is more to disarma-ment than wishing for it. There are inadequacies in international rule-making institutions—which could be corrected. There are faulty inspection mechanisms—which could be perfected by disin-terested scientists. There is Russian intransigency and evasiveness—which do not erase the fact that the Soviet Union, because of a strained econ-omy, an expectant population, fears of Chinese potential, and interest in the colonial revolution, is increasingly disposed to real disarmament with real controls. But there is, too, our own reluctance to face the uncertain world beyond the Cold War, our own shocking assumption that the risks of the present are fewer than the risks of a policy re-orientation to disarmament, our own unwilling-ness to face the implementation of our rhetorical commitments to peace and freedom. . . .

With rare variation, American foreign policy in the Fifties was guided by a concern for foreign investment and a negative anti-communist polit-ical stance linked to a series of military alliances, both undergirded by military threat. We partici-pated unilaterally—usually through the Central Intelligence Agency—in revolutions against gov-ernments in Laos, Guatemala, Cuba, Egypt, Iran. We permitted economic investment to decisively affect our foreign policy: fruit in Cuba, oil in the Middle East, diamonds and gold in South Africa (with whom we trade more than with any African nation). . . .

Ever since the colonial revolution began, American policy makers have reacted to new problems with old "gunboat" remedies, often thinly disguised. The feeble but desirable efforts of the Kennedy administration to be more flexible are coming perhaps too late, and are of too little significance to really change the historical thrust of our policies. The hunger problem is increas-ing rapidly mostly as a result of the worldwide population explosion that cancels out the meager triumphs gained so far over starvation. . . .

The world is in transformation. But America is not. It can race to industrialize the world, tol-erating occasional authoritarianisms, socialisms, neutralisms along the way—or it can slow the pace of the inevitable and default to the eager and self-interested Soviets and, much more importantly, to mankind itself. Only mystics would guess we have opted thoroughly for the first. Consider what our people think of this, the most urgent issue on the human agenda. Fed by a bellicose press, manipulated by economic and political opponents of change, drifting in their own history, they grumble about "the foreign aid waste," or about "that beatnik down in Cuba," or how "things will get us by" . . . thinking confidently, albeit in the usual bewilderment, that Americans can go right on like always, five percent of mankind producing forty percent of its goods.

An unreasoning anti-communism has become a major social problem for those who want to construct a more democratic America. McCarthyism and other forms of exaggerated and conservative anti-communism seriously weaken democratic institutions and spawn movements contrary to the interests of basic freedoms and peace. In such an atmosphere even the most intelligent of Americans fear to join political organizations, sign petitions, speak out on serious issues. Militaristic policies are easily "sold" to a public fearful of a democratic enemy. Political debate is restricted, thought is standardized, action is inhibited by the demands of "unity" and "oneness" in the face of the declared danger. Even many liberals and socialists share static and repititious participation in the anti-communist crusade and often discourage tentative, inquiring discussion about "the Russian question" within their ranks—often by employing "stalinist," "stalinoid," trotskyite" and other epithets in an oversimplifying way to discredit opposition.

Thus much of the American anti-communism takes on the characteristics of paranoia. Not only does it lead to the perversion of democracy and to the political stagnation of a warfare society, but it also has the unintended consequence of preventing an honest and effective approach to the issues. Such an approach would require public analysis and debate of world politics. But almost nowhere in politics is such a rational analysis possible to make.

It would seem reasonable to expect that in America the basic issues of the Cold War should be rationally and fully debated, between persons of every opinion—on television, on platforms and through other media. It would seem, too, that there should be a way for the person or an organization to oppose communism without contributing to the common fear of associations and public actions. But these things do not happen; instead, there is finger-pointing and comical debate about the most serious of issues. This trend of events on the domestic scene, towards greater irrationality on major questions, moves us to greater concern than does the "internal threat" of domestic communism. Democracy, we are convinced, requires every effort to set in peaceful opposition the basic viewpoints of the day; only by conscious, determined, though difficult, efforts in this direction will the issue of communism be met appropriately.

As democrats we are in basic opposition to the communist system. The Soviet Union, as a system, rests on the total suppression of organized opposition, as well as on a vision of the future in the name of which much human life has been sacrificed, and numerous small and large denials of human dignity rationalized. The Communist Party has equated falsely the "triumph of true socialism" with centralized bureaucracy. The Soviet state lacks independent labor organizations and other liberties we consider basic. And despite certain reforms, the system remains almost totally divorced from the image officially promulgated by the Party. Communist parties throughout the rest of the world are generally undemocratic in internal structure and mode of action. Moreover, in most cases they subordinate radical programs to requirements of Soviet foreign policy. The communist movement has failed, in every sense, to achieve its stated intentions of leading a worldwide movement for human emancipation.

But present trends in American anti-communism are not sufficient for the creation of appropriate policies with which to relate to and counter communist movements in the world. In no instance is this better illustrated than in our basic national policy-making assumption that the Soviet Union is inherently expansionist and aggressive, prepared to dominate the rest of the world by military means. On this assumption rests the monstrous American structure of military "preparedness"; because of it we sacrifice values and social programs to the alleged needs of military power.

But the assumption itself is certainly open to question and debate. To be sure, the Soviet state has used force and the threat of force to promote or defend its perceived national interests. But the typical American response has been to equate the use of force—which in many cases might be dispassionately interpreted as a conservative, albeit brutal, action—with the initiation of a world-wide military onslaught. In addition, the Russian-Chinese conflicts and the emergency throughout the communist movement call for a re-evaluation of any monolithic interpretations. And the apparent Soviet disinterest in building a first-strike arsenal of weapons challenges the weight given to protection against surprise attack in formulations of American policy toward the Soviets.

Almost without regard to one's conception of the dynamics of Soviet society and foreign policy, it is evident that the American military response has been more effective in deterring the growth of democracy than communism. Moreover, our prevailing policies make difficult the encouragement of skepticism, anti-war or pro-democratic attitudes in the communist systems. America has done a great deal to foment the easier, opposite tendency in Russia: suspicion, suppression, and stiff military resistance. We have established a system of military alliances which of even dubious deterrence value. It is reasonable of suggest the "Berlin" and "Laos" have been earth-shaking situations partly because rival systems of deterrence make impossible the withdrawal of threats. The "status quo" is not cemented by mutual threat but by mutual fear of receding from pugnacity—since the latter course would undermine the "credibility" of our deterring system. Simultaneously, while billions in military aid were propping up right-wing Laotian, Formosan, Iranian and other regimes, American leadership never developed a purely political policy for offering concrete alternatives to either communism or the status quo for colonial revolutions. The results have been: fulfillment of the communist belief that capitalism is stagnant, its only defense being dangerous military adventurism; destabilizing incidents in numerous developing countries; an image of America allied with corrupt oligarchies counterposed to the Russian-Chinese image of rapid, though brutal, economic development. Again and again, America mistakes the static area of defense, rather than the dynamic area of development, as the master need of two-thirds of mankind.

Our paranoia about the Soviet Union has made us incapable of achieving agreements absolutely necessary for disarmament and the preservation of peace. We are hardly able to see the possibility that the Soviet Union, though not "peace loving," may be seriously interested in disarmament.

Infinite possibilities for both tragedy and progress lie before us. On the one hand, we can continue to be afraid, and out of fear commit suicide. On the other hand, we can develop a fresh and creative approach to world problems which will help to create democracy at home and establish conditions for its growth elsewhere in the world. . . .

How to end the Cold War? How to increase democracy in America? These are the decisive issues confronting liberal and socialist forces today. To us, the issues are intimately related, the struggle for one invariably being a struggle for the other. What policy and structural alternatives are needed to obtain these ends?

Universal controlled disarmament must replace deterrence and arms control as the national defense goal. The strategy of mutual threat can only temporarily prevent thermonuclear war, and it cannot but erode democratic institutions here while consolidating oppressive institutions in the Soviet Union. Yet American leadership, while giving rhetorical due to the ideal of disarmament, persists in accepting mixed deterrence as its policy formula: under Kennedy we have seen first-strike and second-strike weapons, counter-military and counter-population inventions, tactical atomic weapons and guerilla warriors, etc. The convenient rationalization that our weapons potpourri will confuse the enemy into fear of misbehaving is absurd and threatening. Our own intentions, once clearly retaliatory, are now ambiguous since the President has indicated we might in certain circumstances be the first to use nuclear weapons. We can expect that Russia will become more anxious herself, and perhaps even prepare to "preempt" us, and we (expecting the worst from the Russians) will nervously consider "preemption" ourselves. The symmetry of threat and counter-threat lead not to stability but to the edge of hell.

It is necessary that America make disarmament, not nuclear deterrence, "credible" to the

Soviets and to the world. That is, disarmament should be continually avowed as a national goal; concrete plans should be presented at conference tables; real machinery for a disarming and disarmed world—national and international—should be created while the disarming process itself goes on. The long-standing idea of unilateral initiative should be implemented as a basic feature of American disarmament strategy. . . .

Russia cannot be expected to negotiate disarmament treaties for the Chinese. We should not feed Chinese fanaticism with our encirclement but Chinese stomachs with the aim of making war contrary to Chinese policy interests. Every day that we support anti-communist tyrants but refuse to even allow the Chinese Communists representation in the United Nations marks a greater separation of our ideals and our actions, and it makes more likely bitter future relations with the Chinese. . . .

Experiments in disengagement and demilitarization must be conducted as part of the total disarming process. These "disarmament experiments" can be of several kinds, so long as they are consistent with the principles of containing the arms race and isolating specific sectors of the world from the Cold War power-play. First, it is imperative that no more nations be supplied with, or locally produce, nuclear weapons . . .

Second, the United States should reconsider its increasingly outmoded European defense framework, the North Atlantic Treaty Organization. Since its creation in 1949, NATO has assumed increased strength in overall determination of Western military policy, but has become less and less relevant to its original purpose, which was the defense of Central Europe. . . .

If disengagement could be achieved, a major zone could be removed from the Cold War, the German problem would be materially diminished, and the need for NATO would diminish, and attitudes favorable to disarming would be generated.

Needless to say, those proposals are much different than what is currently being practised and praised. American military strategists are slowly acceding to the NATO demand for an independent deterrent, based on the fear that America might not defend Europe from military attack. These tendencies strike just the opposite chords in Russia than those which would be struck by

disengagement themes: the chords of military alertness, based on the fact that NATO (bulwarked by the German Wehrmacht) is preparing to attack Eastern Europe or the Soviet Union. Thus the alarm which underlies the NATO proposal for an independent deterrent is likely itself to bring into existence the very Russian posture that was the original cause of fear. Armaments spiral and belligerence will carry the day, not disengagement and negotiation.

Many Americans are prone to think of the industrialization of the newly developed countries as a modern form of American noblesse, undertaken sacrificially for the benefit of others. On the contrary, the task of world industrialization, of eliminating the disparity between have and have-not nations, is as important as any issue facing America. The colonial revolution signals the end of an era for the old Western powers and a time of new beginnings for most of the people of the earth. In the course of these upheavals, many problems will emerge: American policies must be revised or accelerated in several ways.

The United States' principal goal should be creating a world where hunger, poverty, disease, ignorance, violence, and exploitation are replaced as central features by abundance, reason, love, and international cooperation. To many this will seem the product of juvenile hallucination: but we insist it is a more realistic goal than is a world of nuclear stalemate. Some will say this is a hope beyond all bounds: but is far better to us to have positive vision than a "hard headed" resignation. Some will sympathize, but claim it is impossible: if so, then, we, not Fate, are the responsible ones, for we have the means at our disposal. We should not give up the attempt for fear of failure.

We should undertake here and now a fifty-year effort to prepare for all nations the conditions of industrialization. Even with far more capital and skill than we now import to emerging areas, serious prophets expect that two generations will pass before accelerating industrialism is a worldwide act. The needs are numerous: every nation must build an adequate infrastructure (transportation, communication, land resources, waterways) for future industrial growth; there must be industries suited to the rapid development of differing raw materials and other resources; education must begin on a continuing basis for everyone in the society, especially including engineering and technical training; technical assistance from outside sources must be adequate to meet present and long-term needs; atomic power plants must spring up to make electrical energy available. With America's idle productive capacity, it is possible to begin this process immediately without changing our military allocations. This might catalyze a "peace race" since it would demand a response of such magnitude from the Soviet Union that arms spending and "coexistence" spending would become strenuous, perhaps impossible, for the Soviets to carry on simultaneously.

We should not depend significantly on private enterprise to do the job. Many important projects will not be profitable enough to entice the investment of private capital. The total amount required is far beyond the resources of corporate and philanthropic concerns. The new nations are suspicious, legitimately, of foreign enterprises dominating their national life. World industrialization is too huge an undertaking to be formulated or carried out by private interests. Foreign economic assistance is a national problem, requiring long range planning, integration with other domestic and foreign policies, and considerable public debate and analysis. Therefore the Federal government should have primary responsibility in this area.

We should not lock the development process into the Cold War: we should view it as a way of ending that conflict. When President Kennedy declared that we must aid those who need aid because it is right, he was unimpeachably correct—now principle must become practice. We should reverse the trend of aiding corrupt anti-communist regimes. To support dictators like Diem while trying to destroy ones like Castro will only enforce international cynicism about American "principle," and is bound to lead to even more authoritarian revolutions, especially in Latin America where we did not even consider foreign aid until Castro had challenged the status quo. We should end the distinction between communist hunger and anti-communist hunger. To feed only anticommunists is to . . . incur the wrath of real democrats, and to distort our own sense of human values. We must cease seeing development in terms of communism and capitalism. To fight communism by capitalism in

the newly-developing areas is to fundamentally misunderstand the international hatred of imperialism and colonialism and to confuse and needs of 19th century industrial America with those of contemporary nations.

Quite fortunately, we are edging away from the Dullesian "either-or" foreign policy ultimatum towards an uneasy acceptance of neutralism and nonalignment. If we really desire the end of the Cold War, we should now welcome nonalignment—that is, the creation of whole blocs of nations concerned with growth and with independently trying to break out of the Cold War apparatus.

Finally, while seeking disarmament as the genuine deterrent, we should shift from financial support of military regimes to support of national development. Real security cannot be gained by propping up military defenses, but only through the hastening of political stability, economic growth, greater social welfare, improved education. Military aid is temporary in nature, a "shoring up" measure that only postpones crisis. . . .

America should show its commitment to democratic institutions not by withdrawing support from undemocratic regimes, but by making domestic democracy exemplary. Worldwide amusement, cynicism and hatred toward the United States as a democracy is not simply a communist propaganda trick, but an objectively justifiable phenomenon. If respect for democracy is to be international, then the significance of democracy must emanate from American shores, not from the "soft sell" of the United States Information Agency . . .

Democratic theory must confront the problems inherent in social revolutions. For Americans concerned with the development of democratic societies, the anti-colonial movements and revolutions in the emerging nations pose serious problems. We need to face these problems with humility: after 180 years of constitutional government we are still striving for democracy in our own society. We must acknowledge that democracy and freedom do not magically occur, but have roots in historical experience; they cannot always be demanded for any society at any time, but must be nurtured and facilitated. We must avoid the arbitrary projection of Anglo-Saxon democratic forms onto different cultures. Instead of democratic capitalism we should anticipate more or less authoritarian variants of socialism and collectivism in many emergent societies. . . .

Every effort to end the Cold War and expand the process of world industrialization is an effort hostile to people and institutions whose interests lie in perpetuation of the East-West military threat and the postponement of change in the "have not" nations of the world. Every such effort, too, is bound to establish greater democracy in America . . .

The broadest movement for peace in several years emerged in 1961-62. In its political orientation and goals it is much less identifiable than the movement for civil rights: it includes socialists, pacifists, liberals, scholars, militant activists, middle-class women, some professionals, many students, a few unionists. Some have been emotionally single-issue: Ban the Bomb. Some have been academically obscurantist. Some have rejected the System (sometimes both systems). Some have attempted, too, to "work within" the System. Amidst these conflicting streams of emphasis, however, certain basic qualities appear. The most important is that the "peace movement" has operated almost exclusively through peripheral institutions—almost never through mainstream institutions. Similarly, individuals interested in peace have nonpolitical social roles that cannot be turned to the support of peace activity. Concretely, liberal religious societies, anti-war groups, voluntary associations, ad hoc committees have been the political unit of the peace movement, and its human movers have been students, teachers, housewives, secretaries, lawyers, doctors, clergy. The units have not been located in spots of major social influence, the people have not been able to turn their resources fully to the issues that concern them. The results are political ineffectiveness and personal alienation.

The organizing ability of the peace movement thus is limited to the ability to state and polarize issues. It does not have an institution or the forum in which the conflicting interests can be debated. The debate goes on in corners; it has little connection with the continuing process of determining allocations of resources. This process is not necessarily centralized, however much the peace movement is estranged from it. National policy, though dominated to a large degree by the "power elites" of the corporations and military, is still partially founded in consensus. It can be altered when there actually begins a shift in the allocation of resources and the listing of priorities by the people in the institutions which have social influence, e.g., the labor unions and the schools. As long as the debates of the peace movement form only a protest, rather than an opposition viewpoint within the centers of serious decision-making, then it is neither a movement of democratic relevance, nor is it likely to have any effectiveness except in educating more outsiders to the issue. It is vital, to be sure, that this educating go on. . . .

But in the long interim before the national political climate is more open to deliberate, goal-directed debate about peace issues, the dedicated peace "movement" might well prepare a local base, especially by establishing civic committees on the techniques of converting from military to peacetime production. To make war and peace relevant to the problems of everyday life, by relating it to the backyard (shelters), the baby (fall-out), the job (military contracts)—and making a turn toward peace seem desirable on these same terms—is a task the peace movement is just beginning, and can profitably continue. . . .

From 1960 to 1962, the campuses experienced a revival of idealism among an active few. Triggered by the impact of the sit-ins, students began to struggle for integration, civil liberties, student rights, peace, and against the fast-rising right wing "revolt" as well. The liberal students, too, have felt their urgency thwarted by conventional channels: from student governments to Congressional committees. Out of this alienation from existing channels has come the creation of new ones; the most characteristic forms of liberal-radical student organizations are the dozens of campus political parties, political journals, and peace marches and demonstrations. In only a few cases have students built bridges to power: an occasional election campaign, the sit-ins, Freedom Rides, and voter registration activities; in some relatively large Northern demonstrations for peace and civil rights, and infrequently, through the United States National Student Association whose notable work has not been focused on political change.

These contemporary social movements—for peace, civil rights, civil liberties, labor—have in common certain values and goals. The fight for peace is one for a stable and racially integrated world; for an end to the inherently volatile exploitation of most of mankind by irresponsible elites; and for freedom of economic, political and cultural organization. The fight for civil rights is also one for social welfare for all Americans; for free speech and the right to protest; for the shield of economic independence and bargaining power; for a reduction of the arms race which takes national attention and resources away from the problems of domestic injustice. Labor's fight for jobs and wages is also one labor; for the right to petition and strike; for world industrialization; for the stability of a peacetime economy instead of the insecurity of the war economy; for expansion of the Welfare State. The fight for a liberal Congress is a fight for a platform from which these concerns can issue. And the fight for students, for internal democracy in the university, is a fight to gain a forum for the issues. . . .

The bridge to political power, though, will be built through genuine cooperation, locally, nationally, and internationally, between a new left of young people, and an awakening community of allies. In each community we must look within the university and act with confidence that we can be powerful, but we must look outwards to the less exotic but more lasting struggles for justice.

To turn these possibilities into realities will involve national efforts at university reform by an alliance of students and faculty. They must wrest control of the educational process from the administrative bureaucracy. They must make fraternal and functional contact with allies in labor, civil rights, and other liberal forces outside the campus. They must import major public issues into the curriculum—research and teaching on problems of war and peace is an outstanding example. They must make debate and controversy, not dull pedantic cant, the common style for educational life. They must consciously build a base for their assault upon the loci of power.

As students for a democratic society, we are committed to stimulating this kind of social movement, this kind of vision and program in campus and community across the country. If we appear to seek the unattainable, as it has been said, then let it be known that we do so to avoid the unimaginable.

BARRY GOLDWATER, "ACCEPTANCE SPEECH" (1964)

Dissent from the postwar foreign policy consensus did not come exclusively from the Left. In 1964, Arizona Senator Barry Goldwater (1909–1998), an unabashed conservative, won the Republican nomination for the presidency. In Goldwater's estimation, the forces of freedom were losing the Cold War. He vowed to win it. In the November election, Lyndon Johnson crushed his Republican challenger. Yet Goldwater's critique of the strategy of containment as timorous and his insistence that communism could be defeated outright lived on.

From this moment, united and determined, we will go forward together, dedicated to the ultimate and undeniable greatness of the whole man. Together we will win. . . .

The good Lord raised this mighty Republic to be a home for the brave and to flourish as the land of the free—not to stagnate in the swampland of collectivism, not to cringe before the bully of communism.

Now, my fellow Americans, the tide has been running against freedom. Our people have followed false prophets. We must, and we shall, return to proven ways—not because they are old, but because they are true. We must, and we shall, set the tide running again in the cause of freedom. And this party, with its every action, every word, every breath, and every heartbeat, has but a single resolve, and that is freedom—freedom made orderly for this nation by our constitutional government; freedom under a government limited by laws of nature and of nature's God; freedom—balanced so that liberty lacking order will not become the slavery of the prison cell; balanced so that liberty lacking order will not become the license of the mob and of the jungle.

Now, we Americans understand freedom. We have earned it, we have lived for it, and we have died for it. This Nation and its people are freedom's model in a searching world. We can be freedom's missionaries in a doubting world. But, ladies and gentlemen, first we must renew freedom's mission in our own hearts and in our own homes.

During four futile years, the administration which we shall replace has distorted and lost that faith. It has talked and talked and talked and talked the words of freedom. Now, failures cement the wall of shame in Berlin. Failures blot the sands of shame at the Bay of Pigs. Failures mark the slow death of freedom in Laos. Failures infest the jungles of Vietnam. And failures haunt the houses of our once great alliances and undermine the greatest bulwark ever erected by free nations—the NATO community. Failures proclaim lost leadership, obscure purpose, weakening wills, and the risk of inciting our sworn enemies to new aggressions and to new excesses. . . .

Rather than useful jobs in our country, people have been offered bureaucratic "make work," rather than moral leadership, they have been given bread and circuses, spectacles, and, yes, they have even been given scandals. Tonight there is violence in our streets, corruption in our highest offices, aimlessness among our youth, anxiety among our elders and there is a virtual despair among the many who look beyond material success for the inner meaning of their lives. Where examples of morality should be set, the opposite is seen. Small men, seeking great wealth or power, have too often and too long turned even the highest levels of public service into mere personal opportunity. . . .

Security from domestic violence, no less than from foreign aggression, is the most elementary and fundamental purpose of any government, and a government that cannot fulfill that purpose is one that cannot long command the loyalty of its citizens. History shows us—demonstrates that nothing—nothing prepares the way for tyranny more than the failure of

public officials to keep the streets from bullies and marauders. . . .

Those who seek absolute power, even though they seek it to do what they regard as good, are simply demanding the right to enforce their own version of heaven on earth. And let me remind you, they are the very ones who always create the most hellish tyrannies. Absolute power does corrupt, and those who seek it must be suspect and must be opposed. Their mistaken course stems from false notions of equality, ladies and gentlemen. Equality, rightly understood, as our founding fathers understood it, leads to liberty and to the emancipation of creative differences. Wrongly understood, as it has been so tragically in our time, it leads first to conformity and then to despotism. . . .

Yesterday it was Korea. Tonight it is Vietnam. Make no bones of this. Don't try to sweep this under the rug. We are at war in Vietnam. And yet the President, who is Commander-in-Chief of our forces, refuses to say—refuses to say, mind you, whether or not the objective over there is victory. And his Secretary of Defense continues to mislead and misinform the American people, and enough of it has gone by.

And I needn't remind you, but I will; it has been during Democratic years that a billion persons were cast into Communist captivity and their fate cynically sealed.

Today in our beloved country we have an administration which seems eager to deal with communism in every coin known—from gold to wheat, from consulates to confidence, and even human freedom itself. . . .

We here in America can keep the peace only if we remain vigilant and only if we remain strong. Only if we keep our eyes open and keep our guard up can we prevent war. And I want to make this abundantly clear—I don't intend to let peace or freedom be torn from our grasp because of lack of strength or lack of will—and that I promise you Americans.

I believe that we must look beyond the defense of freedom today to its extension tomorrow. I believe that the communism which boasts it will bury us will, instead, give way to the forces of freedom. And I can see in the distant and yet recognizable future the outlines of a world worthy our dedication, our every risk, our every effort, our every sacrifice along the way. Yes, a world that will redeem the suffering of those who will be liberated from tyranny. I can see and I suggest that all thoughtful men must contemplate the flowering of an Atlantic civilization, the whole world of Europe unified and free, trading openly across its borders, communicating openly across the world. This is a goal far, far more meaningful than a moon shot.

It's a truly inspiring goal for all free men to set for themselves during the latter half of the twentieth century. I can also see—and all free men must thrill to—the events of this Atlantic civilization joined by its great ocean highway to the United States. What a destiny, what a destiny can be ours to stand as a great central pillar linking Europe, the Americas and the venerable and vital peoples and cultures of the Pacific. I can see a day when all the Americas, North and South, will be linked in a mighty system, a system in which the errors and misunderstandings of the past will be submerged one by one in a rising tide of prosperity and interdependence. We know that the misunderstandings of centuries are not to be wiped away in a day or wiped away in an hour. But we pledge—we pledge that human sympathy—what our neighbors to the South call that attitude of "simpatico"—no less than enlightened self-interest will be our guide.

I can see this Atlantic civilization galvanizing and guiding emergent nations everywhere.

I know this freedom is not the fruit of every soil. I know that our own freedom was achieved through centuries, by unremitting efforts by brave and wise men. I know that the road to freedom is a long and a challenging road. I know also that some men may walk away from it, that some men resist challenge, accepting the false security of governmental paternalism.

And I pledge that the America I envision in the years ahead will extend its hand in health, in teaching and in cultivation, so that all new nations will be at least encouraged to go our way, so that they will not wander down the dark alleys of tyranny or to the dead-end streets of collectivism. My fellow Republicans, we do no man a service by hiding freedom's light under a bushel of mistaken humility.

I seek an American proud of its past, proud of its ways, proud of its dreams, and determined actively to proclaim them. But our example to the world must, like charity, begin at home. . . .

Balance, diversity, creativity—these are the elements of Republican equation. Republicans agree, Republicans agree heartily to disagree on many, many of their applications, but we have never disagreed on the basic fundamental issues of why you and I are Republicans.

This is a party, this Republican Party, a Party for free men, not for blind followers, and not for conformists.

Back in 1858 Abraham Lincoln said this of the Republican party—and I quote him, because he probably could have said it during the last week or so: "It was composed of strained, discordant, and even hostile elements" in 1858. Yet all of these elements agreed on one paramount objective: To arrest the progress of slavery, and place it in the course of ultimate extinction.

Today, as then, but more urgently and more broadly than then, the task of preserving and enlarging freedom at home and safeguarding it from the forces of tyranny abroad is great enough to challenge all our resources and to require all our strength. Anyone who joins us in all sincerity, we welcome. Those who do not care for our cause, we don't expect to enter our ranks in any case. And let our Republicanism, so focused and so dedicated, not be made fuzzy and futile by unthinking and stupid labels.

I would remind you that extremism in the defense of liberty is no vice. And let me remind you also that moderation in the pursuit of justice is no virtue.

The beauty of the very system we Republicans are pledged to restore and revitalize, the beauty of this Federal system of ours is in its reconciliation of diversity with unity. We must not see malice in honest differences of opinion, and no matter how great, so long as they are not inconsistent with the pledges we have given to each other in and through our Constitution. Our Republican cause is not to level out the world or make its people conform in computer regimented sameness. Our Republican cause is to free our people and light the way for liberty throughout the world.

J. William Fulbright, "The Fatal Arrogance of Power" (May 15, 1966)

A Democrat who wielded considerable power as chairman of the Senate Foreign Relations Committee, J. William Fulbright (1905–1995) was a committed Cold Warrior, until breaking with President Johnson over Vietnam. He then emerged as an eloquent and influential critic of American overreach. There are times, he argued, when dissent becomes a duty. This view did not endear Fulbright to his president.

To criticize one's country is to do it a service and pay it a compliment. It is a service because it may spur the country to do better than it is doing; it is a compliment because it evidences a belief that the country can do better than it is doing.

Criticism may embarrass the country's leaders in the short run but strengthen their hand in the long run; it may destroy a consensus on policy while expressing a consensus of values. Woodrow Wilson once said there was "such a thing as being too proud to fight." There is also, or ought to be, such as thing as being too confident to conform, too strong to be silent in the face of apparent error. Criticism, in short, is more than a right: It is an act of patriotism—a higher form of patriotism, I believe, than the familiar rituals of national adulation.

Thus, it is not pejorative but a tribute to say that America is worthy of criticism. If nonetheless one is charged with a lack of patriotism, I would reply with Albert Camus: "No, I didn't love my country, if pointing out what is unjust in what we love amounts to not loving, if insisting that what we love should measure up to the finest image we have of her amounts to not loving."

What is the finest image of America? To me it is the image of a composite—or, better still, a synthesis—of diverse peoples and cultures, come together in harmony, but not identity, in an open, receptive, generous and creative society.

We are an extraordinary nation, endowed with a rich and productive land and a talented and energetic population. Surely a nation so favored is capable of extraordinary achievement, not only in the area of producing and enjoying great wealth—where achievements have indeed been extraordinary—but also in the area of human and international relations—in which area, it seems to me, our achievements have fallen short of our capacity and promise. The question I find intriguing is whether a nation so extraordinarily endowed as the United States can overcome the arrogance of power which has afflicted, weakened, and in some cases, destroyed great nations in the past.

The causes of the malady are a mystery, but its recurrence is one of the uniformities of history: Power tends to confuse itself with virtue and a great nation is peculiarly susceptible to the idea that its power is a sign of God's favor, conferring upon it a special responsibility for other nations—to make them richer, happier and wiser, to remake them, that is, in its own shining image.

Power also tends to take itself for omnipotence. Once imbued with the idea of a mission, a great nation easily assumes that it has the means as well as the duty to do God's work. The Lord, after all, would surely not choose you as His agent and then deny you the sword with which to work His will. German soldiers in the First World War wore belt buckles imprinted with the words "*Got mit uns.*" It was approximately under this kind of infatuation—an exaggerated sense of power and an imaginary sense of mission—that the Athenians attacked Syracuse and Napoleon and then Hitler invaded Russia. In plain words, they overextended their commitments and they came to grief.

My question is whether America can overcome the fatal arrogance of power. My hope and my belief are that it can, that it has the human resources to accomplish what few, if any, great nations have ever accomplished before: to be confident, but also tolerant, and rich but also generous; to be willing to teach but also willing to learn; to be powerful but also wise. I believe that America is capable of all of these things; I also believe it is

J. William Fulbright, "The Fatal Arrogance of Power," *New York Times Magazine* (May 15, 1966).

falling short of them. Gradually but unmistakably we are succumbing to the arrogance of power. In so doing we are living up to our capacity and promise. The measure of our falling short is the measure of the patriot's duty to dissent.

The discharge of that most important duty is handicapped in America by an unworthy tendency to fear serious criticism of our Government. In the abstract we celebrate freedom of opinion as a vital part of our patriotic liturgy. It is only when some Americans exercise the right that other Americans are shocked. No one, of course, ever criticizes the right to dissent; it is always this particular instance of it or its exercise under these certain circumstances or at this particular time that throws people into a blue funk. I am reminded of Samuel Butler's observation: "People in general are equally horrified at hearing the Christian religion doubted, and at seeing it practiced."

No one challenges the value and importance of national consensus, but consensus can be understood in two ways. If it is interpreted to mean unquestioning support of existing policies, its effects can only be pernicious and undemocratic, serving to suppress differences rather than to reconcile them. If, on the other hand, consensus is understood to mean a general agreement on goals and values, but not necessarily on the best means of realizing them, then it becomes a lasting basis of national strength.

It is consensus in this sense that has made America strong in the past. Indeed, much of our national success in combining change with continuity can be attributed to the vigorous competition of men and ideas within a context of shared values and generally accepted institutions. It is only through this vigorous competition of ideas that a consensus of values can sometimes be translated into a true consensus of policy.

The correction of errors in a nation's foreign policy is greatly assisted by the timely raising of voices of criticism within the nation. . . .

A second great advantage of free discussion to democratic policymakers is its bringing to light of new ideas and the supplanting of old myths with new realities. We Americans are much in need of this benefit because we are severely, if not uniquely, afflicted with a habit of policy making by analogy: North Vietnam's involvement in South Vietnam, for example, is equated with

Hitler's invasion of Poland and a parley with the Vietcong would represent another Munich.

The treatment of slight and superficial resemblances as if they were full-blooded analogies—as instances, as it were, of history "repeating itself"—is a substitute for thinking and a misuse of history. The value of history is not what it seems to prohibit or prescribe, but its general indications as to the kinds of policies that are likely to succeed and the kinds that are likely to fail, or, as one historian has suggested, its hints as to what is likely not to happen.

There is a kind of voodoo about American foreign policy. Certain drums have to be beaten regularly to ward off evil spirits—for example, the maledictions that are regularly uttered against North Vietnamese aggression, the "wild men" of Peking, Communism in general and President de Gaulle. Certain pledges must be repeated every day lest the whole free world go to rack and ruin—for example, we will never go back on a commitment no matter how unwise; we regard this alliance or that as absolutely "vital" to the free world; and, of course, we will stand stalwart in Berlin from now until Judgment Day. Certain words must never be uttered except in derision—the word "appeasement," for example, comes as near as any word can to summarizing everything that is regarded by American policy makers as stupid, wicked and disastrous.

I do not suggest that we should heap praise on the Chinese Communists, dismantle NATO, abandon Berlin, and seize every opportunity that comes along to appease our enemies. I do suggest the desirability of an environment in which unorthodox ideas would arouse interest rather than horror, reflection rather than emotion. . . .

Consider the idea of "appeasement." In a free and healthy political atmosphere it would elicit neither horror nor enthusiasm but only interest in what precisely its proponent had in mind. . . .

In addition to its usefulness for redeeming error and introducing new ideas, free and open criticism has a third, more abstract but no less important function in a democracy. It is therapy and catharsis for those who are troubled or dismayed by something their country is doing; it helps to reassert traditional values, to clear the air when it is full of tension and mistrust.

There are times in public life as in private life when one must protest, not solely or even primarily because one's protest will be politic or materially productive, but because one's sense of decency is offended, because one is fed up with political craft and public images, or simply because something goes against the grain. The catharsis thus provided may indeed be the most valuable of freedom's uses.

While not unprecedented, protests against a war in the middle of the war are a rare experience for Americans. I see it as a mark of strength and maturity that an articulate minority have raised their voices against the Vietnamese war and that the majority of Americans are enduring this dissent— not without anxiety, to be sure, but with better grace and understanding than would have been the case with any other war of the 20th century.

It is by no means certain that the relatively healthy atmosphere in which the debate is now taking place will not give way to a new era of McCarthyism. The longer the Vietnamese war goes on without prospect of victory or negotiated peace, the higher the war fever will rise. Past experience provides little basis for confidence that reason can prevail in such an atmosphere. In a contest between a hawk and a dove the hawk has a great advantage, not because it is a better bird but because it is a bigger bird with lethal talons and a highly developed will to use them.

Without illusions as to the prospects of success, we must try nonetheless to bring reason and restraint into the emotionally charged atmosphere in which the Vietnamese war is now being discussed. Instead of trading epithets about the legitimacy of debate, we would do well to focus on the issue itself, recognizing that all of us make mistakes and that mistakes can be corrected only if they are acknowledged and discussed, and recognizing further that war is not its own justification, that it can and must be discussed unless we are prepared to sacrifice our traditional democratic processes to a false image of national unanimity. . . .

Some of our superpatriots assume that any war the United States fights is a just war, if not indeed a holy crusade, but history does not sustain their view. No reputable historian would deny that the United States has fought some wars which were unjust, unnecessary or both—I would suggest the War of 1812, the Civil War and the Spanish-American War as examples. In a historical frame of reference, it seems to me logical and proper to question the wisdom of our present military involvement in Asia.

Protesters against the Vietnamese war have been held up to scorn on the ground that they wish to "select their wars," by which it is apparently meant that it is hypocritical to object to this particular war while not objecting to war in general. I fail to understand what is reprehensible about trying to make moral distinctions between one war and another—between, for example, resistance to Hitler and intervention in Vietnam. . . .

Under the American Constitution, the Congress—especially the Senate—has a particular responsibility in coping with such problems, yet in recent years the Congress has not fully discharged its obligations in the field of foreign relations. The reduced role of the Congress and the enhanced role of the President in the making of foreign policy are not the result merely of President Johnson's ideas of consensus; they are the culmination of a trend in the constitutional relationship between President and Congress that began in 1940—that is to say, at the beginning of this age of crisis.

The cause of the change is crisis itself. The President has the authority and the resources to make decisions in an emergency; the Congress does not. Nor, in my opinion, should it; the proper responsibilities of the Congress are to reflect and review, to advise and criticize, to consent and withhold consent.

In the past 25 years, American foreign policy has encountered a shattering series of crises and inevitably—or almost inevitably—the effort to cope with these has been executive effort, while the Congress, inspired by patriotism, importuned by Presidents and deterred by lack of information, has tended to fall in line. The result has been an unhinging of traditional constitutional relationships; the Senate's constitutional powers of advice and consent have atrophied into what is widely regarded—though never asserted—to be a duty to give prompt consent with a minimum of advice.

. . . on Aug. 5, 1964, the Congress received an urgent request from President Johnson for the immediate adoption of a joint resolution regarding Southeast Asia. On Aug. 7, after perfunctory committee hearings and a brief debate, the Congress, with only two Senators dissenting, adopted the resolution, authorizing the President "to take all necessary steps, including the use of armed force" against aggression in Southeast Asia.

The joint resolution was a blank check signed by the Congress in an atmosphere of urgency that seemed at the time to preclude debate. Since its adoption, the Administration has converted the Vietnamese conflict from a civil war in which some American advisers were involved to a major international war in which the principal fighting unit is an American army of 250,000 men. Each time that Senators have raised questions about successive escalation of the war we have had the blank check of Aug. 7, 1964, waved in our faces as supposed evidence of the overwhelming support of the Congress for a policy in Southeast Asia which, in fact, has been radically changed since the summer of 1964.

All this is very frustrating to some of us in the Senate, but we have only ourselves to blame. . . .

The problem, then, is to find a way by which the Senate and individual Senators can discharge their constitutional duties of advice and consent in an age in which the direction and philosophy of foreign policy are largely shaped by urgent decisions made at moments of crisis.

The Senate as a whole, I think, should undertake to revive and strengthen its deliberative function. Acting on the premise that dissent is not disloyalty, that a true consensus is shaped by airing our differences rather than suppressing them, the Senate should again become, as it used to be, an institution in which the great issues of American politics are contested with thoroughness, energy and candor.

MARTIN LUTHER KING, "DECLARATION OF INDEPENDENCE FROM THE WAR IN VIETNAM" (1967)

Chiefly remembered for leading the civil rights movement of the 1950s and 1960s, Martin Luther King (1929–1968) also became an eloquent critic of the Vietnam War. In a speech delivered in New York's Riverside Church just one year before his assassination, Dr. King explains his reasoning.

I come to this magnificent house of worship tonight because my conscience leaves me no other choice. I join with you in this meeting because I am in deepest agreement with the aims and work of the organization which has brought us together: Clergy and Laymen Concerned about Vietnam. The recent statement of your executive committee are the sentiments of my own heart and I found myself in full accord when I read its opening lines: "A time comes when silence is betrayal." That time has come for us in relation to Vietnam.

The truth of these words is beyond doubt but the mission to which they call us is a most difficult one. Even when pressed by the demands of inner truth, men do not easily assume the task of opposing their government's policy, especially in time of war. Nor does the human spirit move without great difficulty against all the apathy of conformist thought within one's own bosom and in the surrounding world. Moreover when the issues at hand seem as

perplexed as they often do in the case of this dreadful conflict we are always on the verge of being mesmerized by uncertainty; but we must move on.

Some of us who have already begun to break the silence of the night have found that the calling to speak is often a vocation of agony, but we must speak. We must speak with all the humility that is appropriate to our limited vision, but we must speak. And we must rejoice as well, for surely this is the first time in our nation's history that a significant number of its religious leaders have chosen to move beyond the prophesying of smooth patriotism to the high grounds of a firm dissent based upon the mandates of conscience and the reading of history. Perhaps a new spirit is rising among us. If it is, let us trace its movement well and pray that our own inner being may be sensitive to its guidance, for we are deeply in need of a new way beyond the darkness that seems so close around us.

Over the past two years, as I have moved to break the betrayal of my own silences and to speak from the burnings of my own heart, as I have called for radical departures from the destruction of Vietnam, many persons have questioned me about the wisdom of my path. At the heart of their concerns this query has often loomed large and loud: Why are you speaking about war, Dr. King? Why are you joining the voices of dissent? Peace and civil rights don't mix, they say. Aren't you hurting the cause of your people, they ask? And when I hear them, though I often understand the source of their concern, I am nevertheless greatly saddened, for such questions mean that the inquirers have not really known me, my commitment or my calling. Indeed, their questions suggest that they do not know the world in which they live.

In the light of such tragic misunderstandings, I deem it of signal importance to try to state clearly, and I trust concisely, why I believe that the path from Dexter Avenue Baptist Church—the church in Montgomery, Alabama, where I began my pastorate—leads clearly to this sanctuary tonight.

I come to this platform tonight to make a passionate plea to my beloved nation. This speech is not addressed to Hanoi or to the National Liberation Front. It is not addressed to China or to Russia.

Nor is it an attempt to overlook the ambiguity of the total situation and the need for a collective solution to the tragedy of Vietnam. Neither is it an attempt to make North Vietnam or the National Liberation Front paragons of virtue, nor to overlook the role they can play in a successful resolution of the problem. While they both may have justifiable reason to be suspicious of the good faith of the United States, life and history give eloquent testimony to the fact that conflicts are never resolved without trustful give and take on both sides.

Tonight, however, I wish not to speak with Hanoi and the NLF, but rather to my fellow Americans, who, with me, bear the greatest responsibility in ending a conflict that has exacted a heavy price on both continents.

I am convinced that if we are to get on the right side of the world revolution, we as a nation must undergo a radical revolution of values. We must rapidly begin the shift from a "thing-oriented" society to a "person-oriented" society. When machines and computers, profit motives and property rights are considered more important than people, the giant triplets of racism, materialism, and militarism are incapable of being conquered.

Since I am a preacher by trade, I suppose it is not surprising that I have seven major reasons for bringing Vietnam into the field of my moral vision. There is at the outset a very obvious and almost facile connection between the war in Vietnam and the struggle I, and others, have been waging in America. A few years ago there was a shining moment in that struggle. It seemed as if there was a real promise of hope for the poor—both black and white—through the poverty program. There were experiments, hopes, new beginnings. Then came the buildup in Vietnam and I watched the program broken and eviscerated as if it were some idle political plaything of a society gone mad on war, and I knew that America would never invest the necessary funds or energies in rehabilitation of its poor so long as adventures like Vietnam continued to draw men and skills and money like some demonic destructive suction tube. So I was increasingly compelled to see the war as an enemy of the poor and to attack it as such.

Perhaps the more tragic recognition of reality took place when it became clear to me that the war was doing far more than devastating the hopes of the poor at home. It was sending their sons and their brothers and their husbands to fight and to die in extraordinarily high proportions relative to the rest of the population. We were taking the black young men who had been crippled by our society and sending them eight thousand miles away to guarantee liberties in Southeast Asia which they had not found in southwest Georgia and East Harlem. So we have been repeatedly faced with the cruel irony of watching Negro and white boys on TV screens as they kill and die together for a nation that has been unable to seat them together in the same schools. So we watch them in brutal solidarity burning the huts of a poor village, but we realize that they would never live on the same block in Detroit. I could not be silent in the face of such cruel manipulation of the poor.

My third reason moves to an even deeper level of awareness, for it grows out of my experience in the ghettoes of the North over the last three years—especially the last three summers. As I have walked among the desperate, rejected and angry young men I have told them that Molotov cocktails and rifles would not solve their problems. I have tried to offer them my deepest compassion while maintaining my conviction that social change comes most meaningfully through nonviolent action. But they asked—and rightly so—what about Vietnam? They asked if our own nation wasn't using massive doses of violence to solve its problems, to bring about the changes it wanted. Their questions hit home, and I knew that I could never again raise my voice against the violence of the oppressed in the ghettos without having first spoken clearly to the greatest purveyor of violence in the world today—my own government. For the sake of those boys, for the sake of this government, for the sake of hundreds of thousands trembling under our violence, I cannot be silent.

For those who ask the question, "Aren't you a civil rights leader?" and thereby mean to exclude me from the movement for peace, I have this further answer. In 1957 when a group of us formed the Southern Christian Leadership Conference, we chose as our motto: "To save the soul of America." We were convinced that we could not limit our vision to certain rights for black people, but instead affirmed the conviction that America would never be free or saved from itself unless the descendants of its slaves were loosed completely from the shackles they still wear. In a way we were agreeing with Langston Hughes, that black bard of Harlem, who had written earlier:

O, yes, I say it plain, America never was America to me, And yet I swear this oath—America will be!

Now, it should be incandescently clear that no one who has any concern for the integrity and life of America today can ignore the present war. If America's soul becomes totally poisoned, part of the autopsy must read Vietnam. It can never be saved so long as it destroys the deepest hopes of men the world over. So it is that those of us who are yet determined that America will be are led down the path of protest and dissent, working for the health of our land.

As if the weight of such a commitment to the life and health of America were not enough, another burden of responsibility was placed upon me in 1964; and I cannot forget that the Nobel Prize for Peace was also a commission—a commission to work harder than I had ever worked before for "the brotherhood of man." This is a calling that takes me beyond national allegiances, but even if it were not present I would yet have to live with the meaning of my commitment to the ministry of Jesus Christ. To me the relationship of this ministry to the making of peace is so obvious that I sometimes marvel at those who ask me why I am speaking against the war. Could it be that they do not know that the good news was meant for all men—for Communist and capitalist, for their children and ours, for black and for white, for revolutionary and conservative? Have they forgotten that my ministry is in obedience to the one who loved his enemies so fully that he died for them? What then can I say to the "Vietcong" or to Castro or to Mao as a faithful minister of this one? Can I threaten them with death or must I not share with them my life?

Finally, as I try to delineate for you and for myself the road that leads from Montgomery to this place I would have offered all that was most valid if I simply said that I must be true to my conviction that I share with all men the calling to be a son of the living God. Beyond the calling of race or nation or creed is this vocation of sonship and brotherhood, and because I believe that the Father is deeply concerned especially for his suffering and helpless and outcast children, I come tonight to speak for them.

This I believe to be the privilege and the burden of all of us who deem ourselves bound by allegiances and loyalties which are broader and deeper than nationalism and which go beyond our nation's self-defined goals and positions. We are called to speak for the weak, for the voiceless, for victims of our nation and for those it calls enemy, for no document from human hands can make these humans any less our brothers.

And as I ponder the madness of Vietnam and search within myself for ways to understand and respond to compassion my mind goes constantly to the people of that peninsula. I speak now not of the soldiers of each side, not of the junta in Saigon, but simply of the people who have been living under the curse of war for almost three continuous decades now. I think of them too because it is clear to me that there will be no meaningful solution there until some attempt is made to know them and hear their broken cries.

They must see Americans as strange liberators. The Vietnamese people proclaimed their own independence in 1945 after a combined French and Japanese occupation, and before the Communist revolution in China. They were led by Ho Chi Minh. Even though they quoted the American Declaration of Independence in their own document of freedom, we refused to recognize them. Instead, we decided to support France in its reconquest of her former colony.

Our government felt then that the Vietnamese people were not "ready" for independence, and we again fell victim to the deadly Western arrogance that has poisoned the international atmosphere for so long. With that tragic decision we rejected a revolutionary government seeking self-determination, and a government that had been established not by China (for whom the Vietnamese have no great love) but by clearly indigenous forces that included some Communists. For the peasants this new government meant real land reform, one of the most important needs in their lives.

For nine years following 1945 we denied the people of Vietnam the right of independence. For nine years we vigorously supported the French in their abortive effort to recolonize Vietnam.

Before the end of the war we were meeting eighty percent of the French war costs. Even before the French were defeated at Dien Bien Phu, they began to despair of the reckless action, but we did not. We encouraged them with our huge financial and military supplies to continue the war even after they had lost the will. Soon we would be paying almost the full costs of this tragic attempt at recolonization.

After the French were defeated it looked as if independence and land reform would come again through the Geneva agreements. But instead there came the United States, determined that Ho should not unify the temporarily divided nation, and the peasants watched again as we supported one of the most vicious modern dictators—our chosen man, Premier Diem. The peasants watched and cringed as Diem ruthlessly routed out all opposition, supported their extortionist landlords and refused even to discuss reunification with the north. The peasants watched as all this was presided over by U.S. influence and then by increasing numbers of U.S. troops who came to help quell the insurgency that Diem's methods had aroused. When Diem was overthrown they may have been happy, but the long line of military dictatorships seemed to offer no real change—especially in terms of their need for land and peace.

The only change came from America as we increased our troop commitments in support of governments which were singularly corrupt, inept and without popular support. All the while the people read our leaflets and received regular promises of peace and democracy—and land reform. Now they languish under our bombs and consider us—not their fellow Vietnamese—the real enemy. They move sadly and apathetically as we herd them off the land of their fathers into concentration camps where minimal social needs are rarely met. They know they must move or be destroyed by our bombs. So they go—primarily women and children and the aged.

They watch as we poison their water, as we kill a million acres of their crops. They must weep as the bulldozers roar through their areas preparing to destroy the precious trees. They wander into the hospitals, with at least twenty casualties from American firepower for one "Vietcong"-inflicted injury. So far we may have killed a million of them—mostly children. They wander into the towns and see thousands of the children, homeless, without clothes, running in packs on the streets like animals. They see the children, degraded by our soldiers as they beg for food. They see the children selling their sisters to our soldiers, soliciting for their mothers.

What do the peasants think as we ally ourselves with the landlords and as we refuse to put any action into our many words concerning land reform? What do they think as we test our latest weapons on them, just as the Germans tested out new medicine and new tortures in the concentration camps of Europe? Where are the roots of the independent Vietnam we claim to be building? Is it among these voiceless ones?

We have destroyed their two most cherished institutions: the family and the village. We have destroyed their land and their crops. We have cooperated in the crushing of the nation's only non-Communist revolutionary political force—the unified Buddhist church. We have supported the enemies of the peasants of Saigon. We have corrupted their women and children and killed their men. What liberators?

Now there is little left to build on—save bitterness. Soon the only solid physical foundations remaining will be found at our military bases and in the concrete of the concentration camps we call fortified hamlets. The peasants may well wonder if we plan to build our new Vietnam on such grounds as these? Could we blame them for such thoughts? We must speak for them and raise the questions they cannot raise. These too are our brothers.

Perhaps the more difficult but no less necessary task is to speak for those who have been designated as our enemies. What of the National Liberation Front—that strangely anonymous group we call VC or Communists? What must they think of us in America when they realize that we permitted the repression and cruelty of Diem which helped to bring them into being as a resistance group in the south? What do they think of our condoning the violence which led to their own taking up of arms? How can they believe in our integrity when now we speak of "aggression from the north" as if there were nothing more essential to the war? How can they trust us when now we charge them with violence after the murderous reign of Diem and charge them with violence while we pour every new weapon of death into their land? Surely we must understand their feelings even if we do not condone their actions. Surely we must see that the men we supported pressed them to their violence. Surely we must see that our own computerized plans of destruction simply dwarf their greatest acts.

How do they judge us when our officials know that their membership is less than twenty-five percent Communist and yet insist on giving them the blanket name? What must they be thinking when they know that we are aware of their control of major sections of Vietnam and yet we appear ready to allow national elections in which this highly organized political parallel government will have no part? They ask how we can speak of free elections when the Saigon press is censored and controlled by the military junta. And they are surely right to wonder what kind of new government we plan to help form without them—the only party in real touch with the peasants. They question our political goals and they deny the reality of a peace settlement from which they will be excluded. Their questions are frighteningly relevant. Is our nation planning to build on political myth again and then shore it up with the power of new violence?

Here is the true meaning and value of compassion and nonviolence when it helps us to see the enemy's point of view, to hear his questions, to know his assessment of ourselves. For from his view we may indeed see the basic weaknesses of our own condition, and if we are mature, we may learn and grow and profit from the wisdom of the brothers who are called the opposition.

So, too, with Hanoi. In the north, where our bombs now pummel the land, and our mines endanger the waterways, we are met by a deep but understandable mistrust. To speak for them is to explain this lack of confidence in Western words, and especially their distrust of American intentions now. In Hanoi are the men who led the nation to independence against the Japanese and the French, the men who sought membership in the French commonwealth and were betrayed by the weakness of Paris and the willfulness of the colonial armies. It was they who led a second struggle against French domination at tremendous costs, and then were persuaded to give up the land they controlled between the thirteenth and seventeenth parallel as a temporary measure at Geneva. After 1954 they watched us conspire with Diem to prevent elections which would have surely brought Ho Chi Minh to power over a united Vietnam, and they realized they had been betrayed again.

When we ask why they do not leap to negotiate, these things must be remembered. Also it must be clear that the leaders of Hanoi considered the presence of American troops in support of the Diem regime to have been the initial military breach of the Geneva agreements concerning foreign troops, and they remind us that they did not begin to send in any large number of supplies or men until American forces had moved into the tens of thousands.

Hanoi remembers how our leaders refused to tell us the truth about the earlier North Vietnamese overtures for peace, how the president claimed that none existed when they had clearly been made. Ho Chi Minh has watched as America has spoken of peace and built up its forces, and now he has surely heard of the increasing international rumors of American plans for an invasion of the north. He knows the bombing and shelling and mining we are doing are part of traditional pre-invasion strategy. Perhaps only his sense of humor and of irony can save him when he hears the most powerful nation of the world speaking of aggression as it drops thousands of bombs on a poor weak nation more than eight thousand miles away from its shores.

At this point I should make it clear that while I have tried in these last few minutes to give a voice to the voiceless on Vietnam and to understand the arguments of those who are called enemy, I am as deeply concerned about our troops there as anything else. For it occurs to me that what we are submitting them to in Vietnam is not simply the brutalizing process that goes on in any war where armies face each other and seek to destroy. We are adding cynicism to the process of death, for they must know after a short period there that none of the things we claim to be fighting for are really involved. Before long they must know that their government has sent them into a struggle among Vietnamese, and the more sophisticated surely realize that we are on the side of the wealthy and the secure while we create hell for the poor.

Somehow this madness must cease. We must stop now. I speak as a child of God and brother to the suffering poor of Vietnam. I speak for those whose land is being laid waste, whose homes are being destroyed, whose culture is being subverted. I speak for the poor of America who are paying the double price of smashed hopes at home and death and corruption in Vietnam. I speak as a citizen of the world, for the world as it stands aghast at the path we have taken. I speak as an American to the leaders of my own nation. The great initiative in this war is ours. The initiative to stop it must be ours.

This is the message of the great Buddhist leaders of Vietnam. Recently one of them wrote these words: "Each day the war goes on the hatred increases in the heart of the Vietnamese and in the hearts of those of humanitarian instinct. The Americans are forcing even their friends into becoming their enemies. It is curious that the Americans, who calculate so carefully on the possibilities of military victory, do not realize that in the process they are incurring deep psychological and political defeat. The image of America will never again be the image of revolution, freedom and democracy, but the image of violence and militarism."

If we continue, there will be no doubt in my mind and in the mind of the world that we have no honorable intentions in Vietnam. It will become clear that our minimal expectation is to occupy it as an American colony and men will not refrain from thinking that our maximum hope is to goad China into a war so that we may bomb her nuclear installations. If we do not stop our war against the people of Vietnam immediately the world will be left with no other alternative than to see this as some horribly clumsy and deadly game we have decided to play.

The world now demands a maturity of America that we may not be able to achieve. It demands that we admit that we have been wrong from the beginning of our adventure in Vietnam, that we have been detrimental to the life of the Vietnamese people. The situation is one in which we must be ready to turn sharply from our present ways.

In order to atone for our sins and errors in Vietnam, we should take the initiative in bringing a halt to this tragic war. I would like to suggest five concrete things that our government should do immediately to begin the long and difficult process of extricating ourselves from this nightmarish conflict:

- End all bombing in North and South Vietnam.
- Declare a unilateral cease-fire in the hope that such action will create the atmosphere for negotiation.
- Take immediate steps to prevent other battlegrounds in Southeast Asia by curtailing our military buildup in Thailand and our interference in Laos.
- Realistically accept the fact that the National Liberation Front has substantial support in

South Vietnam and must thereby play a role in any meaningful negotiations and in any future Vietnam government.

- Set a date that we will remove all foreign troops from Vietnam in accordance with the 1954 Geneva agreement.

Part of our ongoing commitment might well express itself in an offer to grant asylum to any Vietnamese who fears for his life under a new regime which included the Liberation Front. Then we must make what reparations we can for the damage we have done. We most provide the medical aid that is badly needed, making it available in this country if necessary.

Meanwhile we in the churches and synagogues have a continuing task while we urge our government to disengage itself from a disgraceful commitment. We must continue to raise our voices if our nation persists in its perverse ways in Vietnam. We must be prepared to match actions with words by seeking out every creative means of protest possible.

As we counsel young men concerning military service we must clarify for them our nation's role in Vietnam and challenge them with the alternative of conscientious objection. I am pleased to say that this is the path now being chosen by more than seventy students at my own alma mater, Morehouse College, and I recommend it to all who find the American course in Vietnam a dishonorable and unjust one. Moreover I would encourage all ministers of draft age to give up their ministerial exemptions and seek status as conscientious objectors. These are the times for real choices and not false ones. We are at the moment when our lives must be placed on the line if our nation is to survive its own folly. Every man of humane convictions must decide on the protest that best suits his convictions, but we must all protest.

There is something seductively tempting about stopping there and sending us all off on what in some circles has become a popular crusade against the war in Vietnam. I say we must enter the struggle, but I wish to go on now to say something even more disturbing. The war in Vietnam is but a symptom of a far deeper malady within the American spirit, and if we ignore this sobering reality we will find ourselves organizing clergy- and laymen-concerned committees for the next generation. They will be concerned about Guatemala and Peru. They will be concerned about Thailand and Cambodia. They will be concerned about Mozambique and South Africa. We will be marching for these and a dozen other names and attending rallies without end unless there is a significant and profound change in American life and policy. Such thoughts take us beyond Vietnam, but not beyond our calling as sons of the living God.

In 1957 a sensitive American official overseas said that it seemed to him that our nation was on the wrong side of a world revolution. During the past ten years we have seen emerge a pattern of suppression which now has justified the presence of U.S. military "advisers" in Venezuela. This need to maintain social stability for our investments accounts for the counter-revolutionary action of American forces in Guatemala. It tells why American helicopters are being used against guerrillas in Colombia and why American napalm and green beret forces have already been active against rebels in Peru. It is with such activity in mind that the words of the late John F. Kennedy come back to haunt us. Five years ago he said, "Those who make peaceful revolution impossible will make violent revolution inevitable."

Increasingly, by choice or by accident, this is the role our nation has taken—the role of those who make peaceful revolution impossible by refusing to give up the privileges and the pleasures that come from the immense profits of overseas investment.

I am convinced that if we are to get on the right side of the world revolution, we as a nation must undergo a radical revolution of values. We must rapidly begin the shift from a "thing-oriented" society to a "person-oriented" society. When machines and computers, profit motives and property rights are considered more important than people, the giant triplets of racism, materialism, and militarism are incapable of being conquered.

A true revolution of values will soon cause us to question the fairness and justice of many of our past and present policies. On the one hand we are called to play the good Samaritan on life's roadside; but that will be only an initial act. One day we must come to see that the whole Jericho road must be transformed so that men and women will not be constantly beaten and robbed as they make their journey on life's highway. True compassion is more than flinging a coin to a beggar; it is not haphazard and superficial. It comes to see that an edifice which produces beggars needs restructuring. A true revolution of values will soon look uneasily on the glaring contrast of poverty and wealth. With righteous indignation, it will look across the seas and see individual capitalists of the West investing huge sums of money in Asia, Africa and South America, only to take the profits out with no concern for the social betterment of the countries, and say: "This is not just." It will look at our alliance with the landed gentry of Latin America and say: "This is not just." The Western arrogance of feeling that it has everything to teach others and nothing to learn from them is not just. A true revolution of values will lay hands on the world order and say of war: "This way of settling differences is not just." This business of burning human beings with napalm, of filling our nation's homes with orphans and widows, of injecting poisonous drugs of hate into veins of people normally humane, of sending men home from dark and bloody battlefields physically handicapped and psychologically deranged, cannot be reconciled with wisdom, justice and love. A nation that continues year after year to spend more money on military defense than on programs of social uplift is approaching spiritual death.

America, the richest and most powerful nation in the world, can well lead the way in this revolution of values. There is nothing, except a tragic death wish, to prevent us from reordering our priorities, so that the pursuit of peace will take precedence over the pursuit of war. There is nothing to keep us from molding a recalcitrant status quo with bruised hands until we have fashioned it into a brotherhood.

This kind of positive revolution of values is our best defense against communism. War is not the answer. Communism will never be defeated by the use of atomic bombs or nuclear weapons.

Let us not join those who shout war and through their misguided passions urge the United States to relinquish its participation in the United Nations. These are days which demand wise restraint and calm reasonableness. We must not call everyone a Communist or an appeaser who advocates the seating of Red China in the United Nations and who recognizes that hate and hysteria are not the final answers to the problem of these turbulent days. We must not engage in a negative anti-communism, but rather in a positive thrust for democracy, realizing that our greatest defense against communism is to take offensive action in behalf of justice. We must with positive action seek to remove those conditions of poverty, insecurity and injustice which are the fertile soil in which the seed of communism grows and develops.

These are revolutionary times. All over the globe men are revolting against old systems of exploitation and oppression and out of the wombs of a frail world new systems of justice and equality are being born. The shirtless and barefoot people of the land are rising up as never before. "The people who sat in darkness have seen a great light." We in the West must support these revolutions. It is a sad fact that, because of comfort, complacency, a morbid fear of communism, and our proneness to adjust to injustice, the Western nations that initiated so much of the revolutionary spirit of the modern world have now become the arch anti-revolutionaries. This has driven many to feel that only Marxism has the revolutionary spirit. Therefore, communism is a judgement against our failure to make democracy real and follow through on the revolutions we initiated. Our only hope today lies in our ability to recapture the revolutionary spirit and go out into a sometimes hostile world declaring eternal hostility to poverty, racism, and militarism. With this powerful commitment we shall boldly challenge the status quo and unjust mores and thereby speed the day when "every valley shall be exalted, and every moutain and hill shall be made low, and the crooked shall be made straight and the rough places plain."

A genuine revolution of values means in the final analysis that our loyalties must become ecumenical rather than sectional. Every nation must now develop an overriding loyalty to mankind as a whole in order to preserve the best in their individual societies.

This call for a world-wide fellowship that lifts neighborly concern beyond one's tribe, race, class and nation is in reality a call for an all-embracing and unconditional love for all men. This oft misunderstood and misinterpreted concept—so readily dismissed by the Nietzsches of the world as a weak and cowardly force—has now become an absolute necessity for the survival of man. When I speak of love I am not speaking of some sentimental and weak response. I am speaking of that force which all of the great religions have seen as the supreme unifying principle of life. Love is somehow the key that unlocks the door which leads to ultimate reality. This Hindu-Moslem-Christian-Jewish-Buddhist belief about ultimate reality is beautifully summed up in the first epistle of Saint John: Let us love one another; for love is God and everyone that loveth is born of God and knoweth God. He that loveth not knoweth not God; for God is love. If we love one another God dwelleth in us, and his love is perfected in us.

Let us hope that this spirit will become the order of the day. We can no longer afford to worship the god of hate or bow before the altar of retaliation. The oceans of history are made turbulent by the ever-rising tides of hate. History is cluttered with the wreckage of nations and individuals that pursued this self-defeating path of hate. As Arnold Toynbee says: "Love is the ultimate force that makes for the saving choice of life and good against the damning choice of death and evil. Therefore the first hope in our inventory must be the hope that love is going to have the last word."

We are now faced with the fact that tomorrow is today. We are confronted with the fierce urgency of now. In this unfolding conundrum of life and history there is such a thing as being too late. Procrastination is still the thief of time. Life often leaves us standing bare, naked and dejected with a lost opportunity. The "tide in the affairs of men" does not remain at the flood; it ebbs. We may cry out desperately for time to pause in her passage, but time is deaf to every plea and rushes on. Over the bleached bones and jumbled residue of numerous civilizations are written the pathetic words: "Too late." There is an invisible book of life that faithfully records our vigilance or our neglect. "The moving finger writes, and having writ moves on . . ." We still have a choice today; nonviolent coexistence or violent co-annihilation.

We must move past indecision to action. We must find new ways to speak for peace in Vietnam and justice throughout the developing world—a world that borders on our doors. If we do not act we shall surely be dragged down the long dark and shameful corridors of time reserved for those who possess power without compassion, might without morality, and strength without sight.

Now let us begin. Now let us rededicate ourselves to the long and bitter—but beautiful—struggle for a new world. This is the calling of the sons of God, and our brothers wait eagerly for our response. Shall we say the odds are too great? Shall we tell them the struggle is too hard? Will our message be that the forces of American life militate against their arrival as full men, and we send our deepest regrets? Or will there be another message, of longing, of hope, of solidarity with their yearnings, of commitment to their cause, whatever the cost? The choice is ours, and though we might prefer it otherwise we must choose in this crucial moment of human history.

As that noble bard of yesterday, James Russell Lowell, eloquently stated:

Once to every man and nation
Comes the moment to decide,
In the strife of truth and falsehood,
For the good or evil side;
Some great cause, God's new Messiah,
Off'ring each the bloom or blight,
And the choice goes by forever
Twixt that darkness and that light.
Though the cause of evil prosper,
Yet 'tis truth alone is strong;
Though her portion be the scaffold,
And upon the throne be wrong:
Yet that scaffold sways the future,
And behind the dim unknown,

Standeth God within the shadow
Keeping watch above his own.

And if we will only make the right choice, we will be able to transform this pending cosmic elegy into a creative psalm of peace. If we will make the right choice, we will be able to transform the jangling discords of our world into a beautiful symphony of brotherhood. If we will but make the right choice, we will be able to speed up the day, all over America and all over the world, when "justice will roll down like waters, and righteousness like a mighty stream."

COUNTRY JOE AND THE FISH, "I FEEL LIKE I'M FIXIN' TO DIE RAG" (1967)

The decade of the 1960s saw an explosion of rock and roll, which echoed and amplified the voices of dissent. The lyrics to this song, credited to Country Joe McDonald (1942–), offer a pointed critique of the war in Southeast Asia to which the United States by now had committed several hundred thousand troops.

Well, come on all of you, big strong men,
Uncle Sam needs your help again.
He's got himself in a terrible jam
Way down yonder in Vietnam
So put down your books and pick up a gun,
We're gonna have a whole lotta fun.

And it's one, two, three,
What are we fighting for?
Don't ask me, I don't give a damn,
Next stop is Vietnam;
And it's five, six, seven,
Open up the pearly gates,
Well there ain't no time to wonder why,
Whoopee! we're all gonna die.

Well, come on generals, let's move fast;
Your big chance has come at last.
Now you can go out and get those reds
'Cause the only good commie is the one
    that's dead
And you know that peace can only be won
When we've blown 'em all to kingdom come.

And it's one, two, three,
What are we fighting for?
Don't ask me, I don't give a damn,
Next stop is Vietnam;
And it's five, six, seven,
Open up the pearly gates,
Well there ain't no time to wonder why
Whoopee! we're all gonna die.

Come on Wall Street, don't be slow,
Why man, this is war au-go-go
There's plenty good money to be made
By supplying the Army with the tools of
    its trade,
But just hope and pray that if they drop the bomb,
They drop it on the Viet Cong.

And it's one, two, three,
What are we fighting for?
Don't ask me, I don't give a damn,
Next stop is Vietnam.
And it's five, six, seven,
Open up the pearly gates,
Well there ain't no time to wonder why
Whoopee! we're all gonna die.

Come on mothers throughout the land,
Pack your boys off to Vietnam.
Come on fathers, and don't hesitate
To send your sons off before it's too late.
And you can be the first ones in your block
To have your boy come home in a box.

And it's one, two, three
What are we fighting for?
Don't ask me, I don't give a damn,
Next stop is Vietnam.
And it's five, six, seven,
Open up the pearly gates,
Well there ain't no time to wonder why,
Whoopee! we're all gonna die.

JOHN KERRY, "STATEMENT BEFORE THE SENATE FOREIGN RELATIONS COMMITTEE" (1971)

To sustain the war in Vietnam, the United States relied on conscription. As the war became increasingly unpopular, rising numbers of draft-eligible young men sought to avoid military service, with those attending elite colleges demonstrating a particular aptitude for doing so. John Kerry (1943–), a future U.S. senator, presidential candidate, and secretary of state, chose otherwise. Upon graduating from Yale in 1966, he was commissioned in the U.S. Navy. After brief service in South Vietnam where Kerry was wounded and decorated for valor, he was discharged from the service. Soon thereafter he emerged as a prominent voice among veterans opposing the war.

I would like to say for the record that—and also for the men behind me who are also wearing the uniform and their medals—that my sitting up here is really symbolic. I'm not here as John Kerry. I'm here as one member of a group of 1000, which is a small representation of a very much larger group of veterans in this country. And were it possible for all of them to sit at this table, they would be here and have the same kind of testimony.

I would simply like to speak in very general terms. I apologize if my statement is general because I received notification yesterday you would hear me, and I'm afraid, because of the injunction, I was up most of the night and haven't had a great deal of chance to prepare.

I would like to talk representing of all those veterans and say that several months ago in Detroit we had an investigation at which over 150 honorably discharged, and many very highly dec-orated, veterans testified to war crimes committed in Southeast Asia.

These were not isolated incidents but crimes committed on a day-to-day basis with the full awareness of officers at all levels of command. It's impossible to describe to you exactly what did happen in Detroit—the emotions in the room and the feelings of the men who were reliving their experiences in Vietnam. But they did. They relived the absolute horror of what this country, in a sense, made them do.

They told the stories of times that they had personally raped, cut off ears, cut off heads, taped wires from portable telephones to human geni-tals and turned up the power, cut off limbs, blown up bodies, randomly shot at civilians, razed vil-lages in the fashion reminiscent of Genghis Khan, shot cattle and dogs for fun, poisoned food stocks, and generally ravaged the countryside of South Vietnam in addition to the normal ravage of war and the normal and very particular ravaging which is done by the applied bombing power of this country.

We call this investigation the "Winter Soldier Investigation." The term *Winter Soldier* is a play on words of Thomas Paine's in 1776 when he spoke of the Sunshine Patriot and summertime soldiers who deserted at Valley Forge because the going was rough.

And we who have come here to Washington have come here because we feel we have to be winter soldiers now. We could come back to this country; and we could be quiet; we could hold our silence; we could not tell what went on in Vietnam. But we feel because of what threatens this country, the fact that the crimes threaten it, not reds, not redcoats but the crimes which we're committing are what threaten it; and we have to speak out.

I would like to talk to you a little bit about what the result is of—of the feelings these men carry with them after coming back from Vietnam. The country doesn't know it yet but it's created a monster, a monster in the form of millions of men who have been taught to deal and to trade in violence, and who are given the chance to die for the biggest nothing in history; men who have returned with a sense of anger and a sense of betrayal which no one has yet grasped.

As a veteran, and one who feels this anger, I'd like to talk about it. We're angry because we feel we have been used in the worst fashion by the Administration of this country. In 1970 at West Point, Vice President Agnew said: *Some glamorize the criminal misfits of society while our best men die in Asian rice paddies to preserve the freedoms which those misfits abuse.*

And this was used as a rallying point for our effort in Vietnam.

But for us, his boys in Asia whom the country was supposed to support, his statement is a terrible distortion from which we can only draw a very deep sense of revulsion; and hence the anger of some of the men who are here in Washington today.

It's a distortion because we in no way considered ourselves the best men of this country; because those he calls misfits were standing up for us in a way that nobody else in this country dared to; because so many who have died would have returned to this country to join the misfits in their efforts to ask for an immediate withdrawal from South Vietnam; because so many of those best men have returned as quadriplegics and amputees, and they lie forgotten in Veterans Administration hospitals in this country which fly the flag which so many have chosen as their own personal symbol.

And we cannot consider ourselves America's best men when we were ashamed of and hated what we were called to do in Southeast Asia. In our opinion, and from our experience, there is nothing in South Vietnam, nothing which could happen that realistically threatens the United States of America. And to attempt to justify the loss of one American life in Vietnam, Cambodia, or Laos by linking such loss to the preservation of freedom, which those misfits supposedly abuse, is to us the height of criminal hypocrisy, and it's that kind of hypocrisy which we feel has torn this country apart.

We are probably much more angry than that and I don't want to go into the foreign policy aspects because I'm outclassed here. I know that all of you have talked about every possible—every possible alternative to getting out of Vietnam. We understand that. We know that you've considered the seriousness of the aspects to the utmost level and I'm not going to try and deal on that. But I want to relate to you the feeling which many of the men who've returned to this country express because we are probably angriest about all that we were told about Vietnam and about the mystical war against communism.

We found that not only was it a civil war, an effort by a people who had for years been seeking their liberation from any colonial influence

whatsoever, but also we found that the Vietnamese, whom we had enthusiastically molded after our own image, were hard put to take up the fight against the threat we were supposedly saving them from.

We found that most people didn't even know the difference between communism and democracy. They only wanted to work in rice paddies without helicopters strafing them and bombs with napalm burning their villages and tearing their country apart. They wanted everything to do with the war, particularly with this foreign presence of the United States of America, to leave them alone in peace; and they practiced the art of survival by siding with whichever military force was present at a particular time, be it Vietcong, North Vietnamese, or American.

We found also that all too often American men were dying in those rice paddies for want of support from their allies. We saw first hand how monies from American taxes was used for a corrupt dictatorial regime. We saw that many people in this country had a one-sided idea of who was kept free by our flag, as blacks provided the highest percentage of casualties. We saw Vietnam ravaged equally by American bombs as well as by search and destroy missions, as well as by Vietcong terrorism; and yet we listened while this country tried to blame all of the havoc on the Vietcong.

We rationalized destroying villages in order to save them. We saw America lose her sense of morality as she accepted very coolly a My Lai and refused to give up the image of American soldiers that hand out chocolate bars and chewing gum. We learned the meaning of "free-fire zones," "shoot anything that moves," and we watched while America placed a cheapness on the lives of Orientals. We watched the United States' falsification of body counts, in fact the glorification of body counts. We listened while month after month we were told the back of the enemy was about to break.

We fought using weapons against "oriental human beings," with quotation marks around that. We fought using weapons against those people which I do not believe this country would dream of using were we fighting in a European theater—or let us say a non-third-world people theater. And so we watched while men charged up hills because a general said "That hill has to be taken." And after losing one platoon or two platoons they marched away to leave the hill for the reoccupation by the North Vietnamese; because—because we watched pride allow the most unimportant of battles to be blown into extravaganzas; because we couldn't lose, and we couldn't retreat, and because it didn't matter how many American bodies were lost to prove that point. And so there were Hamburger Hills and Khe Sahns and Hill 881's and Fire Base 6's and so many others.

And now we're told that the men who fought there must watch quietly while American lives are lost so that we can exercise the incredible arrogance of Vietnamizing the Vietnamese.

Each day to facilitate the process by which the United States washes her hands of Vietnam, someone has to give up his life so that the United States doesn't have to admit something that the entire world already knows, so that we can't say that we've made a mistake. Someone has to die so that President Nixon won't be, and these are his words, "the first President to lose a war."

And we are asking Americans to think about that because how do you ask a man to be the last man to die in Vietnam? How do you ask a man to be the last man to die for a mistake? But we're trying to do that, and we're doing it with thousands of rationalizations, and if you read carefully the President's last speech to the people of this country, you can see that he says, and says clearly:

But the issue, gentlemen, the issue is communism, and the question is whether or not we will leave that country to the Communists or whether or not we will try to give it hope to be a free people.

But the point is they're not a free people now—under us. They're not a free people. And we cannot fight communism all over the world, and I think we should have learnt that lesson by now.

But the problem of veterans goes beyond this personal problem, because you think about a poster in this country with a picture of Uncle Sam and the picture says "I want you." And a young man comes out of high school and says, "That's fine. I'm going to serve my country." And he goes to Vietnam and he shoots and he kills and he does his job or maybe he doesn't kill, maybe he just goes and he comes back. When he gets back

to this country he finds that he isn't really wanted, because the largest unemployment figure in the country—it varies depending on who you get it from, the Veterans Administration 15 percent, various other sources 22 percent—but the largest figure of unemployed in this country are veterans of this war. And of those veterans 33 percent of the unemployed are black. That means 1 out of every 10 of the nation's unemployed is a veteran of Vietnam.

The hospitals across the country won't or can't meet their demands. It's not a question of not trying. They haven't got the appropriations. A man recently died after he had a tracheotomy in California, not because of the operation but because there weren't enough personnel to clean the mucous out of his tube and he suffocated to death.

Another young man just died in a New York VA hospital the other day. A friend of mine was lying in a bed two beds away and tried to help him, but he couldn't. They rang a bell and there was no one there to service that man, and so he died of convulsions.

Fifty-seven percent—I understand 57 percent of all those entering VA hospitals talk about suicide. Some 27 percent have tried, and they try because they come back to this country and they have to face what they did in Vietnam, and then they come back and find the indifference of a country that doesn't really care, that doesn't really care.

And suddenly we are faced with a very sickening situation in this country because there's no moral indignation, and if there is it comes from people who are almost exhausted by their past indignancies, and I know that many of them are sitting in front of me. The country seems to have lied—lain down and accepted something as serious as Laos, just as we calmly shrugged off the loss of 700,000 lives in Pakistan, the so-called greatest disaster of all times.

But we are here as veterans to say that we think we are in the midst of the greatest disaster of all times *now* because they are still dying over there, and not just Americans, Vietnamese, and we are rationalizing leaving that country so that those people can go on killing each other for years to come.

Americans seem to have accepted the idea that the war is winding down, at least for

Americans, and they have also allowed the bodies, which were once used by a President for statistics to prove that we were winning this war, to be used as evidence against a man who followed orders and who interpreted those orders no differently than hundreds of other men in South Vietnam.

We veterans can only look with amazement on the fact that this country has not been able to see that there's absolutely no difference between a ground troop and a helicopter crew. And yet, people have accepted the differentiation fed them by the Administration. No ground troops are in Laos, so it's alright to kill Laotians by remote control. But believe me, the helicopter crews fill the same body bags and they wreak the same kind of damage on the Vietnamese and Laotian countryside as anyone else, and the President is talking about allowing that to go on for many years to come. And one can only ask if we will really be satisfied when the troops march in to Hanoi.

We are asking here in Washington for some action, action from the Congress of the United States of America which has the power to raise and maintain armies and which by the Constitution also has the power to declare war. We've come here, not to the President, because we believe that this body can be responsive to the will of the people; and we believe that the will of the people says that we should be out of Vietnam now.

We're here in Washington also to say that the problem of this war is not just a question of war and diplomacy. It's part and parcel of everything that we are trying as human beings to communicate to people in this country: the question of racism, which is rampant in the military; and so many other questions also: the use of weapons; the hypocrisy in our taking umbrage in the . . . Geneva Conventions and using that as justification for continuation of this war, when we are more guilty than any other body of violations of those Geneva Conventions—in the use of free-fire zones, harassment interdiction fire, search and destroy missions, the bombings, the torture of prisoners, the killing of prisoners—accepted policy by many units in South Vietnam. That's what we're trying to say. It's part and parcel of everything.

An American Indian friend of mine who lives on the Indian nation of Alcatraz put it to me very succinctly. He told me how as a boy on an Indian reservation he had watched television and he used to cheer the cowboys when they came in and shot the Indians. And then suddenly one day he stopped in Vietnam and he said, "My God, I'm doing to these people the very same thing that was done to my people,"—and he stopped. And that's what we're trying to say, that we think this thing has to end.

We're also here to ask—We are here to ask and we're here to ask vehemently, Where are the leaders of our country? Where is the leadership? We're here to ask: Where are McNamara, Rostow, Bundy, Kilpatrick, and so many others. Where are they now that we the men whom they sent off to war have returned? These are commanders who have deserted their troops and there is no more serious crime in the law of war. The Army says they never leave their wounded. The Marines say they never leave even their dead. These men have left all the casualties and retreated behind a pious shield of public rectitude. They've left the real stuff of their reputations, bleaching behind them in the sun in this country.

And finally, this Administration has done us the ultimate dishonor. They've attempted to disown us and the sacrifices we made for this country. In their blindness and fear, they have tried to deny that we are veterans or that we served in Nam. We do not need their testimony. Our own scars and stumps of limbs are witness enough for others and for ourselves. We wish that a merciful God could wipe away our own memories of that service as easily as this Administration has wiped their memories of us.

And all that they have done and all that they can do by this denial is to make more clear than ever our own determination to undertake one last mission: to search out and destroy the last vestige of this barbaric war, to pacify our own hearts, to conquer the hate and fear that have driven this country these last 10 years and more—and more.

And so, in 30 years from now our brothers go down the street without a leg, without an arm or a face, and small boys ask why, we will be able to say "Vietnam" and not mean a desert, not a filthy obscene memory but mean instead the place where America finally turned and where soldiers like us helped it in the turning.

JIMMY CARTER, "CRISIS OF CONFIDENCE" (JULY 15, 1979)

The Vietnam War, which ended in defeat, was only one among a series of events that traumatized the American body politic during the 1960s and 1970s. Among the others were the assassinations of Martin Luther King and Senator Robert F. Kennedy, race riots in many American cities, the violence-marred Democratic National Convention of 1968, the shooting of student protestors at Kent State University by National Guard troops, the Watergate scandal that resulted in the forced resignation of President Richard M. Nixon, and a devastating energy shortage. In 1976, Jimmy Carter (1924–) offered himself as a presidential candidate who could end this sequence of bad news and make a fresh beginning. The message worked in enabling Carter to prevail over the incumbent Gerald Ford in November. But his own four years in office produced further disappointment—revolution in Iran that ousted a key ally and resulted in a humiliating hostage crisis, another "oil shock," and a Soviet invasion of Afghanistan, which seemed to suggest that America's chief adversary had gained the upper hand in the Cold War. Here Carter proposes a new strategy to address these challenges. Americans rejected both the strategy and Carter's bid for a second term.

Good evening.

This is a special night for me. Exactly 3 years ago, on July 15, 1976, I accepted the nomination of my party to run for President of the United States. I promised you a President who is not isolated from the people, who feels your pain, and who shares your dreams and who draws his strength and his wisdom from you.

During the past 3 years I've spoken to you on many occasions about national concerns, the energy crisis, reorganizing the Government, our Nation's economy, and issues of war and especially peace. But over those years the subjects of the speeches, the talks, and the press conferences have become increasingly narrow, focused more and more on what the isolated world of Washington thinks is important. Gradually, you've heard more and more about what the Government thinks or what the Government should be doing and less and less about our Nation's hopes, our dreams, and our vision of the future.

Ten days ago I had planned to speak to you again about a very important subject—energy. For the fifth time I would have described the urgency of the problem and laid out a series of legislative recommendations to the Congress. But as I was preparing to speak, I began to ask myself the same question that I now know has been troubling many of you. Why have we not been able to get together as a nation to resolve our serious energy problem?

It's clear that the true problems of our Nation are much deeper—deeper than gasoline lines or energy shortages, deeper even than inflation or recession. And I realize more than ever that as President I need your help. So, I decided to reach out and listen to the voices of America.

I invited to Camp David people from almost every segment of our society—business and labor, teachers and preachers, Governors, mayors, and private citizens. And then I left Camp David to listen to other Americans, men and women like you. It has been an extraordinary 10 days, and I want to share with you what I've heard.

First of all, I got a lot of personal advice. . . .

This kind of summarized a lot of other statements: "Mr. President, we are confronted with a moral and a spiritual crisis."

Several of our discussions were on energy, and I have a notebook full of comments and advice. . . .

These 10 days confirmed my belief in the decency and the strength and the wisdom of the American people, but it also bore out some of my longstanding concerns about our Nation's underlying problems.

I know, of course, being President, that government actions and legislation can be very important. That's why I've worked hard to put my campaign promises into law—and I have to admit, with just mixed success. But after listening to the American people I have been reminded again that all the legislation in the world can't fix what's wrong with America. So, I want to speak to you first tonight about a subject even more serious than energy or inflation. I want to talk to you right now about a fundamental threat to American democracy.

I do not mean our political and civil liberties. They will endure. And I do not refer to the outward strength of America, a nation that is at peace tonight everywhere in the world, with unmatched economic power and military might.

The threat is nearly invisible in ordinary ways. It is a crisis of confidence. It is a crisis that strikes at the very heart and soul and spirit of our national will. We can see this crisis in the growing doubt about the meaning of our own lives and in the loss of a unity of purpose for our Nation.

The erosion of our confidence in the future is threatening to destroy the social and the political fabric of America.

The confidence that we have always had as a people is not simply some romantic dream or a proverb in a dusty book that we read just on the Fourth of July. It is the idea which founded our Nation and has guided our development as a people. Confidence in the future has supported everything else—public institutions and private enterprise, our own families, and the very Constitution of the United States. Confidence has defined our course and has served as a link between generations. We've always believed in something called progress. We've always had a faith that the days of our children would be better than our own.

Our people are losing that faith, not only in government itself but in the ability as citizens to serve as the ultimate rulers and shapers of our democracy. As a people we know our past and we are proud of it. Our progress has been part of the living history of America, even the world. We always believed that we were part of a great movement of humanity itself called democracy, involved in the search for freedom, and that belief has always strengthened us in our purpose. But just as we are losing our confidence in the future, we are also beginning to close the door on our past.

In a nation that was proud of hard work, strong families, close-knit communities, and our faith in God, too many of us now tend to worship self-indulgence and consumption. Human identity is no longer defined by what one does, but by what one owns. But we've discovered that owning things and consuming things does not satisfy our longing for meaning. We've learned that piling up material goods cannot fill the emptiness of lives which have no confidence or purpose.

The symptoms of this crisis of the American spirit are all around us. For the first time in the history of our country a majority of our people believe that the next 5 years will be worse than the past 5 years. Two-thirds of our people do not even vote. The productivity of American workers is actually dropping, and the willingness of Americans to save for the future has fallen below that of all other people in the Western world.

As you know, there is a growing disrespect for government and for churches and for schools, the news media, and other institutions. This is not a message of happiness or reassurance, but it is the truth and it is a warning.

These changes did not happen overnight. They've come upon us gradually over the last generation, years that were filled with shocks and tragedy.

We were sure that ours was a nation of the ballot, not the bullet, until the murders of John Kennedy and Robert Kennedy and Martin Luther King, Jr. We were taught that our armies were always invincible and our causes were always just, only to suffer the agony of Vietnam. We respected the Presidency as a place of honor until the shock of Watergate.

We remember when the phrase "sound as a dollar" was an expression of absolute dependability, until 10 years of inflation began to shrink our dollar and our savings. We believed that our Nation's resources were limitless until 1973, when we had to face a growing dependence on foreign oil.

These wounds are still very deep. They have never been healed.

Looking for a way out of this crisis, our people have turned to the Federal Government and found it isolated from the mainstream of our Nation's life. Washington, D.C., has become an island. The gap between our citizens and our Government has never been so wide. The people are looking for honest answers, not easy answers; clear leadership, not false claims and evasiveness and politics as usual.

What you see too often in Washington and elsewhere around the country is a system of government that seems incapable of action. You see a Congress twisted and pulled in every direction by hundreds of well-financed and powerful special interests. You see every extreme position defended to the last vote, almost to the last breath by one unyielding group or another. You often see a balanced and a fair approach that demands sacrifice, a little sacrifice from everyone, abandoned like an orphan without support and without friends.

Often you see paralysis and stagnation and drift. You don't like it, and neither do I. What can we do?

First of all, we must face the truth, and then we can change our course. We simply must have faith in each other, faith in our ability to govern ourselves, and faith in the future of this Nation. Restoring that faith and that confidence to America is now the most important task we face. It is a true challenge of this generation of Americans.

One of the visitors to Camp David last week put it this way: "We've got to stop crying and start sweating, stop talking and start walking, stop cursing and start praying. The strength we need will not come from the White House, but from every house in America."

We know the strength of America. We are strong. We can regain our unity. We can regain our confidence. We are the heirs of generations who survived threats much more powerful and awesome than those that challenge us now. Our fathers and mothers were strong men and women who shaped a new society during the Great Depression, who fought world wars, and who carved out a new charter of peace for the world.

We ourselves are the same Americans who just 10 years ago put a man on the Moon. We are the generation that dedicated our society to the pursuit of human rights and equality. And we are the generation that will win the war on the energy problem and in that process rebuild the unity and confidence of America.

We are at a turning point in our history. There are two paths to choose. One is a path I've warned about tonight, the path that leads to fragmentation and self-interest. Down that road lies a mistaken idea of freedom, the right to grasp for ourselves some advantage over others. That path would be

one of constant conflict between narrow interests ending in chaos and immobility. It is a certain route to failure.

All the traditions of our past, all the lessons of our heritage, all the promises of our future point to another path, the path of common purpose and the restoration of American values. That path leads to true freedom for our Nation and ourselves. We can take the first steps down that path as we begin to solve our energy problem.

Energy will be the immediate test of our ability to unite this Nation, and it can also be the standard around which we rally. On the battlefield of energy we can win for our Nation a new confidence, and we can seize control again of our common destiny.

In little more than two decades we've gone from a position of energy independence to one in which almost half the oil we use comes from foreign countries, at prices that are going through the roof. Our excessive dependence on OPEC has already taken a tremendous toll on our economy and our people. This is the direct cause of the long lines which have made millions of you spend aggravating hours waiting for gasoline. It's a cause of the increased inflation and unemployment that we now face. This intolerable dependence on foreign oil threatens our economic independence and the very security of our Nation.

The energy crisis is real. It is worldwide. It is a clear and present danger to our Nation. These are facts and we simply must face them: What I have to say to you now about energy is simple and vitally important.

Point one: I am tonight setting a clear goal for the energy policy of the United States. Beginning this moment, this Nation will never use more foreign oil than we did in 1977—never. From now on, every new addition to our demand for energy will be met from our own production and our own conservation. The generation-long growth in our dependence on foreign oil will be stopped dead in its tracks right now and then reversed as we move through the 1980's, for I am tonight setting the further goal of cutting our dependence on foreign oil by one-half by the end of the next decade—a saving of over 4½ million barrels of imported oil per day.

Point two: To ensure that we meet these targets, I will use my Presidential authority to set import quotas. I'm announcing tonight that for 1979 and 1980, I will forbid the entry into this country of one drop of foreign oil more than these goals allow. These quotas will ensure a reduction in imports even below the ambitious levels we set at the recent Tokyo summit.

Point three: To give us energy security, I am asking for the most massive peacetime commitment of funds and resources in our Nation's history to develop America's own alternative sources of fuel—from coal, from oil shale, from plant products for gasohol, from unconventional gas, from the Sun.

I propose the creation of an energy security corporation to lead this effort to replace 2½ million barrels of imported oil per day by 1990. The corporation will issue up to $5 billion in energy bonds, and I especially want them to be in small denominations so that average Americans can invest directly in America's energy security.

Just as a similar synthetic rubber corporation helped us win World War II, so will we mobilize American determination and ability to win the energy war. Moreover, I will soon submit legislation to Congress calling for the creation of this Nation's first solar bank, which will help us achieve the crucial goal of 20 percent of our energy coming from solar power by the year 2000.

These efforts will cost money, a lot of money, and that is why Congress must enact the windfall profits tax without delay. It will be money well spent. Unlike the billions of dollars that we ship to foreign countries to pay for foreign oil, these funds will be paid by Americans to Americans. These funds will go to fight, not to increase, inflation and unemployment.

Point four: I'm asking Congress to mandate, to require as a matter of law, that our Nation's utility companies cut their massive use of oil by 50 percent within the next decade and switch to other fuels, especially coal, our most abundant energy source.

Point five: To make absolutely certain that nothing stands in the way of achieving these goals, I will urge Congress to create an energy mobilization board which, like the War Production Board in World War II, will have the responsibility and authority to cut through the red tape, the delays, and the endless roadblocks to completing key energy projects.

We will protect our environment. But when this Nation critically needs a refinery or a pipeline, we will build it.

Point six: I'm proposing a bold conservation program to involve every State, county, and city and every average American in our energy battle. This effort will permit you to build conservation into your homes and your lives at a cost you can afford.

I ask Congress to give me authority for mandatory conservation and for standby gasoline rationing. To further conserve energy, I'm proposing tonight an extra $10 billion over the next decade to strengthen our public transportation systems. And I'm asking you for your good and for your Nation's security to take no unnecessary trips, to use carpools or public transportation whenever you can, to park your car one extra day per week, to obey the speed limit, and to set your thermostats to save fuel. Every act of energy conservation like this is more than just common sense—I tell you it is an act of patriotism.

Our Nation must be fair to the poorest among us, so we will increase aid to needy Americans to cope with rising energy prices. We often think of conservation only in terms of sacrifice. In fact, it is the most painless and immediate way of rebuilding our Nation's strength. Every gallon of oil each one of us saves is a new form of production. It gives us more freedom, more confidence, that much more control over our own lives.

So, the solution of our energy crisis can also help us to conquer the crisis of the spirit in our country. It can rekindle our sense of unity, our confidence in the future, and give our Nation and all of us individually a new sense of purpose.

You know we can do it. We have the natural resources. We have more oil in our shale alone than several Saudi Arabias. We have more coal than any nation on Earth. We have the world's highest level of technology. We have the most skilled work force, with innovative genius, and I firmly believe that we have the national will to win this war.

I do not promise you that this struggle for freedom will be easy. I do not promise a quick way out of our Nation's problems, when the truth is that the only way out is an all-out effort. What I do promise you is that I will lead our fight, and I will enforce fairness in our struggle, and I will ensure honesty. And above all, I will act.

We can manage the short-term shortages more effectively and we will, but there are no short-term solutions to our long-range problems. There is simply no way to avoid sacrifice.

Twelve hours from now I will speak again in Kansas City, to expand and to explain further our energy program. Just as the search for solutions to our energy shortages has now led us to a new awareness of our Nation's deeper problems, so our willingness to work for those solutions in energy can strengthen us to attack those deeper problems. . . .

We can spend until we empty our treasuries, and we may summon all the wonders of science. But we can succeed only if we tap our greatest resources—America's people, America's values, and America's confidence.

I have seen the strength of America in the inexhaustible resources of our people. In the days to come, let us renew that strength in the struggle for an energy secure nation.

In closing, let me say this: I will do my best, but I will not do it alone. Let your voice be heard. Whenever you have a chance, say something good about our country. With God's help and for the sake of our Nation, it is time for us to join hands in America. Let us commit ourselves together to a rebirth of the American spirit. Working together with our common faith we cannot fail.

X.

GRAPPLING WITH TOTAL WAR

With the strategic bombing campaigns of World War II, culminating in the use of atomic bombs to destroy Hiroshima and Nagasaki in August 1945, wars of annihilation became a possibility. A central feature of the ensuing Cold War was a nuclear arms race, during which both the United States and the Soviet Union assembled arsenals consisting of many thousands of nuclear weapons, each side ready to strike the other on a moment's notice. Lesser nations also acquired the "bomb," which was both unusable for any rational purpose and also the ultimate symbol of military power.

For decades thereafter, American political leaders, strategists, and writers reflected on the potential implications of these opposing arsenals and how they exacerbated or tempered the Soviet-American rivalry. Avoiding further employment of weapons of mass destruction became an abiding concern. Yet the danger that they posed persisted. The documents in this section provide an overview of the debate over nuclear weapons that continues even today.

JOHN CUTHBERT FORD, SJ, "THE MORALITY OF OBLITERATION BOMBING," *THEOLOGICAL STUDIES* (1944)

Even as World II was still underway, John Cuthbert Ford (1902–1989), a Jesuit priest, weighed in on the moral implications of large-scale air campaigns that targeted civilians.

In general the term obliteration bombing is used as the opposite of precision bombing. In precision bombing very definite, limited targets, such as airfields, munitions factories, railroad bridges, etc., are picked out and aimed at. But in obliteration bombing, the target is not a well-defined military objective, as that term has been understood in the past. The target is a large area, for instance, a whole city, or all the built-up part of a city, or at least a very large section of the total built-up area, often including by design residential districts.

In the early days of the present war the British did not make use of obliteration bombing; the government insisted that only military objectives in the narrow sense were to be aimed at. . . . Churchill on Jan. 27, 1940, had condemned Germany's policy of indiscriminate bombing as a "new and odious form of warfare." But with the appointment of Sir Arthur Travers Harris to the control of the Bomber Command, on March 3, 1942, the RAF changed its policy and took up obliteration bombing. According to *Time,* the men responsible for the new policy were Sir Arthur Harris, Chief of the RAF Bomber Command, and Major General Clarence Eaker, commander of the United States Eighth Air Force.

The leaders in England acknowledged the new policy. Churchill no longer condemned this "odious form of warfare," and promised the House of Commons on June 2, 1942, that Germany was to be subjected to an "ordeal the like of which has never been experienced by any country." In July, 1943, he spoke of "the systematic shattering of German cities." On Sept. 21, 1943, he said in the House of Commons: "There are no sacrifices we will not make, no lengths in violence to which we will not go." Brendan Bracken, Minister of Information, speaking to the press in Quebec (August, 1943) echoed the leader, saying: "Our plans are to bomb, burn, and ruthlessly destroy in every way available to us the people responsible for creating the war." And when Sir Archibald Sinclair, Secretary of State for Air, was asked in the House of Commons (March 31, 1943) whether on any occasion instructions had been given to British airmen to engage in area bombing rather than limit their attention to purely military targets, he replied: "The targets of Bomber Command are always military, but night bombing of military objectives necessarily involves bombing the area in which they are situated." Area bombing is another name for obliteration bombing.

Leaders in the United States have approved the bombings. President Roosevelt, replying through his secretary, Mr. Stephen Early, to protests against the bombing did not deny that area or obliteration bombing was the present policy, and defended the kind of bombing going on in Germany on the ground that it is shortening the war. A *New York Times* dispatch quotes Chief of Army Air Forces, General H. H. Arnold, as saying that the combined chiefs of staff at the Casablanca Conference had directed American and British Air Forces to destroy the German military, industrial, and economic systems and to undermine the morale of the people. General Arnold is quoted further:

> I remember a day in the summer of 1941, the day a letter from President Roosevelt came to my desk, a letter written to the Secretary of War, asking us to determine what would be required to defeat Germany if we should become involved in the war. The plan drawn up by the air force in response to that letter is in substance the plan we are successfully carrying out right now.

Because of our bombsight, most of the daytime precision work is assigned to American bombers, while the RAF does the obliteration by night. But the whole strategic plan of wiping out the German cities is agreed on by the leaders of both countries. . . . Accordingly, the moral responsibility for the obliteration attacks is shared by both British and American leaders. . . .

The purpose of this strategic bombing is described by those in charge of it as follows: "The bombing of Germany that is now going on has two main objectives. One is, of course, the destruction of Germany's major industrial cities, with Berlin as the main target because it is the largest as well as the most important of those cities. The other main target is the fighter aircraft factories and all related factories. . . ." Thus Sir Arthur Harris, the organizer and chief executive of the obliteration attack. Another purpose is the destruction of railroads and communications generally. And no secret is made of the direct intent to wipe out residential districts where workmen live with their wives and children, so that absenteeism will interfere with industrial production. The leaders have clearly declared their purpose to bomb very large sections of ninety German cities, with the direct intent of wiping out, if possible, not only the industrial but also the residential built-up districts of these cities. In a speech made on November 6, 1943, Sir Arthur Harris said: "We propose entirely to emasculate every center of enemy production, forty of which are centers vital to his war effort and fifty that can be termed considerably important. We are well on the way to their destruction." And writing in the *New York Times Magazine,* April 16,1944, the same leader declares: "There are only thirty industrial towns in Germany with a population over 200,000. . . . Of these thirty major cities there are now only five . . . which have not been seriously damaged. Twelve of them, not including Berlin, . . . now have had their capacity to produce destroyed." He also tells us: "Many cases involve destruction of about half the total built-up area in a city. . . . But many of these industrial towns which have been knocked out of the war are as much as two-thirds or three-quarters devastated." He calls it a "mass destruction of industrial cities." . . .

It requires only a little imagination to picture the agonies which this obliteration bombing has inflicted on the civil populations. Since the bombs, including incendiaries, are aimed at whole areas, and aimed at residential districts on purpose, and over these districts are dropped blindly and indiscriminately, deaths of civilians, men, women, and children, have been very numerous. At times the bombs have been dropped through heavy banks of clouds so that the target (that is, the city) could not be seen at all. When the navigation instruments told them they were over the city, they dropped their enormous bomb loads. (According to a press report, the Allies dropped 147,000 tons of explosives on Europe during the month of May, 1944.) . . .

I have given these facts and many more, based especially on the assertions of Allied leaders, in order that the phrase obliteration bombing might be given a definite meaning. That definite meaning (or definition) I couch in the following terms: *Obliteration bombing is the strategic bombing, by means of incendiaries and explosives, of industrial centers of population in which the target to be wiped out is not a definite factory, bridge, or similar object, but a large area of a whole city, comprising one-third to two-thirds of its whole built-up area, and including by design the residential districts of workingmen and their families.* If this kind of bombing is not taking place, so much the better. But we have such compelling reasons for thinking it does, that the following discussion of its morality is necessary. . . .

The principal moral problem raised by obliteration bombing, then, is that of the rights of non-combatants to their lives in war time. Rights are protected by laws. The laws in question are the international law, the law of humanity, and the natural law. . . .

The present paper, though not excluding considerations based on international law and the law of humanity, will deal principally with the natural-law rights of non-combatants. And our chief concern will be the right of the non-combatant to life and limb. His right not to have his property taken or destroyed (or his family torn asunder) is also pertinent, but will be mentioned only incidentally. Hence, we can put the moral problem raised by obliteration bombing in the form of the following questions, which the rest of the paper will try to answer:

1) Do the majority of civilians in a modern nation at war enjoy a natural-law right of immunity from violent repression?

2) Does obliteration bombing necessarily involve a violation of the rights of innocent civilians?

It is fundamental in the Catholic view that to take the life of an innocent person is always intrinsically wrong, that is, forbidden absolutely by natural law. Neither the state nor any private individual can thus dispose of the lives of the innocent. The killing of enemy soldiers in warfare was justified by older writers on the theory that they were not innocent but guilty. They were guilty of unjust aggression, or of a violation of rights which could be forcibly vindicated. The individual enemy soldiers might be only materially guilty, but it was this guilt, and their immediate cooperation in violent unjust acts that made them legitimate objects of direct killing. As far as I know, this distinction between the innocent and guilty has never been abandoned by Catholic theologians. They still maintain that it is always intrinsically wrong to kill directly the innocent civilians of the enemy country.

But in the course of time the terms innocent and guilty have been replaced by the terms non-combatant and combatant, or by civilian and soldier. And the definitions of these terms have been clarified by conventions of international law. . . .

The contribution of international law has been to make precise the definition of combatant and non-combatant and to determine just who is a legitimate object of lethal attack and who is not. Thus the natural-law distinction between innocent and guilty received the sanction of explicit pacts. Furthermore, the term non-combatant included *all* who were not bearing arms, whether they were strictly "innocent" or not, and so the number of those who were immune from attack was increased. The present immunity from direct violence, which the entire civilian population enjoys (theoretically), is based partly on natural law and partly on international law.

The thorny question is rather: *Who are to be considered non-combatants in a war like the present one?* . . .

On September 1, 1939, before we became engaged in the war and long before we took up the practice of obliteration bombing, President Roosevelt addressed an appeal to the German and Polish governments. I do not quote the President as one whose opinions on morality would weigh with a professor of that science, but rather as a witness to the conscience of humanity. Speaking as the head of a technically neutral nation, and at any rate before the arguments of military necessity were made to bear heavily on whatever consciences we have, he said:

> The ruthless bombing from the air of civilians in unfortified centres of population during the course of hostilities which have raged in various quarters of the earth in the past few years, which have resulted in the maiming and death of thousands of defenceless women and children, has profoundly shocked the conscience of humanity. If resort is had to this sort of inhuman barbarism during the period of tragic conflagration with which the world is now confronted, hundreds of thousands of innocent human beings, who have no responsibility for, and who are not even remotely participating in, the hostilities which have broken out, now will lose their lives. I am therefore addressing this urgent appeal to every Government which may be engaged in hostilities publicly to affirm its determination that its armed forces shall in no event and under no circumstances undertake bombardment from the air of civilian populations or unfortified cities, upon the understanding that the same rules of warfare will be scrupulously observed by all their opponents. . . .

And so the question arises, who has the burden of proof—the civilian behind the lines, who clings to his traditional immunity, or the military leader with new and highly destructive weapons in his hands, who claims that he can attack civilians because modern industrial and economic conditions have changed the nature of war radically and made them all aggressors. Do we start with the supposition that the whole population of the enemy is presumably guilty, and that anyone who wants to exempt a group from that condemnation is called upon to prove the innocence of the group? Or do we start with the view that only armed soldiers are guilty combatants, and anyone who wants to increase the number of the guilty, and make unarmed civilians legitimate objects of violent repression, has the duty of proving his position? Is it not reasonable to put the burden of proof on those who are innovators? Do we not start from here: "Thou shalt not kill"? Seeing that the wartime rights of civilians to life and property are declared by centuries of tradition to be sacrosanct, what do we presume: a man's right to his life, even in war time, or my right to kill him? his right to his property, or my right to destroy it? . . .

The principal justifications I have seen are worthless. They say: the enemy did it first; or, military necessity demands it; or, it is justified by way of reprisal; or, the present situation is desperately abnormal (as if there were ever a war which was not); or, nowadays the whole nation takes part in the aggression, whereas formerly it was only army against army. As to this last point, it is true that the number of civilians who contribute immediately to the armed prosecution of the war has increased in modern times, but to say that all or nearly all do so is a grave distortion of the facts, as we shall see. And to imply that in the past the general civilian population co-operated not at all or only negligibly is equally far from the facts. Armies in the past had to be supplied with food, clothing, guns, and ammunition, and it was the civilian population who supplied them. . . .

Perhaps the governments would like to enlist the active and immediate participation of all civilians in the war itself; but even this is doubtful. And the fact is that they do not succeed in doing so, and from the very nature of the case cannot. Even in a modern war there remains necessarily a vast field of civilian work and activity which is remote from the armed prosecution of the war.

Let us see for a moment what the abandonment of the distinction between combatants and non-combatants would mean in practice; or what it would mean to say that hardly any civilians are innocent in a modern war, because all are co-operating in the aggression. It would mean, for instance, that all the persons listed below are guilty, and deserve death, or at least are fit objects of violent repression. I should not inflict this long list on my readers (though I really believe one can profit by its careful perusal), unless I were convinced that some have been misled by the propaganda of total-war-mongers, or have taken uncritically at their face value statements about "a nation in arms," or "all co-operate in the aggression," or "the enemy has mobilized the whole population," or "nobody is innocent except the infant." . . .

Do these persons, whom I consider to be, almost without exception, *certainly innocent non-combatants according to natural law,* constitute a large proportion of the general civilian population? Here again, though it is impossible to give accurate figures for the proportion, it can be maintained with complete certitude that they constitute the vast majority of the entire civil population even in war time. . . .

The conclusion of this section of our paper is an answer to the question: Do the majority of civilians in a modern nation at war enjoy a natural-law right of immunity from violent repression? The answer is an emphatic affirmative. . . .

And so the immorality of obliteration bombing, its violation of the rights of these innocent civilians to life, bodily integrity, and property would be crystal clear, and would not be subject to dispute, at least amongst Catholics, were it not for the appeal to the principle of the double effect. This principle can be worded as follows: The foreseen evil effect of a man's action is not morally imputable to him, provided that (1) the action in itself is directed immediately to some other result, (2) the evil effect is not willed either in itself or as a means to the other result, (3) the permitting of the evil effect is justified by reasons of proportionate weight.

Applying the principle to obliteration bombing, it would be argued: The bombing has a good effect, the destruction of war industries, communications, and military installations, leading to the defeat of the enemy; it also has an evil effect, the injury and death of innocent civilians (and the destruction of their property). The damage to civilian life (and property) is not intentional; it is not a means to the production of the good effect, but is merely its incidental accompaniment. Furthermore, the slaughter, maiming, and destruction can be permitted because there are sufficiently weighty excusing causes, such as shortening the war, military necessity, saving our own soldiers' lives, etc. This viewpoint, therefore, would find a simple solution to the moral problem merely by advising the air strategist to let go his bombs, but withhold his intention. In what follows I shall attempt to show that this is an unwarranted application of the principle of the double effect.

The principle of the double effect, though basic in scientific Catholic morality, is not, however, a mathematical formula, nor an analytical principle. It is a practical formula which synthesizes an immense amount of moral experience, and serves as an efficient guide in countless perplexing cases. But just because it is called into play to solve the more difficult cases, it is liable to sophistical abuse. Some applications of it can only be called casuistical in the bad sense of that word. It is a truism among moralists that, though the principle is clear in itself, its application requires "sound moral judgment." It seems to me that the following are the points which require a moral, rather than a mathematical or merely verbal, interpretation of the principle, when it is applied in practice.

As to obliteration bombing, then, is it possible to employ this procedure without directly intending the damage to innocent civilians and their property? Obviously, the destruction of property is directly intended. The leaders acknowledge it as an objective. And on this score alone one could argue with reason against the morality of the practice. But since the property of civilians is not so absolutely immune as their persons and lives from direct attack in war time, I prefer to deal mainly with the latter.

Looking at obliteration bombing as it actually takes place, can we say that the maiming and death of hundreds of thousands of innocent persons, which are its immediate result, are not directly intended, but merely permitted? Is it possible psychologically and honestly for the leaders who have developed and ordered the employment of this strategy to say they do not intend any harm to innocent civilians? To many, I am sure, the distinction between the material fabric of a city, especially the densely populated residential areas, and the hundreds of thousands of human inhabitants of such areas, will seem very unreal and casuistical. They will consider it merely playing with words to say that in dropping a bomb on a man's house, knowing he is there with his family, the intent is merely to destroy the house and interfere with enemy production (through absenteeism), while permitting the injury and death of the family. . . .

It is enough to recall that in a single raid on Cologne (according to Mr. J. M. Spaight, one of the most enthusiastic and articulate defenders of the bombing), 5000 acres of the built-up part of the city was wiped out. That means a territory eight miles square. And the American Army Air Forces' official story of the first year of bombing says of Hamburg: "Well over 2200 British and American aircraft dropped more than 7000 tons of high explosive and incendiaries on a city the size of Detroit. To quote an official report: 'There is nothing in the world to which this concentrated devastation of Hamburg can be compared, for an inferno of this scale in a town of this size has never been experienced, hardly even imagined, before.' "The total weight of the bombs dropped on Hamburg in seven days equaled the tonnage dropped on London during the whole of the 1940-1941 blitz. Mr. Spaight informs us: "What the effect was may be inferred from the ejaculations of one German radio commentator (Dr. Carl Hofman): 'Terror . . . terror . . . terror . . . pure, naked, bloody terror.'"

More than nine square miles of Hamburg (77 per cent of its built-up area), including the largest workers' district in the city, were completely wiped out, according to British reports of the raids. An RAF commentator said: "To all intents and purposes a city of 1,800,000 inhabitants lies in absolute ruins. . . . It is probably the most complete blotting-out of a city that ever happened." This kind of thing is still going on. In July, 1944, General H. H. Arnold, commanding general of our Army Air Forces, announced that latest reports indicated that 40 to 50 per cent of the central

portion of Berlin is "burned out. . . . Berlin is a ruined city." The bomber chief also stated that the Army Air Force plans to continue its air offensive against Germany, "burning out" its industries and war centers.

If these are the facts, what is to be said of the contention that the damage to civilian property and especially to civilian life is only incidental? Is it psychologically and honestly possible for the air strategist in circumstances like these to let go his bombs, and withhold his intention as far as the innocent are concerned? I have grave doubts of the possibility.

But there is another reason for excluding the possibility of such merely indirect intent. At the Casablanca conference, the combined chiefs of staff ordered a joint British-United States air offensive to accomplish "the progressive destruction and dislocation of the German military, industrial and economic system and *the undermining of the* armed resistance is fatally weakened." *Target: Germany,* an official publication of the air forces, tells us that "the two bomber commands lost no time in setting about the job. To the RAF fell the task of destroying Germany's great cities, of silencing the iron heart-beat of the Ruhr, *of dispossessing the working population, of breaking the morale of the people.* The mission of VIII Bomber Command was the destruction of the key industries by which the German military machine was sustained." This same authoritative publication (presented with a foreword by General Arnold himself) makes it clear that the terrorization of civilians is part of our bombing strategy. "Bombs behind the fighting fronts may rob armies of their vital supplies and make war so terrible that civilian populations will refuse to support the armed forces in the field. . . . *The physical attrition of warfare is no longer limited to the fighting forces.* Heretofore the home front has remained relatively secure; armies fought, civil populations worked and waited. This conflict's early air attacks were the first portents of a changing order." And after saying that we now follow the "bloody instructions" given us by the Nazis, and after describing the destruction of Hamburg and other industrial cities, this official account says: "Here, then, we have *terror and devastation* carried to the core of a warring nation."

Now I contend that it is impossible to make civilian terrorization, or the undermining of civilian morale, an object of bombing without having a direct intent to injure and kill civilians. The principal cause of civilian terror, the principal cause of the loss of morale, is the danger to life and limb which accompanies the raids. If one intends the end, terror, one cannot escape intending the principal means of obtaining that end, namely, the injury and death of civilians.

Both from the nature of the obliteration operation itself, then, and from the professed objective of undermining morale, I conclude that it is impossible to adopt this strategy without having the direct intent of violating the rights of innocent civilians. This intent is, of course, gravely immoral. . . .

Furthermore, we continually hear the argument: "They did it first," as a justification of our bombing of Germany. The argument is that since the Germans have attacked our innocent civilian populations on purpose, we can do the same thing to them. Mr. Norman Cousins, editor of the *Saturday Review of Literature,* who has interested himself in the subject of obliteration bombing, apparently believes that any procedure whatever, no matter how brutal, is moral and legitimate for us to adopt once the enemy adopts it: "Once the enemy *starts* it [poison gas, and even, it seems, indiscriminate bacteriological warfare] it becomes no longer a moral but a military question, no longer a matter of argument but a matter of action."

Mr. Churchill's appeal to the popular revenge motive has been public. At the present time there are numerous calls for revenge of the robot bombing. An editorial in the *Boston Herald* asks: "Why not go all out on bombings? . . . *Why be nice about the undefended towns and cities? . . .* The time-honored system of tit for tat is the only one which Hitler and his Germans can understand." The *New York Times* had an editorial along the same lines. . . .

Naturally one does not expect political leaders to assert definitely that they intend to kill women and children. The feelings of the whole civilized world are so completely in accord with the traditional distinction between innocent and guilty, and such a very large number of people (with votes) everywhere consider themselves to be among the innocent, that it would probably be political suicide to announce explicitly such a policy; and even from the military point of view it would provide the enemy with priceless propaganda. Any attack on the innocent civil population will always be covered up by a euphemistic name, like "area" bombing, or simply written off under the general absolution of "military necessity." . . .

The principal reason alleged to justify the infliction of enormous agonies on hundreds of thousands and even millions of innocent persons by obliteration bombing is the reason of military necessity, or of shortening the war. We hear that "it must be done to win the war"; "it will shorten the war and save our soldiers' lives"; "it will liberate Europe and enable us to feed the starving sooner." Major General J. F. C. Fuller, writing long before obliteration bombing was an issue, said: "When however it is realized that to enforce policy, and not to kill, is the objective [in war] and that the policy of a nation though maintained and enforced by her soldiers and sailors is not fashioned by them but by the civil population, surely then if a few civilians get killed in the struggle they have nothing to complain of—

'dulce et decorum est pro patria mori!'. . ."

Now in the practical estimation of proportionate cause it is fundamental to recognize that an evil which is certain and extensive and immediate will rarely be compensated for by a problematical, speculative, future good. The evil wrought by obliteration is certain injury and death, here and now, to hundreds of thousands, and an incalculable destruction of their property. The ultimate good which is supposed to compensate for this evil is of a very speculative character.

When Great Britain first adopted obliteration as a policy, Mr. Churchill called it an experiment. He did not know whether it would work or not. The U. S. Army Air Forces in their account of the first year's work in Germany say: *"Target: Germany* is the story of an experiment," and admit that after a year "the final evaluation is yet to be made," and from the nature of the case cannot be made ahead of time or even at the time of the bombing. The effects on future battles are too far removed— sometimes not felt for six months. To the question, "Will bombing win the war?", *Target Germany* replies: "To the military logician the question is beside the point. Aerial assault is directed both at the enemy's will to resist and his means to resist. One may collapse before the other; either eventuality is desirable. Bombing will be carried out to the fullest extent in either case." Naturally the authors of *Target: Germany* have confidence in the military effectiveness of their strategy, but they are far from talking in terms of certainty, and they are talking of the whole air strategy, both the British and American assignments. . . .

We are told by a competent reporter of facts that Churchill had "powerful critics of the British Bomber command inside his own Air Ministry. . . . [Certain] British airmen. . . have come to distrust his bomber strategy. . . . The night attacks on German industrial populations, they think, are too haphazard, the targets too far back in the production sequence, to affect German military strength *now.* They argue that quite aside from ethical considerations Harris' technique . . . is not necessarily shortening the war."The same writer tells us that there is a "small but influential group of British intellectuals who have been arguing privately that the economic and social problems deriving from the wrecking of German communities will prove more disastrous in the end than the immediate problem which bombing is supposed to bypass." . . .

It remains to be seen, therefore, whether this type of bombing is a military *necessity* in order to win the war sooner and save British and American lives. The bombing of Monte Cassino was called a military necessity in order to save American lives; but the military experts proved to be mistaken. "Military necessity" can become a mere catchword, and a cloak for every sort of excess, especially when the judgment is made entirely on military grounds without taking into account other factors, such as psychology (not to mention morality). Germany's strategic bombing of England was held to be a failure partly because it stiffened the resistance of the English. Who can say to what extent our obliteration will strengthen rather than weaken the German will to resist— or to what excesses of cruel retribution against our soldiers the people will be aroused? There are many military men who still agree with Marshal Foch: "You cannot scare a great nation into submission by destroying her cities." . . .

The next argument—that obliteration bombing will hasten the day when our victorious arms will enable us to feed the starving millions abused by the Axis—seems to contain an element of hypocrisy. If we wanted to feed starving Europe, we (the United States and Great Britain) could feed millions of the innocent right now. Mr. Hoover has pointed out the way. It does not become us to omit to feed the millions we certainly could feed now, and adopt obliteration with its immense torture of the innocent on the plea that it *may* enable us to feed the hungry later on; especially when President Roosevelt's personal envoy, Colonel Donovan, spoke as follows to the French ambassador at Ankara in the spring of 1941: "The American people are prepared to starve every Frenchman if that's necessary to defeat Hitler." . . .

I conclude from all this that it is illegitimate to appeal to the principle of the double effect when the alleged proportionate cause is speculative, future, and problematical, while the evil effect is definite, widespread, certain, and immediate. But my argument can be pressed still further, and on more general grounds. Even if obliteration bombing did shorten this war (and if the war ends tomorrow we shall never know whether it was this type of bombing that ended it), and even if it did save many military lives, we still must consider *what the result for the future will be if this means of warfare is made generally legitimate.*

Can we afford to justify from this time forward obliteration bombing as a legitimate instrument of war? Once it is conceded that this is a lawful means of waging war, then it is equally available to our enemies, present and future. They will have just as much right to use it against us as they have to use guns against our soldiers. I do not believe any shortening of the present war, or any saving of the lives of our soldiers (problematical at best) is a cause sufficient to justify on moral grounds the use of obliteration bombing in the future.

For in practice, though one may adhere verbally to the distinction between innocent and guilty, the obliteration of great sections of cities, including whole districts of workers' residences, means the abandonment of that distinction as an effective moral norm. When the innocent civil population can be wiped out on such a large scale very little is left practically of the rights of the innocent. Each new and more terrifying procedure, with more and more loss of innocent life, can always be defended as a mere extension of the principle, justified by the desperate military necessities of the case. The wiping out of whole cities is a reversion to barbarism as far as civilian rights are concerned. Already there is talk of using gas when we go into the Far East. The present demands of legislators, editors, and others for the indiscriminate bombing of *non-industrial* towns in Germany is a clear example of an inevitable tendency—once you get used to the idea of obliteration, and justify it.

This is another way of saying that the recognition of obliteration bombing will easily and quickly lead to the recognition of total war itself. . . .

I do not think any American or British statesman or leader believes we are waging, or should wage war in this utterly unrestrained and barbaric manner. But I do think the theory of total war, proclaimed unashamedly by some of our enemies, has made an impression on leaders and on the popular mind. The phrase has been tossed about like the phrase "military necessity," and it becomes a cover-all to hide and excuse practices which would otherwise be readily recognized as immoral. The false notion that today whole peoples are waging war against whole peoples is insinuated or openly propagated, and the conclusion is drawn that whole peoples are legitimate objects of attack.

Now the air bombardment of civilian centers is a symbol of total war in its worst sense. It is the first thing that comes to mind when the phrase "total war" is heard. The air bombardment of great centers of population lets down the bars, and opens up enormous categories of persons, hitherto immune, against whom warlike action can now be taken; it changes the scene of war-like activity from the battlefield to the city, and not only to the war factories but to the residential districts of the workers; and it uses explosives and incendiaries to a hitherto unheard of degree, leaving only one more step to go to the use of poison gas or bacteriological war. This means that obliteration bombing has taken us a long step in the direction of immoral total war. . . .

The conclusion of this paper can be stated briefly. Obliteration bombing, as defined, is an immoral attack on the rights of the innocent. It includes a direct intent to do them injury. Even if this were not true, it would still be immoral, because no proportionate cause could justify the evil done; and to make it legitimate would soon lead the world to the immoral barbarity of total war.

HARRY S TRUMAN, "STATEMENT BY THE PRESIDENT ANNOUNCING THE USE OF THE A-BOMB AT HIROSHIMA" (1945)

President Truman justifies the destruction of Hiroshima.

Sixteen hours ago an American airplane dropped one bomb on Hiroshima, an important Japanese Army base. That bomb had more power than 20,000 tons of T.N.T. It had more than two thousand times the blast power of the British "Grand Slam" which is the largest bomb ever yet used in the history of warfare.

The Japanese began the war from the air at Pearl Harbor. They have been repaid many fold. And the end is not yet. With this bomb we have now added a new and revolutionary increase in destruction to supplement the growing power of our armed forces. In their present form these bombs are now in production and even more powerful forms are in development.

It is an atomic bomb. It is a harnessing of the basic power of the universe. The force from which the sun draws its power has been loosed against those who brought war to the Far East.

Before 1939, it was the accepted belief of scientists that it was theoretically possible to release atomic energy. But no one knew any practical method of doing it. By 1942, however, we knew that the Germans were working feverishly to find a way to add atomic energy to the other engines of war with which they hoped to enslave the world. But they failed. We may be grateful to Providence that the Germans got the V-1's and V-2's late and in limited quantities and even more grateful that they did not get the atomic bomb at all.

The battle of the laboratories held fateful risks for us as well as the battles of the air, land and sea, and we have now won the battle of the laboratories as we have won the other battles.

Beginning in 1940, before Pearl Harbor, scientific knowledge useful in war was pooled between the United States and Great Britain, and many priceless helps to our victories have come from that arrangement. Under that general policy the research on the atomic bomb was begun. With American and British scientists working together we entered the race of discovery against the Germans.

The United States had available the large number of scientists of distinction in the many needed areas of knowledge. It had the tremendous industrial and financial resources necessary for the project and they could be devoted to it without undue impairment of other vital war work. In the United States the laboratory work and the production plants, on which a substantial start had already been made, would be out of reach of enemy bombing, while at that time Britain was exposed to constant air attack and was still threatened with the possibility of invasion. For these reasons Prime Minister Churchill and President Roosevelt agreed that it was wise to carry on the project here. We now have two great plants and many lesser works devoted to the production of atomic power. Employment during peak construction numbered 125,000 and over 65,000 individuals are even now engaged in operating the plants. Many have worked there for two and a half years. Few know what they have been producing. They see great quantities of material going in and they see nothing coming out of these plants, for the physical size of the explosive charge is exceedingly small. We have spent two billion dollars on the greatest scientific gamble in history—and won.

But the greatest marvel is not the size of the enterprise, its secrecy, nor its cost, but the achievement of scientific brains in putting together infinitely complex pieces of knowledge held by many men in different fields of science into a workable plan. And hardly less marvelous has been the capacity of industry to design, and of labor to operate, the machines and methods to do things never done before so that the brain child of many minds came forth in physical shape and performed as it was supposed to do. Both science and industry worked under the direction of the United States Army, which achieved a unique success in managing so diverse a problem in the advancement of knowledge in an amazingly short time. It is doubtful if such another combination could be got together in the world. What has been done is the greatest achievement of organized science in history. It was done under high pressure and without failure.

We are now prepared to obliterate more rapidly and completely every productive enterprise the Japanese have above ground in any city. We shall destroy their docks, their factories, and their communications. Let there be no mistake; we shall completely destroy Japan's power to make war.

It was to spare the Japanese people from utter destruction that the ultimatum of July 26 was issued at Potsdam. Their leaders promptly rejected that ultimatum. If they do not now accept our terms they may expect a rain of ruin from the air, the like of which has never been seen on this earth. Behind this air attack will follow sea and land forces in such numbers and power as they have not yet seen and with the fighting skill of which they are already well aware.

The Secretary of War, who has kept in personal touch with all phases of the project, will immediately make public a statement giving further details.

His statement will give facts concerning the sites at Oak Ridge near Knoxville, Tennessee, and at Richland near Pasco, Washington, and an installation near Santa Fe, New Mexico. Although the workers at the sites have been making materials to be used in producing the greatest destructive force in history they have not themselves been in danger beyond that of many other occupations, for the utmost care has been taken of their safety.

The fact that we can release atomic energy ushers in a new era in man's understanding of nature's forces. Atomic energy may in the future supplement the power that now comes from coal, oil, and falling water, but at present it cannot be produced on a basis to compete with them commercially. Before that comes there must be a long period of intensive research.

It has never been the habit of the scientists of this country or the policy of this Government to withhold from the world scientific knowledge. Normally, therefore, everything about the work with atomic energy would be made public.

But under present circumstances it is not intended to divulge the technical processes of production or all the military applications, pending further examination of possible methods of protecting us and the rest of the world from the danger of sudden destruction.

I shall recommend that the Congress of the United States consider promptly the establishment of an appropriate commission to control the production and use of atomic power within the United States. I shall give further consideration and make further recommendations to the Congress as to how atomic power can become a powerful and forceful influence towards the maintenance of world peace.

DOROTHY DAY, "THE CATHOLIC WORKER RESPONSE TO HIROSHIMA," *THE CATHOLIC WORKER* (SEPTEMBER 1945)

A pacifist and cofounder of the radical Catholic Worker movement, Dorothy Day (1897–1980) dissents.

Mr. Truman was jubilant. President Truman. True man; what a strange name, come to think of it. We refer to Jesus Christ as true God and true Man. Truman is a true man of his time in that he was jubilant. He was not a son of God, brother of Christ, brother of the Japanese, jubilating as he did. He went from table to table on the cruiser which was bringing him home from the Big Three conference, telling the great news; "jubilant" the newspapers said. Jubilate Deo. We have killed 318,000 Japanese.

That is, we hope we have killed them, the Associated Press, on page one, column one of the Herald Tribune, says. The effect is hoped for, not known. It is to be hoped they are vaporized, our Japanese brothers—scattered, men, women and babies, to the four winds, over the seven seas. Perhaps we will breathe their dust into our nostrils, feel them in the fog of New York on our faces, feel them in the rain on the hills of Easton.

Jubilate Deo. President Truman was jubilant. We have created. We have created destruction. We have created a new element, called Pluto. Nature had nothing to do with it.

"A cavern below Columbia was the bomb's cradle," born not that men might live, but that men might be killed. Brought into being in a cavern, and then tried in a desert place, in the midst of tempest and lightning, tried out, and then again on the eve of the Feast of the Transfiguration of our Lord Jesus Christ, on a far off island in the eastern hemisphere, tried out again, this "new weapon which conceivably might wipe out mankind, and perhaps the planet itself."

"Dropped on a town, one bomb would be equivalent to a severe earthquake and would utterly destroy the place. A scientific brain trust has solved the problem of how to confine and release almost unlimited energy. It is impossible yet to measure its effects."

"We have spent two billion on the greatest scientific gamble in history and won," said President Truman jubilantly.

The papers list the scientists (the murderers) who are credited with perfecting this new weapon. One outstanding authority "who earlier had developed a powerful electrical bombardment machine called the cyclotron, was Professor O. E. Lawrence, a Nobel prize winner of the University of California. In the heat of the race to unlock the atom, he built the world's most powerful atom smashing gun, a machine whose electrical projectiles carried charges equivalent to 25,000,000 volts. But such machines were found in the end to be unnecessary. The atom of Uranium-235 was smashed with surprising ease. Science discovered that not sledgehammer blows, but subtle taps from slow traveling neutrons managed more on a tuning technique were all that were needed to disintegrate the Uranium-235 atom."

(Remember the tales we used to hear, that one note of a violin, if that note could be discovered, could collapse the Empire State Building. Remember too, that God's voice was heard not in the great and strong wind, not in the earthquake, not in the fire, but "in the whistling of a gentle air.")

Scientists, army officers, great universities (Notre Dame included), and captains of industry—all are given credit lines in the press for their work of preparing the bomb—and other bombs, the President assures us, are in production now.

Great Britain controls the supply of uranium ore, in Canada and Rhodesia. We are making the bombs. This new great force will be used for good, the scientists assured us. And then they wiped out a city of 318,000. This was good. The President was jubilant.

Today's paper with its columns of description of the new era, the atomic era, which this colossal slaughter of the innocents has ushered in, is filled with stories covering every conceivable phase of the new discovery. Pictures of the towns and the industrial plants where the parts are made are spread across the pages. In the forefront of the town of Oak Ridge, Tennessee is a chapel, a large comfortable-looking chapel benignly settled beside the plant. And the scientists making the first tests in the desert prayed, one newspaper account said.

Yes, God is still in the picture. God is not mocked. Today, the day of this so great news, God made a madman dance and talk, who had not spoken for twenty years. God sent a typhoon to damage the carrier Hornet. God permitted a fog to obscure vision and a bomber crashed into the Empire State Building. God permits these things. We have to remember it. We are held in God's hands, all of us, and President Truman too, and these scientists who have created death, but will use it for good. He, God, holds our life and our happiness, our sanity and our health; our lives are in His hands. He is our Creator. . . .

Everyone says, "I wonder what the Pope thinks of it?" How everyone turns to the Vatican for judgement, even though they do not seem to listen to the voice there! But our Lord Himself has already pronounced judgement on the atomic bomb. When James and John (John the beloved) wished to call down fire from heaven on their enemies, Jesus said:

"You know not of what spirit you are. The Son of Man came not to destroy souls but to save." He said also, "What you do unto the least of these my brethren, you do unto me."

BERNARD BRODIE, "IMPLICATIONS FOR MILITARY POLICY" (1946)

Trained as a political scientist, Bernard Brodie (1910–1978) pioneered the field of nuclear strategy. Here, in an essay written in the immediate aftermath of Hiroshima, he spells out the implications of the bomb for future US policy.

The essential change introduced by the atomic bomb is not primarily that it will make war more violent—a city can be as effectively destroyed with TNT and incendiaries—but that it will concentrate the violence in terms of time. A world accustomed to thinking it horrible that wars should last four or five years is now appalled at the prospect that future wars may last only a few days. . . .

Is it worth while even to consider military policy as having any consequence at all in an age of atomic bombs? A good many intelligent people think not. . . . If our cities can be wiped out in a day, if there is no good reason to expect the development of specific defenses against the bomb, if all the great powers are already within striking range of each other, if even substantial superiority in numbers of aircraft and bombs offers no real security, of what possible avail can large armies and navies be? Unless we can strike first and eliminate a threat before it is realized in action—something which our national Constitution apparently forbids—we are bound to perish under attack without even an opportunity to mobilize resistance. Such at least seems to be the prevailing conception among those who, if they give any thought at all to the military implications of the bomb, content themselves with stressing its character as a weapon of aggression. . . .

If it [an aggressor] must fear retaliation, the fact that it destroys its opponent's cities some hours or even days before its own are destroyed may avail it little. . . .

If the aggressor state must fear retaliation, it will know that even if it is the victor it will suffer a degree of physical destruction incomparably greater than that suffered by any defeated nation of history, incomparably greater, that is, than that suffered by Germany in the recent war. Under those circumstances no victory, even if guaranteed in advance—which it never is—would be worth the price. The threat of retaliation does not have to be 100 percent certain; it is sufficient if there is a good chance of it, or if there is belief that there is a good chance of it. The prediction is more important than the fact. . . .

There is happily little disposition to believe that the atomic bomb by its mere existence and by the horror implicit in it "makes war impossible." In the sense that war is something not to be endured if any reasonable alternative remains, it has long been "impossible." But for that very reason we cannot hope that the bomb makes war impossible in the narrower sense of the word. Even without it the conditions of modern war should have been a sufficient deterrent but proved not to be such. If the atomic bomb can be used without fear of substantial retaliation in kind, it will clearly encourage aggression. So much the more reason, therefore, to take all possible steps to assure . . . arrangements to make as nearly certain as possible that the aggressor who uses the bomb will have it used against him.

If such arrangements are made, the bomb cannot but prove in the net a powerful inhibition to aggression. It would make relatively little difference if one power had more bombs and were better prepared to resist them than its opponent. It would in any case undergo incalculable destruction of life and property. It is clear that there existed in the [1930s] a deeper and probably more generalized revulsion against war than in any other era of history. Under those circumstances the breeding of a new war required a situation combining dictators of singular irresponsibility with a notion among them and their general staffs that aggression would be both successful and cheap. The possibility of irresponsible or desperate men again becoming rulers of powerful states cannot under the prevailing system of international politics be ruled out in the future. But it does seem possible to erase the idea—if not among madmen rulers then at least among their military supporters—that aggression will be cheap.

Thus, the first and most vital step in any American security program for the age of atomic bombs is to take measures to guarantee to ourselves in case of attack the possibility of retaliation in kind. The writer in making that statement is not for the moment concerned about who will win the next war in which atomic bombs are used. Thus far the chief purpose of our military establishment has been to win wars. From now on its chief purpose must be to avert them. It can have almost no other useful purpose.

John Foster Dulles, "The Evolution of Foreign Policy" (1954)

As secretary of state under President Eisenhower, John Foster Dulles (1888–1959) saw the threatened use of nuclear weapons as an integral component of US strategy in the Cold War.

We live in a world where emergencies are always possible, and our survival may depend upon our capacity to meet emergencies. Let us pray that we shall always have that capacity. But, having said that, it is necessary also to say that emergency measures—however good for the emergency—do not necessarily make good permanent policies. Emergency measures are costly; they are superficial; and they imply that the enemy has the initiative. They cannot be depended on to serve our long-time interests.

This "long time" factor is of critical importance. The Soviet Communists are planning for what they call "an entire historical era," and we should do the same. They seek, through many types of maneuvers, gradually to divide and weaken the free nations by overextending them in efforts which, as Lenin put it, are "beyond their strength, so that they come to practical bankruptcy." . . .

It is not sound economics, or good foreign policy, to support permanently other countries; for in the long run, that creates as much ill will as good will.

Also, it is not sound to become permanently committed to military expenditures so vast that they lead to "practical bankruptcy." . . .

We need allies and collective security. Our purpose is to make these relations more effective, less costly. This can be done by placing more reliance on deterrent power and less dependence on local defensive power.

This is accepted practice so far as local communities are concerned. We keep locks on our doors, but we do not have an armed guard in every home. We rely principally on a community security system so well equipped to punish any who break in and steal that, in fact, would-be aggressors are generally deterred. That is the modern way of getting maximum protection at a bearable cost. . . .

Local defense will always be important. But there is no local defense which alone will contain the mighty landpower of the Communist world.

Local defenses must be reinforced by the further deterrent of massive retaliatory power. A potential aggressor must know that he cannot always prescribe battle conditions that suit him. Otherwise, for example, a potential aggressor, who is glutted with manpower, might be tempted to attack in confidence that resistance would be confined to manpower. He might be tempted to attack in places where his superiority was decisive.

The way to deter aggression is for the free community to be willing and able to respond vigorously at places and with means of its own choosing.

So long as our basic policy concepts were unclear, our military leaders could not be selective in building our military power. If an enemy could pick his time and place and method of warfare—and if our policy was to remain the traditional one of meeting aggression by direct and local opposition—then we needed to be ready to fight in the Arctic and in the Tropics; in Asia, the Near East, and in Europe; by sea, by land, and by air; with old weapons and with new weapons. . . .

But before military planning could be changed, the President and his advisers, as represented by the National Security Council, had to take some basic policy decisions. This has been done. The basic decision was to depend primarily upon a great capacity to retaliate, instantly, by means and at places of our choosing. . . .

In the ways I outlined we gather strength for the long-term defense of freedom.

We do not, of course, claim to have found some magic formula that insures against all forms of Communist successes. It is normal that at some times and at some places there may be setbacks to the cause of freedom. What we do expect to insure is that any setbacks will have only temporary and local significance, because they will leave unimpaired those free world assets which in the long run will prevail.

If we can deter such aggression as would mean general war, and that is our confident resolve, then we can let time and fundamentals work for us. . . .

If we persist in the courses I outline we shall confront dictatorship with a task that is, in the long run, beyond its strength. For unless it changes, it must suppress the human desires that freedom satisfies—as we shall be demonstrating.

If the dictators persist in their present course, then it is they who will be limited to superficial successes, while their foundation crumbles under the tread of their iron boots. . . .

ALBERT WOHLSTETTER, "DELICATE BALANCE OF TERROR" (1958)

As the Soviet Union acquired its own long-range nuclear strike force, US strategy shifted away from issuing nuclear threats to deterring any possible use of such weapons. Another nuclear strategist, Albert Wohlstetter (1913–1997) specialized in explaining the intricacies of deterrence.

The first shock administered by the Soviet launching of Sputnik has almost dissipated. The flurry of statements and investigations and improvised responses has died down, leaving a small residue: a slight increase in the schedule of bomber and ballistic missile production, with a resulting small increment in our defense expenditures for the current fiscal year, a considerable enthusiasm for space travel, and some stirrings of interest in the teaching of mathematics and physics in the secondary schools. Western defense policy has almost returned to the level of activity and the emphasis suited to the basic assumptions which were controlling before Sputnik.

One of the most important of these assumptions—that a general thermonuclear war is extremely unlikely—is held in common by most of the critics of our defense policy as well as by its proponents. Because of its crucial role in the Western strategy of defense, I should like to examine the stability of the thermonuclear balance which, it is generally supposed, would make aggression irrational or even insane. The balance, I believe, is in fact precarious, and this fact has critical implications for policy. Deterrence in the 1960's will be neither inevitable nor impossible but the product of sustained intelligent effort, attainable only by continuing hard choice. . . .

I emphasize that requirements for deterrence are stringent. We have heard so much about the atomic stalemate and the receding probability of war which it has produced, that this may strike the reader as something of an exaggeration. Is deterrence a necessary consequence of both sides having a nuclear delivery capability, and is all-out war nearly obsolete? Is mutual extinction the only outcome of a general war? This belief, frequently expressed by references to Mr. Oppenheimer's simile of the two scorpions in a bottle, is perhaps the prevalent one. . . . If peace were founded firmly on mutual terror and mutual terror on symmetrical nuclear powers, this would be, as Churchill has said, "a melancholy paradox;" nonetheless a most comforting one.

Deterrence, however, is not automatic. While feasible, it will be much harder to achieve in the 1960's than is generally believed. One of the most disturbing features of current opinion is the underestimation of this difficulty. This is due partly to a misconstruction of the technological

race as a problem in matching striking forces, partly to a wishful analysis of the Soviet ability to strike first. . . .

To deter an attack means being able to strike back in spite of it. It means, in other words, a capability to strike second. In the last year or two there has been a growing awareness of the importance of the distinction between a "strike-first" and a "strike-second" capability, but little, if any, recognition of the implications of this distinction for the balance of terror theory.

Where the published writings have not simply underestimated Soviet capabilities and the advantages of a first strike, they have in general placed artificial constraints on the Soviet use of the capabilities attributed to them. . . .

In treating Soviet strategies it is important to consider Soviet rather than Western advantage and to consider the strategy of both sides quantitatively. The effectiveness of our own choices will depend on a most complex numerical interaction of Soviet and Western plans. Unfortunately, both the privileged and unprivileged information on these matters is precarious. As a result, competent people have been led into critical error in evaluating the prospects for deterrence. Western journalists have greatly overestimated the difficulties of a Soviet surprise attack with thermonuclear weapons and vastly underestimated the complexity of the Western problem of retaliation. . . .

Perhaps the first step in dispelling the nearly universal optimism about the stability of deterrence would be to recognize the difficulties in analyzing the uncertainties and interactions between our own wide range of choices and the moves open to the Soviets. On our side we must consider an enormous variety of strategic weapons which might compose our force, and for each of these several alternative methods of basing and operation. These are the choices that determine whether a weapons system will have any genuine capability in the realistic circumstances of a war. . . .

Some of the complexities can be suggested by referring to the successive obstacles to be hurdled by any system providing a capability to strike second, that is, to strike back. Such deterrent systems must have (a) a stable, "steady-state" peacetime operation within feasible budgets (besides the logistic and operational costs that are, for example, problem of false alarms and accidents). They must have also the ability (b) to survive enemy attacks, (c) to make and communicate the decision to retaliate, (d) to reach enemy territory with fuel enough to complete their mission, (e) to penetrate enemy active defenses, that is fighters and surface-to-air missiles, and (f) to destroy the target in spite of any passive civil defense in the form of dispersal or protective construction or evacuation of the target itself.

Within limits the enemy is free to use his offensive and defensive forces so as to exploit the weaknesses of each of our systems in getting over any of these hurdles between peacetime operation and the completion of a retaliatory strike. He will also be free, within limits, in the Sixties to choose that composition of forces for offense, and for active and passive defense which will make life as difficult as possible for the various systems we might select. As I stressed earlier, much of the contemporary Western confidence on the ease of retaliation is achieved by ignoring the full range of sensible enemy plans. It would be quite wrong to assume that the uncertainties I have described affect a totalitarian aggressor and the party attacked equally. A totalitarian country can preserve secrecy about the capabilities and disposition of his forces very much better than a Western democracy. And the aggressor has, among other enormous advantages of the first strike, the ability to weigh continually our performance at each of the six barriers and to choose a precise known time and circumstance for attack which will reduce uncertainty. It is important not to confuse our uncertainty with his. The fact that we may not know the accuracy and number of his missiles will not deter him. Strangely enough, some military commentators have not made this distinction and have actually founded their belief in the certainty of deterrence on the fact simply that there are uncertainties. . . .

The most important conclusion runs counter to the indications of what I have called "Western-preferred Soviet strategies." It runs counter, that is, to our wishes. A sober analysis of Soviet choice from the standpoint of Soviet interest and the technical alternatives, and taking into account the uncertainties that a Russian planner would insure against, suggests that *we must expect a vast increase in the weight of attack which the Soviets can deliver with little warning, and the growth of a significant Russian capability for an essentially warningless attack. As a result, strategic deterrence, while feasible, will be extremely difficult to achieve, and at critical junctures in the 1960's we may not have the power to deter attack.* . . .

What can we say then on the question as to whether general war is unlikely? The most important thing to say perhaps is that it doesn't make much sense to talk about whether general war is likely or not unless we specify a good deal else about the range of circumstances in which the choice of surprise attack might present itself to the Russians. Deterrence is a matter of comparative risks. How much the Soviets will risk in surprise attack will depend in part on the vulnerability of our future posture. These risks could be smaller than the alternative of not striking.

Would not a general thermonuclear war mean "extinction" for the aggressor as well as the defender? "Extinction" is a state that badly needs analysis. Russian fatalities in World War II were more than 20,000,000. Yet Russia recovered extremely well from this catastrophe. There are several quite plausible circumstances in the future when the Russians might be confident of being able to limit damage to considerably *less* than this number—if they make sensible strategic choices and we do not. On the other hand, the risks of *not* striking might at some juncture appear very great to the Soviets, involving, for example, disastrous defeat in peripheral war, loss of key satellites with danger of revolt spreading—possibly to Russia itself—or fear of an attack by ourselves. Then, striking first, by surprise, would be the sensible choice for them, and from their point of view the smaller risk.

It should be clear that it is not fruitful to talk about the likelihood of general war without specifying the range of alternatives that are pressing on the aggressor and the strategic postures of both the Soviet bloc and the West. The balance is not automatic. First, since thermonuclear weapons give an enormous advantage to the aggressor, it takes great ingenuity and realism at any given level of nuclear technology to devise a stable equilibrium. And second, this technology itself is changing with fantastic speed. Deterrence will require an urgent and continuing effort. . . .

It follows that, though a wider distribution in the ownership of nuclear weapons may be inevitable, or at any rate likely, it is by no means inevitable or even very likely that the power to deter an all-out thermonuclear attack by Russia will be widespread. This is true even though a minor power would not need to guarantee as large a retaliation as we in order to deter attack on itself. Unfortunately, the minor powers have smaller resources as well as poorer strategic locations. A multiplicity of such independent retaliatory powers might be desirable as a substitute for the principal current function of the alliance. But they will not be easy to achieve. Mere membership in the nuclear club might carry with it prestige, as the applicants and nominees expect, but it will be rather expensive, and in time it will be clear that it does not necessarily confer any of the expected privileges enjoyed by the two charter members. The burden of deterring a general war as distinct from limited wars is still likely to be on the United States and therefore, so far as our allies are concerned, on the alliance. . . .

The inadequacy of deterrence is a familiar story. Western forces at the end of the war were larger than those of the Soviet Union and its satellites. We demobilized much more extensively, relying on nuclear weapons to maintain the balance of East-West military power. This was plausible then because nuclear power was all on our side. It was *our* bomb. It seemed only to complete the preponderance of American power provided by our enormous industrial mobilization base and to dispense with the need to keep it mobilized. It would compensate for the extra men kept under arms by the East.

But the notion of massive retaliation as a responsible retort to peripheral provocations vanished in the harsh light of a better understanding here and abroad that the Soviet nuclear delivery capability meant tremendous losses to the United States if we attacked them. And now Europe has begun to doubt that we would make the sacrifice involved in using SAC to answer an attack directed at it but not at ourselves.

The many critics of the massive retaliation policy who advocate a capability to meet limited aggression with a limited response are on firm ground in suggesting that a massive response on such an occasion would be unlikely and the threat to use it therefore not believed. Moreover

this argument is quite enough to make clear the critical need for more serious development of the power to meet limited aggressions. Another argument, which will not hold water and which is in fact dangerous, is sometimes used: Little wars are likely, general war improbable. We have seen that this mistakes a possibility for its fulfillment. The likelihood of both general and little wars is contingent on what we do. Moreover, these probabilities are not independent. A limited war involving the major powers is explosive. In this circumstance the likelihood of general war increases palpably. The danger of general war can be felt in every local skirmish involving the great powers. But because the balance of terror is supposed, almost universally, to assure us that all-out war will not occur, advocates of graduated deterrence have proposed to fix the limits of limited conflict in ways which neglect this danger. A few of the proposals seem in fact quite reckless. . . .

I am inclined to believe that most of those who rely on tactical nuclear weapons as a substitute for disparities in conventional forces have in general presupposed a cooperative Soviet attacker, one who did not use atomic weapons himself. Here again is an instance of Western-preferred Soviet strategies, this time applied to limited war. Ironically, according to reports of Soviet tactical exercises described in the last few years in the military newspaper, *The Red Star*, atomic weapons are in general employed only by the offense, the defender apparently employing Soviet-preferred Western strategies. The symmetry of the optimism of East and West here could be quite deadly.

Whether or not nuclear weapons favor the west in limited war, there still remains the question of whether such limitations could be made stable. Korea illustrated the possibility of a conventional limited war which did not become nuclear, though fought in the era of nuclear weapons. It remains to be seen whether there are any equilibrium points between the use of conventional and all-out weapons. In fact the emphasis on the gradualness of the graduated deterrents may be misplaced. The important thing would be to find some discontinuities if these steps are not to lead too smoothly to general war. Nuclear limited war, simply because of the extreme swiftness and unpredictability of its moves, the necessity of delegating authority to local commanders, and the possibility of sharp and sudden desperate reversals of fortune, would put the greatest strain on the deterrent to all-out thermonuclear war.

For this reason I believe that it would be appropriate to emphasize the importance of expanding a conventional capability realistically and, in particular, research and development in non-nuclear modes of warfare. These have been financed by pitifully small budgets. Yet I would conjecture that if one considers the implications of modern surface-to-air missiles in the context of conventional war in which the attacker has to make many sorties and expose himself to recurring attrition, these weapons would look ever so much better than they do when faced, for example, with the heroic task of knocking down 99 percent of a wave of, say one thousand nuclear bombers. Similarly, advances in anti-tank wire-guided missiles and anti-personnel fragmentation weapons, which have been mentioned from time to time in the press, might help redress the current balance of East-West conventional forces without, however, removing the necessity for spending more money in procurement as well as research and development.

The interdependencies of limited and total war decisions make it clear that the development of any powerful limited war capability, and in particular a nuclear one, only underlines the need, at the same time, for insuring retaliation against all-out attack. An aggressor must constantly weigh the dangers of all-out attack against the dangers of waiting, of not striking "all-out." Sharp reversals in a limited war can increase the dangers of waiting. But finally there is no question at this late date that strategic deterrence is inadequate to answer limited provocation.

Strategic deterrence has other inadequacies besides its limitations in connection with limited war. Some of these concern air defense. The power to deter a rational all-out attack does not relieve us of the responsibility for defending our cities in case deterrence fails. It should be said at once that such a defense is not a satisfactory substitute for deterring a carefully planned surprise attack since defense against such an attack is extraordinarily difficult. I know in fact of no high confidence way of avoiding enormous damage to our cities in a war initiated by an aggressor with a surprise thermonuclear attack. The only way of preventing such damage with high confidence is to prevent the war. But if we could obtain a

leakproof air defense, many things would change. A limited war capability, for example, would be unimportant. Massive retaliation against even minor threats, since it exposed us to no danger, might be credible. Deterring attack would also not be very important. . . .

On the other hand, this does not mean that we can dispense with the defense of cities. In spite of deterrence a thermonuclear war could be tripped by accident or miscalculation. In this case, particularly since the attack might be less well planned, a combination of spoiling counterattacks and active and passive defenses might limit the size of the catastrophe. It might mean, for example, the difference between fifty million survivors and a hundred and twenty million survivors, and it would be quite wrong to dismiss this as an unimportant difference.

If strategic deterrence is not enough, is it really necessary at all? Many sensitive and serious critics of Western defense policy have expressed their deep dissatisfaction with the strategy of deterrence. Moreover, since they have almost all assumed a balance of terror making deterrence nearly effortless, their dissatisfaction with deterrence might very well deepen if they accept the view presented here, that deterrence is most difficult. Distaste for the product should not be lessened by an increase in its cost. I must confess that the picture of the world that I have presented is unpleasant. Strategic deterrence will be hard. It imposes some dangers of its own. . . .

On the whole, I think the burden of the criticism of deterrence has been the inadequacy of a thermonuclear capability and frequently of, what is not really deterrence at all, the threat to strike first. But it would be a fatal mistake to confuse the inadequacy of strategic deterrence with its dispensability. Deterrence is not dispensable. If the picture of the world I have drawn is rather bleak, it could nonetheless be cataclysmically worse. . . .

A deterrent strategy is aimed at a rational enemy. Without a deterrent, general war is likely. With it, however, war might still occur. This is one reason deterrence is only a part and not the whole of a military and foreign policy.

In fact, there is a very unpleasant interaction. In order to reduce the risk of a rational act of aggression, we are being forced to undertake measures (increased alertness, dispersal, mobility) which, to a smaller extent but still significantly, increase the risk of an irrational or unintentional act of war. The accident problem, which has occupied an increasingly prominent place in newspaper headlines during the past year, is a serious one. It would be a great mistake to dismiss the recent Soviet charges on this subject as simply part of the war of nerves. . . .

While "fail-safe" or, as it is now less descriptively called, "positive control" is of great importance, it by no means eliminates the possibility of accident. While it can reduce the chance of miscalculation by governments somewhat by extending the period of final commitment, this possibility nonetheless remains. . . .

The critics of current policy who perceive the inadequacy of the strategy of deterrence are prominent among those urging disarmament negotiations, an end to the arms race, and a reduction of tension. This is a paramount interest of some of our allies. The balance of terror theory is the basis for some of the more light-hearted suggestions: if deterrence is automatic, strategic weapons on one side cancel those of the other, and it should be easy for both sides to give them up. . . .

Indeed if there were no real danger of a rational attack, then accidents and the "n-th" country problem seem the *only* problems. In fact, they are very prominent in the recent literature on the subject of disarmament. As I have indicated, they are serious problems and some sorts of limitation and inspection agreement could diminish them. Almost everyone seems concerned with the need to relax tension. However, relaxation of tension, which everyone thinks is good, is not easily distinguished from relaxing one's guard, which almost everyone thinks is bad. . . .

What can we say then, in sum, on the balance of terror theory of automatic deterrence? It is a contribution to the rhetoric rather than the logic of war in the thermonuclear age. In suggesting that a carefully planned surprise attack can be checkmated almost effortlessly, that in short we may resume our deep pre-Sputnik sleep, it is wrong and its nearly universal acceptance is terribly dangerous. Though deterrence is not enough in itself, it is vital. There are two principal points.

First, even if we can deter general war by a strenuous and continuing effort, this will not be the whole of a military, much less a foreign policy! Such a policy would not of itself remove the danger of accidental outbreak or limit the damage in case deterrence failed, nor would it be at all adequate for crises on the periphery. Moreover, to achieve deterrent balance will entail some new risks requiring insurance—in any case, some foreign policy reorientation.

Second, deterring general war in both the early and late Sixties will be hard at best, and hardest both for ourselves and our allies wherever we use forces based near the enemy.

A generally useful way of concluding a grim argument of this kind would be to affirm that we have the resources, intelligence and courage to make the correct decisions. That is, of course, the case. And there is a good chance that we will do so. But perhaps, as a small aid toward making such decisions more likely, we should contemplate the possibility that they may *not* be made. They *are* hard, involve sacrifice, are affected by great uncertainties, concern matters in which much is altogether unknown and much else must be hedged by secrecy; and, above all, they entail a new image of ourselves in a world of persistent danger. It is by no means *certain* that we shall meet the test.

JOHN F. KENNEDY, "AMERICAN UNIVERSITY SPEECH" (1963)

In 1962, the Cuban Missile Crisis brought the world to the brink of Armageddon. In its aftermath, President Kennedy acknowledged that reducing the likelihood of nuclear war had become an imperative—a vital interest shared by both the United States and the Soviet Union.

"There are few earthly things more beautiful than a university," wrote John Masefield, in his tribute to English universities—and his words are equally true today. He did not refer to spires and towers, to campus greens and ivied walls. He admired the splendid beauty of the university, he said, because it was "a place where those who hate ignorance may strive to know, where those who perceive truth may strive to make others see."

I have, therefore, chosen this time and this place to discuss a topic on which ignorance too often abounds and the truth is too rarely perceived—yet it is the most important topic on earth: world peace.

What kind of peace do I mean? What kind of peace do we seek? Not a Pax Americana enforced on the world by American weapons of war. Not the peace of the grave or the security of the slave. I am talking about genuine peace, the kind of peace that makes life on earth worth living, the kind that enables men and nations to grow and to hope and to build a better life for their children— not merely peace for Americans but peace for all men and women—not merely peace in our time but peace for all time.

I speak of peace because of the new face of war. Total war makes no sense in an age when great powers can maintain large and relatively invulnerable nuclear forces and refuse to surrender without resort to those forces. It makes no sense in an age when a single nuclear weapon contains almost ten times the explosive force delivered by all of the allied air forces in the Second World War. It makes no sense in an age when the deadly poisons produced by a nuclear exchange would be carried by wind and water and soil and seed to the far corners of the globe and to generations yet unborn.

Today the expenditure of billions of dollars every year on weapons acquired for the purpose of making sure we never need to use them is essential to keeping the peace. But surely the acquisition of such idle stockpiles—which can only destroy and never create—is not the only, much less the most efficient, means of assuring peace.

I speak of peace, therefore, as the necessary rational end of rational men. I realize that the pursuit of peace is not as dramatic as the pursuit of war—and frequently the words of the pursuer fall on deaf ears. But we have no more urgent task.

Some say that it is useless to speak of world peace or world law or world disarmament—and that it will be useless until the leaders of the Soviet Union adopt a more enlightened attitude. I hope they do. I believe we can help them do it. But I also believe that we must reexamine our own

attitude—as individuals and as a Nation—for our attitude is as essential as theirs. And every graduate of this school, every thoughtful citizen who despairs of war and wishes to bring peace, should begin by looking inward—by examining his own attitude toward the possibilities of peace, toward the Soviet Union, toward the course of the cold war and toward freedom and peace here at home.

First: Let us examine our attitude toward peace itself. Too many of us think it is impossible. Too many think it unreal. But that is a dangerous, defeatist belief. It leads to the conclusion that war is inevitable—that mankind is doomed—that we are gripped by forces we cannot control.

We need not accept that view. Our problems are manmade—therefore, they can be solved by man. And man can be as big as he wants. No problem of human destiny is beyond human beings. Man's reason and spirit have often solved the seemingly unsolvable—and we believe they can do it again.

I am not referring to the absolute, infinite concept of universal peace and good will of which some fantasies and fanatics dream. I do not deny the value of hopes and dreams but we merely invite discouragement and incredulity by making that our only and immediate goal.

Let us focus instead on a more practical, more attainable peace—based not on a sudden revolution in human nature but on a gradual evolution in human institutions—on a series of concrete actions and effective agreements which are in the interest of all concerned. There is no single, simple key to this peace—no grand or magic formula to be adopted by one or two powers. Genuine peace must be the product of many nations, the sum of many acts. It must be dynamic, not static, changing to meet the challenge of each new generation. For peace is a process—a way of solving problems.

With such a peace, there will still be quarrels and conflicting interests, as there are within families and nations. World peace, like community peace, does not require that each man love his neighbor—it requires only that they live together in mutual tolerance, submitting their disputes to a just and peaceful settlement. And history teaches us that enmities between nations, as between individuals, do not last forever. However fixed our likes and dislikes may seem, the tide of time and events will often bring surprising changes in the relations between nations and neighbors.

So let us persevere. Peace need not be impracticable, and war need not be inevitable. By defining our goal more clearly, by making it seem more manageable and less remote, we can help all peoples to see it, to draw hope from it, and to move irresistibly toward it.

Second: Let us reexamine our attitude toward the Soviet Union. It is discouraging to think that their leaders may actually believe what their propagandists write. It is discouraging to read a recent authoritative Soviet text on Military Strategy and find, on page after page, wholly baseless and incredible claims—such as the allegation that "American imperialist circles are preparing to unleash different types of wars . . . that there is a very real threat of a preventive war being unleashed by American imperialists against the Soviet Union . . . [and that] the political aims of the American imperialists are to enslave economically and politically the European and other capitalist countries. . . [and] to achieve world domination . . . by means of aggressive wars."

Truly, as it was written long ago: "The wicked flee when no man pursueth." Yet it is sad to read these Soviet statements—to realize the extent of the gulf between us. But it is also a warning—a warning to the American people not to fall into the same trap as the Soviets, not to see only a distorted and desperate view of the other side, not to see conflict as inevitable, accommodation as impossible, and communication as nothing more than an exchange of threats.

No government or social system is so evil that its people must be considered as lacking in virtue. As Americans, we find communism profoundly repugnant as a negation of personal freedom and dignity. But we can still hail the Russian people for their many achievements—in science and space, in economic and industrial growth, in culture and in acts of courage.

Among the many traits the peoples of our two countries have in common, none is stronger than our mutual abhorrence of war. Almost unique, among the major world powers, we have never been at war with each other. And no nation in the history of battle ever suffered more than the Soviet Union suffered in the course of the Second World War. At least 20 million lost their lives. Countless millions of homes and farms were burned or sacked. A third of the nation's territory, including nearly two thirds of its industrial base, was turned into a wasteland—a loss equivalent to the devastation of this country east of Chicago.

Today, should total war ever break out again—no matter how—our two countries would become the primary targets. It is an ironic but accurate fact that the two strongest powers are the two in the most danger of devastation. All we have built, all we have worked for, would be destroyed in the first 24 hours. And even in the cold war, which brings burdens and dangers to so many countries, including this Nation's closest allies—our two countries bear the heaviest burdens. For we are both devoting massive sums of money to weapons that could be better devoted to combating ignorance, poverty, and disease. We are both caught up in a vicious and dangerous cycle in which suspicion on one side breeds suspicion on the other, and new weapons beget counter-weapons.

In short, both the United States and its allies, and the Soviet Union and its allies, have a mutually deep interest in a just and genuine peace and in halting the arms race. Agreements to this end are in the interests of the Soviet Union as well as ours—and even the most hostile nations can be relied upon to accept and keep those treaty obligations, and only those treaty obligations, which are in their own interest.

So, let us not be blind to our differences—but let us also direct attention to our common interests and to the means by which those differences can be resolved. And if we cannot end now our differences, at least we can help make the world safe for diversity. For, in the final analysis, our most basic common link is that we all inhabit this small planet. We all breathe the same air. We all cherish our children's future. And we are all mortal.

Third: Let us reexamine our attitude toward the cold war, remembering that we are not engaged in a debate, seeking to pile up debating points. We are not here distributing blame or pointing the finger of judgment. We must deal with the world as it is, and not as it might have been had the history of the last 18 years been different.

We must, therefore, persevere in the search for peace in the hope that constructive changes within the Communist bloc might bring within reach solutions which now seem beyond us. We must conduct our affairs in such a way that it becomes in the Communists' interest to agree on a genuine peace. Above all, while defending our own vital interests, nuclear powers must avert those confrontations which bring an adversary to a choice of either a humiliating retreat or a nuclear war. To adopt that kind of course in the nuclear age would be evidence only of the bankruptcy of our policy—or of a collective death-wish for the world.

To secure these ends, America's weapons are nonprovocative, carefully controlled, designed to deter, and capable of selective use. Our military forces are committed to peace and disciplined in self-restraint. Our diplomats are instructed to avoid unnecessary irritants and purely rhetorical hostility.

For we can seek a relaxation of tensions without relaxing our guard. And, for our part, we do not need to use threats to prove that we are resolute. We do not need to jam foreign broadcasts out of fear our faith will be eroded. We are unwilling to impose our system on any unwilling people—but we are willing and able to engage in peaceful competition with any people on earth.

Meanwhile, we seek to strengthen the United Nations, to help solve its financial problems, to make it a more effective instrument for peace, to develop it into a genuine world security system—a system capable of resolving disputes on the basis of law, of insuring the security of the large and the small, and of creating conditions under which arms can finally be abolished.

At the same time we seek to keep peace inside the non-Communist world, where many nations, all of them our friends, are divided over issues which weaken Western unity, which invite Communist intervention or which threaten to erupt into war. . . .

Speaking of other nations, I wish to make one point clear. We are bound to many nations by alliances. Those alliances exist because our concern and theirs substantially overlap. Our commitment to defend Western Europe and West Berlin, for example, stands undiminished because of the identity of our vital interests. The United States will make no deal with the Soviet Union at the expense of other nations and other peoples, not merely because they are our partners, but also because their interests and ours converge.

Our interests converge, however, not only in defending the frontiers of freedom, but in pursuing the paths of peace. It is our hope—and the purpose of allied policies—to convince the Soviet Union that she, too, should let each nation choose its own future, so long as that choice does not interfere with the choices of others. The Communist drive to impose their political and economic system on others is the primary cause of world tension today. For there can be no doubt that, if all nations could refrain from interfering in the self-determination of others, the peace would be much more assured.

This will require a new effort to achieve world law—a new context for world discussions. It will require increased understanding between the Soviets and ourselves. And increased understanding will require increased contact and communication. . . .

The pursuit of disarmament has been an effort of this Government since the 1920's. It has been urgently sought by the past three administrations. And however dim the prospects may be today, we intend to continue this effort—to continue it in order that all countries, including our own, can better grasp what the problems and possibilities of disarmament are.

The one major area of these negotiations where the end is in sight, yet where a fresh start is badly needed, is in a treaty to outlaw nuclear tests. The conclusion of such a treaty, so near and yet so far, would check the spiraling arms race in one of its most dangerous areas. . . .

I am taking this opportunity, therefore, to announce two important decisions in this regard.

First: Chairman Khrushchev, Prime Minister Macmillan, and I have agreed that high-level discussions will shortly begin in Moscow looking toward early agreement on a comprehensive test ban treaty. . . .

Second: To make clear our good faith and solemn convictions on the matter, I now declare that the United States does not propose to conduct nuclear tests in the atmosphere so long as other states do not do so. . . .

Finally, my fellow Americans, let us examine our attitude toward peace and freedom here at home. . . .

All this is not unrelated to world peace. "When a man's ways please the Lord," the Scriptures tell us, "he maketh even his enemies to be at peace with him." And is not peace, in the last analysis, basically a matter of human rights—the right to live out our lives without fear of devastation—the right to breathe air as nature provided it—the right of future generations to a healthy existence?

While we proceed to safeguard our national interests, let us also safeguard human interests. And the elimination of war and arms is clearly in the interest of both. . . .

The United States, as the world knows, will never start a war. We do not want a war. We do not now expect a war. This generation of Americans has already had enough—more than enough—of war and hate and oppression. We shall be prepared if others wish it. We shall be alert to try to stop it. But we shall also do our part to build a world of peace where the weak are safe and the strong are just. We are not helpless before that task or hopeless of its success. Confident and unafraid, we labor on—not toward a strategy of annihilation but toward a strategy of peace.

CURTIS LEMAY, "GRADUATION ADDRESS, UNITED STATES AIR FORCE ACADEMY" (1964)

U.S. Air Force General Curtis LeMay (1906–1990), who had directed the destruction of Japanese cities in 1945, entertained a different view.

Through development of nuclear energy and advanced aerospace systems, civilization has attained its greatest capacity for progress or for destruction. From many sources, we hear expressions of doubt concerning man's ability to avoid using this power for his destruction.

I do not share that doubt. It seems to me that modern weapons make it clear that the penalties for lapses in vigilance and misuse of power that have marred history are now prohibitive. This means that civilization, in order to survive and progress, must do better than it has in the past. And it is my conviction that, in recent years, civilization has done better, according to standards that are acceptable to our country and to the Free World.

It is also my conviction that the United States Air Force throughout its history has done much to make that improvement possible. My basis for that conviction is the record of Air Force operations through two world wars, the Korean War, and through a long roll of crises such as Lebanon, Formosa, Berlin, and Cuba.

For about the first half of that period, the Air Force was planning, testing, training, and fighting to produce the results that established it by 1945 as a dominant military instrument of national policy. Since that time, we have provided the

major strategic deterrent to general war. In that role, we have convinced the potential enemy that the risks incurred by full-scale aggression are unacceptable. . . .

It is vital to understand that these restraints have not resulted from a sudden and miraculous transformation in the attitude and the aims of world Communism. It is equally important to understand that these restraints have been imposed primarily by the superiority of US strategic forces, teamed with hard-hitting tactical elements. . . .

Your first requirement will be to obtain continuing support for the maintenance of US strategic advantage. That advantage must be maintained as the cornerstone of our deterrent posture. . . .

You therefore must not permit the requirement for strategic advantage to be obscured by arguments that describe the present world situation as a condition of "mutual stalemate" and "mutual deterrence."

There is no evidence of stalemate in the present power balance. It still favors us by a clear margin. It is still determined by relative pace of actions going forward in all the areas of national endeavor—social, economic, and military. . . .

The idea of using force to achieve total defeat of an enemy is now only one of the available choices. When you consider the damage levels that high intensity war can bring even to the nominal "winner," total defeat of the enemy may be the least desirable choice.

For the future we need to improve our methods of using weapons to gain precise, but limited, objectives for particular crisis situations. This would increase our capability to neutralize selected targets which are important to the enemy. If carefully applied, these actions could force him to back down from his initial aggression and negotiate our respective interest. . . .

Now, as a final comment on strategy and operational concepts, I want to stress the importance of a counterforce concept of deterrence. By "counterforce," I mean the ability to destroy selective elements of the aggressor's strategic offensive systems, thereby reducing his capability to attack us.

I believe counterforce provides the best deterrent because it is based on a concept of

destroying or neutralizing the military forces, which the enemy must depend on to gain a victory. And through this effective deterrence we achieve the principal objective of our military forces—that is, the full protection of American lives and property.

If deterrence should fail, counterforce provides for maximum limitation of damage under the worst possible conditions. Thus, counterforce, in situations involving either the success or failure of deterrence, provides the greatest dividend that we can gain from any strategy. . . .

In my 35 years of service, I have seen aerospace power remold or set aside many traditional military concepts. Since 1945, it has compelled action on a broad and continuing basis to meet the hard requirements of our security as determined at the highest levels of national leadership. That action, though discomfiting to some, is essential to all.

DR. STRANGELOVE, A FILM BY STANLEY KUBRICK (1964)

Inherent in the logic of nuclear strategy and nuclear deterrence were expectations of control and rationality—that only the president of the United States could order a nuclear attack and that the president would do so only after having exhausted all other alternatives. *Dr. Strangelove*, a film by Stanley Kubrick (1928–1999), mocked such pretensions. In this exchange between the president and the Air Force chief of staff, the commander-in-chief grapples with the realization that a deranged subordinate has ordered an attack on the Soviet Union with nuclear-armed long-range bombers already on their way to their assigned targets.

MUFFLEY: Now, General Turgidson, what's going on here?

TURGIDSON: Mr. President, about thirty-five minutes ago, General Jack Ripper, the commanding General of Burpleson Air Force Base, issued an order to the 34 B-52's of his wing which were airborne at the time as part of a special exercise we were holding called Operation Dropkick. Now, it appears that the order called for the planes to attack their targets inside Russia. The planes are fully armed with nuclear weapons with an average load of 40 megatons each. Now the central display of Russia will indicate the position of the planes. The triangles are their primary targets, the squares are their secondary targets. The

aircraft will begin penetrating Russian radar cover within 25 minutes.

MUFFLEY: General Turgidson, I find this very difficult to understand. I was under the impression that I was the only one in authority to order the use of nuclear weapons.

TURGIDSON: That's right, sir. You are the only person authorized to do so. And although I hate to judge before all the facts are in, it's beginning to look like General Ripper exceeded his authority.

MUFFLEY: It certainly does. Far beyond the point I would have imagined possible.

TURGIDSON: Well perhaps you're forgetting the provisions of plan R, sir.

MUFFLEY: Plan R?

TURGIDSON: Plan R is an emergency war plan in which a lower echelon commander may order nuclear retaliation after a sneak attack if the normal chain of command is disrupted. You approved it, sir. You must remember. Surely you must recall, sir, when Senator Buford made that big hassle about our deterrent lacking credibility. The idea was for plan R to be a sort of retaliatory safeguard.

MUFFLEY: A safeguard.

TURGIDSON: I admit the human element seems to have failed us here. But the idea was to discourage the Russkies from any hope that they could knock out Washington, and yourself, sir, as part of a general sneak attack, and escape retaliation because of lack of proper command and control.

MUFFLEY: Well I assume then, that the planes will return automatically once they reach their failsafe points.

TURGIDSON: Well, sir, I'm afraid not. You see the planes were holding at their failsafe points when the go code was issued. Now, once they fly beyond failsafe they do not require a second order to proceed. They will fly until they reach their targets.

MUFFLEY: Then why haven't you radioed the planes countermanding the go code?

TURGIDSON: Well, I'm afraid we're unable to communicate with any of the aircraft.

MUFFLEY: Why?

TURGIDSON: As you may recall, sir, one of the provisions of plan R provides that once the go code is received the normal SSB radios in the aircraft are switched into a special coded device, which I believe is designated as CRM114. Now, in order to prevent the enemy from issuing fake or confusing orders, CRM114 is designed not to receive at all, unless the message is preceded by the correct three letter code group prefix.

MUFFLEY: Then do you mean to tell me, General Turgidson, that you will be unable to recall the aircraft?

TURGIDSON: That's about the size of it. However, we are plowing through every possible three letter combination of the code. But since there are seventeen thousand permutations it's going to take us about two and a half days to transmit them all.

MUFFLEY: How soon did you say the planes would penetrate Russian radar cover?

TURGIDSON: About eighteen minutes from now, sir.

MUFFLEY: Are you in contact with General Ripper?

TURGIDSON: Ah... No sir, no, General Ripper sealed off the base and cut off all communications.

MUFFLEY: Where did you get all this information?

TURGIDSON: General Ripper called Strategic Air Command headquarters shortly after he issued the go code. I have a partial transcript of that conversation if you'd like me to read it.

MUFFLEY: Read it.

TURGIDSON: The duty officer asked General Ripper to confirm the fact the he had issued the go code and he said, "Yes gentlemen, they are on their way in and no one can bring them back. For the sake of our country and our way of life, I suggest you get the rest of SAC in after them, otherwise we will be totally destroyed by red retaliation. My boys will give you the best kind of start, fourteen hundred megatons worth, and you sure as hell won't stop them now. So let's get going. There's no other choice. God willing, we will prevail in peace and freedom from fear and in true health through the purity and essence of our natural fluids. God bless you all." Then he hung up. We're still trying to figure out the meaning of that last phrase, sir.

MUFFLEY: There's nothing to figure out, General Turgidson. This man is obviously a psychotic.

TURGIDSON: Well, I'd like to hold off judgment on a thing like that, sir, until all the facts are in.

MUFFLEY, *anger rising:* General Turgidson, when you instituted the human reliability tests, you assured me there was no possibility of such a thing ever occurring.

TURGIDSON: Well I don't think it's quite fair to condemn a whole program because of a single slip up, sir.

MUFFLEY: I want to speak to General Ripper on the telephone, personally.

TURGIDSON: I'm afraid that's impossible, sir.

MUFFLEY: General Turgidson, I am becoming less and less interested in your estimates of what is possible and impossible. General Faceman.

FACEMAN: Yes, sir.

MUFFLEY: Are there any army units stationed anywhere near Burpleson?

FACEMAN: Well ah, I'll just check, sir.

Turgidson's phone beeps

TURGIDSON: Hello. *pause, then whispering* I told you never to call me here; don't you know where I am? *pause* Well look, baby, I can't talk to you now. My president needs me. Of course Bucky would rather be there with you. *pause* Of course it isn't only physical. I deeply respect you as a human being. Someday I'm going to make you Mrs. Buck Turgidson. *pause* Listen, you go back to sleep. Bucky'll be back there just as soon as he can. Alright. Listen, sug', don't forget to say your prayers. *hangs up and composes himself*

FACEMAN: Apparently, the 23rd airborne division is stationed seven miles away at Alvarado.

MUFFLEY: General Faceman, I want them to enter the base, locate General Ripper, and put him in immediate telephone contact with me.

FACEMAN: Yes, sir.

TURGIDSON: Mr. President, if I may advise, under condition red it is standard procedure that the base be sealed off, and the base be defended by base security troops. Any force trying to enter there would certainly encounter very heavy casualties.

FACEMAN: General Turgidson, with all due respect for your defense team, my boys can brush 'em aside without too much trouble.

TURGIDSON: Mr. President, there are one or two points I'd like to make, if I may.

MUFFLEY: Go ahead, General.

TURGIDSON: One, our hopes for recalling the 843rd bomb wing are quickly being reduced to a very low order of probability. Two, in less than fifteen minutes from now the Russkies will be making radar contact with the planes. Three, when the do, they are going to go absolutely ape, and they're gonna strike back with everything they've got. Four, if prior to this time, we have done nothing further to suppress their retaliatory capabilities, we will suffer virtual annihilation. Now, five, if on the other hand, we were to immediately launch an all out and coordinated attack on all their airfields and missile bases we'd stand a damn good chance of catching 'em with their pants down. Hell, we got a five to one missile superiority as it is. We could easily assign three missiles to every target, and still have a very effective reserve force for any other contingency. Now, six, an unofficial study which we undertook of this eventuality, indicated that we would destroy ninety percent of their nuclear capabilities. We would therefore prevail, and suffer only modest and acceptable civilian casualties from their remaining force which would be badly damaged and uncoordinated.

MUFFLEY: General, it is the avowed policy of our country never to strike first with nuclear weapons.

TURGIDSON: Well, Mr. President, I would say that General Ripper has already invalidated that policy. *laughs*

MUFFLEY: That was not an act of national policy and there are still alternatives left open to us.

TURGIDSON: Mr. President, we are rapidly approaching a moment of truth both for ourselves as human beings and for the life of our nation. Now, the truth is not always a pleasant thing, but it is necessary now make a choice, to choose between two admittedly regrettable, but nevertheless, distinguishable post-war environments: one where you got twenty million people killed, and the other where you got a hundred and fifty million people killed.

MUFFLEY: You're talking about mass murder, General, not war.

TURGIDSON: Mr. President, I'm not saying we wouldn't get our hair mussed. But I do say. . . no more than ten to twenty million killed, tops. Uh. . . depending on the breaks.

MUFFLEY: I will not go down in history as the greatest mass murderer since Adolph Hitler!

TURGIDSON: Perhaps it might be better, Mr. President, if you were more concerned with the American people, than with your image in the history books.

RONALD REAGAN, "STAR WARS SPEECH" (1983)

By the late 1960s, US and Soviet leaders began discussing ways to curtail the nuclear arms race. Although these negotiations achieved some modest success, the basic architecture—two massive arsenals each now consisting chiefly of long-range missiles mounting multiple warheads and held in instant readiness—persisted. Following Jimmy Carter as president in 1981, Ronald Reagan (1911–2004) rejected the logic of nuclear deterrence as immoral. He sought a technological alternative to a policy that threatened genocidal violence in order to avert genocidal violence.

The defense policy of the United States is based on a simple premise: The United States does not start fights. We will never be an aggressor. We maintain our strength in order to deter and defend against aggression—to preserve freedom and peace.

Since the dawn of the atomic age, we've sought to reduce the risk of war by maintaining a strong deterrent and by seeking genuine arms control. "Deterrence" means simply this: making sure any adversary who thinks about attacking the United States, or our allies, or our vital interests, concludes that the risks to him outweigh any potential gains. Once he understands that, he won't attack. We maintain the peace through our strength; weakness only invites aggression.

This strategy of deterrence has not changed. It still works. But what it takes to maintain deterrence has changed. It took one kind of military force to deter an attack when we had far more nuclear weapons than any other power; it takes another kind now that the Soviets, for example, have enough accurate and powerful nuclear weapons to destroy virtually all of our missiles on the ground. Now, this is not to say that the Soviet Union is planning to make war on us. Nor do I believe a war is inevitable—quite the contrary. But what must be recognized is that our security is based on being prepared to meet all threats.

There was a time when we depended on coastal forts and artillery batteries, because, with the weaponry of that day, any attack would have had to come by sea. Well, this is a different world, and our defenses must be based on recognition and awareness of the weaponry possessed by other nations in the nuclear age.

We can't afford to believe that we will never be threatened. There have been two world wars in my lifetime. We didn't start them and, indeed, did everything we could to avoid being drawn into them. But we were ill-prepared for both. Had we been better prepared, peace might have been preserved.

For 20 years the Soviet Union has been accumulating enormous military might. They didn't stop when their forces exceeded all requirements of a legitimate defensive capability. And they haven't stopped now. During the past decade and a half, the Soviets have built up a massive arsenal of new strategic nuclear weapons—weapons that can strike directly at the United States. . . .

The final fact is that the Soviet Union is acquiring what can only be considered an offensive military force. They have continued to build far more intercontinental ballistic missiles than they could possibly need simply to deter an attack. Their conventional forces are trained and equipped not so much to defend against an attack as they are to permit sudden, surprise offensives of their own. . . .

I know that all of you want peace, and so do I. I know too that many of you seriously believe that a nuclear freeze would further the cause of peace. But a freeze now would make us less, not more, secure and would raise, not reduce, the risks of war. It would be largely unverifiable and would seriously undercut our negotiations on arms reduction. It would reward the Soviets for their massive military buildup while preventing us from modernizing our aging and increasingly vulnerable forces. With their present margin of superiority, why should they agree to arms reductions knowing that we were prohibited from catching up? . . .

The calls for cutting back the defense budget come in nice, simple arithmetic. They're the same kind of talk that led the democracies to neglect their defenses in the 1930's and invited the tragedy of World War II. We must not let that grim chapter of history repeat itself through apathy or neglect. . . .

Now, thus far tonight I've shared with you my thoughts on the problems of national security we must face together. My predecessors in the Oval Office have appeared before you on other occasions to describe the threat posed by Soviet power and have proposed steps to address that threat. But since the advent of nuclear weapons, those steps have been increasingly directed toward deterrence of aggression through the promise of retaliation.

This approach to stability through offensive threat has worked. We and our allies have succeeded in preventing nuclear war for more than three decades. In recent months, however, my advisers, including in particular the Joint Chiefs of Staff, have underscored the necessity to break out of a future that relies solely on offensive retaliation for our security.

Over the course of these discussions, I've become more and more deeply convinced that the human spirit must be capable of rising above dealing with other nations and human beings by threatening their existence. Feeling this way, I believe we must thoroughly examine every opportunity for reducing tensions and for introducing greater stability into the strategic calculus on both sides. . . .

If the Soviet Union will join with us in our effort to achieve major arms reduction, we will have succeeded in stabilizing the nuclear balance. Nevertheless, it will still be necessary to rely on the specter of retaliation, on mutual threat. And that's a sad commentary on the human condition. Wouldn't it be better to save lives than to avenge them? Are we not capable of demonstrating our peaceful intentions by applying all our abilities and our ingenuity to achieving a truly lasting stability? I think we are. Indeed, we must.

After careful consultation with my advisers, including the Joint Chiefs of Staff, I believe there is a way. Let me share with you a vision of the future which offers hope. It is that we embark on a program to counter the awesome Soviet missile threat with measures that are defensive. Let us turn to the very strengths in technology that spawned our great industrial base and that have given us the quality of life we enjoy today.

What if free people could live secure in the knowledge that their security did not rest upon the threat of instant U.S. retaliation to deter a Soviet attack, that we could intercept and destroy strategic ballistic missiles before they reached our own soil or that of our allies?

I know this is a formidable, technical task, one that may not be accomplished before the end of this century. Yet, current technology has attained a level of sophistication where it's reasonable for us to begin this effort. It will take years, probably decades of effort on many fronts. There will be failures and setbacks, just as there will be successes and breakthroughs. And as we proceed, we must remain constant in preserving the nuclear deterrent and maintaining a solid capability for flexible response. But isn't it worth every investment necessary to free the world from the threat of nuclear war? We know it is. . . .

I clearly recognize that defensive systems have limitations and raise certain problems and ambiguities. If paired with offensive systems, they can be viewed as fostering an aggressive policy, and no one wants that. But with these considerations firmly in mind, I call upon the scientific community in our country, those who gave us nuclear weapons, to turn their great talents now to the cause of mankind and world peace, to give us the means of rendering these nuclear weapons impotent and obsolete.

Tonight, consistent with our obligations of the ABM treaty and recognizing the need for closer consultation with our allies, I'm taking an important first step. I am directing a comprehensive and intensive effort to define a long-term research and development program to begin to achieve our ultimate goal of eliminating the threat posed by strategic nuclear missiles. This could pave the way for arms control measures to eliminate the weapons themselves. We seek neither military superiority nor political advantage. Our only purpose—one all people share—is to search for ways to reduce the danger of nuclear war.

My fellow Americans, tonight we're launching an effort which holds the promise of changing the course of human history. There will be risks, and results take time. But I believe we can do it.

U.S. CATHOLIC BISHOPS, "THE CHALLENGE OF PEACE: A SYNOPSIS" (1983)

The bishops of the American Catholic Church advanced a critique of nuclear strategy that differed from Reagan's. They accepted deterrence, but only as an interim step toward disarmament.

The Second Vatican Council opened its evaluation of modern warfare with the statement: "The whole human race faces a moment of supreme crisis in its advance toward maturity." We agree with the council's assessment; the crisis of the moment is embodied in the threat which nuclear weapons pose for the world and much that we hold dear in the world. We have seen and felt the effects of the crisis of the nuclear age in the lives of people we serve. Nuclear weaponry has drastically changed the nature of warfare, and the arms race poses a threat to human life and human civilization which is without precedent. . . .

Catholic teaching has always understood peace in positive terms. In the words of Pope John Paul II: "Peace is not just the absence of war. . . . Like a cathedral, peace must be constructed patiently and with unshakable faith." (Coventry, England, 1982) Peace is the fruit of order. Order in human society must be shaped on the basis of respect for the transcendence of God and the unique dignity of each person, understood in terms of freedom, justice, truth and love. To avoid war in our day we must be intent on building peace in an increasingly interdependent world. . . .

While pursuing peace incessantly, it is also necessary to limit the use of force in a world comprised of nation states, faced with common problems but devoid of an adequate international political authority. Keeping the peace in the nuclear age is a moral and political imperative. . . .

As bishops in the United States, assessing the concrete circumstances of our society, we have made a number of observations and recommendations in the process of applying moral principles to specific policy choices. . . .

Under no circumstances may nuclear weapons or other instruments of mass slaughter be used for the purpose of destroying population centers or other predominantly civilian targets. Retaliatory action which would indiscriminately and disproportionately take many wholly innocent lives, lives of people who are in no way responsible for reckless actions of their government, must also be condemned. . . .

We do not perceive any situation in which the deliberate initiation of nuclear war, on however restricted a scale, can be morally justified. Non-nuclear attacks by another state must be resisted by other than nuclear means. Therefore, a serious moral obligation exists to develop non-nuclear defensive strategies as rapidly as possible. In this letter we urge NATO to move rapidly toward the adoption of a "no first use" policy, but we recognize this will take time to implement and will require the development of an adequate alternative defense posture. . . .

Our examination of the various arguments on this question makes us highly skeptical about the real meaning of "limited." One of the criteria of the just-war teaching is that there must be a reasonable hope of success in bringing about justice and peace. We must ask whether such a reasonable hope can exist once nuclear weapons have been exchanged. The burden of proof remains on those who assert that meaningful limitation is possible. In our view the first imperative is to prevent any use of nuclear weapons and we hope that leaders will resist the notion that nuclear conflict can be limited, contained or won in any traditional sense. . . .

In concert with the evaluation provided by Pope John Paul II, we have arrived at a strictly conditional moral acceptance of deterrence. In this letter we have outlined criteria and recommendations which indicate the meaning of conditional acceptance of deterrence policy. We cannot consider such a policy adequate as a long-term basis for peace. . . .

In the words of the Holy Father, we need a "moral about-face." The whole world must summon the moral courage and technical means to say no to nuclear conflict; no to weapons of mass destruction; no to an arms race which robs the poor and the vulnerable; and no to the moral danger of a nuclear age which places before humankind indefensible choices of constant terror or surrender. Peacemaking is not an optional commitment. It is a requirement of our faith. We are called to be peacemakers, not by some movement of the moment, but by our Lord Jesus.

CARL SAGAN, "NUCLEAR WAR AND CLIMATIC CATASTROPHE," FOREIGN AFFAIRS (WINTER 1983/1984)

What if deterrence failed and World War III actually occurred? In this article, the scientist Carl Sagan (1934–1996) examines the possible range of effects.

Apocalyptic predictions require, to be taken seriously, higher standards of evidence than do assertions on other matters where the stakes are not as great. Since the immediate effects of even a single thermonuclear weapon explosion are so devastating, it is natural to assume—even without considering detailed mechanisms—that the more or less simultaneous explosion of ten thousand such weapons over the Northern Hemisphere might have unpredictable and catastrophic consequences.

And yet, while it is widely accepted that a full nuclear war might mean the end of civilization at least in the Northern Hemisphere, claims that nuclear war might imply a reversion of the human population to prehistoric levels, or even the extinction of the human species, have, among some policymakers at least, been dismissed as alarmist or, worse, irrelevant. . . .

No one knows, of course, how many warheads with what aggregate yield would be detonated in a nuclear war. . . . On the other hand, it is generally accepted, even among most military planners, that even a "small" nuclear war would be almost impossible to contain before it escalated to include much of the world's arsenals. . . .

Recent estimates of the immediate deaths from blast, prompt radiation, and fires in a major exchange in which cities were targeted range from several hundred million to 1.1 billion. . . . Serious injuries requiring immediate medical attention (which would be largely unavailable) would be suffered by a comparably large number of people, perhaps an additional 1.1 billion.

[I]n the wake of a nuclear war there is likely to be a period, lasting at least for months, of extreme cold in radioactive gloom, followed—after the soot and dust fall out—by an extended period of increased ultraviolet light reaching the surface. . . .

The immediate human consequences of nuclear explosions range from the vaporization of populations near the hypocenter, to blast generated trauma (from flying glass, falling beams, collapsing skyscrapers and the like) to burns, radiation sickness, shock, and psychiatric disorders. But our concern here is with longer-term effects. . . .

In nuclear war scenarios in which a great many cities are burning, a significant pyrotoxin smog might persist for months. The magnitude of this danger is unknown.

The pyrotoxins, low light levels, radioactive fallout, subsequent ultraviolet light, and especially the cold are together likely to destroy almost all Northern Hemisphere agriculture. . . . This would represent by itself an unprecedented global catastrophe: North American grain is the principal reliable source of export food on the planet. . . For many scenarios, the effects will extend . . . into two or more growing seasons. Widespread fires and subsequent runoff of topsoil are among the many deleterious consequences extending for years after the war.

Something like three-quarters of the U.S. population lives in or near cities. In the cities themselves, there is, on average, only about one week's supply of food. After a nuclear war it is conceivable that enough of present grain storage might survive to maintain, on some level, the present population for more than a year. But with the breakdown of civil order and transportation systems in the cold, the dark, and the fallout, these stores would become largely inaccessible. Vast numbers of survivors would soon starve to death.

In addition, the sub-freezing temperatures imply, in many cases, the unavailability of fresh water. The ground will tend to be frozen to about a depth of about a meter—incidentally making it unlikely that the hundreds of millions of dead bodies would be buried, even if the civil organization to do so existed. Fuel stores to melt snow and ice would be in short supply, and ice surfaces and freshly fallen snow would tend to be contaminated by radioactivity and pyrotoxins. . . .

[T]he combination of acute doses from prompt radiation fallout, chronic doses from the delayed intermediate-timescale fallout, and internal doses from food and drink are together likely to kill many more by radiation sickness. Because of acute damage to bone marrow, survivors would have significantly increased vulnerability to infectious diseases. Most infants exposed to 100 rads during the first two trimesters of pregnancy would suffer mental retardation and/or other serious birth defects. . . . Livestock and domesticated animals, with fewer resources, vanishing food supplies and in many cases greater sensitivity to the stresses of nuclear war than human beings, would also perish in large numbers. . . .

We have, by slow and imperceptible steps, been constructing a Doomsday Machine. Until recently—and then only by accident—no one even noticed. And we have distributed its triggers all over the Northern Hemisphere. Every American and Soviet leader since 1945 has made critical decisions regarding nuclear war in total ignorance of the climatic catastrophe. Perhaps this knowledge would have moderated the subsequent course of world events and, especially, the nuclear arms race. Today, at least, we have no excuse for failing to factor the catastrophe into long-term decisions on strategic policy. . . .

No one contends it will be easy to reverse the nuclear arms race. It is required at least for the same reasons that were used to justify the arms race in the first place—the national security of the United States and the Soviet Union. It is necessarily an enterprise of great magnitude. John Stuart Mill said: "Against a great evil a small remedy does not produce a small result. It produces no result at all.". . . .

National security policies that seem prudent or even successful during a term in office or a tour of duty may work to endanger national—or even global security—over longer periods of time. In many respects it is just such short-term thinking that is responsible for the present world crisis. The looming prospect of the climatic catastrophe makes short-term thinking even more dangerous. The past has been the enemy of the present, and the present the enemy of the future. . . .

Our talent, while imperfect, to foresee the future consequences of our present actions and to change our course appropriately is a hallmark of the human species, and one of the chief reasons for our success over the past million years. Our future depends entirely on how quickly and how broadly we can refine this talent. We should plan for and cherish our fragile world as we do our children and our grandchildren: there will be no other place for them to live. It is nowhere ordained that we must remain in bondage to nuclear weapons.

XI.

THE PASSING OF THE COLD WAR

In 1979, when Jimmy Carter delivered his "Crisis of Confidence" speech, the Cold War seemed destined to continue indefinitely. Within a decade, it had essentially ended. In 1979, the United States appeared to be flagging. By 1989, it seemingly reigned supreme. Examining the implications of unprecedented global preeminence had emerged as the question of the day.

The easing of Cold War tensions commenced in the mid-1980s when reform-minded Kremlin leaders decided that competing with the United States and the West no longer served Soviet interests. In the meantime, the Reagan era found Americans recovering from their post-Vietnam funk. President Ronald Reagan had come to office vowing to get tough with what he called the "evil empire." In the end, more pragmatist than ideologue, he proved willing to cut a deal.

Yet calling off the Cold War produced consequences that all parties involved failed to anticipate. By 1989, the Soviet Empire disintegrated, a process symbolized by the fall of the Berlin Wall in November of that year. The disintegration of the Soviet Union itself followed shortly thereafter. By the end of 1991, it had ceased to exist. The appeal of communism as an alternative to capitalism had largely vanished.

American policymakers and public intellectuals vied with one another in spelling out the implications of these developments. All agreed that the United States was now the last superpower standing. What that foretold for the future was less clear.

JEANE J. KIRKPATRICK, "DICTATORSHIPS AND DOUBLE STANDARDS," *COMMENTARY* (NOVEMBER 1979)

When she penned this essay, Jeane Kirkpatrick (1926–2006) was an obscure academic. Her critique of US foreign policy under Jimmy Carter vaulted her to national prominence. Soon enough, President Ronald Reagan appointed her as U.S. ambassador to the United Nations.

The failure of the Carter administration's foreign policy is now clear to everyone except its architects, and even they must entertain private doubts, from time to time, about a policy whose crowning achievement has been to lay the groundwork for a transfer of the Panama Canal from the United States to a swaggering Latin dictator of Castroite bent. In the thirty-odd months since the inauguration of Jimmy Carter as President there has occurred a dramatic Soviet military buildup, matched by the stagnation of American armed forces, and a dramatic extension of Soviet influence in the Horn of Africa, Afghanistan, Southern Africa, and the Caribbean, matched by a declining American position in all these areas. The U.S. has never tried so hard and failed so utterly to make and keep friends in the Third World.

As if this were not bad enough, in the current year the United States has suffered two other major blows—in Iran and Nicaragua—of large and strategic significance. In each country, the Carter administration not only failed to prevent the undesired outcome, it actively collaborated in the replacement of moderate autocrats friendly to American interests with less friendly autocrats of extremist persuasion. It is too soon to be certain about what kind of regime will ultimately emerge in either Iran or Nicaragua, but accumulating evidence suggests that things are as likely to get worse as to get better in both countries. The Sandinistas in Nicaragua appear to be as skillful in consolidating power as the Ayatollah Khomeini is inept, and leaders of both revolutions display an intolerance and arrogance that do not bode well for the peaceful sharing of power or the establishment of constitutional governments, especially since those leaders have made clear that they have no intention of seeking either.

It is at least possible that the SALT debate may stimulate new scrutiny of the nation's strategic position and defense policy, but there are no signs that anyone is giving serious attention to this nation's role in Iranian and Nicaraguan developments—despite clear warnings that the U.S. is confronted with similar situations and options in El Salvador, Guatemala, Morocco, Zaire, and elsewhere. Yet no problem of American foreign policy is more urgent than that of formulating a morally and strategically acceptable, and politically realistic, program for dealing with non-democratic governments who are threatened by Soviet-sponsored subversion. In the absence of such a policy, we can expect that the same reflexes that guided Washington in Iran and Nicaragua will be permitted to determine American actions from Korea to Mexico—with the same disastrous effects on the U.S. strategic position. (That the administration has not called its policies in Iran and Nicaragua a failure—and probably does not consider them such—complicates the problem without changing its nature.)

There were, of course, significant differences in the relations between the United States and each of these countries during the past two or three decades. Oil, size, and proximity to the Soviet Union gave Iran greater economic and strategic import than any Central American "republic," and closer relations were cultivated with the Shah, his counselors, and family than with President Somoza, his advisers, and family. Relations with the Shah were probably also enhanced by our approval of his manifest determination to modernize Iran regardless of the effects of modernization on traditional social and cultural patterns (including those which enhanced his own authority and legitimacy). And, of course, the Shah was much better looking and altogether more dashing than Somoza; his private life was much more romantic, more interesting to the media, popular and otherwise. Therefore, more Americans were more aware of the Shah than of the equally tenacious Somoza.

But even though Iran was rich, blessed with a product the U.S. and its allies needed badly, and led by a handsome king, while Nicaragua was poor and rocked along under a long-tenure president of less striking aspect, there were many similarities between the two countries and our relations with them. Both these small nations were led by men who had not been selected by free elections, who recognized no duty to submit themselves to searching tests of popular acceptability. Both did tolerate limited opposition, including opposition newspapers and political parties, but both were also confronted by radical, violent opponents bent on social and political revolution. Both rulers, therefore, sometimes invoked martial law to arrest, imprison, exile, and occasionally, it was alleged, torture their opponents. Both relied for public order on police forces whose personnel were said to be too harsh, too arbitrary, and too powerful. Each had what the American press termed "private armies," which is to say, armies pledging their allegiance to the ruler rather than the "constitution" or the "nation" or some other impersonal entity.

In short, both Somoza and the Shah were, in central ways, traditional rulers of semi-traditional societies. Although the Shah very badly wanted to create a technologically modern and powerful nation and Somoza tried hard to introduce modern agricultural methods, neither sought to reform his society in the light of any abstract idea of social justice or political virtue. Neither attempted to alter significantly the distribution of goods, status, or power (though the democratization of education and skills that accompanied modernization in Iran did result in some redistribution of money and power there).

Both Somoza and the Shah enjoyed long tenure, large personal fortunes (much of which were no doubt appropriated from general revenues), and good relations with the United States. The Shah and Somoza were not only anti-Communist, they were positively friendly to the U.S., sending their sons and others to be educated in our universities, voting with us in the United Nations, and regularly supporting American interests and positions even when these entailed personal and political cost. The embassies of both governments were active in Washington social life, and were frequented by powerful Americans who occupied major roles in this nation's diplomatic, military, and political life. And the Shah and Somoza themselves were both welcome in Washington, and had many American friends.

Though each of the rulers was from time to time criticized by American officials for violating civil and human rights, the fact that the people of Iran and Nicaragua only intermittently enjoyed the rights accorded to citizens in the Western democracies did not prevent successive administrations from granting—with the necessary approval of successive Congresses—both military and economic aid. In the case of both Iran and Nicaragua, tangible and intangible tokens of U.S. support continued until the regime became the object of a major attack by forces explicitly hostile to the United States.

But once an attack was launched by opponents bent on destruction, everything changed. The rise of serious, violent opposition in Iran and Nicaragua set in motion a succession of events which bore a suggestive resemblance to one another and a suggestive similarity to our behavior in China before the fall of Chiang Kaishek, in Cuba before the triumph of Castro, in certain crucial periods of the Vietnamese war, and, more recently, in Angola. In each of these countries, the American effort to impose liberalization and democratization on a government confronted with violent internal opposition not only failed, but actually assisted the coming to power of new regimes in which ordinary people enjoy fewer freedoms and less personal security than under the previous autocracy—regimes, moreover, hostile to American interests and policies.

The pattern is familiar enough: an established autocracy with a record of friendship with the U.S. is attacked by insurgents, some of whose leaders have long ties to the Communist movement, and most of whose arms are of Soviet, Chinese, or Czechoslovak origin. The "Marxist" presence is ignored and/or minimized by American officials and by the elite media on the ground that U.S. support for the dictator gives the rebels little choice but to seek aid "elsewhere." Violence spreads and American officials wonder aloud about the viability of a regime that "lacks the support of its own people." The absence of an opposition party is deplored and civil-rights violations are reviewed. Liberal columnists question the morality of continuing aid to a "rightist dictatorship" and provide assurances concerning the essential moderation of some insurgent leaders who "hope" for some sign that the U.S. will remember its own revolutionary origins. Requests for help from the beleaguered autocrat go unheeded, and the argument is increasingly voiced that ties should be established with rebel leaders "before it is too late." The President, delaying U.S. aid, appoints a special emissary who confirms the deterioration of the government position and its diminished capacity to control the situation and recommends various measures for "strengthening" and "liberalizing" the regime, all of which involve diluting its power.

The emissary's recommendations are presented in the context of a growing clamor for American disengagement on grounds that continued involvement confirms our status as an agent of imperialism, racism, and reaction; is inconsistent with support for human rights; alienates us from the "forces of democracy"; and threatens to put the U.S. once more on the side of history's "losers." This chorus is supplemented daily by interviews with returning missionaries and "reasonable" rebels.

As the situation worsens, the President assures the world that the U.S. desires only that the "people choose their own form of government"; he blocks delivery of all arms to the government and undertakes negotiations to establish a "broadly based" coalition headed by a "moderate" critic of the regime who, once elevated, will move quickly to seek a "political" settlement to the conflict. Should the incumbent autocrat prove resistant to American demands that he step aside, he will be readily overwhelmed by the military strength of his opponents, whose patrons will have continued to provide sophisticated arms and advisers at the same time the U.S. cuts off military sales. Should the incumbent be so demoralized as to agree to yield power, he will be replaced by a "moderate" of American selection. Only after the insurgents have refused the proffered political solution and anarchy has spread throughout the nation will it be noticed that the new head of government has no significant following, no experience at governing, and no talent for leadership. By then, military commanders, no longer bound by loyalty to the chief of state, will depose the faltering "moderate" in favor of a fanatic of their own choosing.

In either case, the U.S. will have been led by its own misunderstanding of the situation to assist actively in deposing an erstwhile friend and ally and installing a government hostile to American interests and policies in the world. At best we will have lost access to friendly territory. At worst the Soviets will have gained a new base. And everywhere our friends will have noted that the U.S. cannot be counted on in times of difficulty and our enemies will have observed that American support provides no security against the forward march of history. . . .

Yet despite all the variations, the Carter administration brought to the crises in Iran and Nicaragua several common assumptions each of which played a major role in hastening the victory of even more repressive dictatorships than had been in place before. These were, first, the belief that there existed at the moment of crisis a democratic alternative to the incumbent government: second, the belief that the continuation of the status quo was not possible; third, the belief that any change, including the establishment of a government headed by self-styled Marxist revolutionaries, was preferable to the present government. Each of these beliefs was (and is) widely shared in the liberal community generally. Not one of them can withstand close scrutiny.

Although most governments in the world are, as they always have been, autocracies of one kind or another, no idea holds greater sway in the mind of educated Americans than the belief that it is possible to democratize governments, anytime, anywhere, under any circumstances. This notion is belied by an enormous body of evidence based on the experience of dozens of countries which have attempted with more or less (usually less) success to move from autocratic to democratic government. Many of the wisest political scientists of this and previous centuries agree that democratic institutions are especially difficult to establish and maintain—because they make heavy demands on all portions of a population and because they depend on complex social, cultural, and economic conditions.

Two or three decades ago, when Marxism enjoyed its greatest prestige among American intellectuals, it was the economic prerequisites of democracy that were emphasized by social scientists. Democracy, they argued, could function only in relatively rich societies with an advanced economy, a substantial middle class, and a literate population, but it could be expected to emerge more or less automatically whenever these conditions prevailed. Today, this picture seems grossly oversimplified. While it surely helps to have an economy strong enough to provide decent levels of well-being for all, and "open" enough to provide mobility and encourage achievement, a pluralistic society and the right kind of political culture—and time—are even more essential. . . .

Fulfilling the duties and discharging the functions of representative government make heavy demands on leaders and citizens, demands for participation and restraint, for consensus and compromise. It is not necessary for all citizens to be avidly interested in politics or well-informed about public affairs—although far more widespread interest and mobilization are needed than in autocracies. What is necessary is that a substantial number of citizens think of themselves as participants in society's decision-making and not simply as subjects bound by its laws. Moreover, leaders of all major sectors of the society must agree to pursue power only by legal means, must eschew (at least in principle) violence, theft, and fraud, and must accept defeat when necessary. They must also be skilled at finding and creating common ground among diverse points of view and interests, and correlatively willing to compromise on all but the most basic values.

In addition to an appropriate political culture, democratic government requires institutions strong enough to channel and contain conflict. Voluntary, non-official institutions are needed to articulate and aggregate diverse interests and opinions present in the society. Otherwise, the formal governmental institutions will not be able to translate popular demands into public policy. . . .

Although there is no instance of a revolutionary "socialist" or Communist society being democratized, right-wing autocracies do sometimes evolve into democracies—given time, propitious economic, social, and political circumstances, talented leaders, and a strong indigenous demand for representative government. . . .

Vietnam presumably taught us that the United States could not serve as the world's policeman; it should also have taught us the dangers of trying to be the world's midwife to democracy when the birth is scheduled to take place under conditions of guerrilla war.

If the administration's actions in Iran and Nicaragua reflect the pervasive and mistaken assumption that one can easily locate and impose democratic alternatives to incumbent autocracies, they also reflect the equally pervasive and equally flawed belief that change *per se* in such autocracies is inevitable, desirable, and in the American interest. It is this belief which induces the Carter administration to participate actively in the toppling of non-Communist autocracies while remaining passive in the face of Communist expansion.

At the time the Carter administration came into office it was widely reported that the President had assembled a team who shared a new approach to foreign policy and a new conception of the national interest. The principal elements of this new approach were said to be two: the conviction that the cold war was over, and the conviction that, this being the case, the U.S. should give priority to North-South problems and help less developed nations achieve their own destiny.

More is involved in these changes than originally meets the eye. For, unlikely as it may seem, the foreign policy of the Carter administration is guided by a relatively full-blown philosophy of history which includes, as philosophies of history always do, a theory of social change, or, as it is currently called, a doctrine of modernization. Like most other philosophies of history that have appeared in the West since the 18th century, the Carter administration's doctrine predicts progress (in the form of modernization for all societies) and a happy ending (in the form of a world community of developed, autonomous nations). . . .

This perspective on contemporary events is optimistic in the sense that it foresees continuing human progress; deterministic in the sense that it perceives events as fixed by processes over which persons and policies can have but little influence; moralistic in the sense that it perceives history and U.S. policy as having moral ends; cosmopolitan in the sense that it attempts to view the world not from the perspective of American interests or intentions but from the perspective of the modernizing nation with both revolution and morality, and U.S. policy with all three. . . .

No matter that the invasions, coups, civil wars, and political struggles of less violent kinds that one sees all around do not *seem* to be incidents in a global personnel search for someone to manage the modernization process. . . .

So what if the "deep historical forces" at work in such diverse places as Iran, the Horn of Africa, Southeast Asia, Central America, and the United Nations look a lot like Russians or Cubans? Having moved past what the President calls our "inordinate fear of Communism," identified by him with the Cold War, we should, we are told, now be capable of distinguishing Soviet and Cuban "machinations," which anyway exist mainly in the minds of cold warriors and others guilty of oversimplifying the world, from evolutionary changes, which seem to be the only kind that actually occur.

What can a U.S. President faced with such complicated, inexorable, impersonal processes *do*? The answer, offered again and again by the President and his top officials, is, not much. Since events are not caused by human decisions, they cannot be stopped or altered by them. Brzezinski, for example, has said: "We recognize that the world is changing under the influence of forces no government can control. . . ."And Cyrus Vance has cautioned: "The fact is that we can no more stop change than Canute could still the waters."

The Carter administration's essentially deterministic and apolitical view of contemporary events discourages an active American response and encourages passivity. . . .

Where once upon a time an American President might have sent Marines to assure the protection of American strategic interests, there is no room for force in this world of progress and self-determination. Force, the President told us at Notre Dame, does not work; that is the lesson he extracted from Vietnam. It offers only "superficial" solutions. . . .

What *is* the function of foreign policy under these conditions? It is to understand the processes of change and then, like Marxists, to align ourselves with history, hoping to contribute a bit of stability along the way. And this, administration spokesmen assure us, is precisely what we are doing. The Carter administration has defined the

U.S. national interest in the Third World as identical with the putative end of the modernization process. . . .

But there is a problem. The conceivable contexts turn out to be mainly those in which non-Communist autocracies are under pressure from revolutionary guerrillas. Since Moscow is the aggressive, expansionist power today, it is more often than not insurgents, encouraged and armed by the Soviet Union, who challenge the status quo. The American commitment to "change" in the abstract ends up by aligning us tacitly with Soviet clients and irresponsible extremists like the Ayatollah Khomeini or, in the end, Yasir Arafat.

So far, assisting "change" has not led the Carter administration to undertake the destabilization of a *Communist* country. The principles of self-determination and nonintervention are thus both selectively applied. We seem to accept the *status quo* in Communist nations (in the name of "diversity" and national autonomy), but not in nations ruled by "right-wing" dictators or white oligarchies. . . .

Something very odd is going on here. How does an administration that desires to let people work out their own destinies get involved in determined efforts at reform in South Africa, Zaire, Nicaragua, El Salvador, and elsewhere? How can an administration committed to nonintervention in Cambodia and Vietnam announce that it "will not be deterred" from righting wrongs in South Africa? What should be made of an administration that sees the U.S. interest as identical with economic modernization and political independence and yet heedlessly endangers the political independence of Taiwan, a country whose success in economic modernization and egalitarian distribution of wealth is unequaled in Asia? The contrast is as striking as that between the administration's frenzied speed in recognizing the new dictatorship in Nicaragua and its continuing refusal to recognize the elected government of Zimbabwe Rhodesia, or its refusal to maintain any presence in Zimbabwe Rhodesia while staffing a U.S. Information Office in Cuba. Not only are there ideology and a double standard at work here, the ideology neither fits nor explains reality, and the double standard involves the administration in the wholesale contradiction of its own principles.

Inconsistencies are a familiar part of politics in most societies. Usually, however, governments behave hypocritically when their principles conflict with the national interest. What makes the inconsistencies of the Carter administration noteworthy are, first, the administration's moralism, which renders it especially vulnerable to charges of hypocrisy; and, second, the administration's predilection for policies that violate the strategic and economic interests of the United States. The administration's conception of national interest borders on doublethink: it finds friendly powers to be guilty representatives of the status quo and views the triumph of unfriendly groups as beneficial to America's "true interests."

This logic is quite obviously reinforced by the prejudices and preferences of many administration officials. Traditional autocracies are, in general and in their very nature, deeply offensive to modern American sensibilities. The notion that public affairs should be ordered on the basis of kinship, friendship, and other personal relations rather than on the basis of objective "rational" standards violates our conception of justice and efficiency. The preference for stability rather than change is also disturbing to Americans whose whole national experience rests on the principles of change, growth, and progress. The extremes of wealth and poverty characteristic of traditional societies also offend us, the more so since the poor are usually very poor and bound to their squalor by a hereditary allocation of role. Moreover, the relative lack of concern of rich, comfortable rulers for the poverty, ignorance, and disease of "their" people is likely to be interpreted by Americans as moral dereliction pure and simple. The truth is that Americans can hardly bear such societies and such rulers. Confronted with them, our vaunted cultural relativism evaporates and we become as censorious as Cotton Mather confronting sin in New England.

But if the politics of traditional and semi-traditional autocracy is nearly antithetical to our own—at both the symbolic and the operational level—the rhetoric of progressive revolutionaries sounds much better to us; their symbols are much more acceptable. One reason that some modern Americans prefer "socialist" to traditional autocracies is that the former have embraced modernity and have adopted modern modes and perspectives, including an instrumental, manipulative, functional orientation toward most social, cultural, and personal affairs; a profession of universalistic norms; an emphasis on reason, science, education, and progress; a deemphasis of the sacred; and "rational," bureaucratic organizations. They speak our language.

Because socialism of the Soviet/Chinese/Cuban variety is an ideology rooted in a version of the same values that sparked the Enlightenment and the democratic revolutions of the 18th century; because it is modern and not traditional; because it postulates goals that appeal to Christian as well as to secular values (brotherhood of man, elimination of power as a mode of human relations), it is highly congenial to many Americans at the symbolic level. Marxist revolutionaries speak the language of a hopeful future while traditional autocrats speak the language of an unattractive past. Because left-wing revolutionaries invoke the symbols and values of democracy—emphasizing egalitarianism rather than hierarchy and privilege, liberty rather than order, activity rather than passivity—they are again and again accepted as partisans in the cause of freedom and democracy.

Nowhere is the affinity of liberalism, Christianity, and Marxist socialism more apparent than among liberals who are "duped" time after time into supporting "liberators" who turn out to be totalitarians, and among Left-leaning clerics whose attraction to a secular style of "redemptive community" is stronger than their outrage at the hostility of socialist regimes to religion. In Jimmy Carter—egalitarian, optimist, liberal, Christian—the tendency to be repelled by frankly non-democratic rulers and hierarchical societies is almost as strong as the tendency to be attracted to the idea of popular revolution, liberation, and progress. Carter is, *par excellence*, the kind of liberal most likely to confound revolution with idealism, change with progress, optimism with virtue.

Where concern about "socialist encirclement," Soviet expansion, and traditional conceptions of the national interest inoculated his predecessors against such easy equations, Carter's doctrine of national interest and modernization encourages support for all change that takes place in the name of "the people," regardless of its "superficial" Marxist or anti-American content. Any lingering doubt about whether the U.S. should, in case of conflict, support a "tested friend" such as the Shah or a friendly power such as Zimbabwe Rhodesia against an opponent who despises us is resolved by reference to our "true," our "long-range" interests. . . .

To this end, overtures were made looking to the "normalization" of relations with Vietnam, Cuba, and the Chinese People's Republic, and steps were taken to cool relations with South Korea, South Africa, Nicaragua, the Philippines, and others. These moves followed naturally from the conviction that the U.S. had, as our enemies said, been on the wrong side of history in supporting the *status quo* and opposing revolution. . . .

To be sure, neither the President, nor Vance, nor Brzezinski *desires* the proliferation of Soviet-supported regimes. Each has asserted his disapproval of Soviet "interference" in the modernization process. But each, nevertheless, remains willing to "destabilize" friendly or neutral autocracies without any assurance that they will not be replaced by reactionary totalitarian theocracies, totalitarian Soviet client states, or worst of all, by murderous fanatics of the Pol Pot variety.

The foreign policy of the Carter administration fails not for lack of good intentions but for lack of realism about the nature of traditional versus revolutionary autocracies and the relation of each to the American national interest. Only intellectual fashion and the tyranny of Right/Left thinking prevent intelligent men of good will from perceiving the *facts* that traditional authoritarian governments are less repressive than revolutionary autocracies, that they are more susceptible of liberalization, and that they are more compatible with U.S. interests. The evidence on all these points is clear enough.

Surely it is now beyond reasonable doubt that the present governments of Vietnam, Cambodia, Laos are much more repressive than those of the despised previous rulers; that the government of the People's Republic of China is more repressive than that of Taiwan, that North Korea is more repressive than South Korea, and so forth. This is the most important lesson of Vietnam and Cambodia. It is not new but it is a gruesome reminder of harsh facts.

From time to time a truly bestial ruler can come to power in either type of autocracy—Idi Amin, Papa Doc Duvalier, Joseph Stalin, Pol Pot

are examples—but neither type regularly produces such moral monsters (though democracy regularly prevents their accession to power). There are, however, *systemic* differences between traditional and revolutionary autocracies that have a predictable effect on their degree of repressiveness. Generally speaking, traditional autocrats tolerate social inequities, brutality, and poverty while revolutionary autocracies create them.

Traditional autocrats leave in place existing allocations of wealth, power, status, and other resources which in most traditional societies favor an affluent few and maintain masses in poverty. But they worship traditional gods and observe traditional taboos. They do not disturb the habitual rhythms of work and leisure, habitual places of residence, habitual patterns of family and personal relations. Because the miseries of traditional life are familiar, they are bearable to ordinary people who, growing up in the society, learn to cope, as children born to untouchables in India acquire the skills and attitudes necessary for survival in the miserable roles they are destined to fill. Such societies create no refugees.

Precisely the opposite is true of revolutionary Communist regimes. They create refugees by the million because they claim jurisdiction over the whole life of the society and make demands for change that so violate internalized values and habits that inhabitants flee by the tens of thousands in the remarkable expectation that their attitudes, values, and goals will "fit" better in a foreign country than in their native land. . . .

Moreover, the history of this century provides no grounds for expecting that radical totalitarian regimes will transform themselves. At the moment there is a far greater likelihood of progressive liberalization and democratization in the governments of Brazil, Argentina, and Chile than in the government of Cuba; in Taiwan than in the People's Republic of China; in South Korea than in North Korea; in Zaire than in Angola; and so forth.

Since many traditional autocracies permit limited contestation and participation, it is not impossible that U.S. policy could effectively encourage this process of liberalization and democratization, provided that the effort is not made at a time when the incumbent government is fighting for its life against violent adversaries, and that proposed reforms are aimed at producing gradual change rather than perfect democracy overnight. To accomplish this, policymakers are needed who understand how actual democracies have actually come into being. History is a better guide than good intentions.

A realistic policy which aims at protecting our own interest and assisting the capacities for self-determination of less developed nations will need to face the unpleasant fact that, if victorious, violent insurgency headed by Marxist revolutionaries is unlikely to lead to anything but totalitarian tyranny. Armed intellectuals citing Marx and supported by Soviet-bloc arms and advisers will almost surely not turn out to be agrarian reformers, or simple nationalists, or democratic socialists. However incomprehensible it may be to some, Marxist revolutionaries are not contemporary embodiments of the Americans who wrote the Declaration of Independence, and they will not be content with establishing a broad-based coalition in which they have only one voice among many.

It may not always be easy to distinguish between democratic and totalitarian agents of change, but it is also not too difficult. Authentic democratic revolutionaries aim at securing governments based on the consent of the governed and believe that ordinary men are capable of using freedom, knowing their own interest, choosing rulers. They do not, like the current leaders in Nicaragua, assume that it will be necessary to postpone elections for three to five years during

which time they can "cure" the false consciousness of almost everyone.

If, moreover, revolutionary leaders describe the United States as the scourge of the 20th century, the enemy of freedom-loving people, the perpetrator of imperialism, racism, colonialism, genocide, war, then they are not authentic democrats or, to put it mildly, friends. Groups which define themselves as enemies should be treated as enemies. The United States is not in fact a racist, colonial power, it does not practice genocide, it does not threaten world peace with expansionist activities. In the last decade especially we have practiced remarkable forbearance everywhere and undertaken the "unilateral restraints on defense spending" recommended by Brzezinski as appropriate for the technetronic era. We have also moved further, faster, in eliminating domestic racism than any multiracial society in the world or in history.

For these reasons and more, a posture of continuous self-abasement and apology *vis-a-vis* the Third World is neither morally necessary nor politically appropriate. No more is it necessary or appropriate to support vocal enemies of the United States because they invoke the rhetoric of popular liberation. It is not even necessary or appropriate for our leaders to forswear unilaterally the use of military force to counter military force. Liberal idealism need not be identical with masochism, and need not be incompatible with the defense of freedom and the national interest.

RONALD REAGAN, "TIME TO RECAPTURE OUR DESTINY" (JULY 17, 1980)

Reagan dominated American politics in the 1980s. Here in accepting the Republican nomination in 1980, he emphasizes his adherence to the tradition of American exceptionalism.

Three hundred and sixty years ago, in 1620, a group of families dared to cross a mighty ocean to build a future for themselves in a new world. When they arrived at Plymouth, Massachusetts, they formed what they called a "compact"; an agreement among themselves to build a community and abide by its laws.

The single act—the voluntary binding together of free people to live under the law—set the pattern for what was to come.

A century and a half later, the descendants of those people pledged their lives, their fortunes and their sacred honor to found this nation. Some forfeited their fortunes and their lives; none sacrificed honor.

Four score and seven years later, Abraham Lincoln called upon the people of all America to renew their dedication and their commitment to a government of, for and by the people.

Isn't it once again time to renew our compact of freedom; to pledge to each other all that is best in our lives; all that gives meaning to them—for the sake of this, our beloved and blessed land?

Together, let us make this a new beginning. Let us make a commitment to care for the needy; to teach our children the values and the virtues handed down to us by our families; to have the courage to defend those values and the willingness to sacrifice for them. . . .

The first Republican president once said, "While the people retain their virtue and their vigilance, no administration by any extreme of wickedness or folly can seriously injure the government in the short space of four years."

If Mr. Lincoln could see what's happened in these last three-and-a-half years, he might hedge a little on that statement. But, with the virtues that our legacy as a free people and with the vigilance that sustains liberty, we still have time to use our renewed compact to overcome the injuries that have been done to America these past three-and-a-half years. . . .

Those who preside over the worst energy shortage in our history tell us to use less, so that we will run out of oil, gasoline, and natural gas a little more slowly. Conservation is desirable, of course, for we must not waste energy. But conservation is not the sole answer to our energy needs.

America must get to work producing more energy. The Republican program for solving economic problems is based on growth and productivity.

Large amounts of oil and natural gas lay beneath our land and off our shores, untouched because the present administration seems to believe the American people would rather see more regulation, taxes and controls than more energy.

Coal offers great potential. So does nuclear energy produced under rigorous safety standards. It could supply electricity for thousands of industries and millions of jobs and homes. It must not be thwarted by a tiny minority opposed to economic growth which often finds friendly ears in regulatory agencies for its obstructionist campaigns.

Make no mistake. We will not permit the safety of our people or our environment heritage to be jeopardized, but we are going to reaffirm that the economic prosperity of our people is a fundamental part of our environment. . . .

When we move from domestic affairs and cast our eyes abroad, we see an equally sorry chapter on the record of the present administration.

- A Soviet combat brigade trains in Cuba, just 90 miles from our shores.
- A Soviet army of invasion occupies Afghanistan, further threatening our vital interests in the Middle East.
- America's defense strength is at its lowest ebb in a generation, while the Soviet Union is vastly outspending us in both strategic and conventional arms.
- Our European allies, looking nervously at the growing menace from the East, turn to us for leadership and fail to find it.
- And, incredibly more than 50 of our fellow Americans have been held captive for over eight months by a dictatorial foreign power that holds us up to ridicule before the world.

Adversaries large and small test our will and seek to confound our resolve, but we are given weakness when we need strength; vacillation when the times demand firmness.

The Carter Administration lives in the world of make-believe. Every day, drawing up a response to that day's problems, troubles, regardless of what happened yesterday and what will happen tomorrow.

The rest of us, however, live in the real world. It is here that disasters are overtaking our nation without any real response from Washington.

This is make-believe, self-deceit and—above all—transparent hypocrisy.

For example, Mr. Carter says he supports the volunteer army, but he lets military pay and benefits slip so low that many of our enlisted personnel are actually eligible for food stamps. Re-enlistment rates drop and, just recently, after he fought all week against a proposal to increase the pay of our men and women in uniform, he helicoptered to our carrier, the U.S.S. Nimitz, which was returning from long months of duty. He told the crew that he advocated better pay for them and their comrades! Where does he really stand, now that he's back on shore?

I'll tell you where I stand. I do not favor a peacetime draft or registration, but I do favor pay and benefit levels that will attract and keep highly motivated men and women in our volunteer forces and an active reserve trained and ready for an instant call in case of an emergency.

There may be a sailor at the helm of the ship of state, but the ship has no rudder. Critical decisions are made at times almost in comic fashion, but who can laugh? Who was not embarrassed when the administration handed a major propaganda victory in the United Nations to the enemies of Israel, our staunch Middle East ally for three decades, and them claim that the American vote was a "mistake," the result of a "failure of communication" between the president, his secretary of state, and his U.N. ambassador?

Who does not feel a growing sense of unease as our allies, facing repeated instances of an amateurish and confused administration, reluctantly conclude that America is unwilling or unable to fulfill its obligations as the leader of the free world?

Who does not feel rising alarm when the question in any discussion of foreign policy is no longer, "Should we do something?", but "Do we have the capacity to do anything?"

The administration which has brought us to this state is seeking your endorsement for four more years of weakness, indecision, mediocrity and incompetence. No American should vote until he or she has asked, is the United States stronger and more respected now than it was three-and-a-half years ago? Is the world today a safer place in which to live?

It is the responsibility of the president of the United States, in working for peace, to insure that the safety of our people cannot successfully be threatened by a hostile foreign power. As president, fulfilling that responsibility will be my number one priority.

We are not a warlike people. Quite the opposite. We always seek to live in peace. We resort to force infrequently and with great reluctance—and only after we have determined that it is absolutely necessary. We are awed—and rightly so—by the forces of destruction at loose in the world in this nuclear era. But neither can we be naive or foolish. Four times in my lifetime America has gone to war, bleeding the lives of its young men into the sands of beachheads, the fields of Europe and the jungles and rice paddies of Asia. We know only too well that war comes not when the forces of freedom are strong, but when they are weak. It is then that tyrants are tempted.

We simply cannot learn these lessons the hard way again without risking our destruction.

Of all the objectives we seek, first and foremost is the establishment of lasting world peace. We must always stand ready to negotiate in good faith, ready to pursue any reasonable avenue that holds forth the promise of lessening tensions and furthering the prospects of peace. But let our friends and those who may wish us ill take note: the United States has an obligation to its citizens and to the people of the world never to let those who would destroy freedom dictate the future course of human life on this planet. I would regard my election as proof that we have renewed our resolve to preserve world peace and freedom. This nation will once again be strong enough to do that. . . .

It is impossible to capture in words the splendor of this vast continent which God has granted as our portion of this creation. There are no words to express the extraordinary strength and character of this breed of people we call Americans.

Everywhere we have met thousands of Democrats, Independents, and Republicans from all economic conditions and walks of life bound together in that community of shared values of family, work, neighborhood, peace and freedom. They are concerned, yes, but they are not frightened. They are disturbed, but not dismayed. They are the kind of men and women Tom Paine had in mind when he wrote—during the darkest days of the American Revolution—"We have it in our power to begin the world over again."

Nearly 150 years after Tom Paine wrote those words, an American president told the generation of the Great Depression that it had a "rendezvous with destiny." I believe that this generation of Americans today has a rendezvous with destiny.

CASPAR WEINBERGER, "THE USES OF MILITARY POWER" (1984)

For Reagan, enhancing US military power figured as a priority. Yet members of his administration, along with many ordinary Americans, remained haunted by Vietnam. How to put US armed might to work without getting dragged into another futile quagmire posed a challenge. Here in what became known as the "Weinberger Doctrine," defense secretary Caspar Weinberger (1917–2006) specifies the criteria that he believes should govern when and how the United States employs its armed might.

In today's world, the line between peace and war is less clearly drawn than at any time in our history. When George Washington, in his farewell address, warned us, as a new democracy, to avoid foreign entanglements, Europe then lay 2-3 months by sea over the horizon. The United States was protected by the width of the oceans. Now in this nuclear age, we measure time in minutes rather than months.

Aware of the consequences of any misstep, yet convinced of the precious worth of the freedom we enjoy, we seek to avoid conflict, while maintaining strong defenses. Our policy has always been to work hard for peace, but to be prepared if war comes. Yet, so blurred have the lines become between open conflict and half-hidden hostile acts that we cannot confidently predict where, or when, or how, or from what direction aggression may arrive. We must be prepared, at any moment, to meet threats ranging in intensity from isolated terrorist acts, to guerrilla action, to full-scale military confrontation.

Alexander Hamilton, writing in the *Federalist Papers,* said that it is impossible to foresee or define the extent and variety of national exigencies, or the correspondent extent and variety of the means which may be necessary to satisfy them. If it was true then, how much more true it is today, when we must remain ready to consider the means to meet such serious indirect challenges to the peace as proxy wars and individual terrorist action. And how much more important is it now, considering the consequences of failing to deter conflict at the lowest level possible. . . .

We find ourselves, then, face to face with a modern paradox: the most likely challenge to the peace—the gray area conflicts—are precisely the most difficult challenges to which a democracy must respond. Yet, while the source and nature of today's challenges are uncertain, our response must be clear and understandable. Unless we are certain that force is essential, we run the risk of inadequate national will to apply the resources needed. . . .

Policies formed without a clear understanding of what we hope to achieve would also earn us the scorn of our troops, who would have an understandable opposition to being used—in every sense of the word—casually and without intent to support them fully. Ultimately this course would reduce their morale and their effectiveness for engagements we *must* win. And if the military were to distrust its civilian leadership, recruitment would fall off and I fear an end to the all-volunteer system would be upon us, requiring a return to a draft, sowing the seeds of riot and discontent that so wracked the country in the '60s. . . .

In maintaining our progress in strengthening America's military deterrent, we face difficult challenges. For we have entered an era where the dividing lines between peace and war are less clearly drawn, the identity of the foe is much less clear. In World Wars I and II, we not only knew who our enemies were, but we shared a clear sense of *why* the principles espoused by our enemies were unworthy.

Since these two wars threatened our very survival as a free nation and the survival of our allies, they were total wars, involving every aspect of our society. All our means of production, all our resources were devoted to winning. Our policies had the unqualified support of the great majority of our people. Indeed, World Wars I and II ended with the unconditional surrender of our enemies. . . . The only acceptable ending when the alternative was the loss of our freedom.

But in the aftermath of the Second World War, we encountered a more subtle form of warfare—warfare in which, more often than not, the face of the enemy was masked. Territorial expansionism could be carried out indirectly by proxy powers, using surrogate forces aided and advised from afar. Some conflicts occurred under the name of "national liberation," but far more frequently ideology or religion provided the spark to the tinder.

Our adversaries can also take advantage of our open society, and our freedom of speech and opinion to use alarming rhetoric and misinformation to divide and disrupt our unity of purpose. While they would never dare to allow such freedoms to their own people, they are quick to exploit ours by conducting simultaneous military and propaganda campaigns to achieve their ends. . . .

Our freedom presents both a challenge and an opportunity. It is true that until democratic nations have the support of the people, they are inevitably at a disadvantage in a conflict. But when they *do* have that support they cannot be defeated. For democracies have the power to send a compelling message to friend and foe alike by the vote of their citizens. . . .

We should only engage *our* troops if we must do so as a matter of our *own* vital national interest. We cannot assume for other sovereign nations the responsibility to defend *their* territory—without their strong invitation—when our freedom is not threatened. . . .

In those cases where our national interests require us to commit combat force we must never let there be doubt of our resolution. When it is necessary for our troops to be committed to combat, we *must* commit them, in sufficient numbers and we *must* support them, as effectively and resolutely as our strength permits. When we commit our troops to combat we must do so with the sole object of winning.

Once it is clear our troops are required, because our vital interests are at stake, then we must have the firm national resolve to commit every ounce of strength necessary to win the fight to achieve our objectives. . . .

Just as clearly, there are other situations where United States combat forces should *not* be used. I believe the postwar period has taught us several

lessons, and from them I have developed *six* major tests to be applied when we are weighing the use of U.S. combat forces abroad. Let me now share them with you:

First, the United States should not commit forces to *combat* overseas unless the particular engagement or occasion is deemed vital to our national interest or that of our allies. That emphatically does not mean that we should *declare* beforehand, as we did with Korea in 1950, that a particular area is outside our strategic perimeter.

Second, if we decide it *is* necessary to put *combat* troops into a given situation, we should do so wholeheartedly, and with the clear intention of winning. If we are unwilling to commit the forces or resources necessary to achieve our objectives, we should not commit them at all. . . .

Third, if we *do* decide to commit forces to combat overseas, we should have clearly defined political and military objectives. And we should know precisely how our forces can accomplish those clearly defined objectives. And we should have and send the forces needed to do just that. As Clausewitz wrote, "no one starts a war—or rather, no one in his senses ought to do so—without first being clear in his mind what he intends to achieve by that war, and how he intends to conduct it." . . .

Fourth, the relationship between our objectives and the forces we have committed—their size, composition and disposition—must be continually reassessed and adjusted if necessary. Conditions and objectives invariably change during the course of a conflict. When they do change, then so must our combat requirements. We must continuously keep as a beacon light before us the basic questions: "is this conflict in our national interest?" "Does our national interest require us to fight, to use force of arms?" If the answers are "yes," then we *must* win. If the answers are "no," then we should not be in combat.

Fifth, before the U.S. commits combat forces abroad, there must be some reasonable assurance we will have the support of the American people and their elected representatives in Congress. This support cannot be achieved unless we are candid in making clear the threats we face; the support cannot be sustained without continuing and close consultation. . . .

Finally, the commitment of U.S. forces to combat should be a last resort.

I believe that these tests can be helpful in deciding whether or not we should commit our troops to combat in the months and years ahead. The point we must all keep uppermost in our minds is that if we ever decide to commit forces to combat, we must support those forces to the *fullest* extent of our national will for as long as it takes to win. So we must have in mind objectives that are clearly defined and understood and supported by the widest possible number of our citizens. And those objectives must be vital to our survival as a free nation and to the fulfillment of our responsibilities as a world power. . . .

LEE GREENWOOD, "GOD BLESS THE USA" (1984)

As a result of the Vietnam War, the reputation of the American soldier took a hit. During the Reagan era, it recovered, in no small part due to the efforts of President Reagan himself. Restoring the soldier's status as a heroic figure and military service as an expression of patriotism helped renew confidence in the effectiveness of the US military itself. The lyrics of this song, written by country music artist Lee Greenwood (1942–), reflect this change in attitudes.

If tomorrow all the things were gone
I'd worked for all my life
And I had to start again
With just my children and my wife

I'd thank my lucky stars
To be living here today
Cause the flag still stands for freedom
And they can't take that away

And I'm proud to be an American
Where at least I know I'm free
And I won't forget the men who died
Who gave that right to me

And I gladly stand up
Next to you and defend her still today
Cause there ain't no doubt I love this land
God bless the USA

From the lakes of Minnesota
To the hills of Tennessee
Across the plains of Texas
From sea to shining sea

From Detroit down to Houston,
And New York to L.A
Well there's pride in every American heart
And its time we stand and say

That I'm proud to be an American
Where at least I know I'm free
And I won't forget the men who died
Who gave that right to me

And I gladly stand up
Next to you and defend her still today
Cause there ain't no doubt I love this land
God bless the USA

And I'm proud to be and American
Where at least I know I'm free
And I won't forget the men who died
Who gave that right to me

And I gladly stand up
Next to you and defend her still today
Cause there ain't no doubt I love this land
God bless the USA

FRANCIS FUKUYAMA, "THE END OF HISTORY?"
THE NATIONAL INTEREST (SUMMER 1989)

In 1985, Mikhail Gorbachev emerged as the top leader in the Kremlin and soon thereafter initiated a bold program of economic and political reform. To implement those reforms, the Soviet leader sought to ease Cold War tensions. President Reagan proved ready to reciprocate. As the Soviet–American rivalry wound down, Soviet control of Eastern Europe unraveled. The end came with stunning rapidity. In November 1989, the Berlin Wall, preeminent symbol of Europe's postwar division, fell. By then, Francis Fukuyama (1952–), a political scientist and former mid-level State Department official, was already explaining what it all meant.

In watching the flow of events over the past decade or so, it is hard to avoid the feeling that something very fundamental has happened in world history. The past year has seen a flood of articles commemorating the end of the Cold War, and the fact that "peace" seems to be breaking out in many regions of the world. Most of these analyses lack any larger conceptual framework for distinguishing between what is essential and what is contingent or accidental in world history, and are predictably superficial. If Mr. Gorbachev were ousted from the Kremlin or a new Ayatollah proclaimed the millennium from a desolate Middle Eastern capital, these same commentators would scramble to announce the rebirth of a new era of conflict.

And yet, all of these people sense dimly that there is some larger process at work, a process that gives coherence and order to the daily headlines. The twentieth century saw the developed world descend into a paroxysm of ideological violence, as liberalism contended first with the remnants of absolutism, then bolshevism and fascism, and finally an updated Marxism that threatened to lead to the ultimate apocalypse of nuclear war. But the century that began full of self-confidence in the ultimate triumph of Western liberal democracy seems at its close to be returning full circle to where it started: not to an "end of ideology" or a convergence between capitalism and socialism, as earlier predicted, but to an unabashed victory of economic and political liberalism.

The triumph of the West, of the Western idea, is evident first of all in the total exhaustion of viable systematic alternatives to Western liberalism. In the past decade, there have been unmistakable changes in the intellectual climate of the world's two largest communist countries, and the beginnings of significant reform movements in both. But this phenomenon extends beyond high politics and it can be seen also in the ineluctable spread of consumerist Western culture in such diverse contexts as the peasants' markets and color television sets now omnipresent throughout China, the cooperative restaurants and clothing stores opened in the past year in Moscow, the Beethoven piped into Japanese department stores, and the rock music enjoyed alike in Prague, Rangoon, and Tehran.

What we may be witnessing is not just the end of the Cold War, or the passing of a particular period of postwar history, but the end of history as such: that is, the end point of mankind's ideological evolution and the universalization of Western liberal democracy as the final form of human government. This is not to say that there will no longer be events to fill the pages of *Foreign Affair*'s yearly summaries of international relations, for the victory of liberalism has occurred primarily in the realm of ideas or consciousness and is as yet incomplete in the real or material world. But there are powerful reasons for believing that it is the ideal that will govern the material world in the long run. . . .

The materialist bias of modern thought is characteristic not only of people on the Left who may be sympathetic to Marxism, but of many passionate anti-Marxists as well. Indeed, there is on the Right what one might label the *Wall Street Journal* school of deterministic materialism that discounts the importance of ideology and culture and sees man as essentially a rational, profit-maximizing individual. It is precisely this kind of individual and his pursuit of material incentives that is posited as the basis for economic life as such in economic textbooks. . . .

As we look around the contemporary world, the poverty of materialist theories of economic development is all too apparent. The *Wall Street Journal* school of deterministic materialism habitually points to the stunning economic success of Asia in the past few decades as evidence of the viability of free market economics, with the implication that all societies would see similar development were they simply to allow their populations to pursue their material self-interest freely. Surely free markets and stable political systems are a necessary precondition to capitalist economic growth. But just as surely the cultural heritage of those Far Eastern societies, the ethic of work and saving and family, a religious heritage that does not, like Islam, place restrictions on certain forms of economic behavior, and other deeply ingrained moral qualities, are equally important in explaining their economic performance. And yet the intellectual weight of materialism is such that not a single respectable contemporary theory of economic development addresses consciousness and culture seriously as the matrix within which economic behavior is formed.

Failure to understand that the roots of economic behavior lie in the realm of consciousness and culture leads to the common mistake of attributing material causes to phenomena that are essentially ideal in nature. For example, it is commonplace in the West to interpret the reform movements first in China and most recently in the Soviet Union as the victory of the material over the ideal—that is, a recognition that ideological incentives could not replace material ones in stimulating a highly productive modern economy, and that if one wanted to prosper one had to appeal to baser forms of self- interest. But the deep defects of socialist economies were evident thirty or forty years ago to anyone who chose to look. Why was it that these countries moved away from central planning only in the 1980s? The answer must be found in the consciousness of the elites and leaders ruling them, who decided to opt for the "Protestant" life of wealth and risk over the "Catholic" path of poverty and security. That change was in no way made inevitable by the material conditions in which either country found itself on the eve of the reform, but instead came about as the result of the victory of one idea over another. . . .

Have we in fact reached the end of history? Are there, in other words, any fundamental "contradictions" in human life that cannot be resolved in the context of modern liberalism, that would be resolvable by an alternative political-economic structure? If we accept the idealist premises laid out above, we must seek an answer to this question in the realm of ideology and consciousness. Our task is not to answer exhaustively the challenges to liberalism promoted by every crackpot messiah around the world, but only those that are embodied in important social or political forces and movements, and which are therefore part of world history. For our purposes, it matters very little what strange thoughts occur to people in Albania or Burkina Faso, for we are interested in what one could in some sense call the common ideological heritage of mankind.

In the past century, there have been two major challenges to liberalism, those of fascism and of communism. The former saw the political weakness, materialism, anomie, and lack of community of the West as fundamental contradictions in liberal societies that could only be resolved by a strong state that forged a new "people" on the basis of national exclusiveness. Fascism was destroyed as a living ideology by World War II. This was a defeat, of course, on a very material level, but it amounted to a defeat of the idea as well. What destroyed fascism as an idea was not universal moral revulsion against it, since plenty of people were willing to endorse the idea as long as it seemed the wave of the future, but its lack of success. After the war, it seemed to most people that German fascism as well as its other European and Asian variants were bound to self-destruct. There was no material reason why new fascist movements could not have sprung up again after the war in other locales, but for the fact that expansionist ultranationalism, with its promise of unending conflict leading to disastrous military defeat, had completely lost its appeal. The ruins of the Reich chancellery as well as the atomic bombs dropped on Hiroshima and Nagasaki killed this ideology on the level of consciousness as well as materially, and all of the pro-fascist movements spawned by the German and Japanese examples like the Peronist movement in Argentina or Subhas Chandra Bose's Indian National Army withered after the war.

The ideological challenge mounted by the other great alternative to liberalism, communism, was far more serious. Marx, speaking Hegel's language, asserted that liberal society contained a fundamental contradiction that could not be resolved within its context, that between capital and labor, and this contradiction has constituted the chief accusation against liberalism ever since. But surely, the class issue has actually been successfully resolved in the West. As Kojève (among others) noted, the egalitarianism of modern America represents the essential achievement of the classless society envisioned by Marx. This is not to say that there are not rich people and poor people in the United States, or that the gap between them has not grown in recent years. But the root causes of economic inequality do not have to do with the underlying legal and social structure of our society, which remains fundamentally egalitarian and moderately redistributionist, so much as with the cultural and social characteristics of the groups that make it up, which are in turn the historical legacy of premodern conditions. Thus black poverty in the United States is not the inherent product of liberalism, but is rather the "legacy of slavery and racism" which persisted long after the formal abolition of slavery.

As a result of the receding of the class issue, the appeal of communism in the developed Western world, it is safe to say, is lower today than any time since the end of the First World War. This can be measured in any number of ways: in the declining membership and electoral pull of the major European communist parties, and their overtly revisionist programs; in the corresponding electoral success of conservative parties from Britain and Germany to the United States and Japan, which are unabashedly pro-market and anti-statist; and in an intellectual climate whose most "advanced" members no longer believe that bourgeois society is something that ultimately needs to be overcome. This is not to say that the opinions of progressive intellectuals in Western countries are not deeply pathological in any number of ways. But those who believe that the future must inevitably be socialist tend to be very old, or very marginal to the real political discourse of their societies.

One may argue that the socialist alternative was never terribly plausible for the North Atlantic world, and was sustained for the last several decades primarily by its success outside of this region. But it is precisely in the non-European world that one is most struck by the occurrence of major ideological transformations. Surely the most remarkable changes have occurred in Asia. Due to the strength and adaptability of the indigenous cultures there, Asia became a battleground for a variety of imported Western ideologies early in this century. Liberalism in Asia was a very weak reed in the period after World War I; it is easy today to forget how gloomy Asia's political future looked as recently as ten or fifteen years ago. It is easy to forget as well how momentous the outcome of Asian ideological struggles seemed for world political development as a whole.

The first Asian alternative to liberalism to be decisively defeated was the fascist one represented by Imperial Japan. Japanese fascism (like its German version) was defeated by the force of American arms in the Pacific war, and liberal democracy was imposed on Japan by a victorious United States. Western capitalism and political liberalism when transplanted to Japan were adapted and transformed by the Japanese in such a way as to be scarcely recognizable.

Many Americans are now aware that Japanese industrial organization is very different from that prevailing in the United States or Europe, and it is questionable what relationship the factional maneuvering that takes place with the governing Liberal Democratic Party bears to democracy. Nonetheless, the very fact that the essential elements of economic and political liberalism have been so successfully grafted onto uniquely Japanese traditions and institutions guarantees their survival in the long run. More important is the contribution that Japan has made in turn to world history by following in the footsteps of the United States to create a truly universal consumer culture that has become both a symbol and an underpinning of the universal homogenous state. . . .

Here again we see the victory of the idea of the universal homogenous state. South Korea had developed into a modern, urbanized society with an increasingly large and well-educated middle class that could not possibly be isolated from the larger democratic trends around them. Under these circumstances it seemed intolerable to a large part of this population that it should be ruled by an anachronistic military regime while Japan, only a decade or so ahead in economic terms, had parliamentary institutions for over forty years. . . .

But the power of the liberal idea would seem much less impressive if it had not infected the largest and oldest culture in Asia, China. The simple existence of communist China created an alternative pole of ideological attraction, and as such constituted a threat to liberalism. But the past fifteen years have seen an almost total discrediting of Marxism-Leninism as an economic system. Beginning with the famous third plenum of the Tenth Central Committee in 1978, the Chinese Communist party set about decollectivizing agriculture for the 800 million Chinese who still lived in the countryside. The role of the state in agriculture was reduced to that of a tax collector, while production of consumer goods was sharply increased in order to give peasants a taste of the universal homogenous state and thereby an incentive to work. The reform doubled Chinese grain output in only five years, and in the process created for Deng Xiaoping a solid political base from which he was able to extend the reform to other parts of the economy. Economic Statistics do not begin to describe the dynamism, initiative, and openness evident in China since the reform began. . . .

What is important about China from the standpoint of world history is not the present state of the reform or even its future prospects. The central issue is the fact that the People's Republic of China can no longer act as a beacon for illiberal forces around the world, whether they be guerrillas in some Asian jungle or middle class students in Paris. Maoism, rather than being the pattern for Asia's future, became an anachronism, and it was the mainland Chinese who in fact were decisively influenced by the prosperity and dynamism of their overseas co-ethnics—the ironic ultimate victory of Taiwan.

Important as these changes in China have been, however, it is developments in the Soviet Union—the original "homeland of the world proletariat"—that have put the final nail in the coffin of the Marxist- Leninist alternative to liberal democracy. It should be clear that in terms of formal institutions, not much has changed in the four years since Gorbachev has come to power: free markets and the cooperative movement represent only a small part of the Soviet economy, which remains centrally planned; the political system is still dominated by the Communist party, which has only begun to democratize internally and to share power with other groups; the regime continues to assert that it is seeking only to modernize socialism and that its ideological basis remains Marxism-Leninism; and, finally, Gorbachev faces a potentially powerful conservative opposition that could undo many of the changes that have taken place to date. Moreover, it is hard to be too sanguine about the chances for success of Gorbachev's proposed reforms, either in the sphere of economics or politics. But my purpose here is not to analyze events in the short-term, or to make predictions for policy purposes, but to look at underlying trends in the sphere of ideology and consciousness. And in that respect, it is clear that an astounding transformation has occurred. . . .

What has happened in the four years since Gorbachev's coming to power is a revolutionary assault on the most fundamental institutions and principles of Stalinism, and their replacement by other principles which do not amount to liberalism per se but whose only connecting thread is liberalism. This is most evident in the economic sphere, where the reform economists around Gorbachev have become steadily more radical in their support for free markets. . . . There is a virtual consensus among the currently dominant school of Soviet economists now that central planning and the command system of allocation are the root cause of economic inefficiency, and that if the Soviet system is ever to heal itself, it must permit free and decentralized decision-making with respect to investment, labor, and prices. . . .

The Soviet Union could in no way be described as a liberal or democratic country now, nor do I think that it is terribly likely that perestroika will succeed such that the label will be thinkable any time in the near future. But at the end of history it is not necessary that all societies become successful liberal societies, merely that they end their ideological pretensions of representing different and higher forms of human society. And in this respect I believe that something very important has happened in the Soviet Union in the past few years: the criticisms of the Soviet system sanctioned by Gorbachev have been so thorough and devastating that there is very little chance of going back to either Stalinism or Brezhnevism in any simple way. Gorbachev has finally permitted people to say what they had privately understood for many years, namely, that the magical incantations of Marxism-Leninism were nonsense, that Soviet socialism was not superior to the West in any respect but was in fact a monumental failure. . . .

If we admit for the moment that the fascist and communist challenges to liberalism are dead, are there any other ideological competitors left? Or put another way, are there contradictions in liberal society beyond that of class that are not resolvable? Two possibilities suggest themselves, those of religion and nationalism.

The rise of religious fundamentalism in recent years within the Christian, Jewish, and Muslim traditions has been widely noted. One is inclined to say that the revival of religion in some way attests to a broad unhappiness with the impersonality and spiritual vacuity of liberal consumerist societies. Yet while the emptiness at the core of liberalism is most certainly a defect in the ideology—indeed, a flaw that one does not need the perspective of religion to recognize—it is not at all clear that it is remediable through politics. Modern liberalism itself was historically a consequence of the weakness of religiously-based societies which, failing to agree on the nature of the good life, could not provide even the minimal preconditions of peace and stability. In the contemporary world only Islam has offered a theocratic state as a political alternative to both liberalism and communism. But the doctrine has little appeal for non-Muslims, and it is hard to believe that the movement will take on any universal significance. Other less organized religious impulses have been successfully satisfied within the sphere of personal life that is permitted in liberal societies.

The other major "contradiction" potentially unresolvable by liberalism is the one posed by nationalism and other forms of racial and ethnic consciousness. It is certainly true that a very large degree of conflict since the Battle of Jena has had its roots in nationalism. Two cataclysmic world wars in this century have been spawned by the nationalism of the developed world in various guises, and if those passions have been muted to a certain extent in postwar Europe, they are still extremely powerful in the Third World. Nationalism has been a threat to liberalism historically in Germany, and continues to be one in isolated parts of "post-historical" Europe like Northern Ireland.

But it is not clear that nationalism represents an irreconcilable contradiction in the heart of liberalism. In the first place, nationalism is not one single phenomenon but several, ranging from mild cultural nostalgia to the highly organized and elaborately articulated doctrine of National Socialism. Only systematic nationalisms of the latter sort can qualify as a formal ideology on the level of liberalism or communism. The vast majority of the world's nationalist movements do not have a political program beyond the negative desire of independence from some other group or people, and do not offer anything like a comprehensive agenda for socio-economic organization. As such, they are compatible with doctrines and ideologies that do offer such agendas. While they may constitute a source of conflict for liberal societies, this conflict does not arise from liberalism itself so much as from the fact that the liberalism in question is incomplete. Certainly a great deal of the world's ethnic and nationalist tension can be explained in terms of peoples who are forced to live in unrepresentative political systems that they have not chosen.

While it is impossible to rule out the sudden appearance of new ideologies or previously unrecognized contradictions in liberal societies, then, the present world seems to confirm that the fundamental principles of sociopolitical organization have not advanced terribly far since 1806. Many of the wars and revolutions fought since that time have been undertaken in the name of ideologies which claimed to be more advanced than liberalism, but whose pretensions were ultimately unmasked by history. In the meantime, they have helped to spread the universal homogenous state to the point where it could have a significant effect on the overall character of international relations.

What are the implications of the end of history for international relations? Clearly, the vast bulk of the Third World remains very much mired in history, and will be a terrain of conflict for many years to come. But let us focus for the time being on the larger and more developed states of the world who after all account for the greater part of world politics. Russia and China are not likely to join the developed nations of the West as liberal societies any time in the foreseeable future, but suppose for a moment that Marxism-Leninism ceases to be a factor driving the foreign policies of these states—a prospect which, if not yet here, the last few years have made a real possibility. How will the overall characteristics of a de-ideologized world differ from those of the one with which we are familiar at such a hypothetical juncture?

The most common answer is—not very much. For there is a very widespread belief among many observers of international relations that underneath the skin of ideology is a hard core of great power national interest that guarantees a fairly high level of competition and conflict between nations. Indeed, according to one academically popular school of international relations theory, conflict inheres in the international system as such, and to understand the prospects for conflict one must look at the shape of the system—for example, whether it is bipolar or multipolar—rather than at the specific character of the nations and regimes that constitute it. This school in effect applies a Hobbesian view of politics to international relations, and assumes that aggression and insecurity are universal characteristics of human societies rather than the product of specific historical circumstances. . . .

In fact, the notion that ideology is a superstructure imposed on a substratum of permanent great power interest is a highly questionable proposition. For the way in which any state defines its national interest is not universal but rests on some kind of prior ideological basis, just as we saw that economic behavior is determined by a prior state of consciousness. In this century, states have adopted highly articulated doctrines with explicit foreign policy agendas legitimizing expansionism, like Marxism-Leninism or National Socialism.

The expansionist and competitive behavior of nineteenth-century European states rested on no less ideal a basis; it just so happened that the ideology driving it was less explicit than the doctrines of the twentieth century. For one

thing, most "liberal" European societies were illiberal insofar as they believed in the legitimacy of imperialism, that is, the right of one nation to rule over other nations without regard for the wishes of the ruled. The justifications for imperialism varied from nation to nation, from a crude belief in the legitimacy of force, particularly when applied to non-Europeans, to the White Man's Burden and Europe's Christianizing mission, to the desire to give people of color access to the culture of Rabelais and Moliere. But whatever the particular ideological basis, every "developed" country believed in the acceptability of higher civilizations ruling lower ones—including, incidentally, the United States with regard to the Philippines. This led to a drive for pure territorial aggrandizement in the latter half of the century and played no small role in causing the Great War.

The radical and deformed outgrowth of nineteenth-century imperialism was German fascism, an ideology which justified Germany's right not only to rule over non-European peoples, but over all non-German ones. But in retrospect it seems that Hitler represented a diseased bypath in the general course of European development, and since his fiery defeat, the legitimacy of any kind of territorial aggrandizement has been thoroughly discredited. Since the Second World War, European nationalism has been defanged and shorn of any real relevance to foreign policy, with the consequence that the nineteenth-century model of great power behavior has become a serious anachronism. The most extreme form of nationalism that any Western European state has mustered since 1945 has been Gaullism, whose self-assertion has been confined largely to the realm of nuisance politics and culture. International life for the part of the world that has reached the end of history is far more preoccupied with economics than with politics or strategy.

The developed states of the West do maintain defense establishments and in the postwar period have competed vigorously for influence to meet a worldwide communist threat. This behavior has been driven, however, by an external threat from states that possess overtly expansionist ideologies, and would not exist in their absence. To take the "neo-realist" theory seriously, one would have to believe that "natural" competitive behavior would reassert itself among the OECD states were Russia and China to disappear from the face of the earth. That is, West Germany and France would arm themselves against each other as they did in the 1930s, Australia and New Zealand would send military advisers to block each others' advances in Africa, and the U.S.-Canadian border would become fortified. Such a prospect is, of course, ludicrous: minus Marxist-Leninist ideology, we are far more likely to see the "Common Marketization" of world politics than the disintegration of the EEC into nineteenth-century competitiveness. Indeed, as our experiences in dealing with Europe on matters such as terrorism or Libya prove, they are much further gone than we down the road that denies the legitimacy of the use of force in international politics, even in self- defense. . . .

The real question for the future, however, is the degree to which Soviet elites have assimilated the consciousness of the universal homogenous state that is post-Hitler Europe. From their writings and from my own personal contacts with them, there is no question in my mind that the liberal Soviet intelligentsia rallying around Gorbachev have arrived at the end-of-history view in a remarkably short time, due in no small measure to the contacts they have had since the Brezhnev era with the larger European civilization around them. "New political thinking," the general rubric for their views, describes a world dominated by economic concerns, in which there are no ideological grounds for major conflict between nations, and in which, consequently, the use of military force becomes less legitimate. . . .

The Soviet Union, then, is at a fork in the road: it can start down the path that was staked out by Western Europe forty-five years ago, a path that most of Asia has followed, or it can realize its own uniqueness and remain stuck in history. The choice it makes will be highly important for us, given the Soviet Union's size and military strength, for that power will continue to preoccupy us and slow our realization that we have already emerged on the other side of history.

The passing of Leninism first from China and then from the Soviet Union will mean its death as a living ideology of world historical significance. For while there may be some isolated true believers left in places like Managua, Pyongyang, or Cambridge, Massachusetts, the fact that there is not a single large state in which it is a going concern undermines completely its pretensions to being in the vanguard of human history. And the death of this ideology means the growing "Common Marketization" of international relations, and the diminution of the likelihood of large-scale conflict between states.

This does not by any means imply the end of international conflict per se. For the world at that point would be divided between a part that was historical and a part that was post-historical. Conflict between states still in history, and between those states and those at the end of history, would still be possible. There would still be a high and perhaps rising level of ethnic and nationalist violence, since those are impulses incompletely played out, even in parts of the post-historical world. Palestinians and Kurds, Sikhs and Tamils, Irish Catholics and Walloons, Armenians and Azeris, will continue to have their unresolved grievances. This implies that terrorism and wars of national liberation will continue to be an important item on the international agenda. But large-scale conflict must involve large states still caught in the grip of history, and they are what appear to be passing from the scene.

The end of history will be a very sad time. The struggle for recognition, the willingness to risk one's life for a purely abstract goal, the worldwide ideological struggle that called forth daring, courage, imagination, and idealism, will be replaced by economic calculation, the endless solving of technical problems, environmental concerns, and the satisfaction of sophisticated consumer demands. In the post-historical period there will be neither art nor philosophy, just the perpetual caretaking of the museum of human history. I can feel in myself, and see in others around me, a powerful nostalgia for the time when history existed. Such nostalgia, in fact, will continue to fuel competition and conflict even in the post-historical world for some time to come. Even though I recognize its inevitability, I have the most ambivalent feelings for the civilization that has been created in Europe since

1945, with its north Atlantic and Asian off-shoots. Perhaps this very prospect of centuries of boredom at the end of history will serve to get history started once again.

CHARLES KRAUTHAMMER, "THE UNIPOLAR MOMENT," *FOREIGN AFFAIRS* (AMERICA AND THE WORLD 1990/1991)

Fukuyama's was only the first such explanation. According to the journalist Charles Krauthammer (1950–), the United States was now the top dog. As such, it needed to lay down the rules and to enforce them.

Ever since it became clear that an exhausted Soviet Union was calling off the Cold War, the quest has been on for a new American role in the world. Roles, however, are not invented in the abstract; they are a response to a perceived world structure.

Accordingly, thinking about post-Cold War American foreign policy has been framed by several conventionally accepted assumptions about the shape of the post-Cold War environment.

First, it has been assumed that the old bipolar world would beget a multipolar world with power dispersed to new centers in Japan, Germany (and/or "Europe"), China and a diminished Soviet Union/Russia. Second, that the domestic American consensus for an internationalist foreign policy, a consensus radically weakened by the experience in Vietnam, would substantially be restored now that policies and debates inspired by "an inordinate fear of communism" could be safely retired. Third, that in the new post-Soviet strategic environment the threat of war would be dramatically diminished.

All three of these assumptions are mistaken. The immediate post-Cold War world is not multipolar. It is unipolar. The center of world power is the unchallenged superpower, the United States, attended by its Western allies. Second, the internationalist consensus is under renewed assault. The assault this time comes not only from the usual pockets of post-Vietnam liberal isolationism (e.g., the churches) but from a resurgence of 1930s-style conservative isolationism. And third, the emergence of a new strategic environment, marked by the rise of small aggressive states armed with weapons of mass destruction and possessing the means to deliver them (what might be called

Weapon States), makes the coming decades a time of heightened, not diminished, threat of war.

The most striking feature of the post-Cold War world is its unipolarity. No doubt, multipolarity will come in time. In perhaps another generation or so there will be great powers coequal with the United States, and the world will, in structure, resemble the pre-World War I era. But we are not there yet, nor will we be for decades. Now is the unipolar moment.

There is today no lack of second-rank powers. Germany and Japan are economic dynamos. Britain and France can deploy diplomatic and to some extent military assets. The Soviet Union possesses several elements of power—military, diplomatic and political—but all are in rapid decline. There is but one first-rate power and no prospect in the immediate future of any power to rival it.

Only a few months ago it was conventional wisdom that the new rivals, the great pillars of the new multipolar world, would be Japan and Germany (and/or Europe). How quickly a myth can explode. The notion that economic power inevitably translates into geopolitical influence is a materialist illusion. Economic power is a necessary condition for great power status. But it certainly is not sufficient, as has been made clear by the recent behavior of Germany and Japan, which have generally hidden under the table since the first shots rang out in Kuwait. And while a unified Europe may sometime in the next century act as a single power, its initial disarray and disjointed national responses to the crisis in the Persian Gulf again illustrate that "Europe" does not yet qualify even as a player on the world stage.

Which leaves us with the true geopolitical structure of the post-Cold War world, brought sharply into focus by the gulf crisis: a single pole of world power that consists of the United States at the apex of the industrial West. Perhaps it is more accurate to say the United States and behind it the West, because where the United States does not tread, the alliance does not follow. That was true for the reflagging of Kuwaiti vessels in 1987. It has been all the more true of the world's subsequent response to the invasion of Kuwait.

American preeminence is based on the fact that it is the only country with the military, diplomatic, political and economic assets to be a decisive player in any conflict in whatever part of the world it chooses to involve itself. In the Persian Gulf, for example, it was the United States, acting unilaterally and with extraordinary speed, that in August 1990 prevented Iraq from taking effective control of the entire Arabian Peninsula.

Iraq, having inadvertently revealed the unipolar structure of today's world, cannot stop complaining about it. It looks at allied and Soviet support for American action in the gulf and speaks of a conspiracy of North against South. Although it is perverse for Iraqi leader Saddam Hussein to claim to represent the South, his analysis does contain some truth. The unipolar moment means that with the close of the century's three great Northern civil wars (World War I, World War II and the Cold War) an ideologically pacified North seeks security and order by aligning its foreign policy behind that of the United States. That is what is taking shape now in the Persian Gulf. And for the near future, it is the shape of things to come.

The Iraqis are equally acute in demystifying the much celebrated multilateralism of this new world order. They charge that the entire multilateral apparatus (United Nations resolutions, Arab troops, European Community pronouncements, and so on) established in the gulf by the United States is but a transparent cover for what is essentially an American challenge to Iraqi regional hegemony.

But of course. There is much pious talk about a new multilateral world and the promise of the United Nations as guarantor of a new post-Cold War order. But this is to mistake cause and effect, the United States and the United Nations. The United Nations is guarantor of nothing. Except in a formal sense, it can hardly be said to exist. Collective security? In the gulf, without the United States leading and prodding, bribing and blackmailing, no one would have stirred. Nothing would have been done: no embargo, no "Desert Shield," no threat of force. The world would have written off Kuwait the way the last body pledged to collective security, the League of Nations, wrote off Abyssinia.

There is a sharp distinction to be drawn between real and apparent multilateralism. True multilateralism involves a genuine coalition of coequal partners of comparable strength and stature—the World War II Big Three coalition, for example. What we have today is pseudo-multilateralism: a dominant great power acts essentially alone, but, embarrassed at the idea and still worshiping at the shrine of collective security, recruits a ship here, a brigade there, and blessings all around to give its unilateral actions a multilateral sheen. The gulf is no more a collective operation than was Korea, still the classic case study in pseudo-multilateralism.

Why the pretense? Because a large segment of American opinion doubts the legitimacy of unilateral American action but accepts quite readily actions undertaken by the "world community" acting in concert. Why it should matter to Americans that their actions get a Security Council nod from, say, Deng Xiaoping and the butchers of Tiananmen Square is beyond me. But to many Americans it matters. It is largely for domestic reasons, therefore, that American political leaders make sure to dress unilateral action in multilateral clothing. The danger, of course, is that they might come to believe their own pretense.

But can America long sustain its unipolar preeminence? The spectacle of secretaries of state and treasury flying around the world rattling tin cups to support America's Persian Gulf deployment exposed the imbalance between America's geopolitical reach and its resources. Does that not imply that the theorists of American decline and "imperial overstretch" are right and that unipolarity is unsustainable?

It is, of course, true that if America succeeds in running its economy into the ground, it will not be able to retain its unipolar role for long. In which case the unipolar moment will be brief indeed (one decade, perhaps, rather than, say, three or four). But if the economy is run into the ground it will not be because of imperial overstretch, i.e., because America has overreached abroad and drained itself with geopolitical entanglements. The United States today spends 5.4 percent of its GNP on defense. Under John F. Kennedy, when the United States was at its economic and political apogee, it spent almost twice as much. Administration plans have U.S. defense spending on a trajectory down to four percent by 1995, the lowest since Pearl Harbor.

An American collapse to second-rank status will be not for foreign but for domestic reasons. This is not the place to engage in extended debate about the cause of America's economic difficulties. But the notion that we have spent ourselves into penury abroad is simply not sustainable. America's low savings rate, poor educational system, stagnant productivity, declining work habits, rising demand for welfare-state entitlements and new taste for ecological luxuries have nothing at all to do with engagement in Europe, Central America or the Middle East. Over the last thirty years, while taxes remained almost fixed (rising from 18.3 percent to 19.6 percent) and defense spending declined, domestic entitlements nearly doubled. What created an economy of debt unrivaled in American history is not foreign adventures but the low tax ideology of the 1980s, coupled with America's insatiable desire for yet higher standards of living without paying any of the cost.

One can debate whether America is in true economic decline. Its percentage of world GNP is roughly where it has been throughout the twentieth century (between 22 and 26 percent), excepting the aberration of the immediate post–World War II era when its competitors were digging out from the rubble of war. But even if one does argue that America is in economic decline, it is simply absurd to imply that the road to solvency is to, say, abandon El Salvador, evacuate the Philippines or get out of the gulf. There may be other good reasons for doing all of these. But it is nonsense to suggest doing them as a way to get at the root of America's economic problems.

It is, moreover, a mistake to view America's exertions abroad as nothing but a drain on its economy. As can be seen in the gulf, America's involvement abroad is in many ways an essential pillar of the American economy. The United States is, like Britain before it, a commercial, maritime, trading nation that needs an open, stable world environment in which to thrive. In a world of Saddams, if the United States were to shed its unique superpower role, its economy would be gravely wounded.

Insecure sea lanes, impoverished trading partners, exorbitant oil prices, explosive regional instability are only the more obvious risks of an American abdication. Foreign entanglements are indeed a burden. But they are also a necessity. The cost of ensuring an open and safe world for American commerce—5.4 percent of GNP and falling—is hardly exorbitant.

Can America support its unipolar status? Yes. But *will* Americans support such unipolar status? That is a more problematic question. For a small but growing chorus of Americans this vision of a unipolar world led by a dynamic America is a nightmare. Hence the second major element of the post–Cold War reality: the revival of American isolationism.

I have great respect for American isolationism. First, because of its popular appeal and, second, because of its natural appeal. On the face of it, isolationism seems the logical, God-given foreign policy for the United States. It is not just geography that inclines us to it—we are an island continent protected by two vast oceans, bordered by two neighbors that could hardly be friendlier—but history. America was founded on the idea of cleansing itself of the intrigues and irrationalities, the dynastic squabbles and religious wars, of the Old World. One must have respect for a strain of American thinking so powerful that four months before Pearl Harbor the vote to extend draft enlistments passed the House of Representatives by a single vote.

Isolationists say rather unobjectionably that America should confine its attentions in the world to defending vital national interests. But the more extreme isolationists define vital national interests to mean the physical security of the United States, and the more elusive isolationists take care never to define them at all.

Isolationists will, of course, say that this is unfair, that they do believe in defending vital national interests beyond the physical security of the United States. We have a test case. Iraq's invasion of Kuwait and hegemonic designs on Arabia posed as clear a threat to American interests as one can imagine—a threat to America's oil-based economy, to its close allies in the region, and ultimately to American security itself. The rise of a hostile power, fueled by endless oil income, building weapons of mass destruction and the means to deliver them regionally and eventually intercontinentally (Saddam has already tested a three-stage rocket) can hardly be a matter of indifference to the United States.

If under these conditions a cadre of influential liberals and conservatives finds that upon reflection (and in contradiction to the doctrine enunciated by the most dovish president of the postwar era, Jimmy Carter) the Persian Gulf is not, after all, a vital American interest, then it is hard to see what "vital interest" can mean. If the Persian Gulf is not a vital interest, then nothing is. All that is left is preventing an invasion of the Florida Keys. And for that you need a Coast Guard—you do not need a Pentagon and you certainly do not need a State Department.

Isolationism is the most extreme expression of the American desire to return to tend its vineyards. But that desire finds expression in another far more sophisticated and serious foreign policy school: not isolationism but realism, the school that insists that American foreign policy be guided solely by interests and that generally defines these interests in a narrow and national manner.

Many of realism's practitioners were heroic in the heroic struggles against fascism and communism. Now, however, some argue that the time for heroism is passed. For example, Jeane J. Kirkpatrick wrote, to be sure before the gulf crisis, that "It is time to give up the dubious benefits of superpower status," time to give up the "unusual burdens" of the past and "return to 'normal' times." That means taking "care of pressing problems of education, family, industry and technology" at home. That means that we should not try to be the balancer of power in Europe or in Asia, nor try to shape the political evolution of the Soviet Union. We should aspire instead to be "a normal country in a normal time.'"

This is a rather compelling vision of American purpose. But I am not sure there is such a thing as normal times. If a normal time is a time when there is no evil world empire on the loose, when the world is in ideological repose, then even such a time is not necessarily peacetime. Saddam has made this point rather emphatically. If a normal time is a time when the world sorts itself out on its own, leaving America relatively unmolested— say, for America, the nineteenth century—then I would suggest that there are no normal times. The world does not sort itself out on its own. In the nineteenth century, for example, international stability was not achieved on its own but, in large part, as the product of Britain's unrelenting exertions on behalf of the balance of power. America tended her vineyards, but only behind two great ocean walls patrolled by the British navy. Alas, the British navy is gone.

International stability is never a given. It is never the norm. When achieved, it is the product of self-conscious action by the great powers, and most particularly of the greatest power, which now and for the foreseeable future is the United States. If America wants stability, it will have to create it. Communism is indeed finished; the last of the messianic creeds that have haunted this century is quite dead. But there will constantly be new threats disturbing our peace.

What threats? Everyone recognizes one great change in the international environment, the collapse of communism. If that were the only change, then this might be a normal time and the unipolar vision I have outlined would seem at once unnecessary and dangerous.

But there is another great change in international relations. And here we come to the third and most crucial new element in the post-Cold War world: the emergence of a new strategic environment marked by the proliferation of weapons of mass destruction. It is a certainty that in the near future there will be a dramatic increase in the number of states armed with biological, chemical and nuclear weapons and the means to deliver them anywhere on earth. "By the year 2000," estimates Defense Secretary Dick Cheney, "more than two dozen developing nations will have ballistic missiles, 15 of those countries will have the scientific skills to make their own, and half of them either have or are near to getting nuclear capability, as well. Thirty countries will have chemical weapons and ten will be able to deploy biological weapons."

It is of course banal to say that modern technology has shrunk the world. But the obvious corollary, that in a shrunken world the divide between regional superpowers and great powers is radically narrowed, is rarely drawn. Missiles shrink distance. Nuclear (or chemical or biological) devices multiply power. Both can be bought at market. Consequently the geopolitical map is irrevocably altered. Fifty years ago, Germany— centrally located, highly industrial and heavily populated—could pose a threat to world security and to the other great powers. It was inconceivable that a relatively small Middle Eastern state with an almost entirely imported industrial base could do anything more than threaten its neighbors. The central truth of the coming era is that this is no longer the case: relatively small, peripheral and backward states will be able to emerge rapidly as threats not only to regional, but to world, security.

Iraq, which (unless disarmed by Desert Storm) will likely be in possession of intercontinental missiles within the decade, is the prototype of this new strategic threat, what might be called the "Weapon State." . . .

The current Weapon States have deep grievances against the West and the world order that it has established and enforces. They are therefore subversive of the international status quo, which they see as a residue of colonialism. These resentments fuel an obsessive drive to high-tech military development as the only way to leapfrog history and to place themselves on a footing from which to challenge a Western-imposed order.

The Weapon State need not be an oil state. North Korea, hard at work on nuclear technology, is a candidate Weapon State: it has about as much legitimacy as a nation-state as the German Democratic Republic; its state apparatus totally dominates civil society by virtue not of oil but of an exquisitely developed Stalinism; its anti-Western grievances run deep.

The danger from the Weapon State is posed today by Iraq, tomorrow perhaps by North Korea or Libya. In the next century, however, the proliferation of strategic weapons will not be restricted to Weapon States. Windfall wealth allows oil states to import high-technology weapons in the absence of a mature industrial base. However, it is not hard to imagine maturer states—say, Argentina, Pakistan, Iran, South Africa—reaching the same level of weapons development by means of ordinary industrialization. (Today most of these countries are friendly, but some are unstable and potentially hostile.)

The post-Cold War era is thus perhaps better called the era of weapons of mass destruction. The proliferation of weapons of mass destruction and their means of delivery will constitute the greatest single threat to world security for the rest of our lives. That is what makes a new international order not an imperial dream or a Wilsonian fantasy but a matter of the sheerest prudence. It is slowly dawning on the West that there is a need to establish some new regime to police these weapons and those who brandish them. . . .

To do what exactly? There is no definitive answer, but any solution will have to include three elements: denying, disarming, and defending. . . .

There might be better tactics, but the overall strategy is clear. With the rise of the Weapon State, there is no alternative to confronting, deterring and, if necessary, disarming states that brandish and use weapons of mass destruction. And there is no one to do that but the United States, backed by as many allies as will join the endeavor.

The alternative to such robust and difficult interventionism—the alternative to unipolarity— is not a stable, static multipolar world. It is not an eighteenth-century world in which mature powers like Europe, Russia, China, America, and Japan jockey for position in the game of nations. The alternative to unipolarity is chaos.

I do not mean to imply that weapons of mass destruction are the only threat facing the post-Cold War world. They are only the most obvious. Other threats exist, but they are more speculative and can be seen today only in outline: the rise, for example, of intolerant aggressive nationalism in a disintegrating communist bloc (in one extreme formulation, the emergence of a reduced but resurgent, xenophobic and resentful "Weimar" Russia). And some threats to the peace of the 21st century are as invisible today as was, say, Nazism in 1920. They will make themselves known soon enough. Only a hopeless utopian can believe otherwise.

We are in for abnormal times. Our best hope for safety in such times, as in difficult times past, is in American strength and will—the strength and will to lead a unipolar world, unashamedly laying down the rules of world order and being prepared to enforce them. Compared to the task of defeating fascism and communism, averting chaos is a rather subtle call to greatness. It is not a task we are any more eager to undertake than the great twilight struggle just concluded. But it is just as noble and just as necessary.

SAMUEL HUNTINGTON, "THE CLASH OF CIVILIZATIONS?" *FOREIGN AFFAIRS* (SUMMER 1993)

A renowned political scientist at Harvard, Samuel Huntington (1927–2008) saw a more daunting future, with new sources of conflict emerging in the Cold War's wake.

World politics is entering a new phase, and intellectuals have not hesitated to proliferate visions of what it will be—the end of history, the return of traditional rivalries between nation states, and the decline of the nation state from the conflicting pulls of tribalism and globalism, among others. Each of these visions catches aspects of the emerging reality. Yet they all miss a crucial, indeed a central, aspect of what global politics is likely to be in the coming years.

It is my hypothesis that the fundamental source of conflict in this new world will not be primarily ideological or primarily economic. The great divisions among humankind and the dominating source of conflict will be cultural. Nation states will remain the most powerful actors in world affairs, but the principal conflicts of global politics will occur between nations and groups of different civilizations. The clash of civilizations will dominate global politics. The fault lines between civilizations will be the battle lines of the future.

Conflict between civilizations will be the latest phase in the evolution of conflict in the modern world. For a century and a half after the emergence of the modern international system with the Peace of Westphalia, the conflicts of the Western world were largely among princes—emperors, absolute monarchs and constitutional monarchs attempting to expand their bureaucracies, their armies, their mercantilist economic strength and, most important, the territory they ruled. In the process they created nation states, and beginning with the French Revolution the principal lines of conflict were between nations rather than princes. In 1793, as R. R. Palmer put it, "The wars of kings were over; the wars of peoples had begun." This nineteenth-century pattern lasted until the end of World War I. Then, as a result of the Russian Revolution and the reaction against it, the conflict of nations yielded to the conflict of ideologies, first among communism, fascism–Nazism and liberal democracy, and then between communism and liberal democracy. During the Cold War, this latter conflict became embodied in the struggle between the two superpowers, neither of which was a nation state in the classical European sense and each of which defined its identity in terms of its ideology.

These conflicts between princes, nation states and ideologies were primarily conflicts within Western civilization, "Western civil wars," as William Lind has labeled them. This was as true of the Cold War as it was of the world wars and the earlier wars of the seventeenth, eighteenth and nineteenth centuries. With the end of the Cold War, international politics moves out of its Western phase, and its centerpiece becomes the interaction between the West and non-Western civilizations and among non-Western civilizations. In the politics of civilizations, the peoples and governments of non-Western civilizations no longer remain the objects of history as targets of Western colonialism but join the West as movers and shapers of history.

During the Cold War the world was divided into the First, Second and Third Worlds. Those divisions are no longer relevant. It is far more meaningful now to group countries not in terms of their political or economic systems or in terms of their level of economic development but rather in terms of their culture and civilization.

What do we mean when we talk of a civilization? A civilization is a cultural entity. Villages, regions, ethnic groups, nationalities, religious groups, all have distinct cultures at different levels of cultural heterogeneity. The culture of a village in southern Italy may be different from that of a village in northern Italy, but both will share in a common Italian culture that distinguishes them from German villages. European communities, in turn, will share cultural features that distinguish them from Arab or Chinese communities. Arabs, Chinese and Westerners, however, are not part of any broader cultural entity. They constitute civilizations. A civilization is thus the highest cultural grouping of people and the broadest level of cultural identity people have short of that which distinguishes humans from other species. It is defined both by common objective elements, such as language, history, religion, customs, institutions, and by the subjective self-identification of people. People have levels of identity: a resident of Rome may define himself with varying degrees of intensity as a Roman, an Italian, a Catholic, a Christian, a European, a Westerner. The civilization to which he belongs is the broadest level of identification with which he intensely identifies. People can and do redefine their identities and, as a result, the composition and boundaries of civilizations change.

Civilizations may involve a large number of people, as with China ("a civilization pretending to be a state," as Lucian Pye put it), or a very small number of people, such as the Anglophone Caribbean. A civilization may include several nation states, as is the case with Western, Latin American and Arab civilizations, or only one, as is the case with Japanese civilization. Civilizations obviously blend and overlap, and may include sub-civilizations. Western civilization has two major variants, European and North American, and Islam has its Arab, Turkic and Malay subdivisions. Civilizations are nonetheless meaningful entities, and while the lines between them are seldom sharp, they are real. Civilizations are dynamic; they rise and fall; they divide and merge. And, as any student of history knows, civilizations disappear and are buried in the sands of time.

Westerners tend to think of nation states as the principal actors in global affairs. They have been that, however, for only a few centuries. The broader reaches of human history have been the history of civilizations. In *A Study of History*, Arnold Toynbee identified 21 major civilizations; only six of them exist in the contemporary world.

Civilization identity will be increasingly important in the future, and the world will be shaped in large measure by the interactions among seven or eight major civilizations. These include Western, Confucian, Japanese, Islamic, Hindu, Slavic-Orthodox, Latin American and possibly African civilization. The most important conflicts of the future will occur along the cultural fault lines separating these civilizations from one another.

Why will this be the case?

First, differences among civilizations are not only real; they are basic. Civilizations are differentiated from each other by language, culture, tradition and, most important, religion. The people of different civilizations have different views on the relations between God and man, the individual and the group, the citizen and the state, parents and children, husband and wife, as well as differing views of the relative importance of rights and responsibilities, liberty and authority, equality and hierarchy. These differences are the product of centuries. They will not soon disappear. They are far more fundamental than differences among political ideologies and political regimes. Differences do not necessarily mean conflict, and conflict does not necessarily mean violence. Over the centuries, however, differences among civilizations have generated the most prolonged and the most violent conflicts.

Second, the world is becoming a smaller place. The interactions between peoples of different civilizations are increasing; these increasing interactions intensify civilization consciousness and awareness of differences between civilizations and commonalities within civilizations. North African immigration to France generates hostility among Frenchmen and at the same time increased receptivity to immigration by "good" European Catholic Poles. Americans react far more negatively to Japanese investment than to larger investments from Canada and European countries. Similarly, as Donald Horowitz has pointed out, "An Ibo may be . . . an Owerri Ibo or an Onitsha Ibo in what was the Eastern region of Nigeria. In Lagos, he is simply an Ibo. In London, he is a Nigerian. In New York, he is an African." The interactions among peoples of different civilizations enhance the civilization-consciousness of people that, in turn, invigorates differences and animosities stretching or thought to stretch back deep into history. Third, the processes of economic modernization and social change throughout the world are separating people from longstanding local identities. They also weaken the nation state as a source of identity. In much of the world religion has moved in to fill this gap, often in the form of movements that are labeled "fundamentalist." Such movements are found in Western Christianity, Judaism, Buddhism and Hinduism, as well as in Islam. In most countries and most religions the people active in fundamentalist movements are young, college-educated, middle-class technicians, professionals and business persons. The "unsecularization of the world," George Weigel has remarked, "is one of the dominant social facts of life in the late twentieth century." The revival of religion, "la revanche de Dieu," as Gilles Kepel labeled it, provides a basis for identity and commitment that transcends national boundaries and unites civilizations.

Fourth, the growth of civilization-consciousness is enhanced by the dual role of the West. On the one hand, the West is at a peak of power. At the same time, however, and perhaps as a result, a return to the roots phenomenon is occurring among non-Western civilizations. Increasingly one hears references to trends toward a turning inward and "Asianization" in Japan, the end of the Nehru legacy and the "Hinduization" of India, the failure of Western ideas of socialism and nationalism and hence "re-Islamization" of the Middle East, and now a debate over Westernization versus Russianization in Boris Yeltsin's country. A West at the peak of its power confronts non-Wests that increasingly have the desire, the will and the resources to shape the world in non-Western ways.

In the past, the elites of non-Western societies were usually the people who were most involved with the West, had been educated at Oxford, the Sorbonne or Sandhurst, and had absorbed Western attitudes and values. At the same time, the populace in non-Western countries often remained deeply imbued with the indigenous culture. Now, however, these relationships are being reversed. A de-Westernization and indigenization of elites is occurring in many non-Western countries at the same time that Western, usually American, cultures, styles and habits become more popular among the mass of the people.

Fifth, cultural characteristics and differences are less mutable and hence less easily compromised and resolved than political and economic ones. In the former Soviet Union, communists can become democrats, the rich can become poor and the poor rich, but Russians cannot become Estonians and Azeris cannot become Armenians. In class and ideological conflicts, the key question was "Which side are you on?" and people could and did choose sides and change sides. In conflicts between civilizations, the question is "What are you?" That is a given that cannot be changed. And as we know, from Bosnia to the Caucasus to the Sudan, the wrong answer to that question can mean a bullet in the head. Even more than ethnicity, religion dis-criminates sharply and exclusively among people. A person can be half-French and half-Arab and simultaneously even a citizen of two countries. It is more difficult to be half-Catholic and half-Muslim.

Finally, economic regionalism is increasing. The proportions of total trade that were intra-regional rose between 1980 and 1989 from 51 percent to 59 percent in Europe, 33 percent to 37 percent in East Asia, and 32 percent to 36 percent in North America. The importance of regional economic blocs is likely to continue to increase in the future. On the one hand, successful economic regionalism will reinforce civilization-consciousness. On the other hand, economic regionalism may succeed only when it is rooted in a common civilization. The European Community rests on the shared foundation of European culture and Western Christianity. The success of the North American Free Trade Area depends on the convergence now underway of Mexican, Canadian and American cultures. Japan, in contrast, faces difficulties in creating a comparable economic entity in East Asia because Japan is a society and civilization unique to itself However strong the trade and investment links Japan may develop with other East Asian countries, its cultural differences with those countries inhibit and perhaps preclude its promoting regional economic integration like that in Europe and North America.

Common culture, in contrast, is clearly facilitating the rapid expansion of the economic relations between the People's Republic of China and Hong Kong, Taiwan, Singapore and the overseas Chinese communities in other Asian countries. With the Cold War over, cultural commonalities increasingly overcome ideological differences, and mainland China and Taiwan move closer together. If cultural commonality is a prerequisite for economic integration, the principal East Asian economic bloc of the future is likely to be centered on China. This bloc is, in fact, already coming into existence. . . .

Culture and religion also form the basis of the Economic Cooperation Organization, which brings together ten non-Arab Muslim countries: Iran, Pakistan, Turkey, Azerbaijan, Kazakhstan, Kyrgyzstan, Turkmenistan, Tadjikistan, Uzbekistan and Afghanistan. One impetus to the revival and expansion of this organization, founded originally in the 1960s by Turkey, Pakistan and Iran, is the realization by the leaders of several of these countries that they had no chance of admission to the European Community. . . .

As people define their identity in ethnic and religious terms, they are likely to see an "us" versus "them" relation existing between themselves and people of different ethnicity or religion. The end of ideologically defined states in Eastern Europe and the former Soviet Union permits traditional ethnic identities and animosities to come to the fore. Differences in culture and religion create differences over policy issues, ranging from human rights to immigration to trade and commerce to the environment. Geographical propinquity gives rise to conflicting territorial claims from Bosnia to Mindanao. Most important, the efforts of the West to promote its values of democracy and liberalism as universal values, to maintain its military predominance and to advance its economic interests engender countering responses from other

civilizations. Decreasingly able to mobilize support and form coalitions on the basis of ideology, governments and groups will increasingly attempt to mobilize support by appealing to common religion and civilization identity.

The clash of civilizations thus occurs at two levels. At the micro-level, adjacent groups along the fault lines between civilizations struggle, often violently, over the control of territory and each other. At the macro-level, states from different civilizations compete for relative military and economic power, struggle over the control of international institutions and third parties, and competitively promote their particular political and religious values.

The fault lines between civilizations are replacing the political and ideological boundaries of the Cold War as the flashpoints for crisis and bloodshed. The Cold War began when the Iron Curtain divided Europe politically and ideologically. The Cold War ended with the end of the Iron Curtain. As the ideological division of Europe has disappeared, the cultural division of Europe between Western Christianity, on the one hand, and Orthodox Christianity and Islam, on the other, has reemerged. The most significant dividing line in Europe, as William Wallace has suggested, may well be the eastern boundary of Western Christianity in the year 1500. This line runs along what are now the boundaries between Finland and Russia and between the Baltic states and Russia, cuts through Belarus and Ukraine separating the more Catholic western Ukraine from Orthodox eastern Ukraine, swings westward separating Transylvania from the rest of Romania, and then goes through Yugoslavia almost exactly along the line now separating Croatia and Slovenia from the rest of Yugoslavia. In the Balkans this line, of course, coincides with the historic boundary between the Hapsburg and Ottoman empires. The peoples to the north and west of this line are Protestant or Catholic; they shared the common experiences of European history—feudalism, the Renaissance, the Reformation, the Enlightenment, the French Revolution, the Industrial Revolution; they are generally economically better off than the peoples to the east; and they may now look forward to increasing involvement in a common European economy and to the consolidation of democratic political systems. The peoples to the east and south of this line are Orthodox or Muslim; they historically belonged to the Ottoman or Tsarist empires and were only lightly touched by the shaping events in the rest of Europe; they are generally less advanced economically; they seem much less likely to develop stable democratic political systems. The Velvet Curtain of culture has replaced the Iron Curtain of ideology as the most significant dividing line in Europe. As the events in Yugoslavia show, it is not only a line of difference; it is also at times a line of bloody conflict.

Conflict along the fault line between Western and Islamic civilizations has been going on for 1,300 years. After the founding of Islam, the Arab and Moorish surge west and north only ended at Tours in 732. From the eleventh to the thirteenth century the Crusaders attempted with temporary success to bring Christianity and Christian rule to the Holy Land. From the fourteenth to the seventeenth century, the Ottoman Turks reversed the balance, extended their sway over the Middle East and the Balkans, captured Constantinople, and twice laid siege to Vienna. In the nineteenth and early twentieth centuries as Ottoman power declined Britain, France, and Italy established Western control over most of North Africa and the Middle East.

After World War II, the West, in turn, began to retreat; the colonial empires disappeared; first Arab nationalism and then Islamic fundamentalism manifested themselves; the West became heavily dependent on the Persian Gulf countries for its energy; the oil-rich Muslim countries became money-rich and, when they wished to, weapons-rich. Several wars occurred between Arabs and Israel (created by the West). France fought a bloody and ruthless war in Algeria for most of the 1950s; British and French forces invaded Egypt in 1956; American forces went into Lebanon in 1958; subsequently American forces returned to Lebanon, attacked Libya, and engaged in various military encounters with Iran; Arab and Islamic terrorists, supported by at least three Middle Eastern governments, employed the weapon of the weak and bombed Western planes and installations and seized Western hostages. This warfare between Arabs and the West culminated in 1990, when the United States sent a massive army to the Persian Gulf to defend some Arab countries against aggression by another. In its aftermath NATO planning is increasingly

directed to potential threats and instability along its "southern tier."

This centuries-old military interaction between the West and Islam is unlikely to decline. It could become more virulent. The Gulf War left some Arabs feeling proud that Saddam Hussein had attacked Israel and stood up to the West. It also left many feeling humiliated and resentful of the West's military presence in the Persian Gulf, the West's overwhelming military dominance, and their apparent inability to shape their own destiny. Many Arab countries, in addition to the oil exporters, are reaching levels of economic and social development where autocratic forms of government become inappropriate and efforts to introduce democracy become stronger. Some openings in Arab political systems have already occurred. The principal beneficiaries of these openings have been Islamist movements. In the Arab world, in short, Western democracy strengthens anti-Western political forces. This may be a passing phenomenon, but it surely complicates relations between Islamic countries and the West.

Those relations are also complicated by demography. The spectacular population growth in Arab countries, particularly in North Africa, has led to increased migration to Western Europe. The movement within Western Europe toward minimizing internal boundaries has sharpened political sensitivities with respect to this development. In Italy, France and Germany, racism is increasingly open, and political reactions and violence against Arab and Turkish migrants have become more intense and more widespread since 1990.

On both sides the interaction between Islam and the West is seen as a clash of civilizations. The West's "next confrontation," observes M. J. Akbar, an Indian Muslim author, "is definitely going to come from the Muslim world. It is in the sweep of the Islamic nations from the Maghreb to Pakistan that the struggle for a new world order will begin." Bernard Lewis comes to a similar conclusion:

> We are facing a mood and a movement far transcending the level of issues and policies and the governments that pursue them. This is no less than a clash of civilizations—the perhaps irrational but surely historic reaction of an ancient rival against our Judeo-Christian heritage, our secular present, and the worldwide expansion of both.

Historically, the other great antagonistic inter-action of Arab Islamic civilization has been with the pagan, animist, and now increasingly Christian black peoples to the south. In the past, this antagonism was epitomized in the image of Arab slave dealers and black slaves. It has been reflected in the on-going civil war in the Sudan between Arabs and blacks, the fight-ing in Chad between Libyan-supported insur-gents and the government, the tensions between Orthodox Christians and Muslims in the Horn of Africa, and the political conflicts, recurring riots and communal violence between Muslims and Christians in Nigeria. The modernization of Africa and the spread of Christianity are likely to enhance the probability of violence along this fault line. Symptomatic of the intensifica-tion of this conflict was the Pope John Paul II's speech in Khartoum in February 1993 attacking the actions of the Sudan's Islamist government against the Christian minority there.

On the northern border of Islam, conflict has increasingly erupted between Orthodox and Muslim peoples, including the carnage of Bosnia and Sarajevo, the simmering violence between Serb and Albanian, the tenuous relations between Bulgarians and their Turkish minority, the vio-lence between Ossetians and Ingush, the unre-mitting slaughter of each other by Armenians and Azeris, the tense relations between Russians and Muslims in Central Asia, and the deployment of Russian troops to protect Russian interests in the Caucasus and Central Asia. Religion reinforces the revival of ethnic identities and restimulates Russian fears about the security of their southern borders. . . .

The conflict of civilizations is deeply rooted elsewhere in Asia. The historic clash between Muslim and Hindu in the subcontinent mani-fests itself now not only in the rivalry between Pakistan and India but also in intensifying reli-gious strife within India between increasingly militant Hindu groups and India's substantial Muslim minority. The destruction of the Ayodhya mosque in December 1992 brought to the fore the issue of whether India will remain a secu-lar democratic state or become a Hindu one. In East Asia, China has territorial disputes with most of its neighbors. It has pursued a ruthless policy toward the Buddhist people of Tibet, and it

is pursuing an increasingly ruthless policy toward its Turkic-Muslim minority. With the Cold War over, the underlying differences between China and the United States have reasserted themselves in areas such as human rights, trade and weap-ons proliferation. These differences are unlikely to moderate. A "new cold war," Deng Xaioping reportedly asserted in 1991, is under way between China and America.

The same phrase has been applied to the increasingly difficult relations between Japan and the United States. Here cultural difference exacerbates economic conflict. People on each side allege racism on the other, but at least on the American side the antipathies are not racial but cultural. The basic values, attitudes, behav-ioral patterns of the two societies could hardly be more different. The economic issues between the United States and Europe are no less serious than those between the United States and Japan, but they do not have the same political salience and emotional intensity because the differences between American culture and European culture are so much less than those between American civilization and Japanese civilization.

The interactions between civilizations vary greatly in the extent to which they are likely to be characterized by violence. Economic competition clearly predominates between the American and European subcivilizations of the West and between both of them and Japan. On the Eurasian conti-nent, however, the proliferation of ethnic conflict, epitomized at the extreme in "ethnic cleansing," has not been totally random. It has been most fre-quent and most violent between groups belong-ing to different civilizations. In Eurasia, the great historic fault lines between civilizations are once more aflame. This is particularly true along the boundaries of the crescent-shaped Islamic bloc of nations from the bulge of Africa to central Asia. Violence also occurs between Muslims, on the one hand, and Orthodox Serbs in the Balkans, Jews in Israel, Hindus in India, Buddhists in Burma and Catholics in the Philippines. Islam has bloody borders.

Groups or states belonging to one civilization that become involved in war with people from a different civilization naturally try to rally support from other members of their own civilization. As the post-Cold War world evolves, civilization commonality, what H. D. S. Greenway has termed the "kin-country" syndrome, is replacing political ideology and traditional balance of power considerations as the principal basis for cooperation and coalitions. It can be seen gradually emerging in the post-Cold War conflicts in the Persian Gulf, the Caucasus and Bosnia. None of these was a full-scale war between civilizations, but each involved some elements of civilizational rallying, which seemed to become more important as the conflict continued and which may provide a foretaste of the future.

First, in the Gulf War one Arab state invaded another and then fought a coalition of Arab, Western and other states. While only a few Muslim governments overtly supported Saddam Hussein, many Arab elites privately cheered him on, and he was highly popular among large sections of the Arab publics. Islamic fundamentalist movements universally supported Iraq rather than the Western-backed governments of Kuwait and Saudi Arabia. Forswearing Arab nationalism, Saddam Hussein explicitly invoked an Islamic appeal. He and his supporters attempted to define the war as a war between civilizations. "It is not the world against Iraq," as Safar Al-Hawali, dean of Islamic Studies at the Umm Al-Qura University in Mecca, put it in a widely circulated tape. "It is the West against Islam." Ignoring the rivalry between Iran and Iraq, the chief Iranian religious leader, Ayatollah Ali Khamenei, called for a holy war against the West: "The struggle against American aggression, greed, plans and policies will be counted as a jihad, and anybody who is killed on that path is a martyr." "This is a war," King Hussein of Jordan argued, "against all Arabs and all Muslims and not against Iraq alone."

The rallying of substantial sections of Arab elites and publics behind Saddam Hussein caused those Arab governments in the anti-Iraq coalition to moderate their activities and temper their public statements. Arab governments opposed or distanced themselves from subsequent Western efforts to apply pressure on Iraq, including enforcement of a no-fly zone in the summer of 1992 and the bombing of Iraq in January 1993. The Western-Soviet-Turkish-Arab anti-Iraq coalition of 1990 had by 1993 become a coalition of almost only the West and Kuwait against Iraq.

Muslims contrasted Western actions against Iraq with the West's failure to protect Bosnians against Serbs and to impose sanctions on Israel for violating U.N. resolutions. The West, they alleged, was using a double standard. A world of clashing civilizations, however, is inevitably a world of double standards: people apply one standard to their kin-countries and a different standard to others.

Second, the kin-country syndrome also appeared in conflicts in the former Soviet Union. Armenian military successes in 1992 and 1993 stimulated Turkey to become increasingly supportive of its religious, ethnic and linguistic brethren in Azerbaijan. "We have a Turkish nation feeling the same sentiments as the Azerbaijanis," said one Turkish official in 1992. "We are under pressure. Our newspapers are full of the photos of atrocities and are asking us if we are still serious about pursuing our neutral policy. Maybe we should show Armenia that there's a big Turkey in the region." President Turgut Ozal agreed, remarking that Turkey should at least "scare the Armenians a little bit." Turkey, Ozal threatened again in 1993, would "show its fangs." Turkish Air Force jets flew reconnaissance flights along the Armenian border; Turkey suspended food shipments and air flights to Armenia; and Turkey and Iran announced they would not accept dismemberment of Azerbaijan. . . .

Third, with respect to the fighting in the former Yugoslavia, Western publics manifested sympathy and support for the Bosnian Muslims and the horrors they suffered at the hands of the Serbs. Relatively little concern was expressed, however, over Croatian attacks on Muslims and participation in the dismemberment of Bosnia-Herzegovina. In the early stages of the Yugoslav breakup, Germany, in an unusual display of diplomatic initiative and muscle, induced the other 11 members of the European Community to follow its lead in recognizing Slovenia and Croatia. As a result of the pope's determination to provide strong backing to the two Catholic countries, the Vatican extended recognition even before the Community did. The United States followed the European lead. Thus the leading actors in Western civilization rallied behind their coreligionists. Subsequently Croatia was reported to be receiving substantial quantities of arms from Central European and other Western countries.

Boris Yeltsin's government, on the other hand, attempted to pursue a middle course that would be sympathetic to the Orthodox Serbs but not alienate Russia from the West. Russian conservative and nationalist groups, however, including many legislators, attacked the government for not being more forthcoming in its support for the Serbs. By early 1993 several hundred Russians apparently were serving with the Serbian forces, and reports circulated of Russian arms being supplied to Serbia.

Islamic governments and groups, on the other hand, castigated the West for not coming to the defense of the Bosnians. Iranian leaders urged Muslims from all countries to provide help to Bosnia; in violation of the U.N. arms embargo, Iran supplied weapons and men for the Bosnians; Iranian-supported Lebanese groups sent guerrillas to train and organize the Bosnian forces. In 1993 up to 4,000 Muslims from over two dozen Islamic countries were reported to be fighting in Bosnia. The governments of Saudi Arabia and other countries felt under increasing pressure from fundamentalist groups in their own societies to provide more vigorous support for the Bosnians. By the end of 1992, Saudi Arabia had reportedly supplied substantial funding for weapons and supplies for the Bosnians, which significantly increased their military capabilities vis-a-vis the Serbs.

In the 1930s the Spanish Civil War provoked intervention from countries that politically were fascist, communist and democratic. In the 1990s the Yugoslav conflict is provoking intervention from countries that are Muslim, Orthodox and Western Christian. The parallel has not gone unnoticed. "The war in Bosnia-Herzegovina has become the emotional equivalent of the fight against fascism in the Spanish Civil War," one Saudi editor observed. "Those who died there are regarded as martyrs who tried to save their fellow Muslims."

Conflicts and violence will also occur between states and groups within the same civilization. Such conflicts, however, are likely to be less intense and less likely to expand than conflicts between civilizations. Common membership in a civilization reduces the probability of violence in situations where it might otherwise occur. In 1991 and 1992 many people were alarmed by the possibility of violent conflict between Russia and Ukraine over territory, particularly Crimea, the Black Sea fleet, nuclear weapons and economic issues. If civilization is what counts, however, the likelihood of violence between Ukrainians and Russians should be low. They are two Slavic, primarily Orthodox peoples who have had close relationships with each other for centuries. As of early 1993, despite all the reasons for conflict, the leaders of the two countries were effectively negotiating and defusing the issues between the two countries. While there has been serious fighting between Muslims and Christians elsewhere in the former Soviet Union and much tension and some fighting between Western and Orthodox Christians in the Baltic states, there has been virtually no violence between Russians and Ukrainians.

Civilization rallying to date has been limited, but it has been growing, and it clearly has the potential to spread much further. As the conflicts in the Persian Gulf, the Caucasus and Bosnia continued, the positions of nations and the cleavages between them increasingly were along civilizational lines. Populist politicians, religious leaders and the media have found it a potent means of arousing mass support and of pressuring hesitant governments. In the coming years, the local conflicts most likely to escalate into major wars will be those, as in Bosnia and the Caucasus, along the fault lines between civilizations. The next world war, if there is one, will be a war between civilizations.

The West is now at an extraordinary peak of power in relation to other civilizations. Its superpower opponent has disappeared from the map. Military conflict among Western states is unthinkable, and Western military power is unrivaled. Apart from Japan, the West faces no economic challenge. It dominates international political and security institutions and with Japan international economic institutions. Global political and security issues are effectively settled by a directorate of the United States, Britain and France, world economic issues by a directorate of the United States, Germany and Japan, all of which maintain extraordinarily close relations with each other to the exclusion of lesser and largely non-Western countries. Decisions made at the U.N. Security Council or in the International Monetary Fund that reflect the interests of the West are presented to the world as reflecting the desires of the world community. The very phrase "the world community" has become the euphemistic collective noun (replacing "the Free World") to give global legitimacy to actions reflecting the interests of the United States and other Western powers. Through the IMF and other international economic institutions, the West promotes its economic interests and imposes on other nations the economic policies it thinks appropriate. In any poll of non-Western peoples, the IMF undoubtedly would win the support of finance ministers and a few others, but get an overwhelmingly unfavorable rating from just about everyone else. . . .

Western domination of the U.N. Security Council and its decisions, tempered only by occasional abstention by China, produced U.N. legitimation of the West's use of force to drive Iraq out of Kuwait and its elimination of Iraq's sophisticated weapons and capacity to produce such weapons. It also produced quite unprecedented action by the United States, Britain and France in getting the Security Council to demand that Libya hand over the Pan Am 103 bombing suspects and then to impose sanctions when Libya refused. After defeating the largest Arab army, the West did not hesitate to throw its weight around in the Arab world. The West in effect is using international institutions, military power and economic resources to run the world in ways that will maintain Western predominance, protect Western interests and promote Western political and economic values.

That at least is the way in which non-Westerners see the new world, and there is a significant element of truth in their view. Differences in power and struggles for military, economic and institutional power are thus one source of conflict between the West and other civilizations. Differences in culture, that is basic values and beliefs, are a second source of conflict. V. S. Naipaul has argued that Western civilization is the "universal civilization" that "fits all men." At a superficial level much of Western culture has indeed permeated the rest of the world. At a more basic level, however, Western concepts differ fundamentally from those prevalent in other civilizations. Western ideas of individualism, liberalism, constitutionalism, human rights, equality, liberty, the rule of law, democracy, free markets, the separation of church and state, often have little resonance in Islamic, Confucian, Japanese, Hindu, Buddhist or Orthodox cultures. Western efforts to propagate such ideas produce instead a reaction against "human rights imperialism" and a reaffirmation of indigenous values, as can be seen in the support for religious fundamentalism by the younger generation in non-Western cultures. The very notion that there could be a "universal civilization" is a Western idea, directly at odds with the particularism of most Asian societies and their emphasis on what distinguishes one people from another. Indeed, the author of a review of 100 comparative studies of values in different societies concluded that "the values that are most important in the West are least important worldwide." In the political realm, of course, these differences are most manifest in the efforts of the United States and other Western powers to induce other peoples to adopt Western ideas concerning democracy and human rights. Modern democratic government originated in the West. When it has developed in non-Western societies it has usually been the product of Western colonialism or imposition.

The central axis of world politics in the future is likely to be, in Kishore Mahbubani's phrase, the conflict between "the West and the Rest" and the responses of non-Western civilizations to Western power and values. Those responses generally take one or a combination of three forms. At one extreme, non-Western states can, like Burma and North Korea, attempt to pursue a course of isolation, to insulate their societies from penetration or "corruption" by the West, and, in effect, to opt out of participation in the Western-dominated global community. The costs of this course, however, are high, and few states have pursued it exclusively. A second alternative, the equivalent of "bandwagoning" in international relations theory, is to attempt to join the West and accept its values and institutions. The third alternative is to attempt to "balance" the West by developing economic and military power and cooperating with other non-Western societies against the West, while preserving indigenous values and institutions; in short, to modernize but not to Westernize.

In the future, as people differentiate themselves by civilization, countries with large numbers of peoples of different civilizations, such as the Soviet Union and Yugoslavia, are candidates for dismemberment. Some other countries have a fair degree of cultural homogeneity but are divided over whether their society belongs to one civilization or another. These are torn countries. Their leaders typically wish to pursue a band-wagoning strategy and to make their countries members of the West, but the history, culture and traditions of their countries are non-Western. The most obvious and prototypical torn country is Turkey. The late twentieth-century leaders of Turkey have followed in the Attaturk tradition and defined Turkey as a modern, secular, Western nation state. They allied Turkey with the West in NATO and in the Gulf War; they applied for membership in the European Community. At the same time, however, elements in Turkish society have supported an Islamic revival and have argued that Turkey is basically a Middle Eastern Muslim society. In addition, while the elite of Turkey has defined Turkey as a Western society, the elite of the West refuses to accept Turkey as such. Turkey will not become a member of the European Community, and the real reason, as President Ozal said, "is that we are Muslim and they are Christian and they don't say that." Having rejected Mecca, and then being rejected by Brussels, where does Turkey look? Tashkent may be the answer. The end of the Soviet Union gives Turkey the opportunity to become the leader of a revived Turkic civilization involving seven countries from the borders of Greece to those of China. Encouraged by the West, Turkey is making strenuous efforts to carve out this new identity for itself.

During the past decade Mexico has assumed a position somewhat similar to that of Turkey. Just as Turkey abandoned its historic opposition to Europe and attempted to join Europe, Mexico has stopped defining itself by its opposition to the United States and is instead attempting to imitate the United States and to join it in the North American Free Trade Area. Mexican leaders are engaged in the great task of redefining Mexican identity and have introduced fundamental economic reforms that eventually will lead to fundamental political change. In 1991 a top adviser to President Carlos Salinas de Gortari described at length to me all the changes the Salinas government was making. When he finished, I remarked: "That's most impressive. It seems to me that basically you want to change Mexico from a Latin American country into a North American country." He looked at me with surprise and exclaimed: "Exactly! That's precisely what we are trying to do, but of course we could never say so publicly." As his remark indicates, in Mexico as in Turkey, significant elements in society resist the redefinition of their country's identity. . . .

Historically Turkey has been the most profoundly torn country. For the United States, Mexico is the most immediate torn country. Globally the most important torn country is Russia. The question of whether Russia is part of the West or the leader of a distinct Slavic-Orthodox civilization has been a recurring one in Russian history. That issue was obscured by the communist victory in Russia, which imported a Western ideology, adapted it to Russian conditions and then challenged the West in the name of that ideology. The dominance of communism shut off the historic debate over Westernization versus Russification. With communism discredited Russians once again face that question.

President Yeltsin is adopting Western principles and goals and seeking to make Russia a "normal" country and a part of the West. Yet both the Russian elite and the Russian public are divided on this issue. Among the more moderate dissenters, Sergei Stankevich argues that Russia should reject the "Atlanticist" course, which would lead it "to become European, to become a part of the world economy in rapid and organized fashion, to become the eighth member of the Seven, and to put particular emphasis on Germany and the United States as the two dominant members of the Atlantic alliance." While also rejecting an exclusively Eurasian policy, Stankevich nonetheless argues that Russia should give priority to the protection of Russians in other countries, emphasize its Turkic and Muslim connections, and promote "an appreciable redistribution of our resources, our options, our ties, and our interests in favor of Asia, of the eastern direction." People of this persuasion criticize Yeltsin for subordinating Russia's interests to those of the West, for reducing Russian military strength, for failing to support traditional friends such as Serbia, and for pushing economic and political reform in ways injurious to the Russian people. Indicative of this trend is the new popularity of the ideas of Petr Savitsky, who in the

1920s argued that Russia was a unique Eurasian civilization. More extreme dissidents voice much more blatantly nationalist, anti-Western and anti-Semitic views, and urge Russia to redevelop its military strength and to establish closer ties with China and Muslim countries. . . .

To redefine its civilization identity, a torn country must meet three requirements. First, its political and economic elite has to be generally supportive of and enthusiastic about this move. Second, its public has to be willing to acquiesce in the redefinition. Third, the dominant groups in the recipient civilization have to be willing to embrace the convert. All three requirements in large part exist with respect to Mexico. The first two in large part exist with respect to Turkey. It is not clear that any of them exist with respect to Russia's joining the West. The conflict between liberal democracy and Marxism-Leninism was between ideologies which, despite their major differences, ostensibly shared ultimate goals of freedom, equality and prosperity. A traditional, authoritarian, nationalist Russia could have quite different goals. A Western democrat could carry on an intellectual debate with a Soviet Marxist. It would be virtually impossible for him to do that with a Russian traditionalist. If, as the Russians stop behaving like Marxists, they reject liberal democracy and begin behaving like Russians but not like Westerners, the relations between Russia and the West could again become distant and conflictual.

The obstacles to non-Western countries joining the West vary considerably. They are least for Latin American and East European countries. They are greater for the Orthodox countries of the former Soviet Union. They are still greater for Muslim, Confucian, Hindu and Buddhist societies. Japan has established a unique position for itself as an associate member of the West: it is in the West in some respects but clearly not of the West in important dimensions. Those countries that for reason of culture and power do not wish to, or cannot, join the West compete with the West by developing their own economic, military and political power. They do this by promoting their internal development and by cooperating with other non-Western countries. The most prominent form of this cooperation is the Confucian-Islamic connection that has emerged to challenge Western interests, values and power.

Almost without exception, Western countries are reducing their military power; under Yeltsin's leadership so also is Russia. China, North Korea and several Middle Eastern states, however, are significantly expanding their military capabilities. They are doing this by the import of arms from Western and non-Western sources and by the development of indigenous arms industries. One result is the emergence of what Charles Krauthammer has called "Weapon States," and the Weapon States are not Western states. Another result is the redefinition of arms control, which is a Western concept and a Western goal. During the Cold War the primary purpose of arms control was to establish a stable military balance between the United States and its allies and the Soviet Union and its allies. In the post-Cold War world the primary objective of arms control is to prevent the development by non-Western societies of military capabilities that could threaten Western interests. The West attempts to do this through international agreements, economic pressure and controls on the transfer of arms and weapons technologies.

The conflict between the West and the Confucian-Islamic states focuses largely, although not exclusively, on nuclear, chemical and biological weapons, ballistic missiles and other sophisticated means for delivering them, and the guidance, intelligence and other electronic capabilities for achieving that goal. The West promotes nonproliferation as a universal norm and nonproliferation treaties and inspections as means of realizing that norm. It also threatens a variety of sanctions against those who promote the spread of sophisticated weapons and proposes some benefits for those who do not. The attention of the West focuses, naturally, on nations that are actually or potentially hostile to the West.

The non-Western nations, on the other hand, assert their right to acquire and to deploy whatever weapons they think necessary for their security. They also have absorbed, to the full, the truth of the response of the Indian defense minister when asked what lesson he learned from the Gulf War: "Don't fight the United States unless you have nuclear weapons." Nuclear weapons, chemical weapons and missiles are viewed, probably erroneously, as the potential equalizer of superior Western conventional power. China, of course, already has nuclear weapons; Pakistan and India have the capability to deploy them. North Korea, Iran, Iraq, Libya and Algeria appear to be attempting to acquire them. A top Iranian official has declared that all Muslim states should acquire nuclear weapons, and in 1988 the president of Iran reportedly issued a directive calling for development of "offensive and defensive chemical, biological and radiological weapons."

Centrally important to the development of counter-West military capabilities is the sustained expansion of China's military power and its means to create military power. Buoyed by spectacular economic development, China is rapidly increasing its military spending and vigorously moving forward with the modernization of its armed forces. It is purchasing weapons from the former Soviet states; it is developing long-range missiles; in 1992 it tested a one-megaton nuclear device. It is developing power-projection capabilities, acquiring aerial refueling technology, and trying to purchase an aircraft carrier. Its military buildup and assertion of sovereignty over the South China Sea are provoking a multilateral regional arms race in East Asia. China is also a major exporter of arms and weapons technology. It has exported materials to Libya and Iraq that could be used to manufacture nuclear weapons and nerve gas. It has helped Algeria build a reactor suitable for nuclear weapons research and production. China has sold to Iran nuclear technology that American officials believe could only be used to create weapons and apparently has shipped components of 300-mile-range missiles to Pakistan. North Korea has had a nuclear weapons program under way for some while and has sold advanced missiles and missile technology to Syria and Iran. The flow of weapons and weapons technology is generally from East Asia to the Middle East. There is, however, some movement in the reverse direction; China has received Stinger missiles from Pakistan.

A Confucian-Islamic military connection has thus come into being, designed to promote acquisition by its members of the weapons and weapons technologies needed to counter the military power of the West. . . . A new form of arms competition is thus occurring between Islamic-Confucian states and the West. In an old-fashioned arms race, each side developed its own arms to balance or to achieve superiority against the other side. In this new form of arms competition, one side is developing its arms and the other side is attempting not to balance but to limit and prevent that arms build-up while at the same time reducing its own military capabilities.

This article does not argue that civilization identities will replace all other identities, that nation states will disappear, that each civilization will become a single coherent political entity, that groups within a civilization will not conflict with and even fight each other. This paper does set forth the hypotheses that differences between civilizations are real and important; civilization-consciousness is increasing; conflict between civilizations wall supplant ideological and other forms of conflict as the dominant global form of conflict; international relations, historically a game played out within Western civilization, will increasingly be de-Westernized and become a game in which non-Western civilizations are actors and not simply objects; successful political, security and economic international institutions are more likely to develop within civilizations than across civilizations; conflicts between groups in different civilizations will be more frequent, more sustained and more violent than conflicts between groups in the same civilization; violent conflicts between groups in different civilizations are the most likely and most dangerous source of escalation that could lead to global wars; the paramount axis of world politics will be the relations between "the West and the Rest"; the elites in some torn non-Western countries will try to make their countries part of the West, but in most cases face major obstacles to accomplishing this; a central focus of conflict for the immediate future will be between the West and several Islamic-Confucian states. This is not to advocate the desirability of conflicts between civilizations. It is to set forth descriptive hypotheses as to what the future may be like. If these are plausible hypotheses, however, it is necessary to consider their implications for Western policy. These implications should be divided between short-term advantage and long-term accommodation. In the short term it is clearly in the interest of the West to promote greater cooperation and unity within its own civilization, particularly between its European and North American components; to incorporate into the West societies in Eastern Europe and

Latin America whose cultures are close to those of the West; to promote and maintain cooperative relations with Russia and Japan; to prevent escalation of local inter-civilization conflicts into major inter-civilization wars; to limit the expansion of the military strength of Confucian and Islamic states; to moderate the reduction of Western military capabilities and maintain military superiority in East and Southwest Asia; to exploit differences and conflicts among Confucian and Islamic states; to support in other civilizations groups sympathetic to Western values and interests; to strengthen international institutions that reflect and legitimate Western interests and values and to promote the involvement of non-Western states in those institutions.

In the longer term other measures would be called for. Western civilization is both Western and modern. Non-Western civilizations have attempted to become modern without becoming Western. To date only Japan has fully succeeded in this quest. Non-Western civilizations will continue to attempt to acquire the wealth, technology, skills, machines and weapons that are part of being modern. They will also attempt to reconcile this modernity with their traditional culture and values. Their economic and military strength relative to the West will increase. Hence the West will increasingly have to accommodate these non-Western modern civilizations whose power approaches that of the West but whose values and interests differ significantly from those of the West. This will require the West to maintain the economic and military power necessary to protect its interests in relation to these civilizations. It will also, however, require the West to develop a more profound understanding of the basic religious and philosophical assumptions underlying other civilizations and the ways in which people in those civilizations see their interests. It will require an effort to identify elements of commonality between Western and other civilizations. For the relevant future, there will be no universal civilization, but instead a world of different civilizations, each of which will have to learn to coexist with the others.

ROBERT KAPLAN, "THE COMING ANARCHY," *THE ATLANTIC MONTHLY* (FEBRUARY 1994)

A journalist who specialized in exploring some of the world's more distressed precincts, Robert Kaplan (1952–) expected the end of the Cold War to give rise to unprecedented disorder, as under developed nations struggled to cope with the effects of overpopulation, urban sprawl, economic distress, and environmental degradation.

West Africa is becoming the symbol of worldwide demographic, environmental, and societal stress, in which criminal anarchy emerges as the real "strategic" danger. Disease, overpopulation, unprovoked crime, scarcity of resources, refugee migrations, the increasing erosion of nation-states and international borders, and the empowerment of private armies, security firms, and international drug cartels are now most tellingly demonstrated through a West African prism. West Africa provides an appropriate introduction to the issues, often extremely unpleasant to discuss, that will soon confront our civilization. . . .

There is no other place on the planet where political maps are so deceptive—where, in fact, they tell such lies—as in West Africa. Start with Sierra Leone. According to the map, it is a nation-state of defined borders, with a government in control of its territory. In truth the Sierra Leonian government, run by a twenty-seven-year-old army captain, Valentine Strasser, controls Freetown by day and by day also controls part of the rural interior. In the government's territory the national army is an unruly rabble threatening drivers and passengers at most checkpoints. In the other part of the country units of two separate armies from the war in Liberia have taken up residence, as has an army of Sierra Leonian rebels. The government force fighting the rebels is full of renegade commanders who have aligned themselves with disaffected village chiefs. A pre-modern form-lessness governs the battlefield, evoking the wars in medieval Europe prior to the 1648 Peace of Westphalia, which ushered in the era of organized nation-states.

As a consequence, roughly 400,000 Sierra Leonians are internally displaced, 280,000 more have fled to neighboring Guinea, and another 100,000 have fled to Liberia, even as 400,000 Liberians have fled to Sierra Leone. The third largest city in Sierra Leone, Gondama, is a displaced-persons camp. With an additional 600,000 Liberians in Guinea and 250,000 in the Ivory Coast, the borders dividing these four countries have become largely meaningless. Even in quiet zones none of the governments except the Ivory Coast's maintains the schools, bridges, roads, and police forces in a manner necessary for functional sovereignty. The Koranko ethnic group in north-eastern Sierra Leone does all its trading in Guinea. Sierra Leonian diamonds are more likely to be sold in Liberia than in Freetown. In the eastern provinces of Sierra Leone you can buy Liberian beer but not the local brand.

In Sierra Leone, as in Guinea, as in the Ivory Coast, as in Ghana, most of the primary rain for-est and the secondary bush is being destroyed at an alarming rate. I saw convoys of trucks bearing majestic hardwood trunks to coastal ports. When Sierra Leone achieved its independence, in 1961, as much as 60 percent of the country was primary rain forest. Now six percent is. In the Ivory Coast the proportion has fallen from 38 percent to eight percent. The deforestation has led to soil erosion, which has led to more flooding and more mos-quitoes. Virtually everyone in the West African interior has some form of malaria.

Sierra Leone is a microcosm of what is occur-ring, albeit in a more tempered and gradual manner, throughout West Africa and much of the underde-veloped world: the withering away of central gov-ernments, the rise of tribal and regional domains, the unchecked spread of disease, and the growing pervasiveness of war. West Africa is reverting to the Africa of the Victorian atlas. It consists now of a series of coastal trading posts, such as Freetown and Conakry, and an interior that, owing to vio-lence, volatility, and disease, is again becoming, as Graham Greene once observed, "blank" and "unexplored." However, whereas Greene's vision

implies a certain romance, as in the somnolent and charmingly seedy Freetown of his celebrated novel *The Heart of the Matter*, it is Thomas Malthus, the philosopher of demographic doomsday, who is now the prophet of West Africa's future. And West Africa's future, eventually, will also be that of most of the rest of the world. . . .

Africa may be as relevant to the future charac-ter of world politics as the Balkans were a hundred years ago, prior to the two Balkan wars and the First World War. Then the threat was the collapse of empires and the birth of nations based solely on tribe. Now the threat is more elemental: nature unchecked. Africa's immediate future could be very bad. The coming upheaval, in which foreign embassies are shut down, states collapse, and con-tact with the outside world takes place through dangerous, disease-ridden coastal trading posts, will loom large in the century we are entering. (Nine of twenty-one U.S. foreign-aid missions to be closed over the next three years are in Africa—a prologue to a consolidation of U.S. embassies themselves.) Precisely because much of Africa is set to go over the edge at a time when the Cold War has ended, when environmental and demo-graphic stress in other parts of the globe is becom-ing critical, and when the post-First World War system of nation-states—not just in the Balkans but perhaps also in the Middle East—is about to be toppled, Africa suggests what war, borders, and ethnic politics will be like a few decades hence.

To understand the events of the next fifty years, then, one must understand environmental scarcity, cultural and racial clash, geographic destiny, and the transformation of war. The order in which I have named these is not accidental. Each con-cept except the first relies partly on the one or ones before it, meaning that the last two—new approaches to mapmaking and to warfare—are the most important. They are also the least understood. . . .

Mention The Environment or "diminishing natural resources" in foreign-policy circles and you meet a brick wall of skepticism or boredom. To conservatives especially, the very terms seem flaky. Public-policy foundations have contrib-uted to the lack of interest, by funding narrowly focused environmental studies replete with tech-nical jargon which foreign-affairs experts just let pile up on their desks.

It is time to understand The Environment for what it is: the national-security issue of the early twenty-first century. The political and strategic impact of surging populations, spreading disease, deforestation and soil erosion, water depletion, air pollution, and, possibly, rising sea levels in critical, overcrowded regions like the Nile Delta and Bangladesh—developments that will prompt mass migrations and, in turn, incite group conflicts—will be the core foreign-policy challenge from which most others will ultimately emanate, arousing the public and uniting assorted interests left over from the Cold War. In the twenty-first century water will be in dangerously short supply in such diverse locales as Saudi Arabia, Central Asia, and the southwestern United States. A war could erupt between Egypt and Ethiopia over Nile River water. Even in Europe tensions have arisen between Hungary and Slovakia over the damming of the Danube, a classic case of how environmental disputes fuse with ethnic and historical ones. The political scientist and erstwhile Clinton adviser Michael Mandelbaum has said, "We have a foreign policy today in the shape of a doughnut—lots of peripheral interests but nothing at the center." The environment, I will argue, is part of a terrifying array of problems that will define a new threat to our security, filling the hole in Mandelbaum's doughnut and allowing a post-Cold War foreign policy to emerge inexorably by need rather than by design.

Our Cold War foreign policy truly began with George F. Kennan's famous article, signed "X," published in *Foreign Affairs* in July of 1947, in which Kennan argued for a "firm and vigilant containment" of a Soviet Union that was imperially, rather than ideologically, motivated. It may be that our post-Cold War foreign policy will one day be seen to have had its beginnings in an even bolder and more detailed piece of written analysis: one that appeared in the journal *International Security*. The article, published in the fall of 1991 by Thomas Fraser Homer-Dixon, who is the head of the Peace and Conflict Studies Program at the University of Toronto, was titled "On the Threshold: Environmental Changes as Causes of Acute Conflict." Homer-Dixon has, more successfully than other analysts, integrated two hitherto separate fields—military-conflict studies and the study of the physical environment.

In Homer-Dixon's view, future wars and civil violence will often arise from scarcities of resources such as water, cropland, forests, and fish. Just as there will be environmentally driven wars and refugee flows, there will be environmentally induced praetorian regimes—or, as he puts it, "hard regimes." Countries with the highest probability of acquiring hard regimes, according to Homer-Dixon, are those that are threatened by a declining resource base yet also have "a history of state [read 'military'] strength." Candidates include Indonesia, Brazil, and, of course, Nigeria. Though each of these nations has exhibited democratizing tendencies of late, Homer-Dixon argues that such tendencies are likely to be superficial "epiphenomena" having nothing to do with long-term processes that include soaring populations and shrinking raw materials. Democracy is problematic; scarcity is more certain. . . .

Over the next fifty years the earth's population will soar from 5.5 billion to more than nine billion. Though optimists have hopes for new resource technologies and free-market development in the global village, they fail to note that, as the National Academy of Sciences has pointed out, 95 percent of the population increase will be in the poorest regions of the world, where governments now—just look at Africa—show little ability to function, let alone to implement even marginal improvements. Homer-Dixon writes, ominously, "Neo-Malthusians may underestimate human adaptability in today's environmental-social system, but as time passes their analysis may become ever more compelling."

While a minority of the human population will be, as Francis Fukuyama would put it, sufficiently sheltered so as to enter a "post-historical" realm, living in cities and suburbs in which the environment has been mastered and ethnic animosities have been quelled by bourgeois prosperity, an increasingly large number of people will be stuck in history, living in shantytowns where attempts to rise above poverty, cultural dysfunction, and ethnic strife will be doomed by a lack of water to drink, soil to till, and space to survive in. In the developing world environmental stress will present people with a choice that is increasingly among totalitarianism (as in Iraq), fascist-tending mini-states (as in Serb-held Bosnia), and road-warrior cultures (as in Somalia). Homer-Dixon concludes that "as environmental degradation proceeds, the size of the potential social disruption will increase.". . . "Think of a stretch limo in the potholed streets of New York City, where homeless beggars live. Inside the limo are the air-conditioned post-industrial regions of North America, Europe, the emerging Pacific Rim, and a few other isolated places, with their trade summitry and computer-information highways. Outside is the rest of mankind, going in a completely different direction."

We are entering a bifurcated world. Part of the globe is inhabited by Hegel's and Fukuyama's Last Man, healthy, well fed, and pampered by technology. The other, larger, part is inhabited by Hobbes's First Man, condemned to a life that is "poor, nasty, brutish, and short." Although both parts will be threatened by environmental stress, the Last Man will be able to master it; the First Man will not.

The Last Man will adjust to the loss of underground water tables in the western United States. He will build dikes to save Cape Hatteras and the Chesapeake beaches from rising sea levels, even as the Maldive Islands, off the coast of India, sink into oblivion, and the shorelines of Egypt, Bangladesh, and Southeast Asia recede, driving tens of millions of people inland where there is no room for them, and thus sharpening ethnic divisions.

Homer-Dixon points to a world map of soil degradation in his Toronto office. "The darker the map color, the worse the degradation," he explains. The West African coast, the Middle East, the Indian subcontinent, China, and Central America have the darkest shades, signifying all manner of degradation, related to winds, chemicals, and water problems. "The worst degradation is generally where the population is highest. The population is generally highest where the soil is the best. So we're degrading earth's best soil." . . .

Outside the stretch limo would be a rundown, crowded planet of skinhead Cossacks and juju warriors, influenced by the worst refuse of Western pop culture and ancient tribal hatreds, and battling over scraps of overused earth in guerrilla conflicts that ripple across continents and intersect in no discernible pattern—meaning there's no easy-to-define threat. Kennan's world of one adversary seems as distant as the world of Herodotus.

Most people believe that the political earth since 1989 has undergone immense change. But it is minor compared with what is yet to come. The breaking apart and remaking of the atlas is only now beginning. The crack-up of the Soviet empire and the coming end of Arab-Israeli military confrontation are merely prologues to the really big changes that lie ahead. Michael Vlahos, a long-range thinker for the U.S. Navy, warns, "We are not in charge of the environment and the world is not following us. It is going in many directions. Do not assume that democratic capitalism is the last word in human social evolution." . . .

To see the twenty-first century truly, one's eyes must learn a different set of aesthetics. One must reject the overly stylized images of travel magazines, with their inviting photographs of exotic villages and glamorous downtowns. There are far too many millions whose dreams are more vulgar, more real—whose raw energies and desires will overwhelm the visions of the elites, remaking the future into something frighteningly new. . . .

To appreciate fully the political and cartographic implications of postmodernism—an epoch of themeless juxtapositions, in which the classificatory grid of nation-states is going to be replaced by a jagged-glass pattern of city-states, shanty-states, nebulous and anarchic regionalisms—it is necessary to consider, finally, the whole question of war.

"Oh, what a relief to fight, to fight enemies who defend themselves, enemies who are awake!" Andre Malraux wrote in Man's Fate. I cannot think of a more suitable battle cry for many combatants in the early decades of the twenty-first century. The intense savagery of the fighting in such diverse cultural settings as Liberia, Bosnia, the Caucasus, and Sri Lanka—to say nothing of what obtains in American inner cities—indicates something very troubling that those of us inside the stretch limo, concerned with issues like middle-class entitlements and the future of interactive cable television, lack the stomach to contemplate. It is this: a large number of people on this planet, to whom the comfort and stability of a middle-class life is utterly unknown, find war and a barracks existence a step up rather than a step down.

"Just as it makes no sense to ask 'why people eat' or 'what they sleep for,'" writes Martin van Creveld, a military historian at the Hebrew

University in Jerusalem, in *The Transformation of War*, "so fighting in many ways is not a means but an end. Throughout history, for every person who has expressed his horror of war there is another who found in it the most marvelous of all the experiences that are vouchsafed to man, even to the point that he later spent a lifetime boring his descendants by recounting his exploits." . . .

The book begins by demolishing the notion that men don't like to fight. "By compelling the senses to focus themselves on the here and now," Van Creveld writes, war "can cause a man to take his leave of them." As anybody who has had experience with Chetniks in Serbia, "technicals" in Somalia, Tontons Macoutes in Haiti, or soldiers in Sierra Leone can tell you, in places where the Western Enlightenment has not penetrated and where there has always been mass poverty, people find liberation in violence. . . . Physical aggression is a part of being human. Only when people attain a certain economic, educational, and cultural standard is this trait tranquilized. In light of the fact that 95 percent of the earth's population growth will be in the poorest areas of the globe, the question is not whether there will be war (there will be a lot of it) but what kind of war. And who will fight whom?

Debunking the great military strategist Carl von Clausewitz, Van Creveld, who may be the most original thinker on war since that early-nineteenth-century Prussian, writes, "Clausewitz's ideas . . . were wholly rooted in the fact that, ever since 1648, war had been waged overwhelmingly by states." But, as Van Creveld explains, the period of nation-states and, therefore, of state conflict is now ending, and with it the clear "threefold division into government, army, and people" which state-directed wars enforce. Thus, to see the future, the first step is to look back to the past immediately prior to the birth of modernism—the wars in medieval Europe which began during the Reformation and reached their culmination in the Thirty Years' War.

Van Creveld writes, "In all these struggles political, social, economic, and religious motives were hopelessly entangled. Since this was an age when armies consisted of mercenaries, all were also attended by swarms of military entrepreneurs. . . . Many of them paid little but lip service to the organizations for whom they had

contracted to fight. Instead, they robbed the countryside on their own behalf. . . ." . . .

Back then, in other words, there was no Politics as we have come to understand the term, just as there is less and less Politics today in Liberia, Sierra Leone, Somalia, Sri Lanka, the Balkans, and the Caucasus, among other places. . . .

Also, war-making entities will no longer be restricted to a specific territory. Loose and shadowy organisms such as Islamic terrorist organizations suggest why borders will mean increasingly little and sedimentary layers of tribalistic identity and control will mean more. "From the vantage point of the present, there appears every prospect that religious . . . fanaticisms will play a larger role in the motivation of armed conflict" in the West than at any time "for the last 300 years," Van Creveld writes. . . .

Van Creveld's pre-Westphalian vision of worldwide low-intensity conflict is not a superficial "back to the future" scenario. First of all, technology will be used toward primitive ends. In Liberia the guerrilla leader Prince Johnson didn't just cut off the ears of President Samuel Doe before Doe was tortured to death in 1990—Johnson made a video of it, which has circulated throughout West Africa. In December of 1992, when plotters of a failed coup against the Strasser regime in Sierra Leone had their ears cut off at Freetown's Hamilton Beach prior to being killed, it was seen by many to be a copycat execution. Considering, as I've explained earlier, that the Strasser regime is not really a government and that Sierra Leone is not really a nation-state, listen closely to Van Creveld: "Once the legal monopoly of armed force, long claimed by the state, is wrested out of its hands, existing distinctions between war and crime will break down much as is already the case today in . . . Lebanon, Sri Lanka, El Salvador, Peru, or Colombia."

If crime and war become indistinguishable, then "national defense" may in the future be viewed as a local concept. As crime continues to grow in our cities and the ability of state governments and criminal-justice systems to protect their citizens diminishes, urban crime may, according to Van Creveld, "develop into low-intensity conflict by coalescing along racial, religious, social, and political lines." As small-scale violence multiplies at home and abroad, state armies will continue to shrink, being gradually replaced by a booming private security business, as in West Africa, and by urban mafias, especially in the former communist world, who may be better equipped than municipal police forces to grant physical protection to local inhabitants.

Future wars will be those of communal survival, aggravated or, in many cases, caused by environmental scarcity. These wars will be subnational, meaning that it will be hard for states and local governments to protect their own citizens physically. This is how many states will ultimately die. As state power fades—and with it the state's ability to help weaker groups within society, not to mention other states—peoples and cultures around the world will be thrown back upon their own strengths and weaknesses, with fewer equalizing mechanisms to protect them. Whereas the distant future will probably see the emergence of a racially hybrid, globalized man, the coming decades will see us more aware of our differences than of our similarities. To the average person, political values will mean less, personal security more. . . .

Henceforward the map of the world will never be static. This future map—in a sense, the "Last Map"—will be an ever-mutating representation of chaos.

THOMAS L. FRIEDMAN, "A MANIFESTO FOR THE FAST WORLD," NEW YORK TIMES MAGAZINE (MARCH 28, 1999)

For Thomas Friedman (1953–), globetrotting columnist with the *New York Times,* one word sufficed to describe the post–Cold War era: globalization.

Globalization is not just a trend, not just a phenomenon, not just an economic fad. It is the international system that has replaced the cold-war system. And like the cold-war system, globalization has its own rules, logic, structures and characteristics.

Unlike the cold-war system, which was largely static, globalization involves the integration of free markets, nation-states and information technologies to a degree never before witnessed, in a way that is enabling individuals, corporations and countries to reach around the world farther, faster, deeper and cheaper than ever. It is also producing a powerful backlash from those brutalized or left behind.

If all the threats and opportunities of the cold-war system grew out of "division," all the threats and opportunities of the globalization system grow out of "integration." The symbol of the cold-war system was a wall, which divided everyone. The symbol of the globalization system is the World Wide Web, which unites everyone. In the cold war we reached for the hot line between the White House and the Kremlin—a symbol that we were all divided but at least someone, the two superpowers, were in charge. In the era of globalization we reach for the Internet—a symbol that we are all connected but nobody is in charge.

If the cold war had been a sport, it would have been sumo wrestling, says Michael Mandelbaum, a foreign affairs expert at Johns Hopkins University. "It would be two big fat guys in a ring, with all sorts of posturing and rituals and stomping of feet, but actually very little contact until the end of the match, when there is a brief moment of shoving and the loser gets pushed out of the ring, but nobody gets killed."

If globalization were a sport, it would be the 100-yard dash, over and over and over. And no matter how many times you win, you have to race again the next day. And if you lose by just a hundredth of a second it can be as if you lost by an hour.

The driving idea behind globalization is free-market capitalism. The more you let market forces rule and the more you open your economy to free trade and competition, the more efficient and flourishing your economy will be. Globalization means the spread of free-market capitalism to virtually every country in the world.

The defining document of the cold-war system was the Treaty. The defining document of the globalization system is the Deal. While the defining measurement of the cold war was weight, the defining measurement of the globalization system is speed—in commerce, travel, communication and innovation. The cold war was about Einstein's mass-energy equation, $E = mc^2$. Globalization is about Moore's Law, which states that the computing power of silicon chips will double every 18 months.

The cold-war system was built around nation-states, and it was balanced by two superpowers: the United States and the Soviet Union. The globalization system is built around three balances that overlap and affect one another. One is the traditional balance between states and states. The next is the balance between states and "supermarkets"—the huge global stock and bond markets. (The United States can destroy you by dropping bombs, and the supermarkets can destroy you by downgrading your bonds.)

The last is the balance between states and "super-empowered individuals." Because globalization has brought down the walls that limited the movement and reach of people, and because it has simultaneously wired the world into networks, it gives more power to individuals than ever before to directly influence markets and nation-states. For instance, Osama bin Laden, the Saudi millionaire with his own global network (Jihad Online), declared war on America, and the Air Force had to launch cruise missiles at him. We launched cruise missiles at an individual—as though he were another nation-state.

As the country that benefits most from global economic integration, we have the responsibility of making sure that this new system is sustainable. This is particularly important at a time when the world has been—and will continue to be—rocked by economic crises that can spread rapidly from one continent to another. America has had 200 years to invent, regenerate and calibrate the balances that keep markets free without their becoming monsters. We have the tools to make a difference. We have an interest in making a difference. And we have the responsibility to make a difference.

Sustaining globalization is our overarching national interest. The political party that understands that first, the one that comes up with the most coherent, credible and imaginative platform for pursuing it, is the party that will own the real bridge to the future.

Designing a strategy to promote sustainable globalization at home and abroad is no easy task. And it is made even more complicated by the effects of globalization, which have intensified the world's long-running love-hate relationship with America. For the moment, America has many of the most sought-after goods, services and innovations in the global market. What people thought was American decline in the 1980's was actually America adjusting to the new system before anyone else. We're already around the second turn before some others have laced up their shoes. Globalization-is-U.S.

Because we are the biggest beneficiaries and drivers of globalization, we are unwittingly putting enormous pressure on the rest of the world. Americans may think their self-portrait is Grant Wood's "American Gothic," the strait-laced couple, pitchfork in hand, standing stoically outside the barn. But to the rest of the world, Americans actually look like some wild, multicolored Andy Warhol print.

To the rest of the world, American Gothic is actually two 20-something software engineers who come into your country wearing beads and sandals, with rings in their noses and paint on their toes. They kick down your front door, overturn everything in the house, stick a Big Mac in your mouth, fill your kids with ideas you never had or can't understand, slam a cable box onto your television, lock in the channel to MTV, plug an Internet connection into your computer and tell you, "Download or die."

We Americans are the apostles of the Fast World, the prophets of the free market and the high priests of high tech. We want "enlargement" of both our values and our Pizza Huts. We want the world to follow our lead and become democratic and capitalistic, with a Web site in every pot, a Pepsi on every lip, Microsoft Windows in every computer and with everyone, everywhere, pumping their own gas.

No wonder, therefore, that resentment of America is on the rise globally. In 1996 I visited Teheran and stayed in the Homa Hotel. The first thing I noticed was that above the front door in the lobby were the words "Down With U.S.A." It wasn't a banner. It wasn't graffiti. It was tiled into the wall. A short time later, I noticed that Iran's mullahs had begun calling America something other than the "Great Satan." They had begun calling it "the capital of global arrogance."

The Iranian leadership had grasped the important distinction between "global arrogance" and old-fashioned notions of imperialism, when one country physically occupies another. Global arrogance is when your culture and economic clout are so powerful and widely diffused that you don't need to occupy other people to influence their lives. Well, guess what? The Iranians aren't the only ones talking about America as "the capital of global arrogance." The French, Germans, Japanese, Indonesians, Indians and Russians also call us that now.

In most countries, people can no longer distinguish between American power, American exports, American cultural assaults, American cultural exports and plain old globalization. . . .

The trick for America is to lead without being too overbearing, to be generous without overextending ourselves and to be tough without engendering too much resentment. But how?

First, forget about the political labels from the cold-war system. Democrats and Republicans, liberals and conservatives; these terms are meaningless today. Instead, to locate yourself and your opponents in the new era, consider the accompanying chart of globalization identities.

The line across the middle from left to right describes how you feel about globalization. At the far right end of this line are the "Integrationists." These are the people who really welcome globalization because they think it is either good or inevitable and want to see it promoted through more free trade, more Internet commerce, more networking of schools, communities and businesses, so that we can have global integration across 24 time zones and into cyberspace.

At the far left end of the globalization line are the "Separatists." These are people who believe that free trade and technological integration are neither good nor inevitable, because they widen income gaps, lead to jobs being sent abroad, homogenize cultures into global mush and lead to life being controlled by distant, faceless market forces. They want to cut off and kill globalization now.

So the first thing you have to do is locate yourself somewhere on this line. Are you a Separatist? An Integrationist? Or something in between?

Now look at the line running from top to bottom of the matrix. This is the distribution axis. It represents what sort of policies you believe governments should adopt to go along with globalization. At the lower end of this line are the "Social-Safety-Netters." These are people who believe that globalization will be sustainable only if it is democratized, in both the economic and the political sense.

Obviously, not everyone agrees with this approach. That's why at the other extreme from the Social-Safety-Netters are the "Let-Them-Eat-Cakers." These are people who believe that globalization is essentially winner-take-all, loser-take-care-of-yourself. They want to shrink government, taxes and safety nets, and let people reap the fruits of their own labor or pay the price of their own ineptitude.

So next you have to locate yourself on this distribution axis. Are you a Social Safety-Netter? Are you a Let-Them-Eat-Caker? Or something in between? . . .

I'm an extreme Integrationist Social-Safety-Netter. I believe you dare not be a globalizer without being a safety-netter and social democrat, because if you don't equip the have-nots, know-nots and turtles to survive in the new system, they will eventually produce a backlash that will choke off your country from the world. And I believe you dare not be a safety-netter or social democrat without being a globalizer, because without ever-increasing integration, you will never generate the incomes and absorb the technologies needed to keep standards of living rising.

But what does it mean to be an Integrationist Social-Safety-Netter? I think it means articulating a politics, geo-economics and geopolitics of sustainable globalization.

The first thing a politics of sustainable globalization must include is a picture of the world, because no policy is sustainable without a public that understands why it's necessary. This is particularly true with globalization, because the people who are hurt by it know exactly who they are, but the people who benefit from it tend not to understand that at all. After World War II, successive Presidents instructed Americans about the One Big Thing in the world that would be at the center of American politics—containing Communism. Today, globalization and rapid technological change are that Big Thing. And that means virtually every aspect of national policy—health care, welfare, education, job training, the environment, market regulation, Social Security, free-trade expansion and military strategy needs to be adjusted so that we get the most out of the globalization system and cushion its worst aspects. . . .

Integrationist Social-Safety-Netters feel that there are a lot of things we can do to democratize globalization economically, promote social stability and prevent our own society from drifting even further into high walls and tinted windows. These measures need not be all that expensive, nor do they have to involve radical income redistribution—or lavish welfare programs that violate the basic, neoliberal free-market rules of the system.

To that end, I believe that each Administration should offer an annual piece of legislation that I would call the Rapid Change Opportunity Act. It would accompany whatever integrationist policy the White House is pursuing that year—whether it be Nafta expansion or most-favored-nation status for China. The act would vary each year, but its goal would be to create both the reality and perception that the Government understands that globalization spreads its blessings unevenly, and therefore the Government is constantly going to be adjusting its safety nets and trampolines to get as many people as possible up to speed for the Fast World. . . .

I like to compare countries to computers. Today, for the first time in history, we all have the same basic piece of hardware—free markets. The question is, which countries will get the economic operating systems (neoliberal macroeconomics) and software (regulatory institutions and laws) to get the most out of those free markets and cushion them from the worst surges coming from the "electronic herd" of global investors.

Russia is the egregious example of a country that plugged into the herd with no operating system and no software, with predictably horrendous results. Thailand, South Korea and Indonesia plugged into the herd, but with a slow operating system: what I call "DOScapital 2.0" (crony capitalism). It was great for getting these countries

from an average income of $500 per capita to $5,000. But when they wanted to move from $5,000 to $15,000, and the speed of the electronic herd moved from a 286 chip to a Pentium III, and they were still using DOScapital 2.0, a message came up on their screens: "You Have Performed a Series of Irrational Investments. Cannot Save Items. Delete Memory of All Inefficient Banks and Firms, and Download New Software and Operating System." . . .

Some have proposed that we put a little sand in the gears of the global economy to slow it down a bit. My response would be that I don't think it is ever very wise to put sand in the gears of a machine when you don't fully understand how it works. It might not just slow down. It could come to a screeching, metal-bending halt. Also, where do you put the sand when you are dealing with a fund manager sitting in Connecticut using the Internet to invest in Brazil via a bank domiciled offshore in Panama? Ever try to put sand in cyberspace? Well, then, how about setting up a global central bank? That may be a good idea, but it's not something that is going to happen anytime soon—not as long as we all still live in 200-odd different countries.

So does that mean that there is nothing we can do? No. The good news is that in the wake of the crisis of 1998-99 the market on its own is brutally disciplining itself. You see signs of this everywhere. The chief executives of some of the biggest banks in the world—Barclays P.L.C., BankAmerica, United Bank of Switzerland—were all ousted in 1998, after huge losses in high-risk emerging markets.

In the wake of these beheadings, those major banks have restricted leverage, cutting off reckless fund managers, demanding more documentation from those to whom they are still lending and scrutinizing more seriously not just the balance-of-payments figures of emerging markets but also their operating systems, legal systems and overall software.

Banks and investors have started asking fund managers tough questions about their exposure to risks and what defensive measures they have taken. And the International Monetary Fund, the Treasury and fund managers have belatedly started asking emerging-market countries what they are doing to improve their financial and regulatory systems.

The only realistic solution for now is to take this ad hoc approach, intensify it and extend it into the future. If everyone from the I.M.F. to Merrill Lynch to my Aunt Bev would just ask these questions more often, and keep asking them, we'd have a chance of preventing two out of the next five crises and limiting the impact of one of the next five. That's the most we can hope for.

Sure, this doesn't seem very sexy—calling on everyone in the system to become a better regulator, a smarter investor and a more prudent lender. But it's time we stopped kidding ourselves. Today's markets are so big and, with the advent of the Internet, becoming so fast that they can never be immunized from crises.

Global financial crises will be the norm in the coming era. In fact, let me leave you, dear readers, with one piece of advice: Fasten your seat belts and put your seat backs and tray tables into a fixed and upright position. Because the booms and the busts and the recoveries will all be coming faster. So get used to it, and just try to make sure that the leverage in the system doesn't become so great in any one area that it can make the whole system go boom or bust. Anyone who tells you that they have a plan for eliminating these crises is just pulling your leg. In fact, as you are reading these words, the next global financial crisis is already germinating somewhere.

It is not easy for this generation of Americans to grasp how important the United States is to the world in the era of globalization. America today is the Michael Jordan of geopolitics—the overwhelmingly dominant system. Now Jordan was good, and his opponents both loved and hated playing against him. Everyone wanted to be like Mike. But as good as Jordan was, he was nothing without all the other teams in the N.B.A. to showcase his skills—and we're nothing without the rest of the world, which is why managing globalization is a role from which America dare not shrink.

Historically, the United States has either been isolated from world affairs or deeply engaged as part of a moral crusade to fend off an aggressive, threatening power. Isolation is easy to explain and understand. Engagement in a bipolar world—with a menacing, nuclear-armed Soviet bear growling on the other side—was easy to explain

and understand. But what is not easy to explain or understand is engagement in a world in which America is the biggest beneficiary and the sole superpower, with multiple secondary powers and no immediately visible threat, but with many little threats and an abstract globalization system to maintain. But this is the world we have. And in this world we can't afford either to retreat into isolation or to wait around for some smaller adversary to become a life-threatening foe.

As I have noted before, globalization and economic integration will act, to some degree, as a restraint on those states that are plugged into the system and dependent upon the electronic herd. It's true that no two countries that both have a McDonald's have ever fought a war since they each got their McDonald's. (I call this the Golden Arches Theory of Conflict Prevention.) But globalization does not end geopolitics—the enduring quest for power, the fear of neighbors, the tug of history. What globalization does is simply put a different frame around geopolitics, a frame that raises the costs of war but cannot eliminate it.

That is why sustainable globalization still requires a stable, geopolitical power structure, which simply cannot be maintained without the active involvement of the United States. All the technologies that Silicon Valley is designing to carry digital voices, videos and data around the world, all the trade and financial integration it is promoting through its innovations and all the wealth this is generating, are happening in a world stabilized by a benign superpower, with its capital in Washington, D.C.

The hidden hand of the market will never work without a hidden fist—McDonald's cannot flourish without McDonnell Douglas, the builder of the F-15. And the hidden fist that keeps the world safe for Silicon Valley's technologies is called the United States Army, Air Force, Navy and Marine Corps. . . .

This is too easily forgotten today. For too many executives in Silicon Valley, there is no geography or geopolitics anymore. There are only stock options and electrons. Their view that Washington is the enemy, and that any tax dollar paid there is a tax dollar wasted, is grotesque. There is a saying in Silicon Valley that "loyalty is just one mouse-click away." But you can take that too far. Execs there make boasts like: "We are not an American company. We are I.B.M. U.S., I.B.M. Canada, I.B.M. Australia, I.B.M. China." Oh, yeah? Then, the next time I.B.M. China gets in trouble in China, call Jiang Zemin for help. And the next time Congress closes another military base in Asia, call Microsoft's navy to secure the sea lanes of the Pacific. And the next time Congress wants to close more consulates and embassies, call Amazon.com to order a new passport.

This doesn't mean America needs to be involved everywhere all the time. There are big, important places and there are small, unimportant places. Diplomacy is about knowing the difference between the two, and knowing how to mobilize others to act where we cannot or should not act alone.

In such a world, pure realism and pure idealism are rarely the answer. The realists would say, Stay away from Kosovo, even if the conflict could spill over to Greece and Turkey; the idealists argue that we should invade Serbia with NATO forces, break off Kosovo, make it an independent state and defend it forever. Both are wrong. . . .

The next Administration, whether Democratic or Republican, will have to try to bring together the new globalizers—from software writers to Web-page designers, from Iowa farmers to environmental activists, from human rights campaigners to high-tech assembly-line workers—to form a new, 21st-century coalition that can sustain internationalism. This new coalition doesn't exist yet, so someone is going to have to put it together.

This won't be easy. Americans were ready to pay any price and bear any burden in the cold war because there was a compelling and immediate sense that their own homes and way of life were threatened. But a large majority don't feel that way about North Korea, Iraq or Kosovo, and

while Russia may still have the capability to pose a lethal threat, it is not doing so at this time. That's why Americans are in the odd position now of being held responsible for everything, while being reluctant to die for anything. That's why in the globalization era, counterinsurgency is out; babysitting is in. House-to-house fighting is out; cruise missiles are in. Green Berets are out; U.N. blue helmets are in.

America truly is the ultimate benign superpower and reluctant enforcer. But history teaches us that if you take this reluctance too far, you can undermine the whole system. Paul Schroeder, emeritus professor of international history at the University of Illinois, is one of the great international historians of the 20th century. He once remarked to me: "If you look at history, the periods of relative peace are those in which there is a durable, stable and tolerable hegemon, who does the adjusting and preserves the minimal necessary norms and rules of the game. And that hegemon always pays a disproportionate share of the collective costs, even forgoes opportunities for conquest or restrains itself in other ways, so as not to build up resentments and to make sure the system stays tolerable for others.

"The difficulty," Schroeder continued, "comes when the benign hegemonic power, which is responsible for keeping the system stable, is unable or unwilling to pay the disproportionate costs to do so, or its hegemony becomes intolerable and predatory rather than benign, or when enough actors rebel against its rules and insist upon a different kind of system that may not benefit that hegemon."

That is what we must avoid. The global system cannot hold together without an activist and generous American foreign and defense policy. Without America on duty, there will be no America Online.

ANTHONY LAKE, "FROM CONTAINMENT TO ENLARGEMENT" (1993)

While writers and intellectuals speculated as to how the passing of the Cold War should affect US foreign policy, events obliged responsible officials to act and then to devise a rationale for those actions. During the period 1993–2001, the Clinton administration confronted many crises. Here Anthony Lake (1939–), who served as national security adviser during President Bill Clinton's first term, attempts to refurbish US grand strategy.

I have come to speak with you today because I believe our nation's policies toward the world stand at an historic crossroads. For half a century America's engagement in the world revolved around containment of a hostile Soviet Union. Our efforts helped block Soviet expansionism, topple Communist repression and secure a great victory for human freedom.

Clearly, the Soviet Union's collapse enhances our security. But it also requires us to think anew because the world is new.

In particular, with the end of the Cold War, there is no longer a consensus among the American people around why, and even whether our nation should remain actively engaged in the world. Geography and history always have made Americans wary of foreign entanglements. Now economic anxiety fans that wariness. Calls from the left and right to stay at home rather than engage abroad are re-enforced by the rhetoric of Neo-Know-Nothings.

Those of us who believe in the imperative of our international engagement must push back. . . .

Stating our purpose is neither academic nor rhetorical. What we do outside our borders has immediate and lasting consequences for all Americans. As the President often notes, the line between foreign and domestic policy has evaporated. . . .

Let us begin by taking stock of our new era. Four facts are salient. First, America's core concepts—democracy and market economics—are more broadly accepted than ever. Over the past ten years the number of democracies has nearly doubled. Since 1970, the number of significant command economies dropped from 10 to 3.

This victory of freedom is practical, not ideological: billions of people on every continent are simply concluding, based on decades of their own hard experience, that democracy and markets are the most productive and liberating ways to organize their lives.

Their conclusion resonates with America's core values. We see individuals as equally created with a God-given right to life, liberty and the pursuit of happiness. So we trust in the equal wisdom of free individuals to protect those rights: through democracy, as the process for best meeting shared needs in the face of competing desires; and through markets as the process for best meeting private needs in a way that expands opportunity.

Both processes strengthen each other: democracy alone can produce justice, but not the material goods necessary for individuals to thrive; markets alone can expand wealth, but not that sense of justice without which civilized societies perish.

Democracy and market economics are ascendant in this new era, but they are not everywhere triumphant. There remain vast areas in Asia, Africa, the Middle East and elsewhere where democracy and market economics are at best new arrivals—most likely unfamiliar, sometimes vilified, often fragile.

But it is wrong to assume these ideas will be embraced only by the West and rejected by the rest. Culture does shape politics and economics. But the idea of freedom has universal appeal. Thus, we have arrived at neither the end of history nor a clash of civilizations, but a moment of immense democratic and entrepreneurial opportunity. We must not waste it.

The second feature of this era is that we are its dominant power. Those who say otherwise sell America short. The fact is, we have the world's strongest military, its largest economy and its most dynamic, multiethnic society. We are setting a global example in our efforts to reinvent our democratic and market institutions. Our leadership is sought and respected in every corner of the world. . . .

Moreover, absent a reversal in Russia, there is now no near-term threat to America's existence. Serious threats remain: terrorism, proliferating weapons of mass destruction, ethnic conflicts and the degradation of our global environment. Above all, we are threatened by sluggish economic growth, which undermines the security of our people as well as that of allies and friends abroad. Yet none of these threats holds the same immediate dangers for us as did Nazi conquest or Soviet expansionism.

America's challenge today is to lead on the basis of opportunity more than fear.

The third notable aspect of this era is an explosion of ethnic conflicts. . . . [T]he end of the Cold War and the collapse of various repressive regimes has removed the lid from numerous caldrons of ethnic, religious or factional hatreds. In many states of the former Soviet Union and elsewhere, there is a tension between the desire for ethnic separatism and the creation of liberal democracy, which alone can safely accommodate and even celebrate differences among citizens. A major challenge to our thinking, our policies and our international institutions in this era is the fact that most conflicts are taking place *within* rather than *among* nations.

These conflicts are typically highly complex; at the same time, their brutality will tug at our consciences. We need a healthy wariness about our ability to shape solutions for such disputes, yet at times our interests or humanitarian concerns will impel our unilateral or multilateral engagement.

The fourth feature of this new era is that the pulse of the planet has accelerated dramatically and with it the pace of change in human events. Computers, faxes, fiber optic cables and satellites all speed the flow of information. The measurement of wealth, and increasingly wealth itself, consists in bytes of data that move at the speed of light.

The accelerated pace of events is neither bad nor good. Its sharp consequences can cut either way. It means both doctors and terrorists can more quickly share their technical secrets. Both prodemocracy activists and skinhead anarchists can more broadly spread their views. Ultimately, the world's acceleration creates new and diverse ways for us to exert our influence, if we choose to do so—but increases the likelihood that, if we do not, rapid events, instantly reported, may overwhelm us. As the President has suggested, we must decide whether to make change our ally or allow ourselves to become its victims.

In such a world, our interests and ideals compel us not only to be engaged, but to lead. And in a real-time world of change and information, it is all the more important that our leadership be steadied around our central purpose.

That purpose can be found in the underlying rationale for our engagement throughout this century. As we fought aggressors and contained communism, our engagement abroad was animated both by calculations of power and by this belief: to the extent democracy and market economics hold sway in other nations, our own nation will be more secure, prosperous and influential, while the broader world will be more humane and peaceful.

The expansion of market-based economics abroad helps expand our exports and create American jobs, while it also improves living conditions and fuels demands for political liberalization abroad. The addition of new democracies makes us more secure because democracies tend not to wage war on each other or sponsor terrorism. They are more trustworthy in diplomacy and do a better job of respecting the human rights of their people.

These dynamics lay at the heart of Woodrow Wilson's most profound insights; although his moralism sometimes weakened his argument, he understood that our own security is shaped by the character of foreign regimes. Indeed, most Presidents who followed, Republicans and Democrats alike, understood we must promote democracy and market economics in the world— because it protects our interests and security; and because it reflects values that are both American and universal.

Throughout the Cold War, we contained a global threat to market democracies; now we should seek to enlarge their reach, particularly in places of special significance to us.

The successor to a doctrine of containment must be a strategy of enlargement—enlargement of the world's free community of market democracies.

During the Cold War, even children understood America's security mission; as they looked at those maps on their schoolroom walls, they knew we were trying to contain the creeping expansion of that big, red blob. Today, at great risk of oversimplification, we might visualize our security mission as promoting the enlargement of the "blue areas" of market democracies. The difference, of course, is that we do not seek to expand the reach of our institutions by force, subversion or repression.

We must not allow this overarching goal to drive us into overreaching actions. To be successful, a strategy of enlargement must provide distinctions and set priorities. It must combine our broad goals of fostering democracy and markets with our more traditional geostrategic interests. And it must suggest how best to expend our large but nonetheless limited national security resources: financial, diplomatic and military.

In recent years, discussions about when to use force have turned on a set of vital questions, such as whether our forces match our objectives; whether we can fight and win in a time that is acceptable;

whether we have a reasonable exit if we do not; whether there is public and congressional support. But we have overlooked a prior, strategic question—the question of "where"—which sets the context for such military judgments.

I see four components to a strategy of enlargement.

First, we should strengthen the community of major market democracies—including our own—which constitutes the core from which enlargement is proceeding.

Second, we should help foster and consolidate new democracies and market economies, where possible, especially in states of special significance and opportunity.

Third, we must counter the aggression—and support the liberalization—of states hostile to democracy and markets.

Fourth, we need to pursue our humanitarian agenda not only by providing aid, but also by working to help democracy and market economics take root in regions of greatest humanitarian concern . . .

Centralized power defends itself. It not only wields tools of state power such as military force, political imprisonment and torture, but also exploits the intolerant energies of racism, ethnic prejudice, religious persecution, xenophobia, and irredentism. Those whose power is threatened by the spread of democracy and markets will always have a personal stake in resisting those practices with passionate intensity.

When such leaders sit atop regional powers, such as Iran and Iraq, they may engage in violence and lawlessness that threatens the United States and other democracies. Such reactionary, "backlash" states are more likely to sponsor terrorism and traffic in weapons of mass destruction and ballistic missile technologies. They are more likely to suppress their own people, foment ethnic rivalries and threaten their neighbors.

In this world of multiplying democracies, expanding markets and accelerating commerce, the rulers of backlash states face an unpleasant choice. They can seek to isolate their people from these liberating forces. If they do, however, they cut themselves off from the very forces that create wealth and social dynamism. Such states tend to rot from within both economically and spiritually.

But as they grow weaker, they also may become more desperate and dangerous.

Our policy toward such states, so long as they act as they do, must seek to isolate them diplomatically, militarily, economically, and technologically. It must stress intelligence, counterterrorism, and multilateral export controls. It also must apply global norms regarding weapons of mass destruction and ensure their enforcement. . . .

While some backlash states may seek to wall themselves off from outside influence, other antidemocratic states will opt to pursue greater wealth by liberalizing their economic rules. Sooner or later, however, these states confront the need to liberalize the flow of information into and within their nation, and to tolerate the rise of an entrepreneurial middle-class. Both developments weaken despotic rule and lead over time to rising demands for democracy. . . .

We cannot impose democracy on regimes that appear to be opting for liberalization, but we may be able to help steer some of them down that path while providing penalties that raise the costs of repression and aggressive behavior. These efforts have special meaning for our relations with China. . . .

Our policies toward the Islamic world prove another example. Let me emphasize this point: our nation respects the many contributions Islam has made to the world over the past 1300 years, and we appreciate the close bonds of values and history between Islam and the Judeo-Christian beliefs of most Americans. We will extend every expression or friendship to those of the Islamic faith who abide in peace and tolerance. But we will provide every resistance to militants who distort Islamic doctrines and seek to expand their influence by force. . . .

I believe there is a more fundamental foreign policy challenge brewing for the United States. It is a challenge over whether we will be significantly engaged abroad at all. As suggested at the outset, in many ways, we are returning to the divisions and debates about our role in the world that are as old as our Republic. On one side is protectionism and limited foreign engagement; on the other is active American engagement abroad on behalf of democracy and expanded trade.

The last time our nation saw that classic division was just after World War I. It pitted those

Democrats and Republicans whose creativity produced the architectures of post-war prosperity and security against those in both parties who would have had us retreat within the isolated shell we occupied in the 1920s and 1930s. The internationalists won those debates, in part because they could point to a unitary threat to America's interests and because the nation was entering a period of economic security.

Today's supporters of engagement abroad have neither of those advantages. The threats and opportunities are diffuse and our people are deeply anxious about their economic fate. Rallying Americans to bear the costs and burdens of international engagement is no less important. But it is much more difficult.

For this reason, those who recognize the value of our leadership in the world should devote far more energy to making the case for sustained engagement abroad and less energy to debates over tactics. . . .

All of us have come out of the Cold War years having learned distinct lessons about what *not* to do—don't go to war without a way to win; don't underestimate the role of ideas; don't minimize the power of nationalism. Yet we have come into the new era with relatively few ways to convince a skeptical public that engagement abroad is a worthwhile investment. That is why a national dialogue over our fundamental purposes is so important.

In a world of extraordinary complexity, it would be too easy for us in the Internationalist camp to become "neo-Marxists"—not after Karl, but after Groucho, who once sang, "Whatever it is, I'm against it."

It is time for those who see the value of American engagement to steady our ranks; to define our purpose; and to rally the American people. In particular, at a time of high deficits and pressing domestic needs, we need to make a convincing case for our engagement or else see drastic reductions in our military, intelligence, peacekeeping and other foreign policy accounts.

In his farewell address in January, 1953, Harry Truman predicted the collapse of Communism. "I have a deep and abiding faith in the destiny of free men," he said. "With patience and courage, we shall some day move on into a new era."

Now that era is upon us. It is a moment of unparalleled opportunity. We have the blessing of living in the world's most powerful and respected nation at a time when the world is embracing our ideals as never before. We casn let this moment slip away. Or we can mobilize our nation in order to enlarge democracy, enlarge markets, and enlarge our future. I am confident that we will choose the road best travelled.

XII.

Impact of 9/11

The terrorist attacks of September 11, 2001 left the American people frightened, angry, and uncertain about what to expect next. To prevent a recurrence of such events, the United States embarked upon what became known as the Global War on Terrorism.

Just weeks after the devastating attack on the World Trade Center and the Pentagon, US forces intervened in Afghanistan, with the intention of destroying Al Qaeda and toppling the Taliban regime that had provided Al Qaeda with sanctuary. Known initially as Operation Enduring Freedom, this campaign achieved only partial success. Despite sustaining significant losses and expending enormous sums of money, the United States struggled unsuccessfully to pacify the Afghan countryside and to create an effective Afghan government. The Taliban persisted. The Afghanistan War was soon on its way to becoming the longest in all of American history.

Further complicating matters, even as events in Afghanistan continued to unfold, the George W. Bush administration decided to invade Iraq, a country uninvolved in the 9/11 conspiracy. The principal argument for doing so was that Saddam Hussein was developing weapons of mass destruction that he could possibly provide to terrorist organizations such as Al Qaeda. In fact, Iraq had no such weapons and was not seriously attempting to develop them.

Operation Iraqi Freedom began in March 2003, with high expectations of winning a decisive and economical victory. Although US forces quickly captured Baghdad and overthrew Saddam's Baathist regime, conclusive success proved elusive. As in Afghanistan, US forces struggled to impose order. Here too insurgents challenged US forces and inflicted heavy losses on the Americans. At home, the war became the least popular since Vietnam, to which it was frequently compared.

GEORGE W. BUSH, "ADDRESS TO A JOINT SESSION OF CONGRESS" (2001)

After a contested election that was ultimately decided by the Supreme Court, George W. Bush became the 43rd U.S. president in January 2001. Although Al Qaeda leader Osama bin Laden had declared war on the United States in 1996, the events of 9/11 caught Bush, members of his inner circle, and the national security apparatus as a whole completely by surprise. Nonetheless, it was left to the president to explain how such a disaster could have occurred and to devise a response. Here he speaks to the Congress just days after the attack.

In the normal course of events, Presidents come to this Chamber to report on the state of the Union. Tonight, no such report is needed. It has already been delivered by the American people.

We have seen it in the courage of passengers, who rushed terrorists to save others on the ground, passengers like an exceptional man named Todd Beamer. . . .

We have seen the state of our Union in the endurance of rescuers, working past exhaustion. We have seen the unfurling of flags, the lighting of candles, the giving of blood, the saying of prayers in English, Hebrew, and Arabic. We have seen the decency of a loving and giving people who have made the grief of strangers their own.

My fellow citizens, for the last 9 days, the entire world has seen for itself the state of our Union, and it is strong.

Tonight we are a country awakened to danger and called to defend freedom. Our grief has turned to anger and anger to resolution. Whether we bring our enemies to justice or bring justice to our enemies, justice will be done.

I thank the Congress for its leadership at such an important time. All of America was touched, on the evening of the tragedy, to see Republicans and Democrats joined together on the steps of this Capitol, singing "God Bless America." And you did more than sing; you acted, by delivering $40 billion to rebuild our communities and meet the needs of our military. . . .

And on behalf of the American people, I thank the world for its outpouring of support. America will never forget the sounds of our national anthem playing at Buckingham Palace, on the streets of Paris, and at Berlin's Brandenburg Gate. We will not forget South Korean children gathering to pray outside our Embassy in Seoul, or the prayers of sympathy offered at a mosque in Cairo. We will not forget moments of silence and days of mourning in Australia and Africa and Latin America. . . .

On September 11th, enemies of freedom committed an act of war against our country. Americans have known wars, but for the past 136 years, they have been wars on foreign soil, except for one Sunday in 1941. Americans have known the casualties of war, but not at the center of a great city on a peaceful morning. Americans have known surprise attacks, but never before on thousands of civilians. All of this was brought upon us in a single day, and night fell on a different world, a world where freedom itself is under attack.

Americans have many questions tonight. Americans are asking, who attacked our country? The evidence we have gathered all points to a collection of loosely affiliated terrorist organizations known as Al Qaida. They are some of the murderers indicted for bombing American Embassies in Tanzania and Kenya and responsible for bombing the U.S.S. *Cole*. Al Qaida is to terror what the Mafia is to crime. But its goal is not making money. Its goal is remaking the world and imposing its radical beliefs on people everywhere.

The terrorists practice a fringe form of Islamic extremism that has been rejected by Muslim scholars and the vast majority of Muslim clerics, a fringe movement that perverts the peaceful teachings of Islam. The terrorists' directive commands them to kill Christians and Jews, to kill all Americans, and make no distinctions among military and civilians, including women and children.

This group and its leader, a person named Usama bin Laden, are linked to many other organizations in different countries, including the Egyptian Islamic Jihad and the Islamic Movement of Uzbekistan. There are thousands of these terrorists in more than 60 countries. They are recruited from their own nations and neighborhoods and brought to camps in places like Afghanistan, where they are trained in the tactics of terror. They are sent back to their homes or sent to hide in countries around the world to plot evil and destruction.

The leadership of Al Qaida has great influence in Afghanistan and supports the Taliban regime in controlling most of that country. In Afghanistan, we see Al Qaida's vision for the world. Afghanistan's people have been brutalized. Many are starving, and many have fled. Women are not allowed to attend school. You can be jailed for owning a television. Religion can be practiced only as their leaders dictate. A man can be jailed in Afghanistan if his beard is not long enough.

The United States respects the people of Afghanistan—after all, we are currently its largest source of humanitarian aid—but we condemn the Taliban regime. It is not only repressing its own people; it is threatening people everywhere by sponsoring and sheltering and supplying terrorists. By aiding and abetting murder, the Taliban regime is committing murder.

And tonight the United States of America makes the following demands on the Taliban: Deliver to United States authorities all the leaders of Al Qaida who hide in your land. Release all foreign nationals, including American citizens, you have unjustly imprisoned. Protect foreign journalists, diplomats, and aid workers in your country. Close immediately and permanently every terrorist training camp in Afghanistan, and hand over every terrorist and every person in their support structure to appropriate authorities. Give the United States full access to terrorist training camps, so we can make sure they are no longer operating.

These demands are not open to negotiation or discussion. The Taliban must act and act immediately. They will hand over the terrorists, or they will share in their fate.

I also want to speak tonight directly to Muslims throughout the world. We respect your faith. It's practiced freely by many millions of Americans and by millions more in countries that America counts as friends. Its teachings are good and peaceful, and those who commit evil in the name of Allah blaspheme the name of Allah. The terrorists are traitors to their own faith, trying, in effect, to hijack Islam itself. The enemy of America is not our many Muslim friends; it is not our many Arab friends. Our enemy is a radical network of terrorists and every government that supports them.

Our war on terror begins with Al Qaida, but it does not end there. It will not end until every terrorist group of global reach has been found, stopped, and defeated.

Americans are asking, why do they hate us? They hate what we see right here in this Chamber, a democratically elected government. Their leaders are self-appointed. They hate our freedoms— our freedom of religion, our freedom of speech, our freedom to vote and assemble and disagree with each other.

They want to overthrow existing governments in many Muslim countries, such as Egypt, Saudi Arabia, and Jordan. They want to drive Israel out of the Middle East. They want to drive Christians and Jews out of vast regions of Asia and Africa.

These terrorists kill not merely to end lives but to disrupt and end a way of life. With every atrocity, they hope that America grows fearful, retreating from the world and forsaking our friends. They stand against us, because we stand in their way.

We are not deceived by their pretenses to piety. We have seen their kind before. They are the heirs of all the murderous ideologies of the 20th century. By sacrificing human life to serve their radical visions, by abandoning every value except the will to power, they follow in the path of fascism and Nazism and totalitarianism. And they will follow that path all the way, to where it ends, in history's unmarked grave of discarded lies.

Americans are asking, how will we fight and win this war? We will direct every resource at our command—every means of diplomacy, every tool of intelligence, every instrument of law enforcement, every financial influence, and every necessary weapon of war—to the disruption and to the defeat of the global terror network.

This war will not be like the war against Iraq a decade ago, with a decisive liberation of territory and a swift conclusion. It will not look like the air war above Kosovo 2 years ago, where no ground troops were used and not a single American was lost in combat.

Our response involves far more than instant retaliation and isolated strikes. Americans should not expect one battle but a lengthy campaign, unlike any other we have ever seen. It may include dramatic strikes, visible on TV, and covert operations, secret even in success. We will starve terrorists of funding, turn them one against another, drive them from place to place, until there is no refuge or no rest. And we will pursue nations that provide aid or safe haven to terrorism. Every nation, in every region, now has a decision to make: Either you are with us, or you are with the terrorists. From this day forward, any nation that continues to harbor or support terrorism will be regarded by the United States as a hostile regime.

Our Nation has been put on notice: We are not immune from attack. We will take defensive measures against terrorism to protect Americans. Today dozens of Federal departments and agencies, as well as State and local governments, have responsibilities affecting homeland security. These efforts must be coordinated at the highest level. . . .

So tonight I announce the creation of a Cabinet-level position reporting directly to me, the Office of Homeland Security. . . .

These measures are essential. But the only way to defeat terrorism as a threat to our way of life is to stop it, eliminate it, and destroy it where it grows. Many will be involved in this effort, from FBI agents to intelligence operatives to the reservists we have called to active duty. All deserve our thanks, and all have our prayers. And tonight, a few miles from the damaged Pentagon, I have a message for our military: Be ready. I've called the Armed Forces to alert, and there is a reason. The hour is coming when America will act, and you will make us proud.

This is not, however, just America's fight, and what is at stake is not just America's freedom. This is the world's fight. This is civilization's fight. This is the fight of all who believe in progress and pluralism, tolerance and freedom.

We ask every nation to join us. We will ask, and we will need, the help of police forces, intelligence services, and banking systems around the world. The United States is grateful that many nations and many international organizations have already responded with sympathy and with support, nations from Latin America to Asia, to Africa, to Europe, to the Islamic world. Perhaps the NATO Charter reflects best the attitude of the world: An attack on one is an attack on all.

The civilized world is rallying to America's side. They understand that if this terror goes unpunished, their own cities, their own citizens may be next. Terror, unanswered, can not only bring down buildings, it can threaten the stability of legitimate governments. And you know what? We're not going to allow it.

Americans are asking, what is expected of us? I ask you to live your lives and hug your children. I know many citizens have fears tonight, and I ask you to be calm and resolute, even in the face of a continuing threat.

I ask you to uphold the values of America and remember why so many have come here. We are in a fight for our principles, and our first responsibility is to live by them. No one should be singled out for unfair treatment or unkind words because of their ethnic background or religious faith. . . .

I ask your continued participation and confidence in the American economy. Terrorists attacked a symbol of American prosperity. They did not touch its source. America is successful because of the hard work and creativity and enterprise of our people. These were the true strengths of our economy before September 11th, and they are our strengths today.

And finally, please continue praying for the victims of terror and their families, for those in uniform, and for our great country. Prayer has comforted us in sorrow and will help strengthen us for the journey ahead. . . .

Tonight we face new and sudden national challenges. We will come together to improve air safety, to dramatically expand the number of air marshals on domestic flights and take new measures to prevent hijacking. We will come together to promote stability and keep our airlines flying, with direct assistance during this emergency.

We will come together to give law enforcement the additional tools it needs to track down terror here at home. We will come together to strengthen our intelligence capabilities, to know the plans of terrorists before they act and find them before they strike. We will come together to take active steps that strengthen America's economy and put our people back to work. . . .

After all that has just passed, all the lives taken and all the possibilities and hopes that died with them, it is natural to wonder if America's future is one of fear. Some speak of an age of terror. I know there are struggles ahead and dangers to face. But this country will define our times, not be defined by them. As long as the United States of America is determined and strong, this will not be an age of terror; this will be an age of liberty, here and across the world.

Great harm has been done to us. We have suffered great loss. And in our grief and anger, we have found our mission and our moment. Freedom and fear are at war. The advance of human freedom, the great achievement of our time and the great hope of every time, now depends on us. Our Nation—this generation—will lift a dark threat of violence from our people and our future. We will rally the world to this cause by our efforts, by our courage. We will not tire; we will not falter; and we will not fail.

It is my hope that in the months and years ahead, life will return almost to normal. We'll go back to our lives and routines, and that is good.

Even grief recedes with time and grace. But our resolve must not pass. Each of us will remember what happened that day and to whom it happened. We'll remember the moment the news came, where we were, and what we were doing. Some will remember an image of a fire or a story of rescue. Some will carry memories of a face and a voice gone forever. . . .

I will not forget this wound to our country and those who inflicted it. I will not yield; I will not rest; I will not relent in waging this struggle for freedom and security for the American people.

The course of this conflict is not known, yet its outcome is certain. Freedom and fear, justice and cruelty have always been at war, and we know that God is not neutral between them.

Fellow citizens, we'll meet violence with patient justice, assured of the rightness of our cause and confident of the victories to come. In all that lies before us, may God grant us wisdom, and may He watch over the United States of America.

George W. Bush, "State of the Union Address" (2002)

In retaliation for the 9/11 attacks, U.S. forces intervened in Afghanistan in October 2001, targeting Al Qaeda and ousting the Taliban regime that had given bin Laden sanctuary. The initial success achieved in Afghanistan persuaded Bush to expand the war on terrorism. He used the occasion of his State of the Union Address to announce those plans.

As we gather tonight, our Nation is at war; our economy is in recession; and the civilized world faces unprecedented dangers. Yet, the state of our Union has never been stronger.

We last met in an hour of shock and suffering. In 4 short months, our Nation has comforted the victims, begun to rebuild New York and the Pentagon, rallied a great coalition, captured, arrested, and rid the world of thousands of terrorists, destroyed Afghanistan's terrorist training camps, saved a people from starvation, and freed a country from brutal oppression.

The American flag flies again over our Embassy in Kabul. Terrorists who once occupied Afghanistan now occupy cells at Guantanamo Bay. And terrorist leaders who urged followers to sacrifice their lives are running for their own.

America and Afghanistan are now allies against terror. We'll be partners in rebuilding that country. . . .

The last time we met in this Chamber, the mothers and daughters of Afghanistan were captives in their own homes, forbidden from working or going to school. Today, women are free and are part of Afghanistan's new Government. . . .

Our progress is a tribute to the spirit of the Afghan people, to the resolve of our coalition, and to the might of the United States military. When I called our troops into action, I did so with complete confidence in their courage and skill. And tonight, thanks to them, we are winning the war on terror. The men and women of our Armed Forces have delivered a message now clear to every enemy of the United States: Even

7,000 miles away, across oceans and continents, on mountaintops and in caves, you will not escape the justice of this Nation. . . .

Our cause is just, and it continues. Our discoveries in Afghanistan confirmed our worst fears and showed us the true scope of the task ahead. We have seen the depth of our enemies' hatred in videos where they laugh about the loss of innocent life. And the depth of their hatred is equaled by the madness of the destruction they design. We have found diagrams of American nuclear powerplants and public water facilities, detailed instructions for making chemical weapons, surveillance maps of American cities, and thorough descriptions of landmarks in America and throughout the world.

What we have found in Afghanistan confirms that, far from ending there, our war against terror is only beginning. Most of the 19 men who hijacked planes on September the 11th were trained in Afghanistan's camps, and so were tens of thousands of others. Thousands of dangerous killers, schooled in the methods of murder, often supported by outlaw regimes, are now spread throughout the world like ticking timebombs, set to go off without warning.

Thanks to the work of our law enforcement officials and coalition partners, hundreds of terrorists have been arrested. Yet, tens of thousands of trained terrorists are still at large. These enemies view the entire world as a battlefield, and we must pursue them wherever they are. So long as training camps operate, so long as nations harbor terrorists, freedom is at risk. And America and our allies must not and will not allow it.

Our Nation will continue to be steadfast and patient and persistent in the pursuit of two great objectives. First, we will shut down terrorist camps, disrupt terrorist plans, and bring terrorists to justice. And second, we must prevent the terrorists and regimes who seek chemical, biological, or nuclear weapons from threatening the United States and the world.

Our military has put the terror training camps of Afghanistan out of business, yet camps still exist in at least a dozen countries. A terrorist underworld, including groups like Hamas, Hizballah, Islamic Jihad, Jaish-e-Mohammed, operates in remote jungles and deserts and hides in the centers of large cities.

While the most visible military action is in Afghanistan, America is acting elsewhere. We now have troops in the Philippines, helping to train that country's armed forces to go after terrorist cells that have executed an American and still hold hostages. Our soldiers, working with the Bosnian Government, seized terrorists who were plotting to bomb our Embassy. Our Navy is patrolling the coast of Africa to block the shipment of weapons and the establishment of terrorist camps in Somalia.

My hope is that all nations will heed our call and eliminate the terrorist parasites who threaten their countries and our own. Many nations are acting forcefully. Pakistan is now cracking down on terror, and I admire the strong leadership of President Musharraf. But some governments will be timid in the face of terror. And make no mistake about it: If they do not act, America will.

Our second goal is to prevent regimes that sponsor terror from threatening America or our friends and allies with weapons of mass destruction. Some of these regimes have been pretty quiet since September the 11th, but we know their true nature.

North Korea is a regime arming with missiles and weapons of mass destruction, while starving its citizens.

Iran aggressively pursues these weapons and exports terror, while an unelected few repress the Iranian people's hope for freedom.

Iraq continues to flaunt its hostility toward America and to support terror. The Iraqi regime has plotted to develop anthrax and nerve gas and nuclear weapons for over a decade. This is a regime that has already used poison gas to murder thousands of its own citizens, leaving the bodies of mothers huddled over their dead children. This is a regime that agreed to international inspections, then kicked out the inspectors. This is a regime that has something to hide from the civilized world.

States like these and their terrorist allies constitute an axis of evil, arming to threaten the peace of the world. By seeking weapons of mass destruction, these regimes pose a grave and growing danger. They could provide these arms to terrorists, giving them the means to match their hatred. They could attack our allies or attempt to blackmail the United States. In any of these cases, the price of indifference would be catastrophic.

We will work closely with our coalition to deny terrorists and their state sponsors the materials, technology, and expertise to make and deliver weapons of mass destruction. We will develop and deploy effective missile defenses to protect America and our allies from sudden attack. And all nations should know: America will do what is necessary to ensure our Nation's security.

We'll be deliberate; yet, time is not on our side. I will not wait on events while dangers gather. I will not stand by as peril draws closer and closer. The United States of America will not permit the world's most dangerous regimes to threaten us with the world's most destructive weapons.

Our war on terror is well begun, but it is only begun. This campaign may not be finished on our watch; yet, it must be and it will be waged on our watch. We can't stop short. If we stop now, leaving terror camps intact and terrorist states unchecked, our sense of security would be false and temporary. History has called America and our allies to action, and it is both our responsibility and our privilege to fight freedom's fight.

Our first priority must always be the security of our Nation, and that will be reflected in the budget I send to Congress. My budget supports three great goals for America: We will win this war; we will protect our homeland; and we will revive our economy. . . .

It costs a lot to fight this war. We have spent more than a billion dollars a month, over $30 million a day, and we must be prepared for future operations. Afghanistan proved that expensive precision weapons defeat the enemy and spare innocent lives, and we need more of them. We need to replace aging aircraft and make our military more agile to put our troops anywhere in the world quickly and safely. Our men and women in uniform deserve the best weapons, the best equipment, the best training, and they also deserve another pay raise.

My budget includes the largest increase in defense spending in two decades, because while the price of freedom and security is high, it is never too high. Whatever it costs to defend our country, we will pay.

The next priority of my budget is to do everything possible to protect our citizens and strengthen our Nation against the ongoing threat of another attack. Time and distance from the events of September the 11th will not make us safer unless we act on its lessons. America is no longer protected by vast oceans. We are protected from attack only by vigorous action abroad and increased vigilance at home.

My budget nearly doubles funding for a sustained strategy of homeland security, focused on four key areas: bioterrorism, emergency response, airport and border security, and improved intelligence. We will develop vaccines to fight anthrax and other deadly diseases. We'll increase funding to help States and communities train and equip our heroic police and firefighters. We will improve intelligence collection and sharing, expand patrols at our borders, strengthen the security of air travel, and use technology to track the arrivals and departures of visitors to the United States.

Homeland security will make America not only stronger but, in many ways, better. Knowledge gained from bioterrorism research will improve public health. Stronger police and fire departments will mean safer neighborhoods. Stricter border enforcement will help combat illegal drugs. And as government works to better secure our homeland, America will continue to depend on the eyes and ears of alert citizens. . . .

Once we have funded our national security and our homeland security, the final great priority of my budget is economic security for the American people. To achieve these great national objectives—to win the war, protect the homeland, and revitalize our economy—our budget will run a deficit that will be small and short term, so long as Congress restrains spending and acts in a fiscally responsible manner. We have clear priorities, and we must act at home with the same purpose and resolve we have shown overseas. We'll prevail in the war, and we will defeat this recession. . . .

During these last few months, I've been humbled and privileged to see the true character of this country in a time of testing. Our enemies believed America was weak and materialistic, that we would splinter in fear and selfishness. They were as wrong as they are evil.

The American people have responded magnificently, with courage and compassion, strength and resolve. As I have met the heroes, hugged the families, and looked into the tired faces of rescuers, I have stood in awe of the American people. . . .

None of us would ever wish the evil that was done on September the 11th. Yet, after America was attacked, it was as if our entire country looked into a mirror and saw our better selves. We were reminded that we are citizens with obligations to each other, to our country, and to history. We began to think less of the goods we can accumulate and more about the good we can do.

For too long our culture has said, "If it feels good, do it." Now America is embracing a new ethic and a new creed, "Let's roll." In the sacrifice of soldiers, the fierce brotherhood of firefighters, and the bravery and generosity of ordinary citizens, we have glimpsed what a new culture of responsibility could look like. We want to be a nation that serves goals larger than self. We've been offered a unique opportunity, and we must not let this moment pass. . . .

This time of adversity offers a unique moment of opportunity, a moment we must seize to change our culture. Through the gathering momentum of millions of acts of service and decency and kindness, I know we can overcome evil with greater good.

And we have a great opportunity during this time of war to lead the world toward the values that will bring lasting peace. All fathers and mothers, in all societies, want their children to be educated and live free from poverty and violence. No people on Earth yearn to be oppressed or aspire to servitude or eagerly await the midnight knock of the secret police. If anyone doubts this, let them look to Afghanistan, where the Islamic "street" greeted the fall of tyranny with song and celebration. Let the skeptics look to Islam's own rich history, with its centuries of learning and tolerance and progress. America will lead by defending liberty and justice because they are right and true and unchanging for all people everywhere.

No nation owns these aspirations, and no nation is exempt from them. We have no intention of imposing our culture. But America will always stand firm for the nonnegotiable demands of human dignity: the rule of law; limits on the power of the state; respect for women; private property; free speech; equal justice; and religious tolerance.

America will take the side of brave men and women who advocate these values around the world, including the Islamic world, because we have a greater objective than eliminating threats and containing resentment. We seek a just and peaceful world beyond the war on terror.

In this moment of opportunity, a common danger is erasing old rivalries. America is working with Russia and China and India, in ways we have never before, to achieve peace and prosperity. In every region, free markets and free trade and free societies are proving their power to lift lives. Together with friends and allies from Europe to Asia and Africa to Latin America, we will demonstrate that the forces of terror cannot stop the momentum of freedom.

The last time I spoke here, I expressed the hope that life would return to normal. In some ways, it has. In others, it never will. Those of us who have lived through these challenging times have been changed by them. We've come to know truths that we will never question: Evil is real, and it must be opposed. Beyond all differences of race or creed, we are one country, mourning together and facing danger together. Deep in the American character, there is honor, and it is stronger than cynicism. And many have discovered again that even in tragedy—especially in tragedy—God is near.

In a single instant, we realized that this will be a decisive decade in the history of liberty, that we've been called to a unique role in human events. Rarely has the world faced a choice more clear or consequential.

Our enemies send other people's children on missions of suicide and murder. They embrace tyranny and death as a cause and a creed. We stand for a different choice, made long ago on the day of our founding. We affirm it again today. We choose freedom and the dignity of every life.

Steadfast in our purpose, we now press on. We have known freedom's price. We have shown freedom's power. And in this great conflict, my fellow Americans, we will see freedom's victory.

George W. Bush, "West Point Commencement Speech" (2002)

Back in 1983, President Reagan had stated that the United States didn't "start fights." After 9/11, the Bush administration embraced a policy of preventive war. The president unveiled this "Bush Doctrine" in a speech to graduating cadets at West Point in May 2002. The immediate target of the Bush Doctrine was Saddam Hussein's Iraq.

Every West Point class is commissioned to the Armed Forces. Some West Point classes are also commissioned by history to take part in a great new calling for their country. Speaking here to the class of 1942, 6 months after Pearl Harbor, General Marshall said, "We're determined that before the Sun sets on this terrible struggle, our flag will be recognized throughout the world as a symbol of freedom on the one hand and of overwhelming power on the other." Officers graduating that year helped fulfill that mission, defeating Japan and Germany and then reconstructing those nations as allies. West Point graduates of the 1940s saw the rise of a deadly new challenge—the challenge of imperial communism—and opposed it from Korea to Berlin to Vietnam, and in the cold war from beginning to end. And as the Sun set on their struggle, many of those West Point officers lived to see a world transformed.

History has also issued its call to your generation. In your last year, America was attacked by a ruthless and resourceful enemy. You graduate from this Academy in a time of war, taking your place in an American military that is powerful and is honorable. Our war on terror is only begun, but in Afghanistan it was begun well.

I am proud of the men and women who have fought on my orders. America is profoundly grateful for all who serve the cause of freedom and for all who have given their lives in its defense. This Nation respects and trusts our military, and we are confident in your victories to come.

This war will take many turns we cannot predict. Yet, I am certain of this: Wherever we carry it, the American flag will stand not only for our power but for freedom. Our Nation's cause has always been larger than our Nation's defense. We fight, as we always fight, for a just peace, a peace that favors human liberty. We will defend the peace against threats from terrorists and tyrants. We will preserve the peace by building good relations among the great powers. And we will extend the peace by encouraging free and open societies on every continent.

Building this just peace is America's opportunity and America's duty. From this day forward, it is your challenge as well, and we will meet this challenge together. You will wear the uniform of a great and unique country. America has no empire to extend or utopia to establish. We wish for others only what we wish for ourselves, safety from violence, the rewards of liberty, and the hope for a better life.

In defending the peace, we face a threat with no precedent. Enemies in the past needed great armies and great industrial capabilities to endanger the American people and our Nation. The attacks of September the 11th required a few hundred thousand dollars in the hands of a few dozen evil and deluded men. All of the chaos and suffering they caused came at much less than the cost of a single tank. The dangers have not passed. This Government and the American people are on watch. We are ready, because we know the terrorists have more money and more men and more plans.

The gravest danger to freedom lies at the perilous crossroads of radicalism and technology. When the spread of chemical and biological and nuclear weapons, along with ballistic missile technology—when that occurs, even weak states and small groups could attain a catastrophic power to strike great nations. Our enemies have declared this very intention and have been caught seeking these terrible weapons. They want the capability to blackmail us or to harm us or to harm our friends, and we will oppose them with all our power.

For much of the last century, America's defense relied on the cold war doctrines of deterrence and containment. In some cases, those strategies still apply, but new threats also require new thinking. Deterrence—the promise of massive retaliation against nations—means nothing against shadowy terrorist networks with no nation or citizens to defend. Containment is not possible when unbalanced dictators with weapons of mass destruction can deliver those weapons on missiles or secretly provide them to terrorist allies. We cannot defend America and our friends by hoping for the best. We cannot put our faith in the word of tyrants who solemnly sign nonproliferation treaties and then systemically break them. If we wait for threats to fully materialize, we will have waited too long.

Homeland defense and missile defense are part of stronger security; they're essential priorities for America. Yet, the war on terror will not be won on the defensive. We must take the battle to the enemy, disrupt his plans, and confront the worst threats before they emerge. In the world we have entered, the only path to safety is the path of action, and this Nation will act.

Our security will require the best intelligence to reveal threats hidden in caves and growing in laboratories. Our security will require modernizing domestic agencies such as the FBI, so they're prepared to act and act quickly against danger. Our security will require transforming the military you will lead, a military that must be ready to strike at a moment's notice in any dark corner of the world. And our security will require all Americans to be forward-looking and resolute, to be ready for preemptive action when necessary to defend our liberty and to defend our lives.

The work ahead is difficult. The choices we will face are complex. We must uncover terror cells in 60 or more countries, using every tool of finance, intelligence, and law enforcement. Along with our friends and allies, we must oppose proliferation and confront regimes that sponsor terror, as each case requires. Some nations need military training to fight terror, and we'll provide it. Other nations oppose terror but tolerate the hatred that leads to terror, and that must change. We will send diplomats where they are needed, and we will send you, our soldiers, where you're needed.

All nations that decide for aggression and terror will pay a price. We will not leave the safety of America and the peace of the planet at the mercy of a few mad terrorists and tyrants. We will lift this dark threat from our country and from the world.

Because the war on terror will require resolve and patience, it will also require firm moral purpose. In this way our struggle is similar to the cold war. Now, as then, our enemies are totalitarians, holding a creed of power with no place for human dignity. Now, as then, they seek to impose a joyless conformity, to control every life and all of life.

America confronted imperial communism in many different ways, diplomatic, economic, and military. Yet, moral clarity was essential to our victory in the cold war. When leaders like John F. Kennedy and Ronald Reagan refused to gloss over the brutality of tyrants, they gave hope to prisoners and dissidents and exiles and rallied free nations to a great cause.

Some worry that it is somehow undiplomatic or impolite to speak the language of right and wrong. I disagree. Different circumstances require different methods but not different moralities. Moral truth is the same in every culture, in every time, and in every place. Targeting innocent civilians for murder is always and everywhere wrong. Brutality against women is always and everywhere wrong. There can be no neutrality between justice and cruelty, between the innocent and the guilty. We are in a conflict between good and evil, and America will call evil by its name. By confronting evil and lawless regimes, we do not create a problem; we reveal a problem. And we will lead the world in opposing it.

As we defend the peace, we also have an historic opportunity to preserve the peace. We have our best chance since the rise of the nation-state in the 17th century to build a world where the great powers compete in peace instead of prepare for war. The history of the last century, in particular, was dominated by a series of destructive national rivalries that left battlefields and graveyards across the Earth. Germany fought France, the Axis fought the Allies, and then the East fought the West, in proxy wars and tense standoffs, against a backdrop of nuclear Armageddon.

Competition between great nations is inevitable, but armed conflict in our world is not. More and more, civilized nations find ourselves on the same side, united by common dangers of terrorist violence and chaos. America has and intends to keep military strengths beyond challenge, thereby making the destabilizing arms races of other eras pointless and limiting rivalries to trade and other pursuits of peace.

Today, the great powers are also increasingly united by common values, instead of divided by conflicting ideologies. The United States, Japan, and our Pacific friends, and now all of Europe, share a deep commitment to human freedom, embodied in strong alliances such as NATO. And the tide of liberty is rising in many other nations.

Generations of West Point officers planned and practiced for battles with Soviet Russia. I've just returned from a new Russia, now a country reaching toward democracy and our partner in the war against terror. Even in China, leaders are discovering that economic freedom is the only lasting source of national wealth. In time, they will find that social and political freedom is the only true source of national greatness.

When the great powers share common values, we are better able to confront serious regional conflicts together, better able to cooperate in preventing the spread of violence or economic chaos. In the past, great power rivals took sides in difficult regional problems, making divisions deeper and more complicated. Today, from the Middle East to South Asia, we are gathering broad international coalitions to increase the pressure for peace. We must build strong and great power relations when times are good to help manage crisis when times are bad. America needs partners to preserve the peace, and we will work with every nation that shares this noble goal.

And finally, America stands for more than the absence of war. We have a great opportunity to extend a just peace by replacing poverty, repression, and resentment around the world with hope of a better day. Through most of history, poverty was persistent, inescapable, and almost universal. In the last few decades, we've seen nations from Chile to South Korea build modern economies and freer societies, lifting millions of people out of despair and want. And there's no mystery to this achievement.

The 20th century ended with a single surviving model of human progress, based on nonnegotiable demands of human dignity, the rule of law, limits on the power of the state, respect for women, and private property and free speech and equal justice and religious tolerance. America cannot impose this vision, yet we can support and reward governments that make the right choices for their own people. In our development aid, in our diplomatic efforts, in our international broadcasting, and in our educational assistance, the United States will promote moderation and tolerance and human rights. And we will defend the peace that makes all progress possible.

When it comes to the common rights and needs of men and women, there is no clash of civilizations. The requirements of freedom apply fully to Africa and Latin America and the entire Islamic world. The peoples of the Islamic nations want and deserve the same freedoms and opportunities as people in every nation. And their governments should listen to their hopes.

A truly strong nation will permit legal avenues of dissent for all groups that pursue their aspirations without violence. An advancing nation will pursue economic reform, to unleash the great entrepreneurial energy of its people. A thriving nation will respect the rights of women, because no society can prosper while denying opportunity to half its citizens. Mothers and fathers and children across the Islamic world and all the world share the same fears and aspirations: In poverty, they struggle; in tyranny, they suffer; and as we saw in Afghanistan, in liberation, they celebrate.

America has a greater objective than controlling threats and containing resentment. We will work for a just and peaceful world beyond the war on terror.

Bernard Lewis, "A Time for Toppling," *Wall Street Journal* (September 28, 2002)

A scholar specializing in the history of Islam, Bernard Lewis (1916–) argued that overthrowing Saddam Hussein held the key to eliminating terrorism and bringing peace to the Middle East. Bush administration officials concurred.

Among the many arguments that have been adduced for not taking action against the present regime in Iraq, two have received special emphasis.

The first is that the governments and peoples of the Middle East attach far greater importance to the Arab-Israeli conflict than to Iraq or any other problem in the region, and that therefore one should begin by solving that. The second is that even a successful attempt at regime change in Iraq would have a dangerous destabilizing effect on the rest of the region, and could lead to general conflict and chaos.

The conflict with Israel certainly receives overwhelmingly major attention in the Arabic media, but since this is the only specific grievance that may be publicly expressed in a region of numerous and painful problems, that is hardly surprising. One may therefore wonder whether Middle Eastern governments would indeed wish for a peace settlement, which would deprive them of this valuable safety valve, leaving them to face the undeflected anger of their subjects, including those who live under the rule of the Palestine authority. From the almost monotonous regularity with which a series of promising peace processes have failed at the moment when they seemed most likely to succeed, one may be driven to the conclusion that they prefer to keep the conflict unresolved, but at a low level—simmering not boiling, and usefully controllable.

In any case, requiring a settlement of the Palestine question as a prerequisite to dealing with Saddam Hussein sends him a clear signal that he must at all costs prevent such a solution. Saddam Hussein has indeed already responded to that signal in various ways, both secret and open. The most notable of his open responses is the increase of the bounty he pays to the families of suicide bombers from $10,000 to $25,000. This is the most public but probably not the most important of his contributions to the conflict. To make the settlement of that conflict—which even in its present form is more than half a century old—a prerequisite for any action concerning Iraq is a sure formula for indefinite inaction.

The fear of destabilization is both genuine and serious, and it is easy to understand the anxiety provoked in the regimes of the Middle East by the prospect of a regime change in Iraq. The crucial question here is not how or by whom Saddam is removed, but what comes in his place. The clear preference of some influential groups in this country and elsewhere is for his replacement to be a kinder and gentler tyrant, who would be amenable to our interests and requirements, while avoiding the hazards of regime change. This would certainly be the preference of our so-called allies in the region, most of whom would feel mortally threatened by the emergence of anything like a democratic regime in Iraq.

But why should we feel threatened by such a change? The overwhelming evidence is that the majority of our terrorist enemies come from purportedly friendly countries, and their main grievance against us is that, in their eyes, we are responsible for maintaining the tyrannical regimes that rule over them—an accusation that has, to say the very least, some plausibility. Apart from Turkey and Israel, the two countries in the region where the governments are elected and can be dismissed by the people, most of the countries of the Middle East can be divided into two groups: those with what we are pleased to call friendly governments, and therefore increasingly hostile people who hold us responsible for the oppression and depredations of those governments, and, on the other hand, those with bitterly hostile governments, whose people consequently look to us for help and liberation.

The most notable of these are Iraq and Iran. In countries under dictatorship, the political joke is often the only authentic and uncensored expression of political opinion. An Iranian joke, current during the campaign in Afghanistan, related that many Iranians put signs on top of their houses, in English, with the text:"This way please!"

It is noteworthy that after the events of Sept. 11, great numbers of people came out into the streets in Iranian cities, where, in defiance of the authorities, they lit candles and held vigils in sympathy and solidarity with the victims in New York and Washington. This contrasted markedly with the scenes of rejoicing elsewhere. One is often told that if we succeed in overthrowing the regimes of what President Bush has rightly called the "Axis of Evil," the scenes of rejoicing in their cities would even exceed those that followed the liberation of Kabul.

The overthrow of a regime must inevitably raise questions, concerning first what will follow, and then what impact this will have in neighboring countries. A regime change may well be dangerous, but sometimes the dangers of inaction are greater than those of action.

There may indeed be, as is so often said, a link between a settlement of the Palestine conflict and a regime change in the region—but in the reverse order to that usually adduced. It is often said and generally agreed that democracies do not start wars. Democratic governments are elected by the people and are answerable to the people, and with exceedingly rare exceptions, the people prefer peace. Even the great Winston Churchill—certainly no warmonger, but seen by his people as a war leader—was thrown out of power by the British people in the general election of 1945. It is equally true, but less recognized, that dictatorships do not make peace. The world war started by the Axis ended with its defeat. The Cold War started by the Soviet Union ended with its collapse.

In the same way, the dictatorships that rule much of the Middle East today will not, indeed cannot, make peace, because they need conflict to justify their tyrannical oppression of their own people, and to deflect their peoples' anger against an external enemy. As with the Axis and the Soviet Union, real peace will come only with their defeat or, preferably, collapse, and their replacement by governments that have been chosen and can be dismissed by their people and will therefore seek to resolve, not provoke, conflicts.

DAVID FRUM AND RICHARD PERLE, *AN END TO EVIL* (2004)

US and allied forces invaded Iraq in March 2003 and quickly deposed Saddam Hussein. Seemingly, President Bush had won a historic victory. David Frum (1960–) and Richard Perle (1941–), enthusiastic promoters of the war, wasted no time in tallying up all that had been achieved. The Iraq War, in their view, provided a template for future action aimed at furthering America's mission.

By toppling Saddam Hussein, we achieved at least seven great objectives.

1. We put an end to the threat from whatever weapons of mass destruction Saddam actually possessed as of 2003—and, far more important, from those weapons he *would* have possessed had he been left in place.
2. We won a great victory over terrorism by eliminating a Middle Eastern regime that has for thirty years been one of the leading sponsors of terrorism in the region . . .
3. We denied our enemies in the Middle East the huge victory *they* would have won had Saddam been able to claim that he had survived and triumphed over us.
4. We have learned valuable lessons about how to fight wars in the region and how to rebuild afterward. Nobody will pretend that mistakes were not made in the Iraqi campaign and the subsequent occupation. But we have learned from those mistakes, and they will not be repeated. . . .

5. We gave other potential enemies a vivid and compelling demonstration of America's ability to win swift and total victory over significant enemy forces with minimal U.S. casualties. The overwhelming American victory in the battle of Baghdad surely stamped a powerful impression upon the minds of the rulers of Teheran and Pyongyang.
6. We aided the forces of democracy throughout the region by demonstrating that even the most fearful local dictatorships are far more fragile than they look.
7. We eliminated the Arab world's cruelest and most tyrannical ruler. We liberated an entire nation, opening the way to a humane, decent civil society in Iraq—and to reform of the ideological and moral climate of the entire Middle East. . . .

For two hundred years, tyrannical rulers have dreaded America's influence over their subjugated peoples. As long as the United States has existed, that existence has demonstrated that freedom is possible. As long as the United States has prospered, our prosperity has shown that freedom is

David Frum and Richard Perle, *An End to Evil* (2004).

rewarded. And now that the United States has become the greatest of all great powers in world history, its triumph has shown that freedom is irresistible. . . .

No lie lasts forever, and militant Islam is a lie. It proposes to restore the vanished glory of a great civilization through crimes that horrify the conscience of the world. It invokes the language of liberation—but it intends to fasten unthinking, unquestioning slavery on the minds of the people of one-fifth of the world. It claims the authority of God for its own cruelty and evil.

The United States has been reproached even by many who should know better for inserting itself into Iraq rather than letting the Iraqis rule themselves. But it is only because we did insert ourselves into Iraq that the Iraqis have any hope of ruling themselves—and the same will be true in Iran and everywhere else in the Islamic world where we must fight. . . .

We do not show our respect for human difference by shrugging indifferently when people somehow different from ourselves are brutalized in body and spirit. If a foreign people lack liberty, it is not because of some misguided act of cultural choice. It is because they have been seized and oppressed and tyrannized. To say that we are engaged in "imposing American values" when we liberate people is to imply that there are peoples on this earth who value their own subjugation.

It is the terrorists, rather, who intend to impose *their* values, upon Muslims and non-Muslims alike. They inflict misery and death upon Muslims— but promise to compensate by inflicting still greater misery and death upon non-Muslims. The terrorists espouse an ideology of conquest, just as the Nazis and the Soviets did; and as we defeated the Nazis and communists by championing freedom not only for ourselves but also for Germans and Russians, so we must now do the same for the Islamic people who are both terrorism's prime constituency and its principal victims. . . .

To call this "empire" as do some opponents of the war—and some rash supporters, too—is to wrong ourselves. To call it "empire" belittles the many small countries that have turned to the United States for protection, rightly confident that our assistance would not impair their independence and sovereignty. The American record on this score is not perfect. But it is a record to be proud of all the same. . . .

A world at peace; a world governed by law; a world in which all peoples are free to find their own destinies: That dream has not yet come true, it will not come true soon, but if it ever does come true, it will be brought into being by American armed might and defended by American might, too. America's vocation is not an imperial vocation. Our vocation is to support justice with power. It is a vocation that has earned us terrible enemies. It is a vocation that has made us, at our best moments, the hope of the world.

NORMAN PODHORETZ, "WORLD WAR IV: HOW IT STARTED, WHAT IT MEANS, WHY WE HAVE TO WIN," *COMMENTARY* (SEPTEMBER 2004)

An uncompromising neoconservative, the writer and editor Norman Podhoretz (1930–) agreed that the overthrow of Saddam Hussein was merely the first act in a far more ambitious undertaking. Only fools, cowards, and anti-Semites would disagree, he insisted.

[W]e are only in the very early stages of what promises to be a very long war, and Iraq is only the second front to have been opened in that war: the second scene, so to speak, of the first act of a five-act play. In World War II and then in World War III, we persisted in spite of impatience, discouragement, and opposition for as long as it took to win, and this is exactly what

we have been called upon to do today in World War IV.

For today, no less than in those titanic conflicts, we are up against a truly malignant force in radical Islamism and in the states breeding, sheltering, or financing its terrorist armory. This new enemy has already attacked us on our own soil—a feat neither Nazi Germany nor Soviet Russia ever managed to pull off—and openly announces his intention to hit us again, only this time with weapons of infinitely greater and deadlier power than those used on 9/11. His objective is not merely to murder as many of us as possible and to conquer our land. Like the Nazis and Communists before him, he is dedicated to the destruction of everything good for which America stands. . . .

The attack came, both literally and metaphorically, like a bolt out of the blue. Literally, in that the hijacked planes that crashed into the twin towers of the World Trade Center on the morning of September 11, 2001 had been flying in a cloudless sky so blue that it seemed unreal. . . .

But the attack came out of the blue in a metaphorical sense as well. . . .

The sheer audacity of what bin Laden went on to do on September 11 was unquestionably a product of his contempt for American power. Our persistent refusal for so long to use that power against him and his terrorist brethren—or to do so effectively whenever we tried—reinforced his conviction that we were a nation on the way down, destined to be defeated by the resurgence of the same Islamic militancy that had once conquered and converted large parts of the world by the sword. . . .

For these reasons, I agree with one of our leading contemporary students of military strategy, Eliot A. Cohen, who thinks that what is generally called the "cold war" (a term, incidentally, coined by Soviet propagandists) should be given a new name. "The cold war," Cohen writes, was actually "World War III, which reminds us that not all global conflicts entail the movement of multimillion-man armies, or conventional front lines on a map." I also agree that the nature of the conflict in which we are now engaged can only be fully appreciated if we look upon it as World War IV. . . .

As for the second President Bush, before 9/11 he was, to all appearances, as deficient in the "vision thing" as his father before him. If he entertained any doubts about the soundness of the "realist" approach, he showed no sign of it. Nothing he said or did gave any indication that he might be dissatisfied with the idea that his main job in foreign affairs was to keep things on an even keel. Nor was there any visible indication that he might be drawn to Ronald Reagan's more

"idealistic" ambition to change the world, especially with the "Wilsonian" aim of making it "safe for democracy" by encouraging the spread to as many other countries as possible of the liberties we Americans enjoyed.

Which is why Bush's address of September 20, 2001 came as so great a surprise. Delivered only nine days after the attacks on the World Trade Center and the Pentagon, and officially declaring that the United States was now at war, the September 20 speech put this nation, and all others, on notice that whether or not George W. Bush had been a strictly conventional realist in the mold of his father, he was now politically born again as a passionate democratic idealist of the Reaganite stamp.

It was also this speech that marked the emergence of the Bush Doctrine, and that pointed just as clearly to World War IV as the Truman Doctrine had to War World III. . . .

The first pillar of the Bush Doctrine, then, was built on a repudiation of moral relativism and an entirely unapologetic assertion of the need for and the possibility of moral judgment in the realm of world affairs. . . .

Bush had won enthusiastic plaudits from many for the "moral clarity" of his September 20 speech, but he had also provoked even greater dismay and disgust among "advanced" thinkers and "sophisticated" commentators and diplomats both at home and abroad. Now he intensified and exacerbated their outrage by becoming more specific. Having spoken in September only in general terms about the enemy in World War IV, Bush proceeded in his second major wartime pronouncement to single out three such nations—Iraq, Iran, and North Korea—which he described as forming an "axis of evil.". . . .

If the first of the four pillars on which the Bush Doctrine stood was a new moral attitude, the second was an equally dramatic shift in the conception of terrorism as it had come to be defined in standard academic and intellectual discourse.

Under this new understanding—confirmed over and over again by the fact that most of the terrorists about whom we were learning came from prosperous families—terrorism was no longer considered a product of economic factors. The "swamps" in which this murderous plague bred were swamps not of poverty and hunger but of political oppression. It was only by "draining" them, through a strategy of "regime change," that we would be making ourselves safe from the threat of terrorism and simultaneously giving the peoples of "the entire Islamic world" the freedoms "they want and deserve."

In the new understanding, furthermore, terrorists, with rare exceptions, were not individual psychotics acting on their own but agents of organizations that depended on the sponsorship of various governments. Our aim, therefore, could not be merely to capture or kill Osama bin Laden and wipe out the al Qaeda terrorists under his direct leadership. Bush vowed that we would also uproot and destroy the entire network of interconnected terrorist organizations and cells "with global reach" that existed in as many as 50 or 60 countries. No longer would we treat the members of these groups as criminals to be arrested by the police, read their Miranda rights, and brought to trial. From now on, they were to be regarded as the irregular troops of a military alliance at war with the United States, and indeed the civilized world as a whole. . . .

September 11 changed much—if not yet all— of that; still in use were atavistic phrases like "bringing the terrorists to justice." But no one could any longer dream that the American answer to what had been done to us in New York and Washington would begin with an FBI investigation and end with a series of ordinary criminal trials. War had been declared on the United States, and to war we were going to go. . . .

The campaign in Afghanistan demonstrated in the most unmistakable terms what followed from the new understanding of terrorism that formed the second pillar of the Bush Doctrine: countries that gave safe haven to terrorists and refused to clean them out were asking the United States to do it for them, and the regimes ruling these countries were also asking to be overthrown in favor of new leaders with democratic aspirations. Of course, as circumstances permitted and prudence dictated, other instruments of power, whether economic or diplomatic, would be deployed. But Afghanistan showed that the military option was open, available for use, and lethally effective.

The third pillar on which the Bush Doctrine rested was the assertion of our right to preempt. Bush had already pretty clearly indicated on

September 20, 2001 that he had no intention of waiting around to be attacked again ("We will pursue nations that provide aid or safe haven to terrorism"). But in the State of the Union speech in January 2002, he became much more explicit on this point too:

> We'll be deliberate, yet time is not on our side. I will not wait on events, while dangers gather. I will not stand by, as peril draws closer and closer. The United States of America will not permit the world's most dangerous regimes to threaten us with the world's most destructive weapons.

To those with ears to hear, the January speech should have made it abundantly clear that Bush was now proposing to go beyond the fundamentally retaliatory strike against Afghanistan and to take preemptive action. . . .

At this early stage, the Bush administration was still denying that it had reached any definite decision about Saddam Hussein; but everyone knew that, in promising to act, Bush was talking about him. The immediate purpose was to topple the Iraqi dictator before he had a chance to supply weapons of mass destruction to the terrorists. But this was by no means the only or—surprising though it would seem in retrospect—even the decisive consideration either for Bush or his supporters (or, for that matter, his opponents). And in any case, the long-range strategic rationale went beyond the proximate causes of the invasion. Bush's idea was to extend the enterprise of "draining the swamps" begun in Afghanistan and then to set the entire region on a course toward democratization. For if Afghanistan under the Taliban represented the religious face of Middle Eastern terrorism, Iraq under Saddam Hussein was its most powerful secular partner. It was to deal with this two-headed beast that a two-pronged strategy was designed. . . .

Which brings us to the fourth pillar on which the Bush Doctrine was erected.

[E]ven before 9/11 it had been widely and authoritatively reported that Bush was planning to come out publicly in favor of establishing a Palestinian state as the only path to a peaceful resolution of the conflict; and in October, after a short delay caused by 9/11, he became the first American President actually to do so. Yet at some point in the evolution of his thinking over the months that followed, Bush seems to have realized that there was something bizarre about supporting the establishment of a Palestinian state that would be run by a terrorist like Yasir Arafat and his henchmen. Why should the United States acquiesce, let alone help, in adding yet another state to those harboring and sponsoring terrorism precisely at a time when we were at war to rid the world of just such regimes? . . .

With the inconsistency thus removed and the resultant shakiness repaired by the addition of this fourth pillar to undergird it, the Bush Doctrine was now firm, coherent, and complete.

Both as a theoretical construct and as a guide to policy, the new Bush Doctrine could not have been further from the "Vietnam syndrome"—that loss of self-confidence and concomitant spread of neoisolationist and pacifist sentiment throughout the American body politic, and most prominently in the elite institutions of American culture, which began during the last years of the Vietnam war. . . .

On every point, the new Bush Doctrine contrasted sharply with the old Nixon Doctrine. Instead of withdrawal and fallback, Bush proposed a highly ambitious forward strategy of intervention. Instead of relying on local surrogates, Bush proposed an active deployment of our own military power. Instead of deterrence and containment, Bush proposed preemption and "taking the fight to the enemy." And instead of worrying about the stability of the region in question, Bush proposed to destabilize it through "regime change." . . .

The most obvious sign of the new era was that once again we were saluting our now ubiquitously displayed flag. This was the very flag that, not so long ago, leftist radicals had thought fit only for burning. Yet now, even on the old flag-burning Left, a few prominent personalities were painfully wrenching their unaccustomed arms into something vaguely resembling a salute. . . .

Although the vast majority of those who blamed America for having been attacked were on the Left, a few voices on the Right joined this perverted chorus. Speaking on Pat Robertson's TV program, the Reverend Jerry Falwell delivered himself of the view that God was punishing the United States for the moral decay exemplified by a variety of liberal groups among us. Both later apologized for singling out these groups, but each

continued to insist that God was withdrawing His protection from America because all of us had become great sinners. And in the amen corner that quickly formed on the secular Right, commentators like Robert Novak and Pat Buchanan added that we had called the attack down on our heads not so much by our willful disobedience to divine law as by our manipulated obedience to Israel.

Oddly enough, however, within the Arab world itself, there was much less emphasis on Israel as the root cause of the attacks than was placed on it by most, if not all, of Buchanan's fellow paleoconservatives on the Right. Even to Osama bin Laden himself, support of Israel ranked only third on a list of our "crimes" against Islam.

Not, to be sure, that Arabs everywhere—together with most non-Arab Middle Eastern Muslims like the Iranians—had given up their dream of wiping Israel off the map. . . .

Indeed, the hatred of Israel was in large part a surrogate for anti-Americanism, rather than the reverse. Israel was seen as the spearhead of the American drive for domination over the Middle East. As such, the Jewish state was a translation of America into, as it were, Hebrew—the "little enemy," the "little Satan." To rid the region of it would thus be tantamount to cleansing an area belonging to Islam (*dar al-Islam*) of the blasphemous political, social, and cultural influences emanating from a barbaric and murderous force. But the force, so to speak, was with America, of which Israel was merely an instrument. . . .

Some who shared my apprehensions believed that if things went well on the military front, all would be well on the home front, too. And that is how it appeared from the effect wrought by the spectacular success of the Afghanistan campaign, which disposed of the "quagmire" theory and also dampened antiwar activity on at least a number of campuses. Nevertheless, the mopping-up operation in Afghanistan created an opportunity for more subtle forms of opposition to gain traction. There were complaints that the terrorists captured in Afghanistan and then sent to a special facility in Guantanamo were not being treated as regular prisoners of war. And there were also allegations of the threat to civil liberties posed in America itself by measures like the Patriot Act, which had been designed to ward off any further terrorist attacks at home. Although these concerns were mostly based on misreadings of the Geneva Convention and of the Patriot Act itself, some people no doubt raised them in good faith. But there is also no doubt that such issues could—and did—serve as a respectable cover for wholesale opposition to the entire war.

Another respectable cover was the charge that Bush was following a policy of "unilateralism." The alarm over this supposedly unheard-of outrage was first sounded by the chancelleries and chattering classes of Western Europe when Bush stated that, in taking the fight to the terrorists and their sponsors, we would prefer to do so with allies and with the blessing of the UN, but if necessary we would go it alone and without an imprimatur from the Security Council.

This was too much for the Europeans. Having duly offered us their condolences over 9/11, they could barely let a decent interval pass before going back into the ancient family business of showing how vastly superior in wisdom and finesse they were to the Americans, whose primitive character was once again on display in the "simplistic" ideas and crude moralizing of George W. Bush. Now they urged that our military operations end with Afghanistan, and that we leave the rest to diplomacy in deferential consultation with the great masters of that recondite art in Paris and Brussels. . . .

Was there, perhaps, an element of the same twisted sentiment in the willingness of millions upon millions of Europeans to lend de-facto aid and comfort to this monster? Of course, the claim was that most such people were neither pro-Saddam nor anti-American: all they wanted was to "give peace a chance." But this claim was belied by the slogans, the body language, the speeches, and the manifestos of the "peace" party. Though hatred of America may not have been universal among opponents of American military action, it was obviously very widespread and very deep. . . .

After 9/11, most Americans had gradually come to recognize that we were hated by the terrorists who had attacked us and their Muslim cheerleaders not for our failings and sins but precisely for our virtues as a free and prosperous country. But why should we be hated by hordes of people living in other free and prosperous countries? In their case, presumably, it must be for our sins. And yet most of us knew for certain that, whatever sins we might have committed, they were not the ones of which the Europeans kept accusing us. . . .

The "post-historical paradise" into which the Europeans were supposedly moving struck me as nothing more than the web of international institutions that had been created at the end of World War II under the leadership of the United States in the hope that they would foster peace and prosperity. These included the United Nations, the World Bank, the World Court, and others. Then after 1947, and again under the leadership of the United States, adaptations were made to the already existing institutions and new ones like NATO were added to fit the needs of World War III. With the victorious conclusion of World War III in 1989-90, the old international order became obsolete, and new arrangements tailored to a new era would have to be forged. But more than a decade elapsed before 9/11 finally made the contours of the "post-cold-war era" clear enough for these new arrangements to begin being developed.

Looked at from this angle, the Bush Doctrine revealed itself as an extremely bold effort to break out of the institutional framework and the strategy constructed to fight the last war. But it was more: it also drew up a blueprint for a new structure and a new strategy to fight a different breed of enemy in a war that was just starting and that showed signs of stretching out into the future as far as the eye could see. Facing the realities of what now confronted us, Bush had come to the conclusion that few if any of the old instrumentalities were capable of defeating this new breed of enemy, and that the strategies of the past were equally helpless before this enemy's way of waging war. To move into the future meant to substitute preemption for deterrence, and to rely on American military might rather than the "soft power" represented by the UN and the other relics of World War III. Indeed, not even the hard power of NATO—which had specifically been restricted by design to the European continent and whose deployment in other places could, and would be, obstructed by the French—was of much use in the world of the future. . . .

The astonishing success of the campaigns in Afghanistan and Iraq made a hash of the skepticism of the many pundits who had been so sure that we had too few troops or were following the wrong battle plan. Instead of getting bogged down, as they had predicted, our forces raced through these two campaigns in record time; and instead of ten of thousands of body bags being flown home, the casualties were numbered in the hundreds. . . .

True, the aftermath of major military operations, especially in Iraq, turned out to be rougher than the Pentagon seems to have expected. Thanks to the guerrilla insurgency mounted by a coalition of intransigent Saddam loyalists, radical Shiite militias, and terrorists imported from Iran and Syria, American soldiers continued to be killed. Nevertheless, by any historical standard—the more than 6,500 who died on D-Day alone in World War II, to cite only one example—our total losses remained amazingly low.

But it was not military matters that aroused the equally sour skepticism of the realists. Their doubts centered, rather, on the issue of whether the Bush Doctrine was politically viable. Most of all, they questioned the idea that democratization represented the best and perhaps even the only way to defeat militant Islam and the terrorism it was using as its main weapon against us. Bush had placed his bet on a belief in the universality of the desire for freedom and the prosperity that freedom brought with it. But what if he was wrong? What if the Middle East was incapable of democratization? What if the peoples of that region did not wish to be as free and as prosperous as we were? And what if Islam as a religion was by its very nature incompatible with democracy?

These were hard questions about which reasonable men could and did differ. But those of us who backed Bush's bet had our own set of doubts about the doubts of the realists. They seemed to forget that the Middle East of today had not been created by Allah in the 7th century, and that the miserable despotisms there had not evolved through some inexorable historical process powered entirely by internal cultural forces. Instead, the states in question had all been conjured into existence less than a hundred years ago out of the ruins of the defeated Ottoman empire in World War I. Their boundaries were drawn by the victorious British and French with the stroke of an often arbitrary pen, and their hapless peoples were handed over in due course to one tyrant after another.

Mindful of this history, we backers of the Bush Doctrine wondered why it should have been taken as axiomatic that these states would and/or should last forever in their present forms, and why the political configuration of the Middle East should be eternally immune from the democratizing forces that had been sweeping the rest of the world.

And we wondered, too, whether it could really be true that Muslims were so different from most of their fellow human beings that they liked being pushed around and repressed and beaten and killed by thugs—even if the thugs wore clerical garb or went around quoting from the Quran. We wondered whether Muslims really preferred being poor and hungry and ill-housed to enjoying the comforts and conveniences that we in the West took so totally for granted that we no longer remembered to be grateful for them. And we wondered why, if all this were the case, there had been so great an outburst of relief and happiness among the people of Kabul after we drove out their Taliban oppressors.

Yes, came the response, but what about the people of Iraq? Most supporters of the invasion—myself included—had predicted that we would be greeted there with flowers and cheers; yet our troops encountered car bombs and hatred. Nevertheless, and contrary to the impression created by the media, survey after survey demonstrated that the vast majority of Iraqis *did* welcome us, and *were* happy to be liberated from the murderous tyranny under which they had lived for so long under Saddam Hussein. The hatred and the car bombs came from the same breed of jihadists who had attacked us on 9/11, and who, unlike the skeptics in our own country, were afraid that we were actually succeeding in democratizing Iraq. . . .

Those of us who supported the new policy also took issue with the view that democracy and capitalism could grow only in a soil that had been cultivated for centuries. We reminded the realists that in the aftermath of World War II, the United States managed within a single decade to transform both Nazi Germany and imperial Japan into capitalist democracies. And in the aftermath of the defeat of Communism in World War III, a similar process got under way on its own steam in Central and Eastern Europe, and even in the old heartland of the evil empire itself. Why not the Islamic world? The realist answer was that things were different there. To which our answer was that things were different everywhere, and a thousand reasons to expect the failure of any enterprise could always be conjured up to discourage making an ambitious effort. . . .

As with democratization, so with the reform and modernization of Islam. In considering this even more difficult question, we found ourselves asking whether Islam could really go on for all eternity resisting the kind of reformation and modernization that had begun within Christianity and Judaism in the early modern period. Not that we were so naive as to imagine that Islam could be reformed overnight, or from the outside. In its heyday, Islam was able to impose itself on large parts of the world by the sword; there was no chance today of an inverse instant transformation of Islam by the force of American arms.

There was, however, a very good chance that a clearing of the ground, and a sowing of the seeds out of which new political, economic, and social conditions could grow, would gradually give rise to correlative religious pressures from within. Such pressures would take the form of an ultimately irresistible demand on theologians and clerics to find warrants in the Quran and the *sharia* under which it would be possible to remain a good Muslim while enjoying the blessings of decent government, and even of political and economic liberty. In this way a course might finally be set toward the reform and modernization of the Islamic religion itself.

What I have been trying to say is that the obstacles to a benevolent transformation of the Middle East—whether military, political, or religious—are not insuperable. In the long run they can be overcome, and there can be no question that we possess the power and the means and the resources to work toward their overcoming. But do we have the skills and the stomach to do

what will be required? Can we in our present condition play even so limited and so benign an imperial role as we did in occupying Germany and Japan after World War II? . . .

In World War III, we as a nation persisted in spite of the inevitable setbacks and mistakes and the defeatism they generated, until, in the end, we won. To us the reward of victory was the elimination of a military, political, and ideological threat. To the people living both within the Soviet Union itself and in its East European empire, it brought liberation from a totalitarian tyranny. Admittedly, liberation did not mean that everything immediately came up roses, but it would be foolish to contend that nothing changed for the better when Communism landed on the very ash heap of history that Marx had predicted would be the final resting place of capitalism.

Suppose that we hang in long enough to carry World War IV to a comparably successful conclusion. What will victory mean this time around? Well, to us it will mean the elimination of another, and in some respects greater, threat to our safety and security. But because that threat cannot be eliminated without "draining the swamps" in which it breeds, victory will also entail the liberation of another group of countries from another species of totalitarian tyranny. As we can already see from Afghanistan and Iraq, liberation will no more result in the overnight establishment of ideal conditions in the Middle East than it has done in East Europe. But as we can also see from Afghanistan and Iraq, better things will immediately happen, and a genuine opportunity will be opened up for even better things to come. . . .

GEORGE W. BUSH, "SECOND INAUGURAL ADDRESS" (JANUARY 20, 2005)

By the time George W. Bush won reelection in November 2004, the wars in Iraq and Afghanistan were not going well. Undeterred, Bush used the occasion of his second inaugural to mount a full-throated defense of American exceptionalism.

I am grateful for the honor of this hour, mindful of the consequential times in which we live, and determined to fulfill the oath that I have sworn and you have witnessed.

At this second gathering, our duties are defined not by the words I use but by the history we have seen together. For a half a century, America defended our own freedom by standing watch on distant borders. After the shipwreck of communism came years of relative quiet, years of repose, years of sabbatical, and then there came a day of fire.

We have seen our vulnerability, and we have seen its deepest source. For as long as whole regions of the world simmer in resentment and tyranny, prone to ideologies that feed hatred and excuse murder, violence will gather and multiply in destructive power and cross the most defended borders and raise a mortal threat. There is only one force of history that can break the reign of hatred and resentment and expose the pretensions of tyrants and reward the hopes of the decent and tolerant, and that is the force of human freedom.

We are led, by events and common sense, to one conclusion: The survival of liberty in our land increasingly depends on the success of liberty in other lands. The best hope for peace in our world is the expansion of freedom in all the world.

America's vital interests and our deepest beliefs are now one. From the day of our founding, we have proclaimed that every man and woman on this Earth has rights and dignity and match-less value, because they bear the image of the Maker of heaven and Earth. Across the generations, we have proclaimed the imperative of self-government, because no one is fit to be a master and no one deserves to be a slave. Advancing these ideals is the mission that created our Nation. It is the honorable achievement of our fathers. Now, it is the urgent requirement of our Nation's security and the calling of our time.

So it is the policy of the United States to seek and support the growth of democratic movements and institutions in every nation and culture, with the ultimate goal of ending tyranny in our world. This is not primarily the task of arms, though we will defend ourselves and our friends by force of arms when necessary. Freedom, by its nature, must be chosen and defended by citizens and sustained by the rule of law and the protection of minorities. And when the soul of a nation finally speaks, the institutions that arise may reflect customs and traditions very different from our own. America will not impose our own style of government on the unwilling. Our goal instead is to help others find their own voice, attain their own freedom, and make their own way.

The great objective of ending tyranny is the concentrated work of generations. The difficulty of the task is no excuse for avoiding it. America's influence is not unlimited, but fortunately for the oppressed, America's influence is considerable and we will use it confidently in freedom's cause.

My most solemn duty is to protect this Nation and its people from further attacks and emerging threats. Some have unwisely chosen to test America's resolve and have found it firm. We will persistently clarify the choice before every ruler and every nation, the moral choice between oppression, which is always wrong, and freedom, which is eternally right.

America will not pretend that jailed dissidents prefer their chains or that women welcome humiliation and servitude or that any human being aspires to live at the mercy of bullies. We will encourage reform in other governments by making clear that success in our relations will require the decent treatment of their own people. America's belief in human dignity will guide our policies. Yet rights must be more than the grudging concessions of dictators. They are secured by free dissent and the participation of the governed. In the long run, there is no justice without freedom and there can be no human rights without human liberty.

Some, I know, have questioned the global appeal of liberty, though this time in history, four decades defined by the swiftest advance of freedom ever seen, is an odd time for doubt. Americans, of all people, should never be surprised by the power of our ideals. Eventually, the call of freedom comes to every mind and every soul. We do not accept the existence of permanent tyranny because we do not accept the possibility of permanent slavery. Liberty will come to those who love it.

Today, America speaks anew to the peoples of the world. All who live in tyranny and hopelessness can know: The United States will not ignore your oppression or excuse your oppressors. When you stand for your liberty, we will stand with you.

Democratic reformers facing repression, prison, or exile can know: America sees you for who you are, the future leaders of your free country.

The rulers of outlaw regimes can know that we still believe as Abraham Lincoln did: "Those who deny freedom to others deserve it not for themselves and, under the rule of a just God, cannot long retain it."

The leaders of governments with long habits of control need to know: To serve your people, you must learn to trust them. Start on this journey of progress and justice, and America will walk at your side.

And all the allies of the United States can know: We honor your friendship; we rely on your counsel; and we depend on your help. Division among free nations is a primary goal of freedom's enemies. The concerted effort of free nations to promote democracy is a prelude to our enemies' defeat.

Today I also speak anew to my fellow citizens. From all of you I have asked patience in the hard task of securing America, which you have granted in good measure. Our country has accepted obligations that are difficult to fulfill and would be dishonorable to abandon. Yet because we have acted in the great liberating tradition of this Nation, tens of millions have achieved their freedom. And as hope kindles hope, millions more will find it. By our efforts, we have lit a fire as well, a fire in the minds of men. It warms those who feel its power. It burns those who fight its progress. And one day this untamed fire of freedom will reach the darkest corners of our world.

A few Americans have accepted the hardest duties in this cause, in the quiet work of intelligence and diplomacy, the idealistic work of helping raise up free governments, the dangerous and necessary work of fighting our enemies. Some have shown their devotion to our country in deaths that honored their whole lives, and we will always honor their names and their sacrifice.

All Americans have witnessed this idealism and some for the first time. I ask our youngest citizens to believe the evidence of your eyes. You have seen duty and allegiance in the determined faces of our soldiers. You have seen that life is fragile and evil is real and courage triumphs. Make the choice to serve in a cause larger than your wants, larger than yourself, and in your days you will add not just to the wealth of our country but to its character.

America has need of idealism and courage because we have essential work at home, the unfinished work of American freedom. In a world moving toward liberty, we are determined to show the meaning and promise of liberty. . . .

In America's ideal of freedom, the public interest depends on private character, on integrity and tolerance toward others and the rule of conscience in our own lives. Self-government relies, in the end, on the governing of the self. That edifice of character is built in families, supported by communities with standards, and sustained in our national life by the truths of Sinai, the Sermon on the Mount, the words of the Koran, and the varied faiths of our people. Americans move forward in every generation by reaffirming all that is good and true that came before, ideals of justice and conduct that are the same yesterday, today, and forever.

In America's ideal of freedom, the exercise of rights is ennobled by service and mercy and a heart for the weak. Liberty for all does not mean independence from one another. Our Nation relies on men and women who look after a neighbor and surround the lost with love. Americans, at our best, value the life we see in one another and must always remember that even the unwanted have worth. And our country must abandon all the habits of racism, because we cannot carry the message of freedom and the baggage of bigotry at the same time.

From the perspective of a single day, including this day of dedication, the issues and questions before our country are many. From the viewpoint of centuries, the questions that come to us are narrowed and few: Did our generation advance the cause of freedom? And did our character bring credit to that cause?

These questions that judge us also unite us, because Americans of every party and background, Americans by choice and by birth are bound to one another in the cause of freedom. We have known divisions, which must be healed to move forward in great purposes, and I will strive in good faith to heal them. Yet those divisions do not define America. We felt the unity and fellowship of our Nation when freedom came under attack, and our response came like a single hand over a single heart. And we can feel that same unity and pride whenever America acts for good and the victims of disaster are given hope and the unjust encounter justice and the captives are set free.

We go forward with complete confidence in the eventual triumph of freedom, not because history runs on the wheels of inevitability—it is human choices that move events; not because we consider ourselves a chosen nation—God moves and chooses as He wills. We have confidence because freedom is the permanent hope

of mankind, the hunger in dark places, the longing of the soul. When our Founders declared a
new order of the ages, when soldiers died in wave
upon wave for a union based on liberty, when
citizens marched in peaceful outrage under the
banner "Freedom Now," they were acting on an
ancient hope that is meant to be fulfilled. History
has an ebb and flow of justice, but history also has
a visible direction, set by liberty and the Author
of Liberty.

When the Declaration of Independence was
first read in public and the Liberty Bell was
sounded in celebration, a witness said, "It rang
as if it meant something." In our time, it means
something still. America, in this young century,
proclaims liberty throughout all the world and
to all the inhabitants thereof. Renewed in our
strength, tested but not weary, we are ready
for the greatest achievements in the history of
freedom.

XIII.

DISSENT AFTER 9/11

The Bush administration's response to 9/11, and especially the decision to invade Iraq, triggered a firestorm of opposition.

SUSAN SONTAG, "TUESDAY AND AFTER," *THE NEW YORKER* (SEPTEMBER 24, 2001)

Did the 9/11 attacks target an innocent nation? No, says the writer Susan Sontag.

The disconnect between last Tuesday's monstrous dose of reality and the self-righteous drivel and outright deceptions being peddled by public figures and TV commentators is startling, depressing. The voices licensed to follow the event seem to have joined together in a campaign to infantilize the public. Where is the acknowledgment that this was not a "cowardly" attack on "civilization" or "liberty" or "humanity" or "the free world" but an attack on the world's self-proclaimed super-power, undertaken as a consequence of specific American alliances and actions? How many citizens are aware of the ongoing American bombing of Iraq? And if the word "cowardly" is to be used, it might be more aptly applied to those who kill from beyond the range of retaliation, high in the sky, than to those willing to die themselves in order to kill others. In the matter of courage (a morally neutral virtue): whatever may be said of the perpetrators of Tuesday's slaughter, they were not cowards.

Our leaders are bent on convincing us that everything is O.K. America is not afraid. Our spirit is unbroken, although this was a day that will live in infamy and America is now at war. But everything is not O.K. And this was not Pearl Harbor. We have a robotic President who assures us that America still stands tall. A wide spectrum of public figures, in and out of office, who are strongly opposed to the policies being pursued abroad by this Administration apparently feel free to say nothing more than that they stand united behind President

Bush. A lot of thinking needs to be done, and perhaps is being done in Washington and elsewhere, about the ineptitude of American intelligence and counter-intelligence, about options available to American foreign policy, particularly in the Middle East, and about what constitutes a smart program of military defense. But the public is not being asked to bear much of the burden of reality. The unanimously applauded, self-congratulatory bromides of a Soviet Party Congress seemed contemptible. The unanimity of the sanctimonious, reality-concealing rhetoric spouted by American officials and media commentators in recent days seems, well, unworthy of a mature democracy.

Those in public office have let us know that they consider their task to be a manipulative one: confidence-building and grief management. Politics, the politics of a democracy—which entails disagreement, which promotes candor—has been replaced by psychotherapy. Let's by all means grieve together. But let's not be stupid together. A few shreds of historical awareness might help us understand what has just happened, and what may continue to happen. "Our country is strong," we are told again and again. I for one don't find this entirely consoling. Who doubts that America is strong? But that's not all America has to be.

BARACK OBAMA, "WEIGHING THE COSTS OF WAR IN IRAQ" (2002)

A young state senator from Illinois explains his opposition to the prospective invasion of Iraq.

Good afternoon. Let me begin by saying that although this has been billed as an anti-war rally, I stand before you as someone who is not opposed to war in all circumstances. The Civil War was one of the bloodiest in history, and yet it was only through the crucible of the sword, the sacrifice of multitudes, that we could begin to perfect this union, and drive the scourge of slavery from our soil. I don't oppose all wars.

My grandfather signed up for a war the day after Pearl Harbor was bombed, fought in Patton's army. He saw the dead and dying across the fields of Europe; he heard the stories of fellow troops who first entered Auschwitz and Treblinka. He fought in the name of a larger freedom, part of that arsenal of democracy that triumphed over evil, and he did not fight in vain. I don't oppose all wars.

After Sept. 11, after witnessing the carnage and destruction, the dust and the tears, I supported this administration's pledge to hunt down and root out those who would slaughter innocents in the name of intolerance, and I would willingly take up arms myself to prevent such tragedy from happening again. I don't oppose all wars. And I know that in this crowd today, there is no shortage of patriots, or of patriotism.

What I am opposed to is a dumb war. What I am opposed to is a rash war. What I am opposed to is the cynical attempt by Richard Perle and Paul Wolfowitz and other armchair, weekend warriors in this administration to shove their own ideological agendas down our throats, irrespective of the costs in lives lost and in hardships borne.

What I am opposed to is the attempt by political hacks like Karl Rove to distract us from a rise in the uninsured, a rise in the poverty rate, a drop in the median income—to distract us from corporate scandals and a stock market that has just gone through the worst month since the Great Depression. That's what I'm opposed to. A dumb war. A rash war. A war based not on reason but on passion, not on principle but on politics. Now let me be clear—I suffer no illusions about Saddam Hussein. He is a brutal man. A ruthless man. A man who butchers his own people to secure his own power. He has repeatedly defied UN resolutions, thwarted UN inspection teams, developed chemical and biological weapons, and coveted nuclear capacity. He's a bad guy. The world, and the Iraqi people, would be better off without him.

But I also know that Saddam poses no imminent and direct threat to the United States or to his neighbors, that the Iraqi economy is in shambles, that the Iraqi military is a fraction of its former strength, and that in concert with the international community he can be contained until, in the way of all petty dictators, he falls away into the dustbin of history. I know that even a successful war against Iraq will require a U.S. occupation of undetermined length, at undetermined cost, with undetermined consequences. I know that an invasion of Iraq without a clear rationale and without strong international support will only fan the flames of the Middle East, and encourage the worst, rather than best, impulses of the Arab world, and strengthen the recruitment arm of al-Qaida. I am not opposed to all wars. I'm opposed to dumb wars.

So for those of us who seek a more just and secure world for our children, let us send a clear message to the president today. You want a fight, President Bush? Let's finish the fight with bin Laden and al-Qaida, through effective, coordinated intelligence, and a shutting down of the financial networks that support terrorism, and a homeland security program that involves more than color-coded warnings. You want a fight, President Bush?

Let's fight to make sure that the U.N. inspectors can do their work, and that we vigorously enforce a non-proliferation treaty, and that former enemies and current allies like Russia safeguard and ultimately eliminate their stores of nuclear material, and that nations like Pakistan and India never use the terrible weapons already in their possession, and that the arms merchants in our own country stop feeding the countless wars that rage across the globe. You want a fight, President Bush?

Let's fight to make sure our so-called allies in the Middle East, the Saudis and the Egyptians, stop oppressing their own people, and suppressing dissent, and tolerating corruption and inequality, and mismanaging their economies so that their youth grow up without education, without prospects, without hope, the ready recruits of terrorist cells. You want a fight, President Bush? Let's fight to wean ourselves off Middle East oil, through an energy policy that doesn't simply serve the interests of Exxon and Mobil.

Those are the battles that we need to fight. Those are the battles that we willingly join. The battles against ignorance and intolerance. Corruption and greed. Poverty and despair. The consequences of war are dire, the sacrifices immeasurable. We may have occasion in our lifetime to once again rise up in defense of our freedom, and pay the wages of war. But we ought not—we will not—travel down that hellish path blindly. Nor should we allow those who would march off and pay the ultimate sacrifice, who would prove the full measure of devotion with their blood, to make such an awful sacrifice in vain.

STANLEY HAUERWAS, "SEPTEMBER 11, 2001: A PACIFIST RESPONSE," *SOUTH ATLANTIC QUARTERLY* (SPRING 2002)

According to the theologian, Stanley Hauerwas (1940–), the proper response to 9/11 was something other than war.

I want to write honestly about September 11, 2001. But it is not easy. Even now, some months after that horrible event, I find it hard to know what can be said or, perhaps more difficult, what should be said. Even more difficult, I am not sure for what or how I should pray. I am a Christian. I am a Christian pacifist. Being Christian and being a pacifist are not two things for me. I would not be a pacifist if I were not a Christian, and

I find it hard to understand how one can be a Christian without being a pacifist. But what does a pacifist have to say in the face of terror? Pray for peace? I have no use for sentimentality.

Indeed some have suggested pacifists have nothing to say in a time like the time after September 11, 2001. The editors of the magazine *First Things* assert that "those who in principle oppose the use of military force have no legitimate part in the discussion about how military force should be used." They make this assertion because according to them the only form of pacifism that is defensible requires the disavowal by the pacifist of any political relevance. That is not the kind of pacifism I represent. I am a pacifist because I think nonviolence is the necessary condition for a politics not based on death. A politics that is not determined by the fear of death means no strong distinction can be drawn between politics and military force.

Yet I cannot deny that September 11, 2001, creates and requires a kind of silence. We desperately want to "explain" what happened. Explanation domesticates terror, making it part of "our" world. I believe attempts to explain must be resisted. Rather, we should learn to wait before what we know not, hoping to gain time and space sufficient to learn how to speak without lying. I should like to think pacifism names the habits and community necessary to gain the time and place that is an alternative to revenge. But I do not pretend that I know how that is accomplished.

Yet I do know that much that has been said since September 11, 2001, has been false. In the first hours and days following the fall of the towers, there was a stunned silence. President Bush flew from one safe haven to another, unsure what had or was still to happen. He was quite literally in the air. I wish he might have been able to maintain that posture, but he is the leader of the "free world." Something must be done. Something must be said. We must be in control. The silence must be shattered. He knew the American people must be comforted. Life must return to normal.

So he said, "We are at war." Magic words necessary to reclaim the everyday. War is such normalizing discourse. Americans know war. This is our Pearl Harbor. Life can return to normal. We are frightened, and ironically war makes us feel safe. The way to go on in the face of September 11, 2001, is to find someone to kill. Americans are, moreover, good at killing. We often fail to acknowledge how accomplished we are in the art of killing. Indeed we, the American people, have become masters of killing. In our battles, only the enemy has to die. Some in our military are embarrassed by our expertise in war making, but what can they do? They are but following orders.

So the silence created by destruction was soon shattered by the need for revenge—a revenge all the more unforgiving because we cannot forgive those who flew the planes for making us acknowledge our vulnerability. The flag that flew in mourning was soon transformed into a pride-filled thing; the bloodstained flag of victims transformed into the flag of the American indomitable spirit. We will prevail no matter how many people we must kill to rid ourselves of the knowledge Americans died as victims. Americans do not die as victims. They have to be heroes. So the stock trader who happened to work on the seventy-second floor becomes as heroic as the policemen and the firemen who were doing their jobs. No one who died on September 11, 2001, gets to die a meaningless death. That is why their deaths must be revenged.

I am a pacifist, so the American "we" cannot be my "me." But to be alienated from the American "we" is not easy. I am a neophyte pacifist. I never really wanted to be a pacifist. I had learned from Reinhold Niebuhr that if you desire justice you had better be ready to kill someone along the way. But then John Howard Yoder and his extraordinary book *The Politics of Jesus* came along. Yoder convinced me that if there is anything to this Christian "stuff," it must surely involve the conviction that the Son would rather die on the cross than for the world to be redeemed by violence. Moreover, the defeat of death through resurrection makes possible as well as necessary that Christians live nonviolently in a world of violence. Christian nonviolence is not a strategy to rid the world of violence, but rather the way Christians must live in a world of violence. In short Christians are not nonviolent because we believe our nonviolence is a strategy to rid the world of war, but rather because faithful followers of Christ in a world of war cannot imagine being anything else than nonviolent.

But what does a pacifist have to say in the face of the terror September 11, 2001, names? I vaguely knew when I first declared I was a pacifist that there might be some serious consequences. To be nonviolent might even change my life. But I do not really think I understood what that change might entail until September 11. For example after I declared I was a pacifist, I quit singing the "Star-Spangled Banner." I will stand when it is sung, particularly at baseball games, but I do not sing. Not to sing the "Star-Spangled

Banner" is a small thing that reminds me that my first loyalty is not to the United States but to God and God's church. I confess it never crossed my mind that such small acts might over the years make my response to September 11 quite different from that of the good people who sing "God Bless America"—so different that I am left in saddened silence.

That difference, moreover, haunts me. My father was a bricklayer and a good American. He worked hard all his life and hoped his work would not only support his family, but also make some contribution to our common life. He held a war-critical job in World War II, so he was never drafted. Only one of his five bricklaying brothers was in that war, but he was never exposed to combat. My family was never militarized, but as Texans they were good Americans. For most of my life I, too, was a good American, assuming that I owed much to the society that enabled me, the son of a bricklayer, to gain a Ph.D. at Yale—even if the Ph.D. was in theology.

Of course there was Vietnam. For many of us Vietnam was extended training necessary for the development of a more critical attitude toward the government of the United States. Yet most of us critical of the war in Vietnam did not think our opposition to that war made us less loyal Americans. Indeed the criticisms of the war were based on an appeal to the highest American ideals. Vietnam was a time of great tension, but the politics of the antiwar movement did not require those opposed to the war to think of themselves as fundamentally standing outside the American mainstream. Most critics of Vietnam (just as many that now criticize the war in Afghanistan) based their dissent on their adherence to American ideals that they felt the war was betraying. That but indicates why I feel so isolated even among the critics of the war in Afghanistan. I do not even share their allegiance to American ideals.

So I simply did not share the reaction of most Americans to the destruction of the World Trade Center. Of course I recoil from murder on such a scale, but I hope I remember that one murder is too many. That Americans have hurried to call what happened "war" strikes me as self-defeating. If this is war, then bin Laden has won. He thinks he is a warrior not a murderer. Just to the extent the language of war is used, he is honored. But in their hurry to call this war, Americans have no time for careful discriminations.

Where does that leave me? Does it mean, as an estranged friend recently wrote me, that I disdain all "natural loyalties" that bind us together as human beings, even submitting such loyalties to a harsh and unforgiving standard? Does it mean that I speak as a solitary individual, failing to acknowledge that our lives are interwoven with the lives of others, those who have gone before, those among whom we live, those with whom we identify, and those with whom we are in Christian communion? Do I refuse to acknowledge my life is made possible by the gifts of others? Do I forsake all forms of patriotism, failing to acknowledge that we as a people are better off because of the sacrifices that were made in World War II? To this I can only answer, "Yes." If you call patriotism "natural," I certainly do disavow that connection. Such a disavowal, I hope, does not mean I am inattentive to the gifts I have received from past and present neighbors.

In response to my friend I pointed out that because he, too, is a Christian I assumed he also disdained some "natural loyalties." After all he had his children baptized. The "natural love" between parents and children is surely reconfigured when children are baptized into the death and resurrection of Christ. . . .

Of course living a life of nonviolence may be harsh. Certainly you have to imagine, and perhaps even face, that you will have to watch the innocent suffer and even die for your convictions. But that is no different from those that claim they would fight a just war. After all, the just warrior is committed to avoiding any direct attack on noncombatants, which might well mean that more people will die because the just warrior refuses to do an evil that a good may come. For example, on just-war grounds the bombings of Hiroshima and Nagasaki were clearly murder. If you are serious about just war, you must be ready to say that it would be better that more people died on the beaches of Japan than to have committed one murder, much less the bombing of civilian populations.

This last observation may suggest that when all is said and done, a pacifist response to September 11, 2001, is just one more version of the anti-American sentiments expressed by what many consider to be the American Left. I say "what many consider" because it is very unclear if there is a Left left in America. Nowhere is that more apparent than in the support to the war on terrorism given by those who identify as the "Left." Yet much has been made of the injustice of American foreign policy that lends a kind of intelligibility to the hatred given form on September 11. I am no defender of American foreign policy, but the problem with such lines of criticism is that no matter how immoral what the American government may have done in the world, such immorality cannot explain or justify the attack on the World Trade Center.

American imperialism, often celebrated as the new globalism, is a frightening power. It is frightening not only because of the harm such power inflicts on the innocent, but because it is difficult to imagine alternatives. Pacifists are often challenged after an event like September 11 with the question, "Well, what alternative do you have to bombing Afghanistan?" Such a question assumes that pacifists must have an alternative foreign policy. My only response is I do not have a foreign policy. I have something better—a church constituted by people who would rather die than kill.

Indeed I fear that absent a countercommunity to challenge America, bin Laden has given Americans what they so desperately needed—a war without end. America is a country that lives off the moral capital of our wars. War names the time we send the youth to kill and die (maybe) in an effort to assure ourselves the lives we lead are worthy of such sacrifices. They kill and die to protect our "freedom." But what can freedom mean if the prime instance of the exercise of such freedom is to shop? The very fact that we can and do go to war is a moral necessity for a nation of consumers. War makes clear we must believe in something even if we are not sure what that something is, except that it has something to do with the "American way of life."

What a gift bin Laden has therefore given America. Americans were in despair because we won the cold war. Americans won by outspending the USSR, proving that we can waste more money on guns than they can or did. But what do Americans do after they have won a war? The war was necessary to give moral coherence. We had to cooperate with one another because we were

at war. How can America make sense of what it means for us to be "a people" if we have no common enemy? We were in a dangerous funk having nothing better to do than entertain ourselves with the soap opera Bill Clinton was. Now we have something better to do. We can fight the war against terrorism.

The good thing, moreover, about the war on terrorism is it has no end, which makes it very doubtful that this war can be considered just. If a war is just, your enemy must know before the war begins what political purpose the war is to serve. In other words, they need to know from the beginning what the conditions are if they choose to surrender. So you cannot fight a just war if it is "a war to end all wars" (World War I) or for "unconditional surrender" (World War II). But a "war on terrorism" is a war without limit. Americans want to wipe this enemy off the face of the earth. Moreover, America even gets to decide who counts and does not count as a terrorist.

Which means Americans get to have it any way they want it. Some that are captured, for example, are prisoners of war; some are detainees. No problem. When you are the biggest kid on the block, you can say whatever you want to say, even if what you say is nonsense. We all know the first casualty in war is truth. So the conservatives who have fought the war against "postmodernism" in the name of "objective truth," the same conservatives that now rule us, assume they can use language any way they please.

That Americans get to decide who is and who is not a terrorist means that this is not only a war without clear purpose, but also a war without end. From now on we can be in a perpetual state of war. America is always at her best when she is on permanent war footing. Moreover, when our country is at war, it has no space to worry about the extraordinary inequities that constitute our society, no time to worry about poverty or those parts of the world that are ravaged by hunger and genocide. Everything—civil liberties, due process, the protection of the law—must be subordinated to the one great moral enterprise of winning the unending war against terrorism.

At the heart of the American desire to wage endless war is the American fear of death. The American love of high-tech medicine is but the other side of the war against terrorism. Americans are determined to be safe, to be able to get out of this life alive. On September 11, Americans were confronted with their worst fear—a people ready to die as an expression of their profound moral commitments. Some speculate such people must have chosen death because they were desperate or, at least, they were so desperate that death was preferable to life. Yet their willingness to die stands in stark contrast to a politics that asks of its members in response to September 11 to shop.

Ian Buruma and Vishai Margalit observe in their article "Occidentalism" that lack of heroism is the hallmark of a bourgeois ethos. Heroes court death. The bourgeois is addicted to personal safety. They concede that much in an affluent, market-driven society is mediocre, "but when contempt for bourgeois creature comforts becomes contempt for life itself you know the West is under attack." According to Buruma and Margalit, the West (which they point out is not just the geographical West) should oppose the full force of calculating antibourgeois heroism, of which

Al-Qaeda is but one representative, through the means we know best—cutting off their money supply. Of course, Buruma and Margalit do not tell us how that can be done, given the need for oil to sustain the bourgeois society they favor.

Christians are not called to be heroes or shoppers. We are called to be holy. We do not think holiness is an individual achievement, but rather a set of practices to sustain a people who refuse to have their lives determined by the fear and denial of death. We believe by so living we offer our non-Christian brothers and sisters an alternative to all politics based on the denial of death. Christians are acutely aware that we seldom are faithful to the gifts God has given us, but we hope the confession of our sins is a sign of hope in a world without hope. This means pacifists do have a response to September 11, 2001. Our response is to continue living in a manner that witnesses to our belief that the world was not changed on September 11, 2001. The world was changed during the celebration of Passover in A.D. 33. . . .

IMMANUEL WALLERSTEIN, "THE EAGLE HAS CRASH LANDED," *FOREIGN POLICY* (JULY–AUGUST 2002)

According to the sociologist Immanuel Wallerstein (1930–), the Global War on Terrorism would only serve to further American decline.

The United States in decline? Few people today would believe this assertion. The only ones who do are the U.S. hawks, who argue vociferously for policies to reverse the decline. This belief that the end of U.S. hegemony has already begun does not follow from the vulnerability that became apparent to all on September 11, 2001. In fact, the United States has been fading as a global power since the 1970s, and the U.S. response to the terrorist attacks has merely accelerated this decline. To understand why the so-called Pax Americana is on the wane requires examining the geopolitics of the 20th century, particularly of the century's final three decades. This exercise uncovers a simple and inescapable conclusion: The economic, political, and military factors that contributed to U.S. hegemony

are the same factors that will inexorably produce the coming U.S. decline.

The rise of the United States to global hegemony was a long process that began in earnest with the world recession of 1873. At that time, the United States and Germany began to acquire an increasing share of global markets, mainly at the expense of the steadily receding British economy. Both nations had recently acquired a stable political base—the United States by successfully terminating the Civil War and Germany by achieving unification and defeating France in the Franco-Prussian War. From 1873 to 1914, the United States and Germany became the principal producers in certain leading sectors: steel and later automobiles for the United States and industrial chemicals for Germany.

The history books record that World War I broke out in 1914 and ended in 1918 and that World War II lasted from 1939 to 1945. However, it makes more sense to consider the two as a single, continuous "30 years' war" between the United States and Germany, with truces and local conflicts scattered in between. The competition for hegemonic succession took an ideological turn in 1933, when the Nazis came to power in Germany and began their quest to transcend the global system altogether, seeking not hegemony within the current system but rather a form of global empire. Recall the Nazi slogan *ein tausendjähriges Reich* (a thousand-year empire). In turn, the United States assumed the role of advocate of centrist world liberalism—recall former U.S. President Franklin D. Roosevelt's "four freedoms" (freedom of speech, of worship, from want, and from fear)—and entered into a strategic alliance with the Soviet Union, making possible the defeat of Germany and its allies.

World War II resulted in enormous destruction of infrastructure and populations throughout Eurasia, from the Atlantic to the Pacific oceans, with almost no country left unscathed. The only major industrial power in the world to emerge intact—and even greatly strengthened from an economic perspective—was the United States, which moved swiftly to consolidate its position.

But the aspiring hegemon faced some practical political obstacles. During the war, the Allied powers had agreed on the establishment of the United Nations, composed primarily of countries that had been in the coalition against the Axis powers. The organization's critical feature was the Security Council, the only structure that could authorize the use of force. Since the U.N. Charter gave the right of veto to five powers—including the United States and the Soviet Union—the council was rendered largely toothless in practice. So it was not the founding of the United Nations in April 1945 that determined the geopolitical constraints of the second half of the 20th century but rather the Yalta meeting between Roosevelt, British Prime Minister Winston Churchill, and Soviet leader Joseph Stalin two months earlier.

The formal accords at Yalta were less important than the informal, unspoken agreements, which one can only assess by observing the behavior of the United States and the Soviet Union in the years that followed. When the war ended in Europe on May 8, 1945, Soviet and Western (that is, U.S., British, and French) troops were located in particular places—essentially, along a line in the center of Europe that came to be called the Oder-Neisse Line. Aside from a few minor adjustments, they stayed there. In hindsight, Yalta signified the agreement of both sides that they could stay there and that neither side would use force to push the other out. This tacit accord applied to Asia as well, as evinced by U.S. occupation of Japan and the division of Korea. Politically, therefore, Yalta was an agreement on the status quo in which the Soviet Union controlled about one third of the world and the United States the rest.

Washington also faced more serious military challenges. The Soviet Union had the world's largest land forces, while the U.S. government was under domestic pressure to downsize its army, particularly by ending the draft. The United States therefore decided to assert its military strength not via land forces but through a monopoly of nuclear weapons (plus an air force capable of deploying them). This monopoly soon disappeared: By 1949, the Soviet Union had developed nuclear weapons as well. Ever since, the United States has been reduced to trying to prevent the acquisition of nuclear weapons (and chemical and biological weapons) by additional powers, an effort that, in the 21st century, does not seem terribly successful.

Until 1991, the United States and the Soviet Union coexisted in the "balance of terror" of the Cold War. This status quo was tested seriously only three times: the Berlin blockade of 1948–49, the Korean War in 1950–53, and the Cuban missile crisis of 1962. The result in each case was restoration of the status quo. Moreover, note how each time the Soviet Union faced a political crisis among its satellite regimes—East Germany in 1953, Hungary in 1956, Czechoslovakia in 1968, and Poland in 1981—the United States engaged in little more than propaganda exercises, allowing the Soviet Union to proceed largely as it deemed fit.

Of course, this passivity did not extend to the economic arena. The United States capitalized on the Cold War ambiance to launch massive economic reconstruction efforts, first in Western Europe and then in Japan (as well as in South Korea and Taiwan). The rationale was obvious: What was the point of having such overwhelming productive superiority if the rest of the world could not muster effective demand? Furthermore, economic reconstruction helped create clientelistic obligations on the part of the nations receiving U.S. aid; this sense of obligation fostered willingness to enter into military alliances and, even more important, into political subservience.

Finally, one should not underestimate the ideological and cultural component of U.S. hegemony. The immediate post-1945 period may have been the historical high point for the popularity of communist ideology. We easily forget today the large votes for Communist parties in free elections in countries such as Belgium, France, Italy, Czechoslovakia, and Finland, not to mention the support Communist parties gathered in Asia—in Vietnam, India, and Japan—and throughout Latin America. And that still leaves out areas such as China, Greece, and Iran, where free elections remained absent or constrained but where Communist parties enjoyed widespread appeal. In response, the United States sustained a massive anticommunist ideological offensive. In retrospect, this initiative appears largely successful: Washington brandished its role as the leader of the "free world" at least as effectively as the Soviet Union brandished its position as the leader of the "progressive" and "anti-imperialist" camp.

The United States' success as a hegemonic power in the postwar period created the conditions of the nation's hegemonic demise. This process is captured in four symbols: the war in Vietnam, the revolutions of 1968, the fall of the Berlin Wall in 1989, and the terrorist attacks of September 2001. Each symbol built upon the prior one, culminating in the situation in which the United States currently finds itself—a lone superpower that lacks true power, a world leader nobody follows and few respect, and a nation drifting dangerously amidst a global chaos it cannot control.

What was the Vietnam War? First and foremost, it was the effort of the Vietnamese people to end colonial rule and establish their own state. The Vietnamese fought the French, the Japanese, and the Americans, and in the end the Vietnamese won—quite an achievement, actually. Geopolitically, however, the war represented a rejection of the Yalta status quo by populations

then labeled as Third World. Vietnam became such a powerful symbol because Washington was foolish enough to invest its full military might in the struggle, but the United States still lost. True, the United States didn't deploy nuclear weapons (a decision certain myopic groups on the right have long reproached), but such use would have shattered the Yalta accords and might have produced a nuclear holocaust—an outcome the United States simply could not risk.

But Vietnam was not merely a military defeat or a blight on U.S. prestige. The war dealt a major blow to the United States' ability to remain the world's dominant economic power. The conflict was extremely expensive and more or less used up the U.S. gold reserves that had been so plentiful since 1945. Moreover, the United States incurred these costs just as Western Europe and Japan experienced major economic upswings. These conditions ended U.S. preeminence in the global economy. Since the late 1960s, members of this triad have been nearly economic equals, each doing better than the others for certain periods but none moving far ahead.

When the revolutions of 1968 broke out around the world, support for the Vietnamese became a major rhetorical component. "One, two, many Vietnams" and "Ho, Ho, Ho Chi Minh" were chanted in many a street, not least in the United States. But the 1968ers did not merely condemn U.S. hegemony. They condemned Soviet collusion with the United States, they condemned Yalta, and they used or adapted the language of the Chinese cultural revolutionaries who divided the world into two camps—the two superpowers and the rest of the world.

The denunciation of Soviet collusion led logically to the denunciation of those national forces closely allied with the Soviet Union, which meant in most cases the traditional Communist parties. But the 1968 revolutionaries also lashed out against other components of the Old Left—national liberation movements in the Third World, social-democratic movements in Western Europe, and New Deal Democrats in the United States—accusing them, too, of collusion with what the revolutionaries generically termed "U.S. imperialism."

The attack on Soviet collusion with Washington plus the attack on the Old Left further weakened the legitimacy of the Yalta arrangements on which the United States had fashioned the world order. It also undermined the position of centrist liberalism as the lone, legitimate global ideology. The direct political consequences of the world revolutions of 1968 were minimal, but the geopolitical and intellectual repercussions were enormous and irrevocable. Centrist liberalism tumbled from the throne it had occupied since the European revolutions of 1848 and that had enabled it to co-opt conservatives and radicals alike. These ideologies returned and once again represented a real gamut of choices. Conservatives would again become conservatives, and radicals, radicals. The centrist liberals did not disappear, but they were cut down to size. And in the process, the official U.S. ideological position—antifascist, anticommunist, anticolonialist—seemed thin and unconvincing to a growing portion of the world's populations.

The onset of international economic stagnation in the 1970s had two important consequences for U.S. power. First, stagnation resulted in the collapse of "developmentalism"—the notion that every nation could catch up economically if the state took appropriate action—which was the principal ideological claim of the Old Left movements then in power. One after another, these regimes faced internal disorder, declining standards of living, increasing debt dependency on international financial institutions, and eroding credibility. What had seemed in the 1960s to be the successful navigation of Third World decolonization by the United States—minimizing disruption and maximizing the smooth transfer of power to regimes that were developmentalist but scarcely revolutionary—gave way to disintegrating order, simmering discontents, and unchanneled radical temperaments. When the United States tried to intervene, it failed. In 1983, U.S. President Ronald Reagan sent troops to Lebanon to restore order. The troops were in effect forced out. He compensated by invading Grenada, a country without troops. President George H. W. Bush invaded Panama, another country without troops. But after he intervened in Somalia to restore order, the United States was in effect forced out, somewhat ignominiously. Since there was little the U.S. government could actually do to reverse the trend of declining hegemony, it chose simply to ignore this trend—a policy that

prevailed from the withdrawal from Vietnam until September 11, 2001.

Meanwhile, true conservatives began to assume control of key states and interstate institutions. The neoliberal offensive of the 1980s was marked by the Thatcher and Reagan regimes and the emergence of the International Monetary Fund (IMF) as a key actor on the world scene. Where once (for more than a century) conservative forces had attempted to portray themselves as wiser liberals, now centrist liberals were compelled to argue that they were more effective conservatives. The conservative programs were clear. Domestically, conservatives tried to enact policies that would reduce the cost of labor, minimize environmental constraints on producers, and cut back on state welfare benefits. Actual successes were modest, so conservatives then moved vigorously into the international arena. The gatherings of the World Economic Forum in Davos provided a meeting ground for elites and the media. The IMF provided a club for finance ministers and central bankers. And the United States pushed for the creation of the World Trade Organization to enforce free commercial flows across the world's frontiers.

While the United States wasn't watching, the Soviet Union was collapsing. Yes, Ronald Reagan had dubbed the Soviet Union an "evil empire" and had used the rhetorical bombast of calling for the destruction of the Berlin Wall, but the United States didn't really mean it and certainly was not responsible for the Soviet Union's downfall. In truth, the Soviet Union and its East European imperial zone collapsed because of popular disillusionment with the Old Left in combination with Soviet leader Mikhail Gorbachev's efforts to save his regime by liquidating Yalta and instituting internal liberalization (perestroika plus glasnost). Gorbachev succeeded in liquidating Yalta but not in saving the Soviet Union (although he almost did, be it said).

The United States was stunned and puzzled by the sudden collapse, uncertain how to handle the consequences. The collapse of communism in effect signified the collapse of liberalism, removing the only ideological justification behind U.S. hegemony, a justification tacitly supported by liberalism's ostensible ideological opponent. This loss of legitimacy led directly to the Iraqi invasion of Kuwait, which Iraqi leader Saddam Hussein would never have dared had the Yalta arrangements remained in place. In retrospect, U.S. efforts in the Gulf War accomplished a truce at basically the same line of departure. But can a hegemonic power be satisfied with a tie in a war with a middling regional power? Saddam demonstrated that one could pick a fight with the United States and get away with it. Even more than the defeat in Vietnam, Saddam's brash challenge has eaten at the innards of the U.S. right, in particular those known as the hawks, which explains the fervor of their current desire to invade Iraq and destroy its regime.

Between the Gulf War and September 11, 2001, the two major arenas of world conflict were the Balkans and the Middle East. The United States has played a major diplomatic role in both regions. Looking back, how different would the results have been had the United States assumed a completely isolationist position? In the Balkans, an economically successful multinational state (Yugoslavia) broke down, essentially into its component parts. Over 10 years, most of the resulting states have engaged in a process of ethnification, experiencing fairly brutal violence, widespread human rights violations, and outright wars. Outside intervention—in which the United States figured most prominently—brought about a truce and ended the most egregious violence, but this intervention in no way reversed the ethnification, which is now consolidated and somewhat legitimated. Would these conflicts have ended differently without U.S. involvement? The violence might have continued longer, but the basic results would probably not have been too different. The picture is even grimmer in the Middle East, where, if anything, U.S. engagement has been deeper and its failures more spectacular. In the Balkans and the Middle East alike, the United States has failed to exert its hegemonic clout effectively, not for want of will or effort but for want of real power.

Then came September 11—the shock and the reaction. Under fire from U.S. legislators, the Central Intelligence Agency (CIA) now claims it had warned the Bush administration of possible threats. But despite the CIA's focus on al Qaeda and the agency's intelligence expertise, it could not foresee (and therefore, prevent) the execution of the terrorist strikes. Or so would argue CIA Director George Tenet. This testimony can hardly comfort the U.S. government or the American people. Whatever else historians may decide, the attacks of September 11, 2001, posed a major challenge to U.S. power. The persons responsible did not represent a major military power. They were members of a nonstate force, with a high degree of determination, some money, a band of dedicated followers, and a strong base in one weak state. In short, militarily, they were nothing. Yet they succeeded in a bold attack on U.S. soil.

George W. Bush came to power very critical of the Clinton administration's handling of world affairs. Bush and his advisors did not admit—but were undoubtedly aware—that Clinton's path had been the path of every U.S. president since Gerald Ford, including that of Ronald Reagan and George H. W. Bush. It had even been the path of the current Bush administration before September 11. One only needs to look at how Bush handled the downing of the U.S. plane off China in April 2001 to see that prudence had been the name of the game.

Following the terrorist attacks, Bush changed course, declaring war on terrorism, assuring the American people that "the outcome is certain" and informing the world that "you are either with us or against us." Long frustrated by even the most conservative U.S. administrations, the hawks finally came to dominate American policy. Their position is clear: The United States wields overwhelming military power, and even though countless foreign leaders consider it unwise for Washington to flex its military muscles, these same leaders cannot and will not do anything if the United States simply imposes its will on the rest. The hawks believe the United States should act as an imperial power for two reasons: First, the United States can get away with it. And second, if Washington doesn't exert its force, the United States will become increasingly marginalized.

Today, this hawkish position has three expressions: the military assault in Afghanistan, the de facto support for the Israeli attempt to liquidate the Palestinian Authority, and the invasion of Iraq, which is reportedly in the military preparation stage. Less than one year after the September 2001 terrorist attacks, it is perhaps too early to assess what such strategies will accomplish. Thus far, these schemes have led to the overthrow of the Taliban in Afghanistan (without the complete dismantling of al Qaeda or the capture of its top leadership); enormous destruction in Palestine (without rendering Palestinian leader Yasir Arafat "irrelevant," as Israeli Prime Minister Ariel Sharon said he is); and heavy opposition from U.S. allies in Europe and the Middle East to plans for an invasion of Iraq.

The hawks' reading of recent events emphasizes that opposition to U.S. actions, while serious, has remained largely verbal. Neither Western Europe nor Russia nor China nor Saudi Arabia has seemed ready to break ties in serious ways with the United States. In other words, hawks believe, Washington has indeed gotten away with it. The hawks assume a similar outcome will occur when the U.S. military actually invades Iraq and after that, when the United States exercises its authority elsewhere in the world, be it in Iran, North Korea, Colombia, or perhaps Indonesia. Ironically, the hawk reading has largely become the reading of the international left, which has been screaming about U.S. policies—mainly because they fear that the chances of U.S. success are high.

But hawk interpretations are wrong and will only contribute to the United States' decline, transforming a gradual descent into a much more rapid and turbulent fall. Specifically, hawk approaches will fail for military, economic, and ideological reasons. Undoubtedly, the military remains the United States' strongest card; in fact, it is the only card. Today, the United States wields the most formidable military apparatus in the world. And if claims of new, unmatched military technologies are to be believed, the U.S. military edge over the rest of the world is considerably greater today than it was just a decade ago. But does that mean, then, that the United States can invade Iraq, conquer it rapidly, and install a friendly and stable regime? Unlikely. Bear in mind that of the three serious wars the U.S. military has fought since 1945 (Korea, Vietnam, and the Gulf War), one ended in defeat and two in draws—not exactly a glorious record.

Saddam Hussein's army is not that of the Taliban, and his internal military control is far more coherent. A U.S. invasion would necessarily involve a serious land force, one that would have to fight its way to Baghdad and would likely suffer significant casualties. Such a force would also need staging grounds, and Saudi Arabia has made clear that it will not serve in this capacity. Would Kuwait or Turkey help out? Perhaps, if Washington calls in all its chips. Meanwhile, Saddam can be expected to deploy all weapons at his disposal, and it is precisely the U.S. government that keeps fretting over how nasty those weapons might be. The United States may twist the arms of regimes in the region, but popular sentiment clearly views the whole affair as reflecting a deep anti-Arab bias in the United States. Can such a conflict be won? The British General Staff has apparently already informed Prime Minister Tony Blair that it does not believe so.

And there is always the matter of "second fronts." Following the Gulf War, U.S. armed forces sought to prepare for the possibility of two simultaneous regional wars. After a while, the Pentagon quietly abandoned the idea as impractical and costly. But who can be sure that no potential U.S. enemies would strike when the United States appears bogged down in Iraq?

Consider, too, the question of U.S. popular tolerance of nonvictories. Americans hover between a patriotic fervor that lends support to all wartime presidents and a deep isolationist urge. Since 1945, patriotism has hit a wall whenever the death toll has risen. Why should today's reaction differ? And even if the hawks (who are almost all civilians) feel impervious to public opinion, U.S. Army generals, burnt by Vietnam, do not. And what about the economic front? In the 1980s, countless American analysts became hysterical over the Japanese economic miracle. They calmed down in the 1990s, given Japan's well-publicized financial difficulties. Yet after overstating how quickly Japan was moving forward, U.S. authorities now seem to be complacent, confident that Japan lags far behind. These days, Washington seems more inclined to lecture Japanese policymakers about what they are doing wrong.

Such triumphalism hardly appears warranted. Consider the following April 20, 2002, *New York Times* report: "A Japanese laboratory has built the world's fastest computer, a machine so powerful that it matches the raw processing power of the 20 fastest American computers combined and far outstrips the previous leader, an I.B.M.-built machine. The achievement . . . is evidence that a technology race that most American engineers thought they were winning handily is far from over." The analysis goes on to note that there are "contrasting scientific and technological priorities" in the two countries. The Japanese machine is built to analyze climatic change, but U.S. machines are designed to simulate weapons. This contrast embodies the oldest story in the history of hegemonic powers. The dominant power concentrates (to its detriment) on the military; the candidate for successor concentrates on the economy. The latter has always paid off, handsomely. It did for the United States. Why should it not pay off for Japan as well, perhaps in alliance with China?

Finally, there is the ideological sphere. Right now, the U.S. economy seems relatively weak, even more so considering the exorbitant military expenses associated with hawk strategies. Moreover, Washington remains politically isolated; virtually no one (save Israel) thinks the hawk position makes sense or is worth encouraging. Other nations are afraid or unwilling to stand up to Washington directly, but even their foot-dragging is hurting the United States.

Yet the U.S. response amounts to little more than arrogant arm-twisting. Arrogance has its own negatives. Calling in chips means leaving fewer chips for next time, and surly acquiescence

breeds increasing resentment. Over the last 200 years, the United States acquired a considerable amount of ideological credit. But these days, the United States is running through this credit even faster than it ran through its gold surplus in the 1960s. The United States faces two possibilities during the next 10 years: It can follow the hawks' path, with negative consequences for all but especially for itself. Or it can realize that the negatives are too great. Simon Tisdall of the Guardian recently argued that even disregarding international public opinion, "the U.S. is not able to fight a successful Iraqi war by itself without incurring immense damage, not least in terms of its economic interests and its energy supply. Mr. Bush is reduced to talking tough and looking ineffectual." And if the United States still invades Iraq and is then forced to withdraw, it will look even more ineffectual.

President Bush's options appear extremely limited, and there is little doubt that the United States will continue to decline as a decisive force in world affairs over the next decade. The real question is not whether U.S. hegemony is waning but whether the United States can devise a way to descend gracefully, with minimum damage to the world, and to itself.

Wendell Berry, "A Citizen's Response to the *National Security Strategy of the United States of America*," *Orion Magazine* (March/April 2003)

Poet and neoagrarian, Wendell Berry (1934–) took particular offense at the Bush Doctrine of preventive war.

The new National Security Strategy published by the White House in September 2002, if carried out, would amount to a radical revision of the political character of our nation. Its central and most significant statement is this:

> *While the United States will constantly strive to enlist the support of the international community, we will not hesitate to act alone, if necessary, to exercise our right of self defense by acting preemptively against such terrorists. . . (p. 6)*

A democratic citizen must deal here first of all with the question, Who is this "we"? It is not the "we" of the Declaration of Independence, which referred to a small group of signatories bound by the conviction that "governments [derive] their just powers from the consent of the governed." And it is not the "we" of the Constitution, which refers to "*the people* [my emphasis] of the United States."

This "we" of the new strategy can refer only to the president. It is a royal "we." A head of state, preparing to act alone in starting a preemptive war, will need to justify his intention by secret information, and will need to plan in secret and execute his plan without forewarning. The idea of a government acting alone in preemptive war is inherently undemocratic, for it does not require or even permit the president to obtain the consent of the governed. As a policy, this new strategy depends on the acquiescence of a public kept fearful and ignorant, subject to manipulation by the executive power, and on the compliance of an intimidated and office dependent legislature. To the extent that a government is secret, it cannot be democratic or its people free. By this new doctrine, the president alone may start a war against any nation at any time, and with no more forewarning than preceded the Japanese attack on Pearl Harbor.

Would-be participating citizens of a democratic nation, unwilling to have their consent coerced or taken for granted, therefore have no choice but to remove themselves from the illegitimate constraints of this "we" in as immediate and public a way as possible.

The alleged justification for this new strategy is the recent emergence in the United States of international terrorism. But why the events of September 11, 2001, horrifying as they were, should have called for a radical new investiture of power in the executive branch is not clear.

The National Security Strategy defines terrorism as "premeditated, politically motivated violence perpetrated against innocents" (p. 5). This is truly a distinct kind of violence, but to imply by the word "terrorism" that this sort of terror is the work exclusively of "terrorists" is misleading. The "legitimate" warfare of technologically advanced nations likewise is premeditated, politically motivated violence perpetrated against innocents. The distinction between the intention to perpetrate violence against innocents, as in "terrorism," and the willingness to do so, as in "war," is not a source of comfort.

Supposedly, if a nation perpetrates violence officially—whether to bomb an enemy airfield or a hospital—it is not guilty of "terrorism." But there is no need to hesitate over the difference between "terrorism" and any violence or threat of violence that is terrifying. The National Security Strategy wishes to cause "terrorism" to be seen "in the same light as slavery, piracy, or genocide" (p. 6) but not in the same light as war. It accepts and affirms the legitimacy of war.

The war against terrorism is not, strictly speaking, a war against nations, even though it has already involved international war in Afghanistan and presidential threats against other nations. This is a war against "the embittered few" "thousands of trained terrorists"—who are "at large" (p. 5) among many millions of others who are, in the language of this document, "innocents," and thus are deserving of our protection.

Unless we are willing to kill innocents in order to kill the guilty, the need to be lethal will be impeded constantly by the need to be careful. Because we must suppose a new supply of villains to be always in the making, we can expect the war on terrorism to be more or less endless, endlessly costly and endlessly supportive of a thriving bureaucracy.

Unless, that is, we should become willing to ask why, and to do something about the causes. Why do people become terrorists? Such questions arise from the recognition that problems have causes. There is, however, no acknowledgment in The National Security Strategy that terrorism might have a cause that could possibly be discovered and possibly remedied. "The embittered few," it seems, are merely "evil."

Much of the obscurity of our effort so far against terrorism originates in this now official idea that the enemy is evil and that we are (therefore) good, which is the precise mirror image of the official idea of the terrorists.

The epigraph of Part III of The National Security Strategy contains this sentence from President Bush's speech at the National Cathedral on September 14, 2001: "But our responsibility to history is already clear: to answer these attacks and rid the world of evil." A government, committing its nation to rid the world of evil, is assuming necessarily that it and its nation are good.

But the proposition that anything so multiple and large as a nation can be "good" is an insult to common sense. It is also dangerous, because it precludes any attempt at self-criticism or self-correction; it precludes public dialogue. It leads us far indeed from the traditions of religion and democracy that are intended to measure and so to sustain our efforts to be good. Christ said "He that is without sin among you, let him first cast a stone at her." And Thomas Jefferson justified general education by the obligation of citizens to be critical of their government: "for nothing can keep it right but their own *vigilant and distrustful* [my emphasis] superintendence." An inescapable requirement of true patriotism, love for one's land, is a vigilant distrust of any determinative power, elected or unelected, that may preside over it.

And so it is not without reason or precedent that a citizen should point out that, in addition to evils originating abroad and supposedly correctable by catastrophic technologies in "legitimate" hands, we have an agenda of domestic evils, not only those that properly self-aware humans can find in their own hearts, but also several that are indigenous to our history as a nation: issues of economic and social justice, and issues related to the continuing and worsening maladjustment between our economy and our land.

There are kinds of violence that have nothing directly to do with unofficial or official warfare. I mean such things as toxic pollution, land destruction, soil erosion, the destruction of biological diversity and of the ecological supports of agriculture. To anybody with a normal concern for health and sanity, these "externalized costs" are terrible and are terrifying.

I don't wish to make light of the threats and dangers that now confront us. But frightening as these are, they do not relieve us of the responsibility to be as intelligent, principled, and practical as we can be. To rouse the public's anxiety about foreign terror while ignoring domestic terror, and to fail to ask if these terrors are in any way related, is wrong.

It is understandable that we should have reacted to the attacks of September 11, 2001, by curtailment of civil rights, by defiance of laws, and by resort to overwhelming force, for those things are the ready products of fear and hasty thought. But they cannot protect us against the destruction of our own land by ourselves. They cannot protect us against the selfishness, wastefulness, and greed that we have legitimized here as economic virtues, and have taught to the world. They cannot protect us against our government's long-standing disdain for any form of self-sufficiency or thrift, or against the consequent dependence, which for the present at least is inescapable, on foreign supplies, such as oil from the Middle East.

It is no wonder that the National Security Strategy, growing as it does out of unresolved contradictions in our domestic life, should attempt to compound a foreign policy out of contradictory principles.

There is, first of all, the contradiction of peace and war, or of war as the means of achieving and preserving peace. This document affirms peace; it also affirms peace as the justification of war and war as the means of peace and thus perpetuates a hallowed absurdity. But implicit in its assertion of this (and, by implication, any other) nation's right to act alone in its own interest is an acceptance of war as a permanent condition. Either way, it is cynical to invoke the ideas of cooperation, community, peace, freedom, justice, dignity, and the rule of law (as this document repeatedly does), and then proceed to assert one's intention to act alone in making war. One cannot reduce terror by holding over the world the threat of what it most fears.

This is a contradiction not reconcilable except by a self-righteousness almost inconceivably naive. The authors of the strategy seem now and then to be glimmeringly conscious of the difficulty. Their implicit definition of "rogue state," for example, is any nation pursuing national greatness by advanced military capabilities that can threaten its neighbors—except our nation.

If you think our displeasure with "rogue states" might have any underpinning in international law, then you will be disappointed to learn on page 31 that

> We will take the actions necessary to ensure that our efforts to meet our global security commitments and protect Americans are not impaired by the potential for investigations, inquiry, or prosecution by the International Criminal Court (ICC), whose jurisdiction does not extend to Americans and which we do not accept.

The rule of law in the world, then, is to be upheld by a nation that has declared itself to be above the law. A childish hypocrisy here assumes the dignity of a nation's foreign policy.

Further contradiction is that between war and commerce. This issue arises first of all in the war economy, which unsurprisingly regards war as a business and weapons as merchandise. However nationalistic may be the doctrine of the National

Security Strategy, the fact is that the internationalization of the weapons trade is a result inherent in international trade itself. It is a part of globalization. Mr. Bush's addition of this Security Strategy to the previous bipartisan commitment to globalization exposes an American dementia that has not been so plainly displayed before.

The America Whose Business is Business has been internationalizing its economy in haste (for bad reasons, and with little foresight), looking everywhere for "trading partners," cheap labor, and tax shelters. Meanwhile, the America Whose Business is National Defense is withdrawing from the world in haste (for bad reasons, with little foresight), threatening left and right, repudiating agreements, and angering friends. The problem of participating in the Global Economy for the benefit of Washington's corporate sponsors while maintaining a nationalist belligerence and an isolationist morality calls for superhuman intelligence in the secretary of commerce. The problem of "acting alone" in an international war while maintaining simultaneously our ability to import the foreign goods (for instance, oil) on which we have become dependent even militarily will call, likewise, for overtopping genius in the secretary of defense.

After World War II, we hoped the world might be united for the sake of peacemaking. Now the world is being "globalized" for the sake of trade and the so-called free market—for the sake, that is, of plundering the world for cheap labor, cheap energy, and cheap materials. How nations, let alone regions and communities, are to shape and protect themselves within this "global economy" is far from clear. Nor is it clear how the global economy can hope to survive the wars of nations.

For a nation to be, in the truest sense, patriotic, its citizens must love their land with a knowing, intelligent, sustaining, and protective love. They must not, for any price, destroy its health, its beauty, or its productivity. And they must not allow their patriotism to be degraded to a mere loyalty to symbols or any present set of officials.

One might reasonably assume, therefore, that a policy of national security would advocate from the start various practical measures to conserve and to use frugally the nation's resources, the objects of this husbandry being a reduction in the nation's

dependence on imports and a reduction in the competition between nations for necessary goods.

Agriculture, which is the economic activity most clearly and directly related to national security—if one grants that we all must eat—receives such scant and superficial treatment as to amount to a dismissal. The document proposes only:

1. *"a global effort to address new technology, science, and health regulations that needlessly impede farm exports and improved agriculture" (p. 19). This refers, without saying so, to the growing consumer resistance to genetically modified food. A global effort to overcome this resistance would help, not farmers and not consumers, but global agribusiness corporations.*
2. *"transitional safeguards which we have used in the agricultural sector" (p. 19). This refers to government subsidies, which ultimately help the agribusiness corporations, not farmers.*
3. *Promotion of "new technologies, including biotechnology, [which] have enormous potential to improve crop yields in developing countries while using fewer pesticides and less water" (p. 23). This is offered (as usual and questionably) as the solution to hunger, but its immediate benefit would be to the corporate suppliers.*

This is not an agriculture policy, let alone a national security strategy. It has the blindness, arrogance, and foolishness that are characteristic of top-down thinking by politicians and academic experts, assuming that "improved agriculture" would inevitably be the result of catering to the agribusiness corporations, and that national food security can be achieved merely by going on as before. It does not address any agricultural problem as such, and it ignores the vulnerability of our present food system dependent as it is on genetically impoverished monocultures, cheap petroleum, cheap long-distance transportation, and cheap farm labor to many kinds of disruption by "the embittered few," who, in the event of such disruption, would quickly become the embittered many. On eroding, ecologically degraded, increasingly toxic landscapes, worked by failing or subsidy-dependent farmers and by the cheap labor of migrants, we have erected the tottering tower of "agribusiness," which prospers and "feeds the world" (incompletely and temporarily) by undermining its own foundations.

Since the end of World War II, when the terrors of industrial warfare had been fully revealed, many people and, by fits and starts, many governments have recognized that peace is not just a desirable condition, as was thought before, but a practical necessity. But we have not yet learned to think of peace apart from war. We wait, still, until we face terrifying dangers and the necessity to choose among bad alternatives, and then we think again of peace, and again we fight a war to secure it.

At the end of the war, if we have won it, we declare peace; we congratulate ourselves on our victory; we marvel at the newly-proved efficiency of our latest weapons; we ignore the cost in lives, materials, and property, in suffering and disease, in damage to the natural world; we ignore the inevitable residue of resentment and hatred; and we go on as before, having, as we think, successfully defended our way of life.

That is pretty much the story of our victory in the Gulf War of 1991. In the years between that victory and September 11, 2001, we did not alter our thinking about peace and war—that is, we thought much about war and little about peace; we continued to punish the defeated people of Iraq and their children; we made no effort to reduce our dependence on the oil we import from other, potentially belligerent countries; we made no improvement in our charity toward the rest of the world; we made no motion toward greater economic self-reliance; and we continued our extensive and often irreversible damages to our own land. We appear to have assumed merely that our victory confirmed our manifest destiny to be the richest, most powerful, most wasteful nation in the world. After the catastrophe of September 11, it again became clear to us how good it would be to be at peace, to have no enemies, to have no more needless deaths to mourn. And then, our need for war following with the customary swift and deadly logic our need for peace, we took up the customary obsession with the evil of other people.

It is useless to try to adjudicate a long-standing animosity by asking who started it or who is the most wrong. The only sufficient answer is to give up the animosity and try forgiveness, to try to love our enemies and to talk to them and (if we pray) to pray for them. If we can't do any of that, then we must begin again by trying to imagine our enemies' children who, like our children, are in mortal danger because of enmity that they did not cause.

We can no longer afford to confuse peaceability with passivity. Authentic peace is no more passive than war. Like war, it calls for discipline and intelligence and strength of character, though it calls also for higher principles and aims. If we are serious about peace, then we must work for it as ardently, seriously, continuously, carefully, and bravely as we now prepare for war.

ROBERT BYRD, "AMERICA'S IMAGE IN THE WORLD" (2003)

West Virginia Senator Robert Byrd (1917–2010) denounced the Iraq War as a grotesque error.

I believe in this beautiful country. I have studied its roots and gloried in the wisdom of its magnificent Constitution. I have marveled at the wisdom of its founders and framers. Generation after generation of Americans has understood the lofty ideals that underlie our great Republic. I have been inspired by the story of their sacrifice and their strength.

But, today I weep for my country. I have watched the events of recent months with a heavy, heavy heart. No more is the image of America one of strong, yet benevolent peacekeeper. The image of America has changed. Around the globe, our friends mistrust us, our word is disputed, our intentions are questioned.

Instead of reasoning with those with whom we disagree, we demand obedience or threaten recrimination. Instead of isolating Saddam Hussein, we seem to have isolated ourselves. We proclaim a new doctrine of preemption which is understood by few and feared by many. We say that the United States has the right to turn its firepower on any corner of the globe which might be suspect in the war on terrorism. We assert that right without the sanction of any international body. As a result, the world has become a much more dangerous place.

We flaunt our superpower status with arrogance. We treat U.N. Security Council members like ingrates who offend our princely dignity by lifting their heads from the carpet. Valuable alliances are split. After war has ended, the United States will have to rebuild much more than the country of Iraq. We will have to rebuild America's image around the globe.

The case this Administration tries to make to justify its fixation with war is tainted by charges of falsified documents and circumstantial evidence. We cannot convince the world of the necessity of this war for one simple reason. This is a war of choice.

There is no credible information to connect Saddam Hussein to 9/11. The twin towers fell because a world-wide terrorist group, al-Qaida, with cells in over 60 nations, struck at our wealth and our influence by turning our own planes into missiles, one of which would likely have slammed into the dome of this beautiful Capitol except for the brave sacrifice of the passengers on board.

The brutality seen on September 11th and in other terrorist attacks we have witnessed around the globe are the violent and desperate efforts by extremists to stop the daily encroachment of western values upon their cultures. That is what we fight. It is a force not confined to borders. It is a shadowy entity with many faces, many names, and many addresses.

But, this Administration has directed all of the anger, fear, and grief which emerged from the ashes of the twin towers and the twisted metal of the Pentagon towards a tangible villain, one we can see and hate and attack. And villain he is. But, he is the wrong villain. And this is the wrong war. If we attack Saddam Hussein, we will probably drive him from power. But, the zeal of our friends to assist our global war on terrorism may have already taken flight.

The general unease surrounding this war is not just due to "orange alert." There is a pervasive sense of rush and risk and too many questions unanswered. How long will we be in Iraq? What will be the cost? What is the ultimate mission? How great is the danger at home? A pall has fallen over the Senate Chamber. We avoid our solemn duty to debate the one topic on the minds of all Americans, even while scores of thousands of our sons and daughters faithfully do their duty in Iraq.

What is happening to this country? When did we become a nation which ignores and berates our friends? When did we decide to risk undermining international order by adopting a radical and doctrinaire approach to using our awesome military might? How can we abandon diplomatic efforts when the turmoil in the world cries out for diplomacy?

Why can this President not seem to see that America's true power lies not in its will to intimidate, but in its ability to inspire?

War appears inevitable. But, I continue to hope that the cloud will lift. Perhaps Saddam will yet turn tail and run. Perhaps reason will somehow still prevail. I along with millions of Americans will pray for the safety of our troops, for the innocent civilians in Iraq, and for the security of our homeland. May God continue to bless the United States of America in the troubled days ahead, and may we somehow recapture the vision which for the present eludes us.

SHELDON WOLIN, "INVERTED TOTALITARIANISM," THE NATION (MAY 1, 2003)

A prominent political scientist who taught at Princeton, Sheldon Wolin (1922–2015) charged the George W. Bush administration with using the war on terrorism as a pretext to undermine American democracy.

The war on Iraq has so monopolized public attention as to obscure the regime change taking place in the Homeland. We may have invaded Iraq to bring in democracy and bring down a totalitarian regime, but in the process our own system may be moving closer to the latter and further weakening the former. The change has been intimated by the sudden popularity of two political terms rarely applied earlier to the American political system. "Empire" and "superpower" both suggest that a new system of power, concentrated and expansive, has come into existence and supplanted the old terms. "Empire" and "superpower" accurately symbolize the projection of American power abroad, but for that reason they obscure the internal consequences. Consider how odd it would sound if we were to refer to "the Constitution of the American Empire" or "superpower democracy." The reason they ring false is that "constitution" signifies limitations on power, while "democracy" commonly refers to the active involvement of citizens with their government and the responsiveness of government to its citizens. For their part, "empire" and "superpower" stand for the surpassing of limits and the dwarfing of the citizenry.

The increasing power of the state and the declining power of institutions intended to control it has been in the making for some time. The party system is a notorious example. The Republicans have emerged as a unique phenomenon in American history of a fervently doctrinal party, zealous, ruthless, antidemocratic and boasting a near majority. As Republicans have become more ideologically intolerant, the Democrats have shrugged off the liberal label and their critical reform-minded constituencies to embrace centrism and footnote the end of ideology. In ceasing to be a genuine opposition party the Democrats have smoothed the road to power of a party more than eager to use it to promote empire abroad and corporate power at home. Bear in mind that a ruthless, ideologically driven party with a mass base was a crucial element in all of the twentieth-century regimes seeking total power.

Representative institutions no longer represent voters. Instead, they have been short-circuited, steadily corrupted by an institutionalized system of bribery that renders them responsive to powerful interest groups whose constituencies are the major corporations and wealthiest Americans. The courts, in turn, when they are not increasingly handmaidens of corporate power, are consistently deferential to the claims of national security. Elections have become heavily subsidized non-events that typically attract at best merely half of an electorate whose information about foreign and domestic politics is filtered through corporate-dominated media. Citizens are manipulated into a nervous state by the media's reports of rampant crime and terrorist networks, by thinly veiled threats of the Attorney General and by their own fears about unemployment. What is crucially important here is not only the expansion of governmental power but the inevitable discrediting of constitutional limitations and institutional processes that discourages the citizenry and leaves them politically apathetic.

No doubt these remarks will be dismissed by some as alarmist, but I want to go further and name the emergent political system "inverted totalitarianism." By inverted I mean that while the current system and its operatives share with Nazism the aspiration toward unlimited power and aggressive expansionism, their methods and actions seem upside down. For example, in Weimar Germany, before the Nazis took power, the "streets" were dominated by totalitarian-oriented gangs of toughs, and whatever there was of democracy was confined to the government. In the United States, however, it is the streets where democracy is most alive—while the real danger lies with an increasingly unbridled government.

Or another example of the inversion: Under Nazi rule there was never any doubt about "big business" being subordinated to the political regime. In the United States, however, it has been apparent for decades that corporate power has become so predominant in the political establishment, particularly in the Republican Party, and so dominant in its influence over policy, as to suggest a role inversion the exact opposite of the Nazis'. At the same time, it is corporate power, as the representative of the dynamic of capitalism and of the ever-expanding power made available by the integration of science and technology with the structure of capitalism, that produces the totalizing drive that, under the Nazis, was supplied by ideological notions such as *Lebensraum*.

In rebuttal it will be said that there is no domestic equivalent to the Nazi regime of torture, concentration camps or other instruments of terror. But we should remember that for the most part, Nazi terror was not applied to the population generally; rather, the aim was to promote a certain type of shadowy fear—rumors of torture–that would aid in managing and manipulating the populace. Stated positively, the Nazis wanted a mobilized society eager to support endless warfare, expansion and sacrifice for the nation.

While the Nazi totalitarianism strove to give the masses a sense of collective power and strength, *Kraft durch Freude* ("Strength through joy"), inverted totalitarianism promotes a sense of weakness, of collective futility. While the Nazis wanted a continuously mobilized society that would not only support the regime without complaint and enthusiastically vote "yes" at the periodic plebiscites, inverted totalitarianism wants a politically demobilized society that hardly votes at all. Recall the President's words immediately after the horrendous events of September 11: "Unite, consume and fly," he told the anxious citizenry. Having assimilated terrorism to a "war," he avoided doing what democratic leaders customarily do during wartime: mobilize the citizenry, warn it of impending sacrifices and exhort all citizens to join the "war effort." Instead, inverted totalitarianism has its own means of promoting generalized fear; not only by sudden "alerts" and periodic announcements about recently discovered terrorist cells or the arrest of shadowy figures or the publicized heavy-handed treatment of aliens and the Devil's Island that is Guantánamo Bay or the sudden fascination with interrogation methods that employ or border on torture, but by a pervasive atmosphere of fear abetted by a corporate economy of ruthless downsizing, withdrawal or reduction of pension and health benefits; a corporate political system that relentlessly threatens to privatize Social Security and the modest health benefits available, especially to the poor. With such instrumentalities for promoting uncertainty and dependence, it is almost overkill for inverted totalitarianism to employ a system of criminal justice that is punitive in the extreme, relishes the death penalty and is consistently biased against the powerless.

Thus the elements are in place: a weak legislative body, a legal system that is both compliant and repressive, a party system in which one party, whether in opposition or in the majority, is bent upon reconstituting the existing system so as to permanently favor a ruling class of the wealthy, the well-connected and the corporate, while leaving the poorer citizens with a sense of helplessness and political despair, and, at the same time, keeping the middle classes dangling between fear of unemployment and expectations of fantastic rewards once the new economy recovers. That scheme is abetted by a sycophantic and increasingly concentrated media; by the integration of universities with their corporate benefactors; by a propaganda machine institutionalized in well-funded think tanks and conservative foundations; by the increasingly closer cooperation between local police and national law enforcement agencies aimed at identifying terrorists, suspicious aliens and domestic dissidents.

What is at stake, then, is nothing less than the attempted transformation of a tolerably free society into a variant of the extreme regimes of the past century. In that context, the national elections of 2004 represent a crisis in its original meaning, a turning point. The question for citizens is: Which way?

PATRICK BUCHANAN, "NO END TO WAR," *THE AMERICAN CONSERVATIVE* (MARCH 1, 2004)

A hard-nosed Republican political operative from the 1960s to the 1980s, Patrick Buchanan (1938–) reinvented himself after the Cold War as an anti-interventionist pundit. Here he charges David Frum and Richard Perle with supporting the Global War on Terrorism for reasons unrelated to US national security. Buchanan's critics called him an anti-Semite.

On the dust jacket of his book, Richard Perle appends a *Washington Post* depiction of himself as the "intellectual guru of the hard-line neoconservative movement in foreign policy."

The guru's reputation, however, does not survive a reading. Indeed, on putting down Perle's new book the thought recurs: the neoconservative moment may be over. For they are not only losing their hold on power, they are losing their grip on reality.

An End to Evil: How to Win the War on Terror opens on a note of hysteria. In the War on Terror, writes Perle, "There is no middle way for Americans: It is victory or holocaust." "What is new since 9/11 is the chilling realization that the terrorist threat we thought we had contained" now menaces "our survival as a nation."

But how is our survival as a nation menaced when not one American has died in a terrorist attack on U.S. soil since 9/11? Are we really in imminent peril of a holocaust like that visited upon the Jews of Poland?

"[A] radical strain within Islam," says Perle, ". . . seeks to overthrow our civilization and remake the nations of the West into Islamic societies, imposing on the whole world its religion and laws."

Well, yes. Militant Islam has preached that since the 7th century. But what are the odds the Boys of Tora Bora are going to "overthrow our civilization" and coerce us all to start praying to Mecca five times a day? . . .

To suggest Frum and Perle are over the top is not to imply we not take seriously the threat of terror attacks on airliners, in malls, from dirty bombs, or, God forbid, a crude atomic device smuggled in by Ryder truck or container ship. Yet even this will never "overthrow our civilization."

In the worst of terror attacks, we lost 3,000 people. Horrific. But at Antietam Creek, we lost 7,000 in a day's battle in a nation that was one-ninth as populous. Three thousand men and boys perished every week for 200 weeks of that Civil War. We Americans did not curl up and die. We did not come all this way because we are made of sugar candy.

Germany and Japan suffered 3,000 dead every day in the last two years of World War II, with every city flattened and two blackened by atom bombs. Both came back in a decade. Is al-Qaeda capable of this sort of devastation when they are recruiting such scrub stock as Jose Padilla and the shoe bomber?

In the war we are in, our enemies are weak. That is why they resort to the weapon of the weak—terror. And, as in the Cold War, time is on America's side. Perseverance and patience are called for, not this panic.

In 25 years, militant Islam has seized three countries: Iran, Sudan, and Afghanistan. We toppled the Taliban almost without losing a man. Sudan is a failed state. In Iran, a generation has grown up that knows nothing of Savak or the Great Satan but enough about the mullahs to have rejected them in back-to-back landslides. The Iranian Revolution has reached Thermidor. Wherever Islamism takes power, it fails. Like Marxism, it does not work.

Yet, assume it makes a comeback. So what? Taken together, all 22 Arab nations do not have the GDP of Spain. Without oil, their exports are the size of Finland's. Not one Arab nation can stand up to Israel, let alone the United States. The Islamic threat is not strategic, but demographic. If death comes to the West it will be because we embraced a culture of death—birth control, abortion, sterilization, euthanasia. Western man is dying as Islamic man migrates north to await his passing and inherit his estate.

Said young Lincoln in his Lyceum address, "If destruction be our lot, we must ourselves be its author and finisher. As a nation of freemen, we must live through all time, or die by suicide."

In his first inaugural address, FDR admonished, "[T]he only thing we have to fear is fear itself—nameless, unreasoning, unjustified terror which paralyzes needed efforts to convert retreat into advance."

Fear is what Perle and his co-author David Frum are peddling to stampede America into serial wars. Just such fear-mongering got us into Iraq, though, we have since discovered, Iraq had no hand in 9/11, no ties to al-Qaeda, no weapons of mass destruction, no nuclear program, and no plans to attack us. Iraq was never "the clear and present danger" the authors insist she was.

Calling their book a "manual for victory," they declaim:

> For us, terrorism remains the great evil of our time, and the war against this evil, our generation's great cause. We do not believe that Americans are fighting this evil to minimize it or to manage it.

We believe they are fighting to win—to end this evil before it kills again and on a genocidal scale. There is no middle way for Americans: It is victory or holocaust.

But no nation can "end evil." Evil has existed since Cain rose up against his brother Abel and slew him. A propensity to evil can be found in every human heart. And if God accepts the existence of evil, how do Frum and Perle propose to "end" it? Nor can any nation "win the war on terror." Terrorism is simply a term for the murder of non-combatants for political ends.

Revolutionary terror has been around for as long as this Republic. It was used by Robespierre's Committee on Public Safety and by People's Will in Romanov Russia. Terror has been the chosen weapon of anarchists, the IRA, Irgun, the Stern Gang, Algeria's FLN, the Mau Mau, MPLA, the PLO, Black September, the Basque ETA, Hezbollah, Islamic Jihad, Hamas, the Al Aksa Martyrs Brigade, SWAPO, ZANU, ZAPU, the Tupamaros, Shining Path, FARC, the ANC, the V.C., the Huks, Chechen rebels, Tamil Tigers, and the FALN that attempted to assassinate Harry Truman and shot up the House floor in 1954, to name only a few.

Accused terrorists have won the Nobel Peace Prize: Begin, Arafat, Mandela. Three lie in mausoleums in the capitals of nations they created: Lenin, Mao, Ho. Others are the fathers of their countries like Ben Bella and Jomo Kenyatta. A terrorist of the Black Hand ignited World War I by assassinating the Archduke Ferdinand. Yet Gavrilo Princep has a bridge named for him in Sarajevo.

The murder of innocents for political ends is evil, but to think we can "end" it is absurd. Cruel and amoral men, avaricious for power and "immortality," will always resort to it. For, all too often, it succeeds.

But what must America do to attain victory in her war on terror?

Say the authors: "We must hunt down the individual terrorists before they kill our people or others . . . . We must deter all regimes that use terror as a weapon of state against anyone, American or not" [emphasis added].

Astonishing. The authors say America is responsible for defending everyone, everywhere from terror and deterring any and all regimes that might use terror —against anyone, anywhere on earth.

But there are 192 nations. Scores of regimes from Liberia to Congo to Cuba, from Zimbabwe to Syria to Uzbekistan, and from Iran to Sudan to the Afghan warlords of the Northern Alliance who fought on our side—have used torture and terror to punish enemies. Are we to fight them all?

Well, actually, no. Excepting North Korea, the authors' list of nations that need to be attacked reads as though it were drawn up in the Israeli Defense Ministry. By the second paragraph, Perle and Frum have given us a short list of priority targets: "The war on terror is not over, it has barely begun. Al Qaeda, Hezbollah, and Hamas still plot murder."

Now al-Qaeda was responsible for 9/11. But when did Hamas attack us? And if Israel can co-exist and negotiate with Hezbollah, why is it America's duty to destroy Hezbollah? Iran and North Korea, the authors warn, "present intolerable threats to American security. We must move boldly against them both and against all other sponsors of terrorism as well: Syria, Libya and Saudi Arabia. And we don't have much time."

"Why have we put up with [Syria] as long as we have?" the authors demand. They call for a cut-off of Syria's oil and an ultimatum to Assad: Get Syrian troops out of Lebanon, hand over all terrorist suspects, end support for Hezbollah, stop agitating against Israel, and adopt a "Western orientation"—or you, too, get the Saddam treatment.

But what has Syria done to us? And if Assad balks do we bomb Damascus? Invade? Where do we get the troops? What if the Syrians, too, resort to guerrilla war?

Bush's father made Hafez al-Assad an ally in the Gulf War. Ehud Barak offered Assad 99.5 percent of the Golan Heights. Why, then, must Bashir Assad's regime be destroyed—by us?

"We don't have much time," say Frum and Perle. But what is Assad doing that warrants immediate attack? Is he, too, buying yellowcake from Niger?

Colonel Khaddafi is now paying billions in reparations for Pan Am 103, giving up his weapons of mass destruction, and inviting U.S. inspectors in to verify his disarmament. Why is it imperative we overthrow him?

While the Saudis have been diffident allies in the War on Terror, they are not America's enemies. They pumped oil to keep prices down in the first Gulf War. They looked the other way as U.S. fighter-bombers flew out of Prince Sultan Air Base in Operation Iraqi Freedom. Yet the Saudis are directed to provide us "with the utmost cooperation in the war on terror," or we will invade, detach their oil-rich eastern province, and occupy it.

But why? If the monarchy falls and bin Laden's acolytes replace it, how would that make us more secure in our own country?

What did Iran do to justify war against her? According to Perle and Frum, Iran defied the Monroe Doctrine and sponsored murder in our own hemisphere, killing eighty-six people and wounding some three hundred at the Jewish community center in Buenos Aires—and our government did worse than nothing: It opened negotiations with the murderers.

But that atrocity occurred a dozen years ago, long before the reform government of President Mohammad Khatami was elected. And if Iran was behind an attack on a Jewish community center in Buenos Aires, why did Argentina and Israel not avenge these deaths? Why is retribution our responsibility? It was not Americans who were the victims, and the attack occurred 5,000 miles from the United States.

The Frum-Perle invocation of the Monroe Doctrine is both cynical and comical. If they were genuinely concerned about violations of the Monroe Doctrine, why did they not include Cuba on their target list, a "state sponsor of terror" 90 miles from our shores that has hosted Soviet missiles and, according to Undersecretary of State John Bolton, is developing chemical and biological weapons? Why did Saudi Arabia make the cut but not Cuba? Might it have something to do with proximity and propinquity?

For Iran, there can be no reprieve. "The regime must go," say our authors, because Ayatollah Khamenei has. . . no more right to control . . . Iran than any other criminal has to seize control of the persons and property of others. It's not always in our power to do something about such criminals, nor is it always in our interest, but when it is in our power and interest, we should toss dictators aside with no more compunction

than a police sharpshooter feels when he downs a hostage-taker.

But where in the Constitution is the president empowered to "toss dictators aside"? And if it took 150,000 U.S. soldiers to toss Saddam aside, how many troops do Frum and Perle think it will take to occupy the capital of a nation three times as large and populous and toss the ayatollah aside? How many dead and wounded would our war hawks consider an acceptable price for being rid of the mullahs?

As South Korea favors appeasement, they write, we must take the lead, demand that North Korea surrender all nuclear materials and shut down all missile sites. If Kim Jong Il balks, we should move U.S. troops back to safety beyond artillery and rocket range of the DMZ and launch preemptive strikes on known North Korean nuclear sites and impose a naval and air blockade. As for the South Koreans, they should probably brace themselves. "We have no doubt how such a war would end," say the authors. They also had no doubt how the Iraqi war would end.

Is the Perle-Frum vision for the suffering people of North Korea a future of freedom and democracy? Not exactly:

> It may be that the only way out of the decade-long crisis on the Korean peninsula is the toppling of Kim Jong Il and his replacement by a North Korean communist who is more subservient to China. If so, we should accept that outcome.

Swell. America is to fight a second Korean War that could entail a nuclear strike on our troops, but, when we have won, we should accept a communist North Korea that is a vassal of Beijing. How many dead and wounded are our AEI warlords willing to accept to make Pyongyang a puppet of Beijing?

But the Frum-Perle enemies' list is not complete. France, if she does not shape up, is to be treated as an enemy.

From every page of this book there oozes a sense of urgency that borders on the desperate for action this day: "We can feel the will to win ebbing in Washington, we sense the reversion to the bad old habits of complacency and denial."

The neocons are not wrong here. With the cost of war at $200 billion and rising, with deaths mounting, and with the possibility growing that Iraq could collapse in chaos and civil war, President Bush appears to be experiencing buyer's remorse about the lemon he was sold by Perle and friends.

They promised him a "cakewalk," that we would be hailed as "liberators," that democracy would take root in Iraq and flourish in the Middle East, that Palestinians and Israelis would break bread and make peace. With Lord Melbourne, Bush must be muttering, "What all the wise men promised has not happened, and what all the damn fools said would happen has come to pass."

What do Perle and Frum see as our decisive failing in Iraq?

But of all our mistakes, probably the most serious was our unwillingness to allow the Iraqi National Congress, Iraq's leading anti-Saddam resistance movement, to form a provisional government after the fall of Baghdad. In 1944, we took care to let French troops enter Paris before U.S. or British forces. We should have shown equal tact in 2003.

Thus, we are in trouble because Ahmad Chalabi was not allowed to play de Gaulle leading his war-weary, battle-hardened Free Iraqis into Baghdad.

Why was Perle's protégé passed over? Because the "INC terrified the Saudis and therefore terrified those in our government who wished to placate the Saudis." The damned Arabists at State did it again.

Hastily written, replete with errors, with no index, *An End to Evil* is a brief in defense of neoconservatives against their impending indictment on charges they lied us into a war that may prove our greatest disaster since Vietnam. And the charge of deliberate deceit is not without merit.

In mid-December 2001, in a column distributed by Copley News, Perle asserted that Saddam "is busily at work on a nuclear weapon . . . . it's simply a matter of time before he acquires nuclear weapons."

Naming Khidir Hamza, "one of the people who ran the nuclear weapons program for Saddam," as his source, Perle gave credence to Hamza's tale of 400 uranium enrichment facilities spread all over Iraq. "Some of them look like farmhouses, some of them look like classrooms, some of them look like warehouses. You'll never find them." Only "preemptive action" can save us, said Perle.

By the end of 2001, according to Perle, the threat of a nuclear-armed Saddam was imminent:

With each passing day he comes closer to his dream of a nuclear arsenal. We know he has a clandestine program, spread over many hidden sites, to enrich natural uranium to weapons grade . . . . And intelligence sources know he is in the market, with plenty of money, for both weapons material and components as well as finished nuclear weapons. How close is he? We do not know. Two years, three years, tomorrow even?

When he wrote this, Perle, as chairman of the Defense Policy Board, had access to secret intelligence. So the question cannot be evaded: did Hamza deliberately deceive Perle, or did Perle deliberately deceive us?

For those unpersuaded that Saddam was a strategic threat, there were his links to the 9/11 massacre. Saddam's "collaboration with terrorism is well documented," wrote Perle, "Evidence of a meeting in Prague between a senior Iraqi intelligence agent and Mohamed Atta, the September 11 ringleader, is convincing."

Thus did the neocons get the war they wanted. And after America fought the war for which they had beaten the drums, how do Perle & Co. explain why it did not turn out as they assured us it would?

Answer: any disaster in Iraq, the authors argue, will be due to the venality and cowardice of the State Department, CIA, FBI, retired generals, and ex-ambassadors bought off by the Saudis. "We have offered concrete recommendations equal to the seriousness of the threat, and the softliners have not, because we have wanted to fight and they have not."

Which brings us back to the point made at the outset: the neocon moment may be passing, for they appear to be losing their grip on reality as well as their influence on policy. Rather than looking for new wars to involve us more deeply in the Middle East, Bush and Rumsfeld seem to be looking for the next exit ramp out of our Mesopotamian morass. "No war in '04" is said to be the watchword of Karl Rove.

Moreover, Americans are coming to appreciate that, all that bombast about "unipolar" moments and "American empire" aside, there are limits to American power, and we are approaching them.

U.S. ground forces of 480,000 are stretched thin. There is grumbling in Army, Reserve, and National Guard units about too many tours too far from home. Backing off his "axis-of-evil" rhetoric, Bush said in this year's State of the Union, "We have no desire to dominate, no ambitions of empire."

The long retreat of American empire has begun. . . .

Moreover, the radicalism of their schemes for two, three, many wars, seems, given our embroilment in Iraq, not only rash but also rooted in unreality. Before Bush could take us to war with any of these regimes, he would have to convince his country of the necessity of war and persuade Congress to grant him the power to go to war. Yet absent a new atrocity on the magnitude of 9/11, directly traceable to one of the regimes on the Perle-Frum list, the president could not win this authority. Nor does it appear he intends to try. And were the United States to attack Libya, Syria, or Saudi Arabia, we would alienate every ally in the Islamic world and Europe—including Tony Blair's Britain. To fight these wars and occupy these nations would bleed our armed forces and mandate a return to the draft. But how would any of these wars make us more secure from terrorism here at home?

Indeed, it is because Americans cannot see the correlation between the wars the authors demand and security at home that Frum and Perle must resort to fear-mongering about holocausts, the end of civilization, and our demise as a nation.

If it is America we defend, *An End to Evil* makes no sense. The Perle-Frum prescription for permanent war makes sense only if it is the mission of the armed forces of the United States to make the Middle East safe for Sharon—and here we come to the heart of the quarrel between us.

On Sept. 11, al-Qaeda attacked us. Al-Qaeda is our enemy, not Syria, Libya, or Saudi Arabia. And the way to cut off al-Qaeda and kill it is to isolate it from all Arab and Islamic nations and centers of power including Syria, Libya, Saudi Arabia, and Iran.

None of these nations had a hand in 9/11. All have a vital interest in not being linked to an al-Qaeda for whom an enraged superpower is on the mortal hunt. Thus, no matter the character of these regimes, we have interests in common. And if

Bush can use carrots to get Bashir Assad to help us find and finish al-Qaeda—as his father got Assad's father to help us expel Iraq from Kuwait—let us make Syria an ally rather than another enemy of the United States.

But here is the rub: The neocons do not want to narrow our list of enemies. They do not want to confine America's war to those who attacked us. They want to expand our list of enemies to include Israel's enemies. They want to escalate and widen what Chris Matthews calls "the Firemen's War" into a war for hegemony in the Middle East. They had hoped to exploit 9/11 to erect an empire, and as they see the vision vanish, their desperation knows no bounds.

That great American military mind Col. John Boyd once described strategy as appending to yourself as many centers of power as possible and isolating your enemy from as many centers of power as possible. . . .

But what Frum and Perle are pressing on him now is an altogether opposite strategy. They want Bush to expand the war, broaden the theater of operations, multiply our enemies, and ignore our allies. If Bush should adopt this strategy, it would be America and Israel against the Arab and Islamic world with Europe neutral and almost all of Asia rooting for our humiliation.

Let it be said: it is vital to victory over al-Qaeda, to the security of our country, the safety of our people, and our broader interests in an Arab and Islamic world of 57 nations that stretches from Morocco to Malaysia that we not let the neocons conflate our war on terror with their war for hegemony.

Neocons believe the Palestinian Authority must be crushed, Arafat eliminated, and the Golan Heights, West Bank, and East Jerusalem held by Israel forever. They want Hezbollah eradicated, Syria denatured, the Saudi monarchy brought down. Let them so believe. But their agenda is not America's agenda, and their fight is not America's fight.

There is no vital U.S. interest in whose flag flies over the Golan or East Jerusalem, when Barak was willing to give up both. But if we allow the neoconservatives to morph our war on al-Qaeda into Israel's war for Palestine, our war will never end. And that is the hidden agenda of the neoconservatives: permanent war for their permanent empowerment. As Frum and Perle concede, this is "our generation's great cause." . . .

The neocons have also begun to injure their reputations and isolate themselves with the nastiness and irrationality of their attacks. French cannon once bore the inscription ultima ratio regum, the last argument of kings. The toxic charge of "Anti-Semite!" has become the last argument of the neocons. But they have wheeled out that cannon too many times. People are less intimidated now. They have seen men look into its muzzle and walk away. . . .

If the neocons purport to see ethnic hatred in everyone else's motives, is it unfair to explore for an ethnic affinity in their own? Why does every grand strategy neocons advance, from "American empire" to "benevolent global hegemony" to "a Pax Americana" to "world democratic revolution" have as its centerpiece solidarity with Sharon and a vigorous wielding of American power against all the enemies of Israel?

Why is every peace plan proposed or endorsed by a president to give the Palestinians a home of their own—the Rogers Plan, the Oslo accords, Camp David, the Taba Plan, the Saudi Plan, the Mitchell Plan, the Road Map—a Munich sell-out? Why is any American patriot, who demands that Ariel Sharon stop building settlements on Palestinian land and walling off Jerusalem, a State Department Arabist, a pawn of the Texas oil lobby, a Coughlinite, an anti-Semite, or a bought-and-paid-for lickspittle of the Saudis?

The United States remains committed morally and politically to the security and survival of Israel and to providing her with the weaponry to guarantee it. No president is going to back off that commitment. But because Israel is a friend does not mean that the Sharonites have preemptive absolution to settle or seize Arab lands or permanently to deny Arab peoples the rights we preach to the world. In our own national interests, we must say so—in the clear.

This is a time for truth. With a mighty and hostile Soviet Empire no longer militarily present in the Maghreb and Middle East, U.S. and Israeli strategic interests have ceased to coincide. And with nightly pictures of Palestinian suffering on Al Jazeera, they have begun to collide.

Thus between traditional conservatives and neoconservatives a breach has been opened and an irreconcilable conflict has arisen. We of the Old Right only have one country. We believe

U.S. foreign policy must be determined by what is best for America. And what is best for America is what our forefathers taught: If you would preserve this Republic, stay out of foreign wars, avoid "permanent alliances," beware of "passionate attachments" to nations not your own. . . .

With the end of the Cold War, an alliance with Israel has ceased to be central to U.S. interests. Indeed, our reputation as armorers and allies of Israel only damages us as Sharon rampages through the West Bank and Gaza walling off Arab land and denying to Palestinians that very right of self-determination we Americans espouse. Sharon is making hypocrites of us, and we are cowards for permitting it.

To the neocons, however, Zionism is second nature. They cannot conceive of a foreign policy that is good for America that does not entail absolute solidarity with Israel. They are dangerously close to imbibing the poisonous brew that drove Jonathan Pollard to treason: If it is good for Israel, it cannot be bad for America.

To evade admission of the transparent truth, neocons have begun to rationalize their passionate attachment, to sublimate it. "The Arab-Israeli quarrel is not a cause of Islamic extremism," Frum and Perle protest.

But when every returning journalist and diplomat and every opinion survey says it is America's uncritical support for Israeli repression of the Palestinians that makes us hated in the region, how can honest men write this? Have they blinded themselves to the truth because it is too painful?

We stand by Israel, writes Irving Kristol, because America is an "ideological" nation, "like the Soviet Union of yesteryear." We and Israel are democracies, the Arab countries are not, and that is all there is to it.

That is why it was in our national interest to come to the defense of France and Britain in World War II. That is why we feel it necessary to defend Israel today, when its survival is threatened. No complicated geopolitical calculations of national interest are necessary.

But this is nonsense, and Kristol knows it. When Britain and France declared war on Hitler on September 3, 1939, FDR did not "come to the defense of France and Britain." He delivered a fireside chat that night promising the nation America would stay out. There will be "no blackout of peace" here, FDR promised us. When

France fell in May-June of 1940, pleading for planes, FDR sent words of encouragement. Not until 18 months after the fall of France did we declare war on Hitler and not until after Hitler declared war on us. Thus, we did not go to war to defend democracy in Britain or France. We went to war to smash the Japanese Empire that attacked us at Pearl Harbor. Kristol is parroting liberal myths.

In the Cold War the United States welcomed as allies Chiang Kai-shek, Salazar, Franco, Somoza, the Shah, Suharto, Syngman Rhee, Park Chung Hee and the Korean generals, Greek colonels, military regimes in Brazil, Argentina, and Turkey, Marcos, and Pinochet because these autocrats proved far more reliable than democratists like Nehru, Olaf Palme, Willy Brandt, and Pierre Trudeau. When it comes to wars that threaten us, hot or cold, we Americans are at one with Nietzsche, "A state, it is the coldest of all cold monsters."

India is democratic and 200 times the size of Israel. Yet in India's wars with Pakistan, we tilted toward Pakistan. Why? Because the Pakistanis were allies, and India sided with Moscow. That India was democratic and Pakistan autocratic made no difference to us.

As for Israel, has America really given her $100 billion and taken her side in every Arab quarrel because she is a democracy?

Tell it to Tony Judt. When this British historian proposed—given the impossibility of separating Arabs from Jews on the West Bank—that Israel annex the West Bank, become a bi-national state, and give Palestinians equal rights, neocons went berserk. . . .

But if the just solution to the South African problem was to abolish bantustans and create a one-man, one-vote democracy, why is that not even a debatable solution to the Palestinian problem?

In temperament, too, neoconservatives have revealed themselves as the antithesis of conservative. In the depiction of scholar Claes Ryn, they are the "neo-Jacobins" of modernity whose dominant trait is conceit.

Only great conceit could inspire a dream of armed world hegemony. The ideology of benevolent American empire and global democracy dresses up a voracious appetite for power. It signifies the ascent to power of a new kind of American, one profoundly at odds with that older type who aspired to modesty and self-restraint.

The Perle-Frum book is marinated in conceit, which may prove the neocons' fatal flaw. In the run-up to the invasion, when critics were exposing their plotting for war long before 9/11, the neocons did not bother to deny it. They reveled in it. They boasted about who they were, where they came from, what they believed, how they were different, and how they had become the new elite. With Rumsfeld, Cheney and Bush marching to their war drums, one of them bellowed, "We are all neoconservatives now!"

But it is always unwise of courtiers to boast of their influence with the prince. And now the neocons have outed themselves. We all know who they are. We all have the coordinates. We all have them bracketed.

With the heady days of the fall of Baghdad behind us and our country ensnared in a Lebanon of our own, neocons seem fearful that it is they who will be made to take the fall if it all turns out badly in Iraq, as McNamara and his Whiz Kids had to take the fall for Vietnam.

And this one they've got right.

Peter Beinart, "A Fighting Faith," *The New Republic* (December 13, 2004)

The heir to Arthur Schlesinger Jr., the journalist Peter Beinart (1971–) argued that it was incumbent upon American liberals to confront terrorism, much as they had once confronted Nazism and then communism.

On January 4, 1947, 130 men and women met at Washington's Willard Hotel to save American liberalism. A few months earlier, in articles in *The New Republic* and elsewhere, the columnists Joseph and Stewart Alsop had warned that "the liberal movement is now engaged in sowing the seeds of its own destruction." Liberals, they argued, "consistently avoided the great political reality of the present: the Soviet challenge to the West." Unless that changed, "In the spasm of terror which will seize this country . . . it is the right—the very extreme right—which is most likely to gain victory."

During World War II, only one major liberal organization, the Union for Democratic Action (UDA), had banned communists from its ranks. At the Willard, members of the UDA met to expand and rename their organization. The attendees, who included Reinhold Niebuhr, Arthur Schlesinger Jr., John Kenneth Galbraith, Walter Reuther, and Eleanor Roosevelt, issued a press release that enumerated the new organization's principles. Announcing the formation of Americans for Democratic Action (ADA), the statement declared, "[B]ecause the interests of the United States are the interests of free men everywhere," America should support "democratic and freedom-loving peoples the world over." That meant unceasing opposition to communism, an ideology "hostile to the principles of freedom and democracy on which the Republic has grown great."

At the time, the ADA's was still a minority view among American liberals. Two of the most influential journals of liberal opinion, *The New Republic* and *The Nation*, both rejected militant anti-communism. Former Vice President Henry Wallace, a hero to many liberals, saw communists as allies in the fight for domestic and international progress. . . .

But, over the next two years, in bitter political combat across the institutions of American liberalism, anti-communism gained strength. With the ADA's help, Truman crushed Wallace's third-party challenge en route to reelection. The formerly leftist Congress of Industrial Organizations (CIO) expelled its communist affiliates and *The New Republic* broke with Wallace, its former editor. The American Civil Liberties Union (ACLU) denounced communism, as did the NAACP. By 1949, three years after Winston Churchill warned that an "iron curtain" had descended across Europe, Schlesinger could write in *The Vital Center*: "Mid-twentieth century liberalism, I believe, has thus been fundamentally reshaped . . . by the exposure of the Soviet Union, and by the deepening of our knowledge of man. The consequence of this historical re-education has been an unconditional rejection of totalitarianism."

Today, three years after September 11 brought the United States face-to-face with a new totalitarian threat, liberalism has still not "been fundamentally reshaped" by the experience. On the right, a "historical re-education" has indeed occurred—replacing the isolationism of the Gingrich Congress with George W. Bush and Dick Cheney's near-theological faith in the transformative capacity of U.S. military might. But American liberalism, as defined by its activist organizations, remains largely what it was in the 1990s—a collection of domestic interests and concerns. On health care, gay rights, and the environment, there is a positive vision, articulated with passion. But there is little liberal passion to win the struggle against Al Qaeda—even though totalitarian Islam has killed thousands of Americans and aims to kill millions; and even though, if it gained power, its efforts to force every aspect of life into conformity with a barbaric interpretation of Islam would reign terror upon women, religious minorities, and anyone in the Muslim world with a thirst for modernity or freedom.

When liberals talk about America's new era, the discussion is largely negative—against the Iraq war, against restrictions on civil liberties, against America's worsening reputation in the world. In sharp contrast to the first years of the cold war, post-September 11 liberalism has produced leaders and institutions—most notably Michael Moore and MoveOn—that do not put the struggle against America's new totalitarian foe at the center of their hopes for a better world. As a result, the Democratic Party boasts a fairly hawkish foreign policy establishment and a cadre of politicians and strategists eager to look tough. But, below this small elite sits a Wallacite grassroots that views America's new struggle as a distraction, if not a mirage. Two elections, and two defeats, into the September 11 era, American liberalism still has not had its meeting at the Willard Hotel. And the hour is getting late. . . .

In 1950, the journal *The New Leader* divided American liberals into "hards" and "softs." The hards, epitomized by the ADA, believed anti-communism was the fundamental litmus test for a decent left. Non-communism was not enough; opposition to the totalitarian threat was the prerequisite for membership in American liberalism because communism was the defining moral challenge of the age.

The softs, by contrast, were not necessarily communists themselves. But they refused to make anti-communism their guiding principle. For them, the threat to liberal values came entirely from the right—from militarists, from red-baiters, and from the forces of economic reaction. To attack the communists, reliable allies in the fight for civil rights and economic justice, was a distraction from the struggle for progress.

Moore is the most prominent soft in the United States today. Most Democrats agree with him about the Iraq war, about [John] Ashcroft, and about Bush. What they do not recognize, or do not acknowledge, is that Moore does not oppose Bush's policies because he thinks they fail to effectively address the terrorist threat; he does not believe there is a terrorist threat. For Moore, terrorism is an opiate whipped up by corporate bosses. In *Dude, Where's My Country?*, he says it plainly: "There is no terrorist threat." And he wonders, "Why has our government gone to such absurd lengths to convince us our lives are in danger?"

Moore views totalitarian Islam the way Wallace viewed communism: As a phantom, a ruse employed by the only enemies that matter, those on the right. Saudi extremists may have brought down the Twin Towers, but the real menace is the Carlyle Group. Today, most liberals naively consider Moore a useful ally, a bomb-thrower against a right-wing that deserves to be torched. What they do not understand is that his real casualties are on the decent left. When Moore opposes the war against the Taliban, he casts doubt upon the sincerity of liberals who say they opposed the Iraq war because they wanted to win in Afghanistan first. When Moore says terrorism should be no greater a national concern than car accidents or pneumonia, he makes it harder for liberals to claim that their belief in civil liberties does not imply a diminished vigilance against Al Qaeda.

Moore is a non-totalitarian, but, like Wallace, he is not an anti-totalitarian. And, when Democratic National Committee Chairman Terry McAuliffe and Tom Daschle flocked to the Washington premiere of *Fahrenheit 9/11*, and when Moore sat in Jimmy Carter's box at the Democratic

convention, many Americans wondered whether the Democratic Party was anti-totalitarian either.

If Moore is America's leading individual soft, liberalism's premier soft organization is MoveOn. MoveOn was formed to oppose Clinton's impeachment, but, after September 11, it turned to opposing the war in Afghanistan. A MoveOn-sponsored petition warned, "If we retaliate by bombing Kabul and kill people oppressed by the Taliban, we become like the terrorists we oppose."

By January 2002, MoveOn was collaborating with 9-11peace.org. . . . One early 9-11peace.org bulletin urged supporters to "[c]all world leaders and ask them to call off the bombing," and to "[f]ly the UN Flag as a symbol of global unity and support for international law." Others questioned the wisdom of increased funding for the CIA and the deployment of American troops to assist in anti-terrorist efforts in the Philippines. In October 2002, after 9-11peace.org was incorporated into MoveOn, an organization bulletin suggested that the United States should have "utilize[d] international law and judicial procedures, including due process" against bin Laden and that "it's possible that a tribunal could even have garnered cooperation from the Taliban." . . . .

Like the softs of the early cold war, MoveOn sees threats to liberalism only on the right. And thus, it makes common cause with the most deeply illiberal elements on the international left. In its campaign against the Iraq war, MoveOn urged its supporters to participate in protests co-sponsored by International ANSWER, a front for the World Workers Party, which has defended Saddam, Slobodan Milosevic, and Kim Jong Il. . . .

When *The New York Times* asked delegates to this summer's Democratic and Republican conventions which issues were most important, only 2 percent of Democrats mentioned terrorism, compared with 15 percent of Republicans. One percent of Democrats mentioned defense, compared with 15 percent of Republicans. And 1 percent of Democrats mentioned homeland security, compared with 8 percent of Republicans. . . .

Arthur Schlesinger Jr. would not have shared MoveOn's fear of an "endless war" on terrorism. In *The Vital Center*, he wrote, "Free society and totalitarianism today struggle for the minds and hearts of men. . . . If we believe in free society hard enough to keep on fighting for it, we are pledged to a permanent crisis which will test the moral, political and very possibly the military strength of each side. A 'permanent' crisis? Well, a generation or two anyway, permanent in one's own lifetime."

Schlesinger, in other words, saw the struggle against the totalitarianism of his time not as a distraction from liberalism's real concerns, or as alien to liberalism's core values, but as the arena in which those values found their deepest expression. That meant several things. First, if liberalism was to credibly oppose totalitarianism, it could not be reflexively hostile to military force. Schlesinger denounced what he called "doughfaces," liberals with "a weakness for impotence . . . a fear, that is, of making concrete decisions and being held to account for concrete consequences." Nothing better captures Moore, who denounced the Taliban for its hideous violations of human rights but opposed military action against it—preferring pie-in-the-sky suggestions about nonviolent regime change.

For Schlesinger (who, ironically, has moved toward a softer liberalism later in life), in fact, it was conservatives, with their obsessive hostility to higher taxes, who could not be trusted to fund America's cold war struggle. "An important segment of business opinion," he wrote, "still hesitates to undertake a foreign policy of the magnitude necessary to prop up a free world against totalitarianism lest it add a few dollars to the tax rate." After Dwight Eisenhower became president, the ADA took up this line, arguing in October 1953 that the "overriding issue before the American people today is whether the national defense is to be determined by the demands of the world situation or sacrificed to the worship of tax reductions and a balanced budget." . . .

Such a critique might seem unavailable to liberals today, given that Bush, having abandoned the Republican Party's traditional concern with balanced budgets, seems content to cut taxes and strengthen the U.S. military at the same time. But subtly, the Republican Party's dual imperatives have already begun to collide—with a stronger defense consistently losing out. Bush has not increased the size of the U.S. military since September 11—despite repeated calls from hawks in his own party—in part because, given his massive tax cuts, he simply cannot afford to. An

anti-totalitarian liberalism would attack those tax cuts not merely as unfair and fiscally reckless, but, above all, as long-term threats to America's ability to wage war against fanatical Islam . . .

But Schlesinger and the ADA didn't only attack the right as weak on national defense; they charged that conservatives were not committed to defeating communism in the battle for hearts and minds. It was the ADA's ally, Truman, who had developed the Marshall Plan to safeguard European democracies through massive U.S. foreign aid. And, when Truman proposed extending the principle to the Third World, calling in his 1949 inaugural address for "a bold new program for making the benefits of our scientific advances and industrial progress available for the improvement and growth of underdeveloped areas," it was congressional Republicans who resisted the effort.

Support for a U.S.-led campaign to defeat Third World communism through economic development and social justice remained central to anti-totalitarian liberalism throughout the 1950s. Addressing an ADA meeting in 1952, Democratic Senator Brien McMahon of Connecticut called for an "army" of young Americans to travel to the Third World as "missionaries of democracy." In 1955, the ADA called for doubling U.S. aid to the Third World, to blunt "the main thrust of communist expansion" and to "help those countries provide the reality of freedom and make an actual start toward economic betterment." When Kennedy took office, he proposed the Alliance for Progress, a $20 billion Marshall Plan for Latin America. And, answering McMahon's call, he launched the Peace Corps, an opportunity for young Americans to participate "in the great common task of bringing to man that decent way of life which is the foundation of freedom and a condition of peace."

The critique the ADA leveled in the '50s could be leveled by liberals again today. For all the Bush administration's talk about promoting freedom in the Muslim world, its efforts have been crippled by the Republican Party's deep-seated opposition to foreign aid and nation-building, illustrated most disastrously in Iraq. . . .

Many Democratic foreign policy thinkers favor a far more ambitious U.S. effort. . . . But, while an updated Marshall Plan and an expanded Peace Corps for the Muslim world are more naturally liberal than conservative ideas, they have not resonated among post-September 11 liberal activists. A new Peace Corps requires faith in America's ability to improve the world, something that Moore—who has said the United States "is known for bringing sadness and misery to places around the globe"—clearly lacks . . .

What the ADA understood, and today's softs do not, is that, while in a narrow sense the struggle against totalitarianism may divert resources from domestic causes, it also provides a powerful rationale for a more just society at home. During the early cold war, liberals repeatedly argued that the denial of African American civil rights undermined America's anti-communist efforts in the Third World. This linkage between freedom at home and freedom abroad was particularly important in the debate over civil liberties. One of the hallmarks of ADA liberals was their refusal to imply—as groups like MoveOn sometimes do today—that civil liberties violations represent a greater threat to liberal values than America's totalitarian foes. And, whenever possible, they argued that violations of individual freedom were wrong, at least in part, because they hindered the anti-communist effort. Sadly, few liberal indictments of, for instance, the Ashcroft detentions are couched in similar terms today.

For liberals to make such arguments effectively, they must first take back their movement from the softs. We will know such an effort has begun when dissension breaks out within America's key liberal institutions. In the late '40s, the conflict played out in Minnesota's left leaning Democratic Farmer-Labor Party, which Hubert Humphrey and Eugene McCarthy wrested away from Wallace supporters. It created friction within the NAACP. And it divided the ACLU, which split apart in 1951, with anti-communists controlling the organization and non-communists leaving to form the Emergency Civil Liberties Committee.

But, most important, the conflict played out in the labor movement. In 1946, the CIO, which had long included communist-dominated affiliates, began to move against them. Over fierce communist opposition, the CIO endorsed the Marshall Plan, Truman's reelection bid, and the formation of NATO. And, in 1949, the Organization's executive board expelled eleven unions. . . .

Today, however, the U.S. labor movement is largely disconnected from the war against totalitarian Islam, even though independent, liberal-minded unions are an important part of the battle against dictatorship and fanaticism in the Muslim world.

The fight against the Soviet Union was an easier fit, of course, since the unions had seen communism up close. And today's AFL-CIO is not about to purge member unions that ignore national security. But, if elements within American labor threw themselves into the movement for reform in the Muslim world, they would create a base of support for Democrats who put winning the war on terrorism at the center of their campaigns. The same is true for feminist groups, for whom the rights of Muslim women are a natural concern. If these organizations judged candidates on their commitment to promoting liberalism in the Muslim world, and not merely on their commitment to international family planning, they too would subtly shift the Democratic Party's national security image. Challenging the "dough-face" feminists who opposed the Afghan war and those labor unionists with a knee-jerk suspicion of U.S. power might produce bitter internal conflict. And doing so is harder today because liberals don't have a sympathetic White House to enact liberal anti-totalitarianism policies. But, unless liberals stop glossing over fundamental differences in the name of unity, they never will.

Obviously, Al Qaeda and the Soviet Union are not the same. The USSR was a totalitarian superpower; Al Qaeda merely espouses a totalitarian ideology, which has had mercifully little access to the instruments of state power. Communism was more culturally familiar, which provided greater opportunities for domestic subversion but also meant that the United States could more easily mount an ideological response. The peoples of the contemporary Muslim world are far more cynical than the peoples of cold war Eastern Europe about U.S. intentions, though they still yearn for the freedoms the United States embodies.

But, despite these differences, Islamist totalitarianism—like Soviet totalitarianism before it—threatens the United States and the aspirations of millions across the world. And, as long as that threat remains, defeating it must be liberalism's north star. Methods for defeating totalitarian Islam are a legitimate topic of internal liberal debate. But the centrality of the effort is not. The recognition that liberals face an external enemy more grave, and more illiberal, than George W. Bush should be the litmus test of a decent left.

Today, the war on terrorism is partially obscured by the war in Iraq, which has made liberals cynical about the purposes of U.S. power. But, even if Iraq is Vietnam, it no more obviates the war on terrorism than Vietnam obviated the battle against communism. Global jihad will be with us long after American troops stop dying in Falluja and Mosul. And thus, liberalism will rise or fall on

whether it can become, again, what Schlesinger called "a fighting faith."

Of all the things contemporary liberals can learn from their forbearers half a century ago, perhaps the most important is that national security can be a calling. If the struggles for gay marriage and universal health care lay rightful claim to liberal idealism, so does the struggle to protect the United States by spreading freedom in the Muslim world. It, too, can provide the moral purpose for which a new generation of liberals yearn. As it did for the men and women who convened at the Willard Hotel.

ANDREW J. BACEVICH, "TWILIGHT OF THE REPUBLIC?" *COMMONWEAL* (NOVEMBER 27, 2006)

In the midst of George W. Bush's second term, the United States was wrestling with large problems at home and abroad. The historian Andrew Bacevich (1947–) explains the context.

In his 2005 inaugural address, President George W. Bush declared the promulgation of freedom to be "the mission that created our nation." Fulfilling what he described as America's "great liberating tradition" now requires that the United States devote itself to "ending tyranny in our world."

Many Americans find such sentiments compelling. Yet to credit the United States with possessing a "liberating tradition" is like saying that Hollywood has a "tradition of artistic excellence." The movie business is just that—a business. Its purpose is to make money. If once in a while the studios produce a film of aesthetic value, that may be cause for celebration; but profit, not revealing truth and beauty, defines the purpose of the enterprise.

Something of the same can be said of the enterprise launched on July 4, 1776. The hard-headed lawyers, merchants, farmers, and slaveholding plantation owners gathered in Philadelphia that summer did not set out to create a church. They founded a republic. Their purpose was not to save mankind. It was to guarantee for people like themselves "life, liberty, and the pursuit of happiness."

In the years and decades that followed, the United States achieved remarkable success in

making good on those aims. Yet never during America's rise to power did the United States exert itself to liberate others absent an overriding perception that the nation itself had large security or economic interests at stake.

From time to time, although not nearly as frequently as we like to imagine, some of the world's unfortunates managed as a consequence to escape from bondage. The Civil War did produce emancipation. Yet to explain the conflagration of 1861–65 as a response to the plight of enslaved African Americans is to engage in vast oversimplification. Near the end of World War II, GIs did liberate the surviving inmates of Nazi death camps. Yet for those who directed the American war effort of 1941–45, the fate of European Jews never figured as more than an afterthought.

Crediting America with a "great liberating tradition" sanitizes the past and obscures the actual motive force behind American politics and U.S. foreign policy. It transforms history into a morality tale and thereby provides a rationale for dodging serious moral analysis. To insist that the liberation of others has never been more than an ancillary motive of U.S. policy is not cynicism; it is a prerequisite to self-understanding.

If the young United States had a mission, it was not to liberate but to expand. "Of course," declared Theodore Roosevelt in 1899, as if explaining the self-evident to the obtuse, "our whole national history has been one of expansion." He spoke truthfully. The Founders viewed stasis as tantamount to suicide. From the outset, Americans evinced a compulsion to acquire territory and to extend their commercial reach abroad.

How was expansion achieved? On this point, the historical record leaves no room for debate: by any means necessary. Depending on the circumstances, the United States relied on diplomacy, hard bargaining, bluster, chicanery, intimidation, or naked coercion. We infiltrated land belonging to our neighbors and then brazenly proclaimed it our own. We harassed, filibustered, and, when the situation called for it, launched full-scale invasions. We engaged in ethnic cleansing. At times, we insisted that treaties be considered sacrosanct. On other occasions, we blithely jettisoned agreements that had outlived their usefulness.

As the methods employed varied, so did the rationale offered to justify action. We touted our status as God's new Chosen People, erecting a "city upon a hill" destined to illuminate the world. We acted at the behest of providential guidance and responded to the urgings of our "manifest destiny." We declared our obligation to spread the gospel of Jesus Christ and to uplift Little Brown Brother. With Woodrow Wilson as our tutor, we shouldered our responsibility to "show the way to the nations of the world how they shall walk in the paths of liberty." Critics who derided these claims as bunkum—the young Lincoln during the war with Mexico, Mark Twain after 1898, Robert LaFollette in 1917—scored points but lost the argument. Periodically revised and refurbished, the concept of American Exceptionalism (which implied exceptional American prerogatives) persisted.

Meanwhile, when it came to action rather than talk, the architects of U.S. policy, even the most idealistic, remained fixated on one overriding aim: enhancing American influence, wealth, and power. The narrative of American foreign relations from the earliest colonial encounters with Native Americans until, say, the end of the cold war reveals a record that is neither uniquely high-minded nor uniquely hypocritical and exploitive.

In this sense, the interpretations of America's past offered by George W. Bush and by Osama bin Laden fall equally wide of the mark. As a rising power, the United States adhered to the iron laws of international politics, which allow little space for altruism. If the tale contains a moral theme, that theme is necessarily one of ambiguity.

To be sure, America's ascent did not occur without missteps: opéra bouffe incursions into Canada; William McKinley's ill-advised annexation of the Philippines; complicity in China's "century of humiliation"; disastrous interwar economic policies that paved the way for the Depression; Harry Truman's decision in 1950 to send U.S. forces north of Korea's 38th Parallel, to name only some. Most of these mistakes Americans have long since shrugged off. A few, like Vietnam, we find impossible to forget even as we persistently disregard their implications.

Yet, however embarrassing, these missteps pale in significance when compared to the masterstrokes of American statecraft. In purchasing Louisiana from the French, Thomas Jefferson may have overstepped the bounds of his authority and in seizing California from Mexico, James Polk may have perpetrated a war of conquest, but their actions ensured that the United States would one day become a great power. To secure the isthmus of Panama, Theodore Roosevelt orchestrated an outrageous swindle. The result affirmed America's hemispheric dominion. In collaborating with Josef Stalin, FDR made common cause with an indisputably evil figure. But in doing so he destroyed the murderous Hitler while simultaneously vaulting the United States to a position of unquestioned economic supremacy. A similar collaboration forged by Richard Nixon with the murderous Mao Zedong helped bring down the Soviet empire, thereby elevating the United States to the self-proclaimed position of sole superpower.

The achievements of these preeminent American statesmen derived not from their common devotion to a liberating tradition but from boldness unburdened by excessive scruples. Notwithstanding the high-sounding pronouncements that routinely emit from the White House and the State Department, the defining characteristic of U.S. foreign policy is not idealism. It is pragmatism, sometimes laced with pragmatism's first cousin, opportunism.

This remains true today even when President Bush has declared without qualification that "America's vital interests and our deepest beliefs are now one." In practice, this dictum allows the Bush administration to hector Iran or North Korea about their undemocratic ways while giving a pass to Egypt and Pakistan. It provides a rationale for military intervention in energy-rich Iraq, but finds no application in Darfur, Burma, and Zimbabwe. (On a flight, shortly after the U.S. invasion of Iraq, I sat beside a retired Zimbabwean supreme court justice. Lamenting the dire situation in his country, he remarked, "Ah, if only we had oil. Then you would come rescue us.")

Bush's critics charge him with abandoning principles that long governed American statecraft. A fairer judgment would credit him with having seized on 9/11 to reinterpret those principles, thereby claiming for the United States new prerogatives (such as waging preventive war) while shedding constraints (such as respect for the sensibilities of key allies) that had seemingly lost their utility. In this regard, the president was adhering to a well-established tradition.

In the annals of history, the rise of the United States to the pinnacle of world power is an epic story worthy of Thucydides or Tacitus. It represents a stunning achievement. Yet those who see America's ascent as an affirmation of virtue are indulging in self-deluding sentimentality. Although sentimentality may sell greeting cards, it ill becomes a great nation that, having reached that pinnacle, now finds itself beset with challenges.

For those fortunate enough to be Americans, this rise to global power yielded rich rewards. Expansion made the United States the land of opportunity. From expansion came abundance. Out of abundance came substantive freedom. Documents drafted in Philadelphia promised liberty. Making good on those promises required a political economy that facilitated the creation of wealth on an enormous scale.

Writing over a century ago, Frederick Jackson Turner made the essential point. "Not the Constitution, but free land and an abundance of natural resources open to a fit people," he argued, made American democracy possible. A half-century later, the historian David Potter discovered a similar symbiosis between affluence and liberty. Potter credited "a politics of abundance"

with creating the American way of life, "a politics which smiled both on those who valued abundance as a means to safeguard freedom and those who valued freedom as an aid in securing abundance."

In short, American prosperity underwrote American freedom. The relationship between the two was reciprocal. Especially as the Industrial Revolution took hold, Americans looked to material abundance to ameliorate domestic tensions and anesthetize the unruly. Money became the preferred lubricant for keeping social and political friction within tolerable limits. As Reinhold Niebuhr once observed, "we seek a solution for practically every problem of life in quantitative terms," certain that more is better. Over time, prosperity also recast freedom, modifying the criteria for eligibility and broadening its claims.

Running in tandem with the chronicle of American expansion abroad is a second narrative of expansion. The theme of this second narrative relates to the transformation of freedom at home. It too is a story of epic achievement overlaid with ambiguity.

Who merits the privileges of citizenship? The answer prevailing in 1776-white male freeholders-was never satisfactory. By the stroke of a Jeffersonian pen, the Declaration of Independence had rendered such a definition untenable. Pressures to amend that restricted conception of citizenship emerged almost immediately.

Until World War II, progress achieved on this front was real but fitful. During the years of the postwar economic boom, and especially during the 1960s, the floodgates opened. Barriers fell. The circle of freedom widened appreciably. The percentage of Americans marginalized as "second-class citizens" dwindled.

Political credit for this achievement lies squarely with the Left. Abundance sustained in no small measure by a postwar presumption of American "global leadership" made possible the expansion of freedom at home. Possibility became reality thanks to progressive political activism.

Pick the group: blacks, Jews, women, Asians, Hispanics, working stiffs, gays, the handicapped— in every case, the impetus for providing equal access to the rights guaranteed by the Constitution originated among radicals, pinks, liberals, and bleeding-heart fellow-travelers. When it comes to ensuring that every American should get a fair shake, the contribution of modern conservatism has been essentially nil. Had Martin Luther King in the 1950s and 1960s counted on William F. Buckley and the *National Review* to take up the fight against racial segregation, Jim Crow would still be alive and well.

Granting the traditionally marginalized access to freedom constitutes the central theme of American politics since World War II. It does not diminish the credit due to those who engineered this achievement to note that their success stemmed in part from the fact that the United States was simultaneously asserting its claim to unquestioned global leadership. The reformers who pushed and prodded for racial equality and women's rights did so in tacit alliance with the officials presiding over the postwar rehabilitation of Germany and Japan, with oil executives pressing to bring the Persian Gulf into America's sphere of influence, and with defense contractors promoting expensive new weapons programs.

The creation of what became by the 1950s an informal American empire of global proportions was not a conspiracy designed to benefit the few. Postwar foreign policy derived its legitimacy from the widely shared perception that the exercise of power abroad was making possible a more perfect union at home. In this sense, a proper understanding of contemporary history requires that we acknowledge an ironic kinship linking cold warriors like Curtis LeMay to feminists like Betty Friedan. General LeMay's Strategic Air Command—both as manifestation of American might and as central component of the postwar military-industrial complex—helped to foster the conditions from which Friedan's National Organization for Women emerged.

During the same postwar period, but especially since the 1960s, the nation's abiding cultural preoccupation focused on reassessing what freedom actually means. The political project was long the exclusive preserve of the Left (although belatedly endorsed by the Right). From the outset, the cultural project has been a collaborative one to which both Left and Right contributed, albeit in different ways. The very real success of the political project lies at the heart of the Bush administration's insistence that the United States today offers a proper model for other nations—notably

those in the Islamic world—to follow. The largely catastrophic results of the cultural project belie that claim.

The postwar political project sought to end discrimination. The postwar cultural project focused on dismantling constraints, especially on matters touching however remotely on sexuality and self-gratification. "Men are qualified for civil liberty," Edmund Burke once observed, "in exact proportion to their disposition to put moral chains upon their appetites." In the aftermath of World War II, Americans rejected that counsel and set out to throw off their manacles. Freedom came increasingly to imply unfettered self-indulgence.

The Left contributed to this effort by promoting a radical new ethic of human sexuality. Removing chains in this regard meant normalizing behavior once viewed as immoral, unnatural, or inconsistent with the common good. On the cutting edge of American culture, removing impediments to the satisfaction of sexual desire emerged as an imperative.

Laws, traditions, and social arrangements impeding the fulfillment of this imperative became obsolete. As a direct consequence, homosexuality, abortion, divorce, out-of-wedlock pregnancies, and children raised in single-parent homes—all once viewed as problematic—lost much of their stigma. Pornography—including child pornography—reached epidemic proportions. Pop culture became a titillating arena for promoting sexual license and celebrating sexual perversity. And popular music became, in the words of cultural critic Martha Bayles, a "masturbatory fantasy."

Some Americans lament this revolution. Many others view it as inevitable or necessary or positively swell. Regardless, the foreign-policy implications of the sexual revolution loom large. The ideals that President Bush eagerly hopes to propagate throughout the Islamic world—those contained in Jefferson's Declaration and in the Bill of Rights—today come packaged with the vulgar exhibitionism of Madonna and the debased sensibility of Robert Mapplethorpe.

Note, however, that the metamorphosis of freedom has had a second aspect, one that has proceeded in harmony with—and even reinforced—the sexual revolution. Here the effect has been to foster a radical new conception of freedom's economic dimension. Increasingly, during the decades of the postwar boom, citizens came to see personal liberty as linked inextricably to the accumulation of "stuff."

Here, the enthusiasm for throwing off moral chains came from the Right. The forces of corporate capitalism relentlessly promoted the notion that liberty correlates with choice and that the key to human fulfillment (not to mention sexual allure and sexual opportunity) is to be found in conspicuous consumption—acquiring a bigger house, a fancier car, the latest fashions, the niftiest gadgets.

By the end of the twentieth century, many Americans had concluded, in the words of the historian Gary Cross, that "to consume was to be free." The events of 9/11 did not dislodge that perception. In early 2006—with the nation locked in what President Bush insisted was an epic confrontation with "Islamofascism"—an article in the *New York Times Magazine* posed the question "Is Freedom Just Another Word for Many Things to Buy?" In the conduct their daily affairs, countless Americans, most of them oblivious to Bush's war, answer that question in the affirmative.

Along the way, consumption eclipsed voting or military service as the nearest thing to an acknowledged civic obligation. If citizenship today endows "the sovereign shopper with the right to select from store shelves," Cross comments, it also imposes "the duty to spend for the 'good of the economy.'" Americans once assessed the nation's economic health by tallying up the output of the nation's steel mills or the tons of bullion locked away in Fort Knox. Today, consumer demand has emerged as the favored metric of overall economic wellbeing. In recent years "Black Friday" has taken its place among notable dates on the national calendar—the willingness of consumers to open their pocketbooks on the day after Thanksgiving having become a key indicator of economic vigor. Woe betide the nation, should holiday shoppers spend less this year than last.

American globalism did little to foster this radical change in American culture. But the cultural revolution—both the sexual liberation demanded by the Left and the conspicuous consumption promoted by the Right—massively complicates our relations with those beyond our borders, who

see our reigning conceptions of freedom as shallow and corrosive.

Still, this consumer's paradise retains considerable appeal for outsiders looking in. The many millions from south of the border or across the seas seeking entry testify to this fact. In the eyes of the typical Third Worlder, to be American is to be rich, pampered, and profligate. Entrance into the United States implies the prospect of being well-fed, well-housed, and well-clothed—to walk where streets are paved with gold.

But how real are our riches? In a recent book *Among Empires*, Charles Maier, professor of history at Harvard, has chronicled the shift from what he calls America's postwar Empire of Production—when we made the steel, the cars, and the TVs—to today's Empire of Consumption—when goods pour in from Japan and China. The implications of this shift for foreign policy are profound. If we are still paving our streets with gold, we're doing so with someone else's money.

In paradise, it turns out, the books don't balance. The federal budget is perpetually in the red. The current account deficit mounts from one year to the next, now topping $800 billion per annum. The national debt is closing in on $9 trillion. The Republican-controlled Congress of the past decade has dealt with this troubling problem precisely as Congress did back when Democrats called the shots: it has routinely raised the ceiling to allow the debt to balloon ever upward.

Despite these alarming trends, we Americans refuse to live within our means. We have discarded old-fashioned notions of thrift, deferred gratification, and putting up for a rainy day. We have forgotten how to save. We won't trim entitlements. We adamantly ignore what President Bush himself refers to as our "addiction" to foreign oil. To sustain the Empire of Consumption we are acquiring a mountain of debt, increasingly owed to foreign countries. The unspoken assumption is that our credit line is endless and that the bills won't ever come due.

Once upon a time, Americans would have dismissed such thinking as twaddle. No more. Having made a fetish of freedom-as-consumption, we have become beholden to others. Dependence, wrote Jefferson two centuries ago, "begets subservience and venality, suffocates the germ of virtue and prepares fit tools for the design of ambition."

As our dependence has deepened, the autonomy that from 1776 through the 1950s ranked as the nation's greatest strategic asset has withered away.

Although periodically bemoaning this slide toward dependence, the nation's political leaders have done little to restore our economic house to order. In practice, ensuring the uninterrupted flow of foreign oil and borrowing from abroad to feed the consumer's insatiable appetite for cheap imports have become categorical imperatives. Back in 1992, when the immediate issue related to curbing greenhouse gases, President George Herbert Walker Bush cut to the heart of the matter: "The American way of life is not up for negotiation." Compromise, accommodation, trimming back the expectations implied by that way of life —none of these are to be countenanced.

Dependence has large foreign-policy consequences. It circumscribes freedom of action. A week after 9/11, Donald Rumsfeld spelled out the implications. In formulating a response to the terrorist attack, the United States had only two options. "We have a choice," Rumsfeld remarked, "either to change the way we live, which is unacceptable, or to change the way that they live, and we chose the latter."

The global "war on terror" represents the Bush administration's effort to do just that-to change the way that they live. "They," of course, are the 1.4 billion Muslims who inhabit an arc stretching from North Africa to Southeast Asia.

The overarching strategic aim of that war is to eliminate the Islamist threat by pacifying the Islamic world, with particular attention given to the energy-rich Persian Gulf. Pacification implies not only bringing Muslims into compliance with American norms. It also requires the establishment of unassailable American hegemony, affirming the superiority of U.S. power beyond the shadow of doubt and thereby deterring attempts to defy those norms. Hegemony means presence, evidenced by the proliferation of U.S. military bases throughout strategically critical regions of the Islamic world. Seen in relation to our own history, the global "war on terror" signifies the latest phase in an expansionist project that is now three centuries old.

This effort to pacify Islam has foundered in Iraq. The Bush administration's determination to change the way Iraqis live has landed us in a quagmire. Today the debate over how to salvage something positive from the Iraq debacle consumes the foreign-policy apparatus. Just beyond lie concerns about how events in Iraq are affecting the overall "war on terror." Expressing confidence that all will come out well, President Bush insists that historians will eventually see the controversies surrounding his Iraq policy as little more than a comma.

Rather than seeing Iraq as a comma, we ought to view it as a question mark. The question posed, incorporating but also transcending the larger "war on terror," is this: Are ongoing efforts to "change the way that they live" securing or further distorting the American way of life? To put it another way, will the further expansion of American dominion abroad enhance the freedom we profess to value? Or have we now reached a point where expansion merely postpones and even exacerbates an inevitable reckoning with the cultural and economic contradictions to which our pursuit of freedom has given rise?

If the survival of American freedom does require pacification of the Islamic world, as adherents of the old expansionist tradition believe, then this must be said: Exertions made up to this point have been laughably inadequate. Changing the way they live presumes a seriousness hitherto lacking on the part of the American people or their elected representatives, including the president himself.

If we intend to transform not only Iraq but also Syria, Iran, Pakistan, Egypt, and Saudi Arabia, prudence dictates that we stop kidding ourselves that the intended beneficiaries of our ministrations will welcome us with open arms. Why bamboozle ourselves with claims of righteousness that few others believe? Better to acknowledge, as the hawkish military analyst Ralph Peters has done, that we are actually engaged "in an effort to keep the world safe for our economy and open to our cultural assault." Doing so will prevent us from being surprised by the intensity of resistance that awaits us as we enforce President Bush's so-called Freedom Agenda across the broad expanse of Islam.

Mounting such a campaign implies mobilization, commitment, sacrifice, and reordering national priorities with the prerequisites of victory rising to first place. It will necessarily require the allocation of additional resources to satisfy the mushrooming requirements of "national security." We will have to hire many more soldiers. A serious attempt to pacify the Islamic world means the permanent militarization of U.S. policy. Almost inevitably, it will further concentrate authority in the hands of an imperial presidency.

This describes the program of the "faster, please" ideologues keen to enlarge the scope of U.S. military action. To paraphrase Che Guevara, it is a program that calls for "one, two, many Iraqs," ignoring the verdict already rendered by the actually existing Iraq. The fact is that events there have definitively exposed the very real limits of American hard power, financial reserves, and will. Leviathan has shot his wad.

Seeking an escape from our predicament through further expansion points toward bankruptcy and the dismantling of what remains of the American republic. Genuine pragmatism—and the beginning of wisdom—lies in paying less attention to "the way that they live" and more attention to the way we do. Ultimately, conditions within American society determine the prospects of American liberty. As early multiculturalist Randolph Bourne observed nearly a century ago, ensuring that authentic freedom will flourish at home demands that we attend in the first instance to "cultivating our own garden."

This does not imply assuming a posture of isolationism, although neoconservative and neoliberal proponents of the global "war on terror" will be quick to level that charge. Let us spare no effort to track down those who attacked us on 9/11, beginning with Osama bin Laden, still at large more than five years later. But let us give up once and for all any pretensions about an "indispensable nation" summoned to exercise "benign global hegemony" in the midst of a uniquely opportune "unipolar moment." For too long now these narcissistic and fallacious claims, the source of the pretensions expressed by President Bush since September 2001, have polluted our discussion of foreign policy, and thereby prevented us from seeing ourselves as we are.

Cultivating our own garden begins with taking stock of ourselves. Thoughtful critics have for decades been calling for just such a critical self-examination. Among the very first canaries to venture into the deteriorating mineshaft of postwar American culture was the writer Flannery O'Connor. "If you live today," she observed with characteristic bluntness a half-century ago, "you breathe in nihilism."

O'Connor correctly diagnosed the disease and other observers bore witness to its implications. Her fellow Southerner Walker Percy wondered if freedom American-style was not simply becoming the "last and inalienable possession in a sick society." The social critic Christopher Lasch derided "the ideology of progress" manipulated by elites contemptuous of the ethnic, social, and religious traditions to which ordinary folk subscribed. Lasch foresaw an impending "dark night of the soul." From his vantage point, Robert Nisbet detected the onset of what he called "a twilight age," marked by "a sense of cultural decay, erosion of institutions . . . and constantly increasing centralization—and militarization—of power." In such an age, he warned, "representative and liberal institutions of government slip into patterns ever more imperial in character. . . . Over everything hangs the specter of war." Towering above them all was Pope John Paul II who, in a message clearly directed toward Americans, pointedly cautioned that a democracy bereft of values "easily turns into a thinly disguised totalitarianism."

Our own self-induced confusion about freedom, reflected in our debased culture and our disordered economy, increases our susceptibility to this totalitarian temptation even as it deadens our awareness of the danger it poses. Escaping its clutches will require something more than presidents intoning clichés about America's historic mission while launching crusades against oil-rich tyrants on the other side of the globe. We are in difficult straits and neither arms (already fully committed) nor treasure (just about used up) will get us out. Our corrupt age requires reformation.

Shedding or at least discrediting the spurious conceptions of freedom to which Americans have lately fallen prey qualifies as a large task. Still, when compared to the megalomania of those who under the guise of "eliminating tyranny" are intent on remaking the entire Islamic world, the restoration of our own culture appears to be a positively modest goal. At the end of the day, as William Pfaff has observed, "The only thing we can remake is ourselves."

And who knows? Should we, as a consequence of such a reformation, actually live up to our professed ideals—restoring to American freedom something of the respect that it once commanded—we may yet become, in some small way, a model worthy of emulation.

XIV.

CHASTENED SUPERPOWER

The post-9/11 effort to reaffirm the validity of American exceptionalism through a concerted demonstration of US military supremacy yielded frustration and disappointment. Americans grew tired of long and costly wars. A decade after the United States had invaded Iraq, the public mood was shifting in favor of retrenchment. Tending to matters at home was once more becoming a priority. The frustrations caused by America's post-9/11 wars helped create the conditions resulting in Donald Trump's election to the presidency in November 2016. Trump took office promising to overturn policies put in place by the foreign policy establishment.

ROBERT KAGAN, "SUPERPOWERS DON'T GET TO RETIRE," *THE NEW REPUBLIC* (MAY 26, 2014)

In the aftermath of the Cold War, Robert Kagan (1958–) had been in the forefront of Washington commentators arguing for the United States to exercise outright global hegemony, relying on American power to promote American values worldwide. When the pursuit of hegemony proved more difficult to achieve than anticipated, Kagan insisted that the United States had no alternative but to persist. If America failed to lead, disaster would inevitably ensue.

Almost 70 years ago, a new world order was born from the rubble of World War II, built by and around the power of the United States. Today that world order shows signs of cracking, and perhaps even collapsing. The Russia-Ukraine and Syria crises, and the world's tepid response, the general upheaval in the greater Middle East and North Africa, the growing nationalist and great-power tensions in East Asia, the worldwide advance of autocracy and retreat of democracy—taken individually, these problems are neither unprecedented nor unmanageable. But collectively they are a sign that something is changing, and perhaps more quickly than we may imagine. They may signal a transition into a different world order or into a world disorder of a kind not seen since the 1930s.

If a breakdown in the world order that America made is occurring, it is not because America's power is declining—America's wealth, power, and potential influence remain adequate to meet the present challenges. It is not because the world has become more complex and intractable—the world has always been complex and intractable. And it is not simply war-weariness. Strangely enough, it is an intellectual problem, a question of identity and purpose.

Many Americans and their political leaders in both parties, including President Obama, have either forgotten or rejected the assumptions that undergirded American foreign policy for the past seven decades. In particular, American foreign policy may be moving away from the sense of global responsibility that equated American interests with the interests of many others around the world and back toward the defense of narrower, more parochial national interests. This is sometimes called "isolationism," but that is not the right word. It may be more correctly described as a search for normalcy. At the core of American unease is a desire to shed the unusual burdens of responsibility that previous generations of Americans took on in World War II and throughout the cold war and to return to being a more normal kind of nation, more attuned to its own needs and less to those of the wider world.

If this is indeed what a majority of Americans seek today, then the current period of retrenchment will not be a temporary pause before an inevitable return to global activism. It will mark a new phase in the evolution of America's foreign policy. And because America's role in shaping the world order has been so unusually powerful and pervasive, it will also begin a new phase in the international system, one that promises not to be marginally different but radically different from what we have known these past 70 years. Unless Americans can be led back to an understanding of their enlightened self-interest, to see again how their fate is entangled with that of the world, then the prospects for a peaceful twenty-first century in which Americans and American principles can thrive will be bleak. . . .

The conventional wisdom these days is that Americans are war-weary. But it may be more accurate to say they are world-weary. During the cold war, after all, Americans had much greater reason for war-weariness—Korea and Vietnam were 14 times more costly in terms of American deaths than Afghanistan and Iraq—but they never fully rejected the global anti-communist containment strategy that had gotten them into the wars. Today's mood seems more analogous to the 1920s. . . .

Historians often refer to the "maturing" of American foreign policy since the nineteenth century. But if nations can learn, they can also unlearn. These days it is hard to watch both the conduct and the discussion of American foreign policy and not sense a certain unlearning, a forgetting of the old lessons on which the grand strategy was premised. Perhaps this was inevitable. World War II is as distant from today's "millennials" as the Civil War was from the generation of the 1930s. A generation that does not remember the cold war, but grew up knowing only Iraq and Afghanistan, is going to view America's role in the world differently. Combine that with the older generations that have tired of playing the old role, and it is hardly surprising that enthusiasm is flagging. Americans today are not isolationists, any more than they were in the 1920s. They favor the liberal world order insofar as they can see how it touches them. But they are no longer prepared to sacrifice very much to uphold it.

This is understandable. Americans have been Atlas carrying the world on their shoulders. They can be forgiven for feeling the temptation to put it down. Under the best of circumstances, playing the role of upholder of the liberal world order was always a monumental task. At the dawn of the American era, Truman called it "the most terrible responsibility that any nation ever faced." George Kennan was convinced that the American people were "not fitted, either institutionally or temperamentally, to be an imperial power in the grand manner." Actually, he underestimated them, for Americans maintained their global commitments for decades, better than most nations.

Yet the burden has been immense, and not just the obvious costs in lives and treasure. Americans have spent vast amounts on defense budgets, more than all other major powers combined. Can't

U.S. allies carry more of the burden? The question has been asked since the dawn of the cold war, but the answer has always been: probably not. The same factors that have made the United States uniquely capable of supporting a world order—great wealth and power and the relative security afforded by geography—help explain why American allies have always been less capable and less willing. They have lacked the power and the security to see and act beyond their narrow interests. So where they failed before they will fail again. Even twenty-first-century Europeans, for all the wonders of their union, seem incapable of uniting against a predator in their midst, and are willing, as in the past, to have the weak devoured if necessary to save their own (financial) skins. There are moral costs, too. Like most people, Americans generally like to believe that they are behaving justly in the world, that they are on the side of the right. If possible, they like to have legal or institutional sanctions for their action, or at least the general approval of like-minded nations. On the two occasions in the past 100 years when the United States contemplated taking on a central role in global affairs, in 1918 and 1945, American leaders insisted on simultaneously creating world organizations that could, at least in theory, provide this legitimacy for American actions.

The problem is, the world lacks any genuine overarching legal or institutional authority, much less a democratic authority, to which all nations subordinate themselves. Questions of right and wrong are settled not according to impartial justice but usually according to the distribution of power in the system. Americans have usually had to use their power to enforce their idea of justice without any assurance beyond their own faith that they are right. This is a heavy moral burden for a democratic people to bear. In their domestic lives, Americans are accustomed to having that burden spread evenly across society. The people make the laws, the police enforce the laws, judges and juries mete out justice, and the prison officials carry out the punishment. But in the international sphere, Americans have had to act as judge, jury, police, and, in the case of military action, executioner. What gives the United States the right to act on behalf of a liberal world order? In truth, nothing does, nothing beyond the conviction that the liberal world order is the most just.

This moral conundrum was easier to ignore during the cold war, when every action taken, even in the most obscure corners of the world, was justified as being in defense of vital national interests. But actions taken in defense of world order are fraught with moral complexity. . . .

Who is to say that even defense of the liberal world order is necessarily good? The liberal world order was never put to a popular vote. It was not bequeathed by God. It is not the endpoint of human progress, despite what our Enlightenment education tells us. It is a temporary and transient world order that suits the needs, interests, and above all the ideals of a large and powerful collection of people, but it does not necessarily fit the needs and desires of everyone. For decades many abroad and some Americans at home saw it as a form of Western imperialism, and many still do. Communism may have failed, but authoritarianism and autocracy live on. And it is that form of government, not democracy, that has been the norm throughout history. In recent decades the democracies, led by the United States and Europe, have had the power to shape the world. But who is to say that Putinism in Russia or the particular brand of authoritarianism practiced in China will not survive as far into the future as European democracy, which, outside of Great Britain, is itself only a little over a century old?

A liberal world order, like any world order, is something that is imposed, and as much as we in the West might wish it to be imposed by superior virtue, it is generally imposed by superior power. Putin seeks to impose his view of a world order, at least in Russia's neighborhood, just as Europe and the United States do. Whether he succeeds or fails will probably not be determined merely by who is right and who is wrong. It will be determined by the exercise of power.

This is a disturbing thought for a nation that has grown weary of exercising power. Hans Morgenthau once observed that Americans are attracted to the "illusion that a nation can escape . . . from power politics," that at some point "the final curtain would fall and the game of power politics would no longer be played." Many escapes have been offered over the past two decades. In 1989, Fukuyama told Americans that with the end of history there would be no more "serious ideological competitors left to liberal democracy." Liberal progress was inevitable, and therefore nothing need be done to promote or defend it. Such thoughts were echoed throughout the 1990s. The age of geopolitics had supposedly given way to the age of geoeconomics. What America needed in the new era was less "hard power" and more "soft power."

Such was the reigning conventional wisdom, at least from the end of the cold war until 2008 and the beginning of the financial crisis. Then the paradigm shifted. Suddenly, instead of the end of history, it was the end of America, the end of the West. Triumphalism turned to declinism. From the post-cold-war utopia it became the post-American world. Yet this, too, turned out to be a form of escapism, for remarkably, whether the liberal world order was triumphing or America and the West were declining, the prescription remained the same: There was nothing to be done. Whereas before it had been unnecessary, and even wrong, for the United States to use its power to shape the world, now, suddenly, it was impossible, because the United States no longer had sufficient power. . . .

The sense of futility has affected policymakers, too. Senior White House officials, especially the younger ones, look at problems like the struggle in Syria and believe that there is little if anything the United States can do. This is the lesson of their generation, the lesson of Iraq and Afghanistan: that America has neither the power nor the understanding nor the skill to fix problems in the world.

This is also escapism, however, for there is a myth embedded in this plea of futility. It is that wielding power effectively was ever any easier than it is today. With rose-colored glasses we look back at the cold war and imagine that the United States used to get others to do what it wanted, used to know what it was doing, and used to wield such overwhelming power that the world simply bent to its will or succumbed to its charms. But American policy during the cold war, despite its ultimate success, was filled with errors, folly, many near-disasters, and some disasters. From the beginning, allies proved rebellious, resentful, and unmanageable. American domestic politics made sensible policies difficult and sometimes impossible to sustain. The world economy, and the American economy, lurched from crisis to crisis. American military power was at its

best a most uncertain instrument. In Vietnam, whether inevitably or because of bad policymaking in Washington, it failed miserably. In Korea, it almost suffered a complete catastrophe. The most successful presidents of the era, from Truman to Reagan, did not always seem successful to their contemporaries and suffered significant setbacks in their foreign policies. Can the architects of today's foreign policies really believe that Acheson and his colleagues, or the policymakers in the Johnson or Nixon or Carter administrations, had an easier time of it?

Any nation's foreign policy is bound to fail more often than it succeeds. The attempt to influence the behavior of people even in the domestic setting is difficult enough. To influence other peoples and other nations without simply annihilating them is the most difficult of all human tasks. It is also in the very nature of foreign policy, as in human affairs generally, that all solutions to problems only breed more problems. This is certainly true of all wars. There is no perfect ending to any war, even those fought with the clearest and most straightforward of objectives. The Civil War did not put an end to the terrible plight of blacks in America, though it cost over half a million lives. World War II ended with the Soviet Union in control of half of Europe and opened the way to another four decades of superpower confrontation.

When a nation uses its power to shape a world order, rather than merely for self-defense or conquest, the tenuousness of solutions is even more pronounced. Military actions for world order preservation are almost by definition limited both in scope and objectives. World order maintenance requires operating in the gray areas between victory and defeat. The measure of success is often not how wonderful the end result is, but whether the unsatisfying end result is better or worse than the outcome if there had been no action. To insist on outcomes that always achieve maximum ends at minimal cost is yet another form of escapism.

Today, however, Americans seem overwhelmed by the difficulty and complexity of it all. They yearn to return to what Niebuhr called "the innocency of irresponsibility," or at least to a normalcy in which the United States can limit the scope of its commitments. In this way America has perhaps returned to the mood of the 1920s.

There is a difference, however. In the 1920s, it was not America's world order that needed shoring up. Americans felt, mistakenly as it turned out, that it was Britain's and Europe's job to preserve the world order they had created. Today, it is America's world order that needs propping up. Will Americans decide that it matters this time, when only they have the capacity to sustain it?

You never miss the water 'til the well runs dry, or so the saying goes. One wonders whether Americans, including their representatives and their president, quite understand what is at stake. When President Obama first took office five years ago, Peter Baker of *The New York Times* reported that he intended to deal "with the world as it is rather than as it might be." It is a standard realist refrain and has been repeated time and again by senior Obama officials as a way of explaining why he decided against pursuing some desirable but unreachable "ideal" in this place or that. What fewer and fewer seem to realize, however, is that the last 70 years have offered Americans and many others something of a reprieve from the world "as it is." . . .

In fact, the world "as it is" is a dangerous and often brutal place. There has been no transformation in human behavior or in international relations. In the twenty-first century, no less than in the nineteenth and twentieth centuries, force remains the ultima ratio. The question, today as in the past, is not whether nations are willing to resort to force but whether they believe they can get away with it when they do. If there has been less aggression, less ethnic cleansing, less territorial conquest over the past 70 years, it is because the United States and its allies have both punished and deterred aggression, have intervened, sometimes, to prevent ethnic cleansing, and have gone to war to reverse territorial conquest. The restraint showed by other nations has not been a sign of human progress, the strengthening of international institutions, or the triumph of the rule of law. It has been a response to a global configuration of power that, until recently, has made restraint seem the safer course.

When Vladimir Putin failed to achieve his goals in Ukraine through political and economic means, he turned to force, because he believed that he could. He will continue to use force so long as he believes that the payoff exceeds the cost. Nor is he unique in this respect. What might China do were it not hemmed in by a ring of powerful nations backed by the United States? For that matter, what would Japan do if it were much more powerful and much less dependent on the United States for its security? We have not had to find out the answers to these questions, not yet, because American predominance, the American alliance system, and the economic, political, and institutional aspects of the present order, all ultimately dependent on power, have mostly kept the lid closed on this Pandora's box.

Nor have we had to find out yet what the world "as it is" would do to the remarkable spread of democracy. Skeptics of "democracy promotion" argue that the United States has often tried to plant democracy in infertile soil. They may be right. The widespread flowering of democracy around the world in recent decades may prove to have been artificial and therefore tenuous. As Michael Ignatieff once observed, it may be that "liberal civilization" itself "runs deeply against the human grain and is achieved and sustained only by the most unremitting struggle against human nature." Perhaps this fragile democratic garden requires the protection of a liberal world order, with constant feeding, watering, weeding, and the fencing off of an ever-encroaching jungle. In the absence of such efforts, the weeds and the jungle may sooner or later come back to reclaim the land.

One wonders if even the current economic order reflects the world "as it is." A world in which autocracies make ever more ambitious attempts to control the flow of information, and in which autocratic kleptocracies use national wealth and resources to further their private interests, may prove less hospitable to the kind of free flow of commerce the world has come to appreciate in recent decades.

In fact, from the time that Roosevelt and Truman first launched it, the whole project of promoting and defending a liberal world order has been a concerted effort *not* to accept the world "as it is." The American project has aimed at shaping a world different from what had always been, taking advantage of America's unique situation to do what no nation had ever been able to do. Today, however, because many Americans no longer recall what the world "as it is" really looks like, they cannot imagine it. They bemoan the burdens and failures inherent in the grand strategy but take for granted all the remarkable benefits.

Nor do they realize, perhaps, how quickly it can all unravel. The international system is an elaborate web of power relationships, in which every nation, from the biggest to the smallest, is constantly feeling for shifts or disturbances. Since 1945, and especially since 1989, the web has been geared to respond primarily to the United States. Allies observe American behavior and calculate America's reliability. Nations hemmed in or threatened by American power watch for signs of growing or diminishing power and will. When the United States appears to retrench, allies necessarily become anxious, while others look for opportunities.

In recent years, the world has picked up unmistakable signals that Americans may no longer want to carry the burden of global responsibility. Others read the polls, read the president's speeches calling for "nation-building at home," see the declining defense budgets and defense capabilities, and note the extreme reticence, on the part of both American political parties, about using force. . . .

Meanwhile, the signs of the global order breaking down are all around us. . . . . . In recent years the number of democracies around the world has been steadily declining, while the number of autocracies grows. If these trends continue, in the near future we are likely to see increasing conflict, increasing wars over territory, greater ethnic and sectarian violence, and a shrinking world of democracies. . . .

Looking back on the period before World War II, Robert Osgood, the most thoughtful of realist thinkers of the past century, discerned a critical element missing from the strategic analyses of the day. Mere rational calculations of the "national interest," he argued, proved inadequate. Paradoxically, it was the "idealists," those who were "most sensitive to the Fascist menace to Western culture and civilization," who were "among the first to understand the necessity of undertaking revolutionary measures to sustain America's first line of defense in Europe." Idealism, he concluded, was "an indispensable spur to reason in leading men to perceive and act upon the real imperatives of power politics." This was Roosevelt's message, too, when he asked Americans to defend "not their homes alone, but the tenets of faith and humanity on which their churches, their governments, and their very civilization are founded."

Perhaps Americans can be inspired in this way again, without the threat of a Hitler or an attack on their homeland. But this time they will not have 20 years to decide. The world will change much more quickly than they imagine. And there is no democratic superpower waiting in the wings to save the world if this democratic superpower falters.

DONALD J. TRUMP, "PRESIDENTIAL CAMPAIGN ANNOUNCEMENT" (2015)

When the real estate developer and reality TV host Donald J. Trump (1946–) announced his intention to the run for the presidency, few observers took his candidacy seriously. Yet Trump's critique of recent US foreign policy resonated with many American voters for whom the pursuit of global hegemony had produced few, if any, benefits.

Our country is in serious trouble. We don't have victories anymore. We used to have victories, but we don't have them. When was the last time anybody saw us beating, let's say, China in a trade deal? They kill us. I beat China all the time. All the time.

When did we beat Japan at anything? They send their cars over by the millions, and what do we do? When was the last time you saw a Chevrolet in Tokyo? It doesn't exist, folks. They beat us all the time.

When do we beat Mexico at the border? They're laughing at us, at our stupidity. And now they are beating us economically. They are not our friend, believe me. But they're killing us economically.

The U.S. has become a dumping ground for everybody else's problems. . . .

When Mexico sends its people, they're not sending their best. They're not sending you. They're not sending you. They're sending people that have lots of problems, and they're bringing those problems with us. They're bringing drugs. They're bringing crime. They're rapists. And some, I assume, are good people. . . .

It's coming from more than Mexico. It's coming from all over South and Latin America, and it's coming probably—probably—from the Middle East. But we don't know. Because we have no protection and we have no competence, we don't know what's happening. And it's got to stop and it's got to stop fast.

Islamic terrorism is eating up large portions of the Middle East. They've become rich. I'm in competition with them.

They just built a hotel in Syria. Can you believe this? They built a hotel. When I have to build a hotel, I pay interest. They don't have to pay interest, because they took the oil that, when we left Iraq, I said we should've taken.

So now ISIS has the oil, and what they don't have, Iran has. And in 19—and I will tell you this, and I said it very strongly, years ago, I said—and I love the military, and I want to have the strongest military that we've ever had, and we need it more now than ever. But I said, "Don't hit Iraq," because you're going to totally destabilize the Middle East. Iran is going to take over the Middle East, Iran and somebody else will get the oil, and it turned out that Iran is now taking over Iraq. Think of it. Iran is taking over Iraq, and they're taking it over big league.

We spent $2 trillion in Iraq, $2 trillion. We lost thousands of lives, thousands in Iraq. We have wounded soldiers, who I love, I love—they're great—all over the place, thousands and thousands of wounded soldiers.

And we have nothing. We can't even go there. We have nothing. And every time we give Iraq equipment, the first time a bullet goes off in the air, they leave it.

Last week, I read 2,300 Humvees—these are big vehicles—were left behind for the enemy. 2,000? You would say maybe two, maybe four? 2,300 sophisticated vehicles, they ran, and the enemy took them. . . .

Our labor participation rate was the worst since 1978. But think of it, GDP below zero, horrible labor participation rate.

And our real unemployment is anywhere from 18 to 20 percent. Don't believe the 5.6. Don't believe it.

That's right. A lot of people up there can't get jobs. They can't get jobs, because there are no jobs, because China has our jobs and Mexico has our jobs. They all have jobs. . . .

Our enemies are getting stronger and stronger by the way, and we as a country are getting weaker. Even our nuclear arsenal doesn't work.

It came out recently they have equipment that is 30 years old. They don't know if it worked. And I thought it was horrible when it was broadcast on television, because boy, does that send signals to Putin and all of the other people that look at us and they say, "That is a group of people, and that is a nation that truly has no clue. They don't know what they're doing. They don't know what they're doing.". . . .

Well, you need somebody, because politicians are all talk, no action. Nothing's gonna get done. They will not bring us—believe me—to the promised land. They will not. . . .

I watch the speeches of these people, and they say the sun will rise, the moon will set, all sorts of wonderful things will happen. And people are saying, "What's going on? I just want a job. Just get me a job. I don't need the rhetoric. I want a job." . . .

So I've watched the politicians. I've dealt with them all my life. If you can't make a good deal with a politician, then there's something wrong with you. You're certainly not very good. And that's what we have representing us. They will never make America great again. They don't even have a chance. They're controlled fully—they're controlled fully by the lobbyists, by the donors, and by the special interests, fully. . . .

Now, our country needs—our country needs a truly great leader, and we need a truly great leader now. We need a leader that wrote "The Art of the Deal."

We need a leader that can bring back our jobs, can bring back our manufacturing, can bring back our military, can take care of our vets. Our vets have been abandoned. . . .

We need somebody that can take the brand of the United States and make it great again. It's not great again.

We need—we need somebody—we need somebody that literally will take this country and make it great again. We can do that. . . .

It can happen. Our country has tremendous potential. We have tremendous people.

We have people that aren't working. We have people that have no incentive to work. But they're going to have incentive to work, because the greatest social program is a job. And they'll be proud, and they'll love it, and they'll make much more than they would've ever made, and they'll be—they'll be doing so well, and we're going to be thriving as a country, thriving. It can happen.

I will be the greatest jobs president that God ever created. I tell you that.

I'll bring back our jobs from China, from Mexico, from Japan, from so many places. I'll bring back our jobs, and I'll bring back our money.

Right now, think of this: We owe China $1.3 trillion. We owe Japan more than that. So they come in, they take our jobs, they take our money, and then they loan us back the money, and we pay them in interest, and then the dollar goes up so their deal's even better.

How stupid are our leaders? How stupid are these politicians to allow this to happen? How stupid are they? . . .

Our president doesn't have a clue. He's a bad negotiator. . . .

Take a look at the deal he's making with Iran. He makes that deal, Israel maybe won't exist very long. It's a disaster, and we have to protect Israel. . . .

I'm a free trader. But the problem with free trade is you need really talented people to negotiate for you. . . .

Free trade can be wonderful if you have smart people, but we have people that are stupid. We have people that aren't smart. And we have people that are controlled by special interests. And it's just not going to work. . . .

People say, "Oh, you don't like China?"

No, I love them. But their leaders are much smarter than our leaders, and we can't sustain ourself with that. . . .

They are ripping us. We are rebuilding China. We're rebuilding many countries. China, you go there now, roads, bridges, schools, you never saw anything like it. They have bridges that make the George Washington Bridge look like small potatoes. And they're all over the place.

We have all the cards, but we don't know how to use them. We don't even know that we have the cards, because our leaders don't understand the game. We could turn off that spigot by charging them tax until they behave properly.

Now they're going militarily. They're building a military island in the middle of the South China sea. A military island. Now, our country could never do that because we'd have to get environmental clearance, and the environmentalist wouldn't let our country—we would never build in an ocean. They built it in about one year, this massive military port.

They're building up their military to a point that is very scary. You have a problem with ISIS. You have a bigger problem with China.

And, in my opinion, the new China, believe it or not, in terms of trade, is Mexico. . . .

Believe me, folks. We will do very, very well, very, very well. . . .

It sounds crass. Somebody said, "Oh, that's crass." It's not crass.

We got $18 trillion in debt. We got nothing but problems.

We got a military that needs equipment all over the place. We got nuclear weapons that are obsolete.

And I'm the one that made all of the right predictions about Iraq. . . .

How are these people gonna lead us? How are we gonna—how are we gonna go back and make it great again? We can't. They don't have a clue. They can't lead us. They can't. They can't even answer simple questions. . . .

There is so much wealth out there that can make our country so rich again, and therefore make it great again. Because we need money. We're dying. We're dying. We need money. We have to do it. And we need the right people. . . .

I'm doing that to say that that's the kind of thinking our country needs. We need that thinking. We have the opposite thinking.

We have losers. We have losers. We have people that don't have it. We have people that are morally corrupt. We have people that are selling this country down the drain. . . .

So, just to sum up, I would do various things very quickly. I would repeal and replace the big lie, Obamacare.

I would build a great wall, and nobody builds walls better than me, believe me, and I'll build them very inexpensively, I will build a great, great wall on our southern border. And I will have Mexico pay for that wall.

Mark my words.

Nobody would be tougher on ISIS than Donald Trump. Nobody.

I will find—within our military, I will find the General Patton or I will find General MacArthur, I will find the right guy. I will find the guy that's going to take that military and make it really work. Nobody, nobody will be pushing us around.

I will stop Iran from getting nuclear weapons. . . .

I will immediately terminate President Obama's illegal executive order on immigration, immediately. . . .

Renegotiate our foreign trade deals.

Reduce our $18 trillion in debt, because, believe me, we're in a bubble. . . .

And strengthen our military and take care of our vets. So, so important.

Sadly, the American dream is dead.

But if I get elected president I will bring it back bigger and better and stronger than ever before, and we will make America great again.

John J. Mearsheimer and Stephen M. Walt, "The Case for Offshore Balancing," *Foreign Affairs* (July/August 2016)

To his critics, Trump's views smacked of "isolationism." They insisted that no alternative exists to the continued exercise of American global leadership. In this essay, the scholars John Mearsheimer (1947–) of the University of Chicago and Stephen Walt (1955–) of Harvard argue to the contrary, outlining an approach to grand strategy based on pragmatism, restraint, and a sober appreciation of actual US interests.

For the first time in recent memory, large numbers of Americans are openly questioning their country's grand strategy. An April 2016 Pew poll found that 57 percent of Americans agree that the United States should "deal with its own problems and let others deal with theirs the best they can." . . .

Americans' distaste for the prevailing grand strategy should come as no surprise, given its abysmal record over the past quarter century. In Asia, India, Pakistan, and North Korea are expanding their nuclear arsenals, and China is challenging the status quo in regional waters. In Europe, Russia has annexed Crimea, and U.S. relations with Moscow have sunk to new lows since the Cold War. U.S. forces are still fighting in Afghanistan and Iraq, with no victory in sight. Despite losing most of its original leaders, al Qaeda has metastasized across the region. The Arab world has fallen into turmoil—in good part due to the United States' decisions to effect regime change in Iraq and Libya and its modest efforts to do the same in Syria—and the Islamic State, or ISIS, has emerged out of the chaos. Repeated U.S. attempts to broker Israeli-Palestinian peace have failed, leaving a two-state solution further away than ever.

Meanwhile, democracy has been in retreat worldwide, and the United States' use of torture, targeted killings, and other morally dubious practices has tarnished its image as a defender of human rights and international law.

The United States does not bear sole responsibility for all these costly debacles, but it has had a hand in most of them. The setbacks are the natural consequence of the misguided grand strategy of liberal hegemony that Democrats and Republicans have pursued for years. This approach holds that the United States must use its power not only to solve global problems but also to promote a world order based on international institutions, representative governments, open markets, and respect for human rights. As "the indispensable nation," the logic goes, the United States has the right, responsibility, and wisdom to manage local politics almost everywhere. At its core, liberal hegemony is a revisionist grand strategy: instead of calling on the United States to merely uphold the balance of power in key regions, it commits American might to promoting democracy everywhere and defending human rights whenever they are threatened.

There is a better way. By pursuing a strategy of "offshore balancing," Washington would forgo ambitious efforts to remake other societies and concentrate on what really matters: preserving U.S. dominance in the Western Hemisphere and countering potential hegemons in Europe, Northeast Asia, and the Persian Gulf. Instead of policing the world, the United States would encourage other countries to take the lead in checking rising powers, intervening itself only when necessary. This does not mean abandoning the United States' position as the world's sole superpower or retreating to "Fortress America." Rather, by husbanding U.S. strength, offshore balancing would preserve U.S. primacy far into the future and safeguard liberty at home.

The United States is the luckiest great power in modern history. Other leading states have had to live with threatening adversaries in their own backyards—even the United Kingdom faced the prospect of an invasion from across the English Channel on several occasions—but for more than two centuries, the United States has not. Nor do distant powers pose much of a threat, because two giant oceans are in the way. As Jean-Jules Jusserand, the French ambassador to the United States from 1902 to 1924, once put it, "On the north, she has a weak neighbor; on the south, another weak neighbor; on the east, fish, and the west, fish." Furthermore, the United States boasts an abundance of land and natural resources and a large and energetic population, which have enabled it to develop the world's biggest economy and most capable military. It also has thousands of nuclear weapons, which makes an attack on the American homeland even less likely.

These geopolitical blessings give the United States enormous latitude for error; indeed, only a country as secure as it would have the temerity to try to remake the world in its own image. But they also allow it to remain powerful and secure without pursuing a costly and expansive grand strategy. Offshore balancing would do just that. Its principal concern would be to keep the United States as powerful as possible—ideally, the dominant state on the planet. Above all, that means maintaining hegemony in the Western Hemisphere.

Unlike isolationists, however, offshore balancers believe that there are regions outside the Western Hemisphere that are worth expending American blood and treasure to defend. Today, three other areas matter to the United

States: Europe, Northeast Asia, and the Persian Gulf. The first two are key centers of industrial power and home to the world's other great powers, and the third produces roughly 30 percent of the world's oil.

In Europe and Northeast Asia, the chief concern is the rise of a regional hegemon that would dominate its region, much as the United States dominates the Western Hemisphere. Such a state would have abundant economic clout, the ability to develop sophisticated weaponry, the potential to project power around the globe, and perhaps even the wherewithal to outspend the United States in an arms race. Such a state might even ally with countries in the Western Hemisphere and interfere close to U.S. soil. Thus, the United States' principal aim in Europe and Northeast Asia should be to maintain the regional balance of power so that the most powerful state in each region—for now, Russia and China, respectively—remains too worried about its neighbors to roam into the Western Hemisphere. In the Gulf, meanwhile, the United States has an interest in blocking the rise of a hegemon that could interfere with the flow of oil from that region, thereby damaging the world economy and threatening U.S. prosperity.

Offshore balancing is a realist grand strategy, and its aims are limited. Promoting peace, although desirable, is not among them. This is not to say that Washington should welcome conflict anywhere in the world, or that it cannot use diplomatic or economic means to discourage war. But it should not commit U.S. military forces for that purpose alone. Nor is it a goal of offshore balancing to halt genocides, such as the one that befell Rwanda in 1994. Adopting this strategy would not preclude such operations, however, provided the need is clear, the mission is feasible, and U.S. leaders are confident that intervention will not make matters worse.

Under offshore balancing, the United States would calibrate its military posture according to the distribution of power in the three key regions. If there is no potential hegemon in sight in Europe, Northeast Asia, or the Gulf, then there is no reason to deploy ground or air forces there and little need for a large military establishment at home. And because it takes many years for any country to acquire the capacity to dominate its region, Washington would see it coming and have time to respond.

In that event, the United States should turn to regional forces as the first line of defense, letting them uphold the balance of power in their own neighborhood. Although Washington could provide assistance to allies and pledge to support them if they were in danger of being conquered, it should refrain from deploying large numbers of U.S. forces abroad. It may occasionally make sense to keep certain assets overseas, such as small military contingents, intelligence-gathering facilities, or prepositioned equipment, but in general, Washington should pass the buck to regional powers, as they have a far greater interest in preventing any state from dominating them.

If those powers cannot contain a potential hegemon on their own, however, the United States must help get the job done, deploying enough firepower to the region to shift the balance in its favor. Sometimes, that may mean sending in forces before war breaks out. During the Cold War, for example, the United States kept large numbers of ground and air forces in Europe out of the belief that Western European countries could not contain the Soviet Union on their own. At other times, the United States might wait to intervene after a war starts, if one side seems likely to emerge as a regional hegemon. Such was the case during both world wars: the United States came in only after Germany seemed likely to dominate Europe.

In essence, the aim is to remain offshore as long as possible, while recognizing that it is sometimes necessary to come onshore. If that happens, however, the United States should make its allies do as much of the heavy lifting as possible and remove its own forces as soon as it can.

Offshore balancing has many virtues. By limiting the areas the U.S. military was committed to defending and forcing other states to pull their own weight, it would reduce the resources Washington must devote to defense, allow for greater investment and consumption at home, and put fewer American lives in harm's way. Today, allies routinely free-ride on American protection, a problem that has only grown since the Cold War ended. Within NATO, for example, the United States accounts for 46 percent of the alliance's aggregate GDP yet contributes about 75 percent of its military spending. As the political scientist Barry Posen has quipped, "This is welfare for the rich."

Offshore balancing would also reduce the risk of terrorism. Liberal hegemony commits the United States to spreading democracy in unfamiliar places, which sometimes requires military occupation and always involves interfering with local political arrangements. Such efforts invariably foster nationalist resentment, and because the opponents are too weak to confront the United States directly, they sometimes turn to terrorism. (It is worth remembering that Osama bin Laden was motivated in good part by the presence of U.S. troops in his homeland of Saudi Arabia.) In addition to inspiring terrorists, liberal hegemony facilitates their operations: using regime change to spread American values undermines local institutions and creates ungoverned spaces where violent extremists can flourish.

Offshore balancing would alleviate this problem by eschewing social engineering and minimizing the United States' military footprint. U.S. troops would be stationed on foreign soil only when a country was in a vital region and threatened by a would-be hegemon. In that case, the potential victim would view the United States as a savior rather than an occupier. And once the threat had been dealt with, U.S. military forces could go back over the horizon and not stay behind to meddle in local politics. By respecting the sovereignty of other states, offshore balancing would be less likely to foster anti-American terrorism.

Offshore balancing may seem like a radical strategy today, but it provided the guiding logic of U.S. foreign policy for many decades and served the country well. During the nineteenth century, the United States was preoccupied with expanding across North America, building a powerful state, and establishing hegemony in the Western Hemisphere. After it completed these tasks at the end of the century, it soon became interested in preserving the balance of power in Europe and Northeast Asia. Nonetheless, it let the great powers in those regions check one another, intervening militarily only when the balance of power broke down, as during both world wars.

During the Cold War, the United States had no choice but to go onshore in Europe and Northeast

Asia, as its allies in those regions could not contain the Soviet Union by themselves. So Washington forged alliances and stationed military forces in both regions, and it fought the Korean War to contain Soviet influence in Northeast Asia.

In the Persian Gulf, however, the United States stayed offshore, letting the United Kingdom take the lead in preventing any state from dominating that oil-rich region. After the British announced their withdrawal from the Gulf in 1968, the United States turned to the shah of Iran and the Saudi monarchy to do the job. When the shah fell in 1979, the Carter administration began building the Rapid Deployment Force, an offshore military capability designed to prevent Iran or the Soviet Union from dominating the region. The Reagan administration aided Iraq during that country's 1980–88 war with Iran for similar reasons. The U.S. military stayed offshore until 1990, when Saddam Hussein's seizure of Kuwait threatened to enhance Iraq's power and place Saudi Arabia and other Gulf oil producers at risk. To restore the regional balance of power, the George H. W. Bush administration sent an expeditionary force to liberate Kuwait and smash Saddam's military machine.

For nearly a century, in short, offshore balancing prevented the emergence of dangerous regional hegemons and preserved a global balance of power that enhanced American security. Tellingly, when U.S. policymakers deviated from that strategy—as they did in Vietnam, where the United States had no vital interests—the result was a costly failure.

Events since the end of the Cold War teach the same lesson. In Europe, once the Soviet Union collapsed, the region no longer had a dominant power. The United States should have steadily reduced its military presence, cultivated amicable relations with Russia, and turned European security over to the Europeans. Instead, it expanded NATO and ignored Russian interests, helping spark the conflict over Ukraine and driving Moscow closer to China.

In the Middle East, likewise, the United States should have moved back offshore after the Gulf War and let Iran and Iraq balance each other. Instead, the Clinton administration adopted the policy of "dual containment," which required keeping ground and air forces in Saudi Arabia to check Iran and Iraq simultaneously. The George W. Bush administration then adopted an even more ambitious strategy, dubbed "regional transformation," which produced costly failures in Afghanistan and Iraq. The Obama administration repeated the error when it helped topple Muammar al-Qaddafi in Libya and when it exacerbated the chaos in Syria by insisting that Bashar al-Assad "must go" and backing some of his opponents. Abandoning offshore balancing after the Cold War has been a recipe for failure.

Defenders of liberal hegemony marshal a number of unpersuasive arguments to make their case. One familiar claim is that only vigorous U.S. leadership can keep order around the globe. But global leadership is not an end in itself; it is desirable only insofar as it benefits the United States directly.

One might further argue that U.S. leadership is necessary to overcome the collective-action problem of local actors failing to balance against a potential hegemon. Offshore balancing recognizes this danger, however, and calls for Washington to step in if needed. Nor does it prohibit Washington from giving friendly states in the key regions advice or material aid.

Other defenders of liberal hegemony argue that U.S. leadership is necessary to deal with new, transnational threats that arise from failed states, terrorism, criminal networks, refugee flows, and the like. Not only do the Atlantic and Pacific Oceans offer inadequate protection against these dangers, they claim, but modern military technology also makes it easier for the United States to project power around the world and address them. Today's "global village," in short, is more dangerous yet easier to manage.

This view exaggerates these threats and overstates Washington's ability to eliminate them. Crime, terrorism, and similar problems can be a nuisance, but they are hardly existential threats and rarely lend themselves to military solutions. Indeed, constant interference in the affairs of other states—and especially repeated military interventions—generates local resentment and fosters corruption, thereby making these transnational dangers worse. The long-term solution to the problems can only be competent local governance, not heavy-handed U.S. efforts to police the world.

Nor is policing the world as cheap as defenders of liberal hegemony contend, either in dollars spent or in lives lost. The wars in Afghanistan and Iraq cost between $4 trillion and $6 trillion and killed nearly 7,000 U.S. soldiers and wounded more than 50,000. Veterans of these conflicts exhibit high rates of depression and suicide, yet the United States has little to show for their sacrifices.

Defenders of the status quo also fear that offshore balancing would allow other states to replace the United States at the pinnacle of global power. On the contrary, the strategy would prolong the country's dominance by refocusing its efforts on core goals. Unlike liberal hegemony, offshore balancing avoids squandering resources on costly and counterproductive crusades, which would allow the government to invest more in the long-term ingredients of power and prosperity: education, infrastructure, and research and development. Remember, the United States became a great power by staying out of foreign wars and building a world-class economy, which is the same strategy China has pursued over the past three decades. Meanwhile, the United States has wasted trillions of dollars and put its long-term primacy at risk.

Another argument holds that the U.S. military must garrison the world to keep the peace and preserve an open world economy. Retrenchment, the logic goes, would renew great-power competition, invite ruinous economic rivalries, and eventually spark a major war from which the United States could not remain aloof. Better to keep playing global policeman than risk a repeat of the 1930s.

Such fears are unconvincing. For starters, this argument assumes that deeper U.S. engagement in Europe would have prevented World War II, a claim hard to square with Adolf Hitler's unshakable desire for war. Regional conflicts will sometimes occur no matter what Washington does, but it need not get involved unless vital U.S. interests are at stake. Indeed, the United States has sometimes stayed out of regional conflicts—such as the Russo-Japanese War, the Iran-Iraq War, and the current war in Ukraine—belying the claim that it inevitably gets dragged in. And if the country is forced to fight another great power, better to arrive late and let other countries bear the brunt of the costs. As the last major power to enter both world wars, the United States emerged stronger from each for having waited.

Furthermore, recent history casts doubt on the claim that U.S. leadership preserves peace. Over the past 25 years, Washington has caused or supported several wars in the Middle East and fueled minor conflicts elsewhere. If liberal hegemony is supposed to enhance global stability, it has done a poor job.

Nor has the strategy produced much in the way of economic benefits. Given its protected position in the Western Hemisphere, the United States is free to trade and invest wherever profitable opportunities exist. Because all countries have a shared interest in such activity, Washington does not need to play global policeman in order to remain economically engaged with others. In fact, the U.S. economy would be in better shape today if the government were not spending so much money trying to run the world.

Proponents of liberal hegemony also claim that the United States must remain committed all over the world to prevent nuclear proliferation. If it reduces its role in key regions or withdraws entirely, the argument runs, countries accustomed to U.S. protection will have no choice but to protect themselves by obtaining nuclear weapons.

No grand strategy is likely to prove wholly successful at preventing proliferation, but offshore balancing would do a better job than liberal hegemony. After all, that strategy failed to stop India and Pakistan from ramping up their nuclear capabilities, North Korea from becoming the newest member of the nuclear club, and Iran from making major progress with its nuclear program. Countries usually seek the bomb because they fear being attacked, and U.S. efforts at regime change only heighten such concerns. By eschewing regime change and reducing the United States' military footprint, offshore balancing would give potential proliferators less reason to go nuclear.

Moreover, military action cannot prevent a determined country from eventually obtaining nuclear weapons; it can only buy time. The recent deal with Iran serves as a reminder that coordinated multilateral pressure and tough economic sanctions are a better way to discourage proliferation than preventive war or regime change.

To be sure, if the United States did scale back its security guarantees, a few vulnerable states might seek their own nuclear deterrents. That outcome is not desirable, but all-out efforts to prevent it would almost certainly be costly and probably be unsuccessful. Besides, the downsides may not be as grave as pessimists fear. Getting the bomb does not transform weak countries into great powers or enable them to blackmail rival states. Ten states have crossed the nuclear threshold since 1945, and the world has not turned upside down. Nuclear proliferation will remain a concern no matter what the United States does, but offshore balancing provides the best strategy for dealing with it.

Other critics reject offshore balancing because they believe the United States has a moral and strategic imperative to promote freedom and protect human rights. As they see it, spreading democracy will largely rid the world of war and atrocities, keeping the United States secure and alleviating suffering.

No one knows if a world composed solely of liberal democracies would in fact prove peaceful, but spreading democracy at the point of a gun rarely works, and fledgling democracies are especially prone to conflict. Instead of promoting peace, the United States just ends up fighting endless wars. Even worse, force-feeding liberal values abroad can compromise them at home. The global war on terrorism and the related effort to implant democracy in Afghanistan and Iraq have led to tortured prisoners, targeted killings, and vast electronic surveillance of U.S. citizens.

Some defenders of liberal hegemony hold that a subtler version of the strategy could avoid the sorts of disasters that occurred in Afghanistan, Iraq, and Libya. They are deluding themselves. Democracy promotion requires large-scale social engineering in foreign societies that Americans understand poorly, which helps explain why Washington's efforts usually fail. Dismantling and replacing existing political institutions inevitably creates winners and losers, and the latter often take up arms in opposition. When that happens, U.S. officials, believing their country's credibility is now at stake, are tempted to use the United States' awesome military might to fix the problem, thus drawing the country into more conflicts.

If the American people want to encourage the spread of liberal democracy, the best way to do so is to set a good example. Other countries will more likely emulate the United States if they see it as a just, prosperous, and open society. And that means doing more to improve conditions at home and less to manipulate politics abroad.

Then there are those who believe that Washington should reject liberal hegemony but keep sizable U.S. forces in Europe, Northeast Asia, and the Persian Gulf solely to prevent trouble from breaking out. This low-cost insurance policy, they argue, would save lives and money in the long run, because the United States wouldn't have to ride to the rescue after a conflict broke out. This approach—sometimes called "selective engagement"—sounds appealing but would not work either.

For starters, it would likely revert back to liberal hegemony. Once committed to preserving peace in key regions, U.S. leaders would be sorely tempted to spread democracy, too, based on the widespread belief that democracies don't fight one another. This was the main rationale for expanding NATO after the Cold War, with the stated goal of "a Europe whole and free." In the real world, the line separating selective engagement from liberal hegemony is easily erased.

Advocates of selective engagement also assume that the mere presence of U.S. forces in various regions will guarantee peace, and so Americans need not worry about being dragged into distant conflicts. In other words, extending security commitments far and wide poses few risks, because they will never have to be honored.

But this assumption is overly optimistic: allies may act recklessly, and the United States may provoke conflicts itself. Indeed, in Europe, the American pacifier failed to prevent the Balkan wars of the 1990s, the Russo-Georgian war in 2008, and the current conflict in Ukraine. In the Middle East, Washington is largely responsible for several recent wars. And in the South China Sea, conflict is now a real possibility despite the U.S. Navy's substantial regional role. Stationing U.S. forces around the world does not automatically ensure peace.

Nor does selective engagement address the problem of buck-passing. Consider that the United Kingdom is now withdrawing its army from continental Europe, at a time when NATO faces what it considers a growing threat from Russia. Once again, Washington is expected to deal with the problem, even though peace in Europe should matter far more to the region's own powers.

What would offshore balancing look like in today's world? The good news is that it is hard to foresee a serious challenge to American hegemony in the Western Hemisphere, and for now, no potential hegemon lurks in Europe or the Persian Gulf. Now for the bad news: if China continues its impressive rise, it is likely to seek hegemony in Asia. The United States should undertake a major effort to prevent it from succeeding.

Ideally, Washington would rely on local powers to contain China, but that strategy might not work. Not only is China likely to be much more powerful than its neighbors, but these states are also located far from one another, making it harder to form an effective balancing coalition. The United States will have to coordinate their efforts and may have to throw its considerable weight behind them. In Asia, the United States may indeed be the indispensable nation.

In Europe, the United States should end its military presence and turn NATO over to the Europeans. There is no good reason to keep U.S. forces in Europe, as no country there has the capability to dominate that region. The top contenders, Germany and Russia, will both lose relative power as their populations shrink in size, and no other potential hegemon is in sight. Admittedly, leaving European security to the Europeans could increase the potential for trouble there. If a conflict did arise, however, it would not threaten vital U.S. interests. Thus, there is no reason for the United States to spend billions of dollars each year (and pledge its own citizens' lives) to prevent one.

In the Gulf, the United States should return to the offshore-balancing strategy that served it so well until the advent of dual containment. No local power is now in a position to dominate the region, so the United States can move most of its forces back over the horizon.

With respect to ISIS, the United States should let the regional powers deal with that group and limit its own efforts to providing arms, intelligence, and military training. ISIS represents a serious threat to them but a minor problem for the United States, and the only long-term solution to it is better local institutions, something Washington cannot provide.

In Syria, the United States should let Russia take the lead. A Syria stabilized under Assad's control, or divided into competing ministates, would pose little danger to U.S. interests. Both Democratic and Republican presidents have a rich history of working with the Assad regime, and a divided and weak Syria would not threaten the regional balance of power. If the civil war continues, it will be largely Moscow's problem, although Washington should be willing to help broker a political settlement.

For now, the United States should pursue better relations with Iran. It is not in Washington's interest for Tehran to abandon the nuclear agreement and race for the bomb, an outcome that would become more likely if it feared a U.S. attack—hence the rationale for mending fences. Moreover, as its ambitions grow, China will want allies in the Gulf, and Iran will likely top its list. (In a harbinger of things to come, this past January, Chinese President Xi Jinping visited Tehran and signed 17 different agreements.) The United States has an obvious interest in discouraging Chinese-Iranian security cooperation, and that requires reaching out to Iran.

Iran has a significantly larger population and greater economic potential than its Arab neighbors, and it may eventually be in a position to dominate the Gulf. If it begins to move in this direction, the United States should help the other Gulf states balance against Tehran, calibrating its own efforts and regional military presence to the magnitude of the danger.

Taken together, these steps would allow the United States to markedly reduce its defense spending. Although U.S. forces would remain in Asia, the withdrawals from Europe and the Persian Gulf would free up billions of dollars, as would reductions in counterterrorism spending and an end to the war in Afghanistan and other overseas interventions. The United States would maintain substantial naval and air assets and modest but capable ground forces, and it would stand ready to expand its capabilities should circumstances require. But for the foreseeable future, the U.S. government could spend more money on domestic needs or leave it in taxpayers' pockets.

Offshore balancing is a grand strategy born of confidence in the United States' core traditions and a recognition of its enduring advantages. It exploits the country's providential geographic position and recognizes the powerful incentives other states have to balance against overly powerful or ambitious neighbors. It respects the power of nationalism, does not try to impose American values on foreign societies, and focuses on setting an example that others will want to emulate. As in the past, offshore balancing is not only the strategy that hews closest to U.S. interests; it is also the one that aligns best with Americans' preferences.

DONALD J. TRUMP, "INAUGURAL ADDRESS" (JANUARY 20, 2017)

In an upset victory, Trump won the presidential election of November 2016. In laying out his foreign policy vision, the 45th president of the United States revived the phrase "America First."

The oath of office I take today is an oath of allegiance to all Americans.

For many decades we've enriched foreign industry at the expense of American industry, subsidized the armies of other countries while allowing for the very sad depletion of our military. We've defended other nations' borders while refusing to defend our own and spent trillions and trillions of dollars overseas while America's infrastructure has fallen into disrepair and decay. We've made other countries rich while the wealth, strength and confidence of our country has dissipated over the horizon.

One by one, the factories shuttered and left our shores with not even a thought about the millions and millions of American workers that were left behind. The wealth of our middle class has been ripped from their homes and then redistributed all across the world. But that is the past and now we are looking only to the future.

We assembled here today are issuing a new decree to be heard in every city, in every foreign capital and in every hall of power. From this day forward, a new vision will govern our land. From this day forward, it's going to be only America first. America first.

Every decision on trade, on taxes, on immigration, on foreign affairs will be made to benefit American workers and American families. We must protect our borders from the ravages of other countries making our products, stealing our companies and destroying our jobs. Protection will lead to great prosperity and strength.

I will fight for you with every breath in my body, and I will never, ever let you down. America will start winning again. Winning like never before. We will bring back our jobs. We will bring back our borders. We will bring back our wealth. And we will bring back our dreams.

We will build new roads and highways and bridges and airports and tunnels and railways all across our wonderful nation. We will get our people off of welfare and back to work rebuilding our country with American hands and American labor.

We will follow two simple rules: Buy American and hire American. We will seek friendship and good will with the nations of the world, but we do so with the understanding that it is the right of all nations to put their own interests first.

We do not seek to impose our way of life on anyone, but rather to let it shine as an example. We will shine for everyone to follow. We will reinforce old alliances and form new ones and unite the civilized world against radical Islamic terrorism, which we will eradicate completely from the face of the earth.

At the bedrock of our politics will be a total allegiance to the United States of America, and through our loyalty to our country, we will rediscover our loyalty to each other. When you open your heart to patriotism, there is no room for prejudice. The Bible tells us how good and pleasant it is when God's people live together in unity.

We must speak our minds openly, debate our disagreements honestly, but always pursue solidarity. When America is united, America is totally unstoppable. There should be no fear. We are protected, and we will always be protected. We will be protected by the great men and women of our military and law enforcement and most importantly, we will be protected by God.

INDEX